Pathways and Patterns in History

Essays on Baptists, Evangelicals, and the Modern World
in Honour of David Bebbington

Pathways and Patterns in History

Essays on Baptists, Evangelicals, and the Modern World in Honour of David Bebbington

Edited by
Anthony R. Cross, Peter J. Morden,
and Ian M. Randall

WIPF & STOCK · Eugene, Oregon

Wipf and Stock Publishers
199 W 8th Ave, Suite 3
Eugene, OR 97401

Pathways and Patterns in History
Essays on Baptists, Evangelicals, and the Modern World
in Honour of David Bebbington
By Cross, Anthony R. and Mordern, Peter J.
Copyright © 2015 by Cross, Anthony R. All rights reserved.
Softcover ISBN-13: 978-1-7252-8766-2
Hardcover ISBN-13: 978-1-7252-8767-9
eBook ISBN-13: 978-1-7252-8768-6
Publication date 9/2/2020
Previously published by Spurgeon's College, 2015

Contents

Contributors ix

Preface and Acknowledgements xi

Introduction
Ian M. Randall, Anthony R. Cross, and Peter J. Morden xiii

Chapter 1
The Nottingham Legacy
Eileen Bebbington 1

Baptist Studies 13

Chapter 2
Performing Religious Nonconformity: Conversion, Debate and
the Republic of Letters
Alison Searle 15

Chapter 3
'Go down to the potter's house': Baptists and the Pottery Industry
John H.Y. Briggs 35

Chapter 4
The Early Bristol Tradition as a Seedbed for Evangelical Reception among
British Baptists, c.1720–1770
Anthony R. Cross 50

Chapter 5
The Annual Tent Meetings of the Suffolk and Norfolk Strict Baptists
Tim Grass 78

Chapter 6
'The Forgotten Spurgeon': A Reappraisal of the Life and Ministry of
James Archer Spurgeon (1837–99)
Peter J. Morden 99

Chapter 7
'Citizens of No Mean City': A Study of Women in Two Baptist Churches
in Late Victorian and Early Edwardian Bristol
Linda Wilson 122

Chapter 8
Spreading the Good News from Scotland: Scottish Baptists and
Overseas Mission in the First Three Decades of the Twentieth Century
Brian R. Talbot 145

Chapter 9
Patterns, Mentalités and the Possibilities for Baptist History
Martin Sutherland 172

Evangelical Studies 185

Chapter 10
Evangelical Revival in Enlightenment Britain: James Erskine of Grange
and the Pietist Turn
John Coffey 187

Chapter 11
'The Grand Point': George Whitefield, Anglo-American Evangelicals,
and the Holy Spirit
Thomas Kidd 215

Chapter 12
A Microcosm of the Community of the Saints: John Erskine's
Relationship with the English Particular Baptists, John Collett Ryland
and his Son John Ryland, Jr
Jonathan Yeager 231

Chapter 13
The East African Revival and British Evangelical Spirituality,
from the 1930s to the 1950s
Ian M. Randall 255

Chapter 14
American Evangelical Transformation in the Aftermath of World War II
Mark A. Noll 278

Socio-Political Studies 297

Chapter 15
British Evangelicals and the United States of America, c.1775–c.1820
Emma Macleod 299

Chapter 16
Hands Joined in Brotherhood: The Rise and Decline of a Movement
for Faith and Social Change, 1875–2000
David Killingray 319

Chapter 17
Taking Leave of Gladstone
John Wolffe 340

Chapter 18
Gardening for the Gospel: Horticulture and Mission in the Life
of Robert Moffat of Kuruman
Brian Stanley 354

Chapter 19
How Evangelical Biblicism Saved Western Civilization
Timothy Larsen 369

Bibliography of the Writings of David William Bebbington 385

General Index 399

Contributors

Eileen Bebbington graduated from Girton College, Cambridge, in 1970. She qualified as a teacher a year later, the same year in which she married David.

John H.Y. Briggs is an Emeritus Professor in History, the University of Birmingham, and Research Professor, International Baptist Theological Study Centre, Amsterdam.

John Coffey is Professor of Early Modern History, University of Leicester.

Anthony R. Cross is a Member of the Faculty of Theology and Religion, University of Oxford.

Tim Grass is a Senior Research Fellow at Spurgeon's College, London, and Assistant Editor for the Ecclesiastical History Society.

Thomas S. Kidd is Professor of History, Baylor University, Texas.

David Killingray is Emeritus Professor of Modern History at Goldsmiths London, and a Senior Research Fellow, School of Advanced Study, University of London.

Timothy Larsen is the Carolyn and Fred McManis Professor of Christian Thought, Wheaton College.

Emma Macleod is Lecturer in History, University of Stirling.

Peter J. Morden is Vice Principal and Lecturer in Church History and Spirituality, Spurgeon's College, London.

Mark A. Noll is Francis A. McAnaney Professor of History, University of Notre Dame.

Ian M. Randall is a Senior Research Fellow, Spurgeon's College, London, and a Research Associate, Cambridge Centre for Christianity Worldwide.

Alison Searle is a Postdoctoral Fellow, Australian Research Council Discovery Early Career Researcher Award, University of Sydney.

Brian Stanley is Professor of World Christianity, University of Edinburgh.

Martin Sutherland is Vice Principal, Laidlaw College, New Zealand.

Brian R. Talbot is Minister of Broughty Ferry Baptist Church, Dundee, Tutor, Greenwich School of Theology, and Extraordinary Professor, Department of Theology, North-West University, South Africa.

Linda Wilson is Senior Lecturer in Church History, University of Gloucestershire.

John Wolffe is Professor of Religious History, The Open University.

Jonathan Yeager is Assistant Professor of Religion, University of Tennessee at Chattanooga.

Preface and Acknowledgements

It has been both a privilege and a joy to co-edit *Pathways and Patterns in History* in honour of David Bebbington, who, in different ways, has been an example and a friend to each of us. To honour David truly, we wanted a volume which made a substantial contribution to the work of ongoing historical scholarship to which he is so committed. Consequently, we are excited by the high quality of the essays we have received. What you will find in these pages is a series of ground-breaking chapters by established scholars from both sides of the Atlantic and the Antipodes. We express warm gratitude to all our contributors for taking time out of their busy schedules to research and to write, for meeting the tight deadlines they were set, and for producing such excellent essays. Editors and writers are thus united in a desire to pay tribute to an outstanding historian and gracious friend by presenting him a volume which interacts with his own work and contributes significantly to the existing historiography in a number of important areas. Together we offer this Festschrift as a mark of our esteem for him in his sixty-fifth year.

Pathways and Patterns seemed a highly appropriate title for this volume of essays. First, David's work has regularly been path-breaking, as it was when he generated a new way of understanding evangelicalism in his seminal *Evangelicalism in Modern Britain*, a volume which has had an extraordinary impact on the subsequent historiography of this crucial global religious movement. Secondly, he has so often brilliantly and provocatively traced 'patterns in history', for example in his book of the same name which sets out a distinctively Christian approach to the philosophy of history.[1] As far as the subtitle of this present work is concerned, *Baptists, Evangelicals and the Modern World* conveys the scope of this present book and also points to the way it is structured. After an Introduction and biographical sketch by the editors and a stand-alone essay by Eileen Bebbington which is more personal, chapters are grouped under three headings, 'Baptist Studies', 'Evangelical Studies', and 'Socio-Political Studies'. These headings reflect the primary foci of David's own body of work. Nevertheless, many essays cross the boundaries implied by these categories and some could plausibly have been grouped in any of the three sections. This too is appropriate, for one of the particular features of David's writing is his ability to connect religious history with socio-political and cultural history in a way that illuminates the whole. The Festschrift concludes with a bibliography of David's publications. Those who have engaged with his written output will be unsurprised to learn that this covers thirteen pages. David has been astonishingly prolific. Yet it is the uniformly high standard of his work which is most remarkable.

Many people and organisations have helped with this book. We especially acknowledge our debt to Eileen Bebbington who has not only contributed her

---

[1] For similar comments, made five years ago, see Tim Larson, 'Reflections on David Bebbington Occasioned by his 60th Birthday', http://esrh.blogspot.co.uk/2009/10/reflections-on-david-bebbington.html, accessed 13 March 2015.

chapter but given wise advice and encouragement from the project's inception. Eileen's fine biography of her husband, *A Patterned Life: Faith, History, and David Bebbington* (Eugene, OR: Wipf and Stock, 2014), should be regarded as a complementary volume to our own. We recommend that all who engage with the essays which make up *Pathways and Patterns* also read *A Patterned Life* which sheds much light on David's career and the influences which shaped him. As well as writing a chapter, Emma McLeod worked hard to obtain the cover image and get permission to use it from the photographer, Jane Massey. We express our thanks to Micky Munro for the lovely cover design. The Baptist Historical Society and Spurgeon's College, who jointly publish this Festschrift, have offered much support. We are particularly grateful to the past and current Presidents of the Society, Prof. John H.Y. Briggs and Dr Keith G. Jones, to the Principal of Spurgeon's College, Dr Roger Standing, and the College's Business Manager, Helen Stokley. A grant from the Whitley Trust, established in honour of W.T. Whitley, a Baptist historian of a previous generation, helped finance publication. Whilst we express our thanks to all those mentioned in this Preface, any errors which remain in this book are the responsibility of the editors.

Finally, we unite to express the wish that David continues to research and write for many years to come. He has helped raise up a new generation of scholars who have been shaped by his example, and encouraged by his personal friendship and wise guidance, and these scholars are part of his legacy. Yet his own writing also continues apace and we hope for many more books and articles. Five years ago, at a dinner given to celebrate David's sixtieth birthday at Baylor University, one of our contributors, Tim Larsen, declared, 'I fully expect that there will be another such occasion on David's 90th birthday when the table will be abuzz with talk about a recent monograph of his. I just hope that I somehow manage to live to be there as well.'[2] We say a hearty Amen! We hope David enjoys this present volume and goes on to write many more of his own.

---

[2] Larson, 'Reflections on David Bebbington Occasioned by his 60th Birthday'.

Introduction

As co-editors we are delighted to be able to introduce this volume of essays in honour of Professor David Bebbington. When we approached a number of colleagues to talk about the possibility of this volume there was unanimous and enthusiastic affirmation. There was also very ready willingness on the part of busy people to write contributory essays. In the light of this warm support, the production of this Festschrift has been a joyful undertaking. One of the three of us (Ian) was a PhD student of David's, another (Peter) had David as a PhD examiner, and for each of us David has been and is a friend, an exemplar, an encourager and a guide. In this introduction we are drawing from what several other contributors to this collection of essays have offered to us as reflections on David's work. Each contributor has found David to be an important influence and a much-valued conversation partner.

An extended sketch of David Bebbington's life is not needed in this volume, since in 2014 Eileen Bebbington produced a splendid biography of her husband, *A Patterned Life*.[1] David was born on 25 July 1949 in Nottingham, where he lived until the end of his secondary school education, and Eileen has contributed to this volume a fascinating study of 'The Nottingham Legacy'. In *A Patterned Life*, chapter 1 is 'The Nottingham Years', followed by a chapter on 'The Cambridge Years'. During those Cambridge years David was an Exhibitioner and then a Scholar of Jesus College, becoming a Research Student of the College in 1971 and a Research Fellow of Fitzwilliam College in 1973. David's first teaching post was at Stirling University, Scotland, and Eileen's third chapter is 'The Stirling Years'. From Lecturer in History at Stirling, David became Senior Lecturer in 1989, Reader two years later, and Professor in 1999. From 2003 he has also been Visiting Distinguished Professor, Department of History, Baylor University, Texas, USA, and has spent the autumn every two years at Baylor.

In the Foreword to *A Patterned Life*, Timothy Larsen, at Wheaton College, Illinois (himself a former PhD student of David's and someone who has helped significantly with this volume), begins in this way:

> David Bebbington is a highly honored historian – one thinks immediately of his personal professorial chair at the University of Stirling, his presidency of the Ecclesiastical History Society, his long association with Baylor University as a Distinguished Visiting Professor, the numerous endowed lecture series that he has been chosen to deliver, and much more. He is also a popular historian: his name is often evoked even by undergraduate students in a whole variety of countries and he is frequently sought out by members of the media to comment on current news stories.[2]

---

[1] Eileen Bebbington, *A Patterned Life: Faith, History, and David Bebbington* (Eugene, OR: Wipf and Stock, 2014).

[2] Timothy Larsen, 'Foreword', in Eileen Bebbington, *A Patterned Life*, p. vii.

It is sometimes the case that although a prophet is accorded many honours, this is not the case 'in his own country', but that is not true of David. One of David's colleagues at Stirling, Dr Emma Macleod, a Lecturer in History at the University and a contributor to the present volume, speaks of David's contributions to the Division of History and Politics at the University as 'many and very substantial'. She continues,

> His international reputation as a scholar of political and religious history is a very important asset to the University, and his contributions to its Research Assessment Exercise and Research Excellence Framework from his prolific research and writing career have been depended upon for their weight and quality.

As well as teaching nineteenth-century British social and religious history, the history of British political thought, and a long-running special subject on Gladstone Studies, Emma notes that David has successfully supervised an unusually large number of doctoral research students, many of them from the United States of America.[3]

David's own involvement in research and writing began early. At age nine his first book appeared: a discerning primary teacher had set him an individual project on the ancient world, and the result was a four-volume book by the young student, complete with footnotes, entitled *A History of the Ancient World with Which Is Incorporated Classical Mythology*.[4] His next book, some years later, was local in its focus. In his final year at Nottingham High School, David investigated the history of the church where he and his family worshipped, Queensberry Street Baptist Church, in Old Basford, Nottingham. It was David's work on the church's story which was published when in 1977 the church was celebrating the centenary of its founding.[5]

John H.Y. Briggs recalls that it was in 1968 that he first met David. The occasion was the Baptist Historical Society's first ever Summer School, held that year at Spurgeon's College in south London. David had been baptized a few weeks earlier, on Whit Sunday, and would enter Cambridge University in October of that year. Dr Ernest A. Payne, a fine historian who had been General Secretary of the Baptist Union of Great Britain and Ireland, and who was then a Vice-President of the World Council of Churches, indicated to John Briggs and others that 'David was a young man of great promise who needed to be encouraged'. At Cambridge, David readily identified himself with the activities of the Cambridge Inter-Collegiate Christian Union (CICCU) and thought hard about how the practice of history could provide a helpful arena in which to engage those uncommitted to Christianity. It was in this area that David's first book, *Patterns in History: A Christian View* (1979) was published. John Briggs recalls discussions about the content: it seemed to John 'that David was adopting a John Henry Newman-like approach [*disciplina arcani* or

---

[3] Emma Macleod email, 31 October 2014.
[4] Eileen Bebbington, *A Patterned Life*, p. 28.
[5] D.W. Bebbington, *A History of Queensberry Street Baptist Church, Old Basford, Nottingham* (Nottingham: Privately printed, 1977).

the method of keeping sacred things secret] in suggesting that Christian historians would be aware of levels of causation which they were not bound to share with their non-Christian colleagues.' John adds that David – as would be expected – defended his position on the historian's craft robustly![6] Tim Larsen observes that *Patterns in History* created a 'dramatic splash' and 'quickly became the standard book to assign or recommend for anyone interested in the integration of faith and the discipline of history'.[7]

David is also a very considerable political historian. John Briggs comments that the book which emerged from David's PhD thesis, *The Nonconformist Conscience: Chapel and Politics, 1870–1914* (1982), was 'an excellent piece of work', which is still a standard treatment of the subject, and he notes that among David's many articles for the *Baptist Quarterly* (the journal of the Baptist Historical Society) are substantial articles – that began under John Briggs' editorship of the *Quarterly* – on Baptist Members of Parliament. To fulfil the necessary requirements to be on David Bebbington's list as a Baptist, John Briggs judges, was to be compared to getting one's name written in the Lamb's book of life. However, in matters of soteriology (by contrast with issues connected with being a genuinely Baptist MP), David was always firmly committed to salvation by grace.[8]

Not only does David understand divine activity as gracious, he is also someone who exhibits grace in his dealings with others. Emma Macleod, as a colleague, speaks of how David is 'respected and held in affection by students and colleagues alike', not only for 'the extraordinary breadth and depth of his historical knowledge' and 'the rigour of his thinking (and questioning of others)', but also 'his kindness and sense of humour'. She further comments, 'He is generous with his time and advice, and whatever administrative tasks he is asked to take on, whether apparently trivial or heavyweight, are attended to with meticulous efficiency and good grace.'[9]

David's ability as a lecturer is also a notable feature of his contribution to the scholarly community. David Killingray has summed up the experience of very many as they have listened to David's lectures: they are

> rigorously composed, comprehensive in content, delivered with firm authority, and in a clear strong voice. But lecturing is not only about conveying ideas and analyses and stimulating the minds of listeners, it is also about being prepared to answer questions from an audience. It has been a delight, and a model to be copied, to see how David

---

[6] John H.Y. Briggs email, 7 November 2014.

[7] Larsen, 'Foreword', pp. ix and x. See D.W. Bebbington, *Patterns in History: A Christian View* (Downers Grove, IL: InterVarsity Press, 1979). The title chosen for this *Festschrift* is intended to reflect the way in which David has explored pathways and patterns in history.

[8] Briggs email. See D.W. Bebbington, *The Nonconformist Conscience: Chapel and Politics, 1870–1914* (London: George Allen & Unwin, 1982). So impressed were other denominations by the articles on Baptist MPs that David was asked to undertake similar research for the Congregationalists and the Unitarians. See the Bibliography.

[9] Macleod email.

responds to such questions: pencil poised as if in anticipation that the questioner will say something of real value, followed by a "thank you", and then a measured and gracious response which invariably acts to encourage the questioner or to firmly point them in the right direction.[10]

It is time now to turn in this short introduction to the book which has, above all, made David Bebbington so influential: *Evangelicalism in Modern Britain: A History from the 1730s to the 1980s* (1989).[11] Leading historians soon saw the significance of this work when it was first published. Callum Brown, later to become best known for his book, *The Death of Christian Britain* (2001), claimed that *Evangelicalism in Modern Britain* was 'little short of an indispensable guidebook for the social historian'.[12] In similar vein, Colin Matthew stated that Bebbington had 'written what will be the standard history of the subject for many years to come'.[13] By the early twenty-first century *Evangelicalism in Modern Britain*, often by now denoted a 'magisterial study', was being used by Kenneth Brown in the *American Historical Review* as a standard for evaluating other contributions.[14]

The definition of evangelicalism which David offered – that the movement's four distinguishing characteristics have been conversionism, activism, biblicism, and crucicentrism – has become so famous and so closely associated with David himself that it is often referred to as the Bebbington Quadrilateral. John Wolffe wrote as early as 1990 that *Evangelicalism in Modern Britain* was

> especially helpful in presenting and applying a working definition of evangelicalism that represents a satisfactory middle course between the theological innocence of some social historians and the excessive ideological rigour of party theologians. Bebbington is thus able to explore the internal diversity of the phenomenon while maintaining overall coherence.[15]

There are many examples of the way David Bebbington's approach has been taken up in more popular and influential books, for instance Derek Tidball's *Who Are the Evangelicals?: Tracing the Roots of Today's Movements* (1994).[16] Tim Larsen has set out evidence for the 'near monopoly position' that the Bebbington Quadrilateral has in the defining of evangelicalism.[17]

---

[10] David Killingray email, 17 December 2014.

[11] D.W. Bebbington, *Evangelicalism in Modern Britain: A History from the 1730s to the 1980s* (London: Unwin Hyman, 1989).

[12] Callum G. Brown, *Scottish Economic and Social History* 10 (1990), p. 100.

[13] H.C.G. Matthew, *Journal of Theological Studies* n.s. 41 (October, 1990), pp. 765-66.

[14] Kenneth Brown, 'Europe: Early Modern and Modern', *American Historical Association* 108.1 (2003), p. 923.

[15] John Wolffe, *History* 75 (1990), pp. 346-47.

[16] Derek Tidball, *Who Are the Evangelicals?: Tracing the Roots of Today's Movements* (London: Marshall Pickering, 1994).

[17] See Timothy Larsen, 'The reception given *Evangelicalism in Modern Britain* since its publication in 1989', in Michael A.G. Haykin and Kenneth J. Stewart (eds), *The Emergence*

What then was David's achievement in *Evangelicalism in Modern Britain*? Tim Larsen has offered a penetrating analysis. He argues for the significance of the connection David has made between religious history and intellectual history. The central task undertaken so brilliantly in the book was, as Larsen puts it, 'uncovering the connections between the history of evangelicalism and the great intellectual movements of the Enlightenment, Romanticism, and Modernism'. He continues,

> Hitherto evangelicalism had often been viewed – even by evangelical scholars – as a kind of intellectual backwater that was largely cut off from the main intellectual currents of society and which was usually hostile and obstructionist when it did encounter them. Evangelicalism was the gigantic, obscurantist Party of No: the Enlightenment was too rationalistic, Modernism was too relativistic, and Romanticism was, well, too romantic. Bebbington demonstrated that the evangelical movement was not only much more in touch with the main ideas of the times than had been assumed, but also impressively skilled at imbibing them and making use of them for its own ends.[18]

Those who simply see this interpretation of the evangelical movement as a 'given', might not know that before David's work on the movement this was certainly not the case.

Another evaluation of David's achievement in *Evangelicalism in Modern Britain* comes from Mark Noll, a contributor to this volume and someone who has worked closely with David on many transatlantic historical projects. He writes, 'I find the research for everything he [David] attempts so extensive, the documentation so precise, the architectonics so clear, and the overall effect so exceedingly useful that no difference in back-ground presuppositions qualifies my heart-felt appreciation.' Noll places *Evangelicalism in Modern Britain* alongside Timothy L. Smith's *Revivalism and Social Reform: American Protestantism on the Eve of the Civil War* (1957) and George Marsden's *Fundamentalism and American Culture* (1980) as the three books most responsible for fuelling the general renewal of historical scholarship on evangelical Christian expressions in the English-speaking world.[19]

It is not the case that everyone has embraced the argument set out in *Evangelicalism in Modern Britain*. In particular a number of authors of the essays in Michael A.G. Haykin and Kenneth J. Stewart (eds), *The Emergence of Evangelicalism: Exploring Historical Continuities* (2008), sought to show that there were more continuities between eighteenth-century evangelicalism and earlier Reformers and Puritans than David Bebbington had recognised. Some of these critiques were the product of confessional presuppositionalism and in the years since the volume was produced (in North America with the title *The Advent of*

---

of Evangelicalism: Exploring Historical Continuities (Nottingham: Apollos, 2008), pp. 21-36.

[18] Larsen, 'Foreword', pp. xi-xii.

[19] Talk by Mark Noll at the Conference on Faith and History Fall meeting, Pepperdine University, 26 September 2014. Quoted with permission.

Evangelicalism) there is no indication that either in scholarly or wider circles has David's overarching argument been undermined. As Larsen puts it,

> in *Evangelicalism in Modern Britain*, David Bebbington made as significant and substantial a contribution to scholarship as the author of any book could ever hope for, in the ambitious way that he related church history to other forms of history and wider cultural developments. Along the way, he also happened to provide us with the standard definition of evangelicalism.[20]

Mark Noll speaks of *Evangelicalism in Modern Britain* being followed by 'an immense amount of subsequent scholarship' from David, not least *Victorian Religious Revivals*, with its 'unprecedented scope of geographical investigation'.[21] The Bibliography at the end of this volume shows David's enormous output of articles, as well as books and edited volumes. In the twenty-first century there have been three highly significant works from David on evangelical and Baptist history: *The Dominance of Evangelicalism: The Age of Spurgeon and Moody* (2005), *Baptists Through the Centuries: A History of a Global People* (2010), and *Victorian Religious Revivals*. Larsen comments on his achievement in his work on revivals,

> The history of religious revivals had been a dubious, if not discredited, field which was seen as embarrassingly old-fashioned and fatally tainted with pious legends, wishful thinking, rigged providentialism, and polemical special pleading. Bebbington brilliantly set it back on its academic footing as an up-to-date, credible, scholarly field of inquiry.

Furthermore, David showed that participants in revivals, who had 'been stereotyped as ignorant fanatics, were often well read, sophisticated, and intellectually current'. Larsen rightly sees *Victorian Religious Revivals* as 'a splendid example of Bebbington's macro/micro approach to history, connecting charming, meticulously researched local case studies with the grand themes sweeping across the continents and the centuries'.[22] David's early interest in political history has continued, with a particular focus on W.E. Gladstone: his seminal work on Gladstone is *The Mind of Gladstone: Religion, Homer, and Politics* (2004).[23]

Alongside his major scholarly contribution through writing, David has been known for his work as a supervisor of many PhD students and an examiner of even more. One of his former PhD students, Dr Linda Wilson, describes how 'David has been involved in producing further generations of historians. His sympathetic yet rigorous supervision of PhDs has resulted in women and men working in related fields both in the UK and the US.' Linda, whose PhD was on women in mid-nineteenth-century Nonconformist churches, also notes that through his research into

---

[20] Larsen, 'The reception given *Evangelicalism in Modern Britain*', p. 36.

[21] D.W. Bebbington, *Victorian Religious Revivals: Culture and Piety in Local and Global Contexts* (Oxford: Oxford University Press, 2012).

[22] Larsen, 'Foreword', p. xii.

[23] D.W. Bebbington, *The Mind of Gladstone: Religion, Homer, and Politics* (Oxford: Oxford University Press, 2004).

Introduction xix

evangelicalism David 'has been instrumental in pioneering the study of an area of religious history previously neglected by mainstream historians, one which helped to shape Victorian Britain'.[24] Dr Tim Grass recalls the experience of having David as his PhD examiner. The length of the vivas conducted by David is legendary. Tim writes,

> The viva lasted a good three hours, and I had got to the point of being pretty convinced I had failed (the experience was rather like taking a driving test); I was a bit surprised, therefore, to be told that I and the thesis had passed muster, and that all I needed to do was sit in the corridor outside the office with the three copies, a bottle of correcting fluid, and a list of about 30 corrections, mostly to punctuation, supplied by David.[25]

Many people seeking to make a contribution in the field of history speak with gratitude of David's personal encouragement and his stimulus to them in their ongoing work.[26] David Killingray aptly describes David as a 'great encourager', and continues,

> Anything that I have written on what might broadly be called 'ecclesiastical or church' history is due to his inspiration and encouragement: an invitation to offer a paper at a conference, suggested sources to read, a ready willingness to answer enquiries and to provide bibliographical advice, and gentle and gracious critical correction – all have come from him over the years, for which I am most grateful.[27]

David's library and his collection (and collecting) of books are – like his PhD examinations – legendary. Emma Macleod writes, 'His carefully and expansively collected library, which has for many years overflowed the capacity of his own well-filled university office, has inspired awe in his students, anxiety in university administrators, and good-natured ribbing from his colleagues, poorly masking their admiration and envy.'[28] David Killingray comments,

> It is always a great occasion when David comes to stay. The first time he arrived I wondered why he had so much luggage and why it was so heavy. Books, of course! Whereas other seasoned bibliophiles would be content with a volume or two, perhaps half a box, David will buy by the dozen, boxes that is.[29]

Another feature noted by those who have had David visiting them is his keen interest in localities – the streets, the buildings and above all the people, not least the people who make up worshipping communities. Tim Grass describes hosting David for a week's research on the Isle of Man. 'He was working on Manx Methodism, and

---

[24] Linda Wilson email, 16 October 2014.
[25] Tim Grass email, 8 December 2014.
[26] E.g., Alison Searle email, 15 October 2014.
[27] Killingray email.
[28] Macleod email.
[29] Killingray email.

as part of his investigations was keen to get the feel of the distinctive island culture.' This interrogative interest is typical of David, wherever he travels. Also typically, the Isle of Man experience included second-hand bookshops. Tim Grass recalls, 'My wife Ann was glad to give him lifts into the Manx National Heritage archive in Douglas on her way to work; being Manx, she was fully questioned about the island's history and culture. On the Sunday, he wanted to attend three Methodist services, the more Manx the better.'[30] Undoubtedly those three services would have seen David occupied with another of his well-known commitments when visiting a worshipping community: the recording of all the details of the services in a small notebook – perhaps source material for a future book.

David's interest in Methodism is an example of the way in which he has investigated a wide range of Christian traditions. Nonconformity has certainly received particularly detailed attention. John Coffey comments that

> Having spent so much time among Victorian Nonconformists, and been raised in the evangelical Nonconformist tradition, David embodies its best characteristics, and avoids the worst. He manages to be scrupulous, without being censorious; faithful, without being unreasonable; and serious, but never dour. Indeed, he has a very sharp ear for amusing quotes and anecdotes. His lectures have a certain Spurgeonesque quality – they invariably educate and entertain.[31]

Yet despite his immersion in Nonconformity, David is equally at home in the history of other Protestant traditions. Nor are his interests confined to Protestantism. In one PhD examination, where the focus of the thesis was a Russian Baptist and evangelical figure, David asked the candidate to comment on the possible parallels between this particular Russian Baptist and a Russian Orthodox thinker with whose work David was clearly familiar. Indeed one of the joys of hearing David give a lecture at a conference is not only the masterly presentation of the topic and his interest in the questioners (as noted above), but the way in which, as he fields questions, it seems that his knowledge extends into virtually every conceivable field.

This is not to say that David ever gives the impression that he has little more to learn. Quite the reverse is the case. John Coffey makes the pertinent observation that

> David has the insatiable curiosity which is a hallmark of the best historians. He is not just a very fine lecturer, he is a remarkably attentive listener. He takes copious notes at academic conferences, and he will pay as close attention to a paper from a new graduate student as to one delivered by an eminent professor. Once the paper is finished, he will pose a pithy and pertinent question, one that always opens up new lines of enquiry. Some academics cultivate an air of superiority, as if they have nothing left to learn. David is not like that at all. He is admirably unassuming and open to new ideas and information.[32]

---

[30] Grass email.
[31] John Coffey email, 20 December 2014.
[32] Coffey email.

Alongside David's wide-ranging ecclesial interests and sympathies, his commitment to Baptist life has been a wholehearted one. When *Evangelicalism in Modern Britain* was produced the back cover stated, 'David Bebbington writes as a participant observer, for he is a Baptist deacon and lay preacher.' John Briggs writes,

> Throughout his distinguished career, when there have been so many calls upon his time, David has proved himself an immensely loyal member of the Baptist denomination – in his support of his local church, in supporting the Baptist Historical Society (BHS) as a committee member, in attending and speaking at BHS Summer Schools, in instituting and masterminding the very important International Conference on Baptist Studies (ICOBS – held every three years in different parts of the world), and in writing Baptist history from the local to the global.[33]

David has also been involved in various ways over the years with Spurgeon's College's work, and it is a privilege for the BHS and the College to be the joint publishers of this volume. We hope that the essays in it express to some degree the profound affection and respect felt towards David by colleagues and friends working in the field of evangelical, Baptist studies and/or socio-political studies. The contributors to this volume are thankful for the way in which David Bebbington has had an impact on our lives.

Ian M. Randall, Anthony R. Cross, and Peter J. Morden
May 2015

---

[33] Briggs email.

Professor David Bebbington.

CHAPTER 1

The Nottingham Legacy

Eileen Bebbington

The city of Nottingham in the East Midlands, where David was born in July 1949, had survived the Second World War with less damage than many other industrial areas. The lace, hosiery, and textile factories that had brought great wealth to the city at the end of the nineteenth century had not been considered a prime target for German bombers, which concentrated their attention on heavier industrial centres such as Derby and Coventry. Nottingham had long been fortunate to have a diversity of businesses which had helped it survive previous downturns in the economy. In 1950 three major firms, Boots the Chemist, Raleigh Cycles, and Players (Imperial Tobacco) supplemented the traditional sources of employment. David, therefore, grew up in a reasonably flourishing civic environment with the public resources that went with it. This economic resilience had provided the specific reason for both David's grandfathers moving to the city where they later married local girls. First came Alec Urquhart, David's maternal grandfather, at the very end of the nineteenth century. After his childhood in Carrbridge in Inverness-shire in Scotland, he trained as a gardener, but high unemployment in the Highlands meant that he could not find a job locally. After trying other places, he eventually arrived in Nottingham where he started work as a salesman who took orders for bespoke men's suits. As a Scot he felt at home at St Andrew's Presbyterian Church where he met and married the organist's daughter, Clarice Evelyn Martindale. They had a son, Roy, and then, in 1912, a daughter, Clarice Vera, always known as Vera, David's mother.

For similar reasons, Nottingham had also managed to navigate the First World War and the difficult years that followed, although unemployment ran high in some sectors. In the 1920s, therefore, the County Borough Council could afford to continue its policy of clearing the city's slums which had become notorious at the end of the previous century. The authorities would erect council estates, hailed as the modern solution to the housing problem, consisting of brick-built family homes with three bedrooms, a bathroom, and a garden. Tenants would then rent their new homes from the Council which would solve the problem of unscrupulous landlords exploiting the poor. This policy resulted in a great need for builders which attracted the attention of David's paternal grandfather. Harold Leach Bebbington, always known in the family as 'Pop', had been working in the Vickers shipyards of Barrow-in-Furness, now in Cumbria. The firm had enjoyed prosperous years during the war, but once the need for warships dwindled, many skilled workmen needed to look for other jobs as, unlike the situation in Nottingham, few other openings existed in the town. On his appointment as a manager in a building firm, Pop moved his wife and family of three children to the East Midland city. His oldest son, William, known as Bill, subsequently became David's father. The family worshipped at the central Brethren assembly in Nottingham where Bill and Vera met. Some years later, in 1939, Pop built a bungalow for them as a wedding present on a development on the outskirts of Sherwood, formerly part of Sherwood Forest, but now a growing suburb two miles north of the city centre. This house, 31 Covedale Road, remained David's home until he left for university in 1968, and Bill and Vera's until their deaths in 1971 and 1997 respectively. David's roots, therefore, lie in Scotland, in Cumbria, and before that in the mid-Cheshire plain where there have been Bebbingtons living since the fourteenth century in the hamlet of Spurstow in the parish of Bunbury, as well as in the local Nottingham area through his two grandmothers.

The preschool years in the bungalow proved quite isolated for David who rarely played with any other children. He spent his days with Vera because Bill would leave early for the family chiropody business in Mansfield, fourteen miles to the north, and not return until after his son's bedtime. The small boy amused himself with his toys for long stretches of time. Despite a meagre education, Vera had a thirst for accurate general knowledge and expected her son to be involved in this quest from an early age. But the young David soon showed himself to be interested in organizing and classifying information, not just in collecting it. He learned two other lessons at home: the need for hard work and application for the serious business of life, and the supreme importance of making a personal commitment to Jesus Christ. Vera, a caring but anxious mother, also taught her son that in the world of practical things danger lurked everywhere; spanners, for example, were almost certainly likely to harm you. There would be occasional 'runs out' in the car into the local area, to Matlock or Dovedale, for example, and David remembers preschool trips to Ingestre Hall in Shropshire, and Belvoir Castle in Leicestershire. Nearer home he would be used to passing the huge variety of local sights such as Wollaton Hall, an Elizabethan mansion actually in the city, and the castle that looked more like somebody's home than a traditional fortification. At this stage, with these buildings simply forming a backdrop to his daily life, he had no idea just how important they would become.

The development of the new council estates around the city directly affected the choice of where the family worshipped on a Sunday. In the 1930s, Pop Bebbington had realized that these new areas of housing could provide new opportunities for Christian witness. He helped to found and build a new Brethren assembly on the Aspley estate, two miles north-west of the centre. David and family attended there until he was eight, and the small boy imbibed many lasting attitudes: a great respect for the sacrament of the Lord's Supper, the need for personal faith, the desirability of standing up for your principles, and of daring to be different when necessary. Becoming frustrated with some of the ways of the Brethren, his parents looked elsewhere, firstly at the Methodists in central Nottingham, and then at Queensberry Street Baptist Church in Old Basford, two miles north west of the centre. Formerly a village, it had been engulfed by industrialization and had become a centre of bleaching and the finishing processes of textiles with good use made of the local river, the Leen. The cause which became Queensberry Street had been started in 1877 among small red-brick houses built for the workers in the local hosiery factories. Bill's sister, Madge, had worshipped there some years previously, and a Welsh preacher, Rev. Glyn Morris, whose parents and grandmother had all been converted in the Welsh Revival of 1904, attracted a large congregation. The family soon settled at the church which still included many workers in the hosiery industry. In this setting Bill and Vera taught David to respect other people, to stand when talking to older people, and various other good manners. Through a lady preacher at the church he committed his life to Christ at the age of ten and it continued as his main place of worship until he left for Cambridge nine years later.

As he grew older he became more and more interested in the history of the Baptist denomination, first in the UK and then worldwide. In these early days, the role that Nottingham had played in Baptist history underlined for him that to be Baptist was normal, not unusual. At the start of the seventeenth century, Thomas Helwys, from the nearby parish of Broxtowe, and John Smyth, from Gainsborough, just across into Lincolnshire, had been leading a Separatist community locally but had escaped to Amsterdam to avoid religious persecution.[1] On his return, Helwys founded the first known Baptist church in England in 1612 in London. Again, in the middle of the seventeenth century, Colonel Hutchinson, the governor of Nottingham Castle, when ordered to arrest some Baptist soldiers, confiscated and then read their literature and became a firm advocate of believer's baptism. All these local 'heroes' confirmed to David that Baptists belonged not to some small sect, but to mainstream society. All kinds of Nonconformists had a strong presence in the Nottingham area and had done so since the time of the Great Ejection in 1662 when any ministers of churches who refused to conform to the Church of England's *Book of Common Prayer* had to leave their churches and livings. Many suffered great hardship and even languished in prison for years. After the arrival of William of Orange in 1688, when this ban was lifted by various acts of Parliament, a huge number of Baptists, Quakers, and Independents came out of hiding and opened places of worship. In the nineteenth century, chapels and Sunday schools flourished across the city. William Booth, from the inner city parish of Sneinton founded the Salvation Army in 1865. Robert Mellors, in his book *Old Nottingham Suburbs* of 1914, records that in a two mile stretch of inner-city Hyson Green, there were 'six Parish or District Churches and seven Mission halls or rooms, three Congregational chapels, four Baptist, three Wesleyan, six United Methodist, five primitives, one Presbyterian, two Salvation Army, two Roman Catholic and one Brotherhood.'[2] Once again, being not just a

---

[1] See, e.g., Fred M.W. Harrison, *It All Began Here: The Story of The East Midland Baptist Association* (London: East Midland Baptist Association, 1986).

[2] R. Mellors, *Old Nottingham Suburbs: Then and Now* (Nottingham: J. & H. Bell, 1914), p. 39.

Baptist but a Nonconformist seemed normal, and many of these people had certainly stood up for their principles.

Not surprisingly, when David first came into contact with the Nottingham education system at the age of five, he felt terrified, becoming an easy target for teasing and scaring. Seely Primary School, a good mile's walk away from Covedale Road, up and down a very steep hill, served the new council estate of Sherwood, one of the innovative housing schemes of which the city felt so proud. Gradually the small boy became more used to the school environment and his general knowledge – increased by the world atlas which he had been given by cousins for his sixth birthday – impressed his teachers. In his fourth year at the school, the education authorities introduced a new idea across the city: group projects. David's small group received the topic 'From Snottingham to Nottingham' on local history in which they were to trace the development of the city from Snot, the Saxon who had settled his people in the local area close to the River Trent, right up to the modern era of the 1950s. Fascinated already by medieval history through a book his much loved Auntie Madge, Bill's sister, had given him for his seventh birthday, David set about this with a will, aided and abetted by his mother who helped track down newspaper and local information. At this point, the richness of the city's history struck him for the first time. For example, he clearly remembers discovering that the Norman market square which he had always thought to be the old centre of town had actually replaced a Saxon original, now in the Lace Market. He soon learned the chronological development of the city. At this very early age the diverse history around him fed his enthusiasm and the enlightened teacher, Mr Fawkes, realising that some spark had been lit, set him his own project later that year on ancient times. This led directly to David's first book entitled *A History of the Ancient world with which is incorporated Classical Mythology*, which had four volumes and, of course, included footnotes!

The prosperity of Nottingham in the sixteenth century determined the course of David's secondary education. In 1513 Dame Agnes Mellers, the widow of a local wealthy bell-founder, Robert Mellors, made an endowment for the 'education, teaching and instruction of boys in good manners and literature'.[3] By 1960 the school had become a public day school, Nottingham High School. The County Borough Council, like most other authorities in England at that time, used the Eleven Plus examination to select which pupils should go to grammar schools and which to more practical secondary moderns. For some years, the top boys in the city and county had attended the High School with their fees paid for them by the Council because of the belief in the value of a good education. David gained an All Saints' Scholarship to the school for 1960 as one of the two top boys in the city exam. David, therefore, can be described as an ex-public schoolboy but from a scholarship background, not one of private wealth. Once at the school he experienced a very high standard of teaching in most subjects from men who now would mostly be teaching in higher education. The classics, English, history, geography, and the

---

[3] A.W. Thomas, *A History of Nottingham High School* (Nottingham: Bell, 1958), p. 23.

religious knowledge all inspired him. Science did not. He remembers being expected to work from thick, unintelligible tomes in smelly laboratories. The values of a liberal education underlay the school curriculum. For example, the senior history master told the boys that civilized people took an interest in architecture, which set David off on many years of visiting medieval parish churches with one of the Pevsner County guides and his one-inch Ordnance Survey Map. He volunteered to work in the school library where he came across and worked with what to him remains the most ingenious system ever created for classifying knowledge, the Dewey Decimal System. Developed first in 1876, it appealed greatly to his love of ordering information. The academic standard of David's class at the school continued to be very high with a great deal of work expected. Geography and history held equal positions in his mind. He actually came top of all the pupils in the country in his examination board at Ordinary Level geography exam. But for Advanced Level he had to choose one, not both. He still maintains that they should not be separated, and likes to know the geography of the area he is studying historically whenever possible.

Nottingham provided rich resources as a background to this education. The excellent public library enabled David in later school years to browse and then borrow many of the great works of Western philosophy. The Thoroton Society, the local history group, provided him with premises to use in the city centre, a library, and regular outings to places of interest. David enjoyed these trips, undeterred by being forty years younger than the others. Plentiful public transport made it easy to get where he wanted to go, although the thick cigarette smoke put him off bus travel for half a century! When trips to parish churches started with his friend, Gordon Waller, they could easily catch trains to take them around the county and into Lincolnshire. The annual Goose Fair, held every autumn as it had been for over 700 years, provided exciting rides and stalls. David's love of Mexican jumping beans, of which he has quite a collection, started in this way! In 1963 the Nottingham Playhouse opened its impressive new building and became the theatre where many aspiring professional actors in the UK wanted to be because of the high standards of its productions. It combined classic plays with some of the more modern 'kitchen sink' type dramas which certainly raised a few eyebrows among the locals. A group of boys from the school would go to most of the productions and hone their skills of critical analysis afterwards which greatly helped David's study of Advanced Level English.

In two other ways Nottingham offered wide opportunities. The city contained shops of all shapes and sizes with impressive stores in the centre and specialist outlets further out. At the age of six, David caught a bus on his own to the stamp shop in the next suburb where he proudly purchased a Bosnia Herzegovina stamp, simply because the name intrigued him and he had then looked up the geography. (That all helped when he later studied the Balkan question as part of his Gladstone studies.) As we shall see, window shopping had been part of his life from an early age, and Nottingham provided ample opportunity. He remains an excellent shopper, unlike the stereotypical male who wishes to minimize time spent in this way. Once his secondhand book collecting started (not at home but while on holiday in Scarborough), he became a frequent visitor to Ian Cowley's bookshop which very conveniently happened to be between the High School and the bus stop. Ian taught him some early principles of book collecting. Apart from shops, the city contained a wide range of places to worship. Apart from annual visits to St Mary's Parish Church in the city centre for the Founder's Day service, David joined the school's Christian Discussion Group which, among other things, made visits to various local churches and religious places such as the Catholic Cathedral and a synagogue. Visiting speakers also came to speak to the group, and on one occasion one of them from a local Brethren assembly mentioned that he took notes on the contents and timings of services he attended. From that day David has kept written records of all the ones he has been to, apart from his own wedding, mainly because he wishes it had been done in the nineteenth century. In all these ways Nottingham gave the young schoolboy rich resources.

Local residents felt a great deal of civic pride in Nottingham which had been made a city only in 1897 at the time of Queen Victoria's diamond jubilee. They did not live in the county borough of the 'Queen of the Midlands' for nothing and tended to feel sorry for the people of nearby Leicester and Derby who did not have such an attractive place in which to live. Lace and hosiery had not turned the buildings into a dark, polluted environment such as in some of the northern mill towns. There had long been an effort to build parks and open spaces into the area partly to help the people from poor housing. In the mid-1920s, Sir Jesse Boot of Boots Chemists, donated land in the Highfields area, just over two miles south west from the centre as a site for Nottingham's civic college. He had been born in a poor area of the city, and on his father's death at the age of ten had had to help his mother run the family herbal business by collecting wildflowers and herbs from the lanes around to sell in the shop. Business had prospered over the years and he chose to give back some of his wealth to the city of his birth. Part of the Highfields site became the home of Nottingham University in 1928 with its impressive Trent building overlooking a lake, and is arguably the most attractive campus of any English university, a title which Stirling University probably holds for Scotland. Certainly Nottinghamians appreciated their University park. They were also served by excellent railway systems which could take you almost anywhere in the country. The city had been a highly desirable prize in the railway stakes of the mid-to-late nineteenth century with five railway companies competing to serve the city and the lucrative coal industry around it. In 1914, Basford parish alone had five stations, and Mellors proudly claimed that 325 passenger trains left Nottingham every day for various destinations. Occasional trains even steamed close to the Covedale Road house. The results of this train activity in Nottingham in the 1950s can lead to David having a *déjà vu* approach nowadays. The Great Central Railway came into being in 1897 when the Manchester, Sheffield, and Lincolnshire railways joined together to extend their lines through Nottingham down through Buckinghamshire and into London. Designed as the high speed rail link of its day to join Manchester, the East Midlands and London, it follows almost the same route as the HS2 system that is planned today. Sadly many of the lines that Nottingham had been so proud of in the 1950s closed in the cuts of the 1960s.

A sharp divide existed between Nottingham and its county which remains with David. He becomes irritated, for example, when the media refer to Notts Forest Football Club because Nottingham Forest is definitely the city's club (and gave David his glory days of football in 1959 when Forest won the FA Cup. Football to David has never been quite the same since then.) Notts County is definitely 'the other'. The county contains huge variety. For many centuries the royal hunting area of Sherwood Forest covered around a quarter of it, but in the seventeenth century areas of the Forest were gifted to various dukes. The area acquired the name The Dukeries and provided another place for the Bebbington family to go for a 'run out'. The Dukes of Newcastle of Clumber Park played a prominent role in the area with the first Duke in the seventeenth century having built a mansion on the site of the medieval Nottingham Castle. When David became interested later in the nineteenth-century prime minister, William Gladstone, his local knowledge of this family proved useful as the 5th Duke was Gladstone's close friend at Eton and Oxford, and persuaded his father to use his patronage to make it possible for the young Gladstone to win his first seat in Parliament. Apart from Sherwood Forest the county was famous for its coal mining which had been going on there certainly from the thirteenth century. As technology improved in the second half of the nineteenth century deeper pits were possible and more investment resulted in large numbers of pits being opened. By the time of David's childhood, when production reached its peak, the headings and coal tips formed an integral part of the landscape he saw. Even the Covedale Road house was built on a site that had been earmarked for mining by its owner but had then been sold off for building instead.

The town that David knew best in the county was Mansfield, very much in the centre of a mining area, and where his parents had their chiropody business. Why Mansfield? The First World War had put a huge strain on Alec Urquhart and family. Having registered as a conscientious objector on religious grounds, he was interned without pay in various places. Penniless at the end of the war, Alec and Clarice took the family to Mansfield, which had a lower cost of living. They turned their hand to anything to make a little money. Clarice and Vera collected roadside flowers and herbs to dry and sell, in just the same way as Jesse Boot had done. Alec took up chiropody, which required little training at that time, and they eked out a living. Several attitudes from this period of hardship remained with Vera, who later taught her son that wasting anything, especially food, should be avoided at all costs. Apart from the herb collecting, Vera started to help her father with the chiropody which became her job on leaving school. Seventeen years later when Bill came back from active service in the Second World War, he did not return to his job as chief clerk with the gas board but joined the practice, as he could not bear to leave his wife again. And so David spent a great deal of time in the surgery in Belvedere Street from the earliest age. With a high proportion of miners coming through the surgery doors, David saw for himself the foot problems that coal mining could cause. As the town had been an integral part of Sherwood Forest, stories of Robin Hood and his struggle against the Sheriff of Nottingham on behalf of the poor abounded, and David regularly was driven past sites connected to the hero, long before historians agreed that Robin Hood actually lived in South Yorkshire, something that never went down well with Vera and her neighbours!

Most of the time on Saturdays and in the holidays David had to sit and amuse himself quietly in the surgery, excellent preparation for historical research, but from the age of six he was told to go round the block to buy a 'quarter of ham' for lunch. The importance of these earliest trips to freedom should not be underestimated. A year later, and by then allowed to go anywhere in the town centre, he learned to spend hours in the shops without spending much money. The market provided a constant source of interest for him with Dutch auctions carried on loudly in which vendors would attract a crowd of (usually) female shoppers and try to persuade them to take advantage of apparently rock-bottom prices. The general store of Woolworths (sadly now closed) became the site of his first independent research when David decided to find out who manufactured the different washing powders on sale. He remembers being surprised to find that Procter and Gamble had a near monopoly. The town at that time had wonderful alleyways and buildings which David came to love. Sadly, many of these disappeared in the 1960s when town developers tended to build straight through ancient town centres. David remains a largely urban person, never happier than when he has a new town to explore, preferably with lots of alleyways, and these days, of course, with a secondhand bookshop. This has all come from his experiences in Mansfield.

The county and its neighbours provided a wealth of opportunities for 'day trips'. Bill and Vera had only a few days holiday a year but these became very important to their son especially when school work caused him pressure. He very soon used Ordnance Survey one-inch maps efficiently and the rhythm of Monday bank holidays during the year came to represent freedom and excitement in what was otherwise a hard, serious life. To start with the family would go on well-known routes, such as into Derbyshire, but gradually David took them further afield until anywhere within a day's journey could be visited. There were exceptions, with Birmingham and its built-up area not considered a suitable destination. Bill and Vera organized a two-week family holiday each summer for their young son, but gradually David took over planning the days' activities, thinking up quite demanding schedules of historical buildings of all sorts to visit. These events assumed huge importance in his life. Nottingham's central position within reach of so many other places assisted this widening of his horizons. Now he travels globally, but it all started in his local area. He still likes to use the maps he used then, often 'last revised in 1958' or even earlier, because they show old chapels and other historical features. Fortunately he does make the concession of using a modern road atlas as well, but certainly not a 'sat nav'. He still gets excited when he can plan 'a trip', however small.

Much of David's life has been spent exploring and thinking about history. What then has been Nottingham's specific legacy to this? It provided him at the age of nine with a rich background when he became interested for his primary school project which led to him writing his first book. By the time he arrived at the High

School at eleven, he already had the story of the city's development in his head. As he went through the British history curriculum in the next seven years, local examples could usually be found which gave a close connection to any subject. For example, the knowledge that Richard III marched out from Nottingham Castle to his death at the Battle of Bosworth in 1485 provided a direct link to the Wars of the Roses. Again, the study of the Civil War of the seventeenth century came alive when the schoolboy knew that Charles I had raised his standard in 1642 to declare war on Parliament on Standard Hill, just near the local general hospital. He was even aware of the huge tension of both sides in that war because of the bravery of Colonel Hutchinson, of Baptist fame, who resolutely refused to hand over his castle to the Royalists despite huge bribes being offered. History came alive in the local context. In his final year at school Queensberry Street Baptist Church provided an excellent body of material which gave him the opportunity to try his hand at local history with its pitfalls and risks.

Once he was reading history at Cambridge, local examples from Nottingham enabled him to consider wider issues rather than simply trying to come to terms with what happened. When studying the medieval period, for example, his awareness of fourteenth- and fifteenth-century Nottingham alabaster that had gone to help decorate churches and private chapels all over Europe, gave him a head start in understanding. Again, in nineteenth-century studies, the Enclosure Act of 1845 could have seemed remote, but David already knew how Nottingham had been effectively strangled by reluctance and refusal to enclose the common land around it. In the industrial boom of the later nineteenth century this had led to huge increases of workers being squeezed into the same small area of land which inevitably led to slums. Enclosure had been highly relevant to his own parish of Basford which had gradually spread out along the Mansfield Road and into Sherwood itself as parts of the forest became added to the town. And so David's own very large parish illustrated the significance of enclosure. Different patterns of town development lay all around him. Arnold, the next parish, had contained large numbers of cottage workers with specialist craftsmen. Basford itself had been a typical village that had been swallowed up in industrialization.

Why then did David not become a specialist in a particular genre of history, such as social or political or the Tudors, which can be said to be more fashionable? His immersion in the many facets of Nottingham's history made him realize that history cannot be neatly divided into different strands. One period illustrates this well. The Luddite Riots began in the city early in the nineteenth century when desperate stockingers took to violence in protest against cuts in wages and the use of unskilled labour during the painful transition from the use of home-based, skilled craftsmen to mass production. Basford saw some serious violence and anger at the stocking frame owners at this time; there was even a fatal shooting. From this example alone, David would have realised the impossibility of separating the strands. The starvation and widespread destitution of the workers and their families highlighted the social dimension of the struggle between workers and owners of the stocking frames. Politically, the whole hosiery industry suffered from the effects of the war with

France. The need for profit and market issues meant that economics certainly impinged on the debate, and David would claim that religious elements always had relevance, as in any period. How could he work in just one of these areas when from such an early age he had realised the integrated wholeness of history? When he became excited at Cambridge about the history of ideas, political thought, and how widespread movements such as Romanticism and the Enlightenment could affect views of history, he launched into big topics. His 1979 *Patterns in History*, in which he traced various views of the historical process, could have been thought ambitious for a young man.[4] Since then he has worked on Baptist history, starting with the local study of Queensberry Street[5] to national[6] and then to global,[7] as well as on the evangelical movement which he first experienced in Nottingham and then studied it nationally[8] and globally.[9] Never one to follow the crowd, he has gradually developed his own particular historical blend, his 'macro/micro' sort of history where he traces the big ideas in the minutiae of daily events so that, for example, in any one area, the playing out of world movements can be seen in the interactions in a debate in one particular church. *Victorian Religious Revivals* is where he succeeds most in blending the macro and micro history with his geographical understanding.[10] This has only been possible for him because of the grounding in all periods of history that Nottingham gave him.

David remains interested in the area, but does not often revisit, feeling that he has more in common with the city of the 1950s than that of the present day where business and commercialism are so to the forefront. He updates his large collection of local books from time to time, keen as always to learn more. He has recently bought two books, one on Roman remains in the county which are far more widespread than he learned at school, and the other on the attempts to drill oil in

---

[4] David Bebbington, *Patterns in History* (Leicester: Inter-Varsity Press, 1979), a second edition of which appeared as *Patterns in History: A Christian Perspective* (Leicester: Apollos, 2nd edn, 1990).

[5] D.W. Bebbington, *A History of Queensberry Street Baptist Church, Old Basford Nottingham, 1877–1977* (Nottingham: For the Church, 1977).

[6] E.g., D.W. Bebbington (ed.), *The Baptists in Scotland: A History* (Glasgow: The Baptist Union of Scotland, 1988).

[7] David W. Bebbington, *Baptists Through the Centuries: A History of a Global People* (Waco, TX: Baylor University Press, 2010). See also his D.W. Bebbington (ed.), *The Gospel in the World: International Baptist Studies* (Studies in Baptist History and Thought, 1; Carlisle: Paternoster Press, 2002).

[8] D.W. Bebbington, *Evangelicalism in Modern Britain: A History from the 1730s to the 1980s* (London: Unwin Hyman, 1989), and David W. Bebbington, *The Dominance of Evangelicalism: The Age of Spurgeon and Moody* (Downers Grove, IL: InterVarsity Press, 2005).

[9] Mark A. Noll, David W. Bebbington, and George A. Rawlyk (eds), *Evangelicalism: Comparative Studies of Popular Protestantism in North America, The British Isles, and Beyond, 1700–1990* (Oxford: Oxford University Press, 1994).

[10] David Bebbington, *Victorian Religious Revivals: Culture and Piety in Local and Global Contexts* (Oxford: Oxford University Press, 2012).

Sherwood Forest during the Second World War. He had been told about that happening by his parents, but had never read about it. The Second World War did not feature largely in his early historical studies as it had been so recent. Stories of his father's experiences in the army in the Far East formed part of ordinary life. Only later did he recognize them as oral history. He still keeps an eye on where Nottingham Forest Football Club is in the FA league. David had the thirst for organizing and shaping information from the earliest years. Nottingham supplied the essential early material for him to start his large-scale historical explorations which he still pursues with application and enthusiasm. The 'Queen of the Midlands' has served him well.[11]

---

[11] See also Eileen Bebbington, *A Patterned Life: Faith, History, and David Bebbington* (Eugene, OR: Wipf and Stock, 2014). For additional background information on Nottingham: with special reference to Boots, see John Beckett, *A Centenary History of Nottingham* (Chichester: Phillimore, 2006); on local history, see Robert Mellors, *In and About Nottinghamshire: A Book for the Young Men and Women of the City and County* (Nottingham: J. & H. Bell, 1908); and for the railways, see Chris Weir, *The Nottinghamshire Heritage* (Chichester: Phillimore, 1991).

Baptist Studies

CHAPTER 2

Performing Religious Nonconformity: Conversion, Debate and the Republic of Letters

Alison Searle

This essay sets out a methodology for exploring the performance of religious nonconformity in seventeenth-century England. Two case studies from the Interregnum that are connected to some of the earliest congregations of open-communion Baptists enable this theoretical premise to be fleshed out. The first examines how M.K. (a prominent member of a separatist congregation in London) performed and narrated her conversion, and its parallels with the popular dramatic genre of tragicomedy. The second explores the performance of a personal and public debate about infant baptism and the right to church membership between Richard Baxter and the Baptist, John Tombes, conducted through the exchange of letters, sermons, and a formal dispute before both their congregations in the parish church at Bewdley. The ways in which M.K., Baxter and Tombes construed themselves as actors, the variegated responses of their contemporary audiences, and the key role these events and transcripts played in subsequent debates about authority, conversion, and the semiotics of belief reveal important aspects about how religious separatism and nonconformity were performed in England.

Towards a Methodology of Performance

The stereotypical puritan or nonconformist was a familiar figure on the English stage from the late sixteenth century. Kristen Poole has demonstrated that far from being the strict and grave figure of later popular and scholarly constructions the stage puritan was, in fact, a licentious character associated with carnival. Poole's monograph covers the period from the late 1580s to the 1660s and offers a crucial revisionary account of the ways in which nonconformity was performed. She contextualises canonical dramatic works and poems by Shakespeare, Jonson and Milton in debates played out in the wider culture through pamphlet literature.[1] Anne Dunan notes that while Poole 'abundantly justifies' her use of puritan, her deployment of nonconformist also used 'to describe sectarians goes almost without explanation. Surely there is ground for thinking that the non-separatist puritan

---

[1] Kristen Poole, *Radical Religion from Shakespeare to Milton: Figures of Nonconformity in Early Modern England* (Cambridge: Cambridge University Press, 2000).

movement is "nonconformist" from a very early date'.² I think Dunan is correct and I use 'nonconformist' in this broader sense here. Such nonconformists were by no means inimical to deploying the metaphor of performance themselves. John Bunyan, for example, imagined

> that a man when he suffereth for Christ, is set upon a *Hill*, upon a *Stage*, as in a *Theater*, to play a part for God in the World. And you know when men are to play their parts upon a Stage, they count themselves, if possible, more bound to circumspection; and *that* for the credit of their Master, the credit of their *Art*, and the credit of *themselves*. For then the eyes of everybody are fixed, they gape and stare upon them. (Ps. 22.17.) and a *trip* here, is as bad as a fall in another place. Also now God himself looks on. Yea, he laugheth, as being pleased to see a good behaviour attending the tryal of the innocent.³

There is also biblical precedent for exploring the experience of suffering Christians through analogical reference to the theatre. Paul writes in his first letter to the church at Corinth (1 Cor. 4.9) that the apostles had become a $\theta\acute{\epsilon}\alpha\tau\rho\text{ov}$ – spectacle, play or theatre – displayed by God to the world, angels and humans. In this formulation, however, God is the director rather than a member of the audience. Similarly, the Epistle to the Hebrews refers to the past experience of its recipients as 'being publicly exposed to reproach and persecution' or more literally 'being exposed in the theatre' (Heb. 10.33).⁴ Understanding themselves as spectacles of suffering was an integral component of nonconformist religious identity in seventeenth-century Britain. The Cavalier Parliament's decision to criminalise corporate nonconformist worship, teaching and print publication transformed even their quotidian religious practice into a political performance and positioned individuals and congregations on a complex continuum between public spectacle and potent sign depending on the attitude of their audience.

Katherine Gillespie explores the important contribution made by nonconformist female prophets to the politics of this period and how these women shaped the cultures of their congregations, local communities and wider networks of influence. She appropriates the language of drama briefly at the beginning of her study modelling a constructive approach for integrating the way in which religious nonconformity was practised within a wider culture of performance in early modern England.

---

[2] Anne Dunan, Review of Poole, Kristen, *Radical Religion from Shakespeare to Milton: Figures of Nonconformity in Early Modern England*, H-Albion, H-Net Reviews, May, 2001: http://www.h-net.org/reviews/showrev.php?id=5116.

[3] John Bunyan, *Seasonable Counsel: or, Advice to Sufferers* (London: Printed for Benjamin Alsop, at the Angel and Bible in the Poultry, 1684), p. 130 (italics original).

[4] For further reflection on this, see Alison Searle, 'Conversion, Incarnation, Performance: Theology and the Future of Imagination', in Trevor Cairney and David Starling (eds), *Theology and the Future: Evangelical Assertions and Explorations* (London: Bloomsbury, 2014), pp. 197-212.

It is possible, then, to say that some of the most compelling drama of the age lay even further outside the Whitehall theatre than did the Earl of Bridgewater's Ludlow Castle. While Milton may have transferred the 'ideal masque world' and its intrinsic project of religious 'reformation' away from the stage-managed gambols of Charles I and his heavenly consort, Henrietta Maria, and on to the perilous pilgrimages of the Protestant elite, self-baptizing sectarians from the lower and middle orders widened this 'disjunction' even further by assuming for themselves the elite aristocratic, religio-mythological, and 'sovereign' roles of Heroic Virtue and Divine Grace.[5]

Separatists and later nonconformists often used the language of performance in a pejorative sense, to indict members of the Church of England for their unbiblical rituals and, by extension, for their unspiritual worship. The theatre provided a cultural analogy for such charges of hypocrisy and this also lies behind the distrust that some had towards the various London playhouses. However, as Katharine Eisaman Maus has demonstrated, an acute awareness of the potential disjunction between internal truth and its external manifestation, and the suspicion this generated, was shared by individuals in all sectors of early modern English society, regardless of their attitude to church ceremonies.

> For the English Renaissance, it is a commonplace that spectacle depends upon, sometimes betrays, but never fully manifests a truth that remains shrouded, indiscernible, or ambiguous. The period's social and religious upheavals arguably provoke a keen, apparently nearly universal suspicion of 'appearances.' Whatever the origins of this distrust, it produces a distinctive way of thinking about human subjectivity that emphasizes the disparity between what a person is and what he or she seems to be to other people ... The frank fakeries of the playhouse, its disguisings and impersonations, stand for the opacities that seem to characterize all relations of human beings to one another.[6]

The concept of performance allows one to explore these inter-relationships between the personal and the public, the interior and exterior, whether they manifest themselves in daily life, or in more specifically defined cultural spaces such as the pulpit or stage. It is not particularly innovative to suggest that methodologies developed in performance studies can be productively applied to the historical

---

[5] Katherine Gillespie, *Domesticity and Dissent in the Seventeenth Century: English Women Writers and the Public Sphere* (Cambridge: Cambridge University Press, 2004), p. 5.

[6] Katharine Eisaman Maus, *Inwardness and Theater in the English Renaissance* (Chicago, IL: The University of Chicago Press, 1995), pp. 210 and 1-2. As Nancy Selleck has noted, the 'psychophysiology of acting must to some extent qualify our sense' of these 'frank fakeries'. 'Certainly Maus is right that the problem of knowing others preoccupies early modern writers, but so does the humorally based, outside-in shaping of identity, which leaves the actor (both on and off the stage) less discrete and self-contained, and more open to the interpersonal environment through the process of his action'. *The Interpersonal Idiom in Shakespeare, Donne and Early Modern Culture* (Basingstoke: Palgrave Macmillan, 2008), p. 64.

analysis of preachers and their congregations; even less so when attempting to reconstruct the performance of plays and audience responses in early modern theatres such as the Globe or the Rose.[7] However, while attention has been paid to canonical preachers such as John Donne or Lancelot Andrewes, and to a lesser extent to the female preachers from the Civil War and Interregnum, very little work has been done on the performance of nonconformity across a range of sects and performance spaces in seventeenth-century Britain.[8] This section sketches out a methodological approach that enables a cross-cultural analysis of religious nonconformity and theatrical performance including their mutual intersections, conflicts and transformations.[9]

The disciplines of performance studies and cultural anthropology offer a range of theoretical approaches to the diverse phenomena under consideration. My method here draws on the sociologist Erving Goffman, literary critics including Kenneth Burke and Nicholas Watson, performance studies theoretician W.B. Worthern, and feminist philosopher, Kelly Oliver. Burke sees 'literature as equipment for living' and begins with a basic question: 'What is involved, when we say what people are doing and why they are doing it?' He elaborates this as follows:

> We shall use five terms as generating principle of our investigation. They are: Act, Scene, Agent, Agency, Purpose. In a rounded statement about motives, you must have some word that names the *act* (names what took place, in thought or deed), and another that names the *scene* (the background of the act, the situation in which it occurred), also, you must indicate what person or kind of person (*agent*) performed the act, what

---

[7] See Kate Armstrong, 'Sermons in Performance', in Peter McCullough, Hugh Adlington and Emma Rhatigan (eds), *The Oxford Handbook of the Early Modern Sermon* (Oxford: Oxford University Press, 2011), pp. 120-36. Armstrong notes, p. 134, 'We should be careful in describing Jacobean preaching as "theatrical". It is, however, indubitable that sermons and plays or masques shared the quality of being performed. Indeed ... during Lent sermons replaced plays as the public events to which Londoners swarmed'. Similarly, in her analysis of church architecture, Emma Rhatigan, 'Preaching Venues: Architecture and Auditories', in McCullough, Adlington and Rhatigan (eds), *Oxford Handbook of the Early Modern Sermon*, p. 92, observes, 'Above all, however, these pulpits were stages, providing an opportunity for sometimes histrionic and emotive performances, as exploited, for example, by John Rogers of Dedham, who was described as "taking hold of the supporters of the canopy over the pulpit with both hands at one time and roaring hideously, to represent the torments of the damned"'.

[8] The importance of the concept of 'sacred space' to the experience of worship, the formation of religious identities and the ways in which the natural landscape is interpreted has been explored in Will Coster and Andrew Spicer (eds), *Sacred Space in Early Modern Europe* (Cambridge: Cambridge University Press, 2005), and Alexandra Walsham, *The Reformation of the Landscape: Religion, Identity, and Memory in Early Modern Britain and Ireland* (Oxford: Oxford University Press, 2011).

[9] This represents a preliminary attempt to outline the methodological approach that informs my current research project *Performing Religious Nonconformity in Britain (c. 1620–1680)*. My thinking to date has been enriched by discussions with Professor Eugene Giddens, Dr Susannah Macready, and Dr Penelope Woods; its limitations are mine alone.

means or instruments he used (*agency*), and the *purpose* ... [A]ny complete statement about motives will offer *some kind of* answers to these five questions: what was done (act), when or where it was done (scene), who did it (agent), how he did it (agency), and why (purpose).[10]

Burke's concept of performance can be applied to daily events, to reconstructions of historical occurrences and to performances of fictional texts. The practical simplicity of his model means that it can be used to illumine the range of spaces and cultural contexts that I wish to explore. W.B. Worthern has further developed Burke's terms to define *dramatic* performance, which, as he notes, 'implies two scenes of acting, the fictive world it represents and the material scene of the theatre'.

Dramatic performance might be captured as a double *pentad*, layering dramatic action on its theatrical motives, as a fictive/material *scene* in which character/actor *agents*, through the *agency* afforded by the material of the play and by the specific regimes of actor training, involve us (watching both the play and the playing), in the duplicitous *purposes* of the particularly ambiguous *act* of dramatic performance ... [T]he redoubling of the [theatrical] *scene* is what enables fictive words to *do things* as part of our *cultural equipment for living* ... performance is 'constitutive,' remaking the rules and meaning of action anew.[11]

Though I do not focus in detail here on the double pentad that Worthern postulates, he offers a necessary critical extension of Burke's thought that allows one to deal with the particular ambiguities introduced by dramatic performance.[12]

The sociologist, Erving Goffman, in his classic study *The Presentation of the Self in Everyday Life* (1959), effectively collapses this distinction by utilising a dramaturgical model in order to understand mundane human interaction and socialisation. Of particular interest in the light of Maus' comment above about early modern England's almost universal distrust of appearances is Goffman's discussion of 'misrepresentation'. He defines 'performance' as 'all the activity of a given participant on a given occasion which serves to influence in any way any of the other participants'. Goffman notes that the 'common-sense view' that 'a patent act of misrepresentation' is something 'an honest performer is able to avoid ... has limited analytical utility'. This is, in part, because the 'social definition of impersonation ... is not itself a very consistent thing'.[13] Goffman offers a way to deal with the

---

[10] Cited by W.B. Worthern, *Drama: Between Poetry and Performance* (Oxford: Wiley-Blackwell, 2010), pp. 23-24 (italics original).

[11] Worthern, *Drama*, pp. 24-25 (italics original)..

[12] Max Harris, *Theatre and Incarnation* (Basingstoke: Macmillan, 1990), *passim*, has argued that theatre, of all the arts, best explicates God's own chosen mode of self-revelation in the incarnation – the Word made flesh. This affinity between theology and performance also informs my theoretical approach; the two spheres are capable of mutually illuminating one another at the levels of historical praxis and theoretical reflection.

[13] Erving Goffman, *The Presentation of the Self in Everyday Life* (New York, NY: Anchor Books, 1959), pp. 15 and 59.

complications introduced by charges of 'hypocrisy' directed at nonconformists – this could be a self-indictment, through scrupulous examination of one's heart, or a criticism levelled by opponents at sectarian thought and practice – by demonstrating its irrelevance in analytical terms. Goffman's development of dramaturgical performance as a critical approach to social interaction also allows a combination of 'fictional' and 'factual' sources to be used when reconstructing the past.

> While we could retain the common-sense notion that fostered appearances can be discredited by a discrepant reality, there is often no reason for claiming that the facts discrepant with the fostered impression are any more real than is the fostered reality they embarrass. A cynical view of everyday performances can be as one-sided as the one that is sponsored by the performer ... Whether an honest performer wishes to convey the truth or whether a dishonest performer wishes to convey a falsehood, both must take care to enliven their performances with appropriate expressions, exclude from their performances expressions that might discredit the impression being fostered, and take care lest the audience impute unintended meanings. Because of the shared dramatic contingencies, we can profitably study performances that are quite false in order to learn about ones that are quite honest.[14]

This means that questions of an historical or fictional actor's actual motivation or degree of authenticity in a particular performance or narration – in theological terms a searching account of whether or not they are hypocrites – can be bracketed in order to focus on how that performance is embodied, mediated or narrated by surviving textual and material artefacts. It is, of course, necessary to acknowledge the distinctive rhetorical, generic and material characteristics of each artefact and the unique ways in which it encodes the past. Worthern's development of Burke's initial pentad is thus critical to facilitating certain analyses of texts and performances, such as identifying the difference between the fictional world proposed by a play-text from the kind of truth-claims embodied in the transcription of a court-hearing, for example.

The context that we create in order to understand and interpret these historical artefacts is inevitably subjective.[15] Nicholas Watson has explored both the dangers and potential that lie in our desire for the past as scholars. He notes that we must account for the inescapable role played by affect and emotion in the way we choose a period to focus on, the selection of sources that we make and how we engage with and represent the past in our work. Watson outlines a hermeneutic that is indebted to medieval female mystics such as Julian of Norwich and maintains a careful balance between empathy and suspicion. The historian or literary critic is consequently able to reconstruct the past with a self-reflexive awareness of the role their own

---

[14] Goffman, *Presentation of the Self*, pp. 65-66.

[15] Frances E. Dolan, *True Relations: Reading, Literature and Evidence in Seventeenth-Century England* (Philadelphia, PA: University of Pennsylvania Press, 2013), and Robert D. Hume, *Reconstructing Contexts: The Aims and Principles of Archaeo-Historicism* (Oxford: Oxford University Press, 1999).

intellectual and emotional engagement plays. Combining empathy with suspicion creates space for an ethics of care that helps to prevent an over-identification of self with other and enriches the concept of experience.[16] Kelly Oliver's insistence on the importance of looking at the other with a critical and loving eye helps to give stronger theoretical weight to Watson's hermeneutic of empathy and suspicion. Oliver transforms the role of the spectator/subject by replacing the concept of 'recognition' (identifying with the other by recognising their sameness with oneself) with 'witness' and 'testimony'. Through witnessing the subjectivity of the other is not objectified but rather incorporated inter-subjectively into the experience and fabric of one's being as one bears testimony to the invisible in narrative form.[17] Empathy, suspicion, witness and testimony critically shape the ways in which I approach trans-historical others through the textual and material traces of the past that remain. These concepts also impact how I reconstruct the role of spectators in the early modern period and represent the inter-subjective relationships established, for example, between speaker and congregation, writer and reader, actors and audience.

M.K. and the 'comicall Tragedy, or ... tragical Comedy' of Her Conversion Experience

In 1653 Henry Walker and Robert Ibbotson printed and distributed a seminal collection of conversion narratives.[18] Vavasor Powell, the well-known Welsh political radical and Baptist preacher, introduced these. It is not clear whether the group represented by this collection of testimonies was explicitly Baptist or not; nor is it certain that they had yet been properly constituted as a separatist congregation. However, their church polity – clearly outlined in a series of articles appended to the collection – along with the choice of endorser, positions them amongst the radical separatists and this could be tentatively narrowed further to a possible identification as open-communion Baptists. The earliest extant copies are designated as a second edition of the text and contain a group of several lengthier, dramatic narratives, followed by a more pro-forma collection of additional testimonies. I focus here on the longest narration of a believer's 'experiences', that of M.K., at the end of the first group. Powell defines experience in affective terms as one of the chief ways in which God teaches the believer:

> for that is the inward sense and feeling, of what is outwardly read and heard; and the spirituall and powerfull enjoyment of what is believed. *Experience* is a Copy written by the Spirit of God upon the hearts of beleevers. It is one of *Faiths* handmaids and

---

[16] Nicholas Watson, 'Desire for the Past/Afterword', in Louise D'Arcens and Juanita Ruys (eds), *Maistresse of My Wit* (Turnhout: Brepols, 2004), pp. 149-88.

[17] Kelly Oliver, *Witnessing: Beyond Recognition* (Minneapolis, MN: University of Minnesota Press, 2001).

[18] Kathleen Lynch, *Protestant Autobiography in the Seventeenth-Century Anglophone World* (Oxford: Oxford University Press, 2012), pp. 136-40.

attendants, and *Hopes* usher, Rom. 5.3 ... Experience is like steel to an edged tool, or like salt to fresh meat, it seasons brain-knowledge, and settles a shaking unsetled soule.[19]

M.K. begins the relation of her experiences with a rather unusual analogy for a separatist. 'When I take a view of my life upon the stage of this world, I may very well compare it to a comicall Tragedy, or a tragical Comedy, or a labyrinth from one sin to another, from one affliction to another'.[20] Theatrical performance and, in particular, the popular genre of tragi-comedy thus becomes part of the language of self-description used by a female separatist in an attempt to communicate her experience as a follower of Jesus Christ in seventeenth-century England. The presentation of oral or written testimonies was a standard part of the membership process for joining a gathered church. Some such occasion was probably the catalyst for the preparation of M.K.'s narrative, though the circumstances remain rather obscure, and the only clear markers of congregational affiliation are provided by the endorsement of Powell and the fact that Walker and Ibbotson published the collection. Kathleen Lynch argues further that M.K.'s testimony

> is a stirring performance, and a reminder of the central role women played in the radical churches ... [T]he confidence, the mastery of the form, and the drama of the story all point to her leadership within the congregation. If this were the narrative of a man, it would surely serve as a coming-out piece, the narrative whereby one demonstrated extraordinary gifts of the spirit, leading to election as a minister ...[21]

As no other congregant appears to have taken this role formally, it is possible that ministerial responsibilities were fulfilled informally by M.K. In a forthcoming study Rachel Adcock has shown the central role women played in the earliest Particular Baptist congregations, often justifying their leadership on the basis of the absence of qualified men and publishing their prophecies, exhortations and vindications when they were unable to present these orally before their churches.[22]

M.K.'s experiences form a tight and carefully structured narrative. She was brought up by godly parents, the favourite child (amongst twelve) of her mother, who 'tooke great delight to instruct me, to heare me read, and ask her questions. She alotted me a portion of Scripture every day, as likewise a part of *Erasmus Rotterdamus* upon the foure Evangelists'.[23] When she was twelve, her mother died, and M.K. marks this as the beginning of her spiritual downfall. Proud at her sudden

---

[19] Vavasor Powell, 'To the Sober and Spirituall Readers of this Booke', in *Spirituall Experiences, of sundry Beleevers* (London: Printed for Robert Ibbitson, 1653), A2^r-A3^v (italics original).

[20] M.K., *Spirituall Experiences*, pp. 160-61.

[21] Lynch, *Protestant Autobiography*, pp. 135-36.

[22] Rachel Adcock, *Baptist Women's Writings in Revolutionary Culture, 1640–1680* (forthcoming with Ashgate). I am grateful to Dr Adcock for allowing me to access her research in manuscript prior to publication.

[23] M.K., *Spirituall Experiences*, p. 161 (italics original).

accession to the status of housekeeper (mother of ten children, and mistress of six servants), she became 'cumbred about many things' (an allusion to the biblical Martha, Luke 10.40) until the death of her father seven years later. This precipitated a spiritual crisis and she believed that her sins of omission were the cause of her father's death. M.K.'s 'excessive sorrow' eventually wearied her friends and they sent her to London with the persuasion that 'the word of God was more plentifully preached there'. She spent three and a half years with the family of the minister, Dr Page, and 'received great comfort'. She then married Page's son and they set up house in Westminster on the proceeds of his inheritance following his father's death. However, rather than taking 'some honest course for a livelihood' as they had planned, they fell into 'company which did not onely cause much time to be spent in idleness, but also almost all our meanes'. Failing to persuade her husband to leave off the company of the man whose influence she most feared, M.K. decided to murder him. In a dream, however, God assured her *'Vengeance is mine'* and she responded biblically: *'And thou wilt repay, O Lord'* (Romans 12.19). This time of backsliding precipitated another intense period of soul-searching. She was convinced that she had broken all of the Ten Commandments, due to her thought-sins, and had sinned in omission by neglecting to pray for her enemies, feed the hungry, clothe the naked and love others.[24]

M.K.'s spiritual despair led to intellectual doubts about the truth of scripture and the existence of God. The torment induced almost broke her: 'I spent many dayes and nights in teares, and sighes, and groanes'. She reached crisis point when she thought a little dog leaping into her bed at night was the devil come to take her to hell. Realising it was just a dog, the sudden shift in perspective caused her to conclude, 'That *surely there was a God that had preserved me all this while*. In a most grevious agony I spent that night weeping, and although it was Winter, yet I sweat that the water ranne from off every part of my body'. Early in the morning she went to the top of the house. Noting that the birds and trees could not have made themselves, she concluded that there must be a God. Falling down and asking forgiveness, she still saw the Lord looking on her with a frowning countenance; this precipitated a period of attempting to earn God's favour. M.K. comments in an aside that demonstrates her awareness of an audience for her testimony: 'But now, I beseech you godly Christians, to take notice of the wonderfull workings of our good God'. This marks the entry of the 'very godly and reverend Divine', Mr Dod. M.K. is probably referring here to the eminent puritan and semi-separatist, John Dod, well known for his skill in casuistry and his exposition of the Ten Commandments.[25] Dod's sermons and counsel may have retrospectively informed M.K.'s own acute sense of both sins of omission and thought-sins against the moral law. She comments, 'for this Minister did not onely preach to the people, but shewed me as it

---

[24] M.K., *Spirituall Experiences*, pp. 161-72.

[25] J. Fielding, 'Dod, John (1550–1645)', *Oxford Dictionary of National Biography*, Oxford University Press, 2004; online edn, Jan 2008, http://www.oxforddnb.com/view/article/7729, accessed 28 June 2012.

were in a looking-glasse mine owne condition ... but after he was sensible of my condition, which I made knowne to him privately, he was very laborious to bring my soule out of the jawes of death, and to raise it to Jesus Christ'. Trusting again in the word of God, she began to search the scriptures. Ultimately, reading John, she gained comfort in an assurance of God's love: 'In the seventeenth of *John*, I heare [Jesus] praying to his Father for mee, whose request I am confident shall not be denied'. The testimony ends with a strong personal assurance of her interest in the saving grace of Christ. She communicates this by providing a visceral cameo of the crucifixion and listing nine marks that demonstrate her regeneration through the work of the Holy Spirit.[26]

Owen Watkins and Kathleen Lynch have considered M.K.'s testimony in detail in terms of the developing genre of puritan autobiography and its significance as a seminal publishing venture in seventeenth-century Anglophone Atlantic culture.[27] I wish to analyse her account from a different angle. The contents of her conversion narrative have been set out here at length because I think M.K.'s self-identification of its genre as a 'comicall Tragedy, or a tragical Comedy' is significant. M.K.'s testimony demonstrates her literacy and her awareness of generic conventions. She was probably reading Erasmus daily at the age of seven with her mother. Tragicomedy was one of the most popular dramatic genres in London during the 1630s and 1640s and, even though she does not record it here, it is entirely plausible that M.K. and her husband attended one or more performances of such plays when, during her early twenties, she was living (according to her own account) in idleness and extravagance in Westminster.

M.K.'s testimony was part of the first collection of conversion narratives to be published in England. This published exemplar was obviously shaped by the oral culture of presenting testimonies in separatist congregations and in many ways by the multiple sermons that M.K. listened to on a weekly basis. Yet it is also important not to overlook other extant literary models, especially for a narrative as complex and in some ways as carefully crafted as M.K.'s. I suggest that she found one in the turns and counter-turns of the dramatic plots of the tragicomedies performed in London during the period when she was experiencing her spiritual journey as a 'labyrinth from one sin to another, from one affliction to another', precisely as did the heroines of plays by James Shirley, William Beaumont and John Fletcher.[28] Literary critics have commented on the affinities of this genre with theological concerns. Michael Neill argues that the 'conventional "turn and counter-turn" of tragicomic design' can be linked to the 'drama of apostasy and conversion' that reflects tensions between Calvinism and Arminianism in the 1630s. Indeed, M.K. writes of how 'my God did not onely make a scourge of small cords, and whipped out the buyers and sellers, but

---

[26] M.K., *Spirituall Experiences*, pp. 172-91 (italics original).

[27] Owen Watkins, *The Puritan Experience* (London: Routledge & Kegan Paul, 1972), p. 43; Lynch, *Protestant Autobiography*, pp. 134-36.

[28] Beaumont and Fletcher's plays were published in an impressive folio edition in 1647 with a foreword by Shirley.

he did over-turn, and over-turne, and over-turne' and 'knocked many times at the door of [her] heart'.²⁹ Bryan Crockett, similarly, suggests that Shakespeare's 'problem' play, *Measure for Measure*, is resolved through 'the audience's acceptance of a paradox: since all human beings, including the audience members, are simultaneously liable to judgment and offered mercy, the only appropriate response is a sense of mercy that paradoxically subsumes judgment'.³⁰ Unsurprisingly, this is precisely how M.K.'s narrative concludes.

Susannah Brietz Monta has articulated the critical position that tragicomedy demands of its audience in her reflections on *The Winter's Tale*.

> The play proposes, then, that a mix of belief and incredulity, faith and doubt, commitment and distance, most properly characterize audience reception of theatrical wonders. We are asked to mingle faith with metadramatic awareness of theatrical trickery, to believe with full awareness and even provocation of doubt in theatrical fiction. If my reading has merit, then the play's insistence that religion and theater are not in opposition that 'faith' and belief in theatrical fiction may be as nuanced as discourses concerning religious faith, constitutes the defense the play mounts of its own dramatic fiction.³¹

This mix of faith and doubt, commitment and distance is equally characteristic of M.K.'s account of her relationship with God, scripture and divine revelation through providence and dreams, and helps to account for why she selected the genre of tragicomedy as an analogue or metaphor for her conversion narrative. During the early 1640s, when Parliament was 'inactive, London theatres constituted alternative spaces and talking-shops for ideas':³² the genre of tragicomedy may be at least partially responsible for the literary shape and rhetorical strategies of the key narrative in the first collection of testimonies published by a gathered congregation in England. As Lynch points out, these diverse individuals met at Somerset House, itself a trophy of the Civil War, 'for reconstitution as an entirely different body politic', indicating the profound nature of the cultural and political upheavals that had occurred during the previous decade.³³

---

²⁹ Michael Neill, 'Turn and Counterturn: Merchanting, Apostasy and Tragicomic Form in Massinger's *The Renegade*', in Subha Mukherji and Raphael Lyne (eds), *Early Modern Tragicomedy* (Woodbridge: Boydell and Brewer, 2007), p. 174. M.K., *Spiritual Experiences*, pp. 177-78.

³⁰ Bryan Crockett, *The Play of Paradox: Stage and Sermon in Renaissance England* (Philadelphia, PA: University of Pennsylvania Press, 1995), p. 113.

³¹ Susannah Brietz Monta, '"It is requir'd you do awake your faith": Belief in Shakespeare's Theater', in Jane Hwang Degenhardt and Elizabeth Williamson (eds), *Religion and Drama in Early Modern England: The Performance of Religion on the Renaissance Stage* (Farnham: Ashgate, 2011), p. 137.

³² Julie Sanders, 'Beggars' Commonwealths and the Pre-Civil War Stage: Suckling's *The Goblins*, Brome's *A Jovial Crew*, and Shirley's *The Sisters*', *The Modern Language Review* 97.1 (2002), pp. 1-14 (p. 4).

³³ Lynch, *Protestant Autobiography*, p. 140.

Richard Baxter and John Tombes: Public Debate and the Republic of Letters

My second case study examines Richard Baxter's correspondence and public debate with the Baptist, John Tombes. It highlights the significance of the letter, generically, textually and materially, in creating and maintaining an epistolary community that was by turns, spiritually nourishing, intellectually curious, inherently disputatious, persecuted and fissured, but irrevocably and influentially literate. Neil Keeble and Geoffrey Nuttall have noted that the 'letters hold a curious position' in Baxter's debates about ecclesiology:

> They often refer to, and continue or are interrupted by, oral debates; they equally often refer to, and continue or are interrupted by, printed animadversions ... Such exchanges ... which involve public disputation, private conference, private correspondence, the publication of private letters, and the composition of letters and tracts written specifically for print, are the product of a culture which has not formulated rigid distinctions between verbal, written, and printed discourses.[34]

Baxter himself was acutely aware of how the differing contexts of speech, manuscript and print shaped the ways in which words, interpersonal relationships and doctrinal truths were expressed and interpreted. He differentiated primarily between the 'presence' of speech and the silent but ready availability of manuscripts or printed texts, rather than between the scribal production of manuscripts and print as alternative modes of dissemination. This distinction between speech and writing resulted directly from his theology of preaching and an associated understanding of the different ways in which speech and text shaped the emotions of the congregation, audience or reader.[35]

---

[34] N.H. Keeble and Geoffrey F. Nuttall, 'Introduction', *Calendar of the Correspondence of Richard Baxter* (Oxford: Clarendon Press, 1991), Vol. 1, xxviii.

[35] See, e.g., the following extract Baxter, *A Christian Directory* (London, 1673). This reflects Baxter's awareness of the political difficulties and constraints facing nonconformist congregations and ministers following the Restoration. 'Vocal preaching hath the preheminence in moving the affections, and being diversified according to the state of the Congregations which attend it: This way the Milk cometh warmest from the breast. But books have the advantage in many other respects: you may read an able Preacher when you have but a mean one to hear. Every *Congregation* cannot hear the most judicious or powerful Preachers: but every *single* person may *read* the *Books* of the most powerful and judicious; *Preachers* may be silenced or banished, when *Books* may be at hand: *Books* may be kept at a smaller charge than Preachers: We may choose Books which treat of that very subject which we desire to hear of; but we cannot choose what subject the Preacher shall treat of. Books we may have at hand every day and hour: when we can have Sermons but seldom, and at set times. If Sermons be forgotten, they are gone. But a Book we may read over and over til we remember it: and if we forget it, may again peruse it at our pleasure, or at our leisure,' p. 60, cited by D.F. McKenzie, 'Speech – Manuscript – Print', in Peter D. McDonald and Michael F. Suarez, Jr (eds), *Making Meaning: 'Printers of the Mind' and Other Essays* (Boston, MA: University of Massachusetts Press, 2002), p. 250.

Baxter and his clerical correspondents were also very conscious of how different venues and formats for oral delivery, such as the public sermon and debate or private conference, with their respective audiences, and varied forms of written media, for example the personal letter or public tract, could shape doctrinal debate, personal conversion, congregational or parish formation and the individual and collective pursuit of truth.[36] Baxter's relationship with John Tombes extended from c.1645[37] through to the 1670s and their epistolary exchange needs to be interpreted within the context of a culture that did not draw rigid distinctions between oral, written and printed discourse. Tombes was a minister at Bewdley about two miles away from where Baxter exercised his celebrated Interregnum ministry in Kidderminster. Tombes appears to have initiated the first doctrinal controversy with a series of letters sent by friends or members of his congregation requesting that Baxter debate the legitimacy or otherwise of infant baptism in writing.

Baxter's relationship with Tombes as it was enacted across these different forms of discourse does not easily map onto models or key terms – such as 'the republic of letters', 'networks' and 'friendship' – often used to analyse correspondence and early modern intellectual exchange. Baxter's epistolary converse with Tombes is marked by an element of aggressive disputation that is characteristic of his correspondence with other key religious dissenters as well. A significant and recurring theme is the need to determine and publicise the truth with clarity and pastoral care: this is a distinguishing mark of nonconformist discourse that was particularly important following the ejection of thousands of ministers from publicly-funded parish pulpits in the state church and the introduction of tight licensing laws which prevented the publication of many nonconformist texts. Such aggression in pursuit of truth has affinities with Pierre Bayle's conception of how friendship worked in the Republic of Letters: 'The only dominion ("empire") recognized is that of truth and reason; under their auspices, war can be innocently waged on anyone. Friends have to be on their guard against friends, fathers against their children, fathers-in-law against their sons-in-law … Everyone is both sovereign and answerable in law to everyone else'.[38] Tombes' insistence on prioritising an uninhibited search for truth despite its impact on personal relationships resonates with Bayle's emphasis on the importance of disagreement 'as a positive sign of critical exchange…a necessary consequence of the open nature of the Republic of Letters'.[39]

---

[36] The significance of the public debate in particular has been examined by Ann Hughes, 'Public Disputations, Pamphlets and Polemic', *History Today* 41.2 (1991), pp. 27-33, and in a recent book-length study by Joshua Rodda, *Public Religious Disputation in England, 1558–1626* (Aldershot: Ashgate, 2014).

[37] Richard Baxter, *Plain Scripture Proof* (London: Robert White, 1651), 210, cited by F.T. Powicke, 'Richard Baxter's Relation to the Baptists and his Proposed Terms of Communion', *Transactions of the Baptist Historical Society* 6.3 (1919), p. 196.

[38] *Dictionnaire historique et critique* (2 vols; Rotterdam: Reinier Leers, 1697), I, entry on Catius; cited and translated by Ian Maclean, 'The Medical Republic of Letters Before the Thirty Years War', *Intellectual History Review*, 18 (2008), p. 15.

[39] Maclean, 'The Medical Republic of Letters', p. 28.

The Aristotelian argument that the 'friend becomes necessary to the self not as reflection, but as the other voice in a dialogic relationship'[40] also has some heuristic value when considering the multiple, interlocking layers of discourse that characterise Baxter's exchanges with the Oxford-educated Tombes. Ronna Burger expresses it as follows in her reading of Book IX of Aristotle's *Nichomachean Ethics*:

> The friend was originally designated an *allos autos*, suggesting the replication of myself as an other; as a partner in dialogue he becomes *heteros autos*, forming a pair with me precisely because of the difference that makes him genuinely other. Sharing speeches and thoughts is motivated by and in turn produces an awareness of one's partial perspective or incompleteness: it introduces into friendship the possibility of some kind of longing, which the friendship of the good seemed to preclude.[41]

This 'awareness of incompleteness' and the 'kind of longing' it introduces is very similar to the implications of a doctrine of original sin and an eschatology that defers human perfectibility and utopian communion to heaven – a theology that both Baxter and Tombes shared. However, this did not result in an idealised form of correspondence and indeed an all-too-human irascibility and touchiness appears to have ended Tombes' extended epistolary exchange with Baxter.

For the sake of brevity, I will focus here on the twelve letters that Baxter and Tombes sent in connection with their initial dispute as to whether or not infant baptism was divinely ordained and prescribed. Baxter and Tombes first met in London during the winter of 1644–45 and Baxter had recommended Tombes for the position he held at Bewdley when their correspondence began in September 1649. Baxter also notes that he '*more rejoyced in Mr. T.'s Neighbourhood, and made more use of it, then of most others*'.[42] The manuscripts of this correspondence are extant, but Baxter also published the letters – with brief segments of explanatory narrative – in his *Plain Scripture Proof of Infants Church Membership and Baptism*. I am drawing on the version of this exchange that the title-page denotes as the third printed edition of the text. I think this, alongside Baxter's running commentary, illuminates key aspects of how the different registers of religious discourse and debate considered in this section functioned within the local Worcestershire context and the broader public sphere implicitly invoked through publication in print.[43] Baxter prefaces a section entitled 'Letters that passed between Mr Baxter and Mr

---

[40] Vanessa Smith and Richard Yeo, 'Friendship in Early Modern Philosophy and Science', *Parergon* 26.2 (2009), p. 3.

[41] Ronna Burger, 'Hunting Together or Philosophizing Together: Friendship and Eros in Aristotle's Nicomachean Ethics', in Eduardo A. Velásquez (ed.), *Love and Friendship: Rethinking Politics and Affection in Modern Times* (Lanham, MD: Lexington Books, 2003), p. 50.

[42] Cited by Keeble and Nuttall, *Calendar*, Vol. 1, p. 47.

[43] Richard Baxter, *Plain Scripture Proof of Infants Church-membership and Baptism* (London: Printed for Robert White, 1653).

Tombes Concerning the Dispute' with the disarming, but somewhat pejorative observation,

> It goes against my mind to trouble the Reader with these following Letters between Mr. T. and me. But his Relations have made it necessary, that it may appear, Whether all my endeavour was not to keep off, if possibly I could, from appearing against him in this Cause in writing; nor did I ever desire the Dispute but meerly to shift off writing, when his followers drove me on to it: and had far rather have been quiet from both: but it was beyond my power to attain without betraying the truth. (p. 404, italics original.)

The printed correspondence originally sent in manuscript two to three years earlier is introduced towards the end of a book which, according to the title-page of the 1651 edition consisted of 'The Arguments prepared for (and partly managed in) the publick Dispute with Mr. Tombes at Bewdley ...With a ful Reply to what he then Answered ... Constrained ... by Mr. Tombes his importunity; by frequent Letters, Messengers, in his Pulpit, and at last in Print, calling out for my Arguments, and charging the denial upon my Conscience'. It is thus somewhat ironic that the first seven letters – which preceded the public debate between the two ministers held on 1 January 1650 – consist primarily of a discussion as to whether it was necessary to dispute the matter at all and, if so, whether it should be done in writing or through an oral defence.

These letters are situated within a local network of congregational relationships and other forms of interpersonal communication. Tombes writes from Bewdley on 2 September 1649, '*I perceive by some speech with* Phillip Munne, *that you propound a disputing the point in difference between me and you about Infant-baptism in some open way of speech....*' (p. 405, italics original). Here a reported conversation with Phillip Munne, who had presumably had a personal meeting with Baxter, is used to supplement information exchanged by letter as to the form their theological debate should take. Tombes continues,

> Open dispute by words for a great number of reasons I affect not: my affairs, and the state of your body and business are likely to make it uncertain, and to protract the time ... The most expedite and surest way I conceive to bring the controversie to an issue, is for you in a Syllogism or two written by you to ... prove a Divine institution of Pedobaptism, which being written may the better be examined; verbal conference is less deliberate, and more unsatisfactory. (p. 405, italics original.)

In his reply, Baxter also references the wider social and pastoral context that is framing their epistolary converse. He tells Tombes that while 'your people my neighbours have much room in my affections' he has no desire 'to play the Bishop in your Diocess, much less to be so rude as to challenge you to a Dispute' (p. 405). He has, however, been solicited 'severall times' by some of Tombes' people 'to do something towards the determining of this controversie'. Though he still thinks 'a dispute the fittest way' he has been told that Tombes refuses it (p. 405). Baxter made an offer to a messenger that came to him in person; he now repeats the same offer to

Tombes via letter with characteristic thoroughness. He does not want a debate but if Tombes and his people consider it 'necessary and desireable' he will 'spend a day or two in publick conference with you'. If there is 'no hope of it' then he suggests that Tombes preach 'two Sermons against it, and I two for it, and so let fall the debate, and leave it to the peoples judgment'. Finally, if 'you absolutely refuse both these (which seem to me the only means) if you can contrive how to make a short dispatch, and give me sufficient assurance of it upon equall terms before we begin, I shall consent to write'. He fears, though, that 'it will never be ended'; it is a comparatively 'small' matter and thus represents a waste of time; there are many more things that Baxter considers it necessary to study first; he has more work already than he is able to complete, including his writing, preaching and 'the practice of physick for the poor'; due to bodily weakness he can only study two to three hours a day; 'I have sweeter and more pleasing work for my thoughts'; many 'tedious volums' will not make 'people more able to discern the truth, then they are from what is already written'; and he will be a poor pastoral example encouraging his parishioners 'to strain at a Gnat and swallow a Camel' (p. 406). Baxter concludes,

> That you should deny an open verball dispute, I cannot but much wonder your affairs will sure give you more leasure for 2 or 3 hours dispute, then many months writing, and so I am sure will the state of my body. Truly Sir the disadvantage on my side is so great, and the advantage on yours, that I should not venture on it, but as urged on for the truths sake, you being a Batchelour of Divinitie of so long standing, and I having scarcely known an Universitie ... (pp. 406-407)

Tombes informed Baxter in his reply on 10 September that some of his neighbours had '*doubts about baptism*' and conceived that the best way to resolve them would be to '*know what arguments*' Baxter '*could bring for Infant-baptism*'. He thus presses upon Baxter the fact that it is a pastoral concern for his own parish that compels him to controversy. Though he does not absolutely refuse it, Tombes is reluctant to agree to an '*open dispute*':

> *... it being fit for schools and not for common Auditories, entered into usually with animosities and eagerness to obtain a supposed victory, managed with heat and multitude of words with Answers and Replies, not so deliberate as were requisite to settle any ones judgment, and usually misapprehended by Auditors, who commonly take him to have the better who speaks most, ending usually in some wrangling ... followed by misreports, accompanyed with disorderly throngings, confused noise, and many other inconveniencies; in so much that except in case of betraying truth by declining it, I can hardly bring myself to yeild to it.* (p. 407, italics original.)

Both Tombes and Baxter are attune to the ways in which the choice of venue and form of delivery whether open debate before a public audience, formal sermons in the parish church, or a scholarly exchange of animadversions in manuscript shape the contours of their theological debate. Neither wants to give the other personal advantage and Tombes points out that Baxter's '*ready wit and speech*' and the '*generall acclamation*' given to the '*superstition of Infant-baptism*' means that outcome of an open debate will be *'crying down truth, and disgrace of my person'* (p. 407, italics original). Personal concern for their professional reputation and detailed consideration of the most appropriate venue or format for discussion is balanced on both sides by a passionate desire to establish the truth and a pastoral concern for the spiritual good of their parishioners. On the latter ground, Tombes argues that Baxter should not dismiss baptism as of *'lesse moment'* than other doctrines for *'this being of frequent practice needs perhaps resolution before other points that come not into so frequent use'*. This echoes more widespread concerns about the relative infrequency with which both sacraments were practised in parishes pastored by scrupulous puritans. Tombes signs himself off tersely, 'Yours as is meet' (p. 408, italics original).

Baxter replied on the following day (11 September) and deals in particular with two matters: Tombes' objections against a public debate and the role of prejudice in pursuit of truth. If their 'verball dispute ... were among the rude Vulgar, much of that you say might fall out; but I have no such desire to be publique, but that if you like it better, before a competent number of the intelligent, I am content'. Baxter here seeks to ensure that Tombes is able to retain his dignity and to prevent a shouting match or public wrangle without being put to the 'inconveniencies of writing' that were 'far greater' (p. 408). To pursue and proclaim the truth was a key imperative for both men. Tombes observed that he did not see how Baxter's *'not denyed prejudice'* could *'suit with an impartiall examination of truth'* (p. 408, italics original). In his response Baxter reveals a sensitivity to the ways in which emotion, in this case prejudice, can shape one's intellectual commitments and the manner in which they are defended: 'For the prejudice you mention, I must confesse I have some, not against this only, but against everything I judge to be an errour. Nor doe I know how any man can debate any point without some prejudice, except where his judgment doth wholly suspend, or hangs in *aequilibrio*' (p. 409). Absence of such emotional investment in one's convictions on this model argues either an apathetic disengagement or genuine indecision, the inference being that neither are an appropriate long-term response where theological error is involved. Baxter also references the terse close of Tombes' letter by signing himself off – *'Sir, I am an unfeigned lover of Truth, Peace, and You, (for I know it is so meet)'* (p. 409, italics original).

Baxter's letter also reveals the important role played by personal messengers in the reception and exchange of manuscript correspondence and the ways in which reported speech and observation of the recipient's physical carriage could shape the interpretation of the written document. Baxter writes,

> What my carriage was that offended you, as you express not, so I know not; and therefore your reproof must needs be vain: I asked your messenger, who answered that he saw no miscarriage, except it were my revealing your Letter to three that were present, which he confesseth to be his own fault, who never told me of any desires of secrecie ... (pp. 408-409).

Shortly after they engaged in the public debate agreed upon via correspondence. Baxter describes it in his autobiography as follows:

> So Mr. *Tombes* and I agreed to meet at his Church on *Jan.* 1. And in great Weakness thither I came, and from Nine of the Clock in the Morning till Five at Night, in a crowded Congregation, we continued our Dispute; which was all spent in managing one Argument, from Infants right to Church-Membership to their Right to Baptism ... In a Word, this Dispute satisfied all my own People and the Country that came in, and Mr. *Tombes*'s own Townsmen, except about Twenty whom he had perverted, who gathered into his Church, which never increased to above Twenty two, that I could learn.[44]

It extended beyond his estimated two to three hours, but Baxter makes no mention of the public disorder that Tombes feared. However, there is a reference in Bewdley's financial accounts to a certain John Weaver being paid five shillings 'for mending the seats & other worke done in the Chappell at the dispute'.[45] Similarly, Anthony Wood notes that Baxter and Tombes 'disputed faced to face, and their followers were like two Armies: And at last it came so to pass that they fell together by the ears, whereby hurt was done, and the Civil Magistrate had much ado to quiet them. All Scholars there and then present, who knew the way of disputing and managing arguments, did conclude that *Tombes* got the better of *Baxter* by far'.[46] Both Baxter and Wood had political agendas that shaped their commentary, but regardless of the actual level of public unrest and personal success the debate certainly heightened the tension and passion with which the epistolary discussion was conducted. In a brief exchange on 3 January, two days after, Baxter claims that Tombes has 'most unworthily and unbrotherly traduced me four times in publick, whereof three in pulpit' indicating that their theological controversy was being carried out publicly in other local forums (p. 413). Tombes replied on the same day with a flat denial: '*In your saying that I have most unworthily and unbrotherly traduced you four times in publick, whereof three in Pulpit, is no truth. After so many told me of your stings at me, I was willing Mr. Davis should tell you no truth is so to be suspended as to be lost for peace*' (p. 414, italics original). He concludes, however, with a puzzling reference to contemporary politics noting '*my fears are that you* go in a slippery path, if you do as your friends imagine, oppose the present government, and dissenting brethren, likely out of mistaken zeal, and others provocation who will abuse you for their own ends' (p. 414, italics original). Baxter never responded personally, but he did reply later in print. This indicates the porous boundaries

---

[44] Richard Baxter, *Reliquiae Baxterianae* (London: Printed for T. Parkhurst, J. Robinson, J. Lawrence, and J. Dunton, 1696), I, p. 96 (italics original).

[45] John R. Burton, *A History of Bewdley* (London: William Reeves, 1883), Appendix, xxxiii. See also Worcestershire Archive & Archaeology Service, Ref. 498 BA 8681/236 (i), 624.

[46] Anthony Wood, *Athenae Oxonienes* (London: Printed for Tho. Bennet at the Half-Moon in S. Pauls Churchyard, 1692), Vol. 2, 409-10 (italics original).

between these two forms of discourse. He evidences a characteristic lack of tact as he reveals his emotional response to Tombes' inflammatory epistolary mixture of theology, politics and professional squabbling.

> This Letter I did not, nor durst not answer, partly because it had in it so many untruths ... partly because his secret friendly threatning ... could not be answered without many inconveniencies: Especially I felt my spirit too prone to have expressed a contempt of his threatnings ... It seemed a strange Diversion to me to turn from a dispute of Infant-baptism so suddenly to State matters; And to intimate my opposing the present Government, because my friends imagine it; and so to join together the present Government and Dissenting Brethren, as if they were conjunct; and it were as dangerous to dispute against Anabaptists, as to oppose the Government! (pp. 414-15)

It is, in its way, a masterly conclusion to this first debate allowing Baxter, temporarily at least, the final word.[47]

Conclusion

These two case studies exemplify some of the ways in which separatist, Baptist, and later nonconformist women and men enacted their religious beliefs and exercised spiritual agency in England following the Civil War. M.K. consciously reworked the conventions of tragicomedy in order to produce a seminal narrative of spiritual experience that authorised her membership of a separatist congregation meeting at Somerset House. Though there is no explicit evidence to demonstrate that she attended any of the regular performances of the highly popular genre of tragicomedy during her time in London, M.K.'s experience drew upon this shared cultural capital in order to help forge the new genre of the conversion narrative which was itself integral to the formation of a different kind of spiritual, political and communal identity in Interregnum London. Rather than categorising M.K.'s actions as a move from 'private' to 'public', I suggest it is more constructive to consider her role as an agent performing her religious belief through communal textual publication in a rapidly shifting social and political scene, where her act of narration was produced for the specific purpose of establishing her credentials as an experiential professor within a particular community of believers – even, perhaps, as a leader amongst them.

---

[47] On the night following the debate, Baxter dreamt that as he was working in his study a hen and chickens came in the door. He was offended by the chickens as 'unmeet company for my chamber', and chased them out. In anger, he 'trod one or two of the chick[e]ns to death'. They turned into 'illuminated Eyes, w[hi]ch gazed in [his] face', and the words of Matthew 23:37 were spoken to him. Baxter concluded that 'it afforded a very cleare Evidence for Infants Church membership under ye Gospell'; this issue was central to his debate with Tombes. British Library Egerton MS 2570 f. 30r. I am indebted to Dr Tom Charlton for drawing this reference to my attention.

The exchange of letters between clerics and their engagement in public debate was a far more traditional and established performance genre for educated males in early modern England. However, the controversy that preoccupied Tombes and Baxter – the nature of baptism and right to church membership – was at the core of political discussions on the national stage during the 1650s in England and played a central role in helping to define the nature of the state and its government. Examining the ways in which the exchange of letters in manuscript and print intersected with personal meetings, weekly sermons and a staged debate demonstrates how gathered and parish congregations performed their religious convictions in the local context of Bewdley and Kidderminster during the Interregnum and, in turn, how this helped to construct, constrain and (to a certain extent) democratise the passionate pursuit of truth in a freshly envisaged, and constantly shifting, public sphere.

CHAPTER 3

'Go down to the potter's house'[1]:
Baptists and the Pottery Industry

John H.Y. Briggs

We have a fair amount of writing on the gathered community; much less on the congregation dispersed. The following study seeks to demonstrate the usefulness of dissenting networks to those engaged in business, in this case the pottery trade.[2] Whilst the establishment principle yielded huge dividends to landed and professional interests, the dissenting network could also offer assistance to increasingly mobile business men as they moved around the nation. Here is an aspect of the layman's world that clericalised studies of religion, which is a bias present in all too much church history, neglect at their peril.

At the time that the Staffordshire Potteries began to develop, the Baptist presence there was relatively small and faltering,[3] but they nevertheless made a significant impact upon the pottery industry. For example, Jacob Phillips,[4] a deacon of the Little Wild Street Church, who belonged to a family that ran a London china dealership in Oxford Street, had, by 1818, moved to The Potteries, where, in partnership with a John Bagster,[5] he purchased the Church Works in Hanley.[6] These works had

---

[1] Jeremiah 18.2.

[2] See also John H.Y. Briggs, 'Nonconformity and the Pottery Industry', in David Bebbington and Timothy Larsen (eds), *Modern Christianity and Cultural Aspirations: In Honour of Professor Clyde Binfield, OBE* (Lincoln Studies in Religion & Society, 5; London: Sheffield Academic Press, 2003), pp. 47-77.

[3] The oldest congregation had assembled in the market town of Newcastle under Lyme, though their seventeenth-century forebears had been virtually taken over by the Quakers. Preaching recommenced at the end of the eighteenth century with places for worship registered in 1814, 1832, and 1839, but the church became extinct in 1854 only to restart in 1867. Hanley started falteringly in 1789 and was re-established in 1820. Burslem began around 1806, Stoke in 1841, and Longton in 1853, the latter two being General Baptist New Connexion churches.

[4] L.F.W. Jewitt, *The Ceramic Art of Great Britain* (London: J.S. Virtue, 1883), p. 482, 'The Phillips of this firm was Jacob, brother to Jonathan Phillips of Oxford Street, London and uncle to the present Messrs Phillips of Oxford Street.'

[5] It would be good if a link could be established between this Bagster and the London Bagsters, printers and Bible publishers: Samuel, the older, 1772–1851, educated at Rylands' school in Northampton, to the benefits of which he bore gracious testimony (Seymour J.

previously been run by James Neale, Robert Wilson and Elijah Mayer.[7] All three were Congregationalists and trustees of Hanley Tabernacle, alongside such Evangelical worthies as Jonathan Scott, Rowland Hill, and John Whitridge. In these exchanges, a dissenting network seems to be facilitating business relationships, exploited by leading London retailers wishing to buy into provincial manufacturing.

In 1819, Phillips invited L.J. Abington (1785–1867), a fellow deacon at Little Wild Street, and, according to Llewellyn Jewitt, a 'clever modeller' and 'a fair chemist', to join him. Deploying his artistic skills, Abington, in his London years, had assisted Benjamin Wyatt with the decoration of Drury Land Theatre and was entrusted by Sir John Soane with much of the ornamental detail on the Bank of England. Abington had been brought up and baptized at the Hammersmith church, but after the death of his first wife, the daughter of a deacon there, he moved to Little Wild Street, marrying again in 1811. Reluctance to undertake Sunday work and health reasons are given as part of the explanation of his move to North Staffordshire. Abington fairly soon entered into partnership with the Congregationalist, Joseph Mayer, son and successor to Elijah Mayer, and cousin to the New Connexion Methodist Ridgways, and by this means subsequently became partner to William Ridgway. Jewitt credits him with being the '& Co' in the Ridgway partnership of 1831, which after 1845 transferred to his son, E.J. Ridgway, the firm trading as Ridgway and Abington from 1848–60, when Abington was able to retire, being the recipient of a substantial legacy from Joseph Mayer.[8]

Preaching widely in all Nonconformist churches, he helped revive the Hanley church, serving it and the church in Burslem in a team ministry with his father and the Rev. J. Hinmers. Subsequently he became pastor at Newcastle-under-Lyme

---

Price, 'Dissenting Academies, 1662–1820', *Baptist Quarterly* 6.3 (July, 1932), 136-38), and Samuel, the younger, 1800-1835, educated by Hinton at Oxford. The former was a member at Keppel Street, and the latter has been identified as sometime a member of Church Street, Blackfriars, which later became Upton Chapel. See H.R. Tedder, rev. J.-M. Alter, 'Bagster, Samuel, the elder (1772–1851), publisher and author', *Oxford Dictionary of National Biography*, Oxford University Press, 2004 [http://www.oxforddnb.com/view/article/1048, accessed 9 January 2015]; and H.R. Tedder, rev. J.-M. Alter, 'Bagster, Samuel, the younger (1800–1835), printer and author', *Oxford Dictionary of National Biography*, Oxford University Press, 2004 [http://www.oxforddnb.com/view/article/1047, accessed 9 January 2015]. There is also a George Bagster of the Eagle Street church who seems to have been involved in the founding of the Baptist Union, see Seymour J. Price, 'The Early Days of the Baptist Union (III)', *Baptist Quarterly* 4.4 (September, 1928), p. 173; and Isaac Mann, 'Calendar of Letters, 1808–1815', *Baptist Quarterly* 6.8 (October, 1933), p. 377. See also Joseph Ivimey, *A History of the English Baptists: including an Investigation of the History of Baptism in England from the Earliest Period to which it can be traced to the close of the Seventeenth Century* (4 vols; London: For the Author, 1811–30), III, p. 252.

[6] The movement of retailers into manufacturing was not uncommon. The most often cited example was that of Miles Mason when the supply of Chinese import wares faltered at the end of the eighteenth century

[7] James Neale was a faithful supporter of the London Missionary Society.

[8] Jewitt, *Ceramic Art of Great Britain*, p. 482.

(1832–36) before returning to Hanley (1834–63). Labelled a Radical by the *Victoria County History*, he for a short time edited *The Pottery Mercury*, and was a leading spirit within the Pottery Philosophical Society. In 1836 he helped bring a long and damaging strike in the pottery industry to an end. In 1834 he was appointed Chief Bailiff of Hanley, which was not incorporated until 1857.[9] He was energetic in campaigning against Nonconformist grievances, supported the work of the Society for the Diffusion of Useful Knowledge, himself contributing to *The Penny Cyclopedia*, lectured to the Mechanics Institute and was active in the Anti-Truck movement. Deeply interested in the founding of the Evangelical Alliance, he was one of the founders of the Hanley Branch of the Religious Tract Society. One of the moving spirits behind the founding of the North Staffordshire Auxiliary of the Sunday School Union, he served the organization as President for many years. With Josiah Wedgwood II and John Ridgway, he helped found the Hanley auxiliary of the British and Foreign Bible Society, whilst also serving as a life governor of the parent society. Welcoming discoveries in geology, he was convinced that 'the investigations of Science would strengthen rather than weaken the evidence of ... Inspiration'.[10] A good example of how faith, conscience and business came together may be found in a fine Anti-Slavery stoneware jug manufactured around 1858 depicting scenes from 'Uncle Tom's Cabin' and obviously aimed at the American market.

In 1845 Abington's partner, William Ridgway, began to simplify his industrial network; the Church Works, in which Abington had an interest, went to his son, E.J. Ridgway, who married Mary Akroyd of the Halifax Methodist New Connexion family that became Anglican, as did E.J. Ridgway himself. The Broad Street Works, which had been purchased in 1835 and operated under the style of Ridgway, Morley, Wear and Co., was transferred to his son-in-law, Francis Morley, of the Nottingham Congregationalist hosiery family, as sole owner. In 1851 on the bankruptcy of C.J. Mason, the patentee of Mason's ironstone, Morley purchased his patents, moulds, copper plates, indeed the entire business.[11] In these marriages the significance of the dissenting network is once more to be seen.

Dissenters were also involved in linking together the clay extraction end of pottery production with its manufacture in Staffordshire. And here I claim a personal connection since, for thirty years, I lived in the house once occupied by the person to

---

[9] J.G. Jenkins (ed.), *Victoria County History: Staffordshire* (London: Oxford University Press, 1963), Volume VIII, p. 165.

[10] Anon., *Personal Recollections of the Late Leonard James Abington, of Hanley, Staffordshire* (Hanley: Allbut and Daniel/Kimbolton: Thomas M. Parker, 1868), p. 12; D. Stuart (ed.), People of the *Potteries: A Dictionary of Local Biography* (Keele: University of Keele, Department of Adult Education, 1985), p. 9.

[11] Jewitt, *Ceramic Art of Great Britain*, pp. 491-92; Geoffrey Godden, *Jewitt's Ceramic Art of Great Britain, 1800–1900* (London: Barrie and Jenkins, [c.1972]), pp. 62-63; Jenkins (ed.), *Victoria County History*, VIII, p. 165. There is confusion as to the chronology here, but the chronology given above is in my judgment more reliable than the variations to be found in the two versions of Jewitt.

whom I wish now to refer. His name was W.H. Grose and he was born near St Austell in 1815. As agent for the West of England China Stone and Clay Company he came to live in Stoke on Trent some time after 1845. Prospering in business, he became the principal in two firms W.H Grose and Sons, Clay Merchants, and Grose and Stocker, who specialised in selling plaster for plaster moulds. He also dabbled in pottery manufacture under the incorporation of Grose and Sons at the Bridge Works in Stoke. Initially one of Abington's deacons in Hanley, in the late 1860s Grose transferred his membership to the Stoke church, nearer to his home in the newly-constructed 'Stokeville', Stoke on Trent's attempt to create an immediate bourgeois neighbourhood in twenty-four houses to the Italianate design of the architect, Charles Lynam.

Nearly every aspect of Baptist life found in him a willing sponsor and the one who frequently provided the finance to bail ailing churches out of debt, his total generosity adding up to a very considerable benefaction. His special delight was his sixty-strong Bible class. Improvement Commissioner and Poor Law Guardian, he was Vice Chairman to the Rev. Lovelace Stamer of the Stoke-on-Trent School Board. Indeed Stamer, by then elevated to be the first Bishop of Shrewsbury, pronounced the benediction at Grose's funeral in 1890, and I wonder whether this may have been the first time that an Anglican bishop participated in a Free-churchman's funeral.[12]

The Stoke Stocker was Grose's son-in-law, but the relationship between the two families was clearly of longer duration, for the West of England (China Clay) Company was largely the creation of Thomas Stocker, which company developed a very considerable reputation for the fair treatment of its workers. A philanthropic Baptist, he largely financed the building of the St Austell Baptist Church. The next generation produced Thomas Medland Stocker who trained at the Camborne School of Mines who was responsible for much technical improvement – the introduction of new filter presses and the application of electricity – in an otherwise conservative industry. Medland Stocker also invented the compacting of clay into granular form, a process that offered considerable economies in things like tile manufacture because the clay did not have to have water added to it for processing, only to have it taken out again in firing. These granules were, in 1985, still known in the trade as 'Stockalite'. Medland Stocker also perceived the need for company amalgamation and so the industrial conglomerate, English China Clays, was his creation, and it has been said that its incarnation was only possible because of his personal high standing in the industry. It was he too who secured the democratic style of management for which English China Clays became renowned. He followed his father in the life of the St Austell church where he served as organist and choirmaster, the organ being his personal gift.[13]

---

[12] J.H.Y. Briggs, 'Civic Engagement and Ecumenical Relations', *Baptist Quarterly* 36.3 (July, 1995), pp. 105-107.

[13] Kenneth Hudson, 'Thomas Medland Stocker', in D.J. Jeremy (ed.), *Dictionary of Business Biography* (London: Butterworths, 1986), Volume 5, pp. 343-44.

A further example of how the dissenting network operated concerns another migrant who came to The Potteries from the wholesale china trade in London. This was Henry Wileman, a wealthy member of what was to become John Clifford's Praed Street congregation. C.T. Bateman makes clear his pivotal role in moving the struggling New Connexion West London causes in Church Street, Marylebone, with Jabez Burns as pastor, and Edward Street, Dorset Square, out of debt. He was a key figure in purchasing the Church Street site and erecting a chapel there, and for the Edward Street congregation he purchased a Calvinistic chapel in Praed Street in 1841, which welcomed John Clifford as pastor in 1858.[14] Sir James Marchant confirms these details and tells the story of Wileman's conversion and of his marriage into the Ludford family in whose home the Paddington church had been founded[15]

Henry Wileman, patron of the New Connexion's move into west London, had by the time of Clifford's arrival moved to The Potteries where he arrived in 1853 as a man of sufficient substance to lease Longton Hall from the banker, Charles Harvey. In the same year he went into partnership with Joseph Knight at the Foley Potteries in Fenton. Alongside new business enterprises, in July 1853 he also took the initiative, supported by the General Baptist Association, in establishing services in the Town Hall, which were immediately successful with a congregation of 200 the first evening. An early set-back occurred when the first minister, the Rev. T Freckleton, seceded to the Unitarians, becoming minister of the Old Meeting in Newcastle, where, though attracting large congregations, he was only paid a modest salary of £78, which 'he eked out by sketching and photography in the services of Wedgwoods'.[16]

Wileman, who also purchased and up to his death ran the Church Gresley Pottery in Derbyshire, became sole partner of the Foley Potteries on Knight's retirement in 1856 and so remained until his death in 1864. In 1860, he built the new Foley China Works for the production of very delicately potted china whilst the old factory continued to produce earthenware, creating a remarkably successful enterprise with tea and dinner ware as fine as any within the industry at that time. His sons joined the firm and continued it after Henry Wileman's death: from 1866 James Wileman ran the earthenware enterprise, which had a very successful export business, and his brother, Charles, ran the china works. On Charles' retirement in 1870 the two businesses were united once more under the control of James, but in 1872 J.B. Shelley became a partner and eventually the Wileman enterprise was subsumed

---

[14] C.T. Bateman, *John Clifford, M.A., B.Sc., LL.B., D.D.: Free Church Leader and Preacher* (London: National Council of the Evangelical Free Churches, 1904), pp. 53-54.

[15] James Marchant, *Dr. John Clifford, C.H.: Life, Letters and Reminiscences* (London: Cassell, 1924), pp. 37-38.

[16] G. Pegler, *A History of the Old Meeting House, Newcastle under Lyme* (Hanley: [unknown], n.d. [but post 1922]), pp. 9-10. An earlier Baptist cause in Longton in the 1820s is referred to by A.G. Matthews, *The Congregational Churches of Staffordshire* (London: The Congregational Union, 1924), p. 176.

under his name.[17] Whilst Henry was much involved with the Longton church, his sons seemed to have conformed to the Church of England. This is, of course, a process worthy of a separate study, but it can certainly be traced in families as significant as the Ridgways and the Doultons.

Four further potting enterprises with Baptist leadership occupied nearby premises on the south bank of the Thames in Lambeth and Blackfriars. The first focused around a remarkable female entrepreneur named Eleanor Coade (1733–1821), who emerged as 'a most benevolent, useful member' of James Upton's chapel in Blackfriars, in south London. This church had been formed in 1785, by a secession from the Mitchell Street Chapel where the minister was Thomas Powell, a man of some substance whose life-style, it was alleged, was hardly that of puritan simplicity. This was financed by his bi-vocational work as minister and leather currier. Therein lay the seeds of dispute, since the issue causing the schism was the minister's decision to prosecute those who had stolen skins and other goods, valued at some £33, from his business. The thief was arrested, convicted and eventually hung at Tyburn. That death some held to be the minister's responsibility for pursuing the offending party at law, so that property loss led to loss of life, that is to a penalty perceived as greatly in excess of the crime committed. Those who thought such behaviour inappropriate to a Christian minister accordingly seceded from Mitchell Street and founded Church Street, later named Upton Chapel after its first minister.[18]

The Coade family came from the West Country where Eleanor, born in Exeter, developed an association with the Baptist chapel in Lyme Regis, which suggests she may have had interests with the supply of West Country clays, though she first appears in London records as a linen draper in 1766. Around 1769 she established 'Coade's Lithodipyra, Terracotta, or Artificial Stone Manufactory' to exploit the patent of the artificial stone that bears her name, a remarkably effective ceramic imitation of natural stone. This impressive creation is to be found in use at Buckingham Palace, St George's Windsor, and the Royal Naval College, Greenwich. Exploiting classical statuary, vases and a variety of forms of architectural embellishment, which were produced for those prominent in the world of fashion who were in possession of substantial wealth, including royal patrons, Coade Stone remains a collector's item to the present day. In fact, Eleanor Coade, who is sometimes allocated to the wrong gender, and sometimes provided with an entrepreneurial sister, seems to have been a member of a group of dissenting or Evangelical craftsmen that worked in association with John Bacon, sculptor and clay modeller, who oscillated between Dissent and Evangelical Anglicanism.[19]

---

[17] Denis Stuart (ed.), *People of the Potteries: A Dictionary of Local Biography* (Keele: University of Keele, Department of Adult Education, 1985), Volume 1, p. 230.

[18] Seymour J. Price, *Upton: The Story of One Hundred and Fifty Years, 1785–1935* (London: Carey Press, 1935), pp. 20-21.

[19] Jewitt, *Ceramic Art of Great Britain*, pp. 93-94; A. Kelly, *Mrs Coade's Stone* (Upton upon Severn: By the Author, 1990); 'Mrs. E. Coade', *Baptist Magazine* 14 (February, 1822), p. 65; Doreen Rosman, *Evangelicals and Culture* (London: Croom Helm, 1984), pp. 158-62, and her entries on both John Bacons, father and son, 'Bacon, John', in Donald M. Lewis

It must be by total accident that the next entry in Jewitt concerns the London Pottery of James Stiff and Sons, in High Street, Lambeth, and subsequently of the Albert Embankment. Stiff's were one of three stoneware manufacturers on the south bank of the Thames often mentioned in the same sentence, and all three had Baptist connections, the other two being Doulton and Watts, and Stephen Green and Company. The Royal Pharmaceutical Society, for example, identifies these, and only these, as the major manufacturers of pharmaceutical ceramics.[20]

The London Pottery passed into the ownership of the Stiff family in the early 1840s, and was described in 1883 as 'among the largest in London' employing about 200 people, occupying a two acre site with its fourteen kilns. Its products extended from sanitary pottery and industrial porcelains and stonewares used by the nation's major utilities, to terracotta ornaments and Bristol stoneware architectural features. They were also quick to see the modern uses of ceramic bodies for their telegraphic and electrical pottery wares secured a prize medal at the Paris Electrical Exhibition in 1878 and other international exhibitions. Another major development was in ceramic water filters. A very extensive export trade was well served by the company's own private dock, developed on the Albert Embankment site. Some Stiff terracotta can still be found, with signature, on London Baptist churches.[21]

The family came from Rougham near Bury St Edmunds in Suffolk where James Stiff's father, Robert, who combined farming with the office of Workhouse Master, was associated with the Baptist church. The young James Stiff did not forget his Suffolk origins and in 1876 endowed six almshouses associated with Rougham chapel for Nonconformist widows. Seeking his fortune in London, where much Suffolk clay was processed, the young James took up an apprenticeship at the Coade factory in 1826, but four years later transferred his employment to Doulton and Watts, thereby remaining in Baptist employment. After ten years there, he set up business on his own, initially taking over the Higgins factory in Ferry Street, manufacturing water filters, extending this in the following year by taking over adjacent premises at 39 Lambeth High Street, producing an ever widening range of products. In 1863 he took his sons, William and Ebenezer, into partnership and the firm became James Stiff and Sons, an enterprise which ceased to trade in 1912, the site being sold to Doulton's in the following year. James Stiff served as one of Spurgeon's deacons at the Metropolitan Tabernacle, whilst William Stiff (1837–99)

(ed.), *The Blackwell Dictionary of Evangelical Biography, 1730–1860* (2 vols; Oxford: Blackwells, 1995), II, pp. 44-45. Robert Parsons, Baptist minister in Bath, provides an example of a distinguished Baptist stone carver/sculptor whose craftsmanship may be seen at Stourhead, Petworth, and a number of other country houses, often alongside examples of Coade stone. Kerry J. Birch, *Waters of the Son: Baptists in Georgian Bath* (n.pl.: Kappa Beta Publications, 2009), pp. 63-68.

[20] The Royal Pharmaceutical Society Museum, Information Sheet No. 22.

[21] Jewitt, *Ceramic Art of Great Britain*, pp. 94-96, where Stiff wares are well illustrated, and information secured on the internet, and a presentation to the Listed Buildings Advisory Committee of the Baptist Union of Great Britain, Case Number 70, September 2000. The autographed building is dated 1884.

became a member of Upton Chapel in 1864, serving twenty-six years as deacon and twenty-one as treasurer, following two years as secretary. His wife, associated with the chapel from birth for nigh on eighty years, contributed a moving testimony to the importance of chapel life at the 150th anniversary of the chapel in 1935, recorded in Seymour Price's history.[22]

Another Baptist Lambeth potter was John Watts who from 1815 until his death in 1858 was partner to John Doulton in his stoneware enterprise founded in Vauxhall. At Vauxhall, Watts had been Martha Jones' foreman, and when John Doulton bought into a partnership with Mrs Jones, John Watts became the third partner. In 1820 Martha Jones withdrew and the company became Doulton and Watts, moving in 1825 the short distance from Vauxhall to Lambeth High Street. The firm specialized in industrial ware, brown stoneware, drain pipes as well as stoneware bottles for chemicals, beer, and other industrial liquids among others. Concern for workers' welfare, as well as the inculcation of pride in their work, is to be seen in the company's arrangement for all its employees to visit the Great Exhibition in 1851. The Doultons at this time were Congregationalists: indeed we are told that it was they who were responsible for persuading Baldwin Brown to become minister of Claylands Congregational Church in 1845. In 1870 this congregation was re-formed as Brixton Independent Church, but by then John's son, Henry Doulton, had abandoned both Dissent and the Liberal Party for conservatism and the Church of England.[23] For his part, John Watts was one of the founders of the Baptist chapel in Gray's Walk, Lambeth (later known as Regent Chapel) founded in 1821 by an amicable and strategic separation from the Church Street, Blackfriars, congregation.[24]

But there were also Baptist Doultons. Frederick Doulton, son of John and brother to Sir Henry Doulton, was also employed by the family firm, serving as a partner in Henry Doulton and Co. from 1846–53, and Doulton and Co from 1854 to the mid-1860s. He was elected MP for Lambeth in 1862 after several unsuccessful attempts at election, serving until 1868. He and his wife had been members of Maze Pond Chapel until 1852, when they became Unitarians.[25]

---

[22] Price, *Upton*, pp. 138-39, 149, 167-68 and 197-99. One of the best local chapel histories we have, it unfortunately tells us nothing of the Bagsters or Miss Coade, and little about Stiff's business activities. A.T. Stiff, of New Street, Covent Garden, appears as a Dissenting Deputy in the *Baptist Magazine* 3 (1811), p. 175, but I have not been able further to trace his identity.

[23] Jeffrey Cox, *The English Churches in a Secular Society, Lambeth 1870–1930* (Oxford: Oxford University Press, 1982), pp. 112 and 145.

[24] See Ian Smith, *The Apprenticeship of a Mountaineer: Edward Whymper's London Diary, 1855–59* (London: London Record Society, 2008), pp. 210 and 129, where his death, aged seventy-three, and his great liberality to the poor is recorded. See also Price, *Upton*, p. 77, for details of the founding of this chapel.

[25] He could, therefore, be added to David Bebbington's lists of 'supposed' Baptist MPs, 'Baptist M.P.s in the Seventeenth and Eighteenth Centuries', *Baptist Quarterly* 28.6 (April, 1980), pp. 245-62, 'Baptist M.P.s in the Nineteenth Century', *Baptist Quarterly* 29.1

Another Maze Pond member, Stephen Green, is described as the manager of a Pottery Works near Blackfriars Bridge, though in fact he was the owner of the Imperial Pottery. The firm, located in Princes Street, had been founded by Stephen's father, James, initially concentrating on the manufacture of common red ware. James Senior died c.1825 when the factory passed to his wife, Sarah, and their son, Stephen. Under Stephen's control the Imperial Pottery flourished, successfully introducing a number of technical innovations, and grew threefold, employing seventy-five persons at its height, when Doulton and Watts employed around 100 persons, with at least half the production going for export. Green thoroughly exploited the chemical and industrial markets, but was also alert to commemorative opportunities such as that provided by the passing of the Reform Bill in 1832 and the accession of Queen Victoria in 1837. The Imperial Pottery was sold to a Mr Cliff, another highly innovative potter, between 1858 and 1860, a year after a widely reported fire had destroyed the newest part of the factory. Mains water was insufficient to control the blaze until eventually a vessel was brought up the Thames which could pump river water onto the blaze. The damage was calculated at £6,000, but Green was well insured with the Unity Fire Office. Green lived in Union Place where he also ran a subsidiary company producing Delft-ware pots for Singleton's Eye Ointment with which there was a family connection. In 1825 Green had married a Miss Selina Folgham, great grand-daughter of Thomas Singleton, after whom the eye ointment was named at the end of the seventeenth century. This business was run from the same address as his Lambeth residence which continued in his name after the sale of the Imperial Pottery. Part of the interest in the recipe for the ointment passed to Stephen Green on Selina's death in 1831, and by 1848 he had sole rights over its manufacture and sale, leading him to take a keen interest in legislation relating to patent medicines. The combination of patent ointment and specially designed pedestal pots contributed considerably to his wealth. In his will he left shares in the Droitwich Salt Company and various railway stocks plus other shares which provided his widow with an income of more than £1,000 p.a. amongst other family legacies. Green was one of several wealthy members of Maze Pond who moved out to Clapham, or other outlying suburbs, or later to the Kent or Surrey countryside.[26]

(January, 1981), pp. 3-23, 'Baptist Members of Parliament, 1847–1914', *Baptist Quarterly* 29.2 (April, 1981), pp. 51-64, and 'Baptist M.P.s in the Twentieth Century', *Baptist Quarterly* 31.6 (April, 1986), pp. 252-87. See also Bebbington's 'The Free Church M.P.s of the 1906 Parliament', in S. Taylor and D.L. Wykes (eds), *Parliament and Dissent* (Edinburgh: Edinburgh University Press, 2005), pp. 136-50. See Smith (ed.), *Apprenticeship of a Mountaineer*, p. 185.

[26] Smith, *Apprenticeship of a Mountaineer*, p. 190 and *passim*, esp. p. 52, where it is said that his third wife, Mary (née Clay), was almost blind at the time of their marriage. Smith considers her Green's second wife being ignorant of his first marriage to Selina Folgham. Jewitt, *Ceramic Art of Great Britain*, pp. 100-102. See 'Stephen Green Limited, patent medicine manufacturer (ointment for eye complaints)', in *London Metropolitan Archives Collections Guide. Business: Unlock the riches of the archives of the London commerce and*

Timothy Whelan identifies Thomas Flight (referred to in letter from James Ashworth to John Sutcliff as raising funds for Mr Hague's chapel in Scarborough – 9-10-1775)[27] as of the same Maze Pond chapel to which Stephen Green and Frederick Doulton later belonged.[28] A life-long messenger to the Particular Baptist Fund, sometime a Dissenting Deputy, as well as being a patron of the Widows' Fund and the Orphan Working School,[29] he was a founder member of the committee of the Baptist Society in London for the Encouragement and Support of Itinerant (and Village) Preaching.[30] Founded in March 1797, the manuscript minutes of this Society, in eminently readable copper-plate handwriting, are to be found in the Angus Library at Regent's Park College in Oxford. The last meeting Flight attended was on 18 August 1797; his name does not appear when the committee was reconstituted in April 1798. The explanation is almost certainly reasons of infirmity,

---

trade with the world A–Z business listing (City of London, n.d.), B/SIN, p. 318. The London Metropolitan Archives have a large collection of business papers which among other things show how his business dealings involved other Maze Pond families

[27] Timothy Whelan, '183 Baptist Autographs in the Rylands University Library, Manchester', TSS, Georgia South University, 2004 p. 34; *Lowndes London Directory, for the year 1787: Containing an alphabetical arrangement of the names and places of abode of the merchants, manufacturers, and principal traders of the cities of London and Westminster* (London: W. Lowndes, 1787); *Kent's Directory for the Year 1800: Containing an Alphabetical List of the Names and Places of Abode of the Directors of Companies, Persons in Public Business, Merchants and Other Eminent Traders in the Cities of London and Westminster, and Borough of Southwark, with the Numbers Affixed to Their Houses, Agreeable to the Late Acts of Parliament* (London: Richard and Henry Causton, 1800).

[28] Another Flight was nominated for the diaconal office at neighbouring Carter Lane, during the early years of Rippon's pastorate, though in December 1773, but he declined to serve. See Ernest A. Payne, 'The Appointment of Deacons: Notes from the Southwark Minute Book, 1719–1802', *Baptist Quarterly* 17.2 (April, 1957), p. 89.

[29] James Dore, *A Sermon, Occasioned by the Death of Mr. Thomas Flight, of Hackney, Middlesex,: Who Departed this Life January 30, 1800, in the Seventy-fourth Year of His Age; Preached at Maze Pond, Southwark, February 9, 1800. To which is Prefixed, the Address Delivered at His Interment in Bunhill Burying Ground, Moorfields, February 7, 1800* (London: C. Whittingham, 1800), p. 17. Flight was the last surviving of the deacons who were in office when Dore became minister and, therefore, the one he knew the best, and 'the more I knew, the more I loved'. With Henry Keene and John Cooper he was one of a powerful triumvirate, which Dore compared to an earlier triumvirate in the Maze Pond story of Tomkins, Heath, and Cox. The minutes of Maze Pond witness him engaged in delicate matters on behalf of the church, for example, Benjamin Staley's denial of the divinity of Christ in 1785, and as church messenger in Isaac Cotham's 'indecent behaviour' case. Both of these were men of stature who, along with Henry Keene, had been part of a committee trying in November 1781 to persuade Robert Robinson to devote some time to writing a history of the English Baptists. Maze Pond Church Book, May 16, 1785, and Ivimey, *History of the English Baptists*, IV, p. 48.

[30] For a brief account of the activities of this society, see Ken R. Manley, *"Redeeming Love Proclaim": John Rippon and the Baptists* (Studies in Baptist History and Thought, 12; Carlisle: Paternoster Press, 2004), pp. 230-35.

for even towards the end of his life he was assigned the task amongst the Maze Pond diaconate of encouraging young men to engage in village preaching. In his memorial address, James Dore referred to the 'long and painful affliction which terminated in death', whilst indicating that until the end he retained 'all his mental energies'. He died on 30 January 1800 in his seventy-fourth year,[31] having been a member at Maze Pond for forty-four years (i.e., from 1756)[32] and a deacon for almost twenty-seven years.[33] Buried in Bunhill Fields, he left £200 in his will for the poor of the church. His eldest son, Bannister, was also a leading member of the church.[34] Two addresses are given for their business, 2 Bread Street as a china warehouse, and 1 Coventry Street, Haymarket, for their retail trade.

Thomas Flight's name, in fact, stands first at the end of that extraordinary diaconal epistle of October 1790 which made a remarkable request of their minister. The occasion was the French Revolution, and it is important to understand that this was no remote event for Thomas Flight, for his son, John, had made several visits to France as late as September 1788 to buy Paris porcelain for his father's London showroom. The same month he was also in Staffordshire looking for artists. We are told that thereafter, towards the end of 1789, Lord Harcourt warned him about returning to France because of the situation created by the Revolution. Thomas Flight evaluated the Revolution differently. With his fellow deacons, he wrote to James Dore about that 'wonderful Revolution, that a neighbouring Nation hitherto groaning under ecclesiastical and civil Tyranny has so recently experienced'. Instead of a nation 'groaning under ecclesiastical and civil Tyranny', the deacons rejoiced in 'The ardour for Liberty extending itself to other countries.' In such a situation, they wrote, 'We desire to unite our voices in thanksgiving to Almighty God for such apparent interpositions of his power and goodness – We cannot but regard them as additional proofs of his providential kindness to his Creatures and as links in that great chain of Events foretold in Scripture, which will finally issue in his Glory and the happiness of Mankind.' Domestic developments were less encouraging:

> we have much to complain of in this;– that the Consciences of Britons are tampered with by the allurements of temporal advantage, and their minds shackled by the terror of persecution – nevertheless we encourage hopes, that by the divine blessing accompanying a steady, temperate and persevering discussion of the subject, such an alteration will be produced in the opinions of the Public, and in the resolves of the Legislature, as may raise us to an eminence on the scale of Freedom, which we have never yet obtained.

With all this in mind, the fifteen signatories confidently requested James Dore, their minister, given his 'repeated exertions to advance the cause of Humanity and

---

[31] Dore, *Sermon on the Death of Thomas Flight*, p. 2.
[32] Maze Pond Church Book confirms the date as 4 April 1756.
[33] Admitted 19 April 1773, Maze Pond Church Book.
[34] He was admitted to church membership on 7 October 1792, seven years after his younger brother, John.

Universal Freedom', to prepare a course of lectures 'on the principles of Nonconformity, and of civil and religious Liberty'.[35]

Llewellyn Jewitt refers to Flight purchasing the Worcester Factory, established by Dr James Wall in 1751, for his sons, John and Joseph, for £3,000, including premises, models, plant, and stock, on 10 April 1783. Whilst Joseph and John are supposed to have moved to Worcester, the father and eldest son seem to have remained in London, looking after retail sales in the capital, though Joseph also remained part of its management, at least until John's untimely death. Thomas had been the Worcester factory's London agent from c.1768. The brothers are recorded as running the porcelain business in Worcester alongside their work as jewellers. Jewitt says 'under their management the works more than regained their former eminence'.[36] In 1786 Joseph Flight, described as 'jeweller and china manufacturer', is recorded as having taken over the shop of Samuel Bradley, who had been one of the partners of Dr Wall, at 33 High Street, shortly afterwards removing to larger premises at 45 High Street,[37] where he later received the king and queen. Some have suggested, with the support of surviving indentures, that Bradley in fact acted as managing director of the factory. Valentine Green, writing in 1795, also identified Bradley, who was a goldsmith/clock seller, as he who 'vended the china when finished'.[38]

Of Thomas Flight's four sons, Joseph (b.c.1762) became a Freeman of Worcester in December 1784 and John (b.c.1766) in November 1788. John Flight was baptized and became a church member at Maze Pond in April 1785. By contrast, I can find no record of Joseph ever becoming a church member. John Sandon says that John had joined Joseph in seeking to bring order to the Worcester situation in 1787, actually taking charge in July of the following year. However, he was still spending sufficient time in London to be reasonably regular at Maze Pond church meetings until 25 May 1789, the last meeting at which his attendance is recorded. These dates indicate the chronology of the Flight's involvement in the Worcester situation. There were problems to be faced to re-secure the reputation of the business, principally overcoming problems in firing the ware and dealing with a works foreman named Shaw who was seriously defrauding the firm. John Flight is described as 'a deeply religious person' and his diary (on display at the Dyson Perrins Museum in Worcester), which runs from 1785–91, is certain evidence for this. Partly written in

---

[35] 'A Diaconal Epistle', *Baptist Quarterly*, VIII, 1936, p. 216. The list of fifteen deacons includes Benjamin Tomkins, John Cooper, John and Joseph Gurney, Henry Keene, Job Heath, and Samuel Beddome. While this paper has suggested the importance of London traders finding partners within the networks of provincial Dissent, there is also considerable evidence of the reverse phenomenon, that is that of provincial Dissenters finding an immediate home within the London churches.

[36] Jewitt, *Ceramic Art of Great Britain*, pp. 137-38.

[37] So says Jewitt, *Ceramic Art of Great Britain*, pp. 138-39, but John Sandon, *The Dictionary of Worcester Porcelain:* Volume I. *1751–1851* (Woodbridge: Antique Collectors' Club, 1993), p. 81, says forty-three though on p. 163 he says forty-five.

[38] Sandon, *Dictionary of Worcester Porcelain*, pp. 81-82.

French, it focuses on his religious ideas and concerns in moral philosophy. It also gives details of his travels to Cornwall in search for clay and stone supplies, his visits to France to promote trade, and the difficulties he encountered in the day-to-day running of the factory. In August 1788, the year in which the larger shop was opened, George III and Queen Charlotte made a much-acclaimed visit to the shop and factory, and granted the firm a royal patent. The only downside was that the older shop was taken over the following year by the Chamberlain family to market their rival wares, in part produced by staff they had enticed away from the Flight enterprise. The royal warrant was in the names of John and Joseph with no mention of Thomas. From 1788, a crown was added to the factory mark. The record also says it was the king who recommended the move of the London showroom to Coventry Street. Noting their role in Worcester as retail jewellers as well as potters, it is clear that John Flight had made a deliberate decision to take the Worcester factory up market, leaving more everyday ware to the Staffordshire potters and others. The Worcester factory now focused on opulence, with an improved body, finely potted with much gilding and hand-executed decoration of great beauty. This was a recipe for success, which reflected Thomas Flight's interest in high quality French imports, and was confirmed in the securing of two important orders for a dessert and a dinner service from the Duke of Clarence in 1789. The axis between serving the tastes of aristocrats and wealthy entrepreneurs and Thomas Flight's sympathies with the achievements of the revolutionaries in France, represents an interesting spread of engagement with both privileged and under-privileged.

John Flight died at a tragically early age in 1791, having only in the previous year married Ann Gillam, daughter of Thomas Gillam of Gillam and Barr 'Drapers, Salesmen, Mercers and Undertakers' of Worcester High Street. The Gillams also had Baptist connexions, for Ivimey records a Mrs Gillam of Worcester as being custodian of a youthful diary of Timothy Thomas, who succeeded his father as minister of the Baptist congregation in neighbouring Pershore c.1717, only to die at the early age of twenty-two. This she entrusted to a London minister who published this in 1752.

James Dore readily paid tribute to the strength of John Flight's character which was well-known to him as one whom he had baptised and admitted to church membership six years earlier. In an allusion to his lack of years, the young Flight was compared to Samuel. He was both well acquainted with the love of God which was a subject on which he delighted to speak, 'a subject that afforded him strong consolation and a good hope, in life and in death'. It would be all too easy for his memorialist to use words which seem too much like a 'panegyrical declaration'. Advantaged by a religious education, he expressed his faith in conventional Calvinist terms – 'a deep sense of his depravity, of the exceeding sinfulness of sin, and of the necessity of faith in Our Lord Jesus Christ for salvation'. To his service he devoted himself, concerned that others share his faith. John Flight confessed that he had been blessed with a remarkably happy life in which he had experienced nothing but mercy and goodness, which made him even more regretful of his sins from which he was anxious to overcome; 'I long to be holy as God is holy.' He was on record as confiding in a friend that he had read scripture for himself 'without any regard to the opinions of men'. Such a reading led him to conclude, 'he could see no other foundation of which a sinner could safely build for eternity than the atonement and righteousness of Christ'. All was the free gift of God with no place for any human merit. In his passing moments, he claimed no angelic vision but was upheld 'in this awful season [by] solid joy and substantial peace'.[39]

The profitability of John Flight's factory can be detected from the fact that this twenty-five year old left his young wife an income of £2,400 a year. It was his wife's father's partner, Martin Barr, Sr, one of his executors,[40] who in 1793 became a partner in the porcelain business on John Flight's early demise. He had already become a Freeman of the City of Worcester in January 1792. He soon became senior partner in the company until his death from 'apoplexy' in 1813, aged fifty-six. Much involved in the affairs of the city, Martin Barr was buried in Angel Street [Independent] Chapel,[41] further evidence of the importance of dissenting networks. On Martin Barr's death, Joseph Flight again became senior partner. It is now known that he himself was an accomplished decorator with at least one marked piece known to exist. He was also an accomplished miniaturist regularly exhibiting at the Royal Academy between 1801 and 1806 until his death in 1838.

Whilst Matthew Arnold might have been inclined to scoff at the vulgarity of Staffordshire figures, there is evidence in Stoke on Trent, Lambeth, and Worcester of high quality craftsmanship which is far from being philistine,[42] and was of sufficient quality to attract the patronage of many aristocratic and metropolitan clients. The two worlds, moreover, are not entirely separate because both Bacon and Coade were involved in the early ceramic representations of the personage of John Wesley. An article in the *Wesleyan Methodist Magazine* for 1896 refers to Coade making a cast of Wesley around 1769, from which undoubtedly copies were produced by this innovator in artificial stone. When, in 1830, Conference wished to commission a life-size replica of the founder, it was to Samuel Manning, a pupil of John Bacon, Jr, that they went. Initial sculpting did not, however, go well and the outcome was deemed unworthy of the founder. Adam Clarke became involved, and on his advice, the famous Enoch Wood bust, of which Clarke possessed a copy, was used for Wesley's head on the full-size figure much to the advantage of the overall presentation. Here are to be noted two inter-related phenomena, first the existence of

---

[39] James Dore, *A Sermon, Occasioned by the Death of Mr. John Flight, who departed this life July 10, 1791, in the Twenty-Fifth year of his Age; Preached in Angel-Street, Worcester, July 24, 1791* (London: L. Wayland, 1791), pp. 23-25. Ivimey, *History of the English Baptists*, IV, p. 334, is doubly misleading in that John Flight is referred to as John Fly and the one sermon becomes two – the sermon occasioned by the death of 'Mr John Fly', and the sermon preached in Angel Street, Worcester, which in fact are both references to the same item.

[40] Sandon, *Dictionary of Worcester Porcelain*, pp. 162-66.

[41] Sandon, *Dictionary of Worcester Porcelain*, pp. 50-54.

[42] For a discussion of Arnold, see Briggs, 'Nonconformity and the Pottery Industry', p. 53.

a network of highly skilled craftsmen and artists associated with Dissent, and through this network the existence of a linkage which connected the world of high art and the more popular productions of The Potteries.[43]

So what is happening through this chain of connections in business enterprise and chapel loyalty? Certainly, as members of the new entrepreneurial classes moved around the country – from the West Country to London, to Staffordshire, to Worcester, and Derby – they used their chapel networks to put down roots in new locations. Thus their participation in the life of Dissent helped them to link together clay extraction, manufacture and sales, both wholesale and retail. The usefulness of their chapel connections to Abington, Coade, and Grose, is clear, as also amongst the Lambeth potters. In the case of Henry Wileman, it looks as if his business move from Paddington to The Potteries, was actually part cause of the establishment of the new General Baptist church in Longton, both occurring in 1853. In the case of the Hanley church, the arrival of London-trained business men and craftsmen helped to revive a faltering cause, and give birth to neighbouring congregations. In South London, the well-established Maze Pond church provided a support to a significant band of emerging entrepreneurs later also to be found at Upton Chapel, whilst also providing leadership for the new church plant at Gray's Walk (later Regent Chapel). Coade and Stiff, as indeed the best work of the Staffordshire dissenting potters and certainly the Flight, and Flight and Barr, products of the Worcester factory, all served to challenge the notion of dissenting philistinism. These thoughtful manufacturers and traders also played their full part in civic institutions, and in the case of Thomas Flight, and may be L.J Abington, were certainly not frightened of espousing radical politics. Whilst the leaders of these enterprises certainly increased their personal wealth, this generation was still part of an alternative society, separately organized from that of parish and landed estate, although it had by this time developed its own effective networks and connections, whilst still bitterly resenting the trappings of establishment, alike in church and state. But when a bishop came to take part in the funeral of a dissenting manufacturer with whom he had shared civic responsibility, it was clear that there was an increasing mutual respect between once hostile interests.

---

[43] A.D. Cummings, *A Portrait in Pottery* (London: Epworth Press, 1962), pp. 21-23, pp 44-45.

CHAPTER 4

The Early Bristol Tradition as a Seedbed for Evangelical Reception among British Baptists, c.1720–c.1770

Anthony R. Cross

The Bristol Education Society (1770)

Founded in 1770, the Bristol Education Society was the realization of the vision of Caleb Evans (1737–91).[1] Its stated goal was to further, support, and encourage the work of the Bristol Baptist Academy at a time when there were 'fome very worthy people, who, from a miftaken view of things, not only call in queftion the importance of fuch an education, but even feem to imagine it is rather prejudicial than ufeful'. If this was true, then 'every fcheme formed for the education of pious youth defigned for the miniftry, ought to be difcountenanced'. However, if it was not true, and 'a learned education' was 'highly ufeful, then every inftitution calculated for that purpofe muft be deferving of the warmeft and moft effectual encouragement'. From this premise, the account of the founding of the Society offered 'a few thoughts on the ufefulnefs and importance of learning to a gofpel minifter.'[2] With his co-founders, his father Hugh among them, Caleb Evans believed that 'The importance of a liberal education, more efpecially to candidates for the Chriftian miniftry, is fo exceedingly obvious, that one might almoft think it impoffible that any confiderate perfon fhould not be convinced of it.'[3]

It is clear from its stated principles that the Bristol Education Society stood firmly within the Evangelical tradition which had first reached Britain from America in the

---

[1] So John Rippon, *A brief essay towards an history of the Baptist Academy at Bristol* (London: s.n., 1796), p. 33; and Joseph Ivimey, *A History of the English Baptists* (4 vols; London: For the Author, 1811–30), III, p. 26. [For the sake of brevity, many book titles have been abbreviated.] See also Norman S. Moon, 'Caleb Evans, Founder of The Bristol Education Society', *Baptist Quarterly* 24.4 (October, 1971), pp. 175-90.

[2] *An Account of the Bristol Education Society: Began Anno 1770* (Bristol: W. Pine, n.d. [1770]), pp. iii-iv. An edited version of the 'Introduction', pp. iii-xii, is reproduced by Norman S. Moon, *Education for Ministry: Bristol Baptist College 1679–1979* (Bristol: Bristol Baptist College, 1979), pp. 129-31. For three studies on the Society, see Norman S. Moon, L.G. Champion, and Harry Mowvley, *The Bristol Education Society 1770–1970* (Bristol: The Bristol Baptist College, n.d. [c.1970]).

[3] *An Account of the Bristol Education Society*, p. iii.

late 1730s, though it was several decades before it really began to influence and rejuvenate Baptist life.⁴

At the centre of this learning was the Bible. The Society readily acknowledged that many had been successful ministers of the gospel despite their lack of 'any of the advantages of learning', but also recognized that 'not a few of thefe' had felt their 'want' of learning and the disadvantages 'they lay under on that account'.⁵ As the days of inspiration had ended and miraculous gifts were not to be expected, 'minifters muft *ftudy* to fhew themfelves approved unto God *workmen that need not to be afhamed*'.⁶ Since apostolic times God's providence had 'in every age, put the greateft honour' upon learning, and the history of the church, 'with *very few* exceptions', demonstrated 'that thofe minifters who have been *the moft laborious* and fuccefsful in their work, have been as eminent for found learning, as for fubftantial piety'. Further, religious revivals saw the raising up of men 'eminent for fpiritual gifts' and also those who 'endeavour zealoufly to improve thofe gifts, for the attainment of all that knowledge, which, with the blefling of God, may render them able minifters of the new teftament'.⁷ While 'the great Head of the church' could continue his work without learned ministers, or any ministers at all, yet 'he fees fit, for the moft part, to fulfil his defigns in the ufe of means', therefore 'it is in this way we are to expect his prefence and blefling'.⁸

The purpose of the Bristol Education Society was, therefore,

> To the end that diffenting congregations, efpecially of the Baptift denomination, in any part of the Britifh dominions, may, if it pleafe God to fucceed our endeavours, be more effectually fupplied with a fucceffion of *able and evangelical minifters*;⁹

---

⁴ See David W. Bebbington, *Baptists Through the Centuries: A History of a Global People* (Waco, TX: Baylor University Press, 2010), pp. 71-81; and Raymond Brown, *The English Baptists of the Eighteenth Century* (A History of the English Baptists, 2; London: The Baptist Historical Society, 1986), pp. 76-82. Roger Hayden's *Continuity and Change: Evangelical Calvinism among Eighteenth-Century Baptist Ministers Trained at Bristol Academy, 1690–1791* (Chipping Norton: Roger Hayden and The Baptist Historical Society, 2006), focuses on Baptists in the South West; while, Ian Sellers (ed.), *Our Heritage: The Baptists of Yorkshire, Lancashire and Cheshire 1647–1987* (Leeds: Yorkshire Baptist Association, 1987), pp. 14-20, examines the Revival's impact in the North from 1750–87, and pp. 21-29 up to 1837. On the capital, see R. Philip Roberts, *Continuity and Change: London Calvinistic Baptists and The Evangelical Revival 1760–1820* (Wheaton, IL: Richard Owen Roberts, 1989).

⁵ *An Account of the Bristol Education Society*, pp. iv-v.

⁶ Caleb Evans, *The Kingdom of God* (Bristol: Printed and sold by W. Pine, T. Cadell, M. Ward, &c., 1775), p. 22 (italics original).

⁷ *An Account of the Bristol Education Society*, p. ix (first italics original, second italics added).

⁸ *An Account of the Bristol Education Society*, p. ix.

⁹ 'An Account of the Constitution of the Bristol Education Society', dated 'June 7, 1770', in *An Account of the Bristol Education Society*, pp. 1-7 (p. 1, italics added). This *Account*

Writing three years after the formation of the Baptist Missionary Society, John Rippon's shortened version of this declaration immediately continued 'and that Missionaries may be sent to those places where there is an opening for the gospel'.[10] The Society, then, called for the churches to assist the Academy led by Hugh Evans with the aid of his son and assistant at the church, Caleb Evans, and also James Newton, assistant minister at the Pithay, Bristol,[11] and established a body of trustees and subscribers who came mainly from the West Country as far south as Bampton in Devon, but extended as far north as Thorpe, Leicestershire, and as far east as London.[12]

This, then, is the Bristol Tradition, and it bears all the marks of Evangelicalism, exhibiting three of the four characteristics identified by David Bebbington as constituting the movement: conversionism, biblicism, and activism, the fourth, crucicentrism,[13] however, lay beyond the scope required by the constituting of the Bristol Education Society, but was implicit within it as a Particular Baptist Society, the Academy subscribing to the *London Confession* of 1688[14] until 1832, when it adopted the doctrinal standard of the newly re-formed Baptist Union.[15]

---

also appears in S.A. Swaine, *Faithful Men: Or, Memorials of Bristol Baptist College* (London: Alexander & Shepheard, 1884), pp. 72-74; and a lightly abbreviated version of it is in Rippon, *A brief essay*, pp. 33-34.

[10] Rippon, *A brief essay*, p. 34. In this he is followed by Ivimey, *History*, III, p. 26.

[11] Newton came from the Maze Pond church, London, having been educated by Dr Thomas Llewelyn. John Tommas' assistant at the Pithay from 1758-90, he also became an assistant tutor at the Academy under both Evans' from 1770. See Caleb Evans' and John Tommas' funeral and interment sermons, *The Faithful Servant Crowned* (Bristol: Printed by William Pine, 1790); John Rippon, *The Baptist Annual Register* (4 vols; s.l.: s.n., 1790-1802), I, pp. 150-54 and 563; Moon, *Education for Ministry*, pp. 11, 13 and 24-25; and 'Newton, James (c.1733–c.1790) (person id: 1191)', Dissenting Academies Online, accessed 20 February 2015. On Tommas (1723/24–1800), see J.G. Fuller, *A Memoir of the Rev. Thomas Roberts, M.A.* (London: Houlston & Stoneman/Bristol: I. Hemmons, 1842), pp. 79-90.

[12] See also the letter sent to London ministers and churches, 'Bristol's Appeal to the Gentlemen of London 1770,' in Moon, *Education for Ministry*, pp. 131-34.

[13] D.W. Bebbington, *Evangelicalism in Modern Britain: A History from the 1730s to the 1980s* (London: Unwin Hyman, 1989), pp. 2-17.

[14] *A Confession of Faith, Put forth by the Elders and Brethren Of many Congregations of Christians* (London: Printed for John Harris, 1688), particularly Chs III, V–XVIII and XX. See, e.g., Nigel G. Wright, 'Election and Predestination in Baptist Confessions of the Seventeenth Century', in Pieter J. Lalleman, Peter J. Morden and Anthony R. Cross (eds), *Grounded in Grace: Essays to Honour Ian M. Randall* (London: Spurgeon's College/Didcot: The Baptist Historical Society, 2013), pp. 16-32 (esp. pp. 24-26).

[15] Roger Hayden, 'Bristol Baptist Academy (1720 to present)', Dissenting Academies Online, accessed 3 September 2014.

Edward Terrill's Vision of a Baptist Academy

Yet the Bristol Tradition did not begin in 1770. In fact, it antedated the rise of Evangelicalism in the 1730s. For generations the foundation of the College has been identified as 1679, and Edward Terrill's (1634–c.85)[16] indenture, dated 3 June 1679,[17] in which accrued income was at 'the use and behoof of the congregation' of which Terrill was a member, Broadmead, Bristol.[18] However, while the 1679 indenture allocated Terrill's own library of 200 books, and provided for the support of a learned minister, fluent in Hebrew and Greek, the only other indication of his intention to establish an academy comes immediately following the provision for the 'pastor or teacher',

> that if it should happen that if any of the young students for the ministry, under the Baptist denomination, should be so poor, that himself, or any of his relations during such study, should be unable to maintain him in food, that such young student, or his assigns, should have the lump sum of 10*l*. [£] paid to him for his maintenance for one year ...[19]

In this, Terrill envisaged an academy similar to those beginning to appear across the country, run by dissenting ministers with the specific aim of providing the next generation of ministers, as well as a level of education otherwise closed to the children of Dissenters.[20]

---

[16] See Ivimey, *History*, II, pp. 522, 529, 538-40, IV, pp. 262-63; Moon's *Education for Ministry*, pp. 1-3 and 105-106; and Hayden, *Continuity and Change*, pp. 8, 17, 21, 26-27, 63-64, 66 and 168.

[17] 'Edward Terrell's Charity', in Thomas John Manchee (ed.), *The Bristol Charities*. Volume 1 (Bristol: T.J. Manchee, 1831), pp. 280-84 (p. 280). See also Terrill's will, 'Will of Edward Terrill made on 25th Sept 1683. Probate given to Dorothy Terrill in P.C.C. 7th April 1685' (G96 Box T, Bristol Baptist College Library).

[18] See J.G. Fuller's *The Rise and Progress of Dissent in Bristol* (Bristol: Hamilton, Adams, 1840), pp. 13-214; R.L. Child and C.E. Shipley, *Broadmead Origins* (London: The Kingsgate Press, 1940); C.S. Hall and H. Mowvley, *Tradition and Challenge: The Story of Broadmead Baptist Church, Bristol from 1685 to 1991* (Bristol: Broadmead Baptist Church, 1991); and Roger Hayden (ed.), *The Records of a Church of Christ in Bristol, 1640–1687* (Bristol Record Society's Publications, 27; Bristol: Bristol Record Society, 1974).

[19] 'Edward Terrell's Charity', pp. 281-82. This provision also extended to the support for needy students for up to four years.

[20] On these academies, see the Dr Williams's Dissenting Academies Online project; Irene Parker, *Dissenting Academies in England: Their Rise and Progress and their Place among the Educational Systems of the Country* (Cambridge: Cambridge University Press, 1914); H. McLachlan, *English Education under the Test Acts: Being the History of the Nonconformist Academies, 1662–1820* (Publications of the University of Manchester, 203/Historical Series, 59; Manchester: Manchester University Press, 1931); and W. Ashley Smith, *The Birth of Modern Education: The Contribution of the Dissenting Academies 1660–1800* (London: Independent Press, 1953).

While Terrill died a quarter of a century before his vision finally came to fruition in 1720,[21] he was 'the man who made possible the beginnings of the Bristol Baptist College',[22] though nothing happened until Terrill's monies were released on the death, around 1697, of his wife, Dorothy Vaux, who had married Thomas Vaux(e),[23] Broadmead's fifth minister (1687-93) after Edward's death. The vision of an academy was finally made possible, with the substantial aid of further bequests,[24] thereby enabling Terrill's plans finally to be realized in 1720,[25] when two Welsh students came under Bernard Foskett's tutelage.[26]

'The venerable Mr. Bernard Fofkett'[27]

Exhibiting a 'considerable proficiency' in learning, Foskett (1685-1758 n.s.)[28] 'was placed under the care of a very able master'.[29] At some point in his youth 'He

---

[21] Dating the foundation of the College as 1679 is, therefore, mistaken. E.g., Moon's *Education for Ministry*, is a tercentenary volume which relates, p. vii, 'the history of the College through three centuries'. Ivimey, *History*, I, p. 548, describes Terrill as 'the founder of the Bristol Education Society', though he dates it from 1686 and Terrill's will. Some four months after the first Particular Baptist Assembly in September 1689, when the setting up of a fund which included the training of young men for the ministry was agreed upon, the church at Plymouth recommended one of its young men, Richard Sampson, to train in Bristol under the Rev. William Thomas. However, since Sampson was not financially supported by the Broadmead Trust, and Thomas is not known to have been a Baptist, Moon, *Education for Ministry*, p. 3, believes he cannot 'legitimately be regarded as the first student of Bristol College'; though Hayden, 'Bristol Baptist Academy (1720 to present)', does list him among its students, giving his dates there as c.1689-c.1692, and as dying c.1716. See Rippon, *A brief essay*, pp. 10-11. For the account of the proceedings of this Assembly, see Ivimey, *History*, I, pp. 480-511.

[22] Hayden (ed.), *Records of a Church of Christ*, p. 5.

[23] On whom, see Ivimey, *History*, II, pp. 530 and 540-41, III, p. 347.

[24] See 'Robert Bodenham's Charity', and 'The Gifts of Dorothy Vaux, Sir John Eyles, and Others', in Manchee (ed.), *Bristol Charities*, pp. 275-80 and 300-302.

[25] See 'Robert Bodenham's Charity', dated 27 August 1720. The date of the deed-poll, p. 277, is 11 January 1715 (1716 n.s.: the year is incorrectly given as 1715 by, e.g., Moon, *Education for Ministry*, p. 106, who fails to account for the change in 1752 to the Gregorian Calendar, prior to which the new year began on 25 March: this change in year is indicated when relevant (though the eleven day discrepancy has not been adjusted) by o.s. (old style) and n.s. (new style).

[26] Thomas Rogers, and John Phillips. See G.F. Nuttall, 'Welsh Students at Bristol Baptist College, 1720-1797', *Transactions of the Honourable Society of Cymmrodorion* (1978), 171-99 (pp. 197, and 196 respectively); and Moon, *Education for Ministry*, p. 4.

[27] So Samuel Stennett and John Tommas, *The Mortality of Minifters contrafted with the Unchangeablenefs of Chrift* (London: Rivington and Marfhall, 1791), p. 25.

[28] See the account of Hugh Evans' unpublished funeral sermon for Foskett, in Caleb Evans, *Elisha's Exclamation!* (Bristol: Printed by W. Pine, 1781), n. * on pp. 22-27. Ivimey, *History*, IV, pp. 266-71, includes some material from the funeral sermon, pp. 267-69, and for additional glimpses into Foskett's life, ministry, and his ongoing influence, see vols III and

became experimentally acquainted with religion',[30] and around the age of seventeen he joined the church at Little Wild Street, London, under the ministry of John Piggott. Here he struck up a lifelong friendship with John Beddome, who had been called to be minister of the church at Horsleydown, Southwark, at which Benjamin Keach and John Gill had both served. In 1711 Foskett left the medical profession to pursue his call to ministry, and Ivimey records that 'he left London for the purpose of assisting his friend [Beddome] ... at Henley Arden'.[31] Whether this suggests that he initially went to train 'on the job' as a minister under Beddome's tutelage is not clear, but it should be considered a possibility as, at this time, there was no Baptist academy, and so a number of Baptist and Nonconformist ministers took young men into their homes to train them for ministry.

Foskett was approached by the Broadmead church, at the time under the ministry of Peter Kitterell (1707/08–27),[32] to succeed Caleb Jope[33] as assistant minister and 'become the tutor of the academy in the room of Mr. Jope'.[34] After preaching twice

---

IV, *passim*. Rippon, *A brief history*, pp. 14-23, also includes much of the sketch Hugh Evans presented at the funeral, pp. 16-20. For Foskett, see also Swaine, *Faithful Men*, *passim*; Moon, *Education for Ministry*, pp. 3-10 and 18-19; Hayden, *Continuity and* Change, pp. 62-103 and *passim*, and 'The Contribution of Bernard Foskett', in W.H. Brackney, P.S. Fiddes and J.H.Y. Briggs (eds), *Pilgrim Pathways: Essays in Baptist History in Honour of B.R. White* (Macon, GA: Mercer University Press, 1999), pp. 189-206; and Michael A.G. Haykin, 'Foskett, Bernard (1685–1758), Particular Baptist minister and college head', *ODNB*, accessed 16 April 2013.

[29] Ivimey, *History*, IV, p. 266.
[30] Rippon, *A brief essay*, p. 14.
[31] Ivimey, *History*, IV, pp. 266-67. See also Rippon, *A brief essay*, pp. 14-15.
[32] See Ivimey, *History*, I, p. 548, II, pp. 124 and 540, IV, pp. 263-64, 266 and 472; and Hayden, *Continuity and Change*, pp. 8-9, 24 and 66-68.

[33] Jope had been called to Broadmead '"to educate young men, as well as to aſſiſt Mr. Kitterell"' in 1710 or 1711. He had close ties with the church in Plymouth, and at the beginning of his studies had lived in Trowbridge, before moving on to Tewkesbury where he studied under the Presbyterian, Samuel Jones. In 1719, Jope moved to the ministry at Exeter, and later on to Plymouth. Rippon notes that none of the names of his students were known, nor the year of his death. On Jope, see Rippon, *A brief essay*, pp. 13-14; Ivimey, *History*, II, p. 463, III, pp. 567-68, IV, pp. 263-66 and 297; Swaine, *Faithful Men*, pp. 30-34; and Hayden, *Continuity and Change*, pp. 8-9, 23-25, 26 and 66-67.

[34] Rippon, *A brief essay*, p. 16. While Rogers and Phillips were the first students of the Academy there were other members of Broadmead whose preaching gifts were recognized. For instance, with the church's consent, in January 1724 (n.s.) those brothers gifted 'in expounding or preaching to a Scripture' were permitted to preach in the room adjoining the meeting house on a Monday evening, see Broadmead Baptist Church Minute Book, 9 January 1724 (n.s.), p. 178. On 10 December 1724, Kitterell proposed that Joseph Gaube be permitted 'to exercise his Gifts' on a scripture consented to by the church (p. 179), and by 6 May 1725 (pp. 179-80), it was recorded that Gaube was permitted to 'expreſs his Gift in Preaching on our days of Prayer whenever either of our Pastors [?] it'. Gaube was the first of a number of members called to ministry but evidently not regarded as students of the Academy. Hayden, 'Contribution of Bernard Foskett', p. 200, believes it difficult to conceive

in 1719, four times in March to April the following year, and later on a further six Sundays, Foskett, after much soul searching, finally agreed to the invitation 'in pursuance of the Design of Mr. Edw. Terrill'.[35] On Kitterell's death in 1726, Foskett became the principal minister of the church and President of the Academy, where he remained until his death on 17 September 1758.[36] The work of the Academy, however, halted and no students were instructed until a new assistant was called.[37] Finding the right assistant, however, did not happen straight away, so for the next six years Foskett was assisted by two younger ministers.

The first of these was Andrew Gifford (1700–84).[38] Following several years as assistant minister to George Eaton at Nottingham, Gifford served at Broadmead (1728–30 n.s.)[39] before moving to the pastorate of Little Wild Street, London. In 1737[40] he formed the Eagle Street church, London, where he remained as pastor until his death. Through provisions made in his 1782 will, he was also a major benefactor to the Bristol Academy.[41]

---

that these men did not receive training from Foskett, their assistant minister. This seems probable when it is remembered that Foskett's predecessor, Jope, was, according to Caleb Evans' 'brief account of Broadmead church' which he sent to John Rippon (see *A brief essay*, p. 13), 'chofen to educate young men, as well as to affift Mr. Kitterell'. There is nothing to suggest that Foskett's call was in any way different. However, the gap between 1687–1720 in the Broadmead records means that, other than Gaube, the names of any of these young men are unknown. The plausibility of this interpretation receives support from Ivimey's version of the conditions set out in Terrill's will, *History*, II, p. 539: '"Provided he be an holy man, well skilled in the Greek and Hebrew tongues, in which the scriptures were originally written; and devote three afternoons in the week to the instruction of any number of young students, not exceeding twelve, who may be recommended by the churches, in the knowledge of the original languages, and other literature"' (original is in italics).

[35] Letter from Joshua Thomas to John Rippon, Letter E. 16 (28), in The Angus Library, Regent's Park College, Oxford, quoted by Hayden, 'Contribution of Bernard Foskett', pp. 192-93. On the death of Emmanuel Gifford in 1721, John Beddome accepted the call to be minister of the Pithay, Bristol.

[36] Rippon, *A brief essay*, p. 20.

[37] See Hayden, 'Contribution of Bernard Foskett', p. 200.

[38] See 'Gifford, Andrew (1700–1784) (person id: 1171)', Dissenting Academies Online, accessed 20 February 2015.

[39] Ivimey, *History*, III, p. 608, records that Gifford had begun as Foskett's assistant on 11 January 1727 (1728 n.s.). See pp. 573-77 for the correspondence between the Little Wild Street church, Andrew Gifford, and the Nottingham church, ranging from 14 December 1729 to 25 January 1730 (n.s.).

[40] The church covenant was agreed and subscribed on 17 February 1736 (1737 n.s.), so the church's minute book quoted by L.G. Champion, *Farthing Rushlight: The Story of Andrew Gifford 1700–1784* (London: The Carey Kingsgate Press, 1961), p. 44.

[41] Chief among which was the first edition of Tyndale's 1526 New Testament. See Ivimey, *History*, III, pp. 608-10; Swaine, *Faithful Men*, pp. 343-68; and Moon, *Education for Ministry*, pp. 135-36.

In December 1730 the Oxford graduate George Braithwaite, MA (1681–1748), came from Bridlington to preach at Broadmead, but he declined the church's invitation on 2 May 1731,[42] though in 1733 he did accept a call to the church at Devonshire Square, London, where he remained until his death.[43] On 24 October, Edward Harrison,[44] who had spent some time at Broadmead, accepted the call and left the church in Newbury. His stay, however, was unhappy and short-lived, returning to Reading in 1733.[45] He was succeeded by Hugh Evans who was invited to become the assistant minister at Broadmead on 7 March 1734 (n.s.).[46] After five years, Evans was called by the church 'to the office of a Teaching Elder',[47] and finally ordained on 7 February 1740 (n.s.).[48]

Foskett's Moderate Calvinism

In many ways Foskett's moderate Calvinism[49] anticipated the emphases of the Evangelical movement less than a generation before the beginning of the Revival.[50] In 1712, a year after Foskett had joined John Beddome (1674–1757) in the ministry of the three Alcester churches (Alcester, Henley in Arden, and Bengeworth, Warwickshire) to which Beddome had originally gone in 1697 as John Willis' (d.1705) assistant, they drew up a confession of faith and a covenant for the widely spread congregation. Following declarations on the oneness of God in Trinity, it declares,

> We believe this God hath revealed his mind and Will to the Sons of Men & this his mind & Will is contained in our Bibles which are the Scriptures of the Old and New

---

[42] See Broadmead Baptist Church Minute Book, pp. 186 and 190.

[43] See S.L. Copson, *Association Life of the Particular Baptists of Northern England 1699–1732* (English Baptist Records, 3; [Didcot]: Baptist Historical Society, 1991), *passim*.

[44] Little is known of Harrison, but see 'Harrison, Edward (?–?) (person id: 2585)', Dissenting Academies Online, accessed 20 February 2015.

[45] Broadmead Baptist Church Minute Book, pp. 190 and 192. On Harrison, see Hayden, 'Contribution of Bernard Foskett', pp. 201-202. Hayden, p. 201, believes that the cause of this unhappiness were his views on particular redemption. See Broadmead Baptist Church Minute Book, p. 191, for 22 July 1733; Ivimey, *History*, IV, p. 428; and Hayden, *Continuity and Change*, pp. 68-70.

[46] See the several entries for 1734–35 in the Broadmead Baptist Church Minute Book, pp. 192-93.

[47] Broadmead Baptist Church Minute Book, p. 196, for 10 May 1739.

[48] For the record of his ordination, see Broadmead Baptist Church Minute Book, p. 197. The delay between being called to the ministry of a church and being ordained was common practice among eighteenth-century Baptists.

[49] Rippon, *A brief history*, p. 18, 'His religious principles, which were thoſe commonly called *Calviniſtical*, he ever maintained with a ſteady Chriſtian zeal. But though he was ſtrenuous for what he apprehended to be the truth, yet he was fond of no extreme' (italics original).

[50] On which, see, e.g., Bebbington, *Evangelicalism in Modern Britain*, pp. 20-74.

Testaments & that these are a compleat and sufficient rule of Faith & obedience exclusive of all those Books commonly called Apocrypha.[51]

Further, as 'King & Head of the Church' Christ 'received all power and authority to appoint Laws & ordinances in & for his Church for their comfort & government & hath accordingly given them a Rule to walk by which is the perceptive part of His Word & his own Example'.[52] Foskett's biblicism receives further testimony in a comment by Caleb Evans, who described him as 'This primitive chriſtian and truly goſpel Biſhop'.[53]

The centrality of the cross and the atonement in God's plan of salvation is also clearly stated. 'God of his own good pleasure hath resolved to glorifie himself by redeeming & eternally saving some of this guilty & corrupted Race of Man'.[54] This is followed by two paragraphs on the doctrine of predestination, then a statement that God's method for making election known is through 'one Mediator ... the Man Christ Jesus' who was qualified by the Father 'to sustain our persons, stand in our room & so have all our iniquities laid upon him in order to make atonement' for the elect, and thereby 'satisfie divine Justice'.[55] It then addresses the Son's taking of 'Flesh and Blood ... & was in every point obedient even to Death of the Cross; that by suffering of Death He might bring many sons to Glory'.[56] The need for personal conversion is implicit in the discussion of the doctrine of baptism,[57] but is later made explicit, for the Saviour 'is able to save to the uttermost all that come unto God'.[58]

The confession then moves from conversion to activism, and though the latter never figures explicitly its presence is unquestionable:

> In order to an enjoyment of these glorious privileges there is an absolute necessity of a Change of heart & nature which change we believe is the result of meer Grace for it is of his own will that He hath begotten us by the Word of Truth & saved & called us with an holy Calling not according to our own works but his own purpose & Grace for

---

[51] 'A Short and Compendius Confession of Faith held by the CHURCH of Christ meeting at Aulcester in the County of WARWICK who are baptized by immersion upon a personal profession of faith do believe ...', in Hayden, *Continuity and Change*, pp. 212-18 (para. 4, p. 212). For the confession, pp. 212-16, and the covenant pp. 217-18, and it is dated 'this seventeenth day of August 1712', p. 218.

[52] 'A Short and Compendius Confession', para. 19, p. 214.

[53] Caleb Evans, *Elisha's Exclamation!*, pp. 22-23.

[54] 'A Short and Compendius Confession', para. 11, p. 213. Cf. para. 17, p. 214, 'making reconciliation for the sins of the people & by once offering up of himself'.

[55] 'A Short and Compendius Confession', paras 12–13, p. 213. See also para. 27, p. 216, which elucidates the doctrine of imputed righteousness.

[56] 'A Short and Compendius Confession', para. 15, p. 214.

[57] 'A Short and Compendius Confession', para. 21, p. 214.

[58] 'A Short and Compendius Confession', para. 25, p. 215. Rippon, *A brief essay*, p. 19, notes the pleasure Foskett got from 'ſeeing his labours crowned with great and happy ſucceſs; of which the very flouriſhing ſtate of his community, at the time of his death, will be conſidered a ſufficient evidence'.

he works in us both to will & to do his own good pleasure & in this change the Arm of the Lord must be revealed ...

The immediately following passage is the closest the confession comes to explicating the mission of the elect: '... He must send the Rod of his Strength out unto the Son except the Father that sent him draw him for it is God alone ... *that translates us into the Kingdom of his Dear son*'.[59]

The importance of 'His Word' has already appeared in the confession, and the declaration of the gospel is again implicit in 'the several standing & stated Ordinances in his House, for the good, growth & increase of his people', first of which is the '*Preaching of His Holy Word*'.[60] For Foskett, however, activism is not confined to preaching the gospel. In a letter to John Rippon in 1795, Joshua Thomas recounted Foskett's close working relationship with John Beddome, and that together they consulted on how 'to spread the tent wider, lengthen the cords and strengthen the stakes'.[61] Further, while deeply committed to what he believed to be true, Hugh Evans reports that Foskett was not extreme in his views, and was deeply concerned that faith be worked out in everyday life: 'While he ſtrongly aſſerted the honours of free grace, he earneſtly contended for the neceſſity of good works; preaching duty as well as privilege, and recommending holineſs as the only way to happineſs.'[62]

The influence of Foskett's Calvinism extended beyond the Academy and the local churches he served to the Western Association.[63] As Roger Hayden has clearly shown,[64] from the time of the Act of Toleration in 1689, the London Baptists[65] were neither able to maintain a national General Assembly nor sustain an Association, its ministers, instead, meeting only amongst themselves in various London coffee

---

[59] 'A Short and Compendius Confession', para. 30, p. 215 (italics added).

[60] 'A Short and Compendius Confession', para. 20, p. 214 (italics added).

[61] Letter from Joshua Thomas to John Rippon, dated 19 March 1795, Letter E. 16 (28) Angus Library, Regent's Park College, Oxford, quoted by Hayden, 'Contribution of Bernard Foskett', p. 191. This same passage, Isa. 54.2-3, was the text used by William Carey in his seminal, and sadly no longer extant, sermon in the history of Baptist and modern missions, preached to the Northamptonshire Association meeting at Nottingham, 30 May 1790. See Rippon, *Baptist Annual Register*, I, pp. 418-19 (p. 419).

[62] Rippon, *A brief essay*, p. 18.

[63] On which, see J.G. Fuller, *A Brief History of the Western Association* (Bristol: I. Hemmons, n.d.).

[64] See especially Hayden, *Continuity and Change*.

[65] Who, Hayden points out, 'Contribution of Bernard Foskett', p. 198, have frequently been portrayed by historians as 'typical of Baptists generally in the eighteenth century', when they were not: e.g., W.T. Whitley, *A History of British Baptists* (London: The Kingsgate Press, 2nd edn, 1932); and A.C. Underwood, *A History of the English Baptists* (London: The Baptist Union Publication Dept., 1947).

houses, which eventually resulted in the founding of the Baptist Board.[66] Further, their prevailing theology became increasingly high Calvinist, of the kind exemplified by John Brine, John Skepp, and John Gill,[67] and while the need for ministerial education was discussed it was never realized.[68] In contrast, and largely as a result of the influence of the Broadmead church, and particularly Foskett,[69] the Western Association between 1689 and 1734[70] maintained its evangelical form of Calvinism, as well as its trinitarianism which had been challenged by the drift towards Socinianism and Arianism exemplified at Salters' Hall in 1719,[71] though in its reformed state General Baptists were excluded along with Unitarians.[72] While not a distinctive of Evangelicalism, Foskett, Broadmead's, the Academy's and Association's orthodox trinitarianism is, nevertheless, a *sine qua non* of Evangelical faith. For example, when Caleb Evans' *The Scripture Doctrine of the Deity of the Son and Holy Spirit* (1766) replied to the Unitarian speculations of a livery servant, George Williams,[73] written two years previously, he was strongly criticized by the Presbyterian, Dr Edward Harwood.[74] Harwood in turn received a reply when Caleb

---

[66] See, Thomas Crosby, *The History of the English Baptists* (4 vols; London: for the Editor, 1738–40), III, pp. 286-89; Ivimey, *History*, III, pp. 178-83; Arthur J. Payne, 'The Baptist Board', *Baptist Quarterly* 1.7 (July, 1923), pp. 321-26.

[67] See, e.g., Brown, *Eighteenth Century*, pp. 72-76.

[68] See, e.g., Ivimey, *History*, I, pp. 478-501 and 327-29, and III, pp. 32-33; and Hayden, *Continuity and Change*, pp. 13-18 and 19-21.

[69] For a detailed discussion of Foskett's influence in the Western Association, see Hayden, 'Contribution of Bernard Foskett', pp. 193-203.

[70] At which time the Association was reformed on the basis of the third edition of the theologically Reformed *London Confession* (1699). See, e.g., Broadmead's 1723 letter, written under Foskett's leadership, which called for the adoption of the third edition of the *London Confession* as the basis of the Association at a time a few years after the Salters' Hall Conference of 1719, and the subsequent drift into Unitarianism of Baptist churches, including those at Trowbridge, Taunton, and Wellington. Foskett and the church's appeal was unsuccessful, though the Confession was eventually adopted in 1732. An extract from the 1723 letter is quoted by J.G. Fuller, *A Brief History of the Western Association*, p. 30. For the letter from the Broadmead church, written by Foskett and Hugh Evans, and dated 'Oct. 22, 1732', which led to the re-establishment of the Association around the *Second London Confession*, see J.G. Fuller, *Brief History of the Western Association*, pp. 33 and 34. See also Ivimey, *History*, III, pp. 160-71, for the period 1719–23; and Hayden's summary covering 1719–34, 'Contribution of Bernard Foskett', pp. 193-99.

[71] E.g., 'Salters' Hall 1719 and the Baptists', *Transactions of the Baptist Historical Society* 5.3 (April, 1917), pp. 172-89.

[72] Cf. Ivimey, *History*, III, p. 168. J.G. Fuller, *Brief History of the Western Association*, pp. 32-33, notes that as a result the General Baptists proposed their own meeting at Morton Hampstead in 1733, though this did not take place.

[73] George Williams, *An Attempt to Restore the Supreme Worship of God The Father Almighty* ([London]: Printed for T. Becket and P.A. De Hont, 1754).

[74] I have only seen the third edition: Caleb Evans, *The Scripture Doctrine of the Deity of the Son and Holy Spirit* (Bristol: Printed and fold by S. Farley, 3rd edn, 1766).

Evans' colleague, James Newton, came to his defence with his own *Reply* (1766),[75] and probably a second one the year after.[76]

Foskett's Students and the Bristol Tradition

During his thirty-eight years as Principal of the Academy, Foskett shared in the preparation for ministry of at least sixty-four Baptist students,[77] half of whom came from the Principality,[78] as well as one other student, the Independent Rev. Herbert Jenkins, who ministered in Maidstone, Kent.[79] Foskett's influence on the churches in which his former students served was considerable. Hugh Evans remarks "'that moſt of those who were under Mr. Foskett's care approved themſelves truly ſerious, and with great reputation filled many of our churches'".[80] At the time of his lecture to the 1795 annual meeting of the Bristol Education Society, John Rippon knew of seven former students under Foskett who were still alive: Benjamin Beddome, AM, son of Foskett's lifelong friend, John Beddome, and minister at Bourton-on-the-Water; John Oulton, AM, of Rawden [sic.], Yorkshire; Edmund Watkins of Usk; John Evans, at that time minister at Northampton; Benjamin Francis, AM, of Horsley; Morgan Jones, LLD, of Hammersmith; and John Evans of Pentre.[81] While Rippon concedes that Foskett had not been 'the firſt of tutors', nevertheless it was right that he be honoured for educating 'ſome good ſcholars, and ſeveral of the greateſt miniſters who have adorned our denomination ſince the days of the reformation'. Leaving aside the six he has just mentioned, Rippon singles out for special mention 'a ſcholar' of whom the Congregationalist Dr Thomas Gibbons had remarked, "'I think ... that Dr. [Thomas] Llewelyn is the firſt ſcholar we have among the Proteſtant diſſenters.'" In addition, Rippon identifies Robert Day, AM, of Wellington, John

---

[75] James Newton, *A Reply to a Letter To the Reverend Mr. Caleb Evans Of Bristol* (Bristol: Printed and Sold by S. Farley, 1766).

[76] By-Stander, *Animadversions on the Rev. Mr. E. Harwood's Affectations and Candid Letter, to the Rev. Mr. Caleb Evans* (Bristol: Printed and ſold by S. Farley, 1767). By-Stander appears to be identified as Newton by Rippon, *Baptist Annual Register*, I, p. 563.

[77] So Rippon, *A brief essay*, p. 20, who said, 'If the liſt of Mr. Foſkett's ſtudents now before me is complete ...'; also Ivimey, *History*, IV, p. 269. See also, Nuttall, 'Welsh Students'. Hayden, 'Contribution of Bernard Foskett', p. 199, gives the number as 'over seventy', and in this is followed by Haykin, 'Foskett, Bernard (1685–1758)'.

[78] Rippon, *A brief essay*, p. 21.

[79] So Rippon, *A brief essay*, p. 20 n. *; and Ivimey, *History*, IV, p. 269.

[80] Quoted by Rippon, *A brief essay*, p. 21. Roger Hayden, 'Bernard Foskett and Abingdon, 1743–5', *Baptist Quarterly* 43.2 (April, 2009), pp. 68-76 (p. 76), says of William Fuller's letter from Abingdon to Foskett, dated 9 February 1744 (n.s. 1745), 'It indicates the pivotal position of Foskett as President of the Bristol Academy in providing ministers for provincial Baptist churches, following the training he had given them', and also provides evidence for the 'close relationship between Foskett and his students'.

[81] Rippon, *A brief essay*, p. 21. For these and other students of Foskett's, see Swaine, *Faithful Men*, pp. 42-69.

Ash, LLD, of Pershore, and John Ryland, AM, at Northampton, but holds up Hugh Evans, AM, for special note.[82]

Foskett's Colleagues and Successors and Moderate Calvinism

Few details are known for Braithwaite's and Harrison's theological convictions, but that cannot be said about Gifford, Hugh Evans, and Newton.

E.F. Clipsham notes that Andrew Gifford was among the few 'influential individuals' who resisted the high-Calvinism of Gill and Brine and 'kept alive in various degrees a moderate evangelical Calvinism'.[83] This is reflected in his lecture on the Holy Spirit, *The Living Water*, just sixteen years after leaving the Academy and Broadmead, in which he appeals to the unconverted to seek divine grace.[84] The Spirit of grace is Christ's gift, and among his many works is to incline saints 'to come to him for life and falvation'.[85] Before conversion 'religion was a burden', but 'Now, the foul being fet at liberty by Chriſt's *free Spirit*', the believer 'delights to do his will'.[86] That his concern for salvation extends beyond the British Isles appears when he exhorts his hearers to pray for Christ's 'intereſt in the world', after which he exclaims, 'Oh, when fhall the Redeemer come to Zion ... and his Spirit be poured out upon all flefh?' From this he infers 'our Obligations to admire, and adore the free grace of God, in the falvation and recovery of fallen man'. As surely as is God's majesty 'fo is his mercy, fo is his love, fo is his grace; like himfelf, infinite, and

---

[82] Rippon, *A brief essay*, pp. 22-23.

[83] E.F. Clipsham, 'Andrew Fuller and Fullerism: A Study in Evangelical Calvinism. 4. Fuller as a Theologian', *Baptist Quarterly* 20.6 (April, 1964), pp. 268-76 (p. 268). Others include Alverey Jackson of Barnoldswick, e.g., in his *The Question Answered* (London: Printed for J. Ward, 1752), which elicited the reply from John Brine, *Motives to Love and Unity among Calvinists* (London: Printed and Sold by John Ward). See also Jackson's *Religion deſcribed* (London: Printed for John Ward, 1760). Another identified by Clipsham is Robert Hall, Sr, e.g., *Help to Zion's Travellers* (Bristol: Printed by William Pine, 1781). To these should be added Abraham Booth, e.g., *The Death of Legal Hope, the Life of Evangelical Obedience* (London: s.n., 1770), and *Glad Tidings to Perishing Sinners* (London: Printed for the Author, 1796). On Jackson, see Ivimey, *History*, III, pp. 271-72, and IV, p. 286. On Hall, Sr, see Rippon, *Baptist Annual Register*, I, pp. 226-41; Ivimey, *History*, IV, pp. 41-42, 87, 443, 528 and 603-609; and M.A.G. Haykin, 'Robert Hall, Sr. (1728–1791), in M.A.G. Haykin (ed.) *The British Particular Baptists 1638–1910* (3 vols; Springfield, MO: Particular Baptist Press, 1998–2003), I, pp. 203-11. On Booth, see, e.g., M.A.G. Haykin and V.J. Haykin (eds), *The First Counsellor of Our Denomination: Studies in the Life of Abraham Booth (1734–1806)* (Springfield, MO: Particular Baptist Press, 2011); and Ernest A. Payne, 'Abraham Booth, 1734–1806', *Baptist Quarterly* 26.1 (January, 1975), pp. 28-42.

[84] Andrew Gifford, *The Living Water* (London: Printed and Sold by J. Lewis, 1746), on John 4.14.

[85] Andrew Gifford, *The Living Water*, p. 4.

[86] Andrew Gifford, *The Living Water*, p. 5.

therefore incomprehenſible'.[87] Gifford's biblicism is reflected in the sheer number of biblical quotations and references peppered throughout this sermon, and is evident throughout his other works.[88]

Gifford was also one of a small number of Baptist admirers[89] of George Whitefield (1714–70) at a time when the Particular Baptists were predominantly 'quite cool' even 'frigid, towards the revival and its leaders'[90] because Whitefield, even though he was a Calvinist, appeared Arminian when he exhorted people to trust in Christ.[91] Ivimey records that Gifford 'was very intimate' with Whitefield, attending the laying of the foundation stone for Whitefield's Tottenham Court Chapel in May 1756. On one occasion Gifford was met on his way to Tottenham Court Road and was asked if he was going to hear Whitefield. His reply was that '"I am going to light my farthing rushlight at his flaming torch."'[92] Such was his respect for the revivalist that he revised eighteen of Whitefield's sermons which had been transcribed verbatim by Joseph Gurney, the parliamentary shorthand writer and stenographer, who was also a bookseller,[93] a member of the Red Cross Street church before moving to the Maze Pond church, Southwark, under the ministry of another Bristol trained minister, James Dore.[94]

---

[87] Andrew Gifford, *The Living Water*, pp. 18-19 (original italics removed).

[88] E.g., Andrew Gifford, 'The Exhortation', in John Potts, *A Sermon Preached at the Ordination of the Rev. Mr. Joseph Gwennap* (London: Printed by D. Nottage, 1764), pp. 67-84, based on 1 Tim. 4.16; and *Bundle of Myrrh, or Rules for a Christian's daily Meditation and Practice* (Newport, RI: Printed and Sold by Samuel Hall, 1763). This anonymous pamphlet is attributed to Gifford by Ivimey, *History*, III, p. 606.

[89] Another was John Oulton, see Whitefield's 1742 letters to Oulton in George Whitefield, *Letters of George Whitefield: For the Period 1734–1742* (Edinburgh: The Banner of Truth Trust, 1976 [1771]), pp. 381-82 and 393-94. Oulton ministered in Leominster from 1731–48/49, then Liverpool until 1765.

[90] See M.A.G. Haykin, 'The Baptist Identity: A View from the Eighteenth Century', *Evangelical Quarterly* 67.2 (1995), pp. 137-52 (p. 141).

[91] Cf. Ivimey's treatment of both Particular Baptists and other Calvinist Dissenters who rejected Whitefield's preaching, and his own appreciation of it, *History*, III, pp. 279-81.

[92] Ivimey, *History*, III, pp. 600-601.

[93] George Whitefield, *Eighteen Sermons Preached by the Late Rev. George Whitefield, A.M.* (rev. Andrew Gifford; Newburyport [MA]: Edmund M. Blunt, 1797). See 'Joseph Gurney (1744–1815)', in Page Life, 'Gurney, Thomas (1705–1770), stenographer', *ODNB*, accessed 1 April 2015. Gurney defended the accuracy of his transcriptions in his *J. Gurney's Appeal to the Public* ([London]: Printed for Joseph Gurney, [c.1771]).

[94] So Timothy Whelan, 'Martha Gurney and William Fox: Baptist Printer and Radical Reformer, 1791–1794', in John H.Y. Briggs (ed.), *Pulpit and People: Studies in Eighteenth-Century Baptist Life and Thought* (Studies in Baptist History and Thought, 28; Milton Keynes: Paternoster, 2009), pp. 165-201 (p. 169). Dore studied at Bristol under both Hugh and Caleb Evans (1779–82), and on whom see Swaine, *Faithful Men*, pp. 93-99.

Hugh Evans (1712–81)⁹⁵ joined Foskett in 1734, and together they shared in the ministry 'with the moſt perfect mutual harmony and affection' for nearly twenty-four years.⁹⁶ Evans' 'religious ſentiments were perfectly evangelical',⁹⁷ and permeate his three published sermons.⁹⁸ He exhorts congregations to accept a minister's ministry, 'to receive the doctrine taught by him, provided it be agreeable to the word of God, to practiſe the duties recommended by him upon evangelical principles'.⁹⁹

First, the able minister, who must be a converted man,¹⁰⁰ is one with the 'earneſt deſire ... to be made uſe of as an inſtrument of winning [the ſouls of men] to Chriſt'.¹⁰¹ All such ministers' 'ſuceſs is from God' because it is God who convinces and converts sinners.¹⁰² Many came to faith through Evans' testimony 'wherever he went' to 'the glorious goſpel of the grace of God'.¹⁰³ A faithful servant,¹⁰⁴ then, is the one through whom congregations 'hear the glad tidings of ſalvation by a redeemer, ... good-will to ſinful men. You hear of the full and free pardon of all ſin through faith in Chriſt', in whom God was 'reconciling the world unto himſelf, not imputing to them their treſpaſſes, nor their ſins'.¹⁰⁵

Secondly, able ministers preach 'Chriſt and him crucified', and with Paul make 'this the conſtant and chief ſubject' of their ministrations.¹⁰⁶ Their duties include feeding God's flock 'with the wholeſome words of our Lord Jeſus Chriſt, and the doctrine which is according to godlineſs'. They are to be fed

> with the knowledge of Chriſt, the glories of his perſon as God-man the great Mediator, his ſtupendous love and grace in undertaking and executing the great work of

---

⁹⁵ For biographical details, see Caleb Evans, *Elisha's Exclamation!*, pp. 17-43; also in his *God the everlaſting Portion of his People* (Bristol: Printed and ſold by W. Pine, T. Cadell, M. Ward, &c., 1776). See also Swaine, *Faithful Men*, *passim*; Moon, *Education for Ministry*, pp. 4-24; and 'Evans, Hugh (c.1713–1781) (person id: 216)', Dissenting Academies Online, accessed 18 February 2015.

⁹⁶ Caleb Evans, *Elisha's Exclamation!*, pp. 21-22.

⁹⁷ Caleb Evans, *Elisha's Exclamation!*, pp. 34-35. Cf. 34, where the content of Hugh Evans' preaching included 'the aſtoniſhing grace of the gospel!' along with the comment 'How would he lay the ſinner in the very duſt before the throne of a holy God, and magnify the riches of free grace in his ſalvation'.

⁹⁸ Caleb Evans, *Elisha's Exclamation!*, p. 36 n. *.

⁹⁹ Caleb Evans and Hugh Evans, *A Charge and Sermon, delivered at the Ordination of the Rev. Thomas Dunscombe* (Bristol: Printed and ſold by W. Pine, T. Cadell, M. Ward, &c., 1773), p. 31. (Hereafter, Caleb Evans, *A Charge*, and Hugh Evans, *The Sermon*.)

¹⁰⁰ Hugh Evans, *The Able Miniſter* (Bristol: Printed and Sold by W. Pine, T. Cadell, M. Ward, S. Edwards, &c., 1773), pp. 41-42. See also his *The Sermon*, p. 24.

¹⁰¹ Hugh Evans, *The Able Miniſter*, p. 32. So also *The Sermon*, p. 30.

¹⁰² Hugh Evans, *The Able Miniſter*, p. 34.

¹⁰³ Cf. Caleb Evans, *Elisha's Exclamation!*, p. 37.

¹⁰⁴ This is a recurrent emphasis throughout Hugh Evans' sermons: e.g., *The Able Miniſter*, pp. 27, 34, 35 and 40; *The Sermon*, pp. 34-35; and *Miniſters deſcribed*, pp. 31-32.

¹⁰⁵ Hugh Evans, *The Sermon*, p. 35.

¹⁰⁶ Hugh Evans, *The Able Miniſter*, p. 30.

redemption, the infinite value and virtue of his ſacrifice and atonement, and the perfection and excellency of his ſpotleſs righteouſneſs.[107]

Thirdly, Evans' biblicism is clear throughout his sermons in the way they are all expositions of biblical texts,[108] and he constantly supports his arguments from scripture. Most conclusively, for him able ministers are, and can only be, able ministers '*of the new testament*', it has to be 'a *goſpel miniſtry*'.[109]

Fourthly, Evans' Evangelical activism is evident not simply through the exercise of his own ministry at Broadmead, which experienced growth during his ministry there,[110] but also in his preaching. He acknowledged the contemporary mission in which both ministers and the churches shared with the Apostle Paul who, in the context of 2 Corinthians 3.6, 'aſſerts and vindicates the divine miſſion and miniſtry of himſelf and his brethren' against the Judaizers.[111] Faithful ministers are those sent by God 'upon the moſt important errand in the world', sent '*to hold forth the word of life*, to be a ſweet ſavour unto God both in them that believe and in them that periſh, the ſavour of life unto life, or elſe, O dreadful alternative! Of death unto death.' They are 'as an inſtrument in God's hand, for the conviction and converſion of ſinners, and the edification of his ſaints and people'.[112]

Such a commitment to mission was not just theoretical, as students were active preachers. During vacations they regularly itinerated, and mission work was one focus of their labours.[113] In 1773, for example, the Bristol Education Society supported a gospel mission to Cornwall with Benjamin Francis[114] as the itinerant preacher, and this was followed in 1776 by a mission to North Wales, a leading figure in which was Thomas Llewelyn.[115]

---

[107] Hugh Evans, *Miniſters deſcribed*, p. 16.

[108] Hugh Evans, *The Able Miniſter*, on 2 Cor. 3.6; *Miniſters deſcribed*, on Zech. 1.5; and *The Sermon*, on Phil. 2.29.

[109] Hugh Evans, *The Able Miniſter*, p. 3 (first italics added, second italics original).

[110] Caleb Evans, *Elisha's Exclamation!*, pp. 37-38, 'Nor did he labor in vain, or ſpend his ſtrength for nought, but it pleaſed God, both at home and abroad, to give him many ſeals to his miniſtry, many that were his joy here, and will be the crown of his rejoicing in the day of the Lord Jeſus hereafter.'

[111] Hugh Evans, *The Able Miniſter*, p. 4.

[112] Hugh Evans, *The Sermon*, p. 30 (italics original).

[113] Moon, *Education for Ministry*, p. 20.

[114] On whom, see M.A.G. Haykin, 'Benjamin Francis (1734–1799)', in Haykin (ed.), *British Particular Baptists*, II, pp. 16-29; 'Francis, Benjamin (c.1734–1799) (person id: 2532)', Dissenting Academies Online, accessed 2 February 2015. Francis studied at the Academy c.1753–c.1755, and went on to minister at Chipping Sodbury (1756–79) and then Horsley, Gloucestershire (1759–99).

[115] On the Cornwall and other such missions, see, e.g., Hayden, *Continuity and Change*, pp. 129-31; and on the North Wales mission, see T.M. Bassett, *The Welsh Baptists* (Swansea: Ilston House, 1977), pp. 100-107. See also D.L. Thomas, rev. Karen E. Smith, 'Llewelyn, Thomas (c.1720–1783), Particular Baptist minister', *ODNB*, accessed 28 April 2013; and

In the little information we have on Newton,[116] there are strong indications that he shared the Evangelicalism of the Academy and his two colleagues, Hugh and Caleb Evans in his biblicism, crucicentrism, and conversionism. Rippon quoted the preacher at Newton's funeral, an unidentified former student who at the time was a minister in London, to the effect that 'As a Minifter, his sermons were fenfible, ferious, and evangelical'.[117] That 'evangelical' here means more than simply Bible-based is suggested by the closeness and unity in which he worked with Hugh and Caleb Evans. Of these relationships Rippon recounts that

> it is no inconfiderable teftimony to the excellence and amiablenefs of his character, that, during the whole of his connexion in the church and in the academy, the moft perfect unbroken amity mutually subfifited between him and each one of his colleagues.[118]

Further,

> His abilities, as a divine and a preacher of the Gofpel were highly refpectable[.] he was a workman that needed not to be afhamed; he rightly divided the word of truth; and, by an open, clear, faithful manifeftation of the truth, commended himfelf to every man's confcience in the fight of God.[119]

Shortly before his death, Newton declared, '... I find it a comfort to me to reflect, that, according to the beft of my ability, I have preached Chrift crucified'.[120] In fact, Newton's first sermon at the Pithay in 1757 had been on 1 Corinthians 2.2 ('For I determined not to know any thing among you, fave Jefus Chrift, and him crucified'), and his last sermon was similarly on 1 Corinthians 1.23-24 ('But we preach Chrift crucified, unto the Jews a ftumbling," [sic] &c').[121] Rippon also reported that Newton's ministry was not 'without many feals to his miniftry, though his fuccefs was not equal to his wifhes'.[122]

The eldest child of Hugh and Sarah (née Browne, d.1751), Caleb Evans[123] was educated at Mile End Academy,[124] baptized by Dr Joseph Stennett, and accepted into membership of the Little Wild Street church the following Sunday, 1 December

---

'Llewelyn [Llewellyn, Llewelin], Thomas (c.1720–1783), Dissenting Academies Online, accessed 2 February 2015. Llewelyn studied at the Academy c.1740–c.1742.

[116] Additional to that already cited, see Rippon, *A brief essay*, pp. 35 and 36-41 n. *.

[117] Rippon, *A brief essay*, p. 39.

[118] Rippon, *A brief essay*, p. 37.

[119] Rippon, *A brief essay*, p. 39.

[120] Rippon, *A brief essay*, p. 40.

[121] Rippon, *A brief essay*, p. 41.

[122] Rippon, *A brief essay*, p. 40.

[123] On whom, see Swaine, *Faithful Men, passim*; Moon, *Education for Ministry*, pp. 9-26; Roger Hayden, 'Caleb Evans (1737-1791), Particular Baptist minister and college head', *ODNB*, accessed 2 April 2013.

[124] See Roger Hayden, 'Caleb Evans' Ministerial Formation at the Mile End Academy, 1752–58', *Baptist Quarterly* 44.4 (October, 2011), pp. 238-45.

1753.[125] After less than a year as Josiah Thompson's assistant at Unicorn Yard, London, Evans moved back to Bristol as his father's assistant at Broadmead in August 1759, and was ordained eight years later.[126] Until his father's death in 1781, Caleb Evans was a tutor at the Academy, at which time he succeeded his father as Principal until his own death in 1791.[127]

At the time Caleb Evans joined the Academy as a tutor in 1759 the Evangelical Revival was just beginning to find acceptance among sympathetic Baptists, Andrew Gifford and Alverey Jackson among them, but it would be over a decade before this number increased beyond such rare figures, and it would not be until 1766 that Evans began publishing his sermons, his first being his trinitarian response to Edward Harwood. But it wasn't long before he was publishing regularly and with this, his pulpit ministry, and his teaching his influence as an early advocate of Evangelical Calvinism as opposed to moderate Calvinism began to prepare for the major shifts which soon took place with Dan Taylor's forming of the New Connexion of General Baptists[128] and the Bristol Education Society, both in 1770, and the formation of the BMS in 1792.[129] Of Evans' preaching Samuel Stennett says it was 'evangelical, experimental, and practical'.[130]

Such is clear in his 1775 sermon before the Bristol Education Society based on Matthew 6.10, 'Thy kingdom come!', by which time Caleb Evans stood firmly within the Evangelical mainstream, such that no longer need the historian and theologian speak of moderate Calvinism but Evangelical Calvinism among Baptists,[131] of the same kind as later held by the likes of Andrew Fuller, John Ryland, Jr, Robert Hall, Jr, John Sutcliff, Samuel Pearce, and, of course, William Carey, all of whom were in some way associated with the Bristol Academy either

---

[125] From Caleb Evans' personal notebook, the 'Evans Ryland Book', quoted by Hayden, 'Caleb Evans' Ministerial Formation', p. 239.

[126] See *A Charge and Sermon, together with an Introductory Discourse, and Confession of Faith, delivered at the Ordination of the Rev. Mr. Caleb Evans* (Bristol: Printed and Sold by S. Farley, 1767), which includes Hugh Evans' 'Introduction', pp. 3-10, Dr Samuel Stennett's *Charge*, pp. 37-71, and John Tommas' *The duties incumbent on church members*, pp. 73-99.

[127] See Stennett and Tommas, *The Mortality of Miniſters contraſted*. Stennett's *Sermon* includes an outline of Caleb Evans' life and ministry, pp. 25-45.

[128] See, e.g., Frank Rinaldi, *The Tribe of Dan: The New Connexion of General Baptists 1770–1891: A Study in the Transition from Revival Movement to Established Denomination* (Studies in Baptist History and Thought, 10; Milton Keynes: Paternoster 2008).

[129] Brian Stanley, *The History of the Baptist Missionary Society 1792–1992* (Edinburgh: T&T Clark, 1992), pp. 1-35.

[130] Stennett, *Sermon*, p. 28.

[131] In *A Charge*, p. 6, Caleb Evans exhorts the preaching of 'the *ability* of Chriſt to ſave; to ſave the very chief of ſinners, to ſave unto the *uttermoſt*, to ſave *all* that come to God by him. Preach the *willingneſs* of Chriſt to ſave. Tell poor broken-hearted ſinners … that whoſoever cometh to him he will in *no wiſe* caſt out' (italics original).

through their having studied there or being close associates of those who had.[132] For Caleb Evans, the first aim of the Academy was 'The education of pious candidates for the miniſtry', the second 'the encouragement of miſſionaries to preach the goſpel wherever providence opens a door'.[133] The business of the minister is to be 'an inſtrument in God's hand, to *ſave the ſouls* of them that hear you'.[134]

God's kingdom, then, 'is formed' by 'the preaching of Chriſt and him crucified, accompanied with the influences of the bleſſed Spirit'.[135] Later he recounts how the Son of God was apprehended 'and crucified; but upon the croſs he bruiſed the ſerpent's head ... Upon the croſs he ſpoiled principalities and powers and made a ſhew of them openly, triumphing over them in it.'[136] The reason the incarnate Christ did this was because in him the just suffered for the unjust, he lay down his life for the sheep, 'bearing their ſins in his own body upon the tree', demonstrating 'not that we loved God, but that he loved us, and ſent his Son to be a propitiation for us'.[137]

Evans' sermon on the kingdom is filled with the gospel and biblical passages, language and allusions, such that his biblicism is unmistakable, and made explicit when he speaks of the 'miniſtry of the word',[138] and 'a goſpel miniſtry, goſpel means of grace', and that we 'be ready cheerfully to embrace every opportunity of ſpreading the goſpel and encouraging its miniſters'.[139] This concern extends beyond mere proclamation to an ethical activism,[140] for the Christian's 'love is not in word and

---

[132] See, e.g., W.R. Ward, 'The Baptists and the Transformation of the Church, 1780–1830', *Baptist Quarterly* 25.4 (October, 1973), pp. 167-84; and Leonard G. Champion, 'Evangelical Calvinism and the Structures of Baptist Church Life', *Baptist Quarterly* 28.5 (January, 1980), pp. 196-208.

[133] Caleb Evans, *The Kingdom of God*, p. 24.

[134] Caleb Evans, *A Charge*, p. 17 (italics original).

[135] Caleb Evans, *The Kingdom of God*, p. 7. See also, *A Charge*, p. 5.

[136] Caleb Evans, *The Kingdom of God*, pp. 16-17 (original italics removed).

[137] Caleb Evans, *God the everlaſting Portion of his People*, p. 10. In *A Charge*, p. 6, he calls Christ as his people's 'prieſt to atone and intercede for them'. In *A Confession of Faith delivered at his Ordination*, pp. 28-29, the agonies Christ suffered when he expired on the cross are described as 'a vicarious atoning ſacrifice for the ſins of his choſen people', and he is the *'procuring cauſe of the whole of ſalvation ... to all them that believe ...'* (italics original). See the more detailed discussion in Caleb Evans' *Christ Crucified; or the Scripture Doctrine of the Atonement briefly Illustrated and Defended* (Bristol: Printed by William Pine, 1789), in which he declares, pp. 53-55, that to those convinced of their sin and who feel its burden on their consciences 'We lift up before them a crucified Savior, and bid them look and live. We direct them to the bleeding Lamb of God, the ſuffering Savior' and 'teach men, not to think themſelves whole and that they have no need of a phyſician, but to go to Chriſt crucified as alone able to ſave, to ſave to the very uttermoſt all that come to God by him.'

[138] Caleb Evans, *The Kingdom of God*, p. 12. Throughout *A Confession of Faith delivered at his Ordination*, Evans' statements of belief are based, p. 24, on 'that which my bible teaches me'.

[139] Caleb Evans, *The Kingdom of God*, p. 21.

[140] Cf. Caleb Evans in *The Elders, Miniſters and Meſſengers of the Several Baptist Churches meeting at Exeter, Tiverton, Preſcott ...* (s.l.: s.n., [1778]), pp. 1-5 (p. 3), 'A

tongue, but in deed and in truth', and, as well as supporting the work of the Society, embraces 'other fchemes of piety and benevolence'.[141] And though conversion is not specifically discussed in this sermon, it nevertheless permeates it. Evans asks his hearers if they can pray for God's kingdom to come 'without confidering the advancement of this kingdom in the world, as an object highly defirable, infinitely important? ... Our bleffed Savior evidently points it out to us as that which has *the firft claim to our attention and regard*',[142] and this advancement of the kingdom comes from God and includes 'the growth' of the kingdom. 'It is his gofpel that is the power of God unto falvation.' God sends out his ministers to preach this gospel and blesses it when it is preached 'accompanying it with the power of his Spirit to the heart'.[143] In all this he is talking about conversion in all but name. Elsewhere this is made explicit. Preaching focused on Christ is the preaching which God has blessed in every age and 'will blefs to the conviction and converfion of finners'.[144]

'Able and evangelical'

As we have seen, the Bristol Tradition is summed up in the preparation of 'able and evangelical ministers', but the form of this phrase most remembered is 'able, evangelical, lively, zealous ministers of the gospel', first coined, as far as I have been able to determine, by Caleb Evans in 1781 in his funeral sermon for his father.[145] But what did these words mean?

The earliest use of 'able' that I have so far found is in the founding constitution of the Bristol Education Society in 1770 which, though the pioneering vision of Caleb Evans, was clearly the fruit of the two Evans' combined work with their colleagues at the Academy, the Broadmead church, former students and those ministers and churches who subscribed to the new Society. The first 'solo' use of the phrase that I have found to date is Hugh Evans' sermon preached at Broadmead before the Society in 1773, *The Able Minister*, on 2 Corinthians 3.6, in which he translates ἱκάνωσεν 'able' in accordance with the Authorised Version,[146] but in his exposition

---

chriftian fpirit, the fruits of righteoufnefs, and the continued exercife of grace, are the beft evidences of a real converfion.'

[141] Caleb Evans, *The Kingdom of God*, pp. 21-22. He continues, p. 22, 'yet fuch is your love to the gofpel, fuch the honorable and affectionate thoughts you entertain of it, fuch your ardent zeal for the promotion and fpread of it in the world, that with a generofity truly exemplary and noble, you have given birth to a new Institution for the advancement of the kingdom of God.'

[142] Caleb Evans, *The Kingdom of God*, pp. 18-19 (italics added).

[143] Caleb Evans, *The Kingdom of God*, pp. 19-20.

[144] Caleb Evans, *A Charge*, p. 7.

[145] Caleb Evans, *Elisha's Exclamation!*, p. 31. However, it is frequently misattributed. E.g., Moon, *Education for Ministry*, pp. 11 and 115 n. 23, incorrectly attributes this to Caleb Evans' *An Address to the Students in the Academy at Bristol. April 12, 1770*, in Rippon, *Baptist Annual Register*, I, pp. 345-51.

[146] Hugh Evans, *The Able Minister*, p. 3.

of the verse he maintains that it 'properly fignifies *fit* or *sufficient*', as in 2 Corinthians 2.16, thus it represents 'a perfon that is properly qualified for the work of the miniftry'.[147] As such it brings together the foresight of Edward Terrill, the trustees of the Terrill and several other funds bequeathed by members of the Broadmead church, and Foskett, Hugh and Caleb Evans, and their colleagues at the Academy in their commitment to training ministers for the Baptist churches. The impression I have from reading this material is that the Society's constitution brought together 'able and evangelical' in a formal statement of purpose but not for the first time. Over half this key sermon describes the 'one whom God hath made an *able minifter* of the new testament'.[148]

For Hugh Evans an able minister, that is, someone qualified to be such, is a person who 'well underftands the various and extensive duties of the facred office, and has such talents and abilities as furnifh him, in a good degree, for the difcharge of them'.[149] For 'fuch a minister, many important qualifications are neceffary'. First is a sufficient number of natural gifts which form the character, including a good constitution, reasonable physical strength and health, a sound mind, and the ability to speak freely and intelligibly.[150]

This leads to the second, that 'the improvements of *human learning*' are 'highly defirable, if not abfolutely neceffary', because in order for someone to be 'wife and knowing' they 'muft be ready to ftudy', and he used Timothy to demonstrate this (1 Tim. 4.13-15).[151] Responding to those who denied the importance of learning, and reflecting a genuine Baptist biblicism, Evans argues,

> Befides, if a man when he is a minifter is to *read* and *ftudy*, then furely he ought *before* he enters upon the miniftry, to be *able* to read and ftudy. And if he is to *read* and *ftudy* the holy fcriptures, furely it muft be very defirable to be able to read them in the languages in which they were wrote, without being obliged to view them through the medium of fallible and varying tranflations; and to be acquainted with thofe ancient cuftoms and ufages, with other branches of learning, whereby he may be the better able to underftand, explain and defend them. Upon the whole, if a *Timothy*, an extraordinary minifter, was yet to purfue ufeful knowledge in an ordinary way; how much more muft this be incumbent upon *us* who are fo much, in every refpect, his inferiors?[152]

---

[147] Hugh Evans, *The Able Minifter*, p. 6.

[148] Hugh Evans, *The Able Minifter*, pp. 5-30, quotation from p. 5 (italics original).

[149] Hugh Evans, *The Able Minifter*, p. 6.

[150] Hugh Evans, *The Able Minifter*, pp. 6-10. Evans later stated that all natural abilities come from God, p. 30.

[151] Hugh Evans, *The Able Minifter*, pp. 10-11 (italics original).

[152] Hugh Evans, *The Able Minifter*, pp. 11-12 (italics original). On the importance of knowledge of the biblical languages, see also p. 43. While Evans openly declared, p. 43, the intention of the Bristol Education Society as 'to improve the minds of thofe pious perfons who are recommended by the churches to its patronage, by proper cultivation, reading, ftudy and converfation'. However, pp. 42-43, this did not mean that the Academy discouraged 'the calling of thofe who appear to be fitted by God for ufefulnefs in his church, though they may

To this end, Evans and the Academy advanced a liberal, or broad, education on the grounds that whoever reads the Bible 'with the leaſt degree of attention' must know that it contains every type of knowledge – 'natural, hiſtorical, moral, civil and other kinds of knowledge, as well as that which is more immediately theological or religious'. Ministers do not read and mediate upon scripture just for their own faith, but it is their

> province to explain and illuſtrate to others thoſe things which may be hard to be underſtood, to defend the cauſe of God and truth againſt thoſe who may oppoſe it, and to ſeek out for acceptable words, as well as arguments, whereby the great and important truths of God may be moſt effectually impreſſed upon the minds of men.[153]

Such a pursuit of 'uſeful knowledge' is commended by 'the conduct of wiſe and good men of all ages', among them the Old Testament schools of the prophets, the seminaries of learning, the reformers, as well as by Jesus, who himself listened to the teachers in the temple (Lk. 2.46).[154] When 'ſanctified, and humbly devoted to the service of God', such learning had given the English Bible, as well as in various other languages, and it was 'humble learning' which gave 'thoſe valuable commentaries, and expoſitions of the ſcriptures, which have been so eminently uſeful to the people of God in every age', also apologetic works which had defended Christianity, and doctrinal treatises.[155]

Thirdly, divine and supernatural gifts were also necessary for an able minister; for instance, gifts of grace, and someone who is 'apt to teach' (1 Tim. 3.2).[156] Unequivocally, for Evans, 'It is God, and he alone, who makes men able ministers of the new teſtament'.[157] As all natural abilities come from him, so, too, do supernatural

---

not have an opportunity to acquire the advantages of learning, whereby their ſphere of uſefulneſs might be enlarged.' He acknowledged there were 'many of this character' who were 'burning and ſhining lights in the church', and who were greatly respected and honoured. To such the Society was 'ready to give all the countenance and encouragement they can reaſonably deſire'.

[153] Hugh Evans, *The Able Miniſter*, p. 13.

[154] Hugh Evans, *The Able Miniſter*, pp. 15-21, quotations from p. 15. He further expounds on the importance of 'knowledge and experience' in *Miniſters deſcribed*, pp. 9-12 and p. 16. E.g., he asserts, p. 10, that 'Miniſters are expected to bring out of the ſacred repoſitory things new and old, rightly to divide the word of truth, and to give to every one his portion in due ſeaſon', but this is not sufficient, for doing so *'requires much experience in the things of God*, to enable us to deal properly with tempted and diſtreſſed ſouls' (italics added). For this reason, p. 11, he believes that when Paul 'deſcribes a chriſtian biſhop or father, he ſays, – *not a novice*, one lately converted to the Christian faith, a raw, ignorant, unexperienced perſon; but one who has been of ſome ſtanding in the church of God, and has attained a competent ſhare of knowledge and experience' (italics original).

[155] Hugh Evans, *The Able Miniſter*, pp. 18-20.

[156] Hugh Evans, *The Able Miniſter*, pp. 25-29.

[157] Hugh Evans, *The Able Miniſter*, p. 30. See also pp. 35-36.

endowments, and both types of gifts comprise the 'miniſterial gifts'.[158] It follows – or precedes – that it is God who calls to the work of the ministry,[159] and who continues to both assist and help them in their work.[160]

Fourthly, an able minister must be 'a truly *evangelical* miniſter, or a miniſter *not of the letter, but of the ſpirit*'. For Evans, the law is the Mosaic law, and the spirit is the gospel (so 2 Corinthians 3.7-9).

> An *able miniſter* therefore of the new testament, is one that is not a *legal*, but a truly *evangelical* miniſter. One who is led into the true ſpirit of the goſpel, who preaches Chriſt and him crucified, and, with our apoſtle, determines to make this the conſtant and chief ſubject of his miniſtrations.

Evans exclaimed 'how great a bleſſing to the church, and to the world' such an able minister will be.[161]

Evans' final points in his sermon on *The Able Miniſter* is that they should be devoted to Christ, and as *'embassadors for Christ'* they should be humble because 'what have we that we have not *received?* ... Is not *all* our sufficiency of God? Let him then that glorieth, glory only in the Lord!'[162] Further, they should be reliant on God 'for thoſe divine aids which are neceſſary to enable them succeſsfully to diſharge the duties of their office'. The church, then, should look to God to supply these able ministers, and be thankful to him when he does.[163]

The importance of 'able ministers' comes out again and again in the Bristol Tradition. Preaching at Thomas Dunscombe's ordination to the church at Coate, Oxfordshire, Caleb Evans contrasts 'a ſolid, able, faithful, laborious miniſter, and a conceited, idle, meer declaimer', and calls on the churches to be 'ſenſible of the difference there is betwixt' them.[164] Three years later, James Newton applauded the annual meetings of the Bristol Education Society for the purpose 'of encouraging a riſing miniſtry' and the way they had 'repeatedly addreſſed – The qualifications of an Able Miniſter', and that each year the addresses aimed at animating those gathered 'in the noble cauſe' in which they were engaged as well as 'to excite others' to join in the work. To that end, his text was Luke 16.2, 'Give an account of thy Stewardſhip'.[165]

---

[158] Hugh Evans, *The Able Miniſter*, pp. 30-31.
[159] Hugh Evans, *The Able Miniſter*, pp. 31-33.
[160] Hugh Evans, *The Able Miniſter*, pp. 33-34.
[161] Hugh Evans, *The Able Miniſter*, pp. 29-30 (italics original).
[162] Hugh Evans, *The Able Miniſter*, pp. 36-37 (italics original). He further expounds ministers as ambassadors of Christ in *The Sermon*, pp. 25 ('embaſſadors of peace'), 27 and 34, and *Miniſters deſcribed*, p. 33; as does Caleb Evans, *A Charge*, p. 17.
[163] Hugh Evans, *The Able Miniſter*, pp. 37-38.
[164] Caleb Evans, *A Charge*, p. 16.
[165] James Newton, *The Good Steward* (Bristol: W. Pine, and M. Ward, n.d. [1776]), p. 3. Newton was among those described by Rippon, *A brief essay*, p. 40, as 'an able miniſter of the New Teſtament'. Given Rippon's use of 'able' throughout this short essay (fifty-two pages) – in addition to those mentioned elsewhere in this chapter, see pp. 9-10 (which

In 1804 the Northern Baptist Education Society[166] was formed under the inspirational leadership of the non-collegially trained John Fawcett of Hebden Bridge[167] and several former Bristol students, including Thomas Langdon of Stone Chapel, Leeds,[168] and the following year William Steadman,[169] also a former student at the Academy (1788–90) under Caleb Evans, was elected the first President (1805–35) of the Horton Academy.[170] Addressing the Northern Baptist Education Society in 1825, Steadman took 2 Corinthians 3.6 as his text and expounded on *The Able Minister* in three parts which more than echo the Bristol Tradition.[171] In his

---

associates the term with Daniel Dyke, William Collins, Henry Forty, and William Kiffin), and p. 15 (Foskett) – it is clear that by it he identifies those ministers firmly within the Bristol Tradition as Evangelicals. It is possible that in describing Foskett's unnamed teacher as 'a very able mafter', Rippon, p. 14, was suggesting something about his theological convictions: however, this is speculation. It is likely that this master was a minister given the frequency of ministers of different traditions running schools, see, e.g., 'Dissenters' Schools, 1660–1820', *Transactions of the Baptist Historical Society* 4.4 (1914), pp. 220-27; and Seymour J. Price, 'Dissenting Academies, 1662–1820', *Baptist Quarterly* 6.3 (July, 1932), pp. 125-38.

[166] Peter Shepherd, *The Making of a Northern Baptist College* (n.pl.: Northern Baptist College, 2004), pp. 27-29, see also pp. 30-31. Another Bristol student, William Staughton (1770–1829), emigrated and, influenced by Caleb Evans, followed the Bristol Academy as his template in establishing the Philadelphia Education Society in 1812 and Columbian College in 1821, now George Washington University. See William Staughton, *Address delivered at the Opening of the Columbian College in the District of Columbia, January 9, 1822* (Washington City [DC]: Anderson and Meehan, 1822), and 'Circular Letter', in A.D. Gillette (ed.), *Minutes of the Philadelphia Association, from A.D. 1707, to A.D. 1807* (Philadelphia, [PA]: American Baptist Publication Society, 1851), 440–46. On Staughton, see S.W. Lynd, *Memoir of the Rev. William Staughton, D.D.* (Boston [MA]: Lincoln, Edmands, 1834); Roger Hayden, 'William Staughton: Baptist Educator and Missionary Advocate', *Foundations* 10.1 (January–March, 1967), pp. 19-35, and 'Bristol Baptist College and America', *Baptist History and Heritage* 14.4 (October, 1979), pp. 26-33.

[167] John Fawcett, Jr, *An Account of The Life, Ministry and Writings of the late Rev. John Fawcett, D.D.* (London: Baldwin, Craddock, and Joy, 1818); Ian Sellers, 'Other Times, Other Ministries: John Fawcett and Alexander McLaren', *Baptist Quarterly* 32.4 (October, 1987), pp. 181-99 (pp. 181-87); and John A. Hargreaves, 'Fawcett, John (1740–1817), Particular Baptist minister and theological writer', *ODNB*, accessed 16 April 2013.

[168] See Moon, *Education for Ministry*, pp. 47-48. On Langdon (1755–1824), see *A Brief Memoir of the Rev. Thomas Langdon, Baptist Minister, of Leeds ... by His daughter* (Leeds: Simpkin, Marshall, 1837).

[169] See Thomas Steadman, *Memoir of the Rev. William Steadman, D.D.* (London: Thomas Ward, 1838); Shepherd, *Northern Baptist College*, pp. 35-51 and *passim*; Sharon James, 'William Steadman (1764–1837)', in Haykin (ed.), *British Particular Baptists*, II, pp. 163-80; and 'Steadman, William (1764–c.1835) (person id: 167)', Dissenting Academies Online, accessed 2 February 2015.

[170] On which, see Shepherd, *Northern Baptist College*, pp. 39-44.

[171] William Steadman, *The Able Minister* (London: Wightman & Cramp, 1826), pp. iv-v. In the light of what we have already seen on the meaning of 'able' as including 'qualified',

exposition of those elements which constitute an able minister of the New Testament, he observes that 'The able minister must possess the facility of acquiring, as well as of imparting, knowledge', and that the students' studies 'must be such ... as under a divine blessing, will render them *able ministers of the New Testament, not of the letter but of the Spirit*'.[172]

The able minister is also, according to Caleb Evans, to be 'zealous', a word which appears to be practically synonymous with 'lively', which itself receives no conscious discussion by either father or son. For Hugh Evans only God

> can make able miniſters of the new teſtament. But as he is pleaſed to make uſe of inſtruments to effect his own purpoſes, the honor *you* are ambitious of, is that of being employed by him, in the accompliſment of the great and deſirable work of raiſing up *able miniſters* of the goſpel. And there is the greater reaſon for our being ſolicitous about this matter in the preſent day, as able miniſters are much wanted. The harveſt truly is plenteous, but able laborers very few. There are moreover many able and indefatigable adverſaries of the goſpel, and great need therefore of able and zealous miniſters to vindicate and eſtablish the truth as it is in Jeſus.[173]

To whatever services ministers are called they should be attended to 'with diligence and zeal',[174] though he recognizes that those ministers who are 'zealous and faithful in the execution of their office' will often have 'many adverſaries'.[175]

This zeal is emphasized by Caleb Evans when he notes that after his baptism his father 'purſued his ſtudies with redoubtable vigour, being desirous of ſerving God in the goſpel of his ſon', that he was 'diligent in buſineſs, fervent in ſpirit, ſerving the Lord'.[176] Of his father's ministry, Caleb Evans speaks of the 'ſoundness of his underſtanding', his 'expanſive heaven illumin'd mind', that he was 'directed by fervent piety and an ardent zeal for the glory of God and the happineſs of mankind',[177] and that as a minister 'He was not a ſlothful ſervant, but truly active,

---

see also Steadman's *The Qualifications necessary for the Discharge of the Duties of the Christian Ministry* (London: Published and Sold by Button and Son, 1819).

[172] Steadman, *The Able Minister*, pp. 20 and 32 respectively (italics original).

[173] Hugh Evans, *The Able Miniſter*, p. 4 (italics original).

[174] Hugh Evans, *Ministers deſcribed*, p. 4. Cf. Newton, *The Good Steward*, p. 29, 'May we be excited to greater activity in our ſtations.' He looks forward to the pleasure that will come when the Lord approves faithful stewardship with 'Well done good and faithful ſervants! Let this fire our ſouls with an holy zeal.' Caleb Evans, *A Charge*, p. 19, also holds out God's 'Well done good and faithful ſervant' as the minister's reward, adding, 'Surely the thought *will revive* and *rouſe* you!' (italics original).

[175] Hugh Evans, *The Sermon*, p. 36.

[176] Caleb Evans, *Elisha's Exclamation!*, p. 27. Cf.

[177] Caleb Evans, *Elisha's Exclamation!*, pp. 30-31. Steadman, *The Able Minister*, p. v, speaks of 'that zeal for the advancement of his kingdom, and that love to the souls of men, which constitute and adorn the character of a gospel minister'.

zealous, laborious and unwearied in the fervice of his beloved mafter'.[178] Indeed, he was 'ready to fpend and be fpent'.[179] Few 'excelled him as a Tutor', in which he 'labored affiduoufly ... not merely to form fubftantial fcholars, but as far as in him lay was defirous of being made an inftrument in God's hand of forming them able, evangelical, lively, zealous Minifters of the gofpel'.[180] Not long before his death, Hugh Evans said that he was '"happy to fee thefe young men rifing up"' and he hoped for their '"great and eminent ufefulnefs in the Church of God"'.[181] Similarly, Caleb Evans informed students that 'it is the higheft ambition of your Friends and Tutors indulge refpecting you, to fee you able, faithful, and fuccefsful, Minifters of the New Teftament; fo, by uniformly supporting this character, you will moft effectually fecure the peace of your own minds and the approbation of God'.[182]

Hugh and Caleb Evans' Legacies

Among 'a hoft of ... luminaries, who have not been afhamed of the gofpel of Chrift', Caleb Evans includes Jonathan Edwards,[183] and he calls David Brainerd 'that truly great and good man'.[184] In a letter to John Sutcliff in 1778, James Turner of Cannon Street, Birmingham, mentions, though without attribution, Edwards' distinction between the natural and moral inability of the will which had been discussed that year by Caleb Evans in the Western Association's circular letter.[185] Hayden believes

---

[178] Caleb Evans, *Elisha's Exclamation!*, p. 37. Cf. p. 40, when nearing the end of his life he was 'reminded of his former activity and zeal', and, p. 48, where Caleb Evans speaks of how his father 'preached the gofpel of life' to those who heard 'the gofpel from his lips'. So important to Hugh Evans is this characteristic of the minister's 'zeal' that it appears repeatedly throughout this sermon, see *Ministers defcribed*, pp. 19, 28, 29 and 30.

[179] Hugh Evans, *The Able Minifter*, p. 37, and *Ministers defcribed*, p. 29. This phrase occurs repeatedly throughout this period, e.g., e.g., Caleb Evans, *Elisha's Exclamation!*, p. 35, and *A Charge*, p. 17.

[180] Caleb Evans, *Elisha's Exclamation!*, p. 31. Cf. Hugh Evans, *The Able Minifter*, p. 42, 'we alfo know he ufually works by *means*, and fuch means as are fuited to the end, and that we may hope therefore to be made ufse of, as inftruments in his hand, to promote and carry on his great and important defigns' (italics original). Similarly, Hugh Evans closes his *Ministers defcribed*, p. 37, stating that as God had raised up fathers in the past who were 'ornaments to the church and the world' so he could 'and we truft will raife up a succeffion of wife and able men, who fhall, as inftruments in his hand, fuccefsfully carry on the fame glorious caufe in which their predecessors were employed; building up the temple of the Lord ...'

[181] Caleb Evans, *Elisha's Exclamation!*, p. 31.

[182] Caleb Evans, *Address to the Students in the Academy*, p. 351 (italics original).

[183] Caleb Evans, *Christ Crucified*, p. 144.

[184] Caleb Evans, *Christ Crucified*, p. 222.

[185] James Turner to John Sutcliff, 9 September 1778 (Original Letters to J. Sutcliff, in the Baptist Missionary Society Archives, The Angus Library), quoted by Hayden, *Continuity and Change*, p. 126. See Caleb Evans in *The Elders, Minifters and Meffengers of the Several*

that Andrew Fuller,[186] who was not a student at Bristol,[187] was nevertheless influenced by Sutcliff (1772–c.74), and was one of many prominent Baptists influenced directly or indirectly by Hugh and Caleb Evans, their colleagues and students. Others who became key figures in the next generation of Baptists include John Rippon (1769–c.73), Robert Hall, Jr (1778–81), Joseph Kinghorn (c.1784–c.88), Samuel Pearce (c.1786–c.89), and William Steadman (1788–90).[188]

Conclusions

David Bebbington's history of Evangelicalism is the single most important study of the movement's origins. His dating of its rise, his Evangelical quadrilateral and identification of the various wider cultural influences that have shaped it at various stages in its history have been widely accepted,[189] though his work has not gone without challenge, sometimes, sadly, in less than acceptable ways. Often the debate has revolved around issues of continuity and discontinuity with the past, issues which he readily acknowledged in the first edition of his *Evangelicalism in Modern Britain* in 1989.[190] During the course of his discussion of Evangelicalism's

---

Baptist Churches meeting at Exeter, Tiverton, Prefcott ... (s.l.: s.n., [1778]), pp. 1-5 (pp. 2-3).

[186] However, Hayden, *Continuity and Change*, p. 126, followed by, e.g., Chris Chun, *The Legacy of Jonathan Edwards in the Theology of Andrew Fuller* (Studies in the History of Christian Traditions; Leiden: Brill, 2012), pp. 42-45, are mistaken when they attribute Fuller's extensive quotation from *An Address to the Serious and Candid Professors of Christianity* (London: Printed for J. Buckland, 2nd edn, 1773 [1772]), pp. 11-13, to Caleb Evans. See Andrew Fuller, *The Gospel of Christ Worthy of All Acceptation* (Northampton: Printed by T. Dicey, n.d. [1785]), pp. 183-85. The *Address* develops Edwards' explanation between natural and moral ability, which Hayden, Chun and others believe was greatly influential in Fuller's developing thought. The *Address* is anonymous, but attributed by Early English Books Online to the Calvinist, Ambrose Serle (1742–1812), an Evangelical religious writer and naval officer, see H.L. Bennett, rev. Emma Major, 'Serle, Ambrose (1742–1812), colonial officer and religious writer', *ODNB*, accessed 27 March 2015. The probable reason for Hayden's confusion is that copies of the *Appeal* are bound in two volumes comprised of works by Caleb Evans, along with his ordination service.

[187] On Fuller's significance, see, e.g., Peter J. Morden, *Offering Christ to the World: Andrew Fuller (1754–1815) and the Revival of Eighteenth-Century Particular Baptist Life* (Studies in Baptist History and Thought, 8; Carlisle: Paternoster Press, 2003), and *The Life and Thought of Andrew Fuller, 1754–1815* (Milton Keynes: Paternoster, 2015).

[188] All dates in parentheses are to the students' time in the Academy according to Hayden, 'Bristol Baptist Academy (1720–present)'. For discussion of Caleb Evans' students, see, e.g., Swaine, *Faithful Men*, pp. 83-177; Moon, *Education for Ministry*, *passim*; and Hayden, *Continuity and Change*, *passim*.

[189] E.g., Inter-Varsity Press' *A History of Evangelicalism* (5 vols; Leicester/Downers Grove, IL: Inter-Varsity Press, 2004–).

[190] See, e.g., Bebbington, *Evangelicalism in Modern Britain*, pp. 34-42.

continuity with the past he notes the evidence from before the Revival of the 1730s, and observes that

> Bristol Baptist Academy was producing a stream of ministers with vital spirituality, evangelistic concerns and a catholic outlook under the three principals who served from 1720 to 1791, Bernard Foskett, Hugh Evans and Caleb Evans.[191]

The focus of the present study has been on fifty years in the mid-eighteenth century, c.1720–c.1770, the period before the rise of the Evangelical movement, and up to the widely accepted date by which it had become a major force within the Baptist tradition. The evidence we have seen, which coincides with the principalships of Foskett and Hugh Evans, with an eye on the years both before and after these dates, is *not* to argue that Evangelicalism as a movement existed prior to the 1730s, or that the impact of the Evangelical Revival took hold before 1770. What it does show is that, in the form of the Bristol Tradition (with due acknowledgement that there were similar traditions in the North and London) there existed theological emphases which provided a ready seedbed for the growing acceptance of Evangelicalism, through its emphases on an 'able and evangelical' ministry, firmly rooted in the word of God, often read in Hebrew and Greek, with the priority it placed on preaching, evangelism and church growth through both pastoral and itinerant mission work, with the specific aim of converting sinners through faith in the atoning work of Christ on the cross. It also supplied several of the key figures who helped Evangelical religion become firmly established among Baptists. It was through the teaching, preaching and examples of Foskett, Hugh Evans and their assistant tutors that the Academy's former students, serving in the ministry of Baptist churches across the country, made a significant contribution to the reception of Evangelicalism among Particular Baptists and the revitalization of not just the Baptists, but of Christianity across the world.

As such this study substantiates Bebbington's contention that the Bristol Baptist Academy was a 'major bridge' between the Evangelical Revival and the Baptists. Though it was small, and up until 1765 it was the only academy for training ministers in the world, nevertheless

> Its succession of tutors turned out a steady flow of ministers who maintained a form of Calvinism that was friendly to evangelistic work. From the 1750s it received a significant number of candidates, particularly from Wales, who were converts from the revival. At the academy, students added knowledge to their zeal without extinguishing it. In their subsequent ministries many Bristol men synthesized Baptist traditions with revival influences.[192]

---

[191] Bebbington, *Evangelicalism in Modern Britain*, p. 34.
[192] Bebbington, *Baptists Through the Centuries*, pp. 74-75.

CHAPTER 5

The Annual Tent Meetings of the Suffolk and Norfolk Strict Baptists

Tim Grass

'One of the most historic religious events in East Anglia is the annual tent meetings of the Suffolk and Norfolk Association of Strict Baptist Churches.' So claimed a local newspaper, the *East Anglian Daily Times*, in 1968.[1] Visitors have often commented on the unique experience afforded by a visit to these meetings, frequently referred to simply as 'the Association'.[2] Other Baptist associations have had their annual assemblies, even extending them over two days as in this case, but the setting and form of these gatherings (what we might call their social history) have attracted relatively little scholarly attention,[3] and I know of none in Britain which have made regular use of a tent.[4] In the course of his travels, David Bebbington has himself visited these meetings, and I grew up attending them in the 1960s. They played a key role in the development of what became one of the most conspicuously successful examples of Baptist associating, and this essay sets out to explore their history and significance.[5] I have written elsewhere about the role played by the

---

[1] 'Baptist Tent Meetings at Hadleigh', *East Anglian Daily Times* 13 June 1968, p. 2.
[2] Where the word is capitalized, it refers specifically to these meetings.
[3] Two exceptions are Frank Buffard, *Kent and Sussex Baptist Associations* (Faversham: The Association, 1963), ch. 7; Cullen T. Clark, 'Association and Authority: Lancashire Baptists, 1765–1865', *Baptist Quarterly* 45.2 (July, 2013), pp. 132-42, and 45.3 (October 2013), pp. 196-209.
[4] Neither can any be traced among the Congregationalists (Independents): my thanks to Professor Clyde Binfield for his assistance on this point.
[5] For the resurgence of regional Baptist associations during the late eighteenth and early nineteenth centuries, in spite of the continuing isolationism of a proportion of churches, see J.H.Y. Briggs, *The English Baptists of the Nineteenth Century* (A History of the English Baptists, 3; Didcot: Baptist Historical Society, 1994), pp. 199-210. On this particular association, the main sources are Ashley J. Klaiber, *The Story of the Suffolk Baptists* (London: The Kingsgate Press, c.1931), ch. 10; Kenneth Dix, *Strict and Particular: English Particular Baptists in the Nineteenth Century* (Didcot: Baptist Historical Society, 2001), ch. 4; Robert Oliver, *History of the English Calvinistic Baptists 1771–1892* (Edinburgh: Banner of Truth, 2006), pp. 318-22; none have much to say, however, about the 'tent meetings'.

association in the life of the region's Strict Baptist churches;[6] in early decades, at least, it was similar to that of other Baptist associations in England.[7] Here, however, the focus is on its annual gatherings, the 'tent meetings', as they are still known. It should be noted that such meetings are of a different character from evangelistic or revivalist meetings using tents, or camp meetings intended solely to provide teaching for Christians, although it has not been uncommon for evangelistic sermons to be preached or for individuals to be converted to Christ at the Association. The Suffolk meetings are distinctive precisely because they were held in a tent in order to accommodate the numbers attending. The fact that for much of their history a relatively high proportion of the membership of associated churches was present has greatly reinforced their formal role in the association's life, expressing and cementing what holds the churches together; this has enabled the association to function coherently until recent decades.

The Tent

The Norfolk and Suffolk Association of Baptist Churches was formed in 1769, and by the early nineteenth century it was meeting annually over two days. In 1819, 'a large booth was erected for the crowds which flocked to the meetings' at Shelfanger near Diss, the first time any such temporary provision appears to have been made.[8] Division of opinion over aspects of high Calvinist doctrine led to the withdrawal of a number of churches in 1829 and the formation of a new association, the Suffolk and Norfolk. It was explicitly opposed to 'Fullerism', the belief that saving faith was a duty incumbent upon all people, its articles stressing that such faith was the 'sovereign and gracious gift of God'.[9] Notwithstanding the doctrinal divergence, its early meetings adopted the same basic format as those of the old association.[10] Initially the meetings were held in late May, but from 1840 they moved to a Tuesday and Wednesday in early June (Wednesday and Thursday from 1877, apart from some years after 1890).

---

[6] They are now known as 'Grace Baptist' rather than 'Strict Baptist', the stress being on their doctrine rather than their communion practice, which is slowly evolving away from a categorical insistence on believer's baptism as a prerequisite for admission to the Lord's Table.

[7] Tim Grass, *'There my friends and kindred dwell': The Strict Baptist Churches of Norfolk and Suffolk* (Ramsey: Thornhill Media, 2012), Introduction.

[8] Maurice F. Hewett, 'The Church at Shelfanger', *Baptist Quarterly* 12 (1946–48), pp. 331-40 (p. 335).

[9] David Bebbington, *Baptists through the Centuries: A History of a Global People* (Waco, TX: Baylor University Press, 2010), pp. 87-91, notes the theological parallels between this division and the Primitive Baptist split in the State of Georgia, North America, in 1828.

[10] See, e.g., *Circular Letter on the Work of the Spirit, by the Norfolk and Suffolk Association of Baptist Churches ... 1820* (Ipswich: Norfolk and Suffolk Association, 1820), pp. 19-20.

During the 1830s, the number of churches in the association grew, their membership increased, and it became easier for members to take time away from work. Attendance at the annual meetings therefore rapidly outgrew the capacity of any of the chapels, and it became necessary to convene in the open air. At Little Stonham one afternoon in 1835, nine or ten wagons were formed into a semi-circle in the meadow next to the chapel, presumably to enclose a space for the congregation.[11] At Rattlesden in 1844, 1,200 were present during the morning of the second day, with more arriving for the afternoon.[12] A tent was therefore used at Wattisham in 1845 as an overflow for those unable to get into the chapel,[13] but in 1846 it was reported that expensive 'booths' had again been erected to accommodate the congregations, again at Stonham, and so the annual business meeting of the association agreed to purchase a tent for preaching services.[14] A tent committee was formed to raise funds and then to oversee the tent's use. Its first outing was at Occold in 1847; it measured 80 feet by 35 feet, and could accommodate 2,000 people standing.[15] Thereafter a tent has been used each year the meetings were held, apart from 1899, when the Lowestoft church borrowed the Sailors' Bethel, and 1914, when Bethesda, Ipswich, in spite of having the largest (and at that point the newest) chapel in the association, used a public hall.[16] As £31 4s. 9d. of the £70 purchase cost remained outstanding, it was determined at the 1847 meetings that the tent should be erected for special services a few weeks later, when a collection would be taken to defray the debt.[17]

By 1867 the tent was wearing out and, when a thunderstorm passed overhead during the meetings, 'it was amusing to witness the dislike so many Baptists seemed to have to sprinkling'.[18] By the following year it had been repaired using sail-cloth

---

[11] *Circular Letter on the Relative Duties of Church Members, by the Suffolk and Norfolk New Association of Baptist Churches ... 1835* (Bungay: Suffolk and Norfolk New Association, 1835), p. 29.

[12] *Circular Letter on the individual Responsibility of Christians to promote the Extension of the Redeemer's Kingdom; by the Suffolk and Norfolk New Association of Baptist Churches ... 1844* (Beccles: Suffolk and Norfolk New Association, 1844), pp. 19-20.

[13] *Grace*, July 1973, pp. 17-18.

[14] *Circular Letter on the Constitution of a Christian Church, by the Suffolk and Norfolk New Association of Baptist Churches ... 1846* (Beccles: Suffolk and Norfolk New Association, 1846), p. 26.

[15] *Circular Letter on Baptism, in its relation to the Lord's Supper, by the Suffolk and Norfolk New Association of Baptist Churches ... 1847* (Beccles: Suffolk and Norfolk New Association, 1847), p. 21; 'The Association', *Grace*, August 1986, p. 4.

[16] S. Wolstenholme, *These Hundred and Fifty Years* (n.pl.: S&NASBC, [1980]), pp. 17-18.

[17] *Circular Letter 1847*, p. 20.

[18] 'A plain Countryman's Visit to the Anniversary of the Suffolk and Norfolk Association of Baptist Churches, held at Laxfield, June 4th and 5th, 1867', *Earthen Vessel* 23 (1867), pp. 216-20 (p. 219).

canvas, at a cost of £39 19*s*. 6*d*.[19] This must have been done well, for the tent was not replaced until 1907.[20] Before too long, seating had been provided, initially simple forms, but later benches with backs. In 1889, £10 was set aside for purchasing new seats and repairing old ones.[21] Many years later, these were in turn replaced, to evident appreciation![22] And in 1973, a new tent was purchased for use in evangelism, which found employment at the Association for prayer meetings and other smaller gatherings.[23]

It was not many years after the tent had been brought into use before a lack of capacity again became evident: one afternoon at the 1861 Association, an estimated 2,500 gathered at Wattisham; as well as the tent and the chapel, a third preacher was required at an unspecified location.[24] Attendance continued to climb, until at Occold in 1870 it was 3,500 on the second afternoon; that year, membership of the Association was reported as 3,147.[25] At times the sides of the tent would be taken down so that those standing outside could participate in the service.[26] 'The Association' was becoming a fixture in the annual calendar of many church members. During the inter-war period, it was not unknown for 'hundreds to walk miles to be present at the 6 a.m. prayer meetings and for many church members to take two precious and unpaid holidays' to attend.[27] In 1923 the largest attendance for many years – 'nearly 2,000' – was reported on the second afternoon, but this indicates that some decline must have taken place.[28]

---

[19] *Circular Letter, on the Christian walking in the Spirit: by the Suffolk and Norfolk Association of Particular Baptist Churches ... 1868* (Beccles: S&NAPBC, 1868), p. 13.

[20] *Circular Letter on 'The Fall and Redemption of Man', by the Suffolk and Norfolk Association of Particular Baptist Churches ... 1929* (Ipswich: S&NAPBC, 1929), p. 9.

[21] *Circular Letter on 'The Love of Christ,' by the Suffolk and Norfolk Association of Particular Baptist Churches ... 1889* (Eye: S&NAPBC, 1889), p. 20.

[22] *Circular Letter on 'The Acceptable Worship of God,' by the Suffolk and Norfolk Association of Strict Baptist Churches ... 1934* (Ipswich: S&NASBC, 1934), p. 9.

[23] *Handbook of the Suffolk and Norfolk Association of Strict Baptist Churches ... 1973* (Foxton: S&NASBC, 1973), pp. 12, 13.

[24] *Circular Letter on the Constitution of a Gospel Church, by the Suffolk and Norfolk Association of Particular Baptist Churches ... 1861* (Beccles: S&NAPBC, 1861), p. 27.

[25] *Circular Letter, on Christian Watchfulness: by the Suffolk and Norfolk Association of Particular Baptist Churches ... 1870* (Beccles: S&NAPBC, 1870), p. 21; at the end of the service, a resolution calling for education to be secular in character apart from the reading of Scripture without note or comment was passed with just one brave dissentient voice.

[26] E.g. *Circular Letter on 'Our Principles and Practices as Baptists:' by the Suffolk and Norfolk Association of Particular Baptist Churches ... 1883* (Eye: S&NAPBC, 1883), p. 18.

[27] 'The Association', *Grace*, August 1986, p. 4.

[28] *Circular Letter on 'Remedies for a Low State of Church Life,' by the Suffolk & Norfolk Association of Particular Baptist Churches ... 1923* (Ipswich: S&NAPBC, 1923), p. 13. The congregation was even larger the following year: *Circular Letter on 'Work for the Master in the Light of his "Well Done,"' by the Suffolk & Norfolk Association of Particular Baptist Churches ... 1924* (Ipswich: S&NAPBC, 1924), p. 13.

After World War II, attendance declined steadily, to the extent that in 1964 it was around 700 at the best attended service.[29] The same figure was reached in 1984, suggesting that attendance levelled out for some years.[30] By this point, the evening services were the best attended: unavailability during the working day was now more of an issue than the need to travel home in good time to perform farm duties.

The Location

As often with area Baptist association meetings, the tent meetings were peripatetic. One of the reasons for this was that the church hosting the meetings was given a spiritual and psychological boost, as it was seen to be part of something larger. This benefited the church itself, but also gave it a higher profile within its local community at a time when Baptist churches were still emerging from social obscurity and sometimes facing local hostility. In addition, taking turns to host the Association helped to bind the churches together and give them a sense of ownership, not only of the meetings, but also of the network of churches. As an outsider observed in 1955, the ability of the Suffolk Strict Baptists to hold their meetings anywhere by using a tent, and the consequent impact on village churches, was 'undoubtedly one of the secrets of their strength'.[31] The strength of attachment to these meetings is evident from the fact that the country churches which hosted the meetings so willingly incurred considerable expense, extending beyond the cost of hospitality to such things as cartage of the tent from its place of storage.

Until after World War II it seems to have been the practice to work through the list of member churches (until the mid-twentieth century they appeared in the annual circular letter in chronological order of joining the association). Thus, in 1898 the church at Kenninghall was asked if it was willing to host the meetings, as it was the next on the list.[32] Sometimes a church is said to have applied to host the meetings, as Great Blakenham did for 1900,[33] although I suspect that usually a church would offer in response to a suggestion made by the association secretary. However, it is indicative of the association's weakness in Norfolk that the meetings have only been held in the county twice, at Claxton (1838) and Pulham St Mary (1871).

---

[29] *Handbook of the Suffolk and Norfolk Association of Strict Baptist Churches ... 1964* (Hadleigh: S&NASBC, 1964), unpaginated.

[30] *Handbook 1984/85 of the Suffolk and Norfolk Association of Strict Baptist Churches* (Rowhedge: S&NASBC, 1984), p. 11.

[31] Ipswich, Suffolk Record Office, HD1842/2, Oswald Job, Free Church notes (1941–84), 8 June 1955.

[32] Norwich, Norfolk Record Office, FC92/2 (MF1619/1), Kenninghall Strict Baptist Church, Minutes 1871–1904, 8 May 1898.

[33] *Circular Letter on 'Church Officers and their Duties,' by the Suffolk and Norfolk Association of Particular Baptist Churches ... 1899* (London: S&NAPBC, 1899), p. 21. On this occasion they also chose the preachers.

The Meetings

As with the old Association, two days each year were allotted to the meetings, except in 1917 and 1918, when the impossibility of catering for attenders led to their cancellation,[34] and during World War II, when the difficulty of travel meant that district meetings replaced the main gathering.

The first feature of the regular programme to note is the prayer meetings. From 1844 there was one at 6 a.m. on the second day (this had hitherto been another preaching service) and in 1858 another was added before the main morning service.[35] In 1869 that at 6 a.m. was led by the messengers or delegates appointed by the churches to represent them at the business meeting, the ministers taking their turn at 9.30 a.m.; this pattern seems to have continued for some years.[36] Some members would attend the first prayer meeting before going on to work.[37] From around 1930 the character of the second meeting changed to become a devotional service, with greetings being brought from sister associations and fewer prayers; the earlier meeting now saw ministers as well as messengers participating. When the tent meetings resumed in 1946, the 6 a.m. prayer meeting was no longer held.[38] Further change ensued, and a short prayer meeting before the first morning's service was added in 1956.[39] This became a fixture in the programme.

Ladies' prayer meetings made their appearance at Cransford in 1906, at different times to the existing gatherings.[40] A woman is first recorded as praying at one of the united meetings at Otley in 1933, when a missionary from Suffolk, Miss Mowle, was one of thirteen participants.[41] When an unnamed pastor attempted to sit in on one prayer meeting in 1930, he 'was gently asked to retire', but two years later a number

---

[34] *Circular Letter on 'Prayer,' by the Suffolk & Norfolk Association of Particular Baptist Churches, for the year 1917 ...* (Ipswich: S&NAPBC, 1917), p. 3; *Circular Letter on 'Particular Redemption,' by the Suffolk & Norfolk Association of Particular Baptist Churches, for the year 1918 ...* (Ipswich: S&NAPBC, 1918), p. 11. The Church at Bradfield St George regretted this, the meetings being 'a witness to the unique position we hold amongst the various religious bodies': *Circular Letter 1917*, p. 20.

[35] *Circular Letter on the Glorification of the Saints, by the Suffolk and Norfolk Association of Particular Baptist Churches ... 1858* (Beccles: S&NAPBC, 1858), p. 16.

[36] W.D., 'The Suffolk and Norfolk Baptist Association', *Earthen Vessel* 25 (1869), pp. 217-22 (p. 221).

[37] *Circular Letter on the Ascension of Christ: by the Suffolk and Norfolk Association of Particular Baptist Churches ... 1876* (Ipswich: S&NAPBC, 1876), p. 27.

[38] *Suffolk & Norfolk Association of Strict Baptist Churches Circular Letter, 1946* (Hadleigh: S&NASBC, 1946), p. 11.

[39] *Circular Letter of the Suffolk and Norfolk Association of Strict Baptist Churches ... 1956* (Ipswich: S&NASBC, 1956), p. 7.

[40] *Circular Letter on the Atonement, by the Suffolk and Norfolk Association of Particular Baptist Churches: The 76th Annual Meetings ... 1906* (Leiston: S&NAPBC, 1906), p. 17. A number of these meetings before and after World War I were conducted by my great-grandmother, Mrs J.J. Marsh.

[41] *Circular Letter 1933*, p. 10.

of brethren 'invaded' the meeting, perhaps because a missionary was speaking.[42] In 1951, perhaps in response to the success of the ladies' prayer meetings, two men's prayer meetings were introduced at the same times.[43] By 1973, however, we read of 'United Prayer Meetings' being held.[44]

The first morning service was the most formal. It included an address by the moderator chosen to lead the association for that year, who was virtually always one of the pastors. From the 1950s onwards, he was formally inducted into the office by his predecessor, a Bible being handed over. Normally the moderator's address, like the sermons at the other services, was an exposition or application of 'things most surely believed among us', or an affirmation of Nonconformist identity in the face of perceived threats, and in 1895 it was resolved that it should appear in the annual circular letter.[45]

At Wattisham in 1938, however, Roland J. French (1876–1965) of Bethesda, Ipswich, delivered an address on 'Our Present Plight', based on Habakkuk 3.2 and Malachi 3.10, doubtless on the topic of revival. At the end of the business meeting later that day, a large majority resolved that it not be included in the circular letter. It had been some years before French had, like other pastors, become a personal member of the association (his application in 1928 had not been accepted, and he was not received until 1934).[46] A historian of his church suggests that this was because of his insistence on personal responsibility to turn to Christ as well as the doctrine of particular redemption (although the associated churches would have affirmed both doctrines, he probably placed more emphasis than most of them on the former and less on the latter), and it is likely that his address had taken issue with Strict Baptist principles. 'His stirring induction address caused such misgivings that many chose to dissociate themselves from it. Eventually the message was printed so all could read his prophecy of impending national and international disaster. It was a challenge to the church at large.'[47] French was not a young man, and probably did not wish to become entangled in controversy to the detriment of his ministry in a

---

[42] *Circular Letter on 'Sunday Schools: Their Place, Purpose and Prospect in the Present Day,' by the Suffolk and Norfolk Association of Strict Baptist Churches ... 1930* (Ipswich: S&NASBC, 1930), p. 11; *Circular Letter on 'Power of Collective Prayer,' by the Suffolk and Norfolk Association of Strict Baptist Churches ... 1932* (Ipswich: S&NASBC, 1932), p. 8.

[43] *Circular Letter of the Suffolk and Norfolk Association of Strict Baptist Churches ... 1951* (Ipswich: S&NASBC, 1951), p. 6.

[44] *Handbook 1973*, p. 12.

[45] *Circular Letter on the 'Sovereign Work of the Holy Ghost as connected with the Use of Appointed Means,' by the Suffolk and Norfolk Association of Particular Baptist Churches ... 1895* (London: S&NAPBC, 1895), p. 27.

[46] *Circular Letter on 'The Majesty of Christ, and its Influence on the Church,' by the Suffolk & Norfolk Association of Particular Baptist Churches ... 1928* (Ipswich: S&NAPBC, 1928), p. 11; *Circular Letter 1934*, p. 10.

[47] Frederick G. Smith, *The Bethesda Story Retold: A History of Bethesda Baptist Church, Ipswich, 1829–1988* (Ipswich: The Church, 1988), pp. 91-92.

large and demanding church; at a meeting of the executive committee on 8 July, he therefore resigned his office as moderator and his membership of the association.[48]

Another fixture in this service was the reading of the association's articles of faith. For many years the annual letters from each church were also read out during this service. As the association grew, there were more letters to read, and the procedure became time-consuming and wearisome. As early as 1851 it was resolved that messengers should request their sending churches 'to restrict the statements and observations in their future annual letters to a brief, but comprehensive, report of their state and circumstances, so that the public reading of them at the annual meeting will not occupy much above five minutes'.[49] But in 1869 the reading of these letters occupied almost three hours, and one Strict Baptist reporter complained wearily, 'Such letters need not contain an elaborate defence of Gospel doctrines; but a summary of general information about the respective churches, and the usual statistics. The attendance was very scanty ... and no wonder, for people are heartily tired of hearing the letters read ... a good many left before the conclusion, which lessens the collection.'[50] Perhaps this was the last straw, for the report of that year's business meeting laid down that instead of reading letters from churches in full, which occupied too much time and put people off attending, letters should be sent in a fortnight before and a digest prepared for reading.[51] Nevertheless, the custom of reading the letters survived until 1959.[52]

For many years until World War II, the association's annual business meeting was held on the morning of the first day, normally in the host chapel. 'This was where churches were admitted or their withdrawal formalized; where structures were set up to resource congregations in such matters as funds and outreach; and where resolutions were passed which dealt with matters of moment, denominationally or nationally.'[53] Churches failing to send messengers or contributions to association funds were liable to receive a letter of rebuke from the business meeting.

---

[48] *Circular Letter on 'Church Officers: Their Appointment and Obligations,' by the Suffolk and Norfolk Association of Strict Baptist Churches ... 1938* (Ipswich: S&NASBC, 1938), pp. 9, 11, 15. French had been a Methodist local preacher before training at C.H. Spurgeon's Pastors' College, possibly preceded by a short time under the tuition of Oswald Chambers at Dunoon: http://www.middlewall.co.uk/people/french_plus.html, accessed 14 November 2014. I have not managed to trace a copy of his address.

[49] *Circular Letter on Providence, by the Suffolk and Norfolk Association of Baptist Churches ... 1851* (Beccles: S&NABC, 1851), p. 23.

[50] W.D., 'Suffolk and Norfolk', p. 220.

[51] *Circular Letter, on the State of the Unconverted, and the Church's Duty in relation to them: by the Suffolk and Norfolk Association of Particular Baptist Churches ... 1869* (Beccles: S&NAPBC, 1869), p. 30.

[52] *Handbook of the Suffolk and Norfolk Association of Strict Baptist Churches ... 1959* (Hadleigh: S&NASBC, 1959), unpaginated.

[53] Grass, *'There my friends and kindred dwell'*, p. 8.

By 1847 the business meeting was taking place in the afternoon; a preaching service was held at the same time.[54] Thereafter, the preaching service appears to have taken place subsequently rather than concurrently, although increasing business may have been why in some years during the 1890s the two were once more held at the same time; the report of the 1891 meeting recorded that the brethren adjourned for half an hour for tea.[55] By the 1920s, the business meeting was starting half an hour before the afternoon service; some delegates would doubtless have been anxious for the business to be dealt with expeditiously so that they could adjourn to the tent in time for the sermon.

One important business meeting agenda item was the approval of a circular letter to be printed and sent to all the associated churches. This would be on a topic settled on at the previous year's meeting, and written by one of the pastors (or, very rarely, a layman);[56] at first it was the duty of the moderator. Such letters were intended to strengthen the churches in the distinctive doctrines of their faith as high Calvinists, and writers were expected to confine themselves to stating what was generally believed among the churches. Controversy over such a letter, written for the old association by George Wright of Beccles in 1829, had precipitated the division leading to the formation of the new body.[57] As early as 1833, history looked like repeating itself: the moderator for that year, writing on the covenant of grace (Samuel Collins of Grundisburgh) introduced his belief in the pre-existence of Christ's human soul, a topic which was agitating Strict Baptists at the time, and he also expressed himself in terms implying that Christ by his death purchased the blessings enjoyed by the elect, rather than these being freely given by God. This occasioned a strongly worded letter of protest from Wright and the church at Beccles.[58] The controversy thus brought into opposition two of the association's founders, and the following year's business meeting at Hadleigh resolved that 'in future, every writer of a Circular Letter shall pledge himself to avoid, as much as possible, the introduction of any private opinion, upon which the Association is not

---

[54] *Circular Letter 1847*, pp. 19, 21.

[55] *Circular Letter on 'The Cause of Zion's low Condition, and the best Means of her Revival,' by the Suffolk and Norfolk Association of Particular Baptist Churches ... 1890* (London: S&NAPBC, 1890), p. 21; *Circular Letter 1891*, p. 17; *Circular Letter on 'The Inspiration, Authority, and Pre-eminence of the Word of God,' by the Suffolk and Norfolk Association of Particular Baptist Churches ... 1896* (London: S&NAPBC, 1896), p. 20.

[56] It has never been written by a woman, these churches never having recognized women in pastoral ministry.

[57] Summarized by Oliver, *English Calvinistic Baptists*, p. 317.

[58] See *Circular Letter on the Covenant of Grace, by the Suffolk and Norfolk New Association of Baptist Churches ... 1833* (Ipswich: Suffolk and Norfolk New Association, 1833); George Wright et al., *The Baptist Church at Beccles, to the Suffolk & Norfolk New Association of Baptist Churches* [Beccles: The Church, 1833].

unanimously agreed'.[59] On rare occasions, this principle was appealed to subsequently. In 1916, it was agreed that the next year's circular letter should be on the subject of 'The return of the Jews to their own land, according to the Scriptures'.[60] In the event it was replaced by a letter on 'Prayer': the association's executive committee had met on 23 November 1916 to consider the letter, and the proposed subject 'was considered unsuitable and not in accord with the rule regarding Circular Letters'.[61] One wonders what went through the minds of those involved when General Allenby entered Jerusalem on 11 December 1917.

Central to 'the Association', however, were the preaching services, featuring local and visiting pastors, who were always of the same high Calvinist and Baptist convictions. These services provided unparalleled opportunities for exposition of biblical texts or passages treating the 'doctrines of grace'. For the first century of the Association's existence, the preachers of the second day's 'Association sermons' were chosen at the previous year's annual business meeting from among its pastors, but those for the first day's services, who might often be Strict Baptists from other churches or pastors from other Suffolk Baptist churches, were for many years chosen on the day. In 1934 it was first reported that the preachers so chosen were announced at the end of the morning meeting.[62] By this time, the preachers of the Association sermons were being chosen by the host church rather than the business meeting.[63]

The centenary meetings of the association were held at Grundisburgh in 1930, and the pastor, H.H. Gladstone, recalled that about 2,000 attenders were expected, with accommodation needing to be found for 200 of them – no mean task in a modestly-sized village.

> In those days it was customary to invite two visiting ministers to preach the sermons on the first day. There would be a number of Pastors from London and Cambridge, and I never knew one to refuse the invitation, so they must all have had sermon notes in their pockets. ... On the second day Association sermons were preached by those chosen from our own Pastors.[64]

His recollections are confirmed by an article in *Grace*, which cited 'some older brethren' as recalling that 'preachers were nominated only an hour or two before service time', and thus often brought sermon notes with them in case they were

---

[59] *Circular Letter on the Legitimate Consequences of a Spiritual Reception of the Doctrines of the Everlasting Gospel, by the Suffolk and Norfolk New Association of Baptist Churches ... 1834* (Bungay: Suffolk and Norfolk New Association, 1834), p. 22.

[60] *Circular Letter on 'Eternal Punishment' by the Suffolk and Norfolk Association of Particular Baptist Churches ... 1916* (Ipswich: S&NAPBC, 1916), p. 12.

[61] *Circular Letter 1917*, p. 15.

[62] *Circular Letter 1934*, p. 10. After World War II, visiting preachers were chosen for the first evening and second afternoon.

[63] *Handbook 1973*, pp. 11, 12.

[64] H.H. Gladstone, *A Suffolk Interlude: Its Highlights and its Humour* (Romford: privately published, c.1978), p. 8.

needed.[65] The tendency of some preachers to trust to the inspiration of the moment, or at least to adapt their discourse at short notice, could produce memorable results, as in 1955 when a torrential rainstorm forced adjournment to a Presbyterian church in Ipswich, and the preacher that evening took as his text 'waters to swim in' (Ezekiel 47.5).[66]

The first preacher from outside the UK to address the meetings was the continental Baptist apostle J.G. Oncken. At Norton in 1866 he gave 'an earnest and affectionate address, replete with wise counsel and instructive suggestions in relation to our churches, and the importance of greater personal and combined effort, to sustain their practical efficiency, and to promote the great cause of christian missions at home and abroad'. In response to his invitation to the association to send a deputation to the 1867 triennial conference of the German Baptists, it was resolved that Pastors Cooper and Collins be sent to Hamburg. The following morning, Oncken brought greetings, and he preached that afternoon from Acts 11.19–21 about mission, arguing in terms which seem remarkably contemporary that 'missionary work is God's work', illustrating his claim with references to the German mission, and also appealing to impenitent hearers.[67] At the 1868 meetings, the two pastors reported on their visit.[68] From further afield, in 1893 T.B. Pandian, an Indian pastor of a church in Madras planted by the Strict Baptist Mission, addressed the business meeting to 'great interest', and at a service the following day 'greatly cheered the audience by an account of his own conversion and some most interesting incidents of Mission work amongst the natives of Southern India'; he was welcomed by a show of hands of the congregation and given the hand of fellowship.[69] From 1930, a missionary or home staff member from the Strict Baptist Mission (later the Grace

---

[65] 'The Association', *Grace*, August 1986, p. 4.

[66] *Circular Letter of the Suffolk and Norfolk Association of Strict Baptist Churches ... 1955* (Ipswich: S&NASBC, 1955), p. 1. Weather caused problems at other times: in 1979, 'A very fierce wind at the end of the [Sunday School] Rally caused some concern for the safety of the people in the tent, but in spite of the strain all the main ropes held, numerous volunteers secured the sides, and no harm came.' It was indeed 'a remarkable deliverance from harm': *Handbook of the Suffolk & Norfolk Association of Strict Baptist Churches 1979–80* (Rowhedge: S&NASBC, 1979), pp. 10-11; *1980/81 Handbook of the Suffolk & Norfolk Association of Strict Baptist Churches* (Rowhedge: S&NASBC, 1980), p. 13.

[67] *Circular Letter, on Godly Fear: by the Suffolk and Norfolk Association of Particular Baptist Churches ... 1866* (Beccles: S&NAPBC, 1866), pp. 25-26. On Oncken, who would not have shared the association's high Calvinist theology, see Ian M. Randall, '"Every Apostolic Church a Mission Society": European Baptist Origins and Identity', in Anthony R. Cross (ed.), *Ecumenism and History: Studies in Honour of John H.Y. Briggs* (Carlisle: Paternoster, 2002), pp. 281-301.

[68] Klaiber, *Suffolk Baptists*, p. 133.

[69] *Circular Letter on 'The Nature and Character of Apostolic Preaching, from a New Testament Point of View, in Relation to the Ministry of our Churches in the Present Day,' by the Suffolk and Norfolk Association of Particular Baptist Churches ... 1893* (London: S&NAPBC, 1893), pp. 18-19.

Baptist Mission) visited the meetings each year until the war,[70] but a regular slot in one of the main services was not given until 1984.[71] There was no further speaker from abroad until Baptist pastor B.-J. Berge from Brussels in 1971, described (inaccurately) as 'the first man from the Continent ever to preach at these meetings'.[72] Until recent decades, then, overseas mission cannot generally be said to have had a prominent place at these meetings, important though it was in the thinking of many of the churches represented. This was probably because the Strict Baptist Mission had its own meetings each year (for a long period twice a year), until recently held in London. As social occasions, these fulfilled similar functions to the tent meetings and often attracted very large attendances: into the 1980s it was not unknown for the evening congregation to number a thousand or more.

Very occasionally, a sermon was replaced by an address on a particular topic, as at Walsham-le-Willows in 1875, when S.K. Bland (later the association's secretary) spoke about his recent visit to Italy and the opening of a Baptist chapel in Rome 'under the shadow of the Vatican'.[73] In 1899 the business meeting resolved that the first evening's service should in future be a public meeting, 'when addresses shall be given on some important and prominent topic'.[74] However, no change resulted; whether because of inertia or (more likely) because preaching was deemed too important.

Occasionally, however, speakers would be allowed to address the congregation more briefly in connection with a particular cause, as in 1865 (a speaker from the Baptist Sunday School Union) and 1872 (the Rev. Henry Dowson of the Strict Baptist Theological Institute, Bury).[75] Greetings were also brought from sister Strict Baptist associations in the London area (from 1895)[76] and Cambridgeshire (formed in 1927); around 1900 and again from the mid-1950s until after 1980 a speaker would also bring greetings from the Suffolk Baptist Union. Debates within the

---

[70] Philip Reynolds, *'These Hundred Years'*: *A Centenary Memento of the Suffolk and Norfolk Association of Strict Baptist Churches* (Ipswich: S&NASBC, [1930]), pp. 26-27; this was at the ladies' prayer meeting and the Sunday School Branch meeting: *Circular Letter 1930*, pp. 14, 15. Visits had been also made to the main services by missionaries during the preceding decade.

[71] *Handbook 1984/85*, p. 10.

[72] *Handbook of the Suffolk and Norfolk Association of Strict Baptist Churches ... 1971* (Hadleigh: S&NASBC, 1971), p. 8. Berge played a leading role in the affairs of the evangelical grouping of French-speaking Baptist churches: Sébastien Fath, *Les Baptistes en France (1810–1950): Faits, Dates et Documents* (Cléon d'Andran: Excelsis, 2002), p. 101.

[73] *Circular Letter on Christian Work amongst the Young: by the Suffolk and Norfolk Association of Particular Baptist Churches ... 1875* (Ipswich: S&NAPBC, 1875), p. 25. The church in Rome was planted with support from the Baptist Missionary Society, which the association supported for much of the nineteenth century; see S. Mondello and P. Nazzaro, 'The Origins of Baptist Evangelism in Italy, 1848–1920', *American Baptist Quarterly* 7.2 (1988), pp. 110-27.

[74] *Circular Letter 1899*, p. 21.

[75] Klaiber, *Suffolk Baptists*, pp. 139, 140.

[76] Klaiber, *Suffolk Baptists*, pp. 141-42.

Baptist Union of Great Britain after Michael Taylor's 1971 address (which was seen by many as questioning the Christian understanding of the person of Christ as fully God and fully man) led to the association's annual business meeting expressing concern at 'the Union's attitude towards a statement of heretical views made by one of its highly placed members' in 1971.[77] Notwithstanding this, the exchange continued, facilitated by the fact that on various occasions in the 1960s and 1970s the SBU representative was the Rev. F.O. Staddon, whose father had been an association pastor. The wider church was also represented on occasion: at Lowestoft in 1899, for example, greetings were brought by a deputation of local Nonconformist ministers, including two Wesleyans;[78] doubtless such breadth was more acceptable at a period when all Nonconformists felt a sense of unity by virtue of their shared antagonism towards the Established Church and its perceived attempts to dominate religious education in schools. During the inter-war period similar greetings were received on several occasions.

One of the great delights of the tent meetings for many was the singing: congregations were large and four-part harmony was common, reflecting a lively musical tradition in the churches which continued at least into the 1980s. The report of the 1911 meetings refers to singing 'special hymns set to old Union and M.S. tunes';[79] 'Union' was the Union Tune Book, published by the Sunday School Union and widely used among Nonconformists, but I am not aware of any extant hymn tune manuscripts with a Suffolk Strict Baptist provenance. The hymns would often be carefully chosen to reflect the great doctrines which Strict Baptists upheld. One favourite which I recall being sung in 1981 was 'Sovereign grace, o'er sin abounding' to the tune CALCUTTA.[80] Another was 'Blest be the tie that binds', sung since the 1850s at the conclusion of the final service, traditionally to 'the tent tune' (GLASGOW, according to the 1911 report and several others around this time) in which the second and fourth lines of each stanza are repeated.[81] The singing of this hymn was no formality: Samuel Collins, who had been pastor at Grundisburgh 1827–76 and a prime mover in the formation and development of the association, when reading the Scriptures and praying at the 1878 meetings, reduced 'a large proportion of the great congregation ... to tears at the tremulous and tender

---

[77] *Handbook 1972*, p. 17. On this controversy, see I.M. Randall, *The English Baptists of the Twentieth Century* (A History of the English Baptists, 4; Didcot: Baptist Historical Society, 2005), pp. 365-82.

[78] *Circular Letter 1899*, p. 16.

[79] *Circular Letter on 'Faith,' by the Suffolk and Norfolk Association of Particular Baptist Churches ... 1911* (Leiston: S&NAPBC, 1911), p. 16.

[80] Cf. *1981/82 Handbook of the Suffolk & Norfolk Association of Strict Baptist Churches* (Rowhedge: S&NASBC, 1981), p. 10.

[81] *Circular Letter 1911*, p. 16; it was still being sung in 1976: *Handbook of the Suffolk and Norfolk Association of Strict Baptist Churches 1976–77* (Cranleigh: S&NASBC, 1976), p. 9. For the tune, see *Companion Tune Book* (London: C.J. Farncombe, 1927), no. 33. This is not the same tune as that known as GLASGOW or IRISH and sung to 'Behold the mountain of the Lord', which is of a different metre.

experience of passed happy days and "Association experiences"'.[82] A third often sung was 'Kindred in Christ, for his dear sake / a hearty welcome here receive', sometimes set to BRIGHTON NEW, in which the final line of each stanza is repeated.[83] In 1978 this was described as 'the usual opening hymn'.[84] For many years special hymn-sheets were sold; after the words edition of *Grace Hymns* was published in 1975, this was used; more recently special booklets have again been produced, this time for free but not to be taken away. Community hymn singing before some of the services has also featured.

Political issues of the day were occasionally aired, although less often than in some other Baptist associations. The 1895 meetings even saw a prospective parliamentary candidate address the meetings 'on civil and religious liberty', as well as sharing meals with the company – doubtless canvassing for votes.[85] Such close fellowship with the political world does not appear to have occurred again, but the meetings did give expression to Strict Baptist convictions on issues then in the public eye. In 1896, the congregation stood to approve a protest against the 'spirit of priestcraft' evident in the Education Bill then before Parliament.[86] A motion in 1902 expressing strong disapproval of another Education Bill was passed by the business meeting and then put to the congregation, by whom it was carried unanimously.[87] Less controversially, in 1915 a resolution of support for king and forces was carried unanimously by the congregation at Stowmarket.[88] In 1928 a telegram was sent to Sir William Joynson Hicks, MP, assuring him of the Association's support in opposing the draft revision of the Prayer Book then under consideration by Parliament.[89] Even after the business meeting had been moved to a different date, the Association might still express the concerns of the assembled churches, as in 1985, when it was agreed to send a letter to Margaret Thatcher as Prime Minister, asserting that the Bible

---

[82] *Circular Letter on 'Rest,' by the Suffolk and Norfolk Association of Particular Baptist Churches ... 1878* (Ipswich: S&NAPBC, 1878).

[83] *Companion Tune Book*, no. 156; *Grace Hymns* (music edition; London: Grace Publications Trust, 1977), no. 535; my thanks to John Rushbrook for assistance with locating the tunes. The retention of this tune in *Grace* may be due to the fact that one of the book's editors, Jack Hoad, had been pastor at Laxfield after World War II and retained a great affection for Suffolk.

[84] *Handbook 1978–79*, p. 9.

[85] *Earthen Vessel* 51 (1895), p. 216, citing the *Bury Free Press*.

[86] *Circular Letter 1896*, p. 20.

[87] *Circular Letter 1902* (London: S&NABPC, 1902), p. 15. Discussion of educational provision, and of the position of the Strict Baptists as Nonconformists, appeared in the published circular letters most years around the turn of the century, whether in the moderator's address, the circular letter itself, or the report of business transacted. For wider Baptist opposition, including in Norfolk, see Randall, *English Baptists of the Twentieth Century*, pp. 36-40.

[88] *Circular Letter on 'The Vicarious Sacrifice of Christ, as taught by our Lord and His Apostles', by the Suffolk and Norfolk Association of Particular Baptist Churches ... 1915* (Ipswich: S&NAPBC, 1915), p. 16.

[89] *Circular Letter 1928*, p. 12.

contained the answers to current national problems and condemning the proposed revision of Sunday trading legislation.[90]

An inter-war innovation on the evening of the second day was the Sunday School rally. This was not technically part of the meetings, but was arranged by the association's 'Sunday School Branch', formed in 1928, and many stayed on from the main meetings. Once this meeting had become established, they were often joined by coach-loads of children from all over Suffolk; as late as 1969, 1,100 (including 300 children) were present at Stonham.[91] As well as a children's speaker (and at first also a missionary speaker), there were presentations of medals and Bibles for full attendance at Sunday School, diplomas for long service by teachers, and recitations by the winners of Bible memorization competitions. In later years there would also be singing items from a Sunday School.[92] In 1963, the first evening's service was also planned with young people in mind, including singing items and an appropriate message.[93]

The meetings did not go without criticism from some quarters, however. In 1873 attention was drawn to a perceived lack of younger ministers taking part and to the conduct of the meetings:

> ... there are defects in the administration of the affairs of the Association. Is it not a defect when the public exercises are confined to a few of the aged brethren? Why should all the younger brethren be kept on the back ground? Why not appoint them to work, that their talents may be developed and made manifest? There is also a great defect in the length of the exercises. The sermons are much too long; but more especially the prayers. On the Wednesday morning, three brethren occupied about one hour in prayer; or rather, in preaching, for the exercises partook more of the character of preaching, than simply an invocation of the blessing of God. This is a lamentable weakness, and will be only productive of barrenness.[94]

In 1901 the moderator, H.D. Tooke of Lowestoft, suggested that the usefulness of the association was largely confined to its annual meeting, and that among other things it might devote one of the services to 'papers or addresses upon important subjects' as the Metropolitan Association was doing, and also hold a winter meeting.[95] In spite of the approval given in principle two years earlier for including topical addresses, neither suggestion was taken up. The moderator some years later, Pastor C.A. Guy of Norwich, drew on his experience ministering in Norfolk, where

---

[90] *1985/86 Handbook of the Suffolk & Norfolk Association of Strict Baptist Churches* (Rowhedge: S&NASBC, 1986), p. 14.

[91] *Handbook of the Suffolk and Norfolk Association of Strict Baptist Churches ... 1969* (Hadleigh: S&NASBC, 1969), unpaginated.

[92] Rushbrook, 'Tent Meetings'.

[93] *Handbook of the Suffolk and Norfolk Association of Strict Baptist Churches ... 1963* (Hadleigh: S&NASBC, 1963), unpaginated.

[94] 'Report of the Suffolk and Norfolk Association', *Earthen Vessel* 29 (1873), p. 217.

[95] *Circular Letter on Public Worship, by the Suffolk and Norfolk Association of Particular Baptist Churches ... 1901* (London: S&NABPC, 1901), p. 20.

Strict Baptist churches were few and often weak, to challenge the churches to look beyond meeting together each year for a 'cosy time', and to give expression to a desire to reach out and revive dying causes.[96] However, the association has not found church-planting easy during the twentieth century.

Catering

Since another significant attraction of the meetings was the chance to renew fellowship with like-minded believers from churches all over the area, mealtimes played a crucial role in terms of cementing the social cohesiveness of the association. As well as the meeting tent, others were therefore devoted to catering and hospitality (unless a convenient barn was available).[97] In 1872 there were refreshment stalls and also sit-down meals available in a malting converted for the occasion: 'Tables are laden with good beef and mutton, and other earthly benefits, for the comforts of such poor bodies as have pockets rich enough to dine and tea with the "upper class." Here, of course, the Levi tribe and their fortunate wives are an exception on the score of payment.'[98] The last reference is to the special treatment accorded to ministers and their wives. Indeed, until the 1960s or 1970s a separate tent was provided for them in which they could eat.[99] Set meals ceased to be provided with the outbreak of war in 1939, and although some refreshment provision appears to have been made by the late 1960s, they were not offered again until 1976.[100]

During the mid-nineteenth century ancillary provision included, to the disgust of one visitor, the smoking tent,

> containing unnecessary clay and shag, with the usual accompanying superfluities. I care not to enquire from what fund these luxuries are supplied; but if they are to some necessary dainties, sure a whole field need not have its air polluted by persons of all sizes and ages, rich and poor, parson, deacon, and member, strutting about with a long clay pipe, nearly long enough to require other assistance to support it, and this too, during the time service is being carried on hard by.[101]

Evidently some played truant from some of the services!

---

[96] *Circular Letter on 'The Source, Nature and Excellency of Soul Prosperity,' by the Suffolk & Norfolk Association of Particular Baptist Churches ... 1921* (Ipswich: S&NAPBC, 1922), p. 21.

[97] At Beccles in 1891 and Hadleigh the following year, the Town Hall was used: *Circular Letter on 'The Church a Mother: Her Obligations and Privileges', by the Suffolk and Norfolk Association of Particular Baptist Churches ... 1891* (London: S&NAPBC, 1891), p. 16; *Circular Letter of the Suffolk and Norfolk Association of Particular Baptist Churches ... 1892* (London: S&NAPBC, 1892), p. 16.

[98] 'A plain Countryman's Visit', p. 216.

[99] John Rushbrook, 'The Tent Meetings', unpublished MS, 2014.

[100] *Handbook 1976–77*, p. 9.

[101] W.D., 'Suffolk and Norfolk Baptist Association', p. 217.

In the days before mechanized transport (and subsequently, for the railways never reached the locations of most village chapels), accommodation was also required. Initially it was customary for ministers and messengers from the churches to sleep at a local inn, as in 1834, when they were due to put up at the Shoulder of Mutton in Hadleigh.[102] In time, with the growth of temperance convictions, this would doubtless have become unacceptable. Private accommodation therefore had to be located by the church hosting the meetings. This offered an opportunity for local householders to earn a little extra income. A visitor to Somersham in 1869 reported that whilst the inhabitants looked to welcome visitors, 'before night they gave such strangers to understand they had an eye to their own profit'.[103] During the late nineteenth century, the customary vote of thanks to the local community for its hospitality often included the local Anglican clergyman and his flock, who often assisted with the provision of accommodation and catering equipment. This was all the more significant given that at this time Strict Baptists were as vociferous as any other denomination in calling for the disestablishment of the Church of England.[104] Shortly after this, we find Anglican clergy often bringing a word of greeting at the lunch table. National disagreements were evidently not allowed to hinder the development of local relationships.

Changes in Recent Years

The moderator in 1982, Pastor Bryan Brown, in his address noted recent complaints about declining attendance. In his view, as well as changing the days of the week on which the meetings were held, a change in format was called for, and he offered a number of suggestions for developing a residential aspect to the gatherings, from camp-ins to taking over nearby guest houses.[105] His call for change provides a convenient watershed dividing the century and a half of meetings along 'traditional' lines from the recent decades, in which a number of modifications have been made.

In spite of occasional questions, the tent format seems set to continue, a new marquee for the meetings having come into use as recently as 1999.[106] Indeed, it is once again becoming something of an attraction, as a time when groups from the churches can have a day or two away in a different environment. Hosting the meetings had become increasingly burdensome for individual churches, many of which had declined in membership or whose members were no longer able to take time off from work to assist. On several occasions groups of churches shared the responsibility, but even this appears to have proved unworkable, and the meetings

---

[102] *Circular Letter 1833*, p. 2.

[103] W.D., 'Suffolk and Norfolk Baptist Association', p. 217.

[104] E.g. *Circular Letter on 'The Second Coming of Christ:' by the Suffolk and Norfolk Association of Particular Baptist Churches ... 1886* (Eye: S&NAPBC, 1886), p. 22.

[105] *1982/83 Handbook of the Suffolk & Norfolk Association of Strict Baptist Churches* (Rowhedge: S&NASBC, 1983), pp. 5-6.

[106] *1999–2000 Handbook of the Association of Grace Baptist Churches (East Anglia)* (Ipswich: AGBC(EA), 1999), p. 11.

finally ceased to migrate round the churches after it was reported in 1996 that no church had offered to host the meetings for the following year, and that changes to the format had been agreed.[107] Since 1997, then, the meetings have been held either at Wetheringsett Manor (a Christian conference centre) or Athelington Hall. Both sites have a range of ancillary facilities, and the work is now undertaken by a band of volunteers from various churches who are committed to assisting each year, under the direction of a committee. The rural nature of both locations attracts attenders from town churches, who are often first-generation Grace Baptists, but it also expresses continuity with associational tradition and therefore retains the loyalty of the diminishing numbers from old Strict Baptist families or from churches with a strong sense of denominational identity. Even now there are those who make the Association the central feature of a holiday in Suffolk, and stay on the field where the meetings are held. Both venues possess a swimming pool, and a variety of catering options are now offered – including the old-style salad plate beloved of chapels all over England.

In 1987 the meetings moved to a Friday and Saturday, allowing people at work during the week to attend. The result was a slight increase in attendance, with a number of families at the Saturday meetings.[108] After a few years of experimenting with various days, this was the choice settled upon. The Sunday School rallies continued to fill the tent through the 1980s but have declined steeply since then, although additional provision has been made for children's activities in parallel with the main services, and from 1995 to 2006 a late-night youth activity was arranged.[109] Attendance in 1994 was described as poor, although the Sunday School rally on the Saturday evening attracted over 600.[110] Now, after a few years of improving numbers, 200 represents a good congregation for the main services, and the old benches needed to accommodate large numbers have been replaced by plastic patio chairs.

The decline in attendance reflects the decline in the sense of distinctive identity of the associated churches. Increased population movement is one factor contributing to this, and it is matched by the arrival of pastors who are not only not locally born, but also often not familiar with the ethos of these churches, even if they adhere to the same basic doctrinal position.[111] The congregations no longer share quite the same

---

[107] *1996–97 Handbook of the Association of Grace Baptist Churches (East Anglia)* (Ipswich: AGBC(EA), 1996), p. 18.

[108] *Handbook 1987/88 of the Association of Grace Baptist Churches (East Anglia)* (Rowhedge, 1987), p. 9.

[109] *1995–96 Handbook of the Association of Grace Baptist Churches (East Anglia)* (Ipswich: AGBC(EA), 1995), p. 16; *Report & Handbook 2010–2011* (Stowmarket: AGBC(EA), 2010), p. 19.

[110] *1994–95 Handbook of the Association of Grace Baptist Churches (East Anglia)* (Ipswich: AGBC(EA), 1994), pp. 10, 13.

[111] Nationally, something of an identity crisis was evident by the 1970s: see my 'Strict Baptists and Reformed Baptists in England, 1955–76', in Philip E. Thompson and Anthony R. Cross (eds), *Recycling the Past or Researching History?: Studies in Baptist*

cultural bonds and geographical roots. There has not been a moderator since 2005, although a chairman presides at business meetings, and it is significant that during the last twenty-five years of moderators, only about a third had been born in Suffolk, and over half had come into the denomination from other types of church. Current practice is for two sermons to be preached by pastors from the association, and three by a visiting preacher. This allows him, should he so choose, to develop a theme. Preaching, however, is still conceived in traditional terms: the guest speaker in 2000, John Blanchard, provoked mixed reactions by giving what amounted to a lecture on apologetics rather than delivering an expository sermon; by prior agreement with the committee he offered a summary of the argument of his book *Does God believe in Atheists?*[112] The meetings remain dominated by men, although within the last decade or so women have read the Scriptures and even spoken on behalf of the Grace Baptist Mission.

Seminars have been introduced before the afternoon services. These explore issues in church life or personal spirituality, explore the challenges of outreach to a particular group, such as students, or present the work of an organization such as the Christian Institute. There is usually opportunity for questions from the audience or small group discussion. Another innovation is the exhibition featuring the work of various denominational agencies, as well as other Christian organizations, which takes up another tent – something first introduced in 1964.[113] Since 1967 there has also been a bookstall.[114]

Another element of continuity is provided by the reading of the articles of faith at one of the services. These had been shorn of their anti-Fullerite clause in 1950, and have now been revised and expanded, the new version first being read in 2007.[115] Greetings continue to be brought by the other Grace Baptist associations (the designation 'Strict Baptist' dropped out of favour among these churches in the 1980s).

However, there was an ongoing debate during the late 1990s concerning the association's standpoint regarding the restriction of communion to those baptized by immersion as believers. This culminated in a reaffirmation of its traditional position (albeit with the recognition that each church interpreted this differently with regard to visiting Christian believers), but led to the withdrawal from the late 1990s of a number of churches which no longer felt able to support its approach. This has

---

Historiography and Myths (Studies in Baptist History and Thought, 11; Milton Keynes: Paternoster, 2005), pp. 294-316.

[112] *2000–2001 Handbook of the Association of Grace Baptist Churches (East Anglia)* (n.pl.: AGBC(EA), 2000), pp. 13-15; *2001–2002 Handbook of the Association of Grace Baptist Churches (East Anglia)* (n.pl.: AGBC(EA), 2001), p. 23. The matter had been referred to the Annual Business Meeting following the 2000 meetings.

[113] *Handbook 1964*, unpaginated.

[114] *Handbook of the Suffolk and Norfolk Association of Strict Baptist Churches ... 1967* (Hadleigh: S&NASBC, 1967), unpaginated. My father initiated this and ran it for many years.

[115] *Report & Handbook 2008–2009* (Stowmarket: AGBC(EA), 2008), p. 12.

further lessened the number of potential attenders; I would estimate that it accounts for three-quarters of the decline in membership of associated churches during the last two decades.[116]

Moreover, the very principle of associating has been challenged in various ways, here as elsewhere among English Baptists. When the subject of the circular letter was 'Inter-Church Fellowship' (2003), the writer, Timothy Alford, made no mention of the association.[117] The report to that year's annual business meeting wondered whether it had reached a crisis point: apart from the difficulty of finding people to take up office, the pastors' and elders' forum expressed the opinion that there was a lack of fellowship among the churches and even a sense of suspicion rather than a feeling of ownership of the association by church members. Furthermore, the format of the tent meetings was being questioned, even to the extent of whether they should continue to be held in a tent (that year the main tent was sold to the owners of Athelington Hall, the association retaining the right to use it there for ten years if required).[118] The following year a number of changes were made, especially regarding provision for young people, due to the initiative of the Fellowship of Youth.[119] Since then, things appear to have settled down. The meetings continue; they are still held in a tent; and congregations appear to be holding up quite well.

The Role Played by the Tent Meetings

Reports of the nineteenth-century meetings often alluded to the sweetness of fellowship with like-minded believers who did not see one another for the rest of the year. In 1934, Pastor L.R. Garrard, visiting as a delegate from the Metropolitan Association, compared the meetings to the annual gathering of the Jews at Jerusalem.[120] For much of their history, they could aptly be regarded as a gathering of the Strict Baptist tribes of Suffolk and Norfolk. As the *Suffolk Times and Mercury* put it regarding the 1883 meetings at Rattlesden, 'Country people tramped in from all the region round about to hear long sermons, to sing hymns in the rambling old tunes of a century ago, and to hobnob with one another in social intercourse. The event is quite a novelty in its way. Nothing quite like it is heard of in connection with any other denomination'.[121] 'Novelty' might not be the most appropriate word now

---

[116] This includes Bethesda, Ipswich, which in its last year of membership of the Association (1998–99) reported a church roll of 339.

[117] *Report & Handbook 2003–2004* (n.pl.: AGBC(EA), 2003), pp. 6-10. Alford, a retired pastor, had never led an association church but held similar doctrinal views and was in membership at Stowmarket.

[118] *Report 2003–2004*, pp. 20-21.

[119] *Report & Handbook 2004–2005* (n.pl.: AGBC(EA), 2004), p. 18.

[120] *Circular Letter 1934*, p. 12; for a more recent use of the same image, see *1999–2000 Handbook*, p. 11.

[121] Quoted in [William Winters], 'Suffolk and Norfolk Association of Particular Baptist Churches: The Annual Meetings at Rattlesden, Suffolk', *Earthen Vessel* 43 (1887), pp. 206-12 (p. 207).

(nor was it then), but these meetings are certainly unusual nowadays, and the use of a tent unique.

A key function of the meetings was the affirmation of the association's doctrinal standpoint. This was done through the reading of the articles, and in time also the moderator's address, as well as the circular letter: in the centenary year, 1930, the topic was 'The Faith of our Fathers'.[122] Sermons, too, would have upheld this, although it does not appear to me that there was an imbalance towards the 'doctrines of grace' in the themes and texts chosen by the preachers. A more practical purpose was probably also served by these gatherings, especially before the use of the telephone became widespread. Church secretaries would doubtless have attended with their diaries to hand, in order to book preachers for the coming year.

What can we say of the relationship between the popularity of these meetings and the success of the association? Clearly mutual concern was fostered by meeting each year, and by hearing the letters from the churches read, wearisome though the reading might have been.[123] In turn, the existence of a cohesive body of churches enabled vigorous extension work, not so much through the association itself as through the related Suffolk and Norfolk Baptist Home Missionary Society, formed in 1831.[124] That cohesiveness was played out in the life of individual churches: whilst some suffered internal tension and even division, it was relatively unusual, and the association sought to do what it could to promote reconciliation. In addition there was not the diversity of Strict Baptist thinking that could be found in areas such as Kent or Lancashire, where the Gospel Standard churches were much stronger. The churches might have been firmly high Calvinist in doctrine for much of their history, but they did not share the aversion of many high Calvinists to inter-church co-operation, nor the reluctance to adopt effective means to extend their work.

The tent meetings had one further unexpected (and unintended) social function. As John Rushbrook recollects, 'One side effect of the meetings was that romances began there. My own parents would delight to recall the year they first met when the meetings were held at Stoke Ash, probably 1935–6. And I have known of other couples with a similar story.'[125] Bringing people together is what these meetings have done best, aided by their distinctive setting, and it looks as if they will continue to do so for some years yet.

---

[122] *Circular Letter 1930*, pp. 16-22.
[123] Dix, *Strict and Particular*, p. 141.
[124] Dix, *Strict and Particular*, pp. 146-48.
[125] Rushbrook, 'Tent Meetings'.

CHAPTER 6

'The Forgotten Spurgeon': A Reappraisal of the Life and Ministry of James Archer Spurgeon (1837–99)

Peter J. Morden

Introduction

James Archer Spurgeon (1837–99), the subject of this chapter, was the younger brother of Charles Haddon Spurgeon (1834–92), the famous British Baptist minister and Victorian 'celebrity'. As well as being the foremost popular preacher of his generation, C.H. Spurgeon was widely recognised for his educational and philanthropic work. In 1856 he founded the influential Pastors' College, which sent a succession of zealous and practically focused men into both pastorates and pioneering situations, and in 1869 he established what became a large and thriving Orphanage. His fame spread beyond the British Isles; indeed, the widespread circulation of his published sermons made him a global phenomenon.[1] So, when one of C.H. Spurgeon's sons, Thomas, arrived in Australia in 1877 to minister, he found that his father was already a household name there.[2] At a meeting in Adelaide Thomas announced he would read a short extract from a letter his father had written him. The effect was dramatic. Those gathered 'were delighted', he reported to his parents, and 'sat forward in their seats to listen eagerly, as they always do when the magic name is pronounced'.[3] Such was C.H. Spurgeon's fame that he was the subject of numerous nineteenth-century biographies, of varying length and quality. These included a biographical sketch published in America when he was still in his early twenties,[4] and an extensive work by G. Holden Pike, an 1894 edition which ran to

---

[1] For these and other biographical details, see Peter J. Morden, *C.H. Spurgeon: The People's Preacher* (Farnham: CWR, 2009).

[2] *The Sword and The Trowel: A Record of Combat With Sin and Labour For The Lord* (henceforth, *ST*) (London: Passmore and Alabaster, 1865–96), May 1878, pp. 224-25. From 1865–92 *ST* was edited by Charles Haddon Spurgeon.

[3] *ST*, June 1878, p. 306. Cf. the use made of this by Ken R. Manley, *From Woolloomooloo to 'Eternity': A History of Australian Baptists: Growing an Australian Church (1831–1914)* (Studies in Baptist History and Thought, 16.1-2; Milton Keynes: Paternoster, 2006), I, p. 109.

[4] Elias L. Magoon, *'The Modern Whitfield (sic.)': Sermons of the Rev. C.H. Spurgeon of London with an Introduction and Sketch of His Life by E.L. Magoon* (New York, NY: Sheldon and Blakeman, 1857).

six volumes.[5] Popular interest in C.H. Spurgeon shows little sign of abating, with many reprints of his sermons and books available. Although there is scope for much more scholarly work to be done, his importance as the most influential purveyor of popular religion of the Victorian era is increasingly recognised.[6]

By contrast, James Archer Spurgeon has received scant attention, either popular or scholarly. During his lifetime he was the subject of just one hagiography, a slim volume, again by Holden Pike – a prolific rather than profound writer – which was published in 1894.[7] There was no 'tombstone' biography and since James Spurgeon's death he has been almost entirely neglected. Even in the biographies and studies of his brother he tends to appear as a peripheral figure, one who is, I submit, much misunderstood. I am not aware of a single scholarly thesis or even an article which focuses explicitly on him. It is James Archer, rather than Charles Haddon, who deserves the epithet, 'the forgotten Spurgeon'.[8] This is despite James and Charles spending most of their lives working together. James was also a Baptist minister. He became 'co-pastor' of his brother's London congregation and was closely involved in other dimensions of Charles' work. In addition, he exercised a significant pastoral ministry in his own right, especially as pastor of West Croydon Baptist Church.

This short study is an attempt to do some groundwork on James Archer Spurgeon, drawing from both published sources and unpublished materials, including the minute books of West Croydon Baptist Church which are now deposited in the Spurgeon's College Heritage Room. The chapter begins with a brief sketch of James Spurgeon's life, before arguing that the role he played in the day-to-day running of his brother's church was a crucial one. Moreover, throughout their long association Charles and James' working relationship was harmonious, not least because the younger brother was consistently willing to take the second place behind the elder. An appreciation of James Spurgeon's involvement in the multi-faceted life of the Metropolitan Tabernacle, which from 1861 housed his brother's congregation, is crucial if the reasons behind C.H. Spurgeon's sustained success are to be properly understood. James' important ministry at West Croydon is also delineated. The chapter closes by examining the 'battle for succession' which took place at the

---

[5] G. Holden Pike, *The Life and Work of Charles Haddon Spurgeon* (6 vols; London: Cassell, 1894 [1892–93]).

[6] For a survey of the literature, both popular and scholarly, see Peter J. Morden, *'Communion with Christ and his People': The Spirituality of C.H. Spurgeon (1834–92)* (Oxford: Regent's Park College, 2010/Eugene, OR: Wipf and Stock, 2014), pp. 4-8.

[7] G. Holden Pike, *James Archer Spurgeon D.D. LL.D.: Preacher, Philanthropist, and Co-Pastor With C.H. Spurgeon at the Metropolitan Tabernacle* (henceforth, *JAS*) (London: Alexander and Shepheard, 1894). Holden Pike was a long-time associate of the Spurgeon brothers who had done significant work for *The Sword and the Trowel*.

[8] For this phrase, see Iain H. Murray, *The Forgotten Spurgeon* (London: Banner of Truth, 1966). Murray does not argue that C.H. Spurgeon himself had been forgotten. Rather he focuses on particular dimensions of C.H. Spurgeon's ministry, e.g., his Calvinism, and shows how these have been neglected by different biographers and commentators.

Tabernacle following C.H. Spurgeon's death.[9] This dispute did much to sully James Archer's reputation among those who were loyal to the memory of his brother, and contributed to his becoming such a neglected figure.

Biographical Sketch

James Archer Spurgeon was born on 8 June 1837 in Braintree, Essex.[10] His parents, John and Eliza (née Jarvis), were staunch Independents and paedobaptists but, like his brother, James became convinced of the case for believers' baptism and submitted to this rite following his evangelical conversion. In 1855 he entered Stepney/Regent's Park College, London to train for Baptist ministry under the tutelage of Dr Joseph Angus. By this date C.H. Spurgeon, who had not undergone any formal theological training, was already finding fame as pastor of New Park Street Chapel in Southwark, drawing vast crowds to hear his dynamic preaching. James found that the interest in his own emerging ministry derived in significant degree from Charles' reputation. So, when James preached at Little Wild Street Chapel on 15 August 1858, the London *Evening Star* introduced its account of the services with the following headline, 'The Rev. Mr Spurgeon's Brother'. Similarly, the *Hampshire Independent* for 20 November 1858 described him as 'a brother of *the* Mr Spurgeon' in a report of his preaching at Portland Union Chapel, Southampton. While the Hampshire paper praised his ministry, it held – probably correctly – that many in the large crowd who packed the chapel to hear him were present primarily because of his older sibling's burgeoning celebrity status.[11] James' voice, style of delivery and sermon content were regularly contrasted with the preaching of his more illustrious brother.[12] James Archer would have to get used to such comparisons, as they would continue to be made for the rest of his ministry.[13]

James Spurgeon's ministry at Portland Chapel led to an invitation to return to supply what was already a well-known pulpit (Alexander MacLaren had been pastor there for twelve years before moving to Manchester in April 1858).[14] In the spring of 1859 James accepted a call to the pastorate of the Southampton church. This was a charge he resigned after two years, but he continued to lead an offshoot of Portland Chapel until 1863, when he was called to be founding minister of a Baptist church in Cornwall Road, Bayswater.[15] Earlier, in August 1860 he had married Emily Burgoyne, a member of New Park Street, with his brother leading the service and

---

[9] Although the West Croydon church was also known as the 'Tabernacle', when I have used the word in this chapter it always refers to the Metropolitan Tabernacle.

[10] For this and other details in this paragraph, see *JAS*, pp. 9-32.

[11] *JAS*, pp. 34-35.

[12] See, e.g., a report in the *Leicestershire Mercury* on a sermon given in January 1859, as recorded in *JAS*, pp. 35-36.

[13] See, e.g., the American paper the *Buffalo Express*, as cited in *JAS*, pp. 108-110.

[14] David Williamson, *The Life of Alexander MacLaren* (London: James Clark, n.d. [1910]), pp. 26-36.

[15] *JAS*, p. 72.

preaching.[16] The young couple's return to London was of great significance to the subsequent course of James Archer's career. James and Charles enjoyed a strong friendship, and the younger brother was soon giving the elder considerable help, especially in the field of administration. James soon became closely involved in the work of the Pastors' College, which had been founded in 1856, and was also involved in meetings concerning the possibility of an Orphanage from early 1867.[17] James Spurgeon was one of the founding trustees of the Orphanage and, as will be shown, a crucial member of the group from the beginning.

In the closing months of 1867 James received an invitation to join his brother and become 'co-pastor' at the 5,500 seat Metropolitan Tabernacle which from 1861 had housed C.H. Spurgeon's congregation. In October 1867, when the possibility of James' appointment was put before the church, there were over 3,500 in membership and Charles was hard-pressed as pastor, regularly unwell and in considerable need of assistance.[18] The invitation from the deacons, which noted the help James had already given in respect of the College and the proposed Orphanage, was startlingly frank. They wished to 'leave the pulpit entirely in the hands of (the) beloved pastor' (i.e., C.H. Spurgeon). Indeed, James was required to sign a legal disclaimer stating he accepted this arrangement. Moreover, he could be given twelve months' notice at any time – by the decision of his brother alone. Finally, it was made clear he would have absolutely no right of succession to the full pastorate in the 'lamentable event' of C.H. Spurgeon's death. James' role would be to engage in pastoral work, attend church meetings and give such 'brotherly assistance' as their pastor 'might from time to time require'.[19] James wrote on 8 January 1868 accepting all the terms.[20] The language of co-pastor was resolutely maintained by the Spurgeons, but the *Baptist Magazine* was closer to reality when it reported that James Archer Spurgeon had resigned his pastorate at Cornwall Road and been appointed 'assistant minister' at the Metropolitan Tabernacle.[21] He would continue to assist his brother until the latter's death.

James Spurgeon was fully extended by his work at the Metropolitan Tabernacle and its institutions, but at the end of 1869 he took on an additional responsibility. In 1868 a committee had been formed with a view to establishing an open communion

---

[16] *JAS*, pp. 46-51; 128. Emily died in 1881. James then married Ellen Withers in 1882 in a ceremony which was also conducted by his brother. *JAS*, p. 131.

[17] S.(tockwell) O.(rphanage) Minute Book No. 1. March 1867–June 1876, held at 'Spurgeons' (Spurgeon's Childcare), Rushden. The first trustees' meeting took place on 18 March.

[18] Charles Haddon Spurgeon, *Autobiography: Compiled from his Diary, Letters, and Records by his Wife and his Private Secretary* (4 vols; London: Passmore and Alabaster, 1897–99), III, p. 30.

[19] Thomas Olney *et al.* to James A. Spurgeon, n.d. [30 December 1867?], in *JAS*, pp. 87-89.

[20] James A. Spurgeon to 'The Officers of the Church at the Tabernacle', 8 January 1868, in *JAS*, pp. 89-90.

[21] *Baptist Magazine* 60 (January, 1868), p. 46.

Baptist church in Croydon, a suburban town to the south of London.[22] A temporary iron chapel was erected, but the work struggled. C.H. Spurgeon had earlier declined to take a service there due, as the Croydon Committee Minute Book recorded, to his 'failing health'.[23] James Spurgeon was willing and able to be involved, however, and he preached there on 11 July 1869 and again on 1 August. The fledgling cause was by now in something of a 'crisis' as it faced some serious financial difficulties.[24] But James Spurgeon's ministry generated considerable excitement and drew increased numbers. After his preaching in August he offered to supply the pulpit for three months, indicating that he would be willing to give his 'surplus time' to the Croydon cause, continuing with his Metropolitan Tabernacle duties but speaking at Croydon most Sundays and also taking a regular week day evening service 'if necessary'.[25] The committee quickly moved to secure his services. Under James Spurgeon's leadership, the church was formally founded on 19 October 1869, with a membership of twenty-nine, all transferring from other churches.[26] The work flourished and the iron chapel was regularly packed to overflowing, so that alternative temporary premises in the town had to be found. The stone was laid for a new and permanent building in May 1872. This was opened in March 1873 and extended in 1878.[27] After his brother's death in 1892 James' roles in the Metropolitan Tabernacle and Pastors' College ended amidst much controversy. Yet he remained pastor of the West Croydon church and president of the Orphanage until his death. This was on 22 March 1899 due to a suspected heart attack experienced whilst travelling in a railway carriage from Brighton to London.[28] He had been elected Vice President of the Baptist Union, and his death occurred just before he was able to become President. James Spurgeon had been an extremely active evangelical Baptist minister, with a ministry which saw him work concurrently in two churches whilst also being at the heart of some significant institutions which were known around the world. Dimensions of this ministry can now be analysed in more detail, beginning with his work alongside his brother.

---

[22] Proposed Open Communion Baptist Church in Croydon, in Croydon Baptist Free Church Committee Minute Book 1868–70, Spurgeon's College, Heritage Room (R.1.02). See *JAS*, p. 132, for a description of middle class, suburban Croydon in the nineteenth century.
[23] Croydon Baptist ... Minute Book 1868–70, Minutes for 17 November 1868.
[24] *JAS*, p. 133.
[25] West Croydon Baptist ... Minute Book 1868–70, Minutes for 29 June, 27 July, 3 August 1869, Spurgeon's College, Heritage Room (R.1.01). Cf. two letters from James Spurgeon, dated 10 and 29 August 1869, which are loose in the volume, West Croydon Baptist Church, Church Meeting Minutes, 1869–90, Spurgeon's College, Heritage Room (R1.03).
[26] West Croydon Baptist ... Minute Book 1868–70, Minutes for 2 November 1869.
[27] *JAS*, pp. 133-35.
[28] West Croydon Baptist Church, Church Meeting Minutes, 1890–1903, 10 April 1899, Spurgeon's College, Heritage Room (R.1.04).

James Archer Spurgeon, the Metropolitan Tabernacle and its Institutions

Among James Spurgeon's first words to the Tabernacle congregation following his calling as co-pastor in 1868 were, 'I could see very clearly, when this came before me, that there was a great deal of work to be done.'[29] This comment was no exaggeration. He was involved in one-to-one pastoral ministry and extensive administration from the time of his appointment onwards. He even became a specialist in ecclesiastical law so that he could better advise the church and help the various church plants which were being established by Pastors' College students all over London and beyond.[30] In addition to strategic administration he found himself preaching and presiding regularly at a range of midweek meetings, as well as engaging in occasional Sunday ministry at the Tabernacle. His leading such a large number of meetings – many more than were envisaged by the terms of his original call – was partly due to his brother's worsening health. C.H. Spurgeon suffered from rheumatic gout, Bright's disease (i.e., chronic nephritis) and a tendency to depression,[31] and James would often have to stand in for him at short notice.[32] The leading role he played in the midweek baptismal services at the Tabernacle can be analysed as an example of the extensive work he undertook.

Notice of the different baptismal services and the numbers of people baptized were recorded each month in *The Sword and The Trowel*, the house magazine of the Metropolitan Tabernacle, with the name of the person baptizing also given. Because of this, James and Charles Spurgeon's respective involvement in these services can be calculated with some precision. These figures show that Charles hardly ever baptized following James's appointment, and that the vast majority of the baptisms were administered by James. Figures for two different six month periods illustrate the point. In the first six months of 1868 there were nineteen baptismal services at the Metropolitan Tabernacle, with statistics indicating 277 people baptized in total.[33] All the candidates at these services were baptized by James Spurgeon. This was an unusually high number of baptisms even by the Metropolitan Tabernacle's standards, and it appears that a backlog had built up before his appointment as co-pastor. In a later six month period, the second half of 1874, there were twelve baptismal services with a total of 194 baptisms. James was responsible for eleven of these services and 192 of the baptisms.[34] C.H. Spurgeon baptized only two candidates, both of them on 21 September 1874.[35] These were his twin sons, Thomas and Charles.[36] I have not

---

[29] *JAS*, pp. 92-93.

[30] *JAS*, p. 80.

[31] For details, see Peter J. Morden, 'C.H. Spurgeon and Suffering', *Evangelical Review of Theology* 35.4 (Autumn, 2011), pp. 306-25.

[32] *JAS*, p. 142.

[33] *ST* February to September 1868, pp. 94, 142, 191, 286, 333, 383, 431. For a detailed breakdown of the figures and further commentary, see Morden, *'Communion with Christ'*, pp. 181-82.

[34] *ST* October 1874 to December 1874, pp. 491, 543, 582; January to February 1875, pp. 44, 92.

[35] *ST* October 1874, p. 491.

been able to find any other instances of C.H. Spurgeon baptizing at the Metropolitan Tabernacle in the 1870s or, indeed, beyond.[37] If James did not conduct the baptisms, then someone else would be called in to do so.[38] James Archer Spurgeon was, therefore, central to this vital aspect of the Metropolitan Tabernacle's ministry.

James Spurgeon was also crucial to the different agencies that were sponsored by the Tabernacle, as already noted. His work for the Orphanage can be taken as an example, with the Orphanage Minute Book shedding much light on the nature of his role. As an Orphanage Trustee he regularly showed himself to be a gifted administrator, one who combined a sharp eye for detail with an impressive breadth of understanding of the business world.[39] At a crucial early Trustees meeting, on 20 June 1867, complex discussions of technicalities relating to a number of railway bonds given to help finance the new work were necessary. At this point, according to the relevant Orphanage Minute Book, C.H. Spurgeon not only left the chair but also the meeting itself. James took over and, after some debate, undertook to follow up the issues relating to these bonds personally.[40] This was an example of the sort of close, detailed work which he would soon be undertaking for the Orphanage on a regular basis. The Trustees as a body were, from the beginning, anxious to protect C.H. Spurgeon as much as possible from any work he found a strain. There were concerns that he was finding it difficult emotionally to visit boys who had applied, through their relatives, for admittance to the Orphanage (not to mention the drain on his time).[41] Accordingly, it was very unusual, from at least the beginning of 1868, for C.H. Spurgeon to have any role in the application process. All the 'application papers and procedures for admission' had earlier been drawn up by James Spurgeon and another trustee.[42]

Once the Orphanage was established, C.H. Spurgeon relied all the more on his brother to look after the work on a day-to-day basis, and from 1869 onwards was increasingly absent from Trustees meetings.[43] In 1869, of the fourteen Trustees' meetings, C.H. Spurgeon attended eleven. But, in 1873, when there were twenty-four

---

[36] 'Baptism of Mr. Spurgeon's Sons', *South London Press* 26 September 1874, in Spurgeon's Scrapbooks, Numbered Volumes, vol. 1, 1856–January 1879, Heritage Room, Spurgeon's College, p. 6.

[37] From the beginning of 1879 the *ST* stopped naming the person who conducted the Tabernacle baptisms, but I have found no evidence, in newspapers or elsewhere, that C.H. Spurgeon baptized in the period from 1879 to his death. If he did so at all it was a rare occurrence.

[38] E.g., Vernon Charlesworth, the headmaster of the Stockwell Orphanage. See *ST* September 1874, p. 439.

[39] G. Holden Pike, 'Men and Women on Work. The Rev. James Archer Spurgeon, D.D., LL.D', in *Family Friend* 27. 315 (March, 1896), p. 37; *JAS*, p. 80.

[40] Stockwell Orphanage Minute Book No. 1, Minutes for 20 June 1867.

[41] Cf. C.H. Spurgeon, *Autobiography*, III, p. 177; 'Stockwell Orphanage', *ST* March 1869, p. 133.

[42] Stockwell Orphanage Minute Book No. 1, Minutes for 20 June 1867.

[43] Cf. the comments in C.H. Spurgeon, *Autobiography*, III, pp. 176-77.

such meetings, he was present at only four of them. In 1875, when there were again twenty-four meetings, he was in attendance only once, on 28 May 1875, when the group gathered to elect some additional Trustees.[44] C.H. Spurgeon took the chair on this occasion, as he always did when he was present. But, in his absence, the meetings were chaired by his brother. It was James Spurgeon who increasingly took the lead in organising the affairs of the Orphanage. When James was himself away, which was unusual, other Trustees, usually William Higgs or William Olney, two Tabernacle deacons, would step in.[45] The involvement of Higgs and Olney shows that James was not the only helper C.H. Spurgeon relied upon in respect of the Orphanage. Indeed, from the mid-1870s the headmaster, Vernon Charlesworth, who increasingly enjoyed the confidence of the Spurgeons and the rest of the Board, had power to act regarding the day-to-day running of the institution. Nevertheless, the oversight for Charlesworth was provided by James Spurgeon, who often signed off the headmaster's notes and was present at a whole host of meetings.[46] Thus, although the Orphanage was firmly associated in the public mind with C.H. Spurgeon, his involvement in its oversight and running, from as early as 1875, was minimal. By contrast, James Archer Spurgeon's commitment to its day-to-day work was significant, and vital.

In summary, there is much evidence to show that James Spurgeon was a vital figure in the life of the Tabernacle and associated concerns from 1867 onwards. His ministry was such that it freed C.H. Spurgeon to focus on Sunday preaching, helping to prepare his messages for weekly publication, teaching (for example, his much anticipated regular Friday lecture to his students)[47] and writing (for instance, his warmly received multi-volume commentary on the Psalms, *The Treasury of David*).[48] James Spurgeon's contribution to sustaining his brother's ministry was immense. It enabled his brother to give himself to the work he felt called to do, free from the burdens of running a huge church and complex organisations. It follows that those who benefited – and who benefit today – from C.H. Spurgeon's ministry owe James Archer Spurgeon a significant debt.

---

[44] S. (tockwell) O.(rphanage) Minute Book No. 2, 1869–1875, held at Spurgeons (formerly Spurgeon's Childcare) Archive, Rushden, Northants. See especially the entry for 28 May 1875.

[45] See, e.g., Stockwell Orphanage Minute Book No. 2, 25 June 1869. For this meeting, Olney was in the chair.

[46] See, e.g., entries for 1876. Stockwell Orphanage Master's Report, 8 September 1867–28 January 1881, 'Spurgeons' (formerly Spurgeon's Childcare) Archive, Rushden, Northants.

[47] Charles Haddon Spurgeon, *Lectures To My Students* (3 vols; London: Passmore and Alabaster, n.d.).

[48] Charles Haddon Spurgeon, *The Treasury Of David: Containing An Original Exposition Of The Book Of Psalms* ... (7 vols; London and Edinburgh: Marshall Brothers, n.d. [London: Passmore and Alabaster, 1869–1885]).

Reasons for Harmony between the Spurgeon Brothers

What was the working relationship between the brothers like? They worked together harmoniously. This was due to a number of factors. Familial ties were obviously crucial (although this potentially could have made the relationship difficult). Yet as well as their fellow feeling as brothers additional reasons why their working relationship was strong can be adduced. Four principal ones will be noticed here.

Firstly, Charles and James had complementary gifts. The older brother was the best-known popular preacher of his era and a visionary entrepreneur, but he struggled with matters of administrative detail. It was precisely in the area of administration that James was strong. Accordingly, much of this work was conducted behind the scenes. Admittedly, he was not always in the background: the baptismal services over which he presided were well attended, and as Vice President of the College and the Orphanage he occupied recognised, prominent positions. Nevertheless, many of his most important contributions were made in committee and, consequently, few were aware of the sheer magnitude and significance of what he accomplished. C.H. Spurgeon himself was conscious of the immense debt he owed his younger brother. In November 1871 he wrote to him whilst abroad,

> Dear brother, —I am not very demonstrative in gratitude, but I must indulge myself with the pleasure of saying how much I owe to you and how greatly you contribute to my peace of mind. Your loving aid is beyond all thanks, although it desires none. Believe me, dear brother, I value you as God's best gift to me in His work.[49]

The comment that James desired no thanks is important and, on the basis of the available evidence, correct. There were some strains within the wider leadership. One church leader was unhappy that James refused to preach at midweek baptismal services if he was baptizing as well (as he invariably was). A comment was made to this effect to the brothers' father, John, who was visiting London. John Spurgeon proceeded to give the complainant short shrift, later taking the matter up with his eldest son.[50] Nevertheless, there seems to have been genuine harmony most of the time and there is much evidence that Charles and James themselves worked well in concert right up to 1892.[51]

The second reason for the brothers' harmony, therefore, was that the younger was happy to take the second place for as long as the older was alive. In 1884 C.H. Spurgeon was fifty years old, and the Metropolitan Tabernacle commemorated this with a Jubilee celebration. On this occasion James declared, 'Ever since I can remember anything I can remember my big brother, and I am quite content that he should remain my big brother to the end of my days.'[52] All the family had to be

---

[49] *JAS*, pp. 139-40.
[50] *JAS*, p. 125.
[51] See, e.g., the private letters from C.H. Spurgeon to James A. Spurgeon reproduced in *JAS*, pp. 137-171.
[52] *JAS*, p. 102.

willing to accept a position behind Charles; nevertheless, James seemed particularly content with this. He stated,

> I consider it to be the greatest honour God could have conferred upon me to be co-partner in my brother's work. Anything I can do for him makes me feel I am multiplying him, and at the same time I feel that I am multiplying myself to a degree which it would have been impossible for me to have done if I had not been linked to my brother.[53]

The partnership worked for both of them. They were stronger together than they would have been apart.

However, these were not the only reasons the Spurgeons worked in harmony. They shared a common theology and the third reason their relationship worked was their mutual commitment to an essentially Calvinistic understanding of Christian doctrine. C.H. Spurgeon's own Calvinistic thinking has been regularly expounded. Although his Calvinism has not always been well delineated, he certainly espoused a Calvinistic theology, and this remained the essential framework for his thinking right to the end of his ministry.[54] James Spurgeon's own Calvinism was similar to his brother's, and it got him into difficulties in his first pastorate in Southampton. During his brief ministry at Portland Chapel he was able to attract substantial crowds, despite following MacLaren, who even early in his career had a strong reputation. With James Spurgeon as minister the chapel had to be enlarged, with 400 'sittings' added to the existing 500. The new building was opened in January 1860.[55] The nature of Portland as a 'Union Chapel' meant that Baptists and paedobaptists were in leadership together. James Spurgeon's resignation after just two years as pastor, which caused him what he described as 'unspeakable pain',[56] was partly because of his commitment to believers' baptism. Yet it appears his Calvinism was the more important issue.[57] Indeed, it was his desire to introduce a book 'which taught the doctrines of sovereign grace' as a core text for a Bible class which was the specific catalyst for division.[58] He led a breakaway group from the church which met at the Carlton Rooms in the town and which, when formally constituted, was established explicitly as a Calvinistic Baptist chapel.[59] So, with 'the tide of nineteenth-century opinion ... running against religious particularism of any form',[60]

---

[53] *JAS*, p. 102.

[54] See C.H. Spurgeon, *Autobiography*, I, and the chapter, 'A Defence of Calvinism', pp. 167-84, for C.H. Spurgeon's mature thought. For a brief exposition of his Calvinism, see Morden, 'Communion with Christ', pp. 39-45.

[55] *JAS*, pp. 42-43.

[56] James Spurgeon's resignation letter to the church, n.d., in *JAS*, p. 59.

[57] *JAS*, p. 59.

[58] *JAS*, p. 54.

[59] *JAS*, p. 65.

[60] Ian Sellers, 'John Howard Hinton, Theologian', *Baptist Quarterly* 33.3 (July, 1989), pp. 119-32 (p. 123).

the Spurgeons both stood against the prevailing trend and held onto Calvinistic convictions.

The Spurgeons were Calvinistic but it is crucial to recognise they were evangelical Calvinists. Their shared evangelicalism, then, is the fourth and final reason for their harmonious relationship. C.H. Spurgeon's own commitment to evangelical priorities is well documented.[61] Once again, James shared his brother's outlook and this fed through into his practice. In 18 April 1893 he delivered a keynote address for the Pastors' College Evangelical Association on Romans 6.13. What, he asked those present, was the 'subject matter and theme of our preaching?' He answered, 'The atoning sacrifice of Jesus Christ, the necessity for His cross, and for our being crucified with Him upon it. Is not this the very heart and soul of what we proclaim?' He died not merely as a martyr or as an example. Rather, 'he came to die for us in our place and stead, so that we should die in Him and afterwards be accepted in Him.'[62] These themes, the cross, penal substitutionary atonement and, vitally, the importance of living and proclaiming the message mirrored the themes which dominated his recently deceased brother's ministry. Both men stood in the tradition of eighteenth-century evangelical Calvinists who freely proclaimed the message of salvation to all and engaged in a range of expansive evangelistic activity.

This commitment to active evangelism can be shown, in James' case, by reference to his work at West Croydon. Holden Pike's sub-heading for his description of how the church developed, 'Aggressive Christian Work', gives a good flavour of the outward focus James Spurgeon brought to the church.[63] The work grew through evangelism. Granted, many of those received into membership in the early years of his pastorate transferred from other churches, but an increasing number began to join the fellowship via baptism. Some of these had had some previous connection with other churches, but others appear to have had no previous church affiliations.[64] There were many new converts. Testimonies of their 'religious experience' were heard by appointed visitors from the church. These 'messengers' reported back to the church meeting on what they had heard. Soon midweek baptismal services were taking place on a regular basis. So, on Tuesday 10 May 1870 six were baptized, and on Friday 4 October 1872 there was a service for four people.[65] The church tended to avoid Thursdays, presumably so there was no clash with the Metropolitan Tabernacle baptismal services. It is possible that no Victorian minister was involved in as many services of believers' baptism, and baptized as many people, as James Archer Spurgeon.

The church also engaged in much children's ministry. The Annual General Meeting held on 15 February 1899, the last at which James Archer was present,

---

[61] See, e.g., Morden, *'Communion with Christ'*, pp. 47-76; 190-222.

[62] *Freeman* 9 June 1893.

[63] *JAS*, p. 135.

[64] West Croydon Baptist Church, Church Meeting Minutes, 1869–90, Minute for 10 February 1870, cf. the Minute for 11 March 1870.

[65] West Croydon Baptist Church, Church Meeting Minutes, 1869–90, notes inserted in book.

recorded that the church now had 447 members. This was an impressive statistic on its own, but there were also 993 Sunday school scholars and sixty-nine Sunday school teachers. Moreover, West Croydon had established two further mission stations, which when combined added a further thirty-nine teachers and 603 scholars.[66] As at the Metropolitan Tabernacle, a high place was given to ministry among children.[67] The figures for West Croydon, whilst impressive given that the work only began in the late 1860s, are not so unusual in the 'Nonconformist century'. Nevertheless, it should be evident that James Archer's church had become a hub of missional activity, with adults and children alike being reached. In many ways West Croydon mirrored the Metropolitan Tabernacle, albeit on a much smaller scale. Both churches were underpinned by a Calvinistic theological framework, and were evangelical and evangelistic. These priorities reflected the shared emphases of the two brothers. In summary, their working relationship was grounded not only in their complementary gifts and a mutually beneficial relationship, they were like-minded, with a common theology and shared evangelical commitments.

The Downgrade Controversy

Was the unity the brothers enjoyed broken by the downgrade controversy of 1887–88? This was the controversy during which C.H. Spurgeon resigned from the Baptist Union (BU), in protest at what he regarded as a growing liberalism within the ranks of its ministers.[68] Ernest Bacon contends that James Spurgeon's 'attitude' in the downgrade was 'undoubtedly a keen disappointment' to C.H. Spurgeon,[69] and it is true there were differences between the two brothers in terms of their approach. When C.H. Spurgeon resigned from the BU in October 1887, James, in common with the vast majority of his brother's supporters and friends,[70] did not take the same

---

[66] West Croydon Baptist Church, Church Meeting Minutes, 1890–1903, 15 February 1899.

[67] On this, see, e.g., Tom Nettles, *Living by Revealed Truth: The Life and Pastoral Theology of Charles Haddon Spurgeon* (Fearn: Christian Focus, 2013), pp. 274-75.

[68] For a full and outstanding guide to this complex dispute, see Mark Hopkins, *Nonconformity's Romantic Generation Evangelical and Liberal Theologies in Victorian England* (Studies in Evangelical History and Thought; Carlisle: Paternoster, 2004), pp. 193-248, and his 'The Down Grade Controversy: New Evidence', *Baptist Quarterly* 35.6 (April, 1994), pp. 262-78.

[69] Ernest Bacon, *Spurgeon: Heir of the Puritans* (London: George Allen and Unwin, 1967), pp. 139-40.

[70] Former students were divided on C.H. Spurgeon's stance. See, Ian M. Randall, 'Charles Haddon Spurgeon, the Pastors' College and the Downgrade Controversy', in Kate Cooper and Jeremy Gregory (eds), *Discipline and Diversity: Papers Read at the 2005 Summer Meeting and the 2006 Winter Meeting of the Ecclesiastical History Society* (Woodbridge: Boydell, 2007), pp. 366-76. However, even those who agreed with him as to the doctrinal issues tended to remain in the Union.

step.[71] Mark Hopkins has written a reliable treatment of the controversy, and he shows that C.H. Spurgeon's 'main interest in resigning was escape – from fellowship with people who in his view denied the gospel, from the responsibilities involved in membership of the Baptist Union, and even from the effort and pain involved in theological conflict'.[72] In other words, at the time of C.H. Spurgeon's resignation his aims were protest and withdrawal, not reform. By contrast, James, who was a member of the BU Council, was willing to stay and work for change.[73] So, although the brothers were like-minded theologically, as to their ecclesiology there was a difference at this stage of their careers. C.H. Spurgeon had come to espouse what he called the 'isolation of independency'; James had not.[74] On this point, there was a divergence between them.

Nevertheless, Bacon's assertion, that James' 'attitude' during the controversy was a 'keen disappointment' to Charles does not bear scrutiny. Hopkins shows, with reference to a wealth of primary evidence, the extent to which the two brothers consulted and acted together throughout the dispute.[75] James even stormed out of a meeting of the BU Council in December 1887 at which he felt his brother was maligned.[76] Bacon's comments appear to hinge primarily on James Spurgeon seconding a 'declaratory statement' at the BU Council meeting of 20 April 1888, which C.H. Spurgeon later said he would have opposed if he had been present. But C.H. Spurgeon had been fully aware of the motion and the fact that his brother would second it, and ahead of the council meeting had urged his supporters to vote in favour, writing to one, 'I hope you will not oppose the declaration wh[ich] it is sought to pass. That w[oul]d be a disastrous course for the Evangelical brethren.'[77] James Spurgeon was effectively outmanoeuvred by late amendments and the speech of the proposer, Charles Williams, as Hopkins shows. James had grave doubts about what he was doing, even as he spoke in favour of the motion.[78] C.H. Spurgeon's own verdict was that they (i.e., both he and his brother) had been 'entrapped by

---

[71] For announcements of C.H. Spurgeon's resignation, see *Christian World* 27 October 1887, in Loose-Leaf Scrapfolder, September–October 1887, p. 121; *Baptist* 28 October 1887, in Loose-Leaf Scrapfolder, October–November 1887, p. 125.

[72] Hopkins, *Nonconformity's Romantic Generation*, p. 207.

[73] Paradoxically, C.H. Spurgeon became more interested in reform of the BU after he had resigned. Spurgeon's resignation was the cause of deep regret to many who were just as conservative theologically. See, e.g., James Douglas, *Spurgeon: The Prince of Preachers* (London: Morgan and Scott, 1893), p. 166.

[74] *ST* November 1887, p. 560. C.H. Spurgeon did also say this should be 'tempered by the love of the Spirit which binds us all to the faithful in Christ Jesus' and that he hoped for a greater unity of 'lovers of the gospel' at some undetermined future point.

[75] See especially, Hopkins, *Nonconformity's Romantic Generation*, pp. 217-18.

[76] *Christian World* 15 December 1887.

[77] C.H. Spurgeon letter to B. Pifford, 4 April 1888, 'Original Correspondence of Charles Haddon Spurgeon 1851–1893[sic.]', Spurgeon's College, Heritage Room, No. 95.

[78] Hopkins, *Nonconformity's Romantic Generation*, pp. 223-26.

diplomatists'.⁷⁹ There is no evidence I have seen to support the assertion that Charles expressed 'keen disappointment' at James' 'attitude' during the conflict. In fact, the elder brother remained warmly supportive of the younger both during and after the downgrade controversy, and they continued to work in harmony. Letters written from Charles to James during and after the controversy provide ample evidence of this. To cite just one example, on 18 May 1891 C.H. Spurgeon wrote,

> I hear you had a great time last Sunday. The Lord abide with you still, and make you more and more blessed in your work ... God bless you, dear brother. I don't often say much about you for your ever kind generous affection; but I think you know I do value you quite as well as if I were demonstrative.⁸⁰

In respect of the church, the Pastors' College and the Orphanage the two men continued to work together post-1888. Moreover, C.H. Spurgeon's affection for his younger brother remained undimmed.

The 'Tabernacle Tempest': Controversy after C.H. Spurgeon's Death

Harmony appeared to characterise not only the brothers' relationship but also the life of the Metropolitan Tabernacle. Yet after C.H. Spurgeon's death in January 1892, the unity of the church was broken by the search for a successor to the pastorate. Early in 1892 the grieving church officers appointed James 'acting pastor' although, in terms consistent with his original call of 1868, it was made clear that this did not imply that he would eventually succeed to the pastorate. At the time of C.H. Spurgeon's death the American Presbyterian Arthur T. Pierson (1837–1911) had been supplying the Metropolitan Tabernacle pulpit and, at the same meeting that confirmed James' interim appointment, Pierson was called as 'officiating minister' on the same temporary basis.⁸¹ Yet within months James was proposing that this stop-gap arrangement become a permanent one.⁸² This would have been a partnership not dissimilar from the one James and Charles had enjoyed – James would have concerned himself with the day-to-day running of the church and Pierson would have been the preacher. This time, though, James would have been more

---

⁷⁹ See C.H. Spurgeon to letter to [?] Wright, 27 April 1888, as cited in Hopkins, *Nonconformity's Romantic Generation*, p. 226.

⁸⁰ C.H. Spurgeon letter to James A. Spurgeon, 18 May 1891, in Charles Spurgeon [C.H. Spurgeon's son] (ed.), *The Letters of C.H. Spurgeon* (London: Marshall Brothers, n.d. [1923?]), pp. 66-67. Other examples of relevant letters include those dated 7 June 1887, 8 December 1890, pp. 64-65. Cf. C.H. Spurgeon letter to James A. Spurgeon, 31 March 1888, in *JAS*, p. 164.

⁸¹ William Y. Fullerton, *Thomas Spurgeon: A Biography* (London: Hodder and Stoughton, 1919), p. 148. For Pierson, see Roger N. Shuff, 'Pierson, Arthur Tappan', in Timothy Larsen (ed.), *Biographical Dictionary of Evangelicals* (Leicester: Inter-Varsity Press, 2003), pp. 526-28.

⁸² Delavan L. Pierson, *Arthur T. Pierson: A Biography* (London: Nisbet, 1912), p. 244.

prominent. This proposal was badly received by many. Pierson's Presbyterianism was one obvious sticking point, but his ministry was far less doctrinal than C.H. Spurgeon's had been. Moreover, Pierson himself at this stage had serious misgivings about continuing at the Tabernacle.[83] James Spurgeon's authority and standing were significantly weakened by this episode.

In June 1892, Thomas Spurgeon, who was still serving in the Antipodes, was asked by the Tabernacle deacons to return and supply the pulpit for three months, with the invitation being given against James' wishes. What followed was described by William Young Fullerton, in his biography of Thomas, as the 'Tabernacle Tempest'. Thomas' preaching was well received by many at the Tabernacle. Some members – a 'substantial minority' – remained positive about Pierson.[84] After Thomas' three months were up, Pierson returned for a further period of supply and also taught at the Pastors' College.[85] Nevertheless, in March 1893 a proposal was put before a church meeting to invite Thomas Spurgeon to preach for a full year on trial with a view to the pastorate. There were over 2,000 members present at the meeting, and they voted in favour of the proposal by a majority of three to one.[86] At this point James Spurgeon resigned as acting pastor. When Thomas Spurgeon was finally called, eight months later, the voting figures were 2,127 votes for, 649 against.[87] Prominent deacons from his father's era, such as William Higgs and William Olney, were strongly supportive of Thomas, but this was hardly a ringing endorsement.[88] The church that had known such unity under the dominant personality of C.H. Spurgeon was thus badly split after his death. James Spurgeon continued as President of the Pastors' College with Thomas becoming President of the Pastors' College Evangelical Association, the association of former students established at the time of the downgrade with a more restrictive basis than that of the old College Conference. This division of responsibilities between the two men was to prove untenable.

The regard of the West Croydon church for James appears to have continued unabated. The church voted unanimously to hold special 'silver jubilee' celebrations to mark his twenty-five years as pastor at West Croydon.[89] The celebrations included the presentation of a 'testimonial', a monetary gift which James only accepted on

---

[83] D.L. Pierson, *Pierson*, p. 245.

[84] See, e.g., *Christian Herald* 12 March 1896, Maroon Scrapfolders, vol. 2, p. 102.

[85] Notebook: Student Notes of Pastors' College Lectures, 1992–95, Spurgeon's College, Heritage Room. The notes indicate that Pierson gave lectures on, e.g., 18 May, 2 June 9 June 23 June 1893. Draft letters written at the back of the book indicate it belonged to Robert M. Hunter, who left the College in 1895 to become pastor at Grovelands Chapel, Reading.

[86] Fullerton, *Thomas Spurgeon*, p. 156.

[87] Fullerton, *Thomas Spurgeon*, p. 173.

[88] Both spoke in favour in the church meeting that called Thomas Spurgeon. Fullerton, *Thomas Spurgeon*, p. 156.

[89] West Croydon ... Church Meeting Minutes, 1890–1903, Minutes for 15 August 1894.

condition that the money was used to help fund repairs to the church's buildings.[90] The sum of just over £1,005 was eventually collected and presented.[91] The celebrations took place during the week beginning 22 October 1894. There was an anniversary hymn written specially for the occasion by Arthur Pierson, a testimony to his continuing regard.[92] Speakers included James' old tutor, Joseph Angus, and William Cuff, who was President of the London Baptist Association. It was advertised that Thomas Spurgeon would be speaking at one of the weekday evening thanksgiving services,[93] but a report of the occasion in the *Baptist* noted that he failed to appear.[94]

This last comment hints at simmering tensions between Thomas and James, unsurprising given the recent turn of events at the Metropolitan Tabernacle. William Olney had declared at the time of Thomas' call to his father's pulpit, that the son 'worked harmoniously with his uncle',[95] but this was little more than wishful thinking. Behind the public façade, a significant family feud was developing, as well as a deep estrangement between the wider leadership of the Metropolitan Tabernacle and their former co-pastor. Pike's biography of James, which was presented as a gift to all those attending the Pastors' College Conference of 1895,[96] actually fanned the flames. A printed review of Pike's volume, inserted in one of the scrapbooks in the Spurgeon's College Heritage Room, is scathing. Pike's volume was, it declared,

> A painfully laboured endeavour to make a passable book out of a very, very small subject. (It?) must be the verdict of every honest reviewer whose sad lot it is to wade through the extraordinary collection of scraps and extracts flung together and entitled *J.A. Spurgeon* ... Of course there are some elements of interest, for it touches here and there on C.H. Spurgeon, and introduces some of his letters, but apart from this we cannot discover any necessity for its publication. Did Dr Pierson weigh his words in the 'preliminary statement', so-called, in which, speaking of the brothers Spurgeon he says:— 'It fell to Charles to be like Aaron, the mouthpiece, and to James to be like Moses, *the mind behind the mouth?*' If so, we can confidently assure him that universal Christendom is still under the delusion that behind the mouth of Charles Haddon Spurgeon there was a brain that was distinctly his own, and no one else's. This pitiable volume will, however, soon find its proper place among many similar books 'written to order'.[97]

---

[90] See James A. Spurgeon to West Croydon Baptist Church, August 1894, copied into West Croydon ... Church Meeting Minutes, 1890–1903, Minutes for 15 August 1894.

[91] *Baptist* 2 November 1894, in Maroon Scrapbook, vol. 1, p. 27.

[92] For the text, see Maroon Scrapbook, vol. 1, p. 26.

[93] Printed handbill, Thanksgiving Services ... J.A. Spurgeon, in Maroon Scrapbook, vol. 1, p. 26.

[94] *Baptist* 26 October 1894, in Maroon Scrapbook, vol. 1, p. 26.

[95] Fullerton, *Thomas Spurgeon*, p. 156.

[96] *Christian World* 2 May 1895, Maroon Scrapbook, vol. 2, p. 80. The copy of Pike's biography I am working with is one which was given on this occasion.

[97] Review from the 'Book World', Maroon Scrapfolder, vol. 1, p. 26.

Pike's work was regarded as a hastily flung together self-serving apology for James Spurgeon's ministry. Both the author and the subject were shown scant respect by the reviewer. Yet it was Pierson's ill-judged introduction which was singled out for the most cutting criticism. Pierson was regarded as puffing up James whilst at the same time denigrating the reputation of his lately deceased brother. His comments – especially the analogy comparing James and Charles to Moses and Aaron respectively – would be used against him repeatedly. For example, when Pierson was baptized as a believer on 1 February 1896 at West Croydon Tabernacle, the *Baptist* took issue with the proceedings, and also referred to Pierson's introduction to James Spurgeon's biography.

> So Dr Pierson has at last been baptized. He and Dr Spurgeon have once more made their *denouement* to the British and Baptist public and mutually sword [sic.] eternal constancy. Dr Pierson has likened Dr Spurgeon to Moses, as distinguished from his deceased brother, who was but Aaron, and this may possibly go some way to explain the distinguished visitor's desire to submit to the ordinance of believers' baptism at the hands of so conspicuous a modern prophet. But, shame assuredly to say it, the Doctor's baptism – an institution that purports to be, in its essential element, a public confession of faith – was after all only a private affair![98]

The baptism had been administered on a Saturday evening, with only about fourteen people present (later letters to the *Baptist* described the service as 'hole-and-corner' and 'unworthy').[99] The report in the *Baptist* was negative about James and almost contemptuous in regard to Pierson.[100] Furthermore, the fact that the baptism had taken place so near to the fourth anniversary of C.H. Spurgeon's death, and in such close geographical proximity to the Metropolitan Tabernacle, was regarded as deeply provocative.

If the baptismal service itself had caused offence, a reception given to Pierson soon after the baptism was regarded by many as scandalous. James had arranged the reception and invited many from the Metropolitan Tabernacle who had especially appreciated Pierson's ministry. At the reception James spoke of the regard he had for Pierson and about how much the Tabernacle owed him. He then asked a deacon of the Tabernacle who represented, as James was reported to have remarked, 'a certain section' of the church he used to co-pastor, to lead in prayer. With Thomas Spurgeon seeking to unite a badly battered Tabernacle congregation this was unwise indeed. But if James had been imprudent, Pierson's own speech showed a cavalier disregard for the sensitivities of the situation. He spoke much of his time supplying C.H.

---

[98] *Baptist* 7 February 1896, Maroon Scrapfolder, vol. 2, p. 94. For another, earlier reference to Pierson's Moses and Aaron analogy, see *Baptist* 31 January 1896, Maroon Scrapfolder, vol. 2, p. 94.

[99] *Baptist* 7 February 1896, Maroon Scrapfolder, vol. 2, p. 94, *Baptist* 14 February 1896, p. 102.

[100] For a more positive report, see *Freeman*, 7 February 1896, Maroon Scrapfolder, vol. 2, p. 94.

Spurgeon's pulpit. In the course of his rambling address, which was unscripted and impromptu, he declared,

> I now think of that great Tabernacle in London. Just suppose that the Holy Ghost were to come into that place, were to come into the pastor of the church, into the elders ... It does not make any difference to me who is your pastor; I have an interest in you – I cannot help myself; and you have an interest in me and – you cannot help yourselves. Well, I am going to hold onto that interest, and however much people may misrepresent, however much people may misapprehend, it makes no difference.[101]

Unfortunately for both Pierson and James, a reporter from the *Baptist* was present with notebook in hand. He took down what was claimed to be a verbatim report of the proceedings, which was printed in the paper on 7 February. A storm ensued. Pierson sought to defend himself in a letter to the *Baptist* which they printed in their issue of 7 March. Pierson said he had 'no recollection' of using some of the words attributed to him. Nevertheless, he admitted that he 'should have been more guarded'. 'Some sentences in [my] address are, I frankly concede, open to misapprehension.' He did not attempt to deny his comments about the Holy Spirit he had made in connection with the pastor and leaders of the Metropolitan Tabernacle, although he protested they had been 'grievously misunderstood'. He had not meant to imply that the 'pastor and officers of the church [were] destitute of the Holy Spirit', he insisted. Rather his aim had been to encourage 'disciples to appreciate the power of united prayer to bring down ever-increasing blessing'.[102] Unsurprisingly, the *Baptist* was unconvinced by Pierson's defence. The reception, which Pierson insisted had not been his idea, was described as a 'pitiful affair'. Moreover, they returned to Pierson's fateful introduction to James Spurgeon's biography, which they believed Pierson should now take the opportunity to repudiate.[103] The American's impromptu speech had done great damage and was negatively reported as far away as South Africa.[104] Pierson's presence in London and James' continued association with him were regarded as incendiary by those supportive of Thomas Spurgeon.

Some of the letters of protest printed by the *Baptist* immediately after Pierson's baptism and the ensuing reception were from supporters of the Pastors' College and members of the Evangelical Association of former students.[105] According to the *Baptist*, James had planned that, soon after Pierson's baptism, students of the College would present him with an 'illuminated address'. However, the West Croydon pastor had to abandon the idea because it was so unpopular with the students.[106] Trouble was brewing, and the annual meetings of the Pastors' College Evangelical Association for 1896 were anticipated with some concern. Even so,

---

[101] *Baptist* 7 February 1896, Maroon Scrapfolder, vol. 2, p. 102.
[102] *Baptist* 6 March 1896, Maroon Scrapfolder, vol. 2, p. 100.
[103] *Baptist* 6 March 1896, Maroon Scrapfolder, vol. 2, p. 100.
[104] *South African Baptist* April 1896, Maroon Scrapfolder, vol. 2, p. 105.
[105] *Baptist* 14 February 1896, Maroon Scrapfolder, vol. 2, p. 102.
[106] *Baptist* 7 February 1896, Maroon Scrapfolder, vol. 2, p. 100.

James' resignation as College President at the conference's public meeting, which took place at the Metropolitan Tabernacle on the evening of 23 April, came as a surprise to many; indeed, the *Christian Pictorial* described it as a 'thunderbolt'.[107] In announcing his resignation to the startled gathering, James said that he did not have the confidence of the Tabernacle church and described himself as 'bound and fettered' by his fellow trustees. The report in the *Christian Pictorial* stated that as James continued with his resignation speech many present, including 'most of the Pastors' College brethren', 'grew impatient of the announcement and the Doctor'. When James sat down Thomas Spurgeon rose to speak and was greeted with 'enthusiasm'.[108] On the Friday the conference closed with the usual communion service. James Spurgeon was present. Thomas Spurgeon preached and James offered a prayer of thanks for the bread. As was their custom, the conference members linked hands as they sung the final hymn. But the conference had been one of significant disunity.[109] The report of the proceedings that appeared in the June number of *The Sword and the Trowel* did not even mention James' resignation, merely stating that at the evening meeting he was one of those who had given an address.[110] The resignation was recorded later in a note in the magazine, which briefly thanked James for the service he had formerly rendered under their 'beloved founder'. The same note recorded that a special meeting of the remaining trustees of the College, held on 21 May, had unanimously elected Thomas Spurgeon as the new President.[111] The main index of the 1897 volume of *The Sword and the Trowel* carried no references to James Spurgeon at all.[112] With the exception of the Orphanage, his time at the heart of the Tabernacle and its institutions had come to a close.[113]

Reasons for Disharmony

Why had this happened? Most obviously, the Tabernacle and its institutions were always likely to experience difficulties after C.H. Spurgeon's death. He was such a big personality and had dominated his church and its associated concerns, with no important decisions being taken against his wishes. He had been, as one church member put it, 'a purely unselfish and upright autocrat'.[114] Moreover, C.H. Spurgeon

---

[107] *Christian Pictorial* 30 April 1896, Maroon Scrapfolder, vol. 2, p. 103. Fullerton, *Thomas Spurgeon*, p. 179, gives the date of the public meeting as 1 May 1896, but this is an error.

[108] *Christian Pictorial* 30 April 1896, Maroon Scrapfolder, vol. 2, p. 103.

[109] *Christian Pictorial* 30 April 1896, Maroon Scrapfolder, vol. 2, p. 103.

[110] *ST* June 1896, p. 288.

[111] *ST* June 1896, p. 294.

[112] *ST* 1897, p. ix.

[113] So Fullerton, *Thomas Spurgeon*, pp. 179-80. Thomas also became president of the Colportage Society.

[114] Letter to the *Daily Chronicle*, from a 'member [of the Tabernacle] for 34 years', 27 September 1892.

had done little to prepare the church for life after his departure, despite his long illness. Therefore, the church and its officers were ill-equipped for the almost inevitable disagreements over future direction and leadership post-January 1892. C.H. Spurgeon had left hints as to what he thought should happen. So, according to William Y. Fullerton, C.H. Spurgeon had said to him, 'There is no danger of [Pierson] being thought of my successor, since he is a Presbyterian.'[115] Yet it appears this had not been shared with the Tabernacle officers and, if it had been communicated with the brother, then James kept his counsel. It appears that C.H. Spurgeon harboured some thoughts of Thomas succeeding him. But only after his call did Thomas Spurgeon read a letter from his father, written to him in 1885 whilst he was in the Antipodes, which included the line, 'Get very strong, and when I am older and feebler get ready to take my place.'[116] This was not as unequivocal an endorsement as Thomas Spurgeon's supporters suggested it was, but it certainly hinted at the previous pastor's wishes. C.H. Spurgeon had probably held back from making clear statements about the succession because he wanted the Tabernacle officers to make their own decisions following prayer and a process of discernment and debate. However, his own long-standing style of leadership – benevolent autocracy – had left his diaconate unable to function adequately without their leader.

There were additional reasons for James' failure to get his way. It does seem his approach to the Tabernacle and its affairs in the period immediately after his brother's death was rather high-handed.[117] James' advice to Pastors' College students in chairing deacons' meetings included the following, 'Get as much voting with as little talking as possible.'[118] As already noted, C.H. Spurgeon's own approach had never admitted much debate and in many ways James was continuing his older brother's style of leadership. But if Charles had been regarded as an 'unselfish and upright autocrat', James was regarded, at least by some, simply as an autocrat, someone who sought to dictate without any clear mandate to do so. C.H. Spurgeon's ability to guide his church and officers was grounded in their long-standing personal loyalty to him and on his deeply loved public ministry. James did not have the same ministry or engender the same loyalty. Indeed, as one member writing to the *Baptist* remarked, 'we scarcely know him except that we hear his voice for a few minutes at the Monday evening prayer meeting' and 'occasionally' at other times. The member even stated that James' involvement in the Tabernacle's life amounted to little more than 'a few hours during the week'.[119] The church officers knew the crucial nature of James' contribution behind the scenes in a way that ordinary members did not. Yet their patience was also tried by James' approach.

---

[115] Fullerton, *Thomas Spurgeon*, p. 150.

[116] Fullerton, *Thomas Spurgeon*, p. 174.

[117] So Craig Skinner, *Lamplighter and Son: The Forgotten Story of Thomas Spurgeon and ... Charles Haddon Spurgeon* (Nashville, TN: Broadman, 1984), pp. 102-105.

[118] Notebook of Pastors' College Lectures, 16 September 1892. This lecture is recorded five pages from the back of the notebook.

[119] Letter to the *Baptist* 20 August 1892, as cited in Skinner, *Lamplighter and Son*, p. 104.

A further reason for James' inability to guide the church and the College in the ways he wanted was his close association with Pierson. Pierson's unwise statements and actions reflected badly on James. Especially controversial were his use of the Aaron/Moses analogy to describe the relationship between the brothers, the comment about James being 'the mind behind [his brother's] mouth', and his behaviour at the notorious reception following his baptism as a believer. Although these particular events occurred after Thomas' call to be pastor at the Metropolitan Tabernacle, they further soured relations between James and many of the Pastors' College students and alumni. Fullerton's comments on Pierson's character are instructive. Fullerton knew and liked Pierson, with the American later preaching at Fullerton's invitation at Melbourne Hall in Leicester.[120] But he also had some strictures to offer. Pierson was, according to Fullerton, a 'magnetic speaker' but 'volatile' and 'impulsive'. '[H]e was so largely the centre of his world', Fullerton declared, 'that he was rather surprised when he discovered he was not the centre of other people's'.[121] James' friendship and ongoing advocacy of the unpredictable Pierson damaged him in the eyes of many associated with the Metropolitan Tabernacle.

Finally, in respect of the Pastors' College, there was a further issue which contributed to the rift between James and many at the College. The *Baptist* recounted James' words of resignation, at the public meeting of 23 April 1896, in more detail than the *Christian Pictorial* had done. Under the heading, 'THE PUBLIC MEETING/DR JAMES A. SPURGEON – A SCENE', they reported the West Croydon pastor as saying,

> I think that, as we must educate men for the Particular Baptist denomination – that it is our work, and we can do nothing else – that therefore we ought to cultivate the most fraternal relations with all the churches of the Particular Baptist denomination, and with all the ministers belonging to the denomination. My colleagues do not agree with me in this matter; my policy is to unite, their policy is one of isolation.

At this point the *Baptist* recorded that there were cries of 'No! no!', 'Time!' and 'Shame!'[122] James Spurgeon wanted to rebuild links with the Baptist Union, but his fellow trustees, and it appears many students and former students, were not in favour.[123] The downgrade controversy continued to cast a long shadow.

---

[120] When Fullerton was pastor there. Fullerton, *Thomas Spurgeon*, p. 149.

[121] Fullerton, *Thomas Spurgeon*, pp. 148-49.

[122] *Baptist* 1 May 1896, Maroon Scrapfolder. vol. 2 p. 102. Cf. Fullerton, *Thomas Spurgeon*, p. 179, who echoed the *Baptist*'s reportage.

[123] There had been another clash earlier in the conference. The *Christian World* 23 April 1896 reported that six members of the Pastors' College Evangelical Association had 'withdrawn on account of dissatisfaction with the basis of union'. James Spurgeon had wanted to defer accepting the resignation of two of the men, but his amendment proposing this had not carried the day.

James Spurgeon's Final Years

As already noted, James continued as President of the Stockwell Orphanage, a role he fulfilled until his death. As early as 1895 the Orphanage was in serious financial trouble as it sought to adjust to life without its founder and figure-head. James wrote to friends of the Orphanage in June 1895, disclosing that expenditure had exceeded income in the previous year by £1,500,[124] with figures published in the *Baptist Handbook* showing an even greater deficit.[125] Unsurprisingly, the President had 'some anxiety of mind' as to the situation.[126] Further appeal letters followed, for example, for Christmas 1895.[127] James was able to steady the ship and in this he had the support of Thomas Spurgeon, who was a Vice President of the Orphanage. Thomas' involvement in the Orphanage, together with that of his twin brother Charles, showed that family relationships had not broken down completely. And in May 1897 James received a measure of thanks for his work at the Pastors' College in the form of an illuminated address which was presented to him at a special meeting. The Metropolitan Tabernacle deacon Thomas Olney was in the chair and although he spoke as much of James' deceased brother as he did of James, his remarks concerning the latter were positive. 'The students would miss him in the class room ... [James] had held up the hand of his brother, and how kindly that brother had spoken of him.'[128] The meeting took place at the Orphanage, not the Pastors' College, and the current Pastor of the Metropolitan Tabernacle was conspicuous by his absence. Nevertheless, this was a rapprochement of sorts.

James Spurgeon continued at West Croydon Tabernacle and, as already noted, in 1899 he was chosen to be President of the Baptist Union for the following year. His election – like much in James' later career – was not straightforward. Of the 268 delegates present and voting at the annual assembly, only seventy supported James in the first ballot. Nevertheless, he had garnered more support than any other candidate,[129] and was backed by a majority in the second round, enough to secure the nomination. His election was greeted with acclamation by the delegates, especially when Alexander MacLaren crossed the platform to shake the newly elected Vice President by the hand in a public show of fellowship and unity. James Spurgeon's acceptance speech was well received, but it appears the biggest cheer was still

---

[124] James A. Spurgeon printed letter to friends of the Orphanage, June 1895, Maroon Scrapfolder, vol. 2, p. 84.

[125] *Baptist Handbook for 1896* (London: Clarke, 1895), p. 144. The income reported was £11, 129, 14s, 3d, as against an expenditure of £13, 006, 9s, 6d.

[126] James A. Spurgeon printed letter to friends of the Orphanage, June 1895, Maroon Scrapfolder, vol. 2, p. 84.

[127] James A. Spurgeon printed letter to friends of the Orphanage, December 1895, Maroon Scrapfolder, vol. 2, p. 91.

[128] *Freeman* 7 May 1897, Maroon Scrapfolder, vol. 2, p. 115.

[129] In the first round William Cuff and John H. Shakespeare received forty-eight and thirty-eight votes respectively. There were a number of other candidates who poled fewer votes. *Daily Chronicle* 26 April 1898, Maroon Scrapfolder, vol. 3, p. 115.

reserved for a passage in which he mentioned his brother.[130] To the last James Archer Spurgeon lived in the shadow of the magic name.

Conclusion

In accepting the call to be co-pastor of the Metropolitan Tabernacle, James Spurgeon had declared he was 'most cheerfully willing' to give his brother 'precedence' in the relationship.[131] He also stated that he was drawn to the work 'by the consciousness of [our] identity in belief and views of truth.'[132] For the length of their working partnership, James remained willing for his brother to have the first place. Moreover, their relationship continued to be grounded on a theological like-mindedness, as well as complementary gifts. James did the work which his brother had no time for and in many cases was not fitted for or, increasingly as the years wore on, was not well enough to undertake. Consequently, James played a vital role in the continuing ministry of his brother and the institutions he had established, and I hope this chapter has indicated something of the scale of his contribution.

If there was a divergence in thought between the brothers it was in the area of ecclesiology. This divergence contributed to some of the problems James experienced after C.H. Spurgeon's death, although, as I have argued, there were other factors which contributed to these difficulties. The Tabernacle and the Pastors' College would continue without his input, and his reputation took a considerable battering. The West Croydon church remained loyal to him, however, and continued to give him a base from which he could exercise a wider ministry. Whatever mistakes he made, James Archer Spurgeon stands as an example of an evangelical who retained strong theological convictions whilst continuing to work within the Baptist Union of Great Britain and Ireland, doing so at a time when others were advocating the 'isolation of independency'.

---

[130] *Daily Chronicle* 26 April 1898; *British Weekly*, n.d., Maroon Scrapfolder, vol. 3, p. 115.

[131] C.H. Spurgeon, *Autobiography*, III, p. 35

[132] *JAS*, p. 91. Pike is paraphrasing James Spurgeon at this point.

CHAPTER 7

'Citizens of No Mean City': A Study of Women in Two Baptist Churches in Late Victorian and Early Edwardian Bristol

Linda Wilson

Early in 1908, Dorothy Glover, a single woman in her early thirties and a member of Tyndale Baptist Church, Bristol, compiled some notes in preparation for a talk. Her audience was to be a group of young people in another church in the city, Broadmead, arguably the first Baptist congregation in Bristol and one of the earliest in the country.[1] Dorothy's topic was the early history of Nonconformity in Bristol, which she based on a contemporary account by Edward Terrill, recounting his involvement in the beginnings of Broadmead Chapel,[2] a subject which clearly enthused her. In her handwritten notes she celebrated the radical religious history of her home city:

> I hope also that you will, like me, take an interest and pride in this bit of history for Bristol's sake. We are citizens of no mean city, and it may endear it still further to us to have its streets, its churchyards, its rivers, its meeting houses, its street corners, its lanes, its woods, its downs hallowed by the part they have played in the history of the search for truth.[3]

The Baptist heritage of Bristol made it, in her eyes, a significant place to live, to the extent that she used St Paul's words about his home city of Tarsus, 'no mean city', to refer to it. This biblical reference would not have gone unnoticed by her scripturally literate audience and it is easy to imagine that Dorothy's enthusiasm for the topic, and her use of local stories from the past, received a ready response from her audience. In her desire to inspire a new generation, Dorothy drew on a keen sense of place and on specific historical examples. In the twenty-first century, her own life,

---

[1] Roger Hayden (ed.), *The Records of a Church of Christ in Bristol, 1640–1687* (Bristol Record Society's Publications, 27; Bristol: Bristol Record Society, 1974), p. 115.

[2] Edward Terrill's handwritten account of these years, 'Records of a Church of Christ in Broadmead' is still held by the church, see http://www.broadmeadbaptist.org.uk/historypage.php?content=history/terrill.htm (accessed 3 July 2014).

[3] Dorothy Glover, MS of talk for Tyndale Young People's Guild, March 1908, pp. 3-4, in Bristol Baptist College Library, G96 Box G 14732.

and those of her contemporaries, are of as much interest to us as is that earlier history. In particular, the exploration of women's role within Nonconformist churches in the late nineteenth and early twentieth centuries is a rich and interesting area yet to be fully explored. This chapter aims to contribute towards that investigation through a study of women in two contrasting Baptist congregations.

The two congregations are Dorothy's home church of Tyndale, founded in 1869 in the growing middle-class suburb of Redland in the north of Bristol, and Counterslip, a city centre church dating back to the first decade of the nineteenth century. This chapter will consider various aspects of the lives of the female members of these two churches, including their geographical distribution, the number who undertook paid work, the nature of their involvement in their respective churches and the extent to which the two churches functioned as a 'third space' for these women, a place neither private nor public where they could develop skills and abilities.[4] It will also discuss the more public roles, beyond the church community, of selected women. Such a study is needed because, whilst excellent work has been done by Madge Dresser,[5] June Hannam,[6] and others into the lives and role of women in some Nonconformist groups, Bristol women who worshipped in the more conventional, predominantly evangelical churches have been comparatively neglected.[7] Before investigating women in these churches in detail, however, some background about late Victorian and early Edwardian Bristol would be appropriate.

Bristol in this period was a rapidly growing city and Dorothy would have experienced a considerable amount of change in Bristol between her birth in 1875 and the occasion of her talk in 1908.[8] During the thirty years between 1881 and 1911 the population increased by over seventy per cent[9] as new workers were drawn to the

---

[4] L. Wilson, *Constrained by Zeal: Female Spirituality amongst Nonconformists 1825–1875* (Studies in Evangelical History and Thought; Carlisle: Paternoster, 2000), pp. 210-11.

[5] See, for instance, M. Dresser, 'Women in the Bristol Moravian Church in the Eighteenth Century', in J. Bettey (ed.), *Historic Churches and Church Life in Bristol* (Bristol: Bristol and Gloucestershire Archaeological Society, 2001), pp. 134-47.

[6] June Hannam has written about the role of Unitarians and Quakers in late nineteenth-century Bristol politics in '"An Enlarged Sphere of Usefulness": The Bristol Women's Movement, c.1860–1914', in M. Dresser and P. Ollerenshaw (eds), *The Making of Modern Bristol* (Tiverton: Redcliffe Press, 1996), pp. 184-209 (pp. 184-85).

[7] See, however, Linda Wilson, 'Sarah Terrett, Katherine Robinson and Edith Pearce: Three Nonconformist Women and Public Life in Bristol, 1870–1910', in Pieter J. Lalleman, Peter J. Morden and Anthony R. Cross (eds), *Grounded in Grace: Essays to Honour Ian M. Randall* (London and Didcot: Spurgeon's College and The Baptist Historical Society, 2013), pp. 118-32, and '"Domestic charms, business acumen, and devotion to Christian work": Sarah Terrett, the Bible Christian Church, the household and the public sphere in late Victorian Bristol', in John Doran, Charlotte Methuen and Alexandra Walsham (eds), *Religion and the Household* (Studies in Church History, 50; Woodbridge: Boydell and Brewer, 2014), pp. 405-15.

[8] Dorothy F. Glover, 'Not so Long Ago', typewritten MS, 1908, Tyndale Baptist Church archives.

[9] J. Lynch, *A Tale of Three Cities* (Basingstoke: Macmillan, 1988), p. 19.

various enterprises developing in and around the city.[10] Much of this growth occurred beyond the city limits, necessitating a series of boundary changes to incorporate the new areas into Bristol, although Redland, where Tyndale was based, was already part of the city when the church was founded.[11] Part of the city's strength was the wide variety of its businesses, especially those founded after 1880.[12] Several of the significant manufacturing firms which contributed to the city's growth were owned by Nonconformists, including E.S. and A. Robinson, paper bag manufacturers, who were Baptists, W.D. & H.O. Wills, tobacco manufacturers, Congregationalists who mostly became Anglican,[13] and J.S. Fry & Sons, Quaker chocolate and cocoa producers. Many of these business leaders, and sometimes their wives, were also active beyond the church community in city life. The city had a strong Nonconformist presence: Gorsky has noted the 'unusual strength of the city's non-conformist tradition'.[14] This strength included a significant number of Baptist churches: by 1890 there were at least fifteen Baptist chapels in different parts of Bristol, several having congregations numbering in the hundreds. The majority had been founded during the nineteenth century, including Counterslip and Tyndale.

Tyndale and Counterslip

Tyndale was one of several Baptist congregations planted as the city grew, in this case in Redland, part of the development of prosperous suburban residential areas in the north of the city. Elisha Robinson, one of the founding brothers of E.S. and A. Robinson, was instrumental in the founding of the chapel in Redland.[15] He was at the helm of a committee overseeing the appointment of a minister and the development of the building. The latter was opened in 1868, but the church formally began the following year, on 6 April 1869, with thirty-eight members drawn from four other Baptist congregations in and around Bristol, including Counterslip, the other church in this study, which contributed six members to the new venture.[16] The new minister, Richard Glover, was present at the launch, having arrived in the city from Scotland with his wife Anna only the night before.[17] Dr Glover evidently found the post

---

[10] Lynch, *Three Cities*, p. 19.

[11] H.E. Meller, *Leisure and the Changing City, 1870–1914* (London: Routledge & Kegan Paul, 1976), p. 21.

[12] Lynch, *Three Cities*, p. 19.

[13] The Wills family was originally Congregationalist although by the late nineteenth century several of them had become Anglican, a common trajectory amongst upwardly mobile Nonconformists.

[14] Martin Gorsky, *Patterns of Philanthropy in Nineteenth-Century Bristol* (London and Woodbridge: The Royal Historical Society and The Boydell Press, 1999), p. 176.

[15] L.G. Champion, *Tyndale Baptist Church, Bristol, 1868–1968* (n.pl.: n.p., n.d. [1968]), p. 9.

[16] According to Champion, *Tyndale Baptist Church*, p. 9, '24 transferred from Broadmead, six from Counterslip, six from Old King Street and one from Pill'.

[17] Champion, *Tyndale Baptist Church*, p. 9.

congenial, staying until his retirement in 1911. By 1880 there were 245 members, growing to 378 in 1890 – 'after that numbers tended to decline though the church remained strong'.[18] Tyndale members were active in the city throughout this period, contributing two mayors, Herbert Ashman in 1898 and Edward Robinson, son of Elisha, in 1908,[19] as well as an MP, Charles Townsend during 1892–95.[20] As Helen Meller has noted, Tyndale was a significant church, having an influence in the city 'far exceeding its numbers'.[21]

Counterslip was a few decades older, having been formed around 1804 when an older Baptist congregation, the Pithay, divided. In 1810 the new group moved to a purpose-built building located nearby in a street called Counterslip, just by the main thoroughfare of Victoria Street: the chapel called itself 'Counterslip Chapel, Victoria Street'.[22] The area the chapel was based in was close to the heart of the city with docks, offices, shops and manufacturing nearby: for instance, Robinsons had one of their factories close by in Redcliffe Street. Henry Knee was Counterslip's pastor until 1900, and the church developed steadily under his leadership, growing to a membership of 395 in 1888.[23] It was certain that there were considerably more attenders than members in both churches, a ratio estimated by John Briggs at four to one in Baptist chapels in 1851 and in the years following.[24] Both churches were thriving in the late Victorian period.

Much of my work on women in these two churches has been done by correlating the membership lists with the 1891 census. This has made it possible to discover the occupations, ages, and family makeup of a significant percentage of these women, giving insight into their class as well. For Counterslip only two years of membership records survive, for 1888 and 1894, whilst Tyndale has more records available, although not for the identical years. For purposes of comparison the membership lists from Tyndale for 1887 and 1892 have been analysed. The first list was used as the base, and the second to explore how many women had moved house, left or joined membership in the intervening period. Of the Tyndale women in the 1892 membership list, a majority of them, sixty per cent, 112, could be found in the census, a significant proportion, providing useful information about the families and working habits of those women. Working from the Counterslip 1888 membership

---

[18] Champion, *Tyndale Baptist Church*, p. 13.

[19] Edward's father Elisha Smith Robinson had been mayor too, in 1866, before Tyndale was founded.

[20] Charles Townsend was initially a town councilor, part of a group of Liberal Nonconformists who were part of the 'governing elite' in this period, so Meller, *Changing City*, pp. 87-95.

[21] Meller, *Changing City*, p. 81.

[22] Handbook of Counterslip Chapel, 1894, front cover.

[23] Counterslip Chapel was bombed during the Second World War, and most of the church records were lost, but membership lists for 1888 and 1894 were amongst the material salvaged. The congregation later relocated several miles south on the Wells Road (the A37).

[24] John H.Y. Briggs, *The English Baptists of the Nineteenth Century* (A History of English Baptists, 3; Didcot: The Baptist Historical Society, 1994), p. 258.

list, which contained 258 women, only sixty-one could be identified in the census, giving us a smaller sample both proportionally and in absolute terms: twenty-four per cent. This in itself is significant, indicating that Counterslip members were more likely to move frequently, suggesting lower income brackets. However, the information is still extremely valuable, being nearly a quarter of the female members, and gives us insight into the lives of a significant minority of women who were involved with Counterslip. So what can be learnt about the women of these two congregations?

The first point to note is that the proportion of male to female members was similar in both churches and was like those found in the membership of other Baptist and also Congregational churches of the time, where, as David Bebbington notes, 'on average around two-thirds ... were female'.[25] In 1888, Counterslip had 257 female members, comprising sixty-five per cent of the total membership. Six years later, although many people had left and others had become members, the overall numbers were similar: 396 members, 246 of whom were women, sixty-two per cent of the membership. At Tyndale the congregation was about 100 smaller in a comparative year, 1892, with 293 members of whom 188 were women, and 105 men, a proportion of sixty-four to thirty-six per cent. Women made up a substantial proportion of both congregations.

There were significant differences in geography and class both in and between the two churches, demonstrated in the differing lives of the women who belonged to each church. These membership lists allow us to see the geographical distribution of members, and correlation of the lists with the 1891 census reveals occupations, the nature of the places families and individuals were living, and other relevant information. Hugh McLeod has demonstrated that Baptist churches recruited from most social classes in the late Victorian period,[26] and certainly there was a wide range of social status across both churches. However, there were clear differences between them, with Counterslip being largely working-class, with a significant lower middle-class minority and the occasional higher status family, whilst Tyndale was predominantly middle-class, with a working-class minority and some significant upper-middle-class members.[27]

Counterslip was well placed in the centre of the city with many members living within half an hour's walk from the Victoria Street building, although a few were a good hour's walk away. Several people would have passed close by other Baptist

---

[25] David W. Bebbington, *The Dominance of Evangelicalism: The Age of Spurgeon and Moody* (Leicester: Iinter-Varsity Press, 2005), p. 205, quoting Clive D. Field, 'Adam and Eve: Gender in the English Free Church Constituency', *Journal of Ecclesiastical History* 44.1 (January, 1993), pp. 63-79.

[26] Hugh McLeod, *Class and Religion in the Late Victorian City* (London: Croom Helm, 1974), p. 173; also Briggs, *English Baptists*, p. 274.

[27] Whilst there is considerable discussion over the nature and usefulness of such class analysis, it makes sense to use it in this context. See the brief summary in Susie L. Steinbach, *Understanding the Victorians: Politics, Culture and Society in Nineteenth Century Britain* (Abingdon: Routledge, 2012), pp. 113-18.

churches to reach Counterslip. Hannah Worgan, for instance, lived in Philip St, Bedminster, and walked a good twenty minutes to Counterslip, despite the presence of another Baptist chapel in her home street, which opened in 1861.[28] Totterdown Baptist chapel, begun in 1881, was situated on the Wells Road, near to several Counterslip members.[29] In its early years this chapel grew slowly, but as the rate of new building in the area picked up, the numbers increased until by 1906 it was a thriving congregation with 815 members.[30] Perhaps some of them were transfers from Counterslip. However, for Ann, Hannah, and others, loyalty to their existing congregation and preference for its familiar style apparently outweighed issues of convenience.

Yet loyalty could be overcome by other events. It is also interesting to note that although the Counterslip numbers might indicate a fairly static population, in fact a significant proportion of the 1888 membership was no longer connected with the church and the 1894 figures contained several new members. It is unclear why there was such a shift in membership. In addition, many of those who were still members in 1894 had moved house since 1888, sometimes twice. For instance, Ann Oldham, a widowed dressmaker, was living near Brandon Hill, north Bristol, in 1888, but in 1891 was renting rooms in Clifton Wood Crescent, and by 1894 had moved to another address in Clifton Wood, properties within half a mile of each other and incidentally much closer to Tyndale than to Counterslip. Like Ann, individuals or families from Counterslip who moved within the city usually stayed within the same area, a few streets or at most a mile away from their previous location. Single women like Ann were living in rented accommodation with little security, which could also have been true of families, although they might have moved to gain more room as their families grew. Ann Oldham would have had a walk of just over a mile to Counterslip from her first address, slightly further from Clifton Wood. Ann Gabb, one of several women who lived south of the river, in Totterdown, would have had a similar walk of around twenty minutes. This wide distribution was typical of Counterslip at this time: a circle drawn round the chapel of an hour's distance on foot would encompass all the active members. It was, therefore, not a local church in any conventional sense, with one specific local community.

There were concentrations of people in certain areas, however. For instance, several families and individuals lived south of the river in Bedminster, Totterdown, and the Bath Road, where there were slums as well as more respectable accommodation. Parts of Bedminster consisted of slums, whilst Totterdown contained recently-built good quality houses for workers: in 1888 nearly forty families or individuals from the church were based there, with many others nearby. In some instances several members lived in one street. Oxford Street, a short street in

---

[28] Frank Phillips, *The History of Phillip Street Chapel, Bedminster, Bristol* (n.pl.: n.p., 1978), p. 5. The church was founded in 1855, but the building was not completed until 1861.

[29] *Souvenir of Twenty-fifth anniversary of Totterdown Baptist 1881–1906* (n.pl.: n.p., n.d.), p. 3.

[30] *Totterdown Baptist*, p. 47.

Totterdown, was home to five of them in 1888. Elizabeth Webb was at number fifty-nine. Jane East, aged sixty-six, lived with her younger husband William, a baker, their two children (ages fifteen and twenty, both working) and a boarder at number sixty-five. At number seventy-one Georgina Neale (aged twenty-nine) lived with her carpenter husband, and her older single sister Elizabeth Passmore, who was also a member. Further along the street at number ninety-five was Alice Foley, also twenty-nine, her husband who was a postman and their two small children.[31] Whilst there is no way of discovering evidence of friendship, it seems unlikely that these working-class women, living so near to each other and members of the same church, did not offer each other mutual support.[32] Counterslip had small pockets of community, largely working-class.

This class composition was reversed at Tyndale where the congregation comprised a minority of working-class members with a predominance of middle-class families and individuals, with some who were distinctly upper-middle class, such as the Robinsons.[33] The majority of Tyndale members came from the new suburbs surrounding the chapel and from what was once the village of Clifton, although its membership also included servants and others who lived locally in order to service the middle-class families. For instance, Norah Dawson, twenty-one in 1891, was one of two general domestic servants working for a retired grocer of sixty-one, his wife aged fifty-four and their twenty-eight-year-old daughter, living in Westfield Park, the same street as the Glovers. Another woman, Julia Close, thirty-four, was the oldest of three servants working for a Clifton family consisting of a widow in her forties and her four young children.[34] Tyndale was easily accessible to these young women. As was the case with Counterslip, Tyndale members also mostly lived within half an hour's walk of the chapel, with only the occasional person further away, but they were mostly concentrated in the well-to-do areas of Redland, Clifton, and Westbury, with only the occasional individual or family in other areas, and rarely south of the river.[35] A few members, like Norah Dawson, or the Glovers themselves, lived within a few minutes' walk of the chapel. As with Counterslip members, some passed other Baptist chapels on their way to services. Buckingham Baptist chapel, opened in 1847 to redress 'the perceived lack of evangelical teaching within the parish (Clifton) at the time'[36] would have been close to the route of several members walking to services at Tyndale. Mrs F.L. Smith lived in Buckingham Place, round the corner from Buckingham, but chose to attend

---

[31] 1891 Census at Ancestry.co.uk.

[32] For a discussion of the mutual support of working-class women in a neighbourhood, whether or not they shared a church connection, see Elizabeth Roberts, *An Oral History of Working-Class Women* (Oxford: Blackwell, 1984), p. 169.

[33] See Briggs, *English Baptists*, pp. 273-78, for a discussion of class composition of nineteenth-century Baptist churches.

[34] 1891 Census at Ancestry.co.uk.

[35] Then, as now, South Bristol was less prosperous than North Bristol.

[36] See http://www.buckinghamchapel.org.uk/about-us/history/, accessed 24 July 2014.

Tyndale, around fifteen minutes' walk away.[37] As well as the different location, clearly there was something about the ethos or theology, or perhaps the friendships, of Tyndale which appealed to her. Tyndale had open communion and was imaginative and forward thinking, whilst Buckingham had a conservative reputation (which it still maintains), withdrawing from the Baptist Union in 1872 over doctrinal issues, well in advance of the downgrade controversy spearheaded by the famous London Baptist, Charles Haddon Spurgeon.[38] Meanwhile Dr Glover, minister at Tyndale, of a more open-minded inclination, was committed to the Baptist Union, serving as its President in 1884. His son and Dorothy's brother, T.R. (Terrot Reaveley) Glover, became a classical scholar and historian at Cambridge. The men and women who adhered to Tyndale supported a more 'generous' orthodoxy.

The Tyndale members included a few who might be called Nonconformist aristocracy. This is significant because, as historians have noted, Baptist churches had difficulty in keeping hold of upwardly mobile members.[39] Yet Tyndale included an MP, Charles Townsend, MP for North Bristol 1892–95, Dr Frederick Gotch the Principal of the Baptist College, and the extended Robinson family which had largely funded the church building, and were active in Bristol politics (Edward becoming mayor in 1908 as has already been noted). Herbert Ashman, a leather manufacturer who was later knighted, was mayor in 1898. Perhaps it was partly because of the lack of sectarian discrimination in Bristol, where, as Meller has noted, 'the governing elite was drawn from the Church of England, the Quakers, Baptists, Wesleyans, even Roman Catholics'.[40] The women related to these families were often active in the churches, and in some cases beyond, as will be seen later.

Women Supporting Themselves or Contributing to the Family Income

An analysis of the membership lists together with the 1891 census demonstrates the distinctive characteristics noted above of the two churches with regard to class, and in particular differences in women's income. In the Tyndale congregation, a significant percentage of the women identified in the census, eighteen per cent, twenty women in total, were living on their own means, in other words, from pensions, legacies or other means. These were single (i.e., never married) or widowed women, often living with other relatives. These women clearly had a range of incomes: Ann Haddon, fifty-six, a retired servant living on her own means, rented only two rooms in a shared house. At the other end of the scale were Sarah Polglase, seventy-four, and her sister Eliza, sixty-five, both widows, who lived together in a large house in prosperous Pembroke Road and employed three servants. Several

---

[37] 1891 Census at Ancestry.co.uk.
[38] See http://www.buckinghamchapel.org.uk/about-us/history/, accessed 24 July 2014. For Spurgeon and the 'Downgrade', see, for instance, Bebbington, *Dominance of Evangelicalism*, p. 243.
[39] McLeod, *Class and Religion*, p. 150; and Jefferey Cox, *The English Churches in a Secular Society, Lambeth 1870–1930* (Oxford: Oxford University Press, 1982), pp. 229-30.
[40] Meller, *Changing City*, p. 79.

women living on their own means were part of an extended household, such as Eliza Mayer, sixty-eight and single, who lived with her cousin, a lodger, and a servant.[41] Presumably some of their shared income was derived from the lodger, but it is hard to be sure. There was a range of incomes amongst these women, but even those who had rooms in a shared house lived in comparatively prosperous areas of the city.

In Counterslip, by contrast, only three women, five per cent, were living on their own means. Two of these three, Alice Gover, sixty-six, and Mary Ann Swiss, seventy-four, each had two lodgers who presumably were their means of support.[42] Only one woman, Elizabeth Morton, a widow who headed a busy household of her descendants, and employed a servant, had her 'own means' which were not derived from direct earnings.[43] Significantly she lived in Redland, five minutes' walk from Tyndale, but over half an hour from Counterslip. She was more typical of a Tyndale member than a Counterslip one. On this evidence, Tyndale was a more prosperous congregation, but clearly these women were only a small minority.

An investigation of the women who were earning bears out the class differences between the churches noted earlier. It should be noted that the available statistics are unlikely to be the whole story. Historians have observed that female occupations were under-represented in the nineteenth-century censuses, and if this is the case for Bristol, as might reasonably be assumed, then the evidence we have is only partial. According to Ellen Ross, for instance, much married women's work in London (and presumably elsewhere) was 'often unlisted by census enumerators either because the male "household head" failed to mention it or because the census taker viewed the wife's work as insignificant, (and) has remained largely invisible even today'.[44] Yet, as Susie L. Steinbech has observed, 'most working-class women worked for wages for at least part of their lives'.[45] Even bearing this likely under-reporting in mind, the results for the two congregations are still revealing.

Twenty-three individuals, twenty per cent, out of the 112 Tyndale women identified in the census, were earning, compared with forty-two out of sixty-one identified, sixty-nine per cent, at Counterslip. Although there is only evidence for a quarter of Counterslip women, it does indicate that, as might be expected, more of them were in paid occupations either full or part-time, and if one adds under-reporting, it is likely that the majority of Counterslip women were in some kind of paid employment. The majority of Tyndale women earning were either involved in a middle-class occupation such as a teacher, or had taken over their husband's business. Emily Betts, fifty-eight in 1891, was a widow and was an employer, running a retail boot warehouse, almost certainly previously her husband's business. Even the dressmakers were running a business rather than working for others: Julia

---

[41] 1891 Census at Ancestry.co.uk.
[42] 1891 Census at Ancestry.co.uk.
[43] 1891 Census at Ancestry.co.uk.
[44] Ellen Ross, *Love and Toil: Motherhood in Outcast London, 1870–1918*, (Oxford: Oxford University Press, 1993), p. 44.
[45] Steinbech, *Understanding the Victorians*, p. 122.

Gibson, twenty-four, was a dressmaker with a sixteen-year-old apprentice.[46] A few took in boarders to supplement the family income, and a few were servants, of whom half were general servants and the rest were either cooks or parlourmaids, further up the social scale of servants.

Tyndale Women Earning

Job description	Number
Artist	1
Domestic work (general servant, parlourmaid or cook)	9
Dressmaker	2
Employer (business)	2
Housekeeper	2
Income from boarders	3
Teacher (principal, teacher, governess)	4
Total working	**23 (20%)**

If we turn to Counterslip, the pattern is rather different. There was a much greater variety of work done, which has been compressed into selected categories for ease of comparison. There were still some middle-class occupations, with five teachers of various kinds, and one grocer, but the majority were 'respectable' working class: shopgirls, factory workers (two out of three in the typical Bristol businesses of chocolate and paper bag manufacture), and a significant proportion who were involved in garment production. Mary Day, the grocer, is interesting because she was evidently running her own business. Her husband was a sewing machine agent and she had a boarder who was a grocer's warehouseman, although she was not listed as an employer on the census.[47] This intriguing glimpse of an unusual businesswoman is all we know of Mary Day.

Counterslip Women Earning

Job description	Number
Bible woman	1
Domestic work (cooks, general servants)	4
Dressmaking or similar (dressmakers, milleners, tailoresses, staymakers)	14
Factory work (chocolate, paper bag, machinist)	3
Grocer	1
Housekeeper	2
Income from lodgers[48]	2

---

[46] 1891 Census at Ancestry.co.uk.
[47] 1891 Census at Ancestry.co.uk.
[48] This refers to women living 'on their own means' who took in boarders: those who had lodgers in addition to other income are not counted here. For instance, Lydia Chandler was a

Laundress	1
Shop assistants (confectionary, drapers, stationer's, fruiters)	9
Teacher (teacher, governess, music teacher)	5
Total working	**42 (69%)**

The evidence from the census sample is that many of the Counterslip women worked, and it is likely, as noted earlier, that this is an under-representation. What is less clear is the extent to which their work affected their church involvement, a topic to be returned to later.

The Place of Servants

Number of servants in a household	Counterslip	Tyndale
One	7	18
Two	3	18
Three	1	6
Total households with servants	11	42
Percentage of census sample with servants	18%	37.5%
Total number of servants in census sample	16	72

Another indication of the class differences between the two churches is the difference in the number of households in both congregations employing servants. Tyndale Baptist, as already noted, had a number of families living in large houses in prosperous areas. Many of these Tyndale households employed servants, a strong indicator of class along with the husbands' occupations. Forty-two of the individual women or families discovered in the census sample, thirty-seven point five per cent, had at least one servant, with eighteen employing two, and a further six families three, a total of seventy-two servants employed. Often this included a cook, but there might be a housekeeper. Compare this with Counterslip, whose families were much less likely to employ servants, with a total of sixteen servants in eleven households, eighteen per cent of the sample, and only one household employed three servants, with three having two, and seven just one servant. Jessie Widgery, aged thirty-seven, managed a large household consisting of her husband, a provision merchant, four children aged six to sixteen all still at school (itself an indication of comparative wealth), an elderly aunt and a twenty-five-year-old nephew working for his uncle. They employed a housekeeper, a cook, and a general domestic servant in one of the

---

teacher and her brother Joseph was an accountant. They had one servant, but also a lodger: however it is unlikely that the lodger was vital to their family income: as he was a clerk and bookkeeper, it is more likely he was part of her husband's business. 1891 Census at Ancestry.co.uk.

grandest houses in the Bedminster area, on Coronation Road.[49] The house, facing the New Cut (the diversion of the River Avon to allow the formation of Bristol floating harbour in 1809)[50] had several stories and an impressive entrance, and they were clearly not typical Counterslip members. More representative of Counterslip members with servants was Emma Jones, whose husband Edwin was a provision dealer, and who had one thirteen-year old servant, Bessie Amos. Most families had to manage without servants, juggling jobs, children, visitors, and sometimes lodgers. Susan Hussey lived in Totterdown with her husband Samuel who worked for a grocer, their five children ranging in age from twelve to eleven months, and a lodger, Sarah Greenman, a single woman of forty-two, living on her own means.[51] Everyday life must have been a struggle for families like the Husseys.

What did Women do within the Churches?

Analysing census data has given some glimpses into the lives of women who attended Tyndale and Counterslip, but to discover their roles within the churches the historian must turn to other sources. The late nineteenth century was a time of growing opportunities for women, but churches could still function as a 'third sphere', neither public nor private, where women could develop skills in a safe environment. The ideology of 'separate spheres', at its height in the middle of the century, was most relevant for middle class women, but even for working class women, who often found themselves outside the home in order to earn, churches could provide opportunities to develop their skills.

One role, by its nature only open to a few, was as the wife of a minister. Leonard Sweet has argued that in America, marrying a minister in the Victorian period could be regarded as a career, and one way to be actively involved in contemporary culture.[52] His analysis is also relevant to England. Both Mary Knee, wife of Henry Knee of Counterslip, and Anna Glover, married to Richard Glover of Tyndale, could be seen in this light, dedicating their lives to bringing up their families whilst simultaneously supporting their husbands' work in their respective churches. Indeed Mary was entered in the census, presumably by her husband, as 'helpmeet', indicating her primary role as his supporter and helper.[53] The Knee family, unlike most of their congregation, lived in one of the newer areas of Bristol, Cotham, rather nearer to Tyndale than to Counterslip. In 1891 Mary was thirty-three, and the Knees had three children aged nine months, five, and eight.[54] They employed a nurse, presumably to help with the youngest of their three children, as well as a general

---

[49] 1891 Census at Ancestry.co.uk.
[50] See Kenneth Morgan, 'The Economic Development of Bristol', in Dresser and Ollerenshaw (eds), *Making of Modern Bristol*, p. 52.
[51] 1891 Census at Ancestry.co.uk.
[52] Leonard Sweet, *The Minister's Wife* (Philadelphia, PA: Temple University Press, 1983), p. 8.
[53] 1891 Census at Ancestry.co.uk.
[54] 1891 Census at Ancestry.co.uk.

servant for the running of the household: this lifestyle indicates that they were of a higher social class than most of their congregation. Mary was active in a variety of church activities: in 1894, while the children were still quite small, she was a collector for both the Baptist Missionary Society (BMS) and the Tower Street Mission, Counterslip's own local mission. She was also in charge of the Bible Women's Mission with the aid of an 'efficient committee of ladies'. This involved supervising their Bible Woman, Alice Crew, visiting 'poor homes' and encouraging the women who lived there to buy Bibles, and to 'improve the home life, by cleanliness, tidiness, thrift and godliness', as well as organising a regular mothers' meeting on Monday afternoons, running loan schemes, and selling cheap clothes.[55] Mary was clearly an active woman not afraid to take a leading role, but one always within the boundaries of what was acceptable for a pastor's 'helpmeet', or the 'Angel out of the House', a useful category suggested by historian Elizabeth Helsinger.[56]

In contrast, Anna Glover, according to her daughter Dorothy, was by nature a very shy person who did not relish a prominent role within the church.[57] Yet in practice she was almost as active as Mary, although a lot of her activity was home-based. Anna was a keen supporter of foreign mission: her husband Richard is recorded as declaring that his interest in mission was due to his wife.[58] She was instrumental in launching the Bristol Women's Auxiliary of the BMS, according to Dorothy, 'at the same time as she launched me',[59] collecting for that and other causes, and acting as secretary of the Dorcas meeting.[60] Her main strength, however, lay in hospitality, and it seems she was happiest working within the confines of her own home. In a speech given many years later at Tyndale's eightieth anniversary, Dorothy recalled that although her mother had almost no public profile, she was a great support to her father, especially in her particular gift of hospitality. Their home in Westfield Park, Redland, was described by Dorothy as having

> ... morning, noon and night, an ever open door, and an ever spread table. Callers, visitors and friends, and sometimes those we children called 'strays'. People who were lonely, people without family, people in sorrow, people in perplexity, the strangers in a strange land, people who wanted a few weeks [sic] nursing or feeding up, people on the eve of marriage, sometimes the poor that are cast out – she was always there and they were always welcome.[61]

In a personal memoir, Dorothy also made a comment about her mother's hospitality, noting that her mother did not follow the usual convention of set visiting days,

---

[55] Counterslip Handbook, 1894, p. 28.
[56] Elizabeth Helsinger, Robin L. Sheets, and William Veeder, *The Woman Question: Volume 1* (Chicago, IL: University of Chicago Press, 1983), 'Introduction', p. xv.
[57] Glover, 'Not so Long Ago', p. 17.
[58] Glover, 'Not so Long Ago', p. 15.
[59] Glover, 'Not so Long Ago', pp. 15-16.
[60] Handbook of Tyndale Chapel, 1882, p. 2; Handbook of Tyndale Chapel, 1892, p. 25.
[61] Champion, *Tyndale Baptist Church*, p. 13.

because she knew people might want a private conversation with the minister's wife. Instead, visitors were welcome at any time. In her own diary, Anna noted for one day 'A called and stayed to tea, and B came in after. Mrs X brought her work and stayed to supper.' Dorothy recalled 'They added up to crowds on some days'.[62] Dorothy's perception was that her mother's reticence was a generational thing: 'she belonged to a generation not trained to speak, provide, take meetings or classes. But she could co-operate'.[63] Whilst there are examples of women of Anna's generation being active as speakers, it is instructive that this was Dorothy's perception. Her own experience was clearly different.[64] Both Mary Knee and Anna Glover, therefore, were active in support of their husbands' ministries, and took some responsibility within the third sphere of the church, according to their ability and personality, and perhaps, as Dorothy indicated, their own preconceptions of their role. Both Anna Glover and Mary Knee were an integral part of their husbands' ministries. Although by the nature of their role and status, they were different from the other women in the church, they do provide an example of a situation where women could, through the 'third sphere' of the church, find a role, purpose and fulfilment.

Very few women became pastors' wives, but there were still many opportunities for involvement available to them within the 'third sphere' that comprised the life of these two churches, similar to those in many other Nonconformist churches during the nineteenth century, filling roles traditionally seen to belong to women.[65] Women in both churches were active in collecting for various missions at home and abroad, Sunday school teaching, in local mission, and in the inevitable 'Dorcas' meetings where clothes were made for the poor.

Dorothy Glover's comment on these gatherings appears rather condescending: 'for the mature woman there was the Dorcas Society at which 30 to 40 ladies sewed on flannel and unbleached calico "for the poor"'. She blamed its decline partly on the move from meeting in the convivial surroundings of members' houses into the church which was much less hospitable, but also on the change in habits of dress, so that the garments made were no longer suitable for anyone to wear.[66] Counterslip also had a Dorcas Society, although by 1894 support for this seemed to be declining, as the writer of the Dorcas item in the Counterslip yearly booklet was complaining that numbers at the meeting were dropping and asking pointedly for friends 'who can spare *one* afternoon in the month' to come and help.[67] Yet a remark in same booklet noted that 'At this time the Bible Woman's Mission and the Dorcas Society were

---

[62] Glover, 'Not so Long Ago', p. 10.
[63] Champion, *Tyndale Baptist Church*, p. 13.
[64] For instance, in Glover, 'Not so Long Ago', p. 17, she noted that she 'had many engagements to speak' on behalf of the London Baptist Missionary Committee.
[65] Wilson, *Constrained by Zeal*, pp. 187-202.
[66] Glover, 'Not so Long Ago', p. 11.
[67] Handbook of Counterslip Chapel, 1894, p. 29.

being greatly used'.[68] Either this was a meaningless platitude, or despite the drop in numbers, the work the women did was still considered worthwhile.

One of the opportunities open to women at Counterslip, but not, it seems, at Tyndale, was being part of the Ladies' Committee, the role of which was to 'assist the Pastors and officers in visitation among the members'.[69] Of the twenty-three female visitors, eight, approximately one third, can be traced in the census. Most of these appear to have had no occupation and would therefore presumably have had plenty of free time for visiting, but two were earning their own living. Martha Stiles, forty-eight in 1891 and a widow, was a music teacher who also had lodgers, but in addition she had an adult daughter contributing to the family income, so her teaching was probably part-time, allowing her opportunities for visiting.[70] The other working visitor, however, Susanna Gast, was a dressmaker who in 1891 was living in two rented rooms in a house in Langton Street, Redcliffe, a crowded area close to the central, manufacturing and dock areas of the city. Susanna, the youngest of five children, was born in Redcliffe over fifty years earlier, and had already been contributing to the family income as a dressmaker by the age of fourteen.[71] Following her father's death she lived with and supported her widowed mother Jane for over ten years, and this would almost certainly have damaged her opportunity for marriage. Indeed, she always remained single.[72] It seems that following her mother's death, Susanna lived briefly with her brother Philip, a Baptist minister in Islington, and his family, but she soon returned to Bristol and once again took up dressmaking to support herself, a business with notoriously long hours.[73] Her active membership of Counterslip, a short walk from her home, would have given Susanna a place of belonging and a sense of significance: it meant enough to her that she found time in a busy life to take part by becoming a visitor. The same can be said about many women: the church provided a third sphere in which they could be active and develop their skills and abilities.

Women were also active as Sunday school teachers. Counterslip in 1893 had thirty-six Sunday school teachers, fifteen of whom were women, although the office holders were all men.[74] At Tyndale in 1892, the majority of the Sunday school teachers, twelve out of fifteen, were women, including Dorothy Glover. Out of those twelve, however, only one was a married woman, and, as at Counterslip, all the office holders, including a librarian and assistant librarian, were men. Even in the more open and liberal atmosphere of Tyndale, women rarely found themselves in positions of responsibility in the church. However, there was plenty for them to do, and some of them took full advantage of the opportunities offered by the third sphere

---

[68] John K. Frampton, *Counterslip Baptist Church – A Brief History 1804–2004* (n.pl.: n.p., n.d.), p. 45.

[69] Handbook of Counterslip Chapel, 1894, p. 29.

[70] 1891 Census at Ancestry.co.uk.

[71] 1861 Census at Ancestry.co.uk.

[72] 1871 Census at Ancestry.co.uk.

[73] 1881 Census, and 1891 Census at Ancestry.co.uk.

[74] Handbook of Counterslip Chapel, 1894, p. 34.

of the church. Sarah Polglase at Tyndale, and Alice Crew at Counterslip, offer very different types of women active within their respective churches.

Sarah Polglase was the childless widow of a Bristol tea merchant who in 1891 lived in a substantial house, 121 Pembroke Road, Clifton, ten minutes' walk from Tyndale chapel. As already noted, she shared this house with her younger sister Eliza Ravis, also a widow and member of Tyndale. Living on their own means, the sisters were able to employ three servants including a cook.[75] In 1892, despite now being seventy-five, Sarah was still active within the church, as treasurer of the Dorcas Society, which met regularly during October to June on a Thursday in different people's homes. In addition to this, together with Eliza, she hosted a weekly sewing gathering in their home, held every Tuesday at five o'clock, to produce items for a sale to raise funds for the Zenana Society, a missionary organisation directed towards Asian women.[76] Together with a similar sale held by the Sunday school, this project had raised £116.11s.00d the previous year for this cause.[77] One can imagine Sarah, her sister and their friends, sitting around sewing and drinking tea in a friendly and convivial atmosphere. Although both of these church activities were home-based, and connected with sewing and craft, as a treasurer Sarah was also making use on behalf of charity of skills developed over years of running her own domestic establishment. She also contributed a total of £10.5s.6d towards various aspects of mission and support beyond Tyndale itself, and twenty pounds towards the new Tyndale Mission Building (£2,742.6s.1d was raised in total). Her giving indicated someone who was well off without being rich (in comparison, the Robinsons gave £400 towards this project).[78] Tyndale clearly played a large part in her life and presumably her affections. Sarah and her sister, able to offer hospitality in their large house, are an example of a class of women not found at Counterslip.

It is hard, however, to see Sarah Polglase as a pioneer of a new way of doing things, as most of her activities were in her home or those of others, and she was more active in private than in the third sphere of church. Her activities were focused around needlework and craft and were also social, as time would have been spent chatting with her friends as they worked. Although she was also treasurer for the Dorcas Society, the responsibility for a society which stated 'The subscription to its funds is optional' would not have been onerous to a woman used to running a substantial domestic establishment.[79] Despite its traditional expression, however, Sarah's church involvement was clearly a major focus, if not the main focus, of her life and her contribution, together with that of other women like her, in terms of personal and financial support to the church should not be underestimated. They contributed to the success of Tyndale as an enterprise.

---

[75] 1891 Census at Ancestry.co.uk.
[76] Handbook of Tyndale Chapel Bristol, June 1892, p. 25.
[77] Handbook of Tyndale Chapel, 1892, p. 35.
[78] Handbook of Tyndale Chapel, 1892, pp. 58-59.
[79] Handbook of Tyndale Chapel, 1892, p. 25.

Another woman who contributed significantly to the life and impact of her church was Alice Crew, for many years the Counterslip Bible Woman, employed for twenty-five hours a week by the British and Foreign Bible Society to work for the Bible Woman's Mission.[80] Before becoming a Bible woman in 1885, she lived with her elderly mother and earned her living by sewing.[81] Bible Women, a movement started in London by Anglican Ellen Ranyard in 1857, making use of poor women to reach others in their own class, was by this time employing individuals in poor districts all over the country.[82] In 1893 Alice received a total of twenty-six pounds for her work with poor families living near the chapel.[83] As was the usual practice, she was supervised by a middle-class woman who also ran the mothers' meetings, in this case the pastor's wife, Mary Knee, helped by her 'efficient Committee of Ladies'.[84] Alice did the work on the ground, as noted earlier, helping women in their household responsibilities as well as encouraging their church involvement.[85] This mixture was an integral part of being a Bible Woman.[86] She was, 'faithful and conscientious' in this role and in 1894 her work was described as 'being largely blessed', in that numbers attending the weekly Mothers' Meeting held in the chapel on Monday afternoons were increasing.[87]

During these years, Alice, who remained single, never moved far from where she was born, close to the 'New Cut'. For many years she boarded with a succession of families, usually in the area of Totterdown just south of the river, although, by 1911, aged sity-six and still working, she was living on her own in two rented rooms.[88] Alice was one of many working-class women throughout the country who responded to this rare opportunity to earn their living through missional activities, working in a community she already knew well amongst people of her own class. Sarah Lane has noted that the 'main strength of Ellen Raynard's system of Biblewomen' was the use of working-class women to reach their peers, even though in so doing it could be argued that they were 'part of the process of perpetuating a middle-class value structure'.[89] There is no indication, however, of how she regarded her role in either class or gender terms, whether she saw herself as part of a new move of women to

---

[80] Frampton, *Counterslip Baptist Church*, p. 40.

[81] 1881 Census at Ancestry.co.uk.

[82] Frank Prochaska, *Women and Philanthropy in 19th Century England* (Oxford: Clarendon Press, 1980), pp. 126-29.

[83] Handbook of Counterslip Chapel, 1894, p. 28.

[84] Handbook of Counterslip Chapel, 1894, p. 28. See also Prochaska, *Women and Philanthropy*, p. 128.

[85] Frampton, *Counterslip Baptist Church*, p. 40.

[86] Prochaska, *Women and Philanthropy*, p. 128.

[87] Handbook of Counterslip Chapel, 1894, p. 28.

[88] 1911 Census at Ancestry.co.uk.

[89] Sarah Lane, 'Forgotten Labours: Women's Bible Work and the BFBS', in Stephen Batalden, Kathleen Cann and John Dean (eds), *Sowing the Word: The Cultural Impact of the British and Foreign Bible Society 1804–2004* (Sheffield: Sheffield Pheonix Press, 2004), pp. 61-62.

take a more active role in churches, or whether she only thought in terms of personal mission and opportunity. However, she was clearly working in the 'third sphere' of the church, and, unusually, being paid for it.

Involvement in Mission

There were also opportunities for women to be involved in supporting home and foreign mission. Much of this was conventional voluntary work, well within the acceptable role for women, and safely in the third sphere of the churches. Only occasionally were women involved in mission-related work which moved into the public sphere. At the more conventional end of the spectrum, women in both churches were collectors for local and overseas mission. At Tyndale, there was a range of opportunities for becoming involved through organising collections, donations and subscriptions for a variety of causes including foreign mission. Money collected for the latter, including subscriptions collected by different individuals and sales of work came to a substantial total of £901 in 1892.[90] The secretary for missions, and the most successful collector of subscriptions, was Katherine Robinson, wife of Edward, partner with his brother Arthur in the paper-bag manufacturing business, and daughter of Dr Gotch, Principal of the Bristol Baptist College.[91] Counterslip had seven collectors for the BMS, all women. Once again both secretary and treasurer were male.[92] Although larger in numbers than Tyndale, Counterslip's more humble membership is indicated in the total raised between April 1892 and April 1893, £140. This, however, appears to be the only involvement the women of that church had in foreign mission, which had a lower profile than it did at Tyndale.

Both churches ran missions aimed at local people and women took part in these, although their exact role is a little uncertain. In 1892 the Tyndale Mission Church in Deanery Road, in a slum area some six miles from the church, consisted of forty-three members. It maintained 'a spirit of earnest devotion' according to Richard Glover's early report.[93] The management committee of twelve, headed by Edward Robinson, included four women, and slightly over half of its Sunday school teachers, twenty-two out of forty-one, were women. These included one married woman, Mrs Norman, who, strangely given her role, was not a member of Tyndale.[94] It is not clear whether women had any further role in the mission church at Tyndale, but they evidently played their part.

---

[90] Handbook of Tyndale Chapel, 1892, p. 35.

[91] It is worth noting that the Tyndale Chapel Handbook sometimes used the plural 'missions' although it more usually used the singular form. So the section heading on the 1892 Handbook, p. 31, is 'Foreign Missions' whilst on p. 33, the subsection is called 'Zenana Mission', although the accounts are under the heading 'Zenana Missions'. This mixed use is reflected in my own use of the term.

[92] Handbook of Tyndale Chapel, 1894, p. 30.

[93] Handbook of Tyndale Chapel, 1892, p. 43.

[94] Handbook of Tyndale Chapel, 1892, p. 38.

Counterslip's local mission was known as the Tower Street Mission, and they also had a group known the Counterslip Gospel Mission Band, which consisted of '26 brethren and 19 sisters', held open air meetings 'in courts and alleys' and cottage meetings in the winter, as well as distributing tracts, the latter done mainly by the female members.[95] There is no evidence to suggest these women were involved in speaking at outdoor and cottage meetings, but they were likely to have at least been present, and they visited the sick in their homes. The opportunities within home mission for women in both churches were unclear but probably mainly conventional.

Tyndale had a much stronger profile in supporting overseas mission than Counterslip did. Richard Glover had wide sympathies (serving as President of the Baptist Union), and as has already been noted, he was an enthusiastic advocate of mission.[96] Richard even visited China during his pastorate, at the invitation of the BMS, sending back photographs for the family of himself in Chinese dress.[97] His daughter later commented that after his return he 'could not talk about anything but China'.[98] The Principal of Bristol Baptist College, Dr Gotch, was also an advocate of mission; his participation at Tyndale, with his family, added to the high profile of mission in the congregation. His daughter Katherine Gotch, under her married name Mrs Edward Robinson, took an active part in promoting missions, for several years being the secretary of the local branch of the BMS, including the Zenana branch.[99] As Secretary of Foreign Missions in general and the Zenana Mission in particular, she was the only woman who wrote a substantial contribution to the yearly Tyndale Handbook, and was active not only in the third sphere of church, but in the wider life of Bristol. For a time she was the national secretary of the Zenana Mission.

So, a number of women were involved in various activities in both churches. Was there more opportunity in Tyndale, with its contingent of well-educated women in well-to-do families? Both congregations offered the conventional church activities for women, often with a social element: Dorcas societies, Sunday school teaching, collecting for mission at home and abroad, and some involvement in those missions. In both churches these women were crossing over the boundaries between the home and the third sphere of church, and both offered the opportunities to push at those boundaries. It might be truer to say that there were different opportunities. In Counterslip women could be visitors, and in 1892 a woman, Emily Reece, became one of the two chapel keepers.[100] Unusually, for Alice Crew there was an opportunity of paid employment related to the church. Tyndale, however, had a wider range of activities. Perhaps this reflects that the women of Tyndale had more leisure. Even when they were not working, Counterslip women were often bringing up families and managing houses with rather less support from servants than many Tyndale

---

[95] Handbook of Counterslip Chapel, 1894, p. 34.

[96] Champion, *Tyndale Baptist Church*, p. 13 (quoting a speech by Dorothy Glover).

[97] Glover, 'Not so Long Ago', pp. 3-6.

[98] Glover, 'Note so Long Ago', p. 6.

[99] *Bristol Mercury* 16 May 1888, and *Bristol Mercury* 17 September 1898.

[100] *Souvenir of Counterslip Church Centenary 1804–1904* (Bristol: E.H. Webb, n.d.), p. 22.

women enjoyed. In both churches women had opportunity to develop their skills and abilities within the safe walls of the third sphere of the church, but it was only in Tyndale that women found the opportunity and the confidence to move beyond this and into the public arena.

Did any of these Women have a Public Profile?

This was an era when women, especially middle and upper middle class women, were having an increasingly public role.[101] This was less true of working class women,[102] so it is no surprise to find that the few women with a public profile whom we can trace were in Tyndale, not in the predominantly working-class Counterslip. Indeed, it is difficult to find evidence of Counterslip women active in any role beyond home, church, and, in a significant number of cases, workplace. There are some examples of working-class Methodist women pursuing such activities, but it was rare in Baptist churches.[103] One concludes that even in the 1890s, whilst these two churches did provide a significant third sphere for those women able to take advantage of it, this did not lead to the development of wider roles and responsibilities for the average woman. Only those who had other advantages and opportunities, through birth, marriage, or more rarely, their own initiative,[104] moved beyond the church into a wider public life.

A few Tyndale women, however, with connections into the 'Nonconformist aristocracy' of Bristol, through religious, manufacturing and political networks, were able to take advantage of the opportunities for women to push at the boundaries of acceptable behaviour and to be at the forefront of a new way of doing things. One example is Dorothy Glover, who spoke publicly on several occasions. As well as her talk to the Broadmead young people in 1908, after her parents died she 'had many engagements' to speak on behalf of the London Baptist Missionary Committee and later spoke at the eightieth anniversary of Tyndale.[105] In 1939–40 she chaired the BMS. Although this is well beyond our period, her confidence in such a role would have built on the early opportunities she had at Tyndale in the late nineteenth and early twentieth centuries.

Another Tyndale woman who had a significant public role was Katherine Robinson. Katherine's husband Edward and his brother Arthur headed up the prosperous firm, E.S. & A. Robinson, which, as already noted, manufactured paper

---

[101] Simon Morgan, *A Victorian Woman's Place: Public Culture in the Nineteenth Century* (London: Taurus Academic Studies, 2007).

[102] Elizabeth Roberts, *A Woman's Place: An Oral History of Working-class Women 1890-1940* (Blackwell: Oxford, 1984), p. 2, has noted, for instance, that in Lancashire working class women did not generally become involved with the suffrage movement.

[103] Wilson, 'Sarah Terrett, Katherine Robinson and Edith Pearce'.

[104] A rare Bristol example, although not a Baptist, is Sarah Terrett, butcher's wife, Methodist preacher and founder of a temperance society. See Wilson, 'Sarah Terrett', pp. 405-15.

[105] Champion, *Tyndale Baptist Church*, p. 12.

bags and stationery. By 1911 there were 2,500 employees in several factories covering an area of ten and a half acres,[106] and the Robinsons were living in Sneyd Park, one of the most exclusive areas of Bristol. They also had a lively social life and a high profile in the politics of the city. Edward became a councillor and was to become mayor in 1908. As his wife, Katherine had a public role with her activities reported in local newspapers, ranging from opening a church bazaar at Counterslip in April 1888, through helping to cook a Christmas Eve dinner for poor children at Lodge Street Congregational Chapel in 1890. In the same year[107] she helped organise a concert in aid of a working girls' club of which she was president, at which she presented the future professional singer Clara Butt with a gift, on the occasion of Clara leaving Bristol to study at the Royal College of Music.[108] It was even considered newsworthy when at a YWCA party on New Year's Eve, 1891, Katherine sang two solos and then a duet with her husband Edward.[109] The Robinsons fulfilled a role similar to a country squire in a previous century, holding garden parties at their house and gracing social events with their presence:[110] her attendance at weddings and funerals was often noted by the local papers.[111] She was active in a much wider area than that of the church alone.

Her role in promoting mission, whilst clearly made easier by her prominent marriage, was rooted in the household she grew up in, the Gotch household, with her father as Principal of the College and a strong supporter of mission no doubt encouraging an early interest. Katherine's role in the Zenana Mission would have taken up a substantial amount of time and commitment, at a time when her husband was still busy in local politics and business.

In addition, she was for some time one of several vice-presidents of the Bristol Women's Liberal Association, and was thus active in politics on her own account.[112] Katherine was also almost certainly a supporter of women's suffrage, for, although she was absent from a Women's Liberal Association meeting in April 1899 when a resolution was passed in favour of the vote for women,[113] the organisation had been strongly supportive of women's suffrage for many years and she would not have been in the position of vice-president if she had not supported this goal. Katherine Robinson was, like many of the leading Baptist women Karen Smith refers to, both an advocate of women's traditional role, not looking for a place in ministry for herself, and also a supporter of women's suffrage. This is evidence of the connection

---

[106] D. Bateman, 'The Growth of the Printing and Packaging Industry in Bristol, 1800–1914', in C. Harvey and J. Press (eds.), *Studies in the Business History of Bristol* (Bristol: Bristol Academic Press, 1988), pp. 83-107 (p. 99).

[107] *Bristol Mercury* 27 December 1890.

[108] *Bristol Mercury* 26 April 1890.

[109] *Bristol Mercury* 7 January 1891.

[110] *Bristol Mercury* 17 September 1898.

[111] *Bristol Mercury* 8 November 1890. In this account of the funeral of the Rev. Dr Trestail, Mrs Robinson was the only non-family member mentioned by name.

[112] *Bristol Mercury* 26 April 1899.

[113] *Bristol Mercury* 26 April 1899.

Smith has made between the Zenana Mission and suffrage. Smith has argued that 'Feminism and the BZM may not have been so radically removed from one another',[114] and cites the example of Sarah Edwards in Cardiff, a leader of BZM in Wales and an 'outspoken advocate on issues like temperance and women's suffrage'.[115] Katherine Robinson stands out as an example of a woman who moved beyond the third sphere into the public sphere, even if that was largely facilitated by her husband's position. However, the few women who had a public profile were the exceptions: most church members rarely moved beyond the third sphere of church.

Drawing it all Together

June Hannam, who has studied the contribution of Quakers and Unitarians to the development of feminist politics in Bristol, has suggested that women from those churches were more likely to be involved in such ventures than evangelicals, who were less likely to challenge the status quo of gender relations.[116] This study has validated that thesis: Katherine Robinson was a rare example, and even she was a very discreet supporter of female suffrage. However, much has been learned about the lives of many ordinary, and some extraordinary, Baptist women from two churches. Most were doing their best to keep home and family together, sometimes doing paid work in order to do that. As Steinbach has noted, working-class Victorians were 'engaged in a daily struggle not only to survive but to do so with dignity.'[117] These women had a range of incomes, ages, and church involvements, but some clearly found in the church a place not only of belonging, but of opportunity and perhaps fulfilment, whether as the host for a Dorcas meeting, as a pastoral visitor, as a speaker to young people, or as a Bible Woman. Only a small minority moved beyond that third sphere into the public arena; but their opportunity to do so was provided not so much by the church as by their upbringing and situation in the world – daughter of the Principal of a Baptist College, wife of a prominent industrialist who eventually became a mayor. One of these rare women was Dorothy Glover. We do not know how her talk on the early history of Broadmead was received, but we do know that Dorothy herself remained a part of Tyndale, living in the family home until her death in October 1961 at the age of eighty-six. During her lifetime the opportunities for women in church and society changed out of all recognition, if rather more slowly than might have been hoped. A later member of Tyndale described Dorothy in terms of 'her vigorous intellect, her lively personality and her robust faith', meriting special mention in his history of the church.[118] She had a strong awareness of place, and of the lives of men and women of faith who had

---

[114] Karen Smith, 'Women in Cultural Captivity: British Women and the Zenana Mission', *Baptist Quarterly* 42.2:1 (April, 2007), pp. 103-13 (p. 108).

[115] Smith, 'Cultural Captivity', pp. 110-11.

[116] Hannam, '"An Enlarged Sphere"', pp. 184-85.

[117] Steinbach, *Understanding the Victorians*, p. 119.

[118] Champion, *Tyndale Baptist Church*, p. 24.

gone before her. This chapter has followed Dorothy's example and 'taken an interest' in the history of Baptists in Bristol. Her image of walking the streets of the city with an awareness of past inhabitants and events is one that has stayed with me as I prepared my own notes for this chapter, exploring the lives of Baptist women in the late nineteenth century, as I have found myself seeking out the houses where they lived and pondering the nature of their lives and faith. Much more remains to be explored, but I trust that this short piece of work has contributed to the understanding of the variety and nature of the lives of Baptist women across the class spectrum in Bristol during the late nineteenth century.

CHAPTER 8

Spreading the Good News from Scotland: Scottish Baptists and Overseas Mission in the First Three Decades of the Twentieth Century

Brian R. Talbot

Introduction

> The foreign missions movement ... bears witness to the existence of the divine impulse and life within the Church at home and, generation after generation, provides a measure of the Church's readiness to know and do the will of God. The real vitality of the Church at any point in its history is attested by its power of expansion.[1]

These words were taken from the 1935 report of the Foreign Mission Committee of the Church of Scotland, commissioned at the 1932 General Assembly to survey the overseas commitments of the largest Presbyterian Church in Scotland. The concern which led to the generation of this report was the serious and repeated shortfalls in income to accomplish the work in these various mission fields. The implication of the report was that this overseas activity was a vital part of the life and witness of this Scottish denomination. Were those sentiments representative of mainstream Protestant churches in Scotland in the first three decades of the twentieth century? The answer is a clear 'yes' as expectations were very high for the further expansion of the Christian church overseas as the last century unfolded.[2] It must be remembered that Edinburgh, Scotland, had been chosen as the venue for the 1910 World Missionary Conference. It was at that time the largest and most significant gathering of Protestant mission agencies in the world. One of the most notable features of the event was the main address at the opening evening session on Tuesday 14 June 1910, viewed by many delegates as a prophetic utterance from the extremely sober Archbishop of Canterbury, Randall Davidson, who encouraged those present that if they gave foreign missions the central place it deserved that it may well be that '"there be some standing here tonight who shall not taste of death till they see," – here on earth, in a way we know not now, – "the Kingdom of God

---

[1] 'A SURVEY and A CALL', The Report of the Foreign General Assembly of 1935 (Edinburgh: William Blackwood, 1935), pp. 7-8.

[2] An example of a scholar who has drawn attention to this point is J. Cox, *The British Missionary Enterprise since 1700* (London: Routledge, 2008), pp. 171-74.

come with power'".³ Protestant Christian delegates from across the English-speaking world were inspired by his words. A United Free Church of Scotland report the following year was representative of the mindset of Scottish churches at that time. After outlining the tremendous opportunities for that denomination's workers overseas, the authors made a more general call for a missionary advance. 'Never in all her history has the Church received such a call and such a challenge. We must plan an advance or face the shame of a retreat.' The Foreign Mission Committee challenged the wider denomination to provide an additional sum of £10,000 per annum to support the work of an extra twenty-five men and fifteen women who would strengthen the team of workers overseas. They had no doubt about their commitment and the urgency of the need to spread the good news from Scotland.⁴ The report concluded with these words:

> What are churches for but to make missionaries? What is education for but to train them? What is commerce for but to carry them? What is money for but to send them? What is life itself for but to fulfil the purpose of foreign missions – the enthroning of Jesus Christ in the hearts of men?⁵

Rhetoric is one thing, but did the Scottish churches send many workers overseas to spread the Christian faith?

Growth of Mission Numbers throughout the Nineteenth Century

There was an increase in the number of missionaries serving overseas throughout the nineteenth century. It had been Archibald McLean, an Edinburgh Baptist minister, as early as December 1795, who had the honour of being the first Scottish Protestant clergyman since the Reformation to argue that the Great Commission of Jesus in taking the gospel to the world was a duty to be taken seriously by Scottish Christians.⁶ By the following year Evangelicals in different denominations were making a similar proclamation, inspired by the work of William Carey and his Baptist Missionary Society (BMS) colleagues in India.⁷ From a handful of Scottish missionaries overseas prior to the 1830s, it was estimated that the total had risen to

---

³ *World Missionary Conference 1910: The History and Records of the Conference together with Addresses delivered at the evening meetings* (Edinburgh: Oliphant, Anderson and Ferrier, n.d. [1910]), pp. 146-50. For more details on this event, see B. Stanley, *The World Missionary Conference, Edinburgh 1910* (Grand Rapids, MI: Eerdmans, 2009).

⁴ Hubert L. Simpson, *United Free Church of Scotland: Our Mission Fields 1910–1911* (Edinburgh: United Free Church of Scotland, 1911), pp. 71-72.

⁵ Simpson, *Our Mission Fields 1910–1911*, p. 77.

⁶ A. McLean, *The Promise that all Nations shall be brought into Subjection to Christ* (Edinburgh: J. Guthrie, 1796).

⁷ Brian Talbot, '"Rousing the Attention of Christians": Scottish Baptists and the Baptist Missionary Society prior to the Twentieth Century', in John H.Y Briggs and Anthony R. Cross (eds), *Baptists and the World: Renewing the Vision* (Oxford: Centre for Baptist History and Heritage Studies, 8; Oxford: Regent's Park College, 2011), pp. 53-60.

around thirty individuals, of which six were Scottish Baptists, and up to 100 by 1850.[8] At the start of the twentieth century, including missionaries' wives, the Church of Scotland was supporting 115 men and women in the mission field,[9] and the United Free Church of Scotland an impressive total of 406.[10] In the National Church this was approximately equivalent to one missionary for every twelve congregations. By contrast the United Free Church had the equivalent of one missionary for every four of its churches. All of the serving missionaries in the former Free Church of Scotland had chosen to affiliate with the new body comprised of the United Presbyterian Church and the vast majority of the Free Church of Scotland. The latter body continued, but its foreign mission work would have to commence afresh with new staff and fresh opportunities for service. W. Roundsfell Brown, Convenor of its Foreign Missions Committee, reported to the 1901 Free Church of Scotland Assembly the following statement:

> In the circumstances of the Church, the Committee finds itself for the moment not in actual touch with any mission. The United Free Church has been enriched, and we impoverished on many points: on none more than on this. All the Foreign Missionaries have preferred to attach themselves to the larger denomination.[11]

Even a small denomination like the Baptist Union of Scotland had commissioned fifty-one members for overseas service with its own mission agency the BMS,[12] even apart from an unknown number of those serving under the auspices of other, usually non-denominational bodies, prior to 1900. On the threshold of the twentieth century Scottish Christians expected the continued growth in the numbers and success of their overseas workers in spreading the good news from Scotland.

---

[8] Figures taken from the *New Edinburgh Almanac*, cited by E. Breitenbach, *Empire and Scottish Society: The Impact of Foreign Missions at Home c1790–c.1914* (Edinburgh: Edinburgh University Press, 2009), p. 57. For details of Baptist missionaries, see Talbot, 'Rousing the Attention of Christians'; and M. McVicar, *A Great Adventure: Scotland and the BMS* (Glasgow: Baptist Union of Scotland, 1992), p. 14.

[9] *Report of the Schemes of the Church of Scotland* (Edinburgh: William Blackwood, 1900), pp. 80-81.

[10] *United Free Church of Scotland Report to the General Assembly of the United Free Church of Scotland 1901* (Edinburgh: T. & A. Constable, 1901), No. XXX, *Report of Committee on Statistics*, pp. 2-4.

[11] W. Roundsfell Brown, 'Report of the Foreign Missions Committee', *Principal Acts of the General Assembly of the Free Church of Scotland 1901* (Edinburgh: William Nimmo, 1901), p. 371. See also W.D. Graham, 'Beyond the Borders of Scotland: The Church's Missionary Enterprise', in C. Graham (ed.), *Crown Him Lord of All: Essays on the Life and Witness of The Free Church of Scotland* (Edinburgh: The Knox Press, 1993), pp. 101-102.

[12] McVicar, *Great Adventure*, pp. 70-83.

Financial Costs of Mission in the United Kingdom Context

It was a costly exercise to fund both workers' stipends and the associated expenditure for equipment and other materials used in overseas mission. However, British Christians across the United Kingdom were enthusiastic for this work and generous in their financial giving. It has been noted that as early as 1847 the Church Missionary Society (CMS), the British and Foreign Bible Society, and the Society for the Propagation of the Gospel all had incomes in excess of £100,000,[13] as did the Wesleyan Methodist Missionary Society.[14] The London Missionary Society (LMS) more than £64,000 and the BMS over £25,000. By way of contrast, the best supported home mission agency, the London City Mission, had an income barely exceeding £14,000 at that time.[15] Overseas mission work without a doubt was viewed as a higher priority due to a perception of a greater need of evangelistic effort outside the home countries. Over the century since its foundation the agency supported by Scottish Congregationalists, the LMS, had seen its income rise from £11,904 in its first full year of operations in 1797, to £51,509 in 1850, and up to £155,621 at the time of its centenary in 1895.[16] However, the additional funds raised at its centenary were only sufficient to pay off accumulated debts rather than enable the LMS to make further advances in its work.[17] With the exception of the war years, 1914–18, the LMS had some critical financial problems. Annual income in the years around 1910 was approximately £100,000, reaching £120,000 in 1918 and hitting a peak for regular giving of £140,000 in 1935. Yet the deficits remaining when expenditure was put alongside income were unsustainable. In 1925 the accumulated deficit had reached £87,000; special appeals cleared this debt, yet by 1929 it had risen again to £56,000 and nearly £70,000 in 1935. Widespread industrial and economic depression in the 1920s and the death of some of its wealthiest supporters brought a realisation that cuts would need to be made in its budget. The LMS was far from alone in this predicament. The era of growth in its work had come to an end.[18] Methodists likewise in the United Methodist Missionary Society (UMMS) viewed

---

[13] S. Thorne, 'Protestant Ethics and the Spirit of Imperialism: British Congregationalists and the London Missionary Society, 1795-1925' (PhD thesis, University of Michigan, 1990), chs 1 and 2, cited in S. Thorne, *Congregational Missions and the Making of an Imperial Culture in 19th Century England* (Stanford, CA: Stanford University Press, 1999), p. 47.

[14] WMMS exceeded £100,000 in contributions and legacies in 1841. N. Allen Birtwhistle, 'Methodist Missions', in R. Davies, A.R. George and G. Rupp (eds), *A History of the Methodist Church in Great Britain. Volume 3* (London: Epworth Press, 1983), p. 40.

[15] Thorne, 'Protestant Ethics and the Spirit of Imperialism', cited in Thorne, *Congregational Missions*, p. 47.

[16] R. Lovett, *The History of the London Missionary Society 1795-1895. Volume 2* (London: Henry Frowde, 1899), Appendix III.

[17] *Centenary Report of the London Missionary Society* (London, 1895), cited by A. Porter, *Religion versus Empire?: British Protestant Missionaries and Overseas Expansion, 1700-1914* (Manchester: Manchester University Press, 2004), p. 282.

[18] N. Goodall, *A History of the London Missionary Society 1895-1945* (London: Oxford University Press, 1954), pp. 549-52.

the period between 1918 and 1932, the year of the reunion of the majority of Methodist denominations in the United Kingdom, as largely one of recovery and consolidation of their work.[19] Eugene Stock, the Anglican CMS historian, gave a rather downbeat assessment of giving to that society between 1896 and 1899. In response to appeals for a significant increase in funding during those years his summary conclusion was clear, 'That it was received with general enthusiasm in England cannot be affirmed.'[20] Although its income did increase over the next half-century the CMS ran an annual deficit between 1910 and 1941, due to its inability to raise the necessary funds for its increasing number of staff and projects.[21] British Baptists raised a respectable £114,670 in 1892, the centenary year of the commencement of the BMS's work. When the size of their constituency is taken into account and the lack of many wealthy donors, in comparison with some of the other denominations, it was a welcome increase in funding for the Society's work. The office bearers stated, 'the sum of £100,000 contemplated has not only been obtained, but considerably exceeded'.[22] The Protestant Nonconformist denominations in the United Kingdom were more generous in giving than the Established Churches,[23] but all the mainstream churches were supportive of overseas mission work.

Costs for Missions associated with Scottish Churches

In Scotland in particular the figures for Church of Scotland's overseas work grew significantly, in particular in the last quarter of the nineteenth century. The Church of Scotland set aside £10,117 in 1879 for overseas work. This total had risen to £50,691 by the end of the century in 1899,[24] £56,114 by 1911,[25] and £67,889 by 1919.[26] However, this funding came from a small number of individuals and a minority of parishes. It appears that only approximately one-third of its parishes were seriously committed to supporting its overseas work.[27] The financial giving of the United Free Church at home for its overseas mission projects had reached

---

[19] Birtwhistle, 'Methodist Missions', p. 86.

[20] E. Stock, *The History of the Church Missionary Society. Volume 3* (London: Church Missionary Society, 1899), pp. 715-20.

[21] G. Hewitt, *The Problems of Success: A History of the Church Missionary Society 1910–1942. Volume 1* (London: SCM Press, 1971), p. 431.

[22] J.B. Myers (ed.), *The Centenary Celebrations of the Baptist Missionary Society 1892–1893* (London: The Baptist Missionary Society, 1893), pp. vi, 721.

[23] Thorne, *Congregational Missions*, p. 13.

[24] *Report of the Schemes of the Church of Scotland for the Year 1900* (Edinburgh: William Blackwood and Sons, 1900), pp. 82-83.

[25] *Report of the Schemes of the Church of Scotland for the Year 1911* (Edinburgh: William Blackwood and Sons, 1911), pp. 88-89.

[26] *Report of the Schemes of the Church of Scotland for the Year 1919* (Edinburgh: William Blackwood and Sons, 1919), pp. 60-61.

[27] Andrew C. Ross, 'Scottish missionary concern 1874–1914', *Scottish Historical Review* 51.151 (1972), pp. 69-70.

£109,645 as early as 1901,[28] but was only £84,698 in 1910 and relied on legacies to balance the books. It was a cause of real concern to their Foreign Mission Committee.[29] Drastic cutbacks were required during the war years, but encouragement was gained from a respectable £77,135 collected in the year at the end of World War One,[30] and £118,861 in 1925. However, with the annual deficit having increased for a third successive year to £10,839, resources had to be obtained from other denominational funds to balance the books. Tough decisions had to be made to reduce expenditure in the following year.[31] In the last set of figures prior to the 1929 Church Union the general foreign mission fund of the UFC raised £122,048, a slightly higher total than the £113,598 in the Church of Scotland.[32] These Churches had other sources of funding for overseas work as well, but the statistics cited above give good comparative figures for the two largest Presbyterian denominations in the early part of the twentieth century.

The BMS, the agency supported by Scottish Baptists, after the encouragements of funds raised in 1892, its centenary year, saw its regular income drop in the following year leaving a deficit of £15,874 in 1893 alone. £46,000 of the funds raised in the centenary appeal had to be used to erase the accumulated debts of the early 1890s. The highest annual income figures attained occurred in 1897–98 when £78,546 was raised, but it was still some way short of the stated goal of £100,000.[33] As late as 1920–21 it had only attained a total of £80,257.[34] However, in August 1910 the BMS received its largest legacy to date, £466,926, from wealthy benefactor Robert Arthington. This substantial sum of money was used to cover the deficits incurred in the annual accounts in the 1920s which reached as high as £34,565 in 1925–26. Drastic measures had to be taken to reduce costs, including withdrawal from eighteen mission stations in India, requiring BMS hospitals to raise eighty per cent of their running costs on the field and a reduction of missionary allowances by five per cent. Most significant at that time was an accelerated move towards the

---

[28] 'Report of Committee on Statistics', No. XXX, *Reports to the General Assembly of the United Free Church of Scotland 1901* (Edinburgh: T. & A. Constable, 1901), p. 8.

[29] 'Eleventh Report on Foreign Missions', *Reports to the General Assembly of the United Free Church of Scotland 1911* (Edinburgh: T. & A. Constable, 1911), pp. 5-6.

[30] 'Report of the Committee on Statistics', No. XXVIII, *Reports to the General Assembly of the United Free Church of Scotland 1919* (Edinburgh: T. & A. Constable, 1919), pp. 7-8.

[31] 'Twenty-Sixth Report on Foreign Mission', *Reports to the General Assembly of the United Free Church of Scotland 1926* (Edinburgh: T. & A. Constable, 1926), pp. 7-10.

[32] *Church of Scotland Reports to the General Assembly with the Legislative Acts* (Edinburgh: William Blackwood, 1930), pp. 501-505, 612-13, 734-35.

[33] *BMS Annual Report*, 1892–93, pp. 3-4, 92-93; 1893–94, pp. 93-94; 1894–95, p. 98; 1897–98, p. 120, cited by B. Stanley, *The History of the Baptist Missionary Society 1792–1992* (Edinburgh: T&T Clark, 1992), pp. 226-27.

[34] *BMS Annual Report, 1920-21*, cited by Stanley, *Baptist Missionary Society*, p. 381.

autonomy of national churches. The Arlington bequest had bought time to make the necessary changes before its funds for BMS work were exhausted in 1928.[35]

Overall British mission societies continued to see an increase in their incomes, even during the war years and sustained growth in their financial support during the 1920s, although they had to work very hard to ensure sufficient resources were raised.[36] The underlying problems arose from the rapid growth in their work for which they struggled to raise the necessary funds. Many missionaries were doing outstanding work with limited resources, but so much more might have been done with a more generous level of financial support from the churches at home.[37] The picture in Scotland was not too dissimilar to other parts of the United Kingdom with reference to funding for overseas work at that time. In summary, funding for overseas work by Protestant churches in Scotland was increasing in the first quarter of the twentieth century, but the costs of this work were rising at a faster rate, putting serious pressure on those individuals who had to determine priorities on the mission field.

Growth in Missionary Numbers from Scottish Churches in the Twentieth Century

In the twentieth century there was a pattern of steady growth in numbers of missionaries employed by the different Scottish Protestant denominations. Overall from the United Kingdom there were approximately 10,000 Christian missionaries serving overseas by 1900, the greater proportion, of course, on behalf of the numerically larger English churches.[38] In the Church of Scotland from a baseline figure of 115 missionaries engaged in 1899–1900[39] this total grew to 170 in 1910–11,[40] and as high as 190 in 1924–25.[41] To see the extent of the growth of this work in their ranks they had progressed from employing the equivalent of one missionary for every twelve congregations in 1899–1900 to more than one for every eight by 1924–

---

[35] 'BMS General Committee Minutes, 28 April, 1926, pp. 32-33; 27 May 1926, pp. 45-48; cited by Stanley, *Baptist Missionary Society*, pp. 381-85.

[36] K.S. Latourette, *A History of Christian Missions in China* (London, 1929), pp. 765-66, cited by B. Stanley, *The Bible and the Flag: Protestant Missions and British Imperialism in the Nineteenth and Twentieth Centuries* (Leicester: Apollos, 1990), pp. 134-35. The Anglican agency The United Society for the Propagation of the Gospel, e.g., attained both its largest number of missionaries and its highest income in 1926. See D. O'Connor *et al.*, *Three Centuries of Mission: The United Society for the Propagation of the Gospel 1701–2000* (London: Continuum, 2000), pp. 88-89.

[37] Ross, 'Scottish missionary concern 1874–1914', pp. 68-69.

[38] A. Porter, 'An Overview, 1700–1914', in N. Etherington (ed.), *Missions and Empire* (Oxford: Oxford University Press, 2005), p. 40.

[39] *Reports of the Schemes of the Church of Scotland for the Year 1900*, p. 82.

[40] *Reports of the Schemes of the Church of Scotland for the Year 1911*, p. 88.

[41] *Reports of the Schemes of the Church of Scotland for the Year 1925* (Edinburgh: William Blackwood, 1925), pp. 175-77.

25. The United Free Church in 1900–1901 had 406 serving missionaries;[42] a total that reached 506 in 1910–11,[43] and a highpoint of 630 in 1924–25.[44] In the same time period, the UFC had increased from the equivalent of one missionary for every four congregations to just over one for every two congregations by 1924–25. In the case of both bodies this was indisputable proof of a great commitment to the cause of world mission.[45]

Amongst the smaller denominations the Congregational Union of Scotland had thirty missionaries employed overseas in 1920–21, reaching the highest total of thirty-eight in 1925–26; this was growth from the equivalent of one missionary for between every five or six churches in 1920–21 to one for between every four or five congregations in 1925–26.[46] The Free Church of Scotland rebuilt a missionary presence overseas with two supported agents in 1910–11, a Rev. A. Dewar in South Africa, and Miss Elizabeth McLeod in India;[47] a decade later a strong work was established with the school in Lima, Peru,[48] with up to nine individuals supported by 1925–26.[49] The BMS experienced remarkable growth in the number of personnel it employed between 1900–1901 and 1921–22. In the former year it employed 311 people rising to a remarkable 515 two decades later.[50] It is no surprise that this agency struggled to raise the necessary finance to support so many agents in the field. A significant contribution to the increase was the growing medical work under its auspices. The rising cost of medical missions was greater than the home constituency could afford at that time.[51] By 1932–33, the BMS missionaries were reduced in number to 397. Changing circumstances such as rising nationalism in

---

[42] 'Report of Committee on Statistics', No. XXX, *Reports to the General Assembly of the United Free Church of Scotland 1901*, p. 8.

[43] 'Eleventh Report on Foreign Missions', *Reports to the General Assembly of the United Free Church of Scotland 1911*, p. 13.

[44] 'Twenty-Sixth Report on Foreign Mission', *Reports to the General Assembly of the United Free Church of Scotland 1926*, p. 90.

[45] Hilary Carey has pointed out what she considered the 'tragic waste of resources' of the different Presbyterian bodies duplicating 'India Missions', 'Colonial Missions and for the Conversion of the Jews'. Hilary M. Carey, *God's Empire: Religion and Colonialism in the British World, c.1801–1908* (Cambridge: Cambridge University Press, 2011), p. 239.

[46] I am grateful to the Rev. Dr W.D. McNaughton in May 2014 for assistance with the figures from the then Congregational Union of Scotland, and his willingness to discuss the contributions made by the Scottish Congregationalists to overseas mission in the early twentieth century.

[47] *The Principal Acts of the General Assembly of the Free Church of Scotland*, 1901, p. 371.

[48] *The Principal Acts of the General Assembly of the Free Church of Scotland* (Edinburgh: William Nimmo, 1911), pp. 582-83.

[49] *The Principal Acts of the General Assembly of the Free Church of Scotland* (Edinburgh: William Nimmo, 1926), pp. 257-58.

[50] H/96-7, BMS Details of Missionary Staff 1900–1949, cited by Stanley, *Baptist Missionary Society*, p. 383.

[51] Stanley, *Baptist Missionary Society*, p. 383.

India in the wider population, together with the anti-foreigner movement in China in 1927,[52] ensured that BMS staffing levels of missionaries would not attain again the heights of the 1920s.[53] This phenomenon was common amongst the Protestant mission agencies at that time. Scottish Baptists undertook a detailed survey of the overseas workers supported by their churches in 1925. This detailed report published in 1926,[54] which, although incomplete and inaccurate in places, is an invaluable guide to the prominence of overseas evangelistic work amongst this branch of the Scottish Christian family.

This brief survey of a range of Protestant churches in Scotland has shown that both financial giving and the numbers of missionaries engaged in overseas service continued to grow in the first three decades of the twentieth century as had been the case throughout the previous century. Claims that missionary activity declined[55] after the First World War are not sustained by the evidence available from the major Protestant churches in Scotland in the 1920s. The numerical high point may have been reached in this decade, but it would be nearer the middle of the century before a substantial drop in the numbers of serving missionaries was experienced.

Scottish Baptist Commitment to Overseas Mission

After setting the work of Baptist missionaries overseas in its wider context the remainder of this paper will look at the work of Scottish Baptists outside the borders of their own country. At the end of the first quarter of the twentieth century Scottish Baptists were in good heart. In the first official history produced by the Baptist Union of Scotland that appeared in print in 1926, the extent of growth in its ranks was readily apparent. In 1850, it had been noted there were only around 5,500 members of Baptist churches whereas at the time of writing in 1926 it had risen to 22,815. Conscious of the population growth in this era, it was noted that Baptists 'numbered 1 in 460' of the Scottish population in 1850, but now in 1925 it had risen to 1 in 133 of the total.[56] It was clear that innovative and enthusiastic initiatives on the home front were bearing fruit.[57]

But how seriously did Scottish Baptists view evangelistic work outside of their native land? In the nineteenth century Scottish Baptists primarily gave their finances

---

[52] Liu Yi, 'From Christian Aliens to Chinese Citizens: The National Identity of Chinese Christians in the Twentieth Century', *Studies in World Christianity* 16.2 (2010), pp. 147-52.

[53] Stanley, *Baptist Missionary Society*, p. 385.

[54] G. Yuille (ed.), *History of the Baptists in Scotland* (Glasgow: Baptist Union of Scotland Publications Committee, 1926), pp. 290-95.

[55] Contra R.J. Finlay, 'Missions Overseas', in M. Lynch (ed.), *Oxford Companion to Scottish History* (Oxford: Oxford University Press, 2007), pp. 424-25.

[56] A.T. Richardson, 'The Later Advance', in Yuille (ed.), *Baptists in Scotland*, p. 87.

[57] See Brian Talbot, 'First in Jerusalem: Scottish Baptist Home Mission work in Twentieth Century Scotland', in Brian R. Talbot (ed.), *A Distinctive People: A Thematic Study of Aspects of the Witness of Baptists in Scotland in the Twentieth Century* (Milton Keynes: Paternoster, 2014), pp. 203-27.

for missionary work to the BMS, with whom the vast majority of Scottish Baptist overseas missionaries served. However, this situation changed with the formation of a growing number of other mission agencies seeking the support of the wider Christian community, especially during the later decades of the nineteenth century. As a result, by the time of the Baptist Union survey in 1925 looking at the missionaries serving overseas from Scottish Baptist congregations, it was clear that the range of mission agencies and fields of service had multiplied as the twentieth century had progressed. It must be stated at the outset that the results obtained in this paper are provisional due to the incomplete nature of the data. Although Yuille's work is an excellent basis on which to build a more complete picture of Scottish Baptists overseas it soon became obvious that there were significant gaps in the data recorded in that account. The total number of men and women recorded in the 1925 survey came to 207 (actually 215 identified, see above) Scottish Baptists serving overseas from 149 congregations.[58] In preparation of this paper the total number of names identified has risen to 260 individuals. When Marjorie McVicar wrote her 1992 account of Scottish Baptists serving with BMS there were important corrections made to the earlier record.[59] It is possible that the number of BMS affiliated missionaries omitted from the Yuille list may be as high as eighteen Scots, of which eight came from other Scottish denominations and ten from Scottish Baptist causes. However, twenty-nine men and women named by Yuille had completed their service in the twentieth century with BMS before 1925. The tentative number of Scottish Baptists who may have been serving overseas as missionaries in 1925–26 is eighty nine with the BMS and the China Inland Mission (CIM), together with fifty-two named persons retired. Of the remaining 119 individuals it is probable that the majority were in active service at this time and the rest retired from the field. From the certain BMS and CIM data this is equivalent to approximately two missionaries for every three Baptist churches in Scotland. These figures indicate very clearly the strong commitment of Baptists to spreading the good news from Scotland.

Baptist Missionaries Serving with the Baptist Missionary Society

On the basis of the figures given in the previous section there will be an attempt to sketch in broad terms at least some information about these individuals. The largest group identified were associated with the BMS and who had either served in the twentieth century prior to 1925 or were serving overseas in that year. The minimum number on the field in the year of the survey was sixty-one missionaries, with a possibility of up to eight more Scots from other churches in Scotland, whose dates of service with the BMS included that year. In addition, there are forty-three

---

[58] 'Scottish Baptists in the Mission Field', in Yuille (ed.), *Baptists in Scotland*, pp. 290-95. *The Baptist Handbook for 1926* (London: Baptist Union Publications Department, 1926), p. 168.

[59] McVicar, *Great Adventure*, pp. 70-83.

individuals[60] whose service with the BMS was concluded prior to the date of the survey. If their identification as BMS missionaries is correct then 104 of the 260 individuals, forty per cent of the total, was employed in the service of this mission agency. Yuille's list of names can be compared with the official BMS list recorded in *The Baptist Handbook for 1926*.

Missionaries Named by Yuille no longer Overseas with the BMS in 1925

There were thirty BMS missionaries listed by Yuille whose service was complete prior to 1925. Thomas Aitken from Wishaw Baptist Church served in Cape Verde and St Helena with BMS between 1896 and 1902 before engaging in Baptist ministry in South Africa until his retirement in 1935.[61] James Balfour from Westray Baptist Church, Orkney, taught as a tutor in Calabar College, Jamaica, from 1883–99.[62] Charles Brown from Academy Street Baptist Church, Aberdeen, served in Jamaica from 1877, but his length of service is unclear.[63] Dr William Brown from Aberchirder Baptist Church served with BMS in China for four years between 1870 and 1874 until his retirement.[64] George Cameron and his wife from Dennistoun Baptist Church, Glasgow, served in Congo between 1884 and 1915 until they returned home to Scotland to work on a revision of the text of the Congo Bible.[65] Moir Duncan of Adelaide Place Baptist Church, Glasgow, and his wife Jessie from Leslie Baptist Church, Fife, rendered distinguished service with BMS in China, 1887–1902 and 1890–1902 respectively.[66] Rebecca Eekhout from Hillhead Baptist Church, Glasgow, worked in the Zenanas of Agra, India, 1893–1921, until she returned home in retirement.[67] Robert Forsyth from Orangefield Baptist Church, Greenock, joined the BMS team in China in 1884. Annie Maitland from John Street Baptist Church, Glasgow, joined the team there in 1886. They were married serving in the same field until 1911.[68] Edwin and Kate Girling of Duncan Street Baptist

---

[60] Yuille names twenty-nine people, but the omission of Dr Agnes Watson was probably unintended.

[61] See S. Hudson Reed (ed.), *Together for a Century: The History of the Baptist Union of South Africa, 1877–1977* (Pietermaritzburg: South African Baptist Historical Society, 1977), pp. 79, 104.

[62] I.K. Sibley, *The Baptists of Jamaica 1793–1965* (Kingston: Jamaica Baptist Union, 1965), p. 19; McVicar, *Great Adventure*, p. 70.

[63] McVicar, *Great Adventure*, p. 71.

[64] R.F. Moorshead, *'Heal the Sick': The Story of the Medical Mission Auxiliary of the Baptist Missionary Society* (London: The Carey Press, 1929), p. 214. H.R. Williamson, *British Baptists in China* (London: The Carey Kingsgate Press, 1957), p. 363.

[65] J.D. Jamieson, 'Scots in Congo', in James Watson (ed.), *Scotland and the BMS 1792–1942* (London: Carey Press, 1943), pp. 21-22.

[66] 'In Memoriam: Death of Rev. Dr Moir Duncan', *Scottish Baptist Magazine* 32.10 (October, 1906), p. 184. See also Williamson, *British Baptists in China*, pp. 49, 54, 364.

[67] McVicar, *Great Adventure*, p. 73.

[68] Williamson, *British Baptists in China*, p. 343; McVicar, *Great Adventure*, p. 73.

Church, Edinburgh, served in Congo with BMS from 1907 and 1910 respectively until 1922.[69] John Hartley from Marshall Street Baptist Church, Edinburgh, served for one year, 1883-1884, until his death in Congo.[70] Mrs George Harvey from Gilcomston Park Baptist Church, Aberdeen, had served in Congo with BMS but was no longer serving with BMS in 1925.[71] Robert Kirkland from Dunoon Baptist Church served with BMS in China in 1889. He had ceased service there before 1925.[72] Yuille lists two William Milnes serving in India with their wives from the same date. It is possible that the couple reputedly from St Andrews Baptist Church is a duplicate of the couple from Bristo Baptist Church in Edinburgh, as no other information has been found about them.[73] Mr and Mrs William McCurrach from Crown Terrace Baptist Church, Aberdeen, served with BMS in China between 1896 and 1900. They were martyred for their faith in the 1900 Boxer uprising.[74] Mr and Mrs Peter Noble from Gilcomston Park, Aberdeen, served in Dacca, India, from 1903 and 1905 respectively, but were no longer in post in 1925.[75] Frank Oldrieve from Morningside Baptist Church, Edinburgh, served in Congo in 1905, according to Yuille, though McVicar placed him in India that year.[76] Joseph Rogers from Leslie Baptist Church served in Congo with BMS from 1888 until his death in 1901.[77] Dr Margaret Stott from Maxwelltown Baptist Church, Dundee, served in Berhampore, India, from 1908 to 1911.[78] Donald Smith from Adelaide Place Baptist Church, Glasgow, served in China with BMS from 1903 to his death in 1922. Yuille did indicate he had died prior to 1925.[79] W.S Thomson from Bristo Baptist Church, Edinburgh, served in Ceylon from 1893-95.[80] Drs James and Agnes Watson from Wishaw Baptist Church served in China from 1884 to 1923. Yuille omitted Agnes from his list.[81] Helena Watt, originally from a Churches of Christ congregation in Glasgow, served in China from 1908-13, at which time she married Dr Thomas

---

[69] McVicar, *Great Adventure*, p. 74.

[70] McVicar, *Great Adventure*, p. 75.

[71] McVicar, *Great Adventure*, p. 75.

[72] Only Yuille, 'Scottish Baptists in the Mission Field', p. 292, has a reference to his service.

[73] There is no mention in I.G. Docherty, *'Something Very Fine': A History of St Andrews Baptist Church 1841-1991* (St Andrews: St Andrews Baptist Church, 1991). However, there are only occasional references to missionaries in the book so confirmation of the above assumption is still awaited.

[74] Watson, 'Scots in China', p. 29; McVicar, *Great Adventure*, p. 77.

[75] McVicar, *Great Adventure*, p. 79.

[76] Yuille, 'Scottish Baptists in the Mission Field', p. 293. McVicar, *Great Adventure*, p. 15. It is unclear on what basis he is placed in either of these locations.

[77] McVicar, *Great Adventure*, p. 80.

[78] McVicar, *Great Adventure*, p. 81.

[79] Williamson, *British Baptists in China*, pp. 85, 114, 150; Yuille, 'Scottish Baptists in the Mission Field', p. 295; McVicar, *Great Adventure*, p. 81.

[80] McVicar, *Great Adventure*, p. 82.

[81] Yuille, 'Scottish Baptists in the Mission Field', p. 295; Williamson, *British Baptists in China*, pp. 47, 78, 100-101, 242; Stanley, *Baptist Missionary Society*, pp. 235-36, 238.

Scollay, sent out from St Andrews Baptist Church in 1911 to China. She returned home to Scotland after his death in China in 1918.[82] Ann Wilson from Duncan Street Baptist Church, Edinburgh, served in Bolobo, Congo, for a time from 1913 before settling in England at an unknown date prior to 1925.[83] Greta Wylie from the Marshall Street Baptist Church, Edinburgh, served with the Baptist Zenana Mission in Bombay, India, for some years from 1916.[84]

Although outside the dates of this enquiry, because he added so many individuals who had served prior to 1925, Yuille might also have included the following thirteen individuals whose term of service took place in the twentieth century. G.C. Claridge and his wife Helen from Leith Baptist Church, Edinburgh, served in the Congo from 1909 and 1907 respectively until 1920.[85] Also, Dr G.K. Edwards and his wife Ethel who served in China from 1915 until his death in 1919; Ethel, a former member of St Paul's Episcopal Church, York Place, Edinburgh, returned to Scotland in 1919.[86] John Ewing from Ward Road Baptist Church, Dundee, served in Ceylon in 1902.[87] Nellie Joseph, whose home church is not identified by McVicar, served in India between 1906 and 1916.[88] Elizabeth Little from High Blantyre Baptist Church served in India for two years from 1921 to 1923.[89] Ella Lockhart, from an unidentified Edinburgh Baptist Church served in India between 1908 and 1911 as the Finance Secretary for the Zenana Mission in Calcutta.[90] Mrs Ella McLeod was a BMS Zenana missionary in Gaya, India, between 1890 and 1915.[91] William Miller from Perth Baptist Church served in India from 1900–20.[92] Dr Mary Raw, whose home church is unidentified, served in India between 1904 and 1919.[93] Dr Andrew and Charlotte Young from Marshall Street Baptist Church, Edinburgh, served in China from 1905 and 1907 respectively; Charlotte returned home to Scotland when Andrew died in service in 1923.[94]

Missionaries Named by Yuille Serving Overseas with the BMS in 1925

There were forty-nine Scottish Baptists – including three spouses from outside Scotland married on the field and two Scottish spouses omitted by Yuille – in active service overseas counted by Yuille at the time of his survey. Catherine Birrell from

---

[82] McVicar, *Great Adventure*, pp. 80, 82; Williamson, *British Baptists in China*, p. 368.
[83] 'BMS List of Missionaries', *Baptist Handbook for 1926*, p. 298.
[84] Yuille, 'Scottish Baptists in the Mission Field', p. 295.
[85] McVicar, *Great Adventure*, p. 72.
[86] Williamson, *British Baptists in China*, p. 368; McVicar, *Great Adventure*, p. 73.
[87] McVicar, *Great Adventure*, p. 73.
[88] McVicar, *Great Adventure*, p. 75.
[89] McVicar, *Great Adventure*, p. 76.
[90] McVicar, *Great Adventure*, pp. 15, 76.
[91] McVicar, *Great Adventure*, pp. 14, 77.
[92] McVicar, *Great Adventure*, p. 78.
[93] McVicar, *Great Adventure*, p. 79.
[94] Williamson, *British Baptists in China*, p. 366; McVicar, *Great Adventure*, p. 83.

Viewfield Baptist Church, Dunfermline, served first in Congo from 1918 to 1923, then from 1924 to 1950 in the English Baptist Mission at Sianfu, Shensi, in northern China. She married Keith Bryan in 1929 serving with him in the same field until retirement in 1950.[95] Dr Stanley Bethel from Duncan Street Baptist Church, Edinburgh, served from 1915 to 1936 primarily at Chou-Ts'un, the chief medical centre for BMS in Shantung, China.[96] Dr Mary Bisset from Gilcomston Park Baptist Church, Aberdeen, served in Bhiwani, Punjab, India, from 1905 to 1938.[97] James and Elizabeth Clark from Wishaw Baptist Church served in Congo from 1911 and 1914 respectively until 1947.[98] May Collins from Orangefield Baptist Church, Greenock, spent three years between 1923 and 1926 in Barisal (now in Bangladesh) and Calcutta in India.[99] Mrs Mary Cowley served first of all in India between 1909 and 1922, then in Trinidad from 1922 to 1926.[100] William Eadie and his wife Annie from Motherwell Baptist Church worked in Calcutta between 1921 and 1959. Annie served in an administrative capacity for the BMS for the last seven years of this posting.[101] Elizabeth Fergusson from Orangefield Baptist Church, Greenock, served from 1903 to 1908 in Calcutta and then 1918 to 1926 in Dacca, East Bengal, India.[102] Dr William Fleming who came from Duncan Street Baptist Church, Edinburgh, with his wife Euphemia (omitted by Yuille) who came from Hopetown Mission Hall, served in China from 1910 and 1913 respectively until 1926.[103] Margaret Gardiner from the West Baptist Church, Perth, served in India at the time of Yuille's survey, despite the fact he states that she was appointed to her sphere of service only in 1926.[104] Alfred and Edith Glenesk from Union Grove Baptist Church, Aberdeen, served in Bolobo, Congo from 1921 and 1930 respectively until his death in 1946.[105] Mary (May) Gordon from the West Baptist Church, Perth, worked in Berhampur, in the district of Ganjam, Orissa, India, between 1925 and 1947.[106] Dr

---

[95] Williamson, *British Baptists in China*, pp. 170, 370; McVicar, *Great Adventure*, p.71, incorrectly dates the conclusion of her service as 1929.

[96] Moorshead, *'Heal the Sick'*, p. 223. Williamson, *British Baptists in China*, pp. 101, 140.

[97] 'BMS List of Missionaries', *Baptist Handbook for 1926*, p. 288; McVicar, *Great Adventure*, p. 71.

[98] McVicar, *Great Adventure*, p. 72.

[99] McVicar, *Great Adventure*, p. 72.

[100] Yuille, 'Scottish Baptists on the Mission Field', in Yuille (ed.), *Baptists in Scotland*, p. 291; McVicar, *Great Adventure*, p. 73.

[101] McVicar, *Great Adventure*, p. 73.

[102] Yuille, 'Scottish Baptists on the Mission Field', p. 291; McVicar, *Great Adventure*, p. 73.

[103] Williamson, *British Baptists in China*, pp. 247, 367; McVicar, *Great Adventure*, p. 73, dated their resignation from service with BMS too early in 1924.

[104] Yuille, 'Scottish Baptists on the Mission Field', p. 292; McVicar, *Great Adventure*, p. 74.

[105] McVicar, *Great Adventure*, p. 74.

[106] 'BMS List of Missionaries', *Baptist Handbook for 1926*, p. 291. McVicar, *Great Adventure*, p. 74.

Helen (Ella) Gregory from Marshall Street Baptist Church, Edinburgh, worked in Berhampur from 1923, but her length of service there is unknown. She died in 1947.[107] Marion Hasler from Springburn Baptist Church, Glasgow, served with her husband John, an English Baptist, in Bayneston in the Simla district of Punjab, India, from 1908–35. She worked both as a nurse and a Zenana missionary.[108] Peter and Olive Horsburgh from Stirling Baptist Church served from 1907 and 1910 respectively until 1928, in Sambalpur, Orissa, in India.[109] John Jardine from Dumfries Baptist Church had originally gone to India to work with the Regions Beyond Missionary Union (RBMU)[110] in 1907, but transferred to the BMS in 1924, serving between 1924 and 1930, and then 1937 to 1948 in Palwal, South Punjab.[111] Drs Gordon and Mary King from West Baptist Church, Perth, served in Taiyuanfu, Shansi, north China, between 1927 and 1924 respectively until 1940.[112] Agnes Kirkland from Dunoon Baptist Church served in Ch'ing-Chou-Fu, China, from 1893 until her retirement in 1927. She was one of four single ladies assigned to work amongst women and girls, after the BMS accepted that single women could serve under its auspices overseas.[113] Robert and Margaret Kirkland from Bristo Baptist Church, Edinburgh, served from 1893 and 1897 respectively until 1926 in Leopoldville-Est in the Belgian Congo.[114] David and Helen Kyles from St Andrews Baptist Church served at the Baptist Mission Press in Calcutta, India, from 1925–31.[115] Margaret Logan from John Street Baptist Church, Glasgow, served as a nurse in hospitals in Chi-Nan-Fu, where she was responsible for the establishment and

---

[107] McVicar, *Great Adventure*, p. 74.

[108] 'BMS List of Missionaries', *Baptist Handbook for 1926*, p. 292; McVicar, *Great Adventure*, pp. 15, 75.

[109] 'BMS List of Missionaries', *Baptist Handbook for 1926*, p. 292; McVicar, *Great Adventure*, p. 75.

[110] RBMU was founded by Henry Grattan Guinness and his wife Fanny in 1873. It was one of the large number of Faith Missions established in the nineteenth century. It merged with the Evangelical Union of South America (EUSA) in 1991 to form a new body, Latin Link. See Klaus Fiedler, *The Story of the Faith Missions* (Oxford: Regnum Books, 1994), pp. 34-40.

[111] McVicar, *Great Adventure*, p. 75; 'BMS List of Missionaries', *Baptist Handbook for 1926*, p. 293.

[112] McVicar, *Great Adventure*, pp. 73, 76; Williamson, *British Baptists in China*, p. 370. These dates follow Williamson's standard work on missionaries serving in China, rather than McVicar's starting dates of 1925 and 1923 respectively. His work was highly praised in G.H. Choa, *'Heal the Sick' was their motto: The Protestant Medical Missionaries in China* (Hong Kong: The Chinese University Press, 1990), pp. 171-88.

[113] Williamson, *British Baptists in China*, pp. 48, 77, 364; McVicar, *Great Adventure*, p. 76; Yuille, 'Scottish Baptists on the Mission Field', p. 292, is mistaken both in the place and dates of Agnes Kirkland's service with BMS.

[114] 'BMS List of Missionaries', *Baptist Handbook for 1926*, p. 293; McVicar, *Great Adventure*, p. 76.

[115] McVicar, *Great Adventure*, p. 76; 'BMS List of Missionaries', *Baptist Handbook for 1926*, p. 293.

development of the Nursing Training School, and Chou-Ts'un in China from 1909 until her retirement in 1940.[116] Andrew and Emmie MacBeath from Charlotte Baptist Chapel, Edinburgh, served in Bolobo, Congo, from 1924 and 1929 respectively until 1941.[117] William and Jeannie Milne from Bristo Baptist Church, Edinburgh, served in Jessore, Bengal, India, from 1896 and 1899 respectively until 1927.[118] Christina Manson from Queen's Park Baptist Church, Glasgow, served in Calcutta and Rhangamati, East Bengal, India from 1923 to 1963.[119] Dr William and Glendoline Matthewson (Gwendolene was omitted from Yuille's list) from Viewfield Baptist Church Dunfermline, served in India from 1921 until their resignation from service in 1925.[120] Nellie Petrie from Viewfield Baptist Church, Dunfermline, also served at Bolobo in Congo from 1922 to 1947.[121] Isabel Rodger from Kilmarnock Baptist Church (who later married the Rev. F. Jarvis) served for ten years in India from 1926 to 1936.[122] Ann Rogers from Charlotte Baptist Chapel, Edinburgh, served as a nurse in China from 1920 to 1928.[123] Dr Ruth Tait from Gorgie Baptist Church, Edinburgh, served at the English Baptist Mission in Sianfu, Shensi, China, between 1923 and her retirement in 1950.[124] Christina Smith from Rothesay Baptist Church served in China from 1910 to 1923 before returning home due to her husband Donald's illness and then death that year, before being appointed to the mission station at Tsingchowfu, Shantung, under the auspices of the Women's Missionary Auxiliary between 1924 and 1947.[125] Catherine Walker from Hillhead Baptist Church, Glasgow, went to Agra, Uttar Pradesh, India, under the auspices of the Women's Missionary Auxiliary of the BMS from 1921–26.[126] William Wallace from Hamilton Baptist Church, after training at Spurgeon's Baptist College, London, went

---

[116] Williamson, *British Baptists in China*, pp. 140, 157, 247, 367; 'BMS List of Missionaries', *Baptist Handbook for 1926*, p. 293.

[117] Yuille, 'Scottish Baptists on the Mission Field', p. 293; McVicar, *Great Adventure*, p. 76.

[118] McVicar, *Great Adventure*, p. 78; 'BMS List of Missionaries', *Baptist Handbook for 1926*, p. 294.

[119] McVicar, *Great Adventure*, p. 77; 'BMS List of Missionaries', *Baptist Handbook for 1926*, p. 294. Yuille, 'Scottish Baptists on the Mission Field', p. 293, mistakenly calls her 'Chrissie Mansen' and lists her home church as 'Partick Baptist Church'.

[120] Moorshead, *'Heal the Sick'*, p. 213; McVicar, *Great Adventure*, p. 78.

[121] McVicar, *Great Adventure*, p. 79.

[122] McVicar, *Great Adventure*, p. 80.

[123] Williamson, *British Baptists in China*, p. 369; McVicar, *Great Adventure*, p. 80. Yuille, 'Scottish Baptists on the Mission Field', p. 294, mistakenly calls her 'Rodgers'.

[124] Moorshead, *'Heal the Sick'*, p. 215; Williamson, *British Baptists in China*, p. 369; 'BMS List of Missionaries', *Baptist Handbook for 1926*, p. 297.

[125] McVicar, *Great Adventure*, p. 81; 'BMS List of Missionaries', *Baptist Handbook for 1926*, p. 296.

[126] McVicar, *Great Adventure*, p. 82; Yuille, 'Scottish Baptists on the Mission Field', p. 295, mistakenly records her commencement of service as 1911 rather than 1921.

to Wathen, Thysville, in the Belgian Congo in 1921 serving until 1925.[127] Joan Williamson from South Leith Baptist Church, Edinburgh, served in Sianfu, Shensi in China from 1923 to 1951.[128] Dr William and Jean Wilson from High Blantyre Baptist Church served from 1923 to 1933 in Matadi in the Belgian Congo.[129]

Missionaries Serving Overseas with BMS in 1925 Omitted by Yuille

Dr Jean Benzie from Fraserburgh Baptist Church served in India between 1924 and 1951.[130] Mary Collect from Dublin Street Baptist Church, Edinburgh, served in India between 1920 and 1950.[131] Alex Macandrew from Gilcomston Park Baptist Church, Edinburgh, also served for a long time in Agra, Delhi, India, between 1925 and 1948.[132] Angus McNaughton from Charlotte Baptist Chapel, Edinburgh, served first in Congo and then in Jamaica between 1922 and 1933.[133] Alex Mill from the Kelvinside Baptist Church, Glasgow, served in Congo from 1911 to 1947.[134] Dr Thomas Paterson from Dublin Street Baptist Church, Edinburgh, served in China between 1892 and 1928. He was accompanied by his first wife, the former Miss Leet, between 1899 and her death in 1912, together with his second wife Annie from 1913 until their retirement in 1928.[135] George and Leonora Young, who were later associated with Adelaide Place Baptist Church, Glasgow, served in China from 1924 and 1923 respectively until their retirement in 1952.[136] Dr Laurence Ingle, an English Baptist, and his wife Agnes, from Largs, served from 1919 and 1921 respectively until their resignations from the BMS in 1940. It is probable that Yuille omitted them due to a link with a home church in England rather than Scotland. Agnes may have had a different church background in Largs as there was no Baptist

---

[127] 'BMS List of Missionaries', *Baptist Handbook for 1926*, p. 297; McVicar, *Great Adventure*, p. 82.

[128] McVicar, *Great Adventure*, p. 82; 'BMS List of Missionaries', *Baptist Handbook for 1926*, p. 298.

[129] McVicar, *Great Adventure*, p. 82; 'BMS List of Missionaries', *Baptist Handbook for 1926*, p. 298.

[130] McVicar, *Great Adventure*, p. 70; Moorshead, *'Heal the Sick'*, p. 213.

[131] McVicar, *Great Adventure*, p. 72.

[132] McVicar, *Great Adventure*, pp. 16, 77.

[133] McVicar, *Great Adventure*, p. 77.

[134] McVicar, *great Adventure*, p. 78.

[135] Williamson, *British Baptists in China*, pp. 47, 101, 140, 242, 364; Moorshead, *'Heal the Sick'*, p. 214.

[136] Williamson, *British Baptists in China*, pp. 170, 236, 261, 370; see also G.A. Young, *The Living Christ in Modern China* (London: Carey Press, 1947); and G.A. Young, *The Fish or The Dragon* (Glasgow: G.A. Young. 1985). George Young was originally from Osset Baptist Church in Yorkshire and trained at Rawdon Baptist College prior to service in China. This is the probable reason for his omission by Yuille. I am grateful to the Rev. Tony Peck for providing this information in November 2014.

cause there at that time.[137] There were also seven Scottish missionaries from other denominations serving under the auspices of the BMS that Yuille omitted as he specified that his list only included missionaries from Baptist congregations in Scotland. Hannah Beale, originally a member of Springburn United Free Church of Scotland, Glasgow, served with her husband Frederick in Congo between 1909 and 1926, before settling in England.[138] Adam and Marion Black from Dundas Street Congregational Church, Glasgow, served as associate missionaries with the BMS in China between 1923 and 1951.[139] Mrs Margaret Savidge from Gartley United Free Church, Aberdeenshire, served in India between 1904 and 1925.[140] John Shields from Rutherglen United Free Church served in China between 1908 and 1931.[141] Dr Fred Thomas from Morningside Congregational Church, Edinburgh, served in India between 1894 and 1926.[142] Dr Ruth Young, from a Church of Scotland congregation in Broughty Ferry, Dundee, served in India with her husband C.B. Young from 1917 to 1940.[143] In total, eighteen individuals serving with the BMS fit into this category.

Baptist Missionaries Serving with the China Inland Mission

Baptist Missionaries Listed by Yuille and Confirmed as CIM Workers

The second largest group of Scottish Baptists served overseas with the China Inland Mission (CIM). It was this overseas agency that perhaps more than any other organisation was in the vanguard of the growing international network of conservative evangelicalism in the twentieth century.[144] Scottish Protestants were enthusiastic about the work of CIM from its launch when Hudson Taylor took his original party of eighteen people to China, including at least four Scots in their ranks. In the years that followed, with reference to CIM missionaries from Scotland,

---

[137] McVicar, *Great Adventure*, p. 75; Williamson, *British Baptists in China*, p. 368; Moorhead, *'Heal the Sick'*, p. 215. Yuille (ed.), *History of the Baptists*, p. 285; D.W. Bebbington (ed.), *The Baptists in Scotland: A History* (Glasgow: Baptist Union of Scotland, 1988), p. 141.

[138] 'BMS List of Missionaries', *Baptist Handbook for 1926*, p. 288; McVicar, *Great Adventure*, p. 70.

[139] McVicar, *Great Adventure*, p. 71; Williamson, *British Baptists in China*, p. 369.

[140] McVicar, *Great Adventure*, p. 80.

[141] McVicar, *Great Adventure*, p. 81.

[142] McVicar, *Great Adventure*, p. 82.

[143] McVicar, *Great Adventure*, p. 83.

[144] B. Stanley, 'Foreword', in A. Austin, *China's Millions: The China Inland Mission and Late Qing Society, 1832–1905* (Grand Rapids, MI: Eerdmans, 2007), p. xiv. It was the largest of the faith missions, the model for many other smaller ones and comprised one third of all Protestant missionaries in China by the 1930s. A. Austin, 'Only Connect: The China Inland Mission and Transatlantic Evangelicalism', in Wilbert R. Shenk (ed.), *North American Foreign Missions, 1810–1914* (Grand Rapids, MI: Eerdmans, 2004), p. 282.

it has been acknowledged that 'Scotland has always punched above its weight on the mission field.'[145]

Baptist Missionaries who Completed Service with CIM prior to 1925

There were at least seven named missionaries (nine if spouses whose background is unclear are included) whose details are found in the CIM archive who fall into this category. George Bowman from Pittenweem Baptist Church in Fife, worked with CIM in China between 1911 and 1914 when he died by drowning. John Craig from Wishaw Baptist Church worked with CIM in China between 1899 and 1904. Alan Dorward from Victoria Street Baptist Church, Galashiels, served with CIM there between 1878 and 1888. George Duncan, who married Catherine Brown while serving with CIM, was a member of the original party on the Lammermoor who went to China with Hudson Taylor. He served there from 1866 to 1873 when he died after contracting tuberculosis. Dugald Lawson and his wife Jeannie from Orangefield Baptist Church, Greenock, first served with CIM from 1887 to 1916 before returning to Scotland. After Dugald's death, Jeannie returned to China in the 1930s to work with Gladys Aylward. Ina Ross from Kelso Baptist Church married Dr John Anderson serving with CIM from 1893–1921.[146]

CIM Missionaries who were still in Service when Yuille's Report was Written

There were at least eighteen named CIM workers in active service at the time of Yuille's report. Jeannie Lawson counted above returned to the field after her husband's death. If spouses married on the field are added to the total this figure increases by a minimum of three more individuals, making a total of twenty-one. Bolster Maida from Charlotte Baptist Chapel, Edinburgh, served in more than one location with CIM. She married fellow worker Paul Contento during that time. Her date of acceptance by CIM must have been in place at the time of Yuille's survey as he lists her in his work published in 1926, though CIM records show her with them in China from 1927–50, when all missionaries had to leave the country, then elsewhere till retirement in 1982. Miss E. Dovey, from Charlotte Baptist Chapel, Edinburgh, married fellow-missionary George Mackenzie, serving with CIM from 1913 to 1925. Lily (Elizabeth) Fischbacher served with CIM between 1922 and 1935.[147] G.W. Gibb and his wife Margaret from Gilcolmston Park Baptist Church,

---

[145] This quotation is from Marion Osgood, archivist of CIM/Overseas Missionary Fellowship, email dated 9 April 2014. I am grateful to her for assistance in consulting the mission's archives regarding potential Scottish Baptist missionaries serving under CIM's auspices in China. Rather than repeated references in the notes all the names confirmed as CIM workers have had their files checked in the CIM archive in the United Kingdom which is the source for information about them unless otherwise stated.

[146] Yuille, 'Scottish Baptists in the Mission Field', p. 294.

[147] Yuille misspells her name as 'Fischbacker'.

Aberdeen, served in Shanghai with CIM from 1894 to 1940.[148] Jeannie Lawson who we have already noted (see the previous section). Alex Mair from Queen's Park Baptist Church, Glasgow, with his wife Janet served with CIM from 1907–53.[149] Robert Porteous from Hawick Baptist Church and his wife Emma served with CIM from 1904–49.[150] Douglas Robertson and his wife from Charlotte Baptist Chapel, Edinburgh, served with CIM from 1919–52, most of that time in China.[151] Annie Sharp from Hillhead Baptist Church, Glasgow, served from 1907 to 1945. James Stark[152] from Kirkintilloch Baptist Church, who married Christabel Williams during his time in China, served from 1889 to 1939. Alex Wilson from Anstruther Baptist Church was with CIM in China from 1897 to 1933. Hamlet George Thompson, originally from Dublin, was sent out by Hillhead Baptist Church with CIM in 1904, but the length of his service is unclear.[153] David Urquhart served from 1900 to 1928. His wife Mary worked with him for at least twenty-one of those years in China.[154]

Baptist Missionaries Listed by Yuille as CIM Agents but not Confirmed by CIM Records

There are also five people working in China that Yuille thought worked with CIM for whom no records are found in the CIM archives. Mrs Elmslie from Victoria Place Baptist Church, Paisley, was recorded by Yuille as serving with CIM in China in 1896,[155] but CIM has no record of her in their archive. Yuille also lists William Elmslie and his wife from Gilcomston Park Baptist Church, Aberdeen, as serving in China with CIM, but has no further information.[156] Mrs Harrobin also from Gilcolmston Park Baptist Church, Aberdeen, was listed by Yuille as serving with CIM, but they have no records of her.[157] Grace Oldfield from Charlotte Baptist Chapel, Edinburgh, was understood by Yuille to be working with CIM in China, but no traces of her have been located in the CIM archives.[158]

---

[148] Yuille, 'Scottish Baptists in the Mission Field', p. 292.

[149] Yuille, 'Scottish Baptists in the Mission Field', p. 293. Yuille has no record of Janet Mair.

[150] Yuille, 'Scottish Baptists in the Mission Field', p. 293. Yuille has no record of Emma Porteous.

[151] Yuille, 'Scottish Baptists in the Mission Field', p. 294.

[152] Yuille, 'Scottish Baptists in the Mission Field', p. 294, mistakenly lists him as Joseph Stark.

[153] Yuille, 'Scottish Baptists in the Mission Field', p. 295.

[154] Yuille, 'Scottish Baptists in the Mission Field', p. 295.

[155] Yuille, 'Scottish Baptists in the Mission Field', p. 291.

[156] Yuille, 'Scottish Baptists in the Mission Field', p. 291.

[157] Yuille, 'Scottish Baptists in the Mission Field', p. 292.

[158] Yuille, 'Scottish Baptists in the Mission Field', p. 293.

Baptist Missionaries Serving with Other Identified Agencies

Only the BMS and CIM had substantial numbers of Scottish Baptist missionaries serving in their ranks in the period under discussion. The only other mission agency with more than two or three identified workers was the Heart of Africa Mission, later called Worldwide Evangelisation Crusade (WEC) with seven named individuals. Therefore, the other workers with identified societies will be collated in this category. In total there were fifty-four missionaries identified who went overseas with recognised Protestant missionary societies.

Fanny Allan from Viewfield Baptist Church, Dunfermline, went out to Wemba in Congo with the Heart of Africa Mission in 1924.[159] Jack Arnott from South Leith Baptist Church, Edinburgh, was appointed by the South American Missionary Society to serve in Argentina.[160] Elizabeth Baird (later Mrs E. Dick) from Bristo Place Baptist Church, Edinburgh, went to Brazil in 1886 with Brazil Mission.[161] Thomas D. Begg from Gilcomston Park Baptist Church, Aberdeen, served in Shanghai as an agent of the British and Foreign Bible Society (B&FBS), but his dates of service are not known.[162] John Bendalow from Gilcomston Park, Aberdeen, was appointed to serve as an evangelist with the Baptist Home Missionary Society in Canada. Annie Braid (later Mrs A. Fanston) from Bristo Place Baptist Church, Edinburgh, went to Brazil in 1888 to work with the Brazil Mission, presumably in connection with Elizabeth Baird who had gone to Brazil two years earlier from the same home church, through the same small mission agency. Robert Burnet from Bristo Baptist Church, Edinburgh, also worked in China on behalf of the B&FBS in 1878.[163] Grace Chalmers from Charlotte Baptist Chapel, Edinburgh, went to serve in Jerusalem under the auspices of the New York based mission of the Christian and Missionary Alliance denomination, USA. Unfortunately no other information is given as to how these connections came about or what she did in Jerusalem. Thomas Chisholm from Kilmarnock Baptist Church went to work at Angoniland, Northern Rhodesia, through the Baptist Industrial Mission in 1896.[164] Ena Clark from Gilcolmston Park Baptist Church, Aberdeen, went to Lima, Peru, with the

---

[159] Yuille, 'Scottish Baptists in the Mission Field', p. 290. All references in this section are to Yuille's list of missionaries unless otherwise specified.

[160] The South American Missionary South gained this name in 1864, but was founded as the Patagonia Missionary Society in 1844. The name change arose due to work commencing in Bolivia, Paraguay, and Argentina. This Anglican agency became an integral part of the CMS in 2010. See www.cms-uk.org/whoweare/history, accessed 30 September 2014.

[161] I have been unable to trace any information about this mission agency.

[162] Yuille, 'Scottish Baptists in the Mission Field', p. 290.

[163] Yuille, 'Scottish Baptists in the Mission Field', p. 290.

[164] The Baptist Industrial Mission was founded in Glasgow in 1895 to provide a field of service for 'consecrated young men of the artisan class' to spread the gospel in British East Central Africa 'on a self-supporting and self-extending basis', Yuille (ed.), *Baptists in Scotland*, p. 267. The work was handed over to the Churches of Christ around 1930. See also Ernest Gray, *A Short History of the Baptist Industrial Mission of Scotland in Nyassaland, 1895–1930* (n.pl.: Churches of Christ Historical Society, 1987).

Evangelical Union of South America (EUSA).[165] Marjory Coutts, a nurse from Charlotte Baptist Chapel, Edinburgh, went to Livingstonia in Africa with the mission agency of the United Free Church of Scotland. Janet Cuthbertson from Dalkeith Baptist Church was working in China with an American Mission Board; possibly she transferred to that agency after marrying an American missionary.[166] Herbert Dickson from Port Glasgow Baptist Church was placed in West Africa in 1922 by the Iboe Mission.[167] Dr Ian Dovey from Charlotte Baptist Chapel Edinburgh, served in Shanghai with the LMS, but no other information has been found.[168] Dr and Mrs T. Draper from Charlotte Chapel served with a Brethren Mission at Anand in India.[169] Thomas Drever from Westray Baptist Church, Orkney, went to Africa with the Baptist Industrial Mission, but no further information is available. Sarah Ellis from Gilcolmston Park Baptist Church, Aberdeen, went to North Africa with the South[ern] Morocco Mission (SMM).[170] Lilias Fison from Charlotte Chapel also went to North Africa with the mission of that name at an unspecified date. Lydie Garrioch from Charlotte Chapel went to work in the Kenya Colony under the auspices of the mission of the Church of Scotland. Laura Gray from Charlotte Chapel was seconded by the North Africa Mission to work at Pandharphur in India, but no explanation was given. Bessie Hamilton from Charlotte Chapel went to North Africa with the SMM. Esther Hamilton from Partick Baptist Church, Glasgow, likewise went at an unspecified time to Sudan, in her case serving with another small

---

[165] EUSA was formed in 1911 by the Regions Beyond Missionary Union (founded in 1894) and the South American Evangelical Mission (founded in 1895), in response to the Edinburgh 1910 World Mission Conference, RBMU passing responsibility for its South American work to EUSA and continuing its own work elsewhere. EUSA worked in Argentina and Peru. In June 1991 EUSA merged with Peru operations of RBMU to form a new interdenominational mission agency, Latin Link. www.mundus.ac.uk/cats/3/1229.htm, accessed 30 September 2014.

[166] Yuille, 'Scottish Baptists in the Mission Field', p. 291.

[167] No mission with this name has been located. Most probably it should be the Qua Iboe Mission, founded by Samuel Bill, its first missionary whose work began in 1887 at the mouth of the Qua Iboe River. The mission council to support him was set up in Belfast in 1891. Its name changed in 1986 to the Qua Iboe Fellowship and then to Mission Africa in 2002 due to the wider scope of its work which now extends to Burkina Faso, Chad, and Kenya. See Eva Stuart Watt, *The Quest of Souls in Qua Iboe* (Edinburgh: Marshall, Morgan and Scott, 1951).

[168] Yuille, 'Scottish Baptists in the Mission Field', p. 291.

[169] Their dates of service are unclear, but they were in India at least until 1928. W.T Stunt *et al.* (eds), *Turning the World Upside Down: A Century of Missionary Endeavour* (Eastbourne: Upperton Press, 1972), Appendix IV, p. 611.

[170] The Southern Morocco Mission was founded by John Anderson in 1888. Fielder, *Story of the Faith Missions*, pp. 37-38, 58 n. 24, and 136. It merged with the North Africa Mission (NAM) in the 1960s, before two other bodies joined with them to form Arab World Ministries (AWM) in 1987. In January 2011 AWM joined the Pioneers mission network and are now known as AWM Pioneers. See www.awm-pioneers.org/new/our-story/, accessed 30 September 2014. See also Francis R. Steele, *Not in Vain: The Story of the North Africa Mission* (Pasadena, CA: William Carey Library, 1981).

faith mission, the Sudan Interior Mission.[171] Mrs Mary Harrison from Charlotte Chapel was placed in Central Africa with the Heart of Africa Mission, but no additional information was provided. Elsie Henry from Gilcolmston Park Baptist Church, Aberdeen, was described as serving in Palestine with a Jewish Mission.[172] Susan Henderson (later Mrs Dickson) from Wishaw Baptist Church was sent to Jamaica in 1912 with the Anglican Church Missionary Society. Dr Enid Hern from Charlotte Baptist Chapel went to Egypt with the Egypt General Mission.[173] George Kerrigan from Queen's Park Baptist Church, Glasgow, went to Africa with the Heart of Africa Mission, as did Mr and Mrs McIntyre from Dennistoun Baptist Church, Glasgow. The former Miss McPhail (later Mrs Myres) from Gilcolmston Park Baptist Church, Aberdeen, served in Shanghai with an American Presbyterian Mission; again it is possible she married an American missionary on the field.[174] Robert Milne from Gilcolmston Park Baptist Church, Aberdeen, went to Congo with the American Baptist Foreign Missionary Union, the mission agency of the Northern American Baptist Convention (USA), now known as the American Baptist International Ministries. James Moon from Bristo Place Baptist Church, Edinburgh, went to the Belgian Congo with one of the newly founded faith missions, the Congo-Balolo Mission. This mission changed its name to Regions Beyond Missionary Union (RBMU) in 1900.[175] Mrs Mary Newbury went to Congo also with the

---

[171] The Sudan Interior Mission began in 1893 by two Canadian and one American missionary 'to reach the sixty million people of the Sudan'. In the 1980s two other mission agencies joined them to form the 'Society for International Ministries'. In 2000 it was rebranded 'Serving in Mission' but retaining the initials SIM. See www.sim.co.uk/about-us/history, accessed 30 September 2014.

[172] Although no details are given it is most likely that she served with the Free Church of Scotland Jewish Mission because the agents of the Church of Scotland Jewish Mission joined the new body at the Disruption in 1843; and the Free Church had workers in Palestine from the 1880s. Michael Marten, *Attempting to Bring the Gospel Home: Scottish Missions to Palestine, 1839–1917* (London: Taurus Academic Studies, 2006), pp. 35, 39, 63-81. David McDougall, *In Search of Israel: A Chronicle of the Jewish Missions of the Church of Scotland* (London: Thomas Nelson and Sons, 1941), pp. 55-56, 86-90.

[173] The first members of the interdenominational Egypt Mission Band sailed from Liverpool in 1897. The first station was opened at Bilbeis, in the East Delta, in January 1900. In 1903 the name Egypt General Mission was adopted. By 1908 there were seven stations comprising girls' and boys' schools, dispensaries and book depots. Information obtained from www.dvdl.library.yale.edu/missionperiodicals/, accessed 30 September 2014

[174] Yuille, 'Scottish Baptists in the Mission Field', p. 293.

[175] The Congo-Balobo Mission was founded by Harry Guinness in 1889 to expand mission work in the interior of Congo beyond the places where the American Baptist Missionary Union had established a witness. C.W. Mackintosh, *Dr Harry Guinness* (London: The Regions Beyond Missionary Union, 1916), p. 37. This mission changed its name to the Regions Beyond Missionary Union (RBMU) in 1900. Fiedler, *Story of Faith Missions*, pp. 37-38. The North American Councils of RBMU had operated independently of the British branch since 1948. A formal division in to RBMU UK and RBMU International took place in 1979. RBMU International merged with World Team in 1995 with the new agency operating

RBMU.[176] Mary Reid, a nurse from Charlotte Baptist Chapel, Edinburgh, went to Portuguese East Africa with the mission agency of the Church of Scotland. Miss Richardson (later Mrs Taylor) from Marshall Street Baptist Church, Edinburgh, worked in Moukden, China, also with a Presbyterian Mission. Again the most probable explanation is that her husband had been sent to the field with that agency.[177] Mary Ritchie from Gilcolmston Park Baptist Church, Aberdeen, went to North Africa with the SMM. Adam Scott from Kelso Baptist Church was sent to India by the India General Mission, and another Adam Scott from Charlotte Baptist Chapel, Edinburgh, went to Ananapur, India, with the same agency then called the India and Ceylon General Mission (I&CGM).[178] Alex Smith and his wife from Queen's Park Baptist Church, Glasgow, went to Africa with the Baptist Industrial Mission. Colin Smith from South Leith Baptist Church, Edinburgh, went to the Argentine with the South American Missionary Society. George Speedie from Tillicoultry Baptist Church went to Canada with the Sailors' Mission,[179] and Robert Stark from Kirkintilloch Baptist Church went to South America with the B&FBS in 1893. Robert Steedman from Viewfield Baptist Church, Dunfermline, went to Wamba in Congo with the Heart of Africa Mission. A.E. Stephens and his wife went to Assam with the American Baptist Foreign Missionary Union, C. Stewart and his wife went to Livingstonia with the Unevangelised Fields Mission,[180] and Nellie Stewart went to Smyrna (Izmir, Turkey) with the Church of Scotland Jewish Mission,[181] all from Gilcolmston Park Baptist Church, Aberdeen. Dr (Mrs) C.M. Stubbs from Dalkeith Baptist Church served in China with a Christian Union

---

under the World Team name. RBMU UK decided to hand its operations over to other missions, a work completed by 1991. This information was obtained from www.mundas.ac.uk/cats/3/42.htm, accessed 30 September 2014.

[176] McVicar, *Great Adventure*, p. 79. She was omitted from Yuille's list, 'Scottish Baptists in the Mission Field'.

[177] Yuille, 'Scottish Baptists in the Mission Field', p. 294.

[178] The Poona and Indian Village Mission (PIVM) was set up in 1893. In 1968 it merged with the Ceylon and Indian General Mission (CIGM, also founded in 1893) to form the International Christian Fellowship (ICF). In the 1980s the ICF and the SIM and the Andes Evangelical Mission merged to form the Society for International Ministries, SIM.

[179] There are insufficient details to determine which agency George Speedie served with in Canada. There was a significant growth in Seamen's missions in the late nineteenth and early twentieth centuries. See R. Kverndal, *Seamen's Missions: Their Origins and Early Growth: A Contribution to the History of the Church Maritime* (Pasadena, CA: William Carey Library, 1986).

[180] The well-known faith mission with this name was only founded in 1931, five years after Yuille's book was published. Therefore, it is possible that another society is intended here.

[181] The Smyrna Jewish Mission was agreed at the General Assembly of the Church of Scotland in 1856, with the Medical Mission begun there in 1881, with the Beaconsfield Hospital opened in 1886. John A. Trail, 'The Enterprises of the Church IV: The Jewish Mission', *Life and Work* 36.4 (April, 1914), pp. 104-105.

Universities Mission, but no further details are given.[182] Lizzie B. Weir from Hawick Baptist Church went to Congo with the RBMU in 1894. Allan Wilkinson from Harper Memorial Baptist Church, Glasgow, went to East Africa with the Heart of Africa Mission. Mrs Wilkes from Hawick Baptist Church went to Poona, India, with the India Village Mission. She died in 1917. Miss Wills (who later married Dr McKay) from Gilcolmston Park Baptist Church, Aberdeen, served in Lima, Peru, with the Free Church of Scotland Mission.

Baptist Missionaries for whom Details of their Service is Incomplete

This final category covers missionaries, usually with a reference to their home church, of whom little else is know from Yuille's records. There were sixty missionaries in this category, only John Linton mentioned below was not recorded by Yuille. Dr J.W. Arthur from Hillhead Baptist Church went to Kikuyu, Africa.[183] James D. Brown from Crown Terrace Baptist Church, Aberdeen, was listed by Yuille as serving in Manchuria, China, in 1921,[184] but no other details of his record have yet been located. Mary Buchan (later married to James Harrison) from Hillhead Baptist Church, Glasgow, went to serve in Argentina, though no other details are given. Miss Clift from Duncan Street Baptist Church, Edinburgh, served in India prior to 1925, but no other details are given by Yuille. Even less information was given by him for Mr and Mrs Cooper from Orangefield Baptist Church, Greenock. They were simply listed as on the mission field at the time of the survey. Nurse Cowie from Charlotte Baptist Chapel, Edinburgh, worked in Nanning, China, at unspecified dates according to Yuille.[185] A.H. Cruickshank from Dennistoun Baptist Church, Glasgow, went to work in the Congo in 1883, but no more details are available. James Cunningham from Motherwell Baptist Church was listed as serving in South America with no dates specified. Clearly Yuille was working on very little information with some of the individuals he included in his survey. Mr and Mrs James Davidson from Hopeman Baptist Church were appointed to serve in Congo in

---

[182] Yuille, 'Scottish Baptists in the Mission Field', p. 294. In the early twentieth century female doctors were sought by Chinese women thus providing openings for female missionaries with medical qualifications. It is probable that Dr Stubbs served as a medical missionary on this mission team.

[183] All references in this section are to Yuille, 'Scottish Baptists in the Mission Field', unless otherwise specified. It is likely he served with the Church of Scotland mission at Kikuyu. The Anglican Church Missionary Society (CMS), the African Inland Mission (AIM) and the Gospel Missionary Society (originally part of AIM) were the first Christian mission agencies in that area. John Karanja, 'The Role of Kikuyu Christians', in Kevin Ward and Brian Stanley (eds), *The Church Missionary Society and World Christianity 1799–1999* (Grand Rapids, MI: Eerdmans, 2000), p. 258. See also A.F. Walls, 'Missions: East Africa', in N.M. de S. Cameron (ed.), *Dictionary of Scottish Church History and Theology* (Edinburgh: T. & T. Clark, 1993), pp. 576-78.

[184] Yuille, 'Scottish Baptists in the Mission Field', p. 290.

[185] Yuille, 'Scottish Baptists in the Mission Field', p. 291.

1921 and 1923 respectively, but no other facts are stated. Gladys Dick from Hillhead Baptist Church was appointed to serve in Rajputana, in north-west India, a location now part of the state of Rajasthan, India. Mr and Mrs William Dingwall from Gilcolmston Park, Aberdeen, served in Rio Tinto, Spain. Margaret Dodds (later Mrs Chalmers) from Duncan Street Baptist Church, Edinburgh, was a missionary at Lovedale, a little town in the Nilgiri Hills, in the state of Tamil Nadu, India. Mr and Mrs Duncan from Clydebank were listed simply as serving in South America. Lawrence Elder and his wife from Gorgie Baptist Church, Edinburgh, were sent to Badajos in Spain in 1923, though the name of the agency is unknown. Maisie Galbraith from Bellshill Baptist Church was known to be serving in South America, though with no further details of her service. George Gray from Duncan Street Baptist Church, Edinburgh, was stated as working in India, with no further details given. Christina Hay from Bristo Place Baptist Church, Edinburgh, was apparently working in West Africa in 1885. George Henderson from Sanday Baptist Church, Orkney, went to China in 1925, but it is unknown which mission agency supported his endeavours. Alice Huber from Crown Terrace Baptist Church, Aberdeen, went to Spezia in Italy in 1920.

Miss Jack from Hillhead Baptist Church, Glasgow, was reported to be working in Ceylon; Mrs Johnston from Forfar Baptist Church in India; and W. King from John Street Baptist Church, Glasgow, somewhere in South America. Susie Lamont from Hillhead Baptist Church, Glasgow, went to the Gold Coast, now Ghana, and Georgina M. Law from Crown Terrace Baptist Church, Aberdeen, worked in China in 1900, but no other information has been located on their work.[186] James Lindsay from Airdrie Baptist Church went to Bombay, India. Once again there is no indication of agency or dates. John Linton from St Andrews Baptist Church, who was baptized and became a member there on 27 July 1890, went as 'an artisan missionary' to Africa, but died there in 1893.[187] Elsie Lochhead from Gilcolmston Park Baptist Church, Aberdeen, went to Algeria, and D.R. Logan of John Street Baptist Church went to India. Miss McKilligan (later Mrs Bernard) from Elgin Baptist Church went to Brazil. C. Malcolm and his wife went from Duncan Street Baptist Church, Edinburgh to Basutoland, South Africa, again without any additional information. Mrs Margaret Milne from Bristo Place Baptist Church, Edinburgh, went to Ceylon in 1894, but how long she stayed or the nature of her work was not supplied. W. Mitchell of Forfar Baptist Church went to India. William Murdock and a Mr and Mrs Murray from Airdrie Baptist Church went to Congo and Palestine respectively. Margaret Myles from Charlotte Baptist Chapel, Edinburgh, went to Africa. Mr and Mrs David Neave from Gilcolmston Park Baptist Church, Aberdeen, were listed as working in western China by Yuille, but no dates or agency are supplied.[188] John Nisbet from Marshall Street Baptist Church, Edinburgh, went to Jamaica in 1856. Ella Reid (later Mrs Bristow) from Motherwell Baptist Church

---

[186] Yuille, 'Scottish Baptists in the Mission Field', p. 293.
[187] Docherty, *'Something very Fine'*, p. 29.
[188] Yuille, 'Scottish Baptists in the Mission Field', p. 293.

went to Nigeria. Aida Roberts (later Mrs Hill), L. Roberts (later Mrs Amner), and Dr Howard Roberts, all from Duncan Street Baptist Church, Edinburgh, went to China, the Straits Settlement, and Tangiers, Morocco respectively. The Straits Settlement was a former British Colony on the Strait of Malacca, comprising four trade centres, Penang, Singapore, Malacca, and Labuan, which apart from Singapore are now incorporated in Malaysia. Isabella Robertson (later Mrs Ball) from Bristo Place Baptist Church, Edinburgh, was listed by Yuille as having served in China in 1845.[189] Jean Scott from Charlotte Baptist Chapel, Edinburgh, was listed as serving in China, but no details are recorded.[190] Miss Shawer (Mrs Longlands) from Duncan Street Baptist Church, Edinburgh, Yuille reported, had recently returned from Congo. Adelaide D. Smith from Viewfield Baptist Church, Dunfermline, went to Agra, India, in 1919. Arthur Y. Steel from Hillhead Baptist Church went to Egypt at an unknown date. Robert Twaddel from Motherwell Baptist Church went to North Africa. Edith White from Hillhead Baptist Church, Glasgow, served in India before settling in Bournemouth, England in her latter years. Harry Whittington from Dennistoun Baptist Church, Glasgow, went to Brazil in 1907. Georgina Wilson from Motherwell Baptist Church served in North Africa. Elizabeth Wilson from Maxwelltown Baptist Church, Dundee, served in Kalimpong, West Bengal, India. Mary Wishart from Dennistoun Baptist Church, Glasgow, served in India from 1889.

Conclusions

Scottish Baptists were in the mainstream of Scottish Protestant enthusiasm for the cause of spreading the good news from their native land in the first three decades of the twentieth century. George Yuille's survey of Scottish Baptists on the mission field taken in 1925 indicates that many members of this denomination were committed to this cause. His data was far from complete and the total numbers involved were probably higher than those listed. Baptists were most committed to serving with the denominational agency, the BMS, and the best-known faith mission, the CIM. However, a growing number chose to work with the rapidly increasing number of small faith missions across the globe. There was a confident expectation of the advance of the Christian church in this era, in partnership with fellow Christians of other Protestant traditions. What is very clear, though, is that a lot of work remains to be done before a full picture of Scottish Baptist missionary service in this era is completed.

---

[189] Yuille, 'Scottish Baptists in the Mission Field', p. 294.
[190] Yuille, 'Scottish Baptists in the Mission Field', p. 294.

CHAPTER 9

Patterns, Mentalités and the Possibilities for Baptist History

Martin Sutherland

Historians are suspicious of theory. This is especially so in the English-speaking branches of the profession, where most, if pressed, would admit a sneaking admiration for E.P. Thompson's thunderous 1978 polemic *The Poverty of Theory* (although they might then have to concede that they have not read it!). The lessons from Thompson are certainly profound. His principal target was the structuralist Marxist theory of the French theorist Louis Althusser. Althusser had denied the worth of empiricism, locating instead human action in structures and ideologies. For Thompson, this unconscionably denied the possibility of history as a discipline. Althusser and his followers had demonstrated that there was no common ground anymore within Marxism.

> For the gulf that has opened has not been between different accentuations to the vocabulary of concepts, between this analogy and that category, but between idealist and materialist modes of thought, between Marxism as closure and a tradition, derivative from Marx, of open investigation and critique. The first is a tradition of theology. The second is a tradition of active reason.[1]

History, surely, seeks to open up. If theory tends towards closure, it is best left alone.

It is, thus, all the more notable that just at the point in the later 1970s when Thompson was seeking to shore up a lifetime's contribution to historical writing against the eviscerating effects of what he saw as a destructive theory, David Bebbington was beginning his discipline-shaping career with a work of historiographical theory. *Patterns in History: A Christian Perspective on Historical Thought* appeared in 1979, published by Inter-Varsity Press. A 1990 update, with minor additions was later issued by Baker with subsequent reprints by Regent College Publishing, together with a version in Korean. As this publication history suggests, David's work appeared in a different milieu from that of Thompson. *Patterns in History* has been a creature of the evangelical press; Thompson's *The Poverty of Theory* appeared under the socialist Merlin Press imprint. However, the

---

[1] E.P. Thompson, *The Poverty of Theory or an Orrery of Errors* (London: Merlin Press, 1995 [1978]), p. 254.

gulf between the two was perhaps not so wide as might be imagined. From Thompson's point of view at least, it was not as broad as that which he found within Marxism. The once Methodist Thompson goes on from the above passage to declare,

> If I thought that Althusserianism was the logical terminus of Marx's thought, then I could never be a Marxist. I would rather be a Christian (or hope to have the courage of a certain kind of Christian radical). At least I would then be given back a vocabulary within which value choices are allowed, and which permits the defence of the human personality against the invasions of the Unholy Capitalist or Holy Proletarian State.[2]

It is that very Christian 'vocabulary' which David Bebbington explores in *Patterns of History*. It is an important work – at the very least because, as it has been reissued without substantial alteration, we can assume it to have remained programmatic for David's own work. In this essay, as the title suggests, I will seek to engage some of the key ideas in this, David's first major work, making along the way some modest proposals for the expansion of the theory and its application in another major field of his contribution, the history of Baptist communities.

Patterns in History is, itself, primarily a work of history. It outlines a more or less standard interpretation of various ways of discerning a 'pattern' in history. The first is the vision of the ancient world, in which history is cyclical. The rise and fall of empires, or the fall from an Acadian golden age provide the pattern. The key feature of this understanding is that the cycles of fall and rise are inevitable, or at least beyond human control. Some principal of the cosmos, or some flaw in humanity, drives an inexorable process which cannot be redirected by decision or agency, or deflected by unexpected intervention or surprising event.

Although, ironically, the cyclical view has had its minor rises and falls, it became in the Christian West at least, eventually supplanted by the Judaeo-Christian view which has intervention at its heart. Creation itself is a surprising event, an act of divine agency. This fundamental theistic conviction precludes permanent or inexorable cycles. Why, even the seasons will one day pass away. The focus of all history is found in Christ, but only because he is a figure of the End to which God is taking his creation. 'History is seen not as a cycle, but as a straight line.'[3]

The Christian view is open to challenge, however, at its very heart. If 'providence' describes the varieties of divine intervention, how are such moments distinguished from others. Moreover how are extraordinary, though apparently tragic, events such as defeats, earthquakes or plagues to be understood?

Enlightenment history gradually clipped theistic intervention from its vision. Teleology was replaced with the secular concept of progress. As Bebbington suggests, however, its roots were clear.

---

[2] Thompson, *The Poverty of Theory*, p. 254.
[3] David Bebbington, *Patterns in History: A Christian Perspective on Historical Thought* (Grand Rapids, MI: Baker Book House, 1990), p. 18.

Belief in divine intervention was eliminated, but otherwise the structure of the idea of progress betrays its Christian origins. It is linear, offers confidence in the future and entails acceptance of unchanging moral values.[4]

It was against such universalist claims for history that the German historicist schools rebelled. If the idea of univalent progress was typically Enlightenment in character, the historicist schools were the product of the Romantic reaction, in which local cultures and differences were instead the key. The point to history was not its teleological nature but its culture-forming processes. All cultures are shaped in their own way by the specifics of their histories and as such are worthy of study (and respect) in their own terms. Individuals fade in this picture, regarded more as products of their cultures than the agents of history.

Bebbington discerns a fifth school, arising in the nineteenth century, in the historical materialism of Marxist historians. Here the driving force of history is taken to be not inexorable cycles, divine intervention, inevitable progress or cultural ideas. Rather it is the need for production and materials goods. Humans have agency but principally to meet their material needs. There is an implicit hope for progress and ideas remain important, but the principal categories are material. It was this version of Marxist history which Thompson was at pains to defend.

These five models broadly represent, Bebbington suggests, the principal attempts to discern a pattern in history. In his later brief revision he acknowledges that postmodernism is probably a sixth. The five, however, provided the context for twentieth-century, specifically English-speaking historiography in which the debate, he argues, centred less on metaphysical visions of history than on the nature of historical method. Here, nonetheless, the influence of the Enlightenment and Romantic models persist. Bebbington identified a fundamental divide between 'positivist' approaches, which proposed methodologies based on the model of the natural sciences and which downplayed human uniqueness and agency and sought structures and laws in history, with 'idealist' approaches which called for intuitive empathy with the object of enquiry and emphasised ideas, individual choice and event. Described thus, the two approaches clearly derive from the Enlightenment/progress/modernist and Romantic/historicist models respectively. Marxism persisted between these stools, claiming a voice but rarely entering the mainstream.

As is the way with such surveys, the most contemporary chapter is the one which becomes most rapidly dated. So it is with Bebbington's depiction of English-speaking historiography three-quarters of the way through the last century. Thirty-five years later the landscape has changed dramatically. Marxist approaches have almost disappeared. Idealism, as Bebbington described it has faded, or rather, morphed into the various versions (and the variety seems infinite) of what he in 1990 was still calling 'modernism' (out of reference to its roots in the high cultural

---

[4] Bebbington, *Patterns in History*, p. 68.

modernism which appeared in the early twentieth century), but which the rest of us lump together as postmodernism.

Positivism, too, has altered almost beyond recognition. Michael Bentley, preferring 'modernist' to Bebbington's 'positivist', has more recently shown that this style of history was already in decline by 1970. It did not, of course, simply disappear, but its confidence, interests and methods came increasingly under the postmodernist influence, not in its (largely impenetrable) theoretical form perhaps, but in the shifting focus and style of the job of history itself. As Bentley describes it,

> Together, however, internal anxieties about the nature of modernist history in the second half of the century and the presence after 1970 of a penetrating theoretical revision helped turn the wheel of historiography and open the way for a more humane and open form of scholarship, one concerned more with *mentalités* and cultural forms than structures.[5]

As the title of the present essay suggests, I will want to return to the possibilities presented by *mentalités*. However, it is important first to note what is really the main point to David Bebbington's analysis in *Patterns in History*. Namely, that a recovery of a suitably chastened and humbled Christian vision of history enables, first, a methodological 'third way', combining creatively the emphases of positivism and idealism, and, secondly, a vision for the role of the Christian historian.

Lord Elton – in Bentley's terms, the quintessential modernist – was as dismayed and dismissive of Hayden White's 1972 *Metahistory*, the first comprehensive outline of a new approach to history, as the Marxist Thompson was at the proposals of Althusser. Historians are nervous about theory, and many make a living at their craft paying little or no attention to it. Christian historians, aware of the risk of guilt by association with hagiographies, triumphalist denominational histories and the uncritical antiquarianism of the vast plethora of parish and local accounts, have been especially anxious to avoid the implication that their historical writing is second rate, compromised by faith positions and commitments and, therefore, in positivist eyes at least, biased and untrustworthy. All of which makes David Bebbington's programme-setting manifesto in *Patterns in History* the more remarkable. Christian historians, of course, have at their disposal the polar opposite of a 'poverty of theory'. Christianity is an historical faith, standing in a long historical tradition. Not surprisingly Bebbington draws on this tradition in categories familiar to his evangelical readership, pointing to their usefulness for guiding method and for understanding the role of the Christian historian.

In terms of method, Bebbington proposes that the Christian approach can enable a resolution of the conflict between positivism and idealism, each of which at its root has emerged from the Christian view only to deny different aspects of it. The resolution lies in the familiar evangelical convictions about the nature of humanity before God.

---

[5] Michael Bentley, *Modernising England's Past: English Historiography in the Age of Modernism 1870–1970* (Cambridge: Cambridge University Press, 2005), p. 231.

The controversy between the two schools of thought arises from their isolating one or other aspect of Christian thought about man. For positivists he is a creature of circumstance; for idealists he is capable of heroic creativity. From that divergence springs the whole debate. It is therefore when the philosophy of historiography rediscovers its Christian roots that it becomes possible to approach a resolution of the questions at issue. Human beings can then be seen whole, as shaped by their context and as shapers of it. Positivists and idealists alike can be appreciated for being right in what they affirm but wrong in what they deny.[6]

The role of the Christian historian is similarly delineated in classic evangelical terms, focusing primarily on the concept of providence. Whilst he acknowledges that identifying the specific hand of God is problematic, Bebbington nonetheless insists that it must be looked for.

> If a Christian historian tries to write without a thought for providence, he is likely to succumb to some alternative view or blend of views that happens to be in fashion ... His Christian understanding of history will decay. It is far better not to compartmentalize ... A believer should not be a Christian and a historian but a Christian historian.[7]

How, though, is the professional historian to proceed? Bebbington acknowledges that interpretations replete with references to providence are not likely to gain publication in leading journals or garner respect within a resolutely secular profession. Drawing again on familiar evangelical strategies – this time for communication – the answer is to pick your audience. Historical writing is a form of rhetoric, and good rhetoricians tailor their message to their audiences. '[T]he Christian historian is not obliged to tell the whole truth as he sees it in every piece of historical writing. He can write of providence or not according to his judgement of the composition of his audience.'[8]

I confess to finding this the least satisfying of Bebbington's arguments. For a start there is a reverse risk, also justified by the same rhetorical argument. The Christian historian is tempted, as has happened too often, to leave out the uncomfortable secular explanations for their Christian audience. Church and mission history is so littered with this selectivity that its usefulness is often compromised. There are, moreover, deeper reasons to imagine that more integrated historical writing is possible. Attention to the wider riches of Christian theology offers a broader take on methodological issues, and even a rethink on the nature of providence itself.

Bebbington was, of course, writing in an English historiographical context, for an evangelical audience. By his own lights, it is logical to expect he will bring familiar categories to bear in his rhetoric. But in thirty-five years the church (and certainly evangelicalism) has changed, as has the profession of history. It is, therefore, surely appropriate to consider the usefulness of two further sources – one, a body of

---

[6] Bebbington, *Patterns in History*, p. 167.
[7] Bebbington, *Patterns in History*, p. 186.
[8] Bebbington, *Patterns in History*, p. 187.

theology, the other a school of historical practice – notably absent from the pages of *Patterns in History*.

In 1959, the just emerging German theologian Wolfhart Pannenberg delivered a programmatic lecture which would mark the beginning of a new school of theology. It found its English translation in 1970 as 'Redemptive Event and History'.[9] It is, of course, a theology of history, but it is notable also for the attention is pays to the *task* of history – what Bebbington refers to as the philosophy of historiography. It has few peers as a statement of Christian historical theory.

Pannenberg asserts not that theology is the basis for history, but that history is the basis for theology. This history involves God. Indeed, God is known as the living God precisely because he has 'a history with humanity and through humanity with his whole creation'. God is neither detached observer nor occasional interventionist, God is a participant. Old and New Testaments in their apocalyptic frameworks show this revelatory participation by God to be infinite. 'Thus Israel not only discovered history as a particular sphere of reality; it finally drew the whole of creation into history. History is reality in its totality.'[10]

Like Bebbington, Pannenberg clearly distinguishes this Judaeo-Christian view of history from the cyclical models. In those, continuity is the dominant motif – an assurance against vagaries of constant change. 'By way of contrast, Israel is distinguished by the fact that it experienced the reality of its God ... more and more decisively in historical change itself.'[11] It is, however, too simplistic merely to conclude that history is a straight line. It is so only in the negative sense that it is not cyclical. At stake is Israel's (and the church's) experience of God.

> Within the reality characterised by the constantly creative work of God, history arises because God makes promises and fulfils these promises. History is event so suspended in tension between promise and fulfilment that through the promise it is irreversibly pointed toward the goal of future fulfilment.[12]

However, it is a mistake to imagine that this implies a straight line of providential action. Rudolf Bultmann, for instance, seeks a form of continuity between Old and New Testaments which should not even be imagined. '[H]e does not begin with the promises and their structure which for Israel were the foundation of history, and therefore does not understand the events of the history of Israel in their significance as change, as God's "interpretation" of the content of the promises – promises which thus endure precisely in change'.[13] History is inherently particular, specific and contingent. The unity of history will not be found in any straight line image, or an immanent teleology as per the theory of progress. 'The unity of history has its

---

[9] Wolfhart Pannenberg, 'Redemptive Event and History', in *Basic Questions in Theology*, Volume 1 (London: SCM Press, 1970), pp. 15-80.
[10] Pannenberg, 'Redemptive Event and History', p. 21.
[11] Pannenberg, 'Redemptive Event and History', p. 17.
[12] Pannenberg, 'Redemptive Event and History', p. 18.
[13] Pannenberg, 'Redemptive Event and History', pp. 27-28.

ground in something transcending history. The God who by the transcendence of his freedom is the origin of contingency in the world, is also the ground of the unity which comprises the contingencies as history.'[14]

This places pressure on the traditional view of interventionist providence and recasts the role of the Christian historian. '[E]very event in the world stands in the service of the Creator of all things'.[15] The historian should not be looking for some special class of event or miraculous intervention. That in fact would undermine the revealed nature of God. Precisely because God is Creator, 'his will does not occur at the expense of human activity, but precisely through the experience, plans, and deeds of men, despite and in their sinful perversion'.[16] History is, in a word, messy. Pannenberg argues that the motif of fulfilment is entirely compatible, indeed inherently bound up, with contingency and change. Eschatology does not disappear, but we are released from a univalent arrow image in favour of a rich multi-valency which finds its sense in the living God.

My proposal is, further, that Pannenberg's version of the Christian vision of history is particularly empowering of Baptist history. Discussions of providence tend inexorably to discussions of big events, typically beyond the horizons and almost always beyond the power of Baptists. On the other hand the contingency and specificity of God's work in history fits well with gathered, local communities. 'Experience', 'plans', 'human deeds', 'sinful perversion' – sounds like your average members meeting! Such a vision removes the rhetorical temptation of the church historian to leave out the very human elements of most Christian stories. For the Christian historian, leaving them in is no longer a concession, but a compulsion.

It is my contention, then, that more can be drawn from the rich field of Christian theology than Bebbington was able to incorporate for his audience in 1979. A similar claim can surely be made for an omitted historiographical school. *Patterns in History* makes much of English and German language historiographies, but almost entirely ignores the French. Specifically I am suggesting that the twentieth-century *Annales* school has something to offer, again of particular potential benefit in the writing of Baptist history.

The *Annales* movement has two distinct phases, before and after World War II. The later *Annales*, dominated by Fernand Braudel, fits in many ways the confident positivism Bebbington describes. Braudel's constant calls for integration with other disciplines, especially sociology, and his emphasis on the *longue durée* militated against the significance of individual agency, and even events themselves, tending instead to determinism. However, the earlier phase under the leadership of Georges Lefebvre and Marc Bloch adopted from Durkheim the notion of *mentalités*. This calls for the consideration of the nature of communities of belief, shared assumptions, and the rituals and structures which uphold them. As has been so often the case in evangelical thought, Bebbington's discussion, and proposed resolution, of

---

[14] Pannenberg, 'Redemptive Event and History', pp. 74-75.
[15] Pannenberg, 'Redemptive Event and History', p. 79.
[16] Pannenberg, 'Redemptive Event and History', p. 79.

the divide between positivism and idealism is highly individualised. Context is important, but primarily as the shaper of individuals. Communities are hardly mentioned in their own right. This is unhelpful for the study of Baptists for whom the covenanted community is key. As Bentley notes in the passage cited above, *mentalités* present a softer, more open approach, than the drive for laws and structures. The *mentalités* approach presents its own problems, of course. In particular, historians have found it difficult to identify and describe change within these communities of belief. The *Annales* were always seeking structure. Here again Pannenberg comes to our aid. If contingency and change lie at the heart of history itself, then evolving *mentalités* are to be expected. The potential advantages for understanding the polymorphous Baptist international community are clear.

My modest proposal in augmentation of Bebbington's *Patterns in History* is thus threefold, and focused specifically on finding even better historiographical tools for the study of Baptist communities. First, that the messy unpredictability, even the perverseness, of human behaviour need not be apologised away or disguised by bogus claims to identify the supernatural hand of God. Secondly, that Baptist communities can indeed by studied *as* communities and that this is fitting both to Baptist ecclesiology and to the place of these religious groups among wider communities, also with their *mentalités*. Thirdly, that change and contingency should be expected to be evident in the *mentalités*, too, and that this need not represent compromise, but history – indeed, the work of the living God.

I turn now to attempt to illustrate what such a blended approach might look like, through illustrations in the history of the Baptist communities with which I am most familiar, those of New Zealand.

The vast majority of New Zealand Baptist colonists before World War I were from Britain, specifically England. A few years ago, I published a monograph entitled *Conflict and Connection: Baptist Identity in New Zealand*. As the title implies, this was a study focused on the tensions and ties within New Zealand Baptist life. One of the notable early points to be made was that the headline divisions which had characterised English Baptist life – hymn singing, mission, Calvinism and Arminianism – hardly featured in New Zealand debates. The emerging colony presented more urgent problems. Yet New Zealand Baptists were, nonetheless, powerfully shaped by their English heritage. More than two centuries of dissent had created a *mentalité* of alienation, of being the outsider, artificially frustrated in their efforts to establish what New Zealand Maori know as a *turangawaewae* – 'a place to stand'.

This is evident at the very genesis of New Zealand colonisation. A writer in the *Baptist Magazine* in 1842, after considering in some detail the economic opportunities for Baptists considering emigration, nevertheless lamented the recent appointment of George August Selwyn as the first Anglican Bishop of New Zealand.

> In this comparatively uninhabited region there is already the germ of a religious establishment. Already there is a bishop! Alas, that church! It haunts us go whither we will. At home it taxes us; it calls us schismatics, points at us with scorn, and frowns on our worship; it proclaims itself our great benefactress, boasts of its unparalleled

tolerance, and tramples upon us contemptuously. Abroad it meets us at every turn: in India it circumvents us; in the old colonies it has constructed its fortresses; and if there be a spot of earth in another hemisphere to which an Englishman might repair with hope, it watches his movements, follows him instantaneously, or anticipates his arrival. East or west, north or south, there is no possibility of escaping it; if we sail for the antipodes, thither it vaults and meets us on our landing ... [A] bishop recognized by the secular governor as his spiritual colleague, cannot fail to be an object of jealousy to all who, being acquainted with the history of episcopalian ecclesiastics and the claims they are now making, are anxious for the religious liberties of the infant colony.[17]

New Zealand never adopted an established church model but this did not mean that the fears of the writer in the *Baptist Magazine* were completely unfounded. Unofficial concessions to the Church of England were common. Neither were these sentiments limited to Baptists. Recent studies of the origins of the New Zealand land wars of the 1860s have identified a suspicion among a significant body of smallholding colonists of any alliance between the Church of England and hereditary landowners. In England this perceived alliance, reinforced by such structures as the control over Anglican livings by wealthy individuals and institutions, had turned the minds of many to the perceived freely available land in the new colony. Early in the land controversies, key bishops and Anglican leaders expressed support for Maori concerns. Today, such solidarity seems prophetic. To landless English colonists, among them Baptists, it seemed like the betrayal of a promise.[18]

But the experience of life in the new colony would begin a process of change, which would eventually shift the self-understanding of Baptists. The colonial milieu, no matter how energetically it sought to replicate English norms, was itself a fractured society of displacement. In a seminal study, Miles Fairburn posits that New Zealand's social organisation 'was gravely deficient. Community structures were few and weak and the forces of social isolation were many and powerful.'[19] This has been observed more recently in literary studies. The convention of the 'new chum' in colonial novels and stories begins a motif of 'alienation and social distance', of the protagonist as outsider, which imbues the New Zealand literary psyche.[20] Ironically, then, the seeds of change to the nonconformist *mentalité* of colonial Baptists are found in discovering that most in the new society they inhabited were experiencing something analogous. Some degree of alienation, was, perhaps unexpectedly, the norm. The harder edges of sect-like structures began immediately to crumble.

---

[17] 'Reviews', *Baptist Magazine* 34 (1842), pp. 353-60 (p. 358).

[18] See, e.g., John Stenhouse, 'Religion and Society', in G. Byrnes (ed), *The New Oxford History of New Zealand* (Melbourne: Oxford University Press, 2009), pp. 323-56.

[19] Miles Fairburn, *The Ideal Society and its Enemies: The Foundations of Modern New Zealand Society 1850–1900* (Auckland: Auckland University Press, 1989), p. 11.

[20] See, e.g., Janet Wilson, "The 'New Chum': Writings of the English Diaspora in New Zealand, 1860-1914', in Lyndon Fraser and Angela McCarthy (eds), *Far From Home: The English in New Zealand* (Dunedin: Otago University Press, 2012), pp. 165-84.

Memories, and old habits, die hard, however. The first concrete signs of the evolving *mentalité* of New Zealand Baptists emerges in a long-running controversy over religious education in schools.

The 1877 Education Act excluded religious instruction from state primary schools. Various moves had been made to soften or confuse the purity of this principle. In 1890 a Private Schools Bill had been submitted. Regarded as a screen for state funding of Catholic and Anglican schools, this was opposed by other Protestant groups. Nevertheless, some Protestants sought the inclusion of Bible teaching in the state curriculum. In 1893, Baptists, with clear memories and contemporary observations of the marginalisation of Dissenters in British education, largely eschewed any state involvement in religious instruction. Radical minister A.H. Collins captured this sense in a clause of his key motion: 'That it is not the function of the state to teach religion and that it has neither the right to control or enforce it.'[21] Twenty years later, however, the sect like radical separation of church and state had lost the initiative. This shift played itself out in New Zealand Baptist Union Conference debates of the religious instruction issue. Baptists joined other denominations in welcoming a compromise of Bible teaching during school hours. The gradual change from an imported to an indigenous leadership was a crucial factor. In 1893 Collins had just arrived from Britain, as had his key supporter at the Conference that year, the Rev. W. Drew. Both spoke out of their English experience. Others who opposed state involvement had similar backgrounds.

In contrast to these imported ministers, the advocates for compromise were colonials, home grown. These men were comfortable seeking legislative change on the very questions (religious education, prohibition, gambling) which English free radicals wanted kept from state interference. The difference of context is profound. The New Zealanders did not have the automatic bogey of an established church against which to define their approach. On the other hand, by the mid-1890s they did have before them the record of an interventionist Liberal government. Far more than in Britain, the resources of colonial society were concentrated in central government. In the debate over religion in schools, Dunedin layman J.G. Fraser made these differences specific. In the colony, he pointed out, the state was different, more democratic and inclusive, than that in Britain. Moreover, only the state had shown itself capable of providing free, 'commodious and well-equipped' schools.[22]

Engagement on social issues in the New Zealand context would inevitably entail the resources and involvement of the state. Baptists were coming to see the pure separation of religion and state as less critical. In turn this reflects their changing view of themselves. Need they be so fervently outsiders, when the opportunity seemed ripe to approach, even be welcomed into, the main stream?

By the eve of another World War, the evolution of the New Zealand Baptist *mentalité* had profoundly advanced. Again this may be seen to reflect something of the wider emerging *Zeitgeist*. The experience of the Great Depression and the

---

[21] See the account in *New Zealand Baptist* (December 1893), pp. 185, 188.
[22] *New Zealand Baptist* (September 1896), p. 129.

resurgent search for localized solutions by the first Labour government coincided with the rise of a new, more self-confident 'Nationalist' literature. Crucial to this was a development of the motif of dislocation. The 'new chum' had become the 'man alone', an independent, often darkly subversive figure who came to be seen to embody the New Zealand spirit. The dissenter was now the hero. Perhaps Baptists had at last attained respectability.

In 1940 the Baptist Union of New Zealand issued a brief, self-congratulatory profile.[23] Themes of continuity and security dominated. The long unbroken publication of the denominational newspaper, the steady growth 'in churches, membership and institutions', and the international affiliation of the Union with the Baptist World Alliance sent reassuring signals of dependability and virtue. The pamphlet was clearly designed to advance the Union's claims to be taken seriously among the churches. The assurance was given that 'the Baptist church in New Zealand at the present time is vigorous, splendidly organised, and progressive'.

1940 was the centenary of the signing of the key constitutional document in New Zealand's history, the Treaty of Waitangi. It was the occasion for many official commemorations and survey publications. The Baptist pamphlet was no doubt issued in recognition of this national centenary. The denomination was determined to own its place in this story.

New Zealand Baptists had become something different, at least in their perceptions of themselves. The alienated outsiders were making a bid for the main table. War created another moment to demonstrate this solid respectability. Beginning in 1940 the annual assembly began a custom of commencing with a 'Loyal Resolution' – loyal, that is, to the state and the crown. Notable as this is, in a movement which arrived in the colony very clear as to the separation of church and state, it perhaps makes sense at a time of war and unknown threat. What is perhaps more telling is that the practice continued after the cessation of hostilities, only ceasing in 1963.

Baptist history has tended to be the story of individuals and institutions. The *mentalités* approach calls us to a view at once broader and deeper. This does not have to trap us into laws and immobile structures. In New Zealand the 'collective unconsciousness' of Baptists changed with the circumstances and opportunities of a new nation. There is little which can be identified as the intervening providence of God in this narrative. On the other hand it is possible to discern the fulfillment of God's promise in what Baptists saw as a chance to establish themselves closer to the centre rather than continuing to inhabit the margins of society. It was, at least arguably, a flourishing in the hands of the Creator. To be sure, it can also be read as a weakening of vigour, and not all the subsequent impacts can be seen to be desirable. But to discern and interpret the different threads of these stories is the historian's task and privilege.

---

[23] *The Baptist Churches in New Zealand 1851–1940* (Wellington: Baptist Union of N.Z., 1940).

David Bebbington set himself a bold agenda in 1979. His monumental contribution to intellectual and religious history since then demonstrates the power of his vision and the immense possibilities which still remain for Christian historians. I have suggested that *Patterns in History* can profitably be augmented by incorporating further streams of Christian thought and historiographical practice. It was not the last word on the historian's craft. That it was David Bebbington's first major word as a professional historian is testimony to the possibility that historians need not be so suspicious of theory after all.

Evangelical Studies

CHAPTER 10

Evangelical Revival in Enlightenment Britain: James Erskine of Grange and the Pietist Turn[1]

John Coffey

How should we understand the Evangelical Revival? Was it a reaction against the tepid piety and scepticism of the Enlightenment, a return to Reformation principles? Or was Evangelicalism, as David Bebbington has argued, a movement 'created by the Enlightenment'. Bebbington acknowledges that the Revival owed much to seventeenth-century Puritanism, high Church Anglicanism, and continental Pietism, but he maintains that it was 'permeated by Enlightenment influences', reflected in the Evangelical accent on sense experience, doctrinal moderation, inter-denominational ecumenism, and optimistic postmillennialism.[2]

In making this claim, Bebbington was building on the rediscovery of 'the religious Enlightenment'.[3] In the quarter of a century since the publication of his magnum opus, numerous scholars have concurred with his argument that Evangelicalism and Enlightenment could coalesce.[4] Yet many remained unconvinced. Historians of the Enlightenment still tend to treat Evangelicalism as a counter-Enlightenment movement, the polar opposite of English Latitudinarianism or Scottish Moderatism.[5] Scholars sympathetic to the Reformed tradition emphasise that in much of the English-speaking world Evangelicalism was a renewal of

---

[1] For expert comment on this chapter I am most grateful to Boyd Schlenther and Anne Skoczylas. Professor Skoczylas is currently working on the first major biography of Grange, and generously shared her findings on his early career.

[2] D.W. Bebbington, *Evangelicalism in Modern Britain: A History from the 1730s to the 1980s* (London: Unwin Hyman, 1989), pp. 34-35.

[3] A landmark work was Roy Porter and Mikulaus Teich (eds), *The Enlightenment in National Context* (Cambridge: Cambridge University Press, 1981). See more recently, David Sorkin, *The Religious Enlightenment: Protestants, Jews and Catholics from London to Vienna* (Princeton, NJ: Princeton University Press, 2008).

[4] See, e.g., David Hempton, *Methodism: Empire of the Spirit* (New Haven, CT: Yale University Press, 2005), ch. 2; Phyllis Mack, *Heart Religion in the British Enlightenment: Gender and Emotion in Early Methodism* (Cambridge: Cambridge University Press, 2008); Jonathan Yeager, *Enlightened Evangelicalism: The Life and Thought of John Erskine* (New York, NY: Oxford University Press, 2011).

[5] See, e.g., Roy Porter, *Enlightenment: Britain and the Creation of the Modern World* (London: Allen Lane, 2000).

experimental Calvinism.⁶ In response, Bebbington has continued to make the case for the novelty of Evangelicalism, while qualifying his thesis: 'Though not created by the Enlightenment, evangelicalism was embedded in it'.⁷

In a previous essay, I entered this debate by highlighting the continuity between Puritanism and Evangelicalism.⁸ In the present chapter, I approach it through a case study of a single individual, The Honourable James Erskine of Grange.⁹ His story is stranger than fiction. Yet for all his peculiarity, he was a major figure whose life and writings give us a fresh perspective on the Evangelical Revival. Born in 1679, the year of a famous Covenanter rebellion, he died in 1754, in the midst of the era of Enlightenment and Awakening.¹⁰ During his long career, he was associated with many of the leading figures of his day, from Frederick, Prince of Wales to Count Zinzendorf.

Despite being among the most eminent, ardent and well informed patrons of the British Evangelical awakening, Erskine remains a mysterious figure, lurking in the shadows of histories of the revival, if mentioned at all.¹¹ Yet his significance has been recognised by two of the most astute scholars of early Evangelicalism – Geoffrey Nuttall and W.R. Ward.¹² My own research was prompted by Ward's

---

⁶ Michael Haykin and Kenneth J. Stewart (eds), *The Emergence of Evangelicalism: Exploring Historical Continuities* (Nottingham: Apollos, 2008).

⁷ David Bebbington, 'Response', in Haykin and Stewart (eds), *Emergence of Evangelicalism*, pp. 417-32 (p. 427).

⁸ John Coffey, 'Puritanism, Evangelicalism, and the Evangelical Protestant Tradition', in Haykin and Stewart (eds), *Emergence of Evangelicalism*, pp. 252-77.

⁹ 'The Honourable' was a courtesy title derived from his status as the younger son of an Earl. As a judge on the Court of Session from 1706 to 1734 he adopted the courtesy title of Lord Grange (Prestongrange being the name of his estate at Prestonpans). Technically, he ceased to be 'Lord Grange' when he resigned from the Court in 1734, and thereafter he was formally addressed as 'The Honourable James Erskine of Grange Esqr', or simply 'Mr James Erskine'. I shall refer to him interchangeably as Erskine and Grange.

¹⁰ The published biographies of Erskine are tantalisingly brief: Richard Scott, 'James Erskine, Lord Grange', *Oxford Dictionary of National Biography* [hereafter *ODNB*]; Eveline Cruickshanks, 'Erskine, Hon. James (c.1678–1754), of Prestongrange, nr. Prestonpans, East Lothian', in R. Sedgwick (ed.), *The History of Parliament: The House of Commons, 1715–1754* (1970), http://www.historyofparliamentonline.org/volume/1715-1754/member/erskine-hon-james-1678-1754, accessed 5 January 2015.

¹¹ He has no entry in such major reference works as Donald M. Lewis (ed.), *The Blackwell Dictionary of Evangelical Biography 1730–1860* (2 vols; Oxford: Blackwell, 1995), or Nigel M. de S. Cameron (ed.), *Dictionary of Scottish Church History and Theology* (Downers Grove, IL: Inter-Varsity Press, 1990). Other eighteenth-century Erskines are listed (the Seceders, Ralph and Ebenezer; the Calvinistic Methodist, Lady Anne Erskine; and the Church of Scotland's John Erskine) but not James.

¹² Geoffrey F. Nuttall, 'Howell Harris and "The Grand Table": A Note on Religion and Politics, 1744–50', *Journal of Ecclesiastical History* 39 (1988), pp. 531-44; W.R. Ward, *The Protestant Evangelical Awakening* (Cambridge: Cambridge University Press, 1992), pp. 322, 333-35, 339, *Faith and Faction* (London: Epworth Press, 1993), pp. 395-96, and 'Was there

remark that Erskine's 'huge analysis of the religious situation' in Scotland (addressed to Zinzendorf) had 'lain unused' in the Moravian archives in Herrnhut.[13]

The letter to Zinzendorf was merely one part of a large body of Erskine's correspondence, now scattered in archives across Scotland, England, Wales, Germany, and the United States. The sources richly document his religious activism in the decades before and after the Evangelical Revival. His early life is illuminated by various remains: family correspondence from Alloa House (published by the Historical Manuscripts Commission);[14] a multi-volume diary filled with 'endless religious controversial disputations' and 'pious ejaculations' (extracts of which were printed in the nineteenth century);[15] correspondence and conversations with the Scottish divine Robert Wodrow in the 1720s and early 1730s (held at the National Library of Scotland and largely published);[16] correspondence with the English Dissenter Abraham Taylor (deposited in the National Archives of Scotland); and letters from the decade after 1731 (published by the Spalding Club).[17] His correspondence with the leading Evangelicals can be found in the Trevecka Letters at the National Library of Wales; the Laing Papers at Edinburgh University Library; the Methodist archives at the John Rylands University Library; the Moravian archives at Herrnhut and London; the Hastings Letters in the Leicestershire Record Office; and the John Wesley family papers at Emory University.[18] Most of this material remains unpublished, but we do have an excellent calendar of the Trevecka Letters,[19] and Wesley scholars have done fine work on Grange's correspondence with John and Charles.[20]

---

a Methodist Evangelistic Strategy in the Eighteenth Century?', in Nicholas Tyacke (ed.), *England's Long Reformation, 1500-1800* (London: University College London Press, 1998), pp. 285-305.

[13] Ward, *Protestant Evangelical Awakening*, p. 334.

[14] *Historical Manuscripts Commission: Report on the Manuscripts of the Earl of Mar and Kellie, Preserved at Alloa House*, 60 (London: Ben Johnson, 1904). This volume contains letters to and from Erskine beginning in 1706 (p. 246) and ending in 1743 (pp. 552-53). Hereafter HMC, *Mar and Kellie*.

[15] James Maidment (ed.), *Extracts from the Diary of a Senator of the College of Justice, 1717–1718* (Edinburgh: Thomas G. Stevenson, 1843), pp. iii-iv.

[16] Robert Wodrow, *Analecta, or, Materials for a History of Remarkable Providences, Mostly Relating to Scotch Ministers and Christians* (ed. [M. Leishman]; 4 vols; Edinburgh: Maitland Club, 1842–43); Thomas McCrie (ed.), *The Correspondence of the Rev. Robert Wodrow* (3 vols; (Edinburgh: Wodrow Society, 1842-43).

[17] 'Letters of Lord Grange', *Miscellany of the Spalding Club* 3 (1846), pp. 1-67.

[18] Abbreviated below as follows: John Rylands University Library (JRUL); Unity Archives, Herrnhut (UA-Herrnhut); Moravian Church House, London (MCH-London); Leicestershire Record Office (LRO). I am grateful to the Moravian archivists at Herrnhut and London for providing digital copies of the correspondence.

[19] Boyd S. Schlenther and Eryn M. White (eds), *Calendar of the Trevecka Letters* (Aberystwyth: National Library of Wales, 2003).

[20] Frank Baker (ed.), *The Works of John Wesley: Volume 26. Letters II: 1740–1755* (Oxford: Oxford University Press, 1982), pp. 124, 128-30, 132-36, 147; Randy Maddox,

Despite leaving such a rich array of sources, it is easy to see why Erskine has been neglected by historians of early Evangelicalism. He operated in the background, linking up revivalist factions through correspondence and conversation, and published nothing of religious significance. His strategic projects enjoyed limited success and soon faded from memory. Above all, he was (and remains) a man of deeply dubious reputation. The whiff of scandal that hung around him is one reason why he kept a low profile and worked behind the scenes. In both political and personal affairs, he was accused of living a double life. Ostensibly loyal to the Hanoverians, he was always suspected of Jacobite sympathies. His elder brother – John Erskine, the sixth Earl of Mar – led the Jacobite rebellion of 1715.[21] His brother-in-law, Sir Hugh Paterson, was implicated in both the Fifteen and the Forty-Five.[22] His close friend and relative – Simon Fraser, eleventh Lord Lovat – would be executed for his part in the 1745 rebellion.[23] Unlike Mar and Lovatt, Grange never appeared in open rebellion, but the surviving Jacobite correspondence reveals that he was plotting with the Young Pretender and French agents in the years leading up to the Forty-Five. In his personal life, Grange was ostentatiously pious, but allegedly unfaithful to his marriage vows, and definitely guilty (as we shall see) of having his wife abducted and exiled. The scandal grew in the telling – it was already legendary by the time of Boswell and Johnson's visit to the Hebrides.[24] It earned Grange a chapter in *The Historical Gallery of Criminal Portraitures* (1823), where he was placed in the company of Lucretia Borgia and described as 'a monster of depravity', 'a match for old Nick himself!'[25] A more sober writer summarised the received view: Grange 'prayed with the Presbyterians, got drunk with the Jacobites, and sent his wife into exile lest she should expose his inconsistencies'.[26]

'Correspondence between James Erskine and John and Charles Wesley', *Proceedings of the Wesley Historical Society* 58 (2012), pp. 264-75, and 'James Erskine's Critique of John Wesley on Christian Perfection', *Proceedings of the Wesley Historical Society*, 59 (2013), pp. 39-53.

[21] See Edward Gregg, 'The Jacobite Career of John, Earl of Mar', in Eveline Cruickshanks (ed.), *Ideology and Conspiracy: Aspects of Jacobitism, 1689–1759* (Edinburgh: John Donald, 1982), pp. 179–200; Christoph v. Ehrenstein, 'John Erskine, sixth Earl of Mar', *ODNB*.

[22] D.W. Hayton, 'Sir Hugh Paterson', in D. Hayton, S. Handley, E. Cruickshanks (eds), *The History of Parliament: The House of Commons, 1690–1715* (2002): http://www.history ofparliamentonline.org/volume/1690-1715/member/paterson-sir-hugh-1685-1777 (accessed 5 January 2015).

[23] See Edward Furgol, 'Simon Fraser, eleventh Lord Lovat (1667/8–1747)', *ODNB*.

[24] James Boswell, *A Journal of a Tour of the Hebrides, with Samuel Johnson* (1785), pp. 277-78; [William Erskine], *Epistle from Lady Grange* (1798); Harriet Martineau, *The Billow and the Rock: A Tale* (1846).

[25] John Brown (ed.), *The Historical Gallery of Criminal Portraitures* (2 vols; Manchester: J. Gleave, 1823), I, pp. 155-292 (pp. 156, 210).

[26] Charles Rogers, *Scotland: Social and Domestic* (London: Charles Griffin, 1869), pp. 14-15.

Erskine's reputation for hypocrisy was sealed by the Moderate clergyman, Alexander Carlyle, whose character sketch amounts to character assassination. Carlyle had been raised in Prestonpans, where his father William was the minister and Lord Grange the 'leading man'. For all his first-hand knowledge, he was prejudiced against the Popular party in the Kirk. Unlike other witnesses, Carlyle dismissed Erskine as a man of 'neither learning nor ability', 'no lawyer', 'a bad speaker', one who had 'never distinguished himself'. He claimed that the breakup of Erskine's marriage owed much to his keeping a Scottish mistress in London – Fanny Lindsay, the proprietor of a Haymarket coffeehouse. Carlyle's father suspected that Erskine engaged in bouts of debauchery in Edinburgh, 'spending the day in meetings for prayer and pious conversation, and [the] nights in lewdness and revelling'. He was 'a great plotter', suspected of anti-government activity, and his abduction of Lady Grange was 'one of the boldest and most violent projects that ever had been attempted since the nation was governed by laws'.[27] With this kind of bad press, Lord Grange was never a prime candidate for hagiography.

Yet for historians of the Evangelical Revival, Erskine's life and letters shed a flood of light on 'the tunnel period' between the passing of seventeenth-century Covenanters and Puritans and the rise of eighteenth-century Evangelicals. Whatever his faults, Grange was a serious man – highly educated, politically ambitious, theologically literate, and passionately devout. He shows us how the decades-long defence of old-style Reformed religion primed some conservative Protestants to embrace the new-style Evangelical revivalism. He reveals how the Revival was at odds with Enlightenment values and in tune with them, how the turn to Pietism consolidated traditional Protestantism and reshaped it. And he suggests that we need to pay more attention to the political context of the Revival, one in which the Opposition critique of a corrupt Whig ministry could be linked to projects of religious renewal.

Early Career: Calvinism versus Enlightenment

The younger son of a landed family, James Erskine was not a godly youth. He had 'a great esteem' for the writings of 'the Wits', and when he sailed to the Netherlands to study law at the University of Utrecht in 1699, he carried 'the bawdy poems' of Lord Rochester in his pocket. By his own admission, he contracted the clap on three occasions in his late teens and twenties. While he believed in the Deity, he was not preoccupied by his eternal destiny, and had no time for the Calvinist divines of Utrecht or Scotland, who in his youthful mind were 'narrow spirited, and prejudiced creatures'. The only kind of Christianity he could take seriously was the moderate Enlightenment Protestantism articulated by the Amsterdam theologian, Jean Le

---

[27] *Autobiography of the Rev. Dr. Alexander Carlyle* (Edinburgh: William Blackwood & Sons, 2nd edn, 1860), pp. 7-16, 58-61. See also the modern edition, Alexander Carlyle, *Anecdotes and Characters of the Times* (ed. James Kinsey; London: Oxford University Press, 1973).

Clerc, friend and correspondent of John Locke, and leading champion of toleration and liberal Arminianism.[28] His studies abroad turned him into a cosmopolitan European and he would often express frustration at the parochialism of his fellow Scots. He later corresponded with the Moravians in French,[29] and asked them to provide a translation of the Augsburg Confession from German, which he could not read, into one of the five languages he had learnt – 'Latin, or English, or Low Dutch, or French, or Italian'.[30]

Among his fellow students was Archibald Campbell, who was also reading civil law at the Dutch University. Erskine would later remember 'our comradeship, during our studys at Utrecht', and how they had 'lived in friendship' in the years that followed.[31] Campbell would go on to become the most powerful manager in Scottish politics, and the greatest patron of the Scottish literati.[32] He 'promoted polite secular scholarship at the expense of the presbyterian theology with which his family had previously been identified'.[33] Erskine was a cultured man in his own right, but he would take a dramatically different course in politics and religion. He came to be defined by his opposition to his old friend.

Their divergence was not immediately obvious. On their return to Scotland, both rose rapidly on the coattails of their elder brothers, with Erskine enjoying the patronage of his powerful sibling, the Earl of Mar. He became a member of the Faculty of Advocates in 1705, taking the title of Lord Grange in 1706, the same year that saw Campbell ennobled as Earl of Ilay. In 1707, Ilay, Mar and Grange keenly supported the Anglo-Scottish Union.[34] A letter to his brother displays Erskine's firmly Erastian disdain for clericalism – 'both high Church and high Kirk join in their principles as to screwing up the power of the clergy'. He 'heartily' wished for England and Scotland to be free of 'the fury and impertinence of biggots', whether Presbyterian or Episcopal.[35] In subsequent years, Erskine would draw much closer to the orthodox Presbyterian clergy of the Kirk, but he would always retain this commitment to the Union and to good relations between the Church of Scotland and the Church of England.

In 1707, Lord Grange was appointed a lord of justiciary and a member of the Privy Council. Two years later, he became Lord Justice Clerk, a post he held for the

---

[28] *Extracts from the Diary*, pp. 78-84. For Locke's connections and affinities with Le Clerc and Dutch Arminians see John Marshall, *John Locke, Toleration and Early Enlightenment Culture* (Cambridge: Cambridge University Press, 2006).

[29] UA-Herrnhut, R. 13. C. No.6: JE to Isaac Le Long, Fevrier 1744; Erskine to Zinzendorf, Juilet 1744.

[30] MCH-London, AB87 Folder 7: JE to James Hutton, 23 April 1743.

[31] 'Letters of Lord Grange', p. 25.

[32] Roger Emerson, *An Enlightened Duke the Life of Archibald Campbell (1682–1761), Earl of Ilay, 3rd Duke of Argyll* (Kilkerran: Humming Earth, 2013). The catalogue of his library lists many theological works: *Catalogus Librorum, A.C. D. A.* (2 vols; 1758).

[33] Alexander Murdoch, 'Archibald Campbell, third duke of Argyll (1682–1761),' *ODNB*.

[34] HMC, *Mar and Kellie*, p. 424.

[35] HMC, *Mar and Kellie*, p. 426.

remainder of Queen Anne's reign. In 1709, he presided over a ground-breaking trial in Perth, pardoning hundreds of people accused of sexual crime, 'effectively decriminalising adultery and fornication', 'abandoning Scripture as a relevant source of law', and marking 'a stage in the secularisation of Scottish criminal justice'.[36] With the Hanoverian succession in 1714, however, Grange was dismissed from this office, and when his brother was snubbed by the new king, Mar led the Jacobite rebellion of 1715. Its failure resulted in the sequestration of the family's estate. From this point on, salvaging the family's fortunes and rehabilitating its reputation would be one of Lord Grange's consuming passions.

Grange insisted that he deplored the rebellion in 1715 and affirmed that George I alone had a good title to be king.[37] He told the clergyman Allan Logan that 'tho'' all my relations allmost' were known Jacobites, he himself was 'convinced of the justice of the present establishment', and persuaded that 'the safety and preservation of religion depended on it'.[38] His alignment with hard line Presbyterians led the leading Jacobite George Lockhart to describe him as 'a true blue republican' who 'appear'd violently against the Episcopal clergy'.[39]

During the rebellion and in its aftermath, Lord Grange concentrated on developing his estate. His brother, the Earl of Mar, had been a keen promoter of improvement at his Alloa House estate.[40] Grange now followed suit, and 'amused himself in laying out and planting a fine garden' in the latest style, 'full of close walks and labyrinths and wildernesses'; for the next quarter of a century it attracted weekend and summer crowds from Edinburgh.[41] It was a passion shared with Ilay.[42]

Grange and Ilay had broader ambitions for the modernisation of the Scottish economy. In the winter of 1724/25, Erskine produced memoranda on the state of the Highlands for Ilay and Viscount Townshend, setting out proposals for transforming Highland society by abolishing feudalism and introducing commercial society. According to a recent historian, 'the Whig ministry put most of Grange's proposals into effect'. Two hundred and forty miles of roads were constructed in the region, and in 1727 Ilay founded the Royal Bank of Scotland and the Board of Trustees for Fisheries, Manufactures, and Improvements. Legal reforms to abolish feudal lordship would follow, and the Highlands were transformed into 'a commercial, manufacturing, and consuming society', 'in much the way Lord Grange predicted'.[43]

---

[36] Brian Levack, 'The Prosecution of Sexual Crimes in Early Eighteenth-Century Scotland', *Scottish Historical Review* 89 (2010), pp. 172-93 (p. 192).

[37] HMC, *Mar and Kellie*, p. 424.

[38] *Extracts from the Diary*, pp. 59-60.

[39] George Lockhart, *The Lockhart Papers* (2 vols; London: William Anderson, 1817), I, p. 466.

[40] Margaret Stewart, 'John Erskine, 6th and 11th Earl of Mar (1675–1732): Architecture, Landscape and Industry', *Architectural Heritage* 23 (2012), pp. 97-116.

[41] Carlyle, *Autobiography*, pp. 7-8.

[42] Emerson, *An Enlightened Duke*, ch. 8.

[43] Christopher Dudley, 'Party Politics, Political Economy, and Economic Development in Early Eighteenth-Century Britain', *Economic History Review* 66 (2013), pp. 1088-90.

Erskine was pioneering the practice of political economy, a discipline that would flourish during the Scottish Enlightenment.

In religion, by contrast, he was disillusioned with eighteenth-century fashions. The timing and causes of his turn to serious religion remain opaque, but the trauma of the 1715 rebellion may have prompted his embrace of intense Reformed piety. Around this time he was taking an increasingly active role in the affairs of the Kirk, through the Scottish SPCK and the annual meetings of the General Assembly. Turning his back on the fashionable Enlightenment theology he had once admired, he became a keen supporter of 'the zealous orthodox ministers' who were devoted to 'the reviving of decayed piety and zeal'. These ministers opposed the Arminian drift promoted by 'our modish writers' in the Church of England and (more discreetly) in the Kirk; the rise of anti-trinitarianism; the decline of confidence in the 'strict inspiration' of the Bible; and the growing suspicion of creeds and confessions. Although Grange supported the Toleration Act, he set his face against the 'taste of our times'.[44] He opposed the Patronage Act which gave elite patrons the right to appoint clergy, fearing that it would elevate fashionable young divines who were not acceptable to traditional Calvinist congregations.[45] At Prestonpans, he and William Carlyle sat up late in the evenings 'settling the high points of Calvinism; for their creed was that of Geneva'. The young Alexander claimed that he had 'frequently' seen his father's patron 'drowned in tears, during the whole of a sacramental Sunday'.[46]

In resisting the intellectual drift of his own century, Erskine turned for inspiration to the seventeenth century. This was the heroic age of the Kirk, and Wodrow and Erskine regularly corresponded about manuscripts by the Melvilles, David Calderwood, and Covenanters like Robert Blair and Archibald Johnston of Wariston. What they admired about these figures was not just their staunch Calvinist orthodoxy, but their 'vital', 'experimental' religion. The mental world of seventeenth-century Scottish Calvinists seemed increasingly alien to eighteenth-century readers, but Erskine urged Wodrow to publish their writings in full, including instances of 'remarkable providences' and 'extraordinary communications' with God.[47] He was enthralled by contemporary cases of the same phenomena – his diary recorded the 'singular' experiences of a shopkeeper called Jean Brown, who had a vision of Christ. This, he knew, would be dismissed as 'enthusiasm'; he

---

[44] HMC, *Mar and Kellie*, pp. 521, 525; *Correspondence of the Rev. Robert Wodrow*, III, pp. 146, 165, 172, 188, 67-68.

[45] Wodrow, *Analecta*, IV, p. 254. For more on the patronage controversy and Grange's role in it, see Whitley Laurence, *A Great Grievance: Ecclesiastical Lay Patronage in Scotland until 1750* (Eugene, OR: Wipf and Stock, 2013).

[46] Carlyle, *Autobiography*, pp. 13-15.

[47] *Correspondence of the Rev. Robert Wodrow*, III, pp. 62-63, 66-68, 89-91, 167-70, 229-32.

preferred to see it as 'a sort of extacy'.[48] His fascination with the supernatural extended to 'daemonologia', a subject in which he was 'learned'.[49]

Alongside Wodrow and other traditional Calvinist clergy, he coordinated the second campaign against John Simson, a Glasgow divinity professor accused of insinuating the Arian christology of Samuel Clarke into the Church of Scotland. The affair dragged on for several years between 1727 and 1731, and Erskine made a number of major speeches in the General Assembly, enabling the orthodox party to secure the permanent suspension of Simson from academic teaching and preaching.[50] His success in the face of powerful opposition from leading lawyers and courtiers, suggests that Grange was a far more skilful operator than Carlyle cared to admit. Wodrow had no doubts about his importance in the case – 'upon this single man very much depended'.[51]

While Erskine trained his fire on the Kirk's liberal ministers, he was often exasperated by the orthodox. When John Simson had first been tried by the General Assembly in 1716–17, it was on grounds of alleged Arminianism rather than Arianism, and Grange sought to 'prevent farther divisions and heats' and 'heall all factions'. He avoided 'peevish, narrow-minded, and violent men' like the heresy-hunter James Webster, who was 'a man drunk with passion and heat'. Erskine sympathised with the Auchterardour presbytery and the Marrow Men like Thomas Boston, whose 'free grace' teaching attracted charges of antinomianism, but he wished that they would be more careful in their theological formulations.[52] He was also ambivalent about his 'cousins', Ralph and Ebenezer Erskine, who were expelled from the ministry of the Kirk in 1733, and retaliated by setting up the Secession Church. He had been one of the two witnesses to Ralph's contract of marriage in 1732, and Ebenezer kept him informed about how the Secession was developing. He lobbied to 'get the four outed ministers brought in again', but in later years he would lament their bigotry.[53]

He was also concerned to support the cause of orthodoxy in England, where the prosecution of Simson attracted much negative comment: 'church tyranny is cry'd out on. Such as are of another mind speak not openly'.[54] Non-subscribers among the

---

[48] *Extracts from the Diary*, pp. 34-37.

[49] Carlyle, *Autobiography*, p. 9.

[50] The campaign and Erskine's part in it can be followed in Wodrow's *Analecta* and *Correspondence*, and through the exemplary monograph of Anne Skoczylas, *Mr Simson's Knotty Case: Divinity, Politics, and Due Process in Early Eighteenth-Century Scotland* (Montreal: McGill-Queen's University Press, 2001).

[51] Wodrow, *Analecta*, III, pp. 498-503.

[52] *Extracts from a Diary*, pp. 1-15, 39-40. See also *Memoirs of the Life, Time and Writings of Thomas Boston* (1776), pp. 396, 401-02, 487.

[53] Donald Fraser (ed.), *The Life and Diary of the Rev. Ralph Erskine* (Edinburgh: William Oliphant & Son, 1834), p. 429; HMC, *Mar and Kellie*, pp. 530-31; Laurence, *A Great Grievance*.

[54] Robert Wodrow, *Private Letters* (ed. James Maidment; Edinburgh: n.p., 1829), pp. 68-69.

Dissenters were accusing Grange of 'persecuting' Simson.[55] Erskine worried that Queen Caroline was enamoured with Samuel Clarke's low christology, and took comfort from an audience with George I in which the king appeared to disapprove of Simson. He was disturbed that Lord Chancellor King would not affirm the deity of Christ, fearing that he 'has drunk in too much his uncle, Mr [John] Lock's, principles on tolleration of all things, without exception almost. And this principle of latitude will undermine both religion and liberty'.[56] He corresponded with Isaac Watts on the doctrine of the Trinity,[57] and met occasionally with a circle of Calvinist Dissenters in London led by Abraham Taylor, who enjoyed the patronage of the old Earl of Sunderland. Taylor was disturbed by the drift from Reformed orthodoxy in the Scottish universities, and he feared that Watts as well as Simson was tinged with the Arian heresy.[58] Erskine sought to shore up orthodoxy by subscribing to the Congregationalist Thomas Ridgley's *Body of Divinity*, an exposition of the Westminster Catechism.[59] Like Wodrow, Grange was now part of a growing international network of orthodox Calvinists committed to the revival of experimental piety.[60]

Despite his Calvinist credentials, Grange was still suspected of harbouring Jacobite sympathies.[61] He secured the financial rescue of a number of Jacobite families by purchasing their estates,[62] though in doing so he had the support of the Argathelians who sought to reconcile exiled Jacobites to George I and George II. In exile, his brother betrayed the Jacobite case by exposing Bishop Atterbury's part in the plot of 1722, and Grange subsequently lobbied Sir Robert Walpole for a pardon for his brother.[63] In contrast to his Jacobite relatives, Erskine was an ardent exponent of evangelical Presbyterianism who urged 'prosecuting the Papists in the North of Scotland'.[64] He assured Wodrow in 1727 that he knew 'by direct conversation, that the bulk of our Jacobites' were growing disillusioned with the Pretender, and increasingly impressed by King George. Erskine's enemies were unconvinced. During the Simson trial, he complained of being slandered as a 'hypocrite and pretender to religion, as a Jacobite and in the same bottome with his brother, the Earl

---

[55] Skoczylas, *Mr Simson's Knotty Case*, p. 274.

[56] Wodrow, *Analecta*, III, pp. 457-59.

[57] HMC, *Mar and Kellie*, p. 528: 'Letters from Mr. Isaac Watts, minister of the Gospel in London, to Lord Grange, dated 23rd September, 1724, and 14th January, 1725, with copy reply by Lord Grange, dated 17th February, 1725'; Wodrow, *Analecta*, III, p. 206.

[58] Wodrow, *Analecta*, III, 460; *The Correspondence of Rev. Robert Wodrow*, pp. 170, 290, 449, 454, 470.

[59] Thomas Ridgley, *A Body of Divinity* (2 vols; 1731-33), I: List of Subscribers.

[60] On this network, see Mark Noll, *The Rise of Evangelicalism* (Leicester: IVP, 2004), pp. 48-54.

[61] See Carlyle, *Autobiography*, p. 9.

[62] Cruickshanks, 'Erskine, Hon. James (c.1678-1754)'.

[63] Gregg, 'The Jacobite Career of John, Earl of Mar', pp. 190-93.

[64] Wodrow, *Analecta*, III, p. 458.

of Mar'. A libel was affixed to his door in Edinburgh, 'Queries to my Lord Grange. 1. Whither he be a Jesuit or not? 2. Whither he be a pensioner to the Pope?'[65]

Mid-Life Crisis: Broken Marriage and Opposition Politics

Erskine's Jacobite connections would be one factor in the collapse of his marriage, which was but one element of a mid-career crisis in the early 1730s. He and Rachel Chiesley had been swiftly wed around 1706 after a passionate romance. His family and friends disapproved – her father had been executed for the murder of Lord President Lockhart in 1689, and despite her beauty this was seen as a bad match. She went on to bear eight children, but the marriage disintegrated around 1730. In July of that year, the orthodox Presbyterian minister, Robert Wodrow, heard 'the very melancholy account of the open breach in my Lord Grange his family'. His wife had accused him of adultery, set spies upon him during his visits to England, intercepted his letters, and alleged that they revealed treasonous dealings with the Pretender ('without the least shaddou for the inference'). In turn, Erskine accused his wife of being 'that plague of his life' – alcoholic, deranged, and prone to murderous rages. Wodrow, who reckoned Lord Grange 'among the greatest men in this time', observed that even his enemies admitted that he had suffered 'the greatest provocations possible', though they still spread 'calumnies' against him, which the clergyman could only hope were 'very groundless'.[66]

The couple separated, but Lady Grange continued to threaten and harangue him in public. Meanwhile, he was making increasingly desperate efforts to shore up the family finances and secure the pardon and repatriation of his ailing brother. Lady Mar was afflicted by mental illness, and Erskine fought a bitter custody battle in a vain attempt to gain access to her income. He now feared that Rachel's outbursts and allegations could wreck his plans to bring Mar home, especially if she supplied written evidence of his animosity towards Walpole. Convinced that she could ruin the family, Lord Grange and his kinsman Lord Lovat took drastic action.[67] In January 1732, they arranged for her to be abducted from Edinburgh 'by some highlanders'. This was a matter of gossip in the city 'for a few weeks only'; as Carlyle notes, the abduction was ignored by the authorities, supported by her sons and relations, and justified as 'only confining a mad woman in a place of safety'.[68] A verse libel that appears to date from this time chastised 'hypocrit Lord Grange,'

---

[65] Wodrow, *Analecta*, III, p. 410, 506, 510-11.

[66] Wodrow, *Analecta*, IV, pp. 165-66; 'Letters of Lord Grange', p. 8.

[67] For this reading of Erskine's motives, I am indebted to the unpublished work of Anne Skoczylas.

[68] Carlyle, *Autobiography*, pp. 11-13. See John and Charles Edward Sobieski Stuart, *Tales of the Century: Or Sketches of the Romance of History between the Years 1746 and 1846* (Edinburgh: James Marshall, 1847), pp. 233-96; David Laing, 'Mrs Erskine, Lady Grange, in the Island of St Kilda', *Proceedings of the Society* (1874), pp. 722-30; R.W. Seton-Watson, 'The Strange Story of Lady Grange', *History* 16 (1931), pp. 12-24; Margaret Macaulay, *The Prisoner of St Kilda* (Edinburgh: Luath Press, 2009).

declaring that 'Grange kidnapt his wife by noon/And whoors with upcast eyes'.[69] But it was only in later years, when contemporaries discovered the true fate of Lady Grange, that Erskine faced widespread opprobrium.

Within a few months of her abduction, the Earl of Mar died in exile. The fortunes of the family had reached their nadir, and Erskine was furious. For years, he had lobbied Ilay and Walpole on his brother's behalf, and heard them 'profess great friendship to me and the family', but 'when it came to the execution', they did nothing, resorting to 'shifts, tricks, and lies'. Eventually, he had been given permission to attend his brother's deathbed, but on his return, his reception by Ilay was 'very cold and dry', and Erskine 'resolved to deall no more' with him. He told the Earl that he 'had been his friend and humble servant more than thirty years', and Ilay reportedly confessed that Grange's conduct towards him had been 'irreproachable'. But Erskine was now convinced that 'under a very thin mask of friendship, he is an enemy to us all, and was driving at our ruine'. He decided to throw in his lot with the opposition, flourishing in the wake of the Excise Crisis. Walpole had 'rendered himself obnoxious to the law, and hatefull to the bulk of the English', 'high church, whig and dissenter' – 'he and Ilay proceed like men drunk with power and infatuated of heaven'. They were 'oppressors of the family we belong to, and enemys of Britain'.[70]

Walpole reacted swiftly to Grange's defection, framing parliamentary legislation to exclude Scottish judges from sitting in the Commons. Erskine was defiant: 'I will not be trampled on by him, Lord Islay, and his dogs'.[71] He promptly resigned from the bench and ran for election in Stirling, 'one of the most venal constituencies in Scotland', but even the support of Ebenezer Erskine and other 'high flying' clergy opposed to Ilay's policy on lay patronage was not enough to defeat the Argathelian political machine and its presiding officer. Grange was, however, returned for the rural constituency of Clackmannanshire, and would subsequently sit as MP for Stirling Burghs between 1741 and 1747.[72]

He was now a significant player in opposition politics. Allying himself with the Squadrone-Patriot Whigs, he attacked Walpole and the Robinocracy in a periodical, *The Thistle* (1734–36), and in pamphlets. *The Late Excise Scheme Dissected* (1734) maintained that 'the Liberties of this Country depend upon the Frequency and Independency of Parliaments', and it set out measures to secure Parliament from the arbitrary power of royal ministers.[73] *The Fatal Consequences of Ministerial Influence* (1736) bore on its title page a quotation from Addison's play, *Cato*, featuring the incorruptible Roman orator, the self-appointed guardian of the

---

[69] Wodrow, *Private Letters*, pp. 83-84. Carlyle, *Autobiography*, p. 11, suggests that Erskine exaggerated Lady Grange's violence, but even he accepts she was 'stormy and outrageous' and 'led him a miserable life'.

[70] 'Letters of Lord Grange', pp. 25-51.

[71] *A Selection from the Papers of the Earls of Marchmont*, 3 vols (London: John Murray, 1831), II, p. 18.

[72] Scott, 'James Erskine', *ODNB*.

[73] [James Erskine], *The Late Excise Scheme Dissected* (1734), pp. 21-22.

republic's laws, liberties, and civic virtue. It powerfully articulated the neo-Roman distinction between liberty and slavery (being 'obliged to act, or not to act, according to the arbitrary Will and Pleasure of another'), and argued that 'ministerial influence' over elections and Parliament was undermining Britain's mixed constitution and enslaving its citizens.[74] According to John Wilkes, who reprinted extracts many years later, the pamphlet 'made a very great noise'.[75]

In joining with the Patriot opposition, Erskine was able to redouble his assault on Ilay's ecclesiastical policy. From the late 1720s, Ilay emerged as a patron of the moderate clergy: he protected Simson, secured the election of Francis Hutcheson to Glasgow's Chair of Moral Philosophy, and helped to make William Wishart, Jr, Moderator of the General Assembly. One report suggests that under pressure from Ilay, Grange had 'softened with respect to our professor [Simson]'.[76] But in his own eyes, Grange was pitted against Ilay in a battle for the soul of Kirk and nation. In 1735, he supported a measure to reduce the number of playhouses, and in the following year he made his maiden speech as an MP. Characteristically, he set himself against the spirit of the age, opposing the repeal of witchcraft legislation with 'a long canting speech that set the house in a titter of laughter'.[77] According to Ian Bostridge, it was designed as 'an act of resistance to a deistical and irreligious English ministry', albeit one that made little headway in the face of 'the triumph of polite and rational discourse'.[78]

When Prince Frederick was expelled from the royal court in 1737, he became the new focus of the opposition. A year later, Grange was appointed the Prince's Secretary for Scotland. His son, James, was made one of the Prince's Advocates in Scotland in 1739.[79] The Prince's new residence at Leicester House became a

---

[74] [James Erskine], *The Fatal Consequence of Ministerial Influence* (1736), p. 5. See also *A Key for Filling up the Blanks in a Pamphlet Lately Published, intitled, The Fatal Consequences of Ministerial Influence* (n.d.). For further analysis of Grange's arguments, see Colin Kidd, 'North Britishness and the Nature of Eighteenth-Century British Patriotisms', *Historical Journal* 39 (1996), pp. 370-71; Colin Kidd, 'The Ideological Significance of Robertson's *History of Scotland*', in S.J. Brown (ed.), *William Robertson and the Expansion of Empire* (Cambridge: Cambridge University Press, 1997), pp. 126-27; Pasi Ihaleinen, *Agents of the People: Democracy and Popular Sovereignty in British and Swedish Parliamentary Debates, 1734–1800* (Leiden: Brill, 2010), pp. 84-85. On the neo-Roman concept of liberty, see Quentin Skinner, *Liberty before Liberalism* (Cambridge: Cambridge University Press, 1998).

[75] *The North Briton* 3.65 (8 Oct. 1763), pp. 162-67.

[76] Roger Emerson, *Academic Patronage in the Scottish Enlightenment* (Edinburgh: Edinburgh University Press, 2008), p. 92.

[77] Carlyle, *Autobiography*, p. 9. In the absence of contemporary reports of the speech, historians have had to rely on this passing remark from Carlyle, who wrote over six decades later.

[78] Ian Bostridge, 'Witchcraft Repealed', in Jonathan Barry, Marianne Hester, and Gareth Roberts (eds), *Witchcraft in Early Modern Europe* (Cambridge: Cambridge University Press, 1996), pp. 321-28 (p. 328).

[79] *Daily Gazetteer* 25 July 1739.

'shadow court', prepared to take over the government of Britain when the king died and the 'reversionary' interest succeeded to the throne.[80] Yet at the same time, Grange was exploring a more subversive alternative. When Lord Lovat initiated correspondence with the Pretender in 1739, Erskine was kept informed at every stage through another intimate friend, MacGregor of Balhaldy, who conducted the negotiations. The Pretender commended Lord Grange in 1740 for his 'zealous and loyal disposition', and he was tasked with building support for the Stuarts among opposition politicians. He continued in the service of the Prince of Wales, but absented himself from Parliament during divisions over the Hanoverians in 1742 and 1744, and entered into communication with French agents (and Cardinal de Fleury) to prepare for a Jacobite rising.[81]

This was the context in which Erskine began to forge links with the Evangelical revivalists. By the late 1730s, his campaigns for family honour, national virtue, and old-time religion had met with grave setbacks as well as some successes. A younger generation of ministers in the Kirk and in England was increasingly open to fresh currents of Enlightenment thought; in elite circles deistic sentiments were common and traditional beliefs in the demonic were ridiculed. Desperate to revive his family's fortunes and to combat the forces of corruption and irreligion, Grange latched onto oppositional networks – the 'shadow court' around the Prince of Wales, Jacobite conspirators, and the new Evangelicals – all inclined to denounce the Whig order as immoral and impious.[82]

Later Life: The Evangelical Revival

His introduction to the revivalist movement came courtesy of George Whitefield. In November 1739, on a preaching tour of the American colonies, Whitefield embarked on a long distance courtship with the Scottish Seceders.[83] When Grange was shown 'some of their mutual letters', presumably by Ralph and Ebenezer Erskine, he realised that 'they had but a very superficial Knowledge of one another'.[84] Once Whitefield arrived in Scotland in 1741, the Seceders soon realised their mistake –

---

[80] Aubrey Newman, 'The Political Patronage of Frederick Lewis, Prince of Wales', *Historical Journal* 1 (1958), pp. 68-75.

[81] Cruickshanks, 'Erskine, Hon. James (c.1678–1754)'.

[82] On the oppositional political context of early Evangelicalism in England see John Walsh, '"Methodism" and the Origins of English-Speaking Evangelicalism', in Mark Noll, David Bebbington and George Rawlyk (eds), *Evangelicalism: Comparative Studies of Popular Protestantism in North America, the British Isles, and Beyond, 1700–1900* (New York, NY: Oxford University Press, 1994), pp. 24-27; Grayson Ditchfield, *The Evangelical Revival* (London: University College London Press, 1998), pp. 66-68; J.C.D. Clark, 'The Eighteenth-Century Context', in William Abraham and James Kirby (eds), *The Oxford Handbook of Methodism* (Oxford: Oxford University Press, 2009), p. 4.

[83] John Gillies (ed.), *Letters of George Whitefield, 1734–1742* (Edinburgh: Banner of Truth, 1976), pp. 128-29, 139-41, 262-63, 267-68.

[84] UA-Herrnhut, R 13 C no. 6: JE to Count Zinzendorf, 11 April 1743.

Whitefield shared their Calvinist piety but resisted their high Presbyterian ecclesiology, and they denounced him 'as a priest of the superstitious Church of England and as of Latitudinarian Principles'.[85] Grange sided emphatically with the Anglicans against his own cousins, who now went out of their way to avoid him.[86] He heard Whitefield preach at a field meeting outside Edinburgh, denouncing sectarian divisions.[87] From 1741 onwards, he was speaking with Whitefield on a regular basis, in Edinburgh and London; he told James Hutton that the evening before he was 'sitting with Messrs Whitefield and Cennick &c', discussing the plight of lay preachers who had been press ganged into the army.[88]

In Scotland, Erskine keenly followed the revivals at Cambuslang and Kilsyth. Estranged from Ralph and Ebenezer Erskine, he looked to revivalist pastors within the Kirk: William McCulloch of Cambuslang, James Robe of Kilsyth, John MacLaurin of Glasgow, John Erskine of Kirkintilloch, and Alexander Webster.[89] He encouraged McCulloch to publish the testimonies of converts at Cambuslang, where William Carlyle may have been among the preachers.[90] He particularly admired the irenic James Robe; in October 1744 he was full of 'sweet and joyfull' expectation of his forthcoming visit to Kilsyth.[91]

More surprisingly, for a Scottish Calvinist, Erskine fell in with the Moravians. By April 1741, he had already enjoyed two long conversations with August Spangenberg, and the following year, he took the poet John Byrom to hear the Moravian preach at Fetter's Lane.[92] He embarked on a programme of research into Moravian history, reading numerous books and manuscripts, including Zinzendorf's 'short account', on which he drew up a list of queries.[93] When the Count visited London in February–March 1743, Erskine was fully apprised of his meetings with Whitefield (whom Zinzendorf encountered for the first time). Grange had his own personal audience with the Count and arranged with the Speaker and the Bearer of the Mace for his 'ready admittance' to the House of Commons.[94] They discussed the

---

[85] LRO, 14D32/567: JE to Selina, Countess of Huntingdon, 9 October 1744.

[86] *Calendar of the Trevecka Letters*, no. 1016.

[87] MCH-London, AB87 Folder 7: JE to James Hutton, August 1741.

[88] MCH-London, AB87 Folder 7: JE to James Hutton, n.d..

[89] JRUL, DDPr 1/26: JE to Howell Harris, 30 January 1750; MCH-London, AB87 Folder 7: JE to James Hutton, 26 May 1750. On the evangelical clergy in the Kirk, see John R. McIntosh, *Church and Theology in Enlightenment Scotland: The Popular Party, 1740–1800* (East Linton: Tuckwell Press, 1998); Yeager, *Enlightened Evangelicalism*.

[90] Keith Beebe (ed.), *The McCulloch Examinations of the Cambuslang Revival (1742)* (2 vols; Woodbridge: Scottish History Society, 2013), I, lii-liii, p. 351; II, p. 251.

[91] LRO, 14D32/540: JE to Selina Hastings, 9 October 1744.

[92] MCH-London, AB87 Folder 7: JE to James Hutton, 27 April 1741; R. Parkinson (ed.), *The Private Diary and Literary Remains of John Byrom, Vol II: Part I* (Manchester: The Chetham Society, 1856), pp. 318-19.

[93] MCH-London, AB87 Folder 7: JE to James Hutton, 6 May 1742.

[94] UA-Herrnhut, R 13 C no. 6: JE to James Hutton, [1 March 1743]; Colin Podmore, *The Moravian Church in England, 1728–1760* (Oxford: Clarendon Press, 1998), p. 85. The letter

potential for Moravian influence in Scotland, with Zinzendorf floating the idea that a Moravian missionary could instigate 'the study of Arabick in Edinburgh'.[95] Erskine was formally invited to join 'that Illustrious Society', the Order of the Mustard Seed. He wore the ring of the Order with pride, telling anyone who asked that it was a memorial of Count Zinzendorf.[96] It was an honour he shared with the Archbishop of Canterbury, John Potter, whom he knew well, and commended to fellow Evangelicals as a man 'having a reall sense of Christ on his heart, & Love for all who love jesus'.[97]

Meanwhile, he was extending his network among Calvinist Evangelicals. In October 1743, Howell Harris initiated a correspondence, and in February 1744, Whitefield introduced them to each other in person. The following month, Harris arranged a meeting between 'dear Mr Erskine' and the Countess of Huntingdon. He thought that Grange's 'light may be useful to her, & her zeal & warmth to him'.[98] The Congregationalist, Philip Doddridge, was also part of Grange's circle. Doddridge was on friendly terms with James Erskine, Jr,[99] and cited the witness of Grange's chaplain, a Reverend Spears, when he wrote his bestselling *Life of Colonel James Gardiner*, a long-time resident of Prestonpans.[100] And Erskine counted the prolific Calvinistic Baptist writer, Anne Dutton, as his dear friend.[101]

He was just as deeply involved with the Wesleys. He had heard John preach in Newcastle by the early 1740s, and Whitefield had drawn him to John's attention as early as 1742. Charles Wesley was present when Erskine first met the Countess of Huntingdon in 1744, and John was corresponding with Grange by 1745. Wesley (like Howell Harris) used franked sheets of letter paper supplied by the MP to save on postage costs.[102] Erskine was invited to the 1745 Conference in Bristol, and while

---

to Hutton can be dated by its reference to a Monday debate in the House of Commons 'on the Bill for better regulating the English Elections to Parlt', which was debated in the Commons on Monday 4 March 1743. See *The History and Proceedings of the House of Commons ... held in the Years 1742, and 1743* (1744), p. 218.

[95] UA-Hernnhut, R 13 C no. 6: JE to Zinzendorf, 11 April 1743.

[96] MCH-London, AB87 Folder 7: JE to James Hutton, 23 April 1743; UA-Herrnhut, R 13 C no. 6: JE to Zinzendorf, July 1744.

[97] *Calendar of the Trevecka Letters*, no. 1162; MCH-London, AB87 Folder 7: JE to August Spangenberg, 2 November 1742.

[98] *Calendar of the Trevecka Letters*, no. 999, 1150, 1152, 1186; Nuttall, 'Howell Harris and "the Grand Table"', p. 532.

[99] Geoffrey Nuttall (ed.), *Calendar of the Correspondence of Philip Doddridge* (London: HMSO, 1979), pp. 208, 365.

[100] *Some Remarkable Passages in the Life of Colonel James Gardiner* (1747); Carlyle, *Autobiography*, p. 18.

[101] JRUL, DDPr 1/26: JE to Howell Harris, 30 January 1750.

[102] Baker (ed.), *Works of John Wesley:* Volume 26. *Letters II: 1740–1755*, pp. 87, 124, 128-30, 132-36, 147; *Calendar of the Trevecka Letters*, no. 1186. On Wesley's use of letters franked 'Free – James Erskine', see Frank Baker (ed.), *The Works of John Wesley:* Volume 25. *Letters I: 1721–1739* (Oxford: Oxford University Press, 1980), p. 25. See also *Calendar of the Trevecka Letters*, no. 1291.

the participants were 'much disappointed' that he could not attend, they 'universally approved' his letter on 'terms of union'.[103] He did attend the London Conference in June 1748, by which time he had become especially close to Charles Wesley – in a two-year period between June 1745 and May 1747, Charles wrote twenty-six letters to Erskine (most of which have not survived).[104] As Ward observed, they could readily reduce each other to happy tears.[105] In one Sunday in April 1744, Charles observed that the whole congregation at the Foundery 'was in tears under the word. Old Mr Erskine [now in his mid-60s], in particular, was quite broken down'. In 1750, Charles was instrumental in the conversion of Erskine's daughter, who had fallen into Deism – when he brought the two together, 'She fell at his feet', and 'All wept'.[106]

His relationships with the revivalist leaders survived despite fresh rumours about the fate of Lady Grange. In late 1740, a smuggled letter from Rachel Erskine reached the Edinburgh lawyer Thomas Hope. Having assumed that the abducted woman would be 'well entertained and cared for', Hope now learned that she had been exiled far from civilised life to the barren wilds of St Kilda. The 'strange storyes were spread all over the town of Edinburgh, and made the talk of coffee houses and tea tables', and sent 'to several other places of Great Brittain'. Hope prevented the publication of a pamphlet narrative, but the scandal would haunt Erskine for years to come. He vigorously defended his own conduct towards 'that person' – his wife's relations had all consented to her removal, and his informants assured him that his generous allowance had ensured her 'comfortable accommodation'. Along with Lord Lovat, Grange believed that he was the victim of defamation, as his enemies (led by Hope) traduced his good name and his family's honour. Hope did pay for an expedition to find the unfortunate Lady Grange, but she was quickly moved from St Kilda to Assynt and then to the Isle of Skye. Erskine felt no remorse over his wife's plight; he persuaded himself and his godly friends that he was the true victim of 'horrid misfortunes'. Writing to Lovat in 1743, he drew comfort from the fact that Whitefield supported him in prayer during his ordeal.[107] When Lady Grange died in

---

[103] Maddox, 'Correspondence', p. 268. This was probably either the 3–4 April letter which John Wesley published in his *Journal* for 29 May 1745, or the longer letter on 'outward communion' dated 23 April 1745. See *A Collection of Letters on Religious Subject, From Various Eminent Ministers, and Others; to the Rev. John Wesley* (1797), pp. 37-40; Baker (ed.), *The Works of John Wesley: Volume 26. Letters II: 1740–1755*, pp. 129-30, 132-36. See also Kenneth Newport and Gareth Lloyd (eds), *The Letters of Charles Wesley* (2 vols; Oxford: Oxford University Press, 2013), I, p. 119.

[104] Maddox, 'Correspondence', pp. 267-74.

[105] Ward, *Protestant Evangelical Awakening*, p. 334.

[106] S.T. Kimborough and Kenneth Newport (eds), *The Manuscript Journal of Rev Charles Wesley* (2 vols; Nashville, TN: Kingswood Books, 2007), II, p. 403, 595, 597.

[107] Laing, 'Mrs Erskine, Lady Grange', pp. 722-30; 'Letters of Lord Grange', pp. 58-67; letters from Lord Lovat in HMC, *Mar and Kellie*, pp. 551-53 (dated 31 October 1742 and September 1743). See also Sobieski Stuart, *Tales of the Century*, pp. 285-96; Carlyle, *Autobiography*, pp. 8-13; Seton-Watson, 'The Strange Story of Lady Grange', pp. 20-23.

1745, Erskine wasted no time in marrying his long-term companion Frances Lindsay.[108] Meanwhile, Hope pursued Erskine in the courts, and the case was only finally settled in 1751, when Erskine paid Hope's expenses.[109] Writing in 1746, John Wesley sympathised with 'Mr. Erskine's trials'.[110]

That he remained in good standing with his godly friends suggests that he was an esteemed member of the Evangelical network. His elite connections, his legal expertise, and his parliamentary seat, made him a valuable ally. He used his long-standing friendship with the field marshall of the British forces (the Earl of Stair) to secure the release of Methodist lay preachers impressed into military service.[111] In 1744, he provided legal advice when Charles Wesley faced allegations of scandalous behaviour, and together with the Countess of Huntingdon, he interceded with the bishop of London on Wesley's behalf.[112]

But Erskine brought something else to the Revival – a powerful strategic vision that was both intellectually compelling and politically promising. He had amused himself with 'a Variety of Studys and Projects', he confessed to Zinzendorf in 1743, but he now saw these as mere 'moonshine'; for the rest of his life, 'my Desire is to be wholly taken up with the Gospel ... to direct every thing towards the Advancement of it'.[113] He argued that the new Evangelicals should steer a course between confessional dogmatism and latitudinarian compromise. By setting aside their differences and forming a unified revivalist front, they could revive the fortunes of the Reformation gospel in Enlightenment Britain and position themselves to claim the centre ground of British Protestantism.

Grange set out this vision in substantive letters and reports. In April 1743, he sent Zinzendorf a twenty-four-page report on the religious situation in Scotland, analysing each of the key parties – the Episcopalians, the Kirk's Evangelicals, and the Kirk's 'prevailing' 'modish' faction; the Seceders, Cameronians, Independents, Quakers, and Papists. He explained theological controversies over James Fraser of Brea, John Simson, and the Marrow Men, and gave astute advice on how the

---

[108] The marriage took place at St James Duke's Place on 20 June 1745, less than a month after Erskine received the news of Rachel's death. James Erskine was described as a 'widow' of 'ye Parish of St John the Evangelist Westminster', while his new wife was of 'ye Parish of Chelsea' (London Metropolitan Archives, St James Duke's Place, Register of Marriages, 1700-54, P69/JS1/A/002/MS07894, Item 003). Lady Grange died on 10 May and Erskine wrote to acknowledge the news of her death on 1 June (Macaulay, *The Prisoner of St Kilda*, pp. 145-52).

[109] Sobieski Stuart, *Tales of the Century*, pp. 291-96; Macaulay, *The Prisoner of St Kilda*, pp. 160-61.

[110] Maddox, 'Correspondence', pp. 269-71.

[111] MCH-London, AB87 Folder 7: JE to James Hutton, n.d.; *Calendar of the Trevecka Letters*, no. 1186, 1191; *Manuscript Journal of Rev Charles Wesley*, II, pp. 405-06.

[112] *Manuscript Journal of Rev Charles Wesley*, II, pp. 429-30, 434; Maddox, 'Correspondence', p. 266.

[113] UA-Herrnhut, R 13 C no. 6: JE to Zinzendorf, 11 April 1743.

Moravians could overcome the 'Party Biggotrie' of Scottish Presbyterians.[114] For the Wesleys, he drew up a paper ('Of Outward Christian Communion') prepared in the form of a legal brief on eight pages of foolscap.[115] In 1749, he drew up a similar document, filling nine pages of legal-sized notepaper, on John Wesley's doctrine of Christian perfection, a major point of contention among the revivalists.[116]

In some respects, Erskine's conception of the Revival was staunchly traditional – it was a return to Reformation principles. The Moravians appealed to him as descendants of Jan Hus, followers of Luther, and the church of the famous Reformed intellectual, Jan Amos Comenius.[117] He shared with Howell Harris a love of the 'Good old orthodox Reformers and Puritans'.[118] Writing to the Countess of Huntingdon, he recommended the writings of 'that great Evangelical Man Dr [Richard] Sibb[e]s', the Cambridge Puritan renowned for his 'affectionate' divinity.[119] His friendly critique of Wesley's sermon on Christian perfection cited the Westminster Confession as well as the Thirty-Nine Articles.[120] In writing to Zinzendorf he praised 'sound and orthodox' Scottish churchmen who clung to 'the old presbyterian way of Grace' and adhered to 'the Doctrine of the Reformation' or 'the Evangelical reform'd Doctrine'.[121]

What was this 'Doctrine of the Reformation'? In his letter to Zinzendorf, he summarised it in trinitarian terms. Evangelicals were 'sound & orthodox as to the suppream Deity of our Lord jesus & of the Father & Holy Ghost, & as to Salvation Righteousnesse & Holynesse in and through Christ only by the drawing of the Father & Work of the Holy Ghost, and of men's lost Estate by nature, & the impossibility of their Recovery but by jesus only'.[122] Writing to John Wesley, he parsed the Reformation gospel slightly differently, with a greater accent on sanctification. He commended Wesley for 'your doctrine of man's utter ruin by the fall, and utter inability to do any thing for his own recovery; and the necessity of regeneration; and of an interest in Christ by Faith only, that works by love, and produces universal

---

[114] UA-Hernnhut, R 13 C no. 6: JE to Zinzendorf, 11 April 1743.

[115] See Baker (ed.), *The Works of John Wesley:* Volume 26. *Letters II: 1740–1755*, pp. 132-36. For the full version, see Richard Steele, *'Gracious Affection' and 'True Virtue' according to Jonathan Edwards and John Wesley* (Metuchen, NJ: Scarecrow Press, 1994), pp. 369-83.

[116] Maddox, 'James Erskine's Critique', p. 39. The original manuscript is in the Wesleyan Collection of Emory University.

[117] UA-Herrnhut, R 13 C no. 6: JE to Spangenberg, 30 March 1742 (on Hus); MCH-London, AB87 Folder 7: JE to James Hutton, 27 April 1741 (on Comenius); JE to James Hutton, 23 April 1743 (on Luther).

[118] *Calendar of the Trevecka Letters*, no. 1295.

[119] LRO, 14D32/540: JE to Selina Hastings, 9 October 1744.

[120] Maddox, 'James Erskine's Critique', p. 47.

[121] UA-Hernnhut, R 13 C no. 6: JE to Zinzendorf, 11 April 1743.

[122] Unity Archives, Hernnhut, R 13 C no. 6: Erskine to Zinzendorf, 11 April 1743.

holiness in heart, lip and life; and all by the operations of the Holy Spirit'.[123] This gospel – ruin by sin, redemption by Christ, regeneration by the Holy Spirit – turned attention away from natural religion and human moral effort and towards the 'supernatural' work of Christ and the Spirit. It fostered the affective piety that drenched Erskine's letters, where he extolled 'lovely Jesus', 'blessed Jesus', 'sweet Jesus'. This was the kind of effusive piety mocked as 'enthusiasm' by the polite clergy. They would have been equally disdainful of Grange's fascination with seventeenth-century Moravian prophecies predicting 'The Fall of the House of Austria'.[124]

On other issues, Grange still sounded like an unreconstructed Scottish Presbyterian. He held tenaciously to the sabbatarianism that had been a hallmark of Scottish and Puritan piety. He rarely spoke in the House of Commons, but when he did so in June 1746 it was to denounce a proposed clause in the Militia Bill that ordered musters after divine service. When the House voted for it two to one, he declared this 'a new addition to the crying sins of the land'. Around the same time, he sent Harris a sermon against theatre-going.[125] He grumbled about 'our Beaux and Belles & bon Companions', who disliked Whitefield for 'inveighing against Playhouse, dancing Assemblys, meetings for cards & Title tattle, haunting Taverns, gaudy Dress, Levity in behaviour & conversation'.[126]

It is hardly surprising that Erskine often presented the Revival as a counter-Enlightenment movement. In the 1740s, as in the 1710s and 20s, he lamented contemporary intellectual trends. Deism was now 'professed openly by ... the greatest part of our nobility and gentry'.[127] His own daughter 'confessed she had turned many to Deism'.[128] Writing to Zinzendorf and other Moravians, he complained of the rise within the Kirk of 'the meer philosophick moralists', and 'the modish way of moral Philosophy embellished with a few scriptural Thoughts'. He thrilled to the 'supernatural' religion of the Moravians, because their 'Apostolical' missionary successes demonstrated the transformative power of revealed religion and undermined 'some prevailing Schemes wch degrade certain Christian Doctrines into a meer notional Lifeless Philosophy'. The 'new fashion'd Clergy' or 'the fine polite Courtier Clergy' were 'the most prevailing party and most favoured by Statesmen', but 'they love not spirituall evangelical Christianity'. In the pulpit they were cautious 'for fear of the people', but outside it they 'pretended' to have a monopoly on reason and politeness, even though the Evangelicals included men like John Maclaurin, 'Elder Brother of the late eminent Mathematician Colin Maclaurin, and who a few years ago was within one voice of being chosen Professor of

---

[123] Erskine to John Wesley, 4 September 1745, in *A Collection of Letters*, p. 41. Intriguingly, the accent here falls on sanctification, whereas the letter to the Lutheran Zinzendorf emphasises justification by Christ's righteousness.

[124] Moravian Archives, London, AB87 Folder 7: Erskine to James Hutton, 27 April 1741

[125] *Calendar of the Trevecka Letters*, nos. 1474, 1493[b].

[126] Moravian Archives, London, AB87 Folder 7: Erskine to James Hutton, August 1741.

[127] *Calendar of the Trevecka Letters*, no. 1285.

[128] *Manuscript Journal of Rev Charles Wesley*, II, p. 595.

Theology' at Glasgow University. Erskine took the trouble to explain the Simson affair to Zinzendorf, observing that 'the Symsonians' had used the Marrow controversy to attack 'the Doctrine of free Grace', and had abused their academic positions to wean divinity students off the orthodox gospel.[129] The Evangelical Revival was a defence of Reformation doctrine against Enlightenment erosion.

In other ways, however, Erskine's Evangelicalism was a fresh departure. The vocabulary of the movement was a potent mix of the old-fashioned and the fashionable, with the venerable 'language of Canaan' blended with the new-fangled jargon of the literati. Erskine latched onto the concept of 'benevolence', associated with the moral philosophy of Shaftesbury and Hutcheson. He had read Hutcheson's *Inquiry into the Original of our Ideas of Beauty and Virtue* (1725) a year after its publication, and he told Wodrow that he had been 'entertain'd' with its 'many Speculations'. In 'the main' he took its notions to be 'just & solid', and years later he would use Hutchesonian language in a long letter to the Nottingham Methodist, Daniel Saint, setting out a rationale for 'Universal Love & Benevolence to all the Humane Race without Exception'. Yet like Jonathan Edwards, he worried that Hutcheson's argument was 'conducted so litle with regard to God, and with a certain Cast as if Virtue could be established, if not without yet, abstract from the Notion of God'. Shaftesbury's approach was more 'directly' secular, but reading Hutcheson 'tends rather to lead an unwary mind into the full of Shaftsbury's way than to bring God directly into the scheme.' Unsurprisingly, Erskine's own account of benevolence was emphatically theocentric, more Edwardsean than Hutchesonian. It emphasised conformity to the divine being as the end of humanity, the fallenness of human nature, the Devil as 'the grand Pattern' of malice and pride, the power of 'the Blood of God', the 'Heavenly Principle fixed in us by the Holy Ghost', and the 'Social Life' of 'the Kingdom of Grace'. But in his conviction that 'all Mankind are Brethren and Sisters' and his emphasis on 'natural sympathy', Erskine was offering an Evangelical revision of the new ethics rather than a simple reversion to traditional vocabulary.[130]

More importantly, he celebrated the new Evangelical religion for turning its back on the intolerance of post-Reformation Christendom. 'There are few things so astonishing to me', he told Zinzendorf, 'as the bad and mischievous way that those who profess Christ, have almost in all Ages & Places treated one another'. The one-time admirer of Jean Le Clerc still cherished the value of toleration, and was keen to assure Zinzendorf that 'of late very many of the Presbyterians in Scotland, have declared roundly & openly against all sort of Persecution & Severity on account of Religion, & for a Tolleration'. The Seceders still denounced toleration like their

---

[129] UA-Hernnhut, R 13 C no. 6: JE to Spangenberg, 30 March 1742; JE to Zinzendorf, 11 April 1743; MCH-London, AB87 Folder 7: JE to James Hutton, 17 September 1742.

[130] NLS, Advocates Mss 44.6.8: Wodrow Letters, Quarto 3, fo. 10/6: JE to Robert Wodrow, 6 November 1726; Leicestershire Record Office, 14D32/567: Erskine to Daniel Saint, 28 September 1744. See Norman Fiering, *Jonathan Edwards Moral Thought and its British Context* (Chapel Hill, NC: University of North Carolina Press, 1981). I am grateful to Anne Skoczylas for sharing her notes on the Wodrow correspondence.

Covenanter forefathers, and had 'notions of blending the Church and the State together'. 'But this Enmity to Tolleration lessens every day, as the Spirit of Biggotry declines'.[131] Pietist ecumenism was a solvent for clerical bigotry.

He knew that this would be controversial among his fellow Scots, and expected to be censured as 'a Moravian Heretick and underminer of the Gospel'.[132] In letters to Zinzendorf and Wesley he warned of the Scottish temper, quoting the Renaissance poet George Buchanan, 'Perfervidum Scotorum ingenium'.[133] He told Wesley that while Presbyterians comprised 'five-eights of the real Christians' in Scotland, 'I fear three-fifths are woefully bigotted'. To explain why this was so, he turned to John Locke's *Essay concerning Human Understanding* and its concept of 'the Association of Ideas'. People long accustomed to explaining 'the essential things of christianity' in a particular way, tended to 'transfer their zeal for the essential things to their own way of explication'. They assumed 'a necessary connection' between the essentials and their own explication, even though the connection only existed in their heads. This 'association of ideas' had made it very difficult for many Christians to disentangle 'the great essentials' of the gospel, from their 'particular opinions and practices'. It explained why 'even saints act like the most fierce, cruel, and unforgiving, proud, domineering sinner'.[134]

'It grieves my Heart', Erskine told Hutton, 'when honest Christians entertain Mistakes and Prejudices agst one another'.[135] He believed it was the duty of Christians 'to bring all the LORD's people from this bigotry', and he laid out his strategy for doing so in letters to Zinzendorf and Wesley. His aim was to foster 'Harmony' among all those who embraced 'the great things of the Gospel'. Real Christians were united by 'practical' doctrines, and divided by 'speculative' differences over reprobation and universal redemption. Such points were not so much 'Religious as Philosophical, or at least Theologico-Philosophicae'. Erskine embraced 'the Great Things of the Gospel' and distanced himself from elaborate scholastic orthodoxy. 'People should not be troubled about secret Decrees but about the Work of Grace in their own souls'.[136] He was willing to fight over the Trinity, but not over Calvinism and Arminianism.

What concerned Erskine was that the different wings of the Revival were still inclined to major on minors. The Calvinistic Methodists placed such stress on 'free grace' that they fostered antinomianism, a tendency both divisive and demoralising. Erskine expressed shock at instances of sexual abuse among Ranter-like 'antinomians' associated with Whitefield's Tabernacle, where corrupt preachers got 'in to men's houses ... adulterating their wives, fornicating their daughters,

---

[131] UA-Hernnhut, R 13 C no. 6: JE to Zinzendorf, 11 April 1743.

[132] MCH-London, AB87 Folder 7: JE to August Spangenberg, 2 November 1742.

[133] *A Collection of Letters*, p. 41; UA-Hernnhut, R 13 C no. 6: JE to Zinzendorf, 11 April 1743.

[134] Baker (ed.), *The Works of John Wesley:* Volume 26. *Letters II: 1740–1755*, p. 129.

[135] MCH-London, AB87 Folder 7: JE to James Hutton, 6 May 1742.

[136] UA-Hernnhut, R 13 C no. 6: JE to Zinzendorf, 11 April 1743; Baker (ed.), *The Works of John Wesley:* Volume 26. *Letters II: 1740–1755*, pp. 129-30.

sodomitically abusing their boys'.[137] At a less serious level, he was disturbed at Gilbert Tennent's unrestrained attacks on Moravians as 'Enthusiasts', and sympathised with Wesley's complaint that Jonathan Edwards appeared to elevate Calvinist distinctives (like absolute predestination and particular redemption) into prerequisites for sound Christianity. Yet he feared that the Wesleyans made the same mistake with Arminian doctrine, writing universal redemption into their hymns so that Calvinists like Whitefield could not join in singing them.[138] Erskine worried that John Wesley's insistence on his doctrine of Christian perfection was alienating Reformed revivalists, and he asked the Wesleys to refrain from placing the worst construction on Calvinist teaching.[139] As for the Moravians, they could be more proactive in refuting 'misrepresentations' of their teaching, and more cautious in their 'use of Phrases & ways of speaking'. Writing before he had met Zinzendorf, Erskine feared that 'the Count is too rash foreward and positive, & apt to use too strong & sometimes paradoxical Expressions & Thoughts'.[140]

In almost every letter he wrote, Erskine sought to foster love, peace and understanding between the different Evangelical camps. Throughout the 1740s, he was unusual in retaining the friendship and respect of all the major branches of the Revival – English, Welsh and Scottish; Calvinist, Arminian, and Moravian. He moved easily between the Moravians at Fetter Lane, the Wesleys at the Foundery, and Whitefield's Tabernacle. He wrote to Harris with the latest news of Charles Wesley's itinerant ministry, using extracts from Charles' manuscript journal to show that Wesley was doing good work countering antinomian excesses.[141] In writing to Zinzendorf, he found points of contact between the Moravians' doctrine of universal redemption and free grace and similar teaching in James Fraser of Brea and the Marrow Men.[142] He kept the Moravians informed about the successes of Whitefield's ministry and the Scottish revivals and Jonathan Edwards' latest publication on the life of David Brainerd. He sent correspondence from James Robe to Zinzendorf, and donated a 1750 edition of Robe's sermons to the Moravian leader and to Charles Wesley.[143] In letters to John Wesley, Howell Harris, and James Hutton, he promoted the Scottish plan for an international 'concert of prayer' among

---

[137] *Calendar of the Trevecka Letters*, no. 1285, 1306.

[138] Baker (ed.), *The Works of John Wesley:* Volume 26. *Letters II: 1740–1755*, pp. 132-36. On Tennent, see MCH-London, AB87 Folder 7: JE to Spangenberg, 2 November 1742.

[139] Maddox, 'James Erskine's Critique'.

[140] MCH-London, AB87 Folder 7: JE to Spangenberg, 2 November 1742.

[141] *Calendar of the Trevecka Letters*, no. 1480, 1507.

[142] UA-Herrnhut, R 13 C no. 6: JE to Zinzendorf, 11 April 1743.

[143] UA-Herrnhut, R 13 C no. 6: James Robe to JE, 15 April 1743; MCH-London, AB87 Folder 7: JE to James Hutton ['At his Excellence Count Zinzendorf's … Bloomsbury Square], 26 May 1750; Randy Maddox, 'Collection of Books Owned by the Charles Wesley Family in the John Rylands Library', *Bulletin of the John Rylands Library* 88 (2006), p. 149: 'C Wesley 1750. The Gift of my much respected and beloved Friend James Erskine Esqr'.

revivalists.[144] He gave John Wesley a copy of a Scottish devotional classic – *The Sum of Saving Knowledge* – suggesting that Wesley publish 'in a little cheap pamphlet, with a proper preface recommending it to the Scotch Presbyterians', who 'would at once see your soundness in the Faith of Jesus Christ'. When Wesley visited Erskine in his London residence a few days later, he declared the book 'too Calvinistic', but Grange was 'exceeding glad' to hear the evangelist urge his Foundery congregation to 'moderation and brotherly communion' with 'Mr. Whitefield's people'.[145]

For Erskine, the Evangelical Revival was no mere return to seventeenth-century orthodoxy; it was a new moment, when the bitter divisions of the Reformation could be swallowed up in a union of true Christians. Erskine was astonished at Whitefield's positive reception in Scotland. Here was a man who 'avows and owns himself a member & minister of the Church of England'; who denies that Presbytery is by divine right; who declares that the Solemn League and Covenant is a sinful oath; who preaches Calvinism but urges charity towards Arminian brethren. 'That our Presbyterians would hold Communion with such a one, would have appeared incredible 20 or 30 years ago ... Gods ways are wonderful'.[146]

For most of his career, Erskine had lamented declension; in the 1740s, he rejoiced that 'primitive purity' had 'lately revived in a way that seems supernatural'. The Moravians had been honoured with 'the Graces and Gifts of the Spirit beyond what I have heard or read of in modern times'. For all its Calvinist orthodoxy, Scotland had been marked by 'a great deadness & Lifelessness, even among the best people'. But 'the God of Cambuslang' brought an extraordinary 'effusion of the Spirit', drenching the parched land with showers of revival.[147]

In seeking to unite the revivalist factions in a common cause, Erskine hoped to make them credible to patrons at the highest level of British society. As Scottish secretary to the Prince of Wales, he worked to place the revivalists in prime position to take advantage of the eventual succession of Prince Frederick. It may well be due to Erskine's influence that the Prince himself became an occasional hearer of Whitefield in the early 1740s, and that Whitefield was talking from 1743 about 'being made a Bishop'. It is surely no coincidence that Prince Frederick sent for the Countess in March 1744, the same month in which she met Erskine for the first time, and a month after Whitefield had introduced him to Howell Harris. Erskine probably brought Scottish friends like William Kerr, Earl of Lothian, and his relative Lady Frances Erskine into the Leicester House circle, and may have secured the appointment of the Scottish Evangelical Alexander Webster as the Prince's chaplain

---

[144] Baker (ed.), *The Works of John Wesley: Volume 26. Letters II: 1740–1755*, p. 128; *Calendar of the Trevecka Letters*, no. 1305, 3188, 1312; MCH-London, AB87 Folder 7: JE to James Hutton, 26 May 1750.

[145] *A Collection of Letters*, p. 42; *HMC, 15th Report, Appendix, Part II: The Manuscripts of J. Eliot Hodgkin, Esq., F.S.A., of Richmond, Surrey* (London: HMSO, 1897), p. 247.

[146] MCH-London, AB87 Folder 7: JE to James Hutton, August 1741.

[147] UA-Herrnhut, R 13 C no. 6: JE to Spangenberg, 30 March 1742; JE to Zinzendorf, 11 April 1743; MCH-London, AB87 Folder 7: JE to James Hutton, 17 September 1742.

in 1748. His long association with opposition peers like Bolingbroke makes their openness to Whitefield somewhat less surprising.[148] Harris believed that Grange could help the Countess gain the confidence of the Archbishop of Canterbury.[149] As Ward noted, Erskine offered a genuine strategy for 'a mission within the Establishment'. He sought to build a broad-based revivalist coalition bringing together Whitefield, Harris, the Countess of Huntingdon, the Wesleys, and the Moravians 'on a Catholic Christianity and anti-bigotry platform', one that would shift the balance of the power in the Kirk (and the churches of England and Wales) 'ahead of the shift in government to be expected when the accession of the prince brought the reversionary interest to power'.[150]

The leading Evangelicals were no doubt fully apprised of this strategy, but they may well have been in the dark about his communication with the Jacobites. Overtly, Erskine professed his loyalty to the Hanoverians. In 1744, he presented loyal addresses from his constituents in Inverkeithing and Stirling to the king, expressing their 'Abhorrence' at the invasion threat from France and the 'Popish Pretender'.[151] Yet in June 1745, he informed Charles Edward that 'there never was and never can be such a favourable opportunity to attempt your Majesty's restoration'. He lamented the Pretender's 'very rash' decision to mount a rebellion without French troops or arms, and joined other Jacobites in secretly lobbying for French military support.[152]

As in 1715, however, he sat out the rebellion, this time in London, missing the Jacobite victory at Prestonpans, fought alongside his own estate.[153] When he described the battle in two letters to Charles Wesley, he did so as a loyal Hanoverian, referring to 'our King' and 'the young Pretender' and his Highland 'rebels', who fought like 'enraged furys'. While he gave a notably positive account of the Chevalier's personal courage and conduct, he noted the 'popish' allegiances of his aristocratic supporters, and told Wesley of the good death of Colonel Gardiner, who had fallen at Prestonpans fighting the rebels. Gardiner was married to Erskine's 'kinswoman', Lady Frances Erskine, and their estate was literally across the road from his. He was 'a real Christian', Grange assured Wesley, who as he lay dying,

---

[148] Nuttall, 'Howell Harris and "The Grand Table"', pp. 532-33, 541, 543; Boyd Schlenther, *Queen of the Methodists: The Countess of Huntingdon and the Eighteenth-Century Crisis of Faith and Society* (Durham: Durham Academic Press, 1997), pp. 39-43. On Erskine's links to the Earl of Lothian and Lady Frances Erskine, see Carlyle, *Autobiography*, pp. 15-16, 19. On Webster, see Mary Stewart, 'Webster, Alexander (1707–84)', *ODNB*.

[149] *Calendar of the Trevecka Letters*, no. 1152.

[150] Ward, 'Was there a Methodist Evangelistic Strategy in the Eighteenth Century?', pp. 288-91.

[151] *London Gazette*, 31 March–3 April 1744, p. 4; *London Gazette*, 1–5 May 1744, pp. 3-4.

[152] Cruickshanks, 'Erskine, Hon. James (c. 1678–1754)'.

[153] See John Marchant, *History of the Present Rebellion* (1745), p. 98.

told the Chevalier, 'You are come, Sir, to take a temporal crown, and I am going to get a crown of glory'.[154]

Deciding where Erskine's true loyalties lay is difficult, if not impossible. He may well have been a committed Jacobite, dedicated to the restoration of the Stuarts. Alternatively, he may have been a lifelong Presbyterian Whig, operating as a double agent for the Prince of Wales and the Hanoverians. Over against his apparently treasonous correspondence with the Pretender we must set the possibility that he was 'the "Mr. Erskine" drawing a secret service pension of £400 p.a. shown in a list of such pensions saved since April 1754'.[155] Perhaps he was simply a man hedging his bets. Whatever the case, he avoided the fate of his old friend, Lord Lovat, who paid for his leading role in the revolt by becoming the last man to be legally beheaded in the United Kingdom.[156] The Countess of Huntingdon lamented the fate of Lovat and his co-conspirators, and it is intriguing to note that on 9 April 1747 Howell Harris attended the execution of Lord Lovat before spending the rest of the day at 'Lady Huntingdon's' and finishing up at Leicester House.[157] By contrast, Scottish revivalists like Webster and Evangelical Dissenters like Doddridge concurred with George Whitefield, who condemned the rebellion as a 'horrid plot first hatched in hell', one that would have opened the floodgates to popery.[158]

Grange surely knew that many revivalists were hostile to Jacobitism, but he had secured a written pledge from the Pretender to defend British liberties and the Protestant religion.[159] Had the Stuarts returned, he would have been in a strong position to promote the cause of Evangelicalism in both the Kirk and the Church of England. In Zinzendorf and the Moravians, he perhaps saw the potential for an ecumenical Evangelicalism that could flourish under a Catholic monarch. The defeat of Bonnie Prince Charlie in 1746 ended that option, and the death of the Prince of Wales in 1751 scuppered the Leicester House strategy. By then, Grange was a septuagenarian with failing health. When he died in 1754, his visionary schemes were unrealised. Evangelicalism would find other ways to thrive, despite its factions and the absence of royal patronage.

Conclusion

So what, in conclusion, does Erskine tell us about the nature of the Evangelical Revival? Was it 'embedded' in the Enlightenment, or did it reject Enlightenment

---

[154] The letters were listed in a *Catalogue of the Manuscript Library of the Late Dawson Turner* (London: Puttick and Simpson, 1859), p. 221; a partial transcription was provided in HMC, *The Manuscripts of J. Eliot Hodgkin, Esq.*, pp. 245-48, where they are misattributed to 'John Erskine'. These letters are not listed in Maddox, 'Correspondence'.

[155] Cruickshanks, 'Erskine, Hon. James (c. 1678–1754)'.

[156] Furgol, 'Simon Fraser', *ODNB*.

[157] Schlenther, *Queen of the Methodists*, pp. 27-31; Nuttall, 'Howell Harris and "The Grand Table"', p. 533.

[158] George Whitefield, *Britain's Mercies and Britain's Duty* (1746), pp. 6-8.

[159] Cruickshanks, 'Erskine, Hon. James (c.1678–1754)'.

values in favour of Reformation principles? Grange's career can be read as a case study in religious reaction. Like so many early Evangelicals he was driven by 'revulsion from deism and reductionist latitudinarianism'.[160] He saw himself as a defender of traditional Protestant religion against 'the new fashioned clergy'. He deplored their tendency to reduce theology to ethics, their drift towards Arianism, their polite and lukewarm piety. He saw his own struggles on behalf of the orthodox party in the Kirk as preparation for the revival, and believed that the revivalists were recapturing the fervent piety and sense of the supernatural that had been common among Puritans and Covenanters. If the Earl of Ilay was the father of the Scottish Enlightenment (the patron of moderate clergy like Simson, Hutcheson, Robertson and Ferguson), Grange was his Evangelical counterweight, aligning himself with clergy whom Ilay dismissed as 'Levites', 'high-flyers', 'hot brethren'.[161] He suggests that if Evangelicalism was 'created by the Enlightenment', it was more by way of reaction than emulation.

Yet at the same time, Erskine's Evangelicalism did not involve a wholesale repudiation of eighteenth-century values. Carlyle depicted him as a talentless buffoon whose library consisted mainly of works on demonology, but this caricature cannot survive a careful study of his career and his writings. Instead, Erskine confirms one of the central arguments of Bebbington's magnum opus – that the shapers of British Evangelicalism have been closely attuned to trends among cultural elites. Erskine was one of Scotland's leading lawyers, a man versed in the writings of Jean Le Clerc, John Locke, and Francis Hutcheson, and someone who shared the Scottish Enlightenment passion for political economy and improvement.

Moreover, Erskine expressed disdain for 'bigotry' and professed allegiance to the core Enlightenment principles of religious toleration and 'universal benevolence'. He set out to broaden the minds of his fellow Scottish Presbyterians. A suspicion of narrow-minded clericalism was a consistent feature of his correspondence, and he could invoke Locke against heresy-hunters. Fundamentally, however, he was a product of the Pietist turn, an adherent of 'the experiential tradition within post-Reformation Protestantism which emphasizes practical piety as the main concern of the Christian life and leaves questions of speculative theology and polity peripheral'.[162] Disdaining denominational factions, he admired the devotion of Anglican prelates like Bishop Burnet and Archbishop Potter; when in England, he used his own copy of the Book of Common Prayer.[163] Transcending confessional divides, he embraced the Moravians and Wesleyan Arminians, and argued strenuously for making a sharp distinction between 'the great things of the Gospel' and scholastic doctrinal formulations. While he maintained a high regard for the

---

[160] Walsh, '"Methodism" and the Origins of English-speaking Evangelicalism', p. 26.

[161] Emerson, *An Enlightened Duke*, pp. 163-64, 185.

[162] August Lang, cited in Scott Kisker, *Foundation for Revival: Anthony Horneck, the Religious Societies, and the Construction of an Anglican Pietism* (Lanham, MD: Scarecrow Press, 2008), p. xxii.

[163] MCH-London, AB87 Folder 7: JE to James Hutton, 1 November 1742.

Westminster Confession, his emphasis was on 'essentials', the 'practical' doctrines that united 'real Christians' across denominations.

The Evangelical Revival marked a turning point for Erskine, as it did for Protestantism. In the 1720s, he was close to Wodrow and the orthodox Presbyterian clergy; in the 1740s, to the Wesleys and Zinzendorf. In the ecumenical networks of the Revival he felt less cramped than among the 'rigid Calvinists' of the Kirk.[164] In his early career, Lord Grange had looked back wistfully to the seventeenth century; after Cambuslang, this yearning for the past became less strong. He now marvelled at the 'apostolic' achievements of the Moravians, and revelled in the emotional intensity of the new Evangelicalism. Trading nostalgia for hope, he came to see that hot Protestantism could flourish in the conditions of modernity. This was old-time religion, but with an 'eighteenth-century twist'.[165]

---

[164] He uses this expression of the 'sound and orthodox' party in the Kirk: UA-Herrnhut, R 13 C no. 6: JE to Spangenberg, 30 March 1742; JE to Zinzendorf, 11 April 1743.

[165] Douglas Sweeney, *The American Evangelical Story* (Grand Rapids, MI: Baker, 2005), p. 24, 'evangelicals are a movement of orthodox Protestants with an eighteenth-century twist'.

CHAPTER 11

'The Grand Point': George Whitefield, Anglo-American Evangelicals, and the Holy Spirit[1]

Thomas S. Kidd

Five years after Jonathan Edwards' remarkable Northampton revival of 1734–35, the sensational English evangelist George Whitefield came to visit Edwards' family and to preach at his church. Edwards was hoping for Whitefield to 'revive the flame again, even in the darkest times'. Whitefield had seen incredible responses, in crowds and conversions, to his preaching in England and elsewhere in America. Edwards thought that Whitefield's revivals, and the broader unfolding of the Great Awakening, might herald 'the dawning of a day of God's might, power and glorious grace'. Whitefield had known about the Northampton revival for several years, and had begun a correspondence with Edwards well before they met in October 1740. Whitefield's Northampton sermons did not disappoint: Edwards noted that there was a great outbreak of holy grieving and the audience was 'extraordinarily melted'. Edwards himself was not exempt from the emotional scene. 'Dear Mr. Edwards wept during the whole time of exercise', Whitefield wrote. It was a milestone in the course of the revivals: the meeting of the Great Awakening's finest preacher, and finest theologian.[2]

Preaching on four occasions at Northampton, Whitefield spent more time there than he usually did in towns of comparable size. Each assembly grew more fervent and heated, until he gave the Sunday morning sermon where many attendees,

---

[1] See also Thomas S. Kidd, *George Whitefield: America's Spiritual Founding Father* (New Haven, CT; Yale University Press, 2014). Short sections of this essay will also appear in Thomas S. Kidd, 'The Bebbington Quadrilateral and the Work of the Holy Spirit', *Fides et Historia* (forthcoming).

[2] Kidd, *George Whitefield*, p. 106; Henry Abelove (ed.), 'Jonathan Edwards's Letter of Invitation to George Whitefield', *William and Mary Quarterly*, 3rd series, 29.3 (July, 1972), p. 488; Jonathan Edwards to Thomas Prince, December 12, 1743, in *The Christian History* 46 (January 14, 1743/4), p. 368; George Whitefield, *A Continuation of the Reverend Mr. Whitefield's Journal, From a Few Days after his Return to Georgia to his Arrival at Falmouth, on the 11th of March 1741* (London: W. Strahan, 1741), p. 47. Histories of this encounter between Whitefield and Edwards often quote Sarah Edwards describing Whitefield's voice as 'perfect music', but the source used appears to have put words in Sarah's mouth for literary effect. See 'Diary and Letters of Sarah Pierpont', *Hours a Home* 5.4 (August, 1867), p. 301. Credit goes to George Marsden for explaining this to me.

including Edwards, cried with joy and grief. His Sunday afternoon meeting witnessed even more powerful results: 'our Lord seemed to keep the good wine to the last [John 2.10]', Whitefield noted. Preaching on Genesis 3, he likely gave a version of his commonly-delivered sermon 'The Seed of the Woman, and the Seed of the Serpent.' Addressing the return of Christ, the evangelist thundered that 'Satan, the accuser of the brethren ... shall then be cast out ... then shall the righteous shine in the Kingdom of the Father, and sit with Christ on thrones, in majesty on high.' He assured Christian believers in the crowd that 'the Lord Jesus has engaged to make you more than conqueror over all – plead with your Savior, plead – plead the promise in the text – wrestle, wrestle with God in prayer ... Be not any wise terrified by your adversaries – The King of the Church has them all in a chain.'[3]

Hoping that he could assist Northamptonites return to their 'first love', Whitefield's sermons did help bring about a re-awakening there. 'Mr. Whitefield's sermons were suitable to the circumstances of the town', Edwards said, 'containing just reproofs of our backslidings, and, in a most moving and affecting manner, making use of our great profession and great mercies as arguments with us to return to God, from whom we had departed.' A revival that crested at the end of 1740 generated special concern among the congregation's youths. In Edwards' own household, some of the family's children found assurance of salvation in Christ. Edwards requested that Whitefield pray that he 'become fervent, as a flame of fire in my work', and that the Northampton minister would experience the full power of the Holy Spirit in his work and devotion.[4]

As much as they agreed about the work of God in the Great Awakening, the two ministers did not see eye-to-eye about all aspects of Whitefield's tactics and spirituality. Edwards went along with Whitefield on a visit to the nearby congregation of Edwards' father at East Windsor, Connecticut. While they travelled, Edwards informed Whitefield that he should be more circumspect about 'judging other persons to be unconverted', and that he should stop basing so many of his decisions on spiritual impressions via revelatory words or Scripture passages. Although Whitefield did not seem to be personally affronted by Edwards' correction, Edwards believed that the talk soured what in most ways had been a congenial encounter at Northampton. 'Mr. Whitefield liked me not so well, for my opposing

---

[3] Kidd, *George Whitefield*, p. 128; Whitefield, *From Georgia to Falmouth*, p. 47; Daniel Rogers Diary, October 19, 1740, New-York Historical Society; George Whitefield, 'The Seed of the Woman, and the Seed of the Serpent', in George Whitefield, *Nine Sermons Upon the Following Subjects* (London: Sam. Mason, 1742), pp. 64-65. Rogers noted that Whitefield preached on '3. Chaptr. Genesis.'

[4] Whitefield, *From Georgia to Falmouth*, p. 45; Jonathan Edwards to Thomas Prince, Dec. 12, 1743, Edwards to Whitefield, Dec. 14, 1740, in George Claghorn (ed.), *The Works of Jonathan Edwards: Letters and Personal Writings* (New Haven, CT: Yale University Press, 1998), XVI, pp. 116, 87.

these things', Edwards reckoned. Edwards sensed that his friendship with Whitefield was always cool afterwards.[5]

Not long after Whitefield came to town, Edwards gave a series of lessons to his congregation on the story of the sower and the seed from the Gospel of Matthew. Edwards cautioned about the fleeting experiences of those who reacted with elation to their first hearing of the good news about Christ, but ultimately did not demonstrate any lasting devotion. Were his congregants responding mainly to the dramatic oratory of the young Whitefield, or were they experiencing the new birth in authenticity? Those with no spiritual root, he warned, 'are drawn to take some notice of what the minister says, either by the unusualness of the subject, or the unusual manner of treating it, or the loudness of his voice, or his extraordinary earnestness'. Some might cry openly during preaching. But if their fervor was directed primarily toward the preacher, rather than Christ and his grace, they would be at risk of hypocrisy and delusion. The enduring fruits of the Spirit were the surest gauges of one's commitment to God, not the short-term excitement produced by a touring minister.[6]

Even though their relationship would never endure the kind of bitter public feud that Whitefield and John Wesley's did, Edwards did allow his rebuke of Whitefield to come out in print in 1745. Strangely, it emerged in one of Edwards' attempts to refute the critics of the great itinerant. The Northampton pastor was seeking to affirm the legitimacy of Whitefield's work, even if he objected to certain minor aspects of it. (This episode of disputing with Edwards was just one of many points of contention Whitefield had with other major revivalist leaders. As historian George Marsden has noted, the itinerant seemed to have an easier time relating to his non-evangelical business partner Benjamin Franklin than to Edwards, or especially to Wesley.)[7]

Edwards' and Whitefield's disagreement entailed degrees of emphasis, rather than the somewhat more fundamental disagreement over Calvinism that divided Whitefield from John Wesley for decades. But both Edwards and Whitefield had a sense that they were shaping and defining the movement emerging from the new revivals, and both (not just Edwards) were men of staunch theological conviction. It may also be relevant that Edwards, like Wesley, was eleven years Whitefield's senior, and was disposed to chastise the younger preacher for any mistakes he perceived. It was not surprising to find that the role of the Holy Spirit was one of the pivotal areas of disagreement between the two, as that disagreement divided many within the new evangelical camp, as it also distinguished the revivals' critics from their supporters. To participants at the time, disputes over the precise role of the

---

[5] Jonathan Edwards, *Copies of the Two Letters Cited by the Rev. Mr. Clap, Rector of the College at New-Haven* (Boston, MA: S. Kneeland and T. Green, 1745), p. 7.

[6] Ava Chamberlain, 'The Grand Sower of the Seed: Jonathan Edwards's Critique of George Whitefield', *New England Quarterly* 70.3 (September, 1997), pp. 374, 379.

[7] George Marsden, *Jonathan Edwards: A Life* (New Haven, CT: Yale University Press, 2003), p. 213.

Holy Spirit seemed enormously significant, as all evangelicals agreed in principle that the Spirit was the primary instigator of both spiritual regeneration, and of revival.[8]

For all of historians' focus on Whitefield's spectacular ministry and preaching, we may have missed how significant the role of the Holy Spirit was in his personal devotion to God, and in his view of how revival happened. Throughout his career, but especially from his mid-1730s conversion to the revivals of the early 1740s, Whitefield put a strong emphasis on the presence of the Holy Spirit in the revivals generally, and also in the life of the individual believer. His journals (especially before he produced abridged versions of them later in his career) included spiritual phenomena such as impressions of words or Scripture phrases on his mind, or revelatory dreams. For example, as he struggled after his conversion to discern his aptitude to become a pastor, God, Whitefield said, sent him a remarkable dream about having a meeting with the bishop who would ordain him. In particular, he dreamed that the bishop handed him several gold coins. Not long after the dream, the bishop in question did indeed ask to meet with Whitefield, and affirmed that he intended to ordain Whitefield in spite of the young man being less than the normally required age (he was twenty-one, but twenty-three was the standard rule). Finally, the bishop dropped five gold coins into the aspiring minister's hand, in order for him to purchase a book. Whitefield instantly recalled his revelatory dream about the episode, and wrote that his 'heart was filled with a sense of God's love'.[9]

Whitefield's reliance on dreams and spiritual impressions drew fire from critics, including both anti-revivalists and moderate evangelicals. As Whitefield grew in moderation in the mid-1740s, he deleted accounts of revelatory dreams from new, more circumspect editions of his journals. Although he depended on spiritual impressions longer into his ministry, Whitefield seems to have only had revelatory dreams during his conversion ordeal, and the lead-up to his ordination. Among other Methodists, however, especially female leaders, revelatory dreams continued to inform their piety and ministry well after conversion. Such influential Methodist leaders as Hester Roe Rogers and Sarah Boyce prayed and fasted in order to encourage dreaming, believing that dreams were one of the Spirit's primary means of communicating with believers. Whitefield dropped his emphasis on dreams after his appointment as a minister, but clearly the one involving the bishop convinced him to seek ordination.[10]

Whitefield's conversion as a student at Oxford, however, led him into a new world of spiritual experiences which included revelatory dreams and much more. In a rare 1736 unpublished journal, now possessed by the British Library in London, Whitefield mentioned the Holy Spirit in many entries. He repeatedly noted that he

---

[8] Kidd, *George Whitefield*, pp. 128-29.

[9] Kidd, *George Whitefield*, p. 35; George Whitefield, *A Short Account of God's Dealings with the Reverend Mr. George Whitefield* (London: W. Strahan, 1740), pp. 60, 62-64.

[10] Phyllis Mack, *Heart Religion in the British Enlightenment: Gender and Emotion in Early Methodism* (New York, NY: Cambridge University Press, 2008), p. 232.

was 'full of the Holy Ghost', or felt 'joy in the Holy Ghost', sometimes for hours at a time. On May 6 he recorded that he felt 'joy in the Holy Ghost Grace Grace Free Grace'. He felt the Spirit's tangible presence in his body, mind, and heart. As he spoke to small assemblies of Christian acquaintances, Whitefield suggested that the Spirit helped him know what to say. One time, the Spirit assisted him 'to apply all the promises made to the Apostles to us'. On another occasion, the Spirit 'suggested' to him 'things just applicable to what we were discoursing', and the Spirit even 'put words into my mouth', he recalled. One of the Spirit's tasks was 'to point out appropriate particular texts to our particular circumstances' among believers.[11]

Although he would begin to moderate his views about immediate, authoritative impulses from the Spirit in the mid-1740s, the focus on the work of the Holy Spirit would mark Whitefield's career and theology. In this, Whitefield represented a larger trend among early evangelicals. As I argued in my 2007 work, *The Great Awakening*, early evangelicals placed strong emphasis on the Spirit's role in bringing about revivals through periodic 'outpourings', but the Spirit also represented a direct presence in the life of evangelical believers, supplying comfort and strength, and sometimes immediate guidance by words or impressions. In more limited episodes, early evangelicals saw instances of miraculous healings and speaking in tongues.[12]

Pertinent to the focus of this volume, David Bebbington's celebrated quadrilateral has argued that evangelical Christianity is defined by conversionism (the need for a life-transforming encounter with God), activism (the idea that the gospel demands action by believers), biblicism (the conviction that the Bible is the authoritative source of God's truth), and crucicentrism (the centrality of Jesus' death on the cross to win forgiveness of sins for believers). No one has produced a more accurate or serviceable definition of evangelicalism over time and space, but the breadth of Bebbington's definition sets it up for criticism, especially from the perspective of particular places and times in the history of evangelical Christianity. With regard to the Anglo-American evangelicals of the Great Awakening era, the quadrilateral does not reflect the heavy focus that Whitefield and others placed on the role of the Holy Spirit in personal piety, conversions, and revivals. In addition to conversion, the work of the Spirit in individual hearts and broader awakenings, was what seemed so new to Whitefield and many of the Great Awakening's evangelical converts. These evangelicals were marked by biblicism, activism, and crucicentrism, but not in ways that departed significantly from earlier fervent Protestants of the seventeenth century. To degrees unlike most of those earlier Protestants, however, the new

---

[11] Whitefield, diary, Mar. 3, 6, Apr. 6, May 6, 30, 31, June 23, 1736, British Library. On Whitefield and the Holy Spirit, see also David Jull, 'George Whitefield and the Great Awakening: A Pentecostal Perspective', *Asian Journal of Pentecostal Studies* 14.2 (July, 2011), pp. 256-71. On the primacy of the Holy Spirit among evangelicals, see Timothy Larsen, 'Defining and Locating Evangelicalism', in Timothy Larsen and Daniel J. Treier (eds), *The Cambridge Companion to Evangelical Theology* (New York, NY: Cambridge University Press, 2007), pp. 10-12.

[12] Kidd, *George Whitefield*, p. 36, and *The Great Awakening: The Roots of Evangelical Christianity in Colonial America* (New Haven, CT: Yale University Press, 2007), p. xiv.

evangelicals probed the lengths to which the Spirit might offer them immediate guidance and knowledge. Many of the most pointed arguments over the revivals, moreover, concerned objections to the awakeners' claims about the role of the Spirit.[13]

While most evangelicals would concede that the Holy Spirit illuminates the meaning of Scripture for believers, or that the Spirit plays a determinative role in regeneration, I am not simply contending that the Spirit reshapes our understanding of biblicism and conversionism (two of the quadrilateral's points) during the Great Awakening. The work and presence of the Holy Spirit, instead, represented (along with a discernible conversion) the most distinctive and animating dynamic undergirding the new evangelical movement. For new believers such as Whitefield, the presence of the Spirit transformed life itself, ushering them into an unfamiliar world of joy and hope. Antagonists understandably focused on evangelicals' claims about the Spirit, prompting many to subtly downplay that emphasis on the Spirit which had so decidedly marked the height of the revival fervor. Nevertheless, as seen especially in the ministry and thought of George Whitefield, an emphasis on the Spirit remained a 'Distinguishing Mark' of evangelicalism, to borrow Jonathan Edwards' phrase. As Whitefield wrote four years before his death, 'To be filled with the Holy Ghost. That is the grand point.'[14]

So well-known was Whitefield for his claims about the Holy Spirit's work in life that in 1739 he encountered accusations that he had gone crazy and begun saying that he *was* the Holy Ghost. The itinerant definitely did not believe he was the Holy Spirit, but perhaps the critics' rumor-mongering made some sense, as Whitefield certainly emphasized the ministry of the Spirit, and the contrast between those in whom the Spirit dwelled, and those who had not received the Spirit. He commonly spoke of meetings where 'some were so filled with the Holy Ghost, that they were almost unable to support themselves under it. This, I know, is foolishness to the natural and letter-learned men.' His publicist William Seward claimed in 1739 that 'Brother Whitefield has had joy in the Holy Ghost without intermission for three years.'[15]

The itinerant's focus on the Spirit irritated critics, and even disturbed some who might otherwise have supported him. Anglican bishop Joseph Butler, for example, became perturbed by what he was hearing and reading about Whitefield and other Methodists. Meeting with John Wesley in August 1739, he registered his concerns about Methodist enthusiasm, and about Whitefield especially: 'Mr. Whitefield says

---

[13] Kidd, *Great Awakening*, p. xiv; David Bebbington, *Evangelicalism in Modern Britain: A History from the 1730s to the 1980s* (Grand Rapids, MI: Baker Book House, 1992), p. 3.

[14] Whitefield to W.P., Dec. 30, 1766, in George Whitefield, *The Works of the Reverend George Whitefield*. Volume 3 (London: Edward and Charles Dilly, 1771), p. 343.

[15] Kidd, *George Whitefield*, p. 72; George Whitefield, *A Continuation of the Rev. Mr. Whitefield's Journal, From his Arrival at London to his Departure* (London: James Hutton, 1739), pp. 79-80; William Seward to Joseph Stennett, Apr. 17, 1739, in Graham Thomas (ed.), 'George Whitefield and Friends: The Correspondence of Some Early Methodists', *National Library of Wales Journal* 27 (1991–1992), p. 293.

in his *Journal* [for February 11, 1739], "There are promises still to be fulfilled in me.'" Butler complained. 'Sir, the pretending to extraordinary revelations and gifts of the Holy Ghost is a horrid thing, a very horrid thing', he told Wesley.[16]

The Dissenter and well-known hymnist Isaac Watts similarly expressed concern about Whitefield's views on the way that the Holy Spirit guided him. Whitefield had told Watts that he did, in fact, receive personal impressions from the Spirit in the form of words or Scripture passages, typically during times of prayer. Whitefield said he could state with confidence that these messages were from the Lord. Watts was not so sure – he cautioned Whitefield about the 'danger of delusion'.[17]

Watts, and anyone else we might count as an 'evangelical' in this era, was delighted with the legions of converts professing new faith in Christ. But the Methodists' focus on the work of the Holy Spirit in modern times gave some moderate evangelicals pause. Many Protestant commentators held that miraculous interventions of the Spirit had 'long since ceased', as one Anglican bishop asserted in a letter criticizing Whitefield. The passing of the apostolic era, and the fashioning of the canon of the New Testament, had rendered obsolete the need for such wondrous works. Authoritative revelations, tongues, and dramatic healings had primarily functioned to confirm Jesus' messianic identity, and the Spirit uniquely guided the authors of the books of the Bible. Thus, talk of the Spirit's miraculous workings or revelations today seemed dangerous, suggesting that people subject to the Spirit's gifts might have a kind of quasi-apostolic authority. Moderates insisted that such authority was possessed only by Christ's apostles and the biblical authors. All would concede that the Spirit remained at work in the post-apostolic era, but only in his commonly-available benefits such as peace and comfort. A number of the early Methodists, however, determined that the remarkable works of the Spirit were not limited to ancient church history. Whitefield and John Wesley both included dramatic evidence of the Spirit's ministry in their published diaries – that evidence marked the revivals and the Methodists' ministries as distinctive new works of God. Critics like Watts were concerned with the potential for spiritual presumption and overheated enthusiasm that might accompany this attention to the Spirit's work. The early Methodists believed that the work of the Spirit was the only hope for Christians and their churches to break out of their stupor, and to revive.[18]

---

[16] 'Wesley's Interview with Bishop Butler, August 16 and 18, 1739', in W.R. Ward and Richard P. Heitzenrater (eds), *Works of John Wesley* (Nashville, TN: Abingdon, 1990), XIX, p. 471; Arnold A. Dallimore, *George Whitefield: The Life and Times of the Great Evangelist of the Eighteenth-Century Revival* (Carlisle, PA: Banner of Truth, 1970), I, pp. 342-44.

[17] Kidd, *George Whitefield*, p. 73; Isaac Watts to the Bishop of London, Aug. 15, 1739, Thomas Milner (ed.), *The Life, Times, and Correspondence of the Rev. Isaac Watts* (London: Thomas Richardson, 1845), p. 638.

[18] Thomas S. Kidd, 'The Healing of Mercy Wheeler: Illness and Miracles among Early American Evangelicals', *William and Mary Quarterly*, 3rd series, 63.1 (January, 2006), pp. 164-65; Edmund Gibson, *The Bishop of London's Pastoral Letter to the People of His Diocese* (London: S. Buckley, 1739), p. 20; Henry D. Rack, *Reasonable Enthusiast: John Wesley and the Rise of Methodism* (London: Epworth Press, 3rd edn, 2002), p. 113.

It is true that Whitefield, in particular, became more guarded about relating dreams, spiritual impressions, and similar phenomena after the early 1740s. Bruce Hindmarsh has argued that one of the key moments in Whitefield's moderation came in early 1744 when his infant and only son John died, even though Whitefield believed that God had impressed upon him that John would grow up to be a great preacher. Combining that scarring experience with the torrent of criticism he had already received in the five years prior to it, and Whitefield had circumspection about the Spirit's work forced upon him. As early as 1739, he had begun insisting that he had never experienced 'extraordinary operations of working miracles, or of speaking with tongues'.[19] Still, the emphasis on the work of the Spirit continued into the early 1740s (and even beyond, as we shall see). One of the ministers at the Cambuslang, Scotland, revival of 1742 noted that Whitefield himself, while serving communion tables on Sunday evening, 'appeared to be so filled with the love of God, as to be in a kind of ecstasy or transport'. That evening Whitefield preached extemporaneously through a heavy rain. 'There was a great awakening', Whitefield wrote.[20]

Although the sources on laypeople's responses to Whitefield's ministry are often limited or indirect, those who rallied to his meetings seem to have resonated with his themes about the Spirit's work. Testimonies recorded from Scotland's 1742 Cambuslang revival demonstrate the ways in which attendees felt the moving of the Spirit. An unmarried twenty-nine year old woman named Margaret Lap had heard Whitefield speak a year before Cambuslang, and noted that his elaboration of the terrors of hell and judgment weighed on her ever since. She was one of the throng who heard Whitefield preach 'Thy Maker is Thy Husband', a sermon given at Cambuslang and elsewhere in his itinerant ministry. This sermon was based on Isaiah 54.5, and it became perhaps his most impactful sermon text of the many he delivered and published. Lap did not immediately experience conversion, but she also could not get the sermon's message out of her mind. As she moved through her conversion ordeal, she routinely had Bible verses impressed on her mind. Then one morning, before rising from the night's sleep, 'these words, "Thy Maker is thy Husband,"' surged into her mind, along 'with several notes of a sermon of a certain minister'. This was her breakthrough moment: she was so overwhelmed with love for

---

[19] D. Bruce Hindmarsh, 'A Burning and Shining Light: The Zealous Spirituality of George Whitefield', paper delivered at Baylor University's 'Whitefield at 300' symposium, November 2014; George Whitefield, *The Rev. Mr. Whitefield's Answer, to the Bishop of London's Last Pastoral Letter* (London: W. Strahan, 1739), pp. 11-12, 16-17, Whitefield to [the Fetter Lane Society], June 12, 1739, in George Whitefield, *The Letters of Whitefield For the Period 1734–1742* (Carlisle, PA: Banner of Truth, 1976), p. 50, and Whitefield, *The Indwelling of the Spirit* (London: W. Strahan, 1739), p. 7.

[20] Kidd, *George Whitefield*, p. 168; D. MacFarlan, *The Revivals of the Eighteenth Century, Particularly at Cambuslang* (Edinburgh: John Johnston, 1847), p. 72; George Whitefield to [Jonathan] B[arber], Aug. 17, 1742, and Whitefield to Mr. A--, Aug. 27, 1742, in *Letters of Whitefield*, pp. 417, 429; William McCulloch, 'An Account of the Second Sacrament at Cambuslang', *Glasgow Weekly History* 39 (1743), pp. 4, 8.

Christ that she almost felt nauseated. The Spirit, she believed, helped her to know that Jesus could become as a spiritual husband to her.[21]

Another account of a Cambuslang convert, the thirty-two year old and unmarried Anne Wylie, offers a different angle on the effects of Whitefield's sermons and the work of the Spirit. Wylie testified that she broke through to conversion during a sermon delivered by Cambuslang's pastor, William McCulloch, although the printed editions of Whitefield's sermons assisted her in her travail. During the height of her experience at Cambuslang, Wylie said that she fell into an hour-long trance. She did not remember what happened during that time, but her companions at the assembly told her that she repeated out loud almost the complete text of Whitefield's sermon on 1 Kings 17, that of Elisha 'multiplying the widow's oil'. She had read this sermon before the Cambuslang meeting, and now she applied it to herself, 'saying that I was the empty soul the Lord was filling and pouring the oil of His grace into'. The effects on converts of the myriad printed and oral sermons were dizzying: one man recalled that he also had many words and Bible passages given to him by the Spirit during his conversion process. Then during one of the great itinerant's Cambuslang addresses, this convert had the phrase 'a God of love' impressed upon his thoughts. However, the man recalled that this phrase was not one that Whitefield had uttered, but, as he saw it, it came straight from the Holy Spirit. The man was 'swallowed up' in a transcendent reverie, he said, not knowing 'whether [his] soul was in the body or out of the body'. Another male convert said that as he heard Whitefield speak, a Bible passage on which McCulloch had spoken came into his thoughts with such power that he started calling out in worship among the assembled Cambuslang throng.[22]

Visions were less common than spiritual impressions in evangelical conversion testimonies, but they did occur among certain Whitefield converts. A married forty-two year old named Margaret Clark, for example, had struggled for months over whether she could receive God's mercy and forgiveness. During one of Whitefield's orations, however, she related that she witnessed 'with my bodily eyes, Christ as hanging on the cross, and a great light about him in the air, and it was strongly impressed on my mind; that he was suffering there for my sins'. All but the most radical evangelicals balked at claims of visions seen with a person's 'bodily eyes' (visions of the spirit or mind were somewhat more palatable). The cautious pastor interviewing Clark made sure to note that she never did see this vision again, nor did she want to, and that the physical sighting of Jesus on the cross had no bearing on her salvation.[23]

---

[21] Kidd, *George Whitefield*, p. 166; Keith Edward Beebe (ed.), 'The McCulloch Manuscripts of the Cambuslang Revival, 1742: A Critical Edition' (PhD diss., University of Aberdeen, 2003), Appendix ia: 9, 13, see also Appendix ia: 59; Ned Landsman, 'Evangelists and Their Hearers: Popular Interpretation of Revivalist Preaching in Eighteenth-Century Scotland', *Journal of British Studies* 28.2 (April, 1989), p. 133.

[22] Beebe (ed.), 'McCulloch Manuscripts', Appendix ia. 45, 129, 288-89.

[23] Kidd, *George Whitefield*, pp. 166-67; Beebe (ed.), 'McCulloch Manuscripts', Appendix iib: 450; Kidd, *Great Awakening*, p. 285.

Whitefield and followers like Lap, Wylie, and Clark were testing what believers might realistically expect the Spirit to do in their conversions, and in their daily devotions. The itinerant commonly referred to people at his meetings being full of spiritual 'new wine', referring to a phrase that Christ used in Matthew 9.17. Whitefield, as well as some of his followers, speculated about reaching heights of fervor in which they did not know if they were 'in or out of the body'. But Whitefield instinctively knew that there had to be limits to one's experiences in the Spirit. 'It is a good thing', he wrote, 'to know how to manage a manifestation aright.' The 'comforts of the Holy Ghost' were desirable, and even the norm for converted believers, Whitefield taught, but the possibility of self-deception was also real. One point on which Whitefield made his limits clear were miracles, such as instant healings, or the gift of tongues – he also seemed to adhere to the idea that such works had ceased with the apostolic period. Allies such as Scottish minister John Willison seemed to accept such boundaries, too, saying that he had seen the 'Holy Ghost falling upon [Whitefield] and his hearers oftener than once, I don't say in a miraculous, though observable manner'.[24]

The emphasis on the work of the Spirit, then, undergirded the first eight years or so of Whitefield's public ministry. That emphasis would never fundamentally change, but after his son's death, and his return to America in 1744, Whitefield had become much more of a moderate evangelical with regard to the things of the Spirit. He turned thirty that year, and though he did not know it yet, the height of the revivals had passed. He had endured years of attacks on his ministry, and those attacks often focused on the primacy he put on the Spirit. These criticisms came from anti-revivalists, of course, but they also came from moderate evangelicals. He also drew more and more aristocratic and wealthy followers, and he presumably figured that some or most of them might be embarrassed by some of the more exotic spiritual phenomena which marked his early revivals. Of course, the core message of the new birth, as well as his Calvinist emphases such as election, stayed fairly constant through these years. He was still drawn into occasional controversy over the ministry of the Spirit, as well as disputes with Arminians (his feud with the Wesleys did not really heal until the 1760s), but the days of the incendiary, church-splitting, Spirit-guided Whitefield were largely left behind.[25]

In a sense, Whitefield's path to moderation was to be expected, and it has certainly been taken by many other pastors at other times. Some of his Great Awakening colleagues also took the journey to moderation in these years. Arguably the most important radical evangelical preacher in colonial America, Long Island, New York's James Davenport, suffered a medical and ministerial collapse in 1743 when he hosted a book and clothes burning in New London, Connecticut, which

---

[24] Kidd, *George Whitefield*, p. 160; Whitefield to Mr. A--, Nov. 30, 1741 [also printed, with slight variations, in *The Weekly History*, Dec. 5, 1741], in *Letters of Whitefield*, p. 343; John Willison to a friend in Edinburgh, Oct. 8, 1741, in Thomas Prince, *The Christian History*, Nov. 5, 1743.

[25] Kidd, *George Whitefield*, p. 190.

even some of his most devoted followers realized was rank foolishness. Davenport understood that he was at the cusp of losing his pastoral career, so he toured New England and the Middle Colonies, apologizing to those he had offended during his radical phase, and entering a much quieter time of evangelical ministry. New Jersey's Gilbert Tennent likewise stopped itinerating and calling out unconverted pastors, and took a prestigious position in Philadelphia and apologized for the 'excessive heat' of his preaching during the height of the Great Awakening. Tennent had publicly confronted the radicalism of the Moravians, who had established a missionary beachhead in Pennsylvania, as a way to establish his own moderate *bona fides*.[26]

In 1745 Whitefield returned to Northampton, speaking twice at Jonathan Edwards' church on a July Sunday. One of these sermons was a version of his famous 'Thy Maker is Thy Husband' message. The next Thursday, as part of an official Massachusetts day of thanksgiving in observance of the colonists' victory over the French at the fortress of Louisbourg in eastern Canada, Whitefield spoke again at the Northampton church 'at the request of the Rev. Mr. Edwards'.[27]

This second personal meeting between Edwards and Whitefield cooled whatever personal antagonism was left over from their first encounter, and their disagreement over the role of spiritual impressions. Writing to a Scottish correspondent, Edwards lamented the abuse that had been directed toward the itinerant in New England. 'Whitefield was reproached in the most scurrilous and scandalous manner', Edwards wrote. 'I question whether history affords any instance paralleled with this, as so much pains taken in writing to blacken a man's character, and render him odious.' Whitefield's latest visit to New England had precipitated a host of new attacks on him, but Edwards believed that they all dealt only with the itinerant's 'old faults, without anything new worth speaking of'.[28]

Whitefield's time in Northampton convinced Edwards that the itinerant had turned over a new leaf with regard to the things of the Spirit. The itinerant 'behaved himself so, that he endeared himself much to me', Edwards told correspondents in Scotland. 'He appeared in a more desirable temper of mind and more solid and judicious in his thoughts, and prudence in his conduct, than when he was here before.' After his visit with Edwards, Whitefield moved on to eastern Connecticut, a place notorious for radical outbreaks during the Great Awakening. Now Whitefield worked against the enthusiastic excesses of the 'wild and extravagant people there, and has there done a great deal of good', Edwards noted with satisfaction. The

---

[26] Kidd, *George Whitefield*, pp. 190-91; Gilbert Tennent, *The Necessity of Holding Fast the Truth* (Boston: S. Kneeland and T. Green, 1743), p. 2; Kidd, *Great Awakening*, p. 147; Milton J. Coalter, Jr, *Gilbert Tennent, Son of Thunder: A Case Study of Continental Pietism's Impact on the First Great Awakening in the Middle Colonies* (Westport, CT: Greenwood Press, 1986), p. 106.

[27] Kidd, *George Whitefield*, p. 185; *Pennsylvania Gazette*, Aug. 15, 1745.

[28] Kidd, *George Whitefield*, pp. 185-86; Jonathan Edwards to friends in Scotland [after Sept. 16, 1745], in Claghorn (ed.), *Works of Edwards*, XVI, p. 176.

itinerant had once spawned radical frenzy and church splits, but now he 'reclaimed' some Connecticut evangelicals for moderation.[29]

A new version of Whitefield's published journals was another landmark in his turn to moderation. In the late 1740s, he reflected on the reasons for editing a more tempered version of the diaries: 'Alas! Alas! In how many things have I judged and acted wrong. I have been too rash and hasty in giving characters, both of places and persons. Being fond of scripture language, I have often used a style too apostolical, and at the same time I have been too bitter in my zeal. Wild-fire has been mixed with it, and I find that I frequently wrote and spoke in my own spirit, when I thought I was writing and speaking by the assistance of the spirit of God.' Whitefield was now convinced that he had placed too much emphasis on dreams and impressions. God had seasoned him by years of testing in ministry and by 'ripening my judgment a little more'. His circumspection about the things of the Spirit did not obfuscate the Spirit's work altogether, however. The new journals would still feature descriptions of the Spirit's presence in revival meetings, and a believer's need for the 'abiding witness and indwelling of the blessed Spirit of God'.[30]

Whitefield had reached a point where he saw the need to reflect on the difference between works of the flesh and the work of the Spirit, but he would never devote as much time to this difference as Edwards (much more the theologian and writer than Whitefield) did. Most of the participants in the Great Awakening would have to contend with this puzzle, and one of Edwards' most seminal accomplishments as a theologian was creating a cogent framework for testing whether revival experiences really came from the Holy Spirit. This framework was best explained in Edwards' *Religious Affections*, which is perhaps Edwards' most significant treatise.[31]

Far from denying a role for the emotions in true piety, Edwards posited in *Religious Affections* that 'True religion, in great part, consists in holy affections.' The key points of the Christian gospel, especially God's offer of the free gift of salvation through Christ, in order to rescue people from the threat of judgment, should elicit 'lively' feelings of thankfulness and gratitude in sinners who receive God's grace. These lively feelings might produce seemingly enthusiastic behavior or experiences in certain believers, but Christians should not necessarily dismiss these as false shows. They could be authentic works of the Spirit. But most observers knew, especially after the height of the revivals had passed, that revival fervor could also be inauthentic or deceptive. Many pastors, including Edwards, were disappointed at how some of those who exhibited the most public outbursts of spiritual emotion had fallen away from true religion in the years following. Some of the revivalists' opponents used these cases to dismiss the awakenings altogether, but

---

[29] Kidd, *George Whitefield*, p. 186; Jonathan Edwards to friends in Scotland [after Sept. 16, 1745], in Claghorn (ed.), *Works of Edwards*, XVI, p. 178; Marsden, *Jonathan Edwards*, p. 310.

[30] Kidd, *George Whitefield*, p. 204; Whitefield to the Rev. Mr. S--, June 24, 1748, Whitefield to the Countess of H[untingdon], Nov. 14, 1748, Whitefield to the Countess of D--, Feb. 22, 1749, in Whitefield, *Works*, II, pp. 143-44, 202, 237.

[31] Kidd, *George Whitefield*, pp. 204-205.

Edwards thought this was an overreaction. The best means to distinguish between the flesh and the Spirit was to examine the longer-term results of the revivals and people's experiences in them. If the so-called work of the Spirit focused attention to the person alone, and that person did not grow in love and piety, one would have reason to doubt the validity of their experiences. But if a person's dramatic manifestations focused attention on God's majesty and glory, and the convert stayed on course as a devout, growing Christian, then their experiences were likely from God, Edwards averred.[32]

After years of criticism and disappointments, Whitefield himself realized that he too needed to ponder these sorts of questions about discerning the Spirit's work. Of course, he remained convinced that the Spirit precipitated true awakenings and conversions. Unlike some moderate evangelicals, he also maintained contact with even the most radical evangelicals, as well as notorious former radicals including James Davenport. But his enduringly popular journals represented an apt venue for presenting himself in a more cautious stance.[33]

We might ask how Whitefield felt justified in editing (or redacting?) his journals in such a way to remove the more enthusiastic episodes of his conversion and early ministry? More than a simple record of biographical facts, Whitefield intended his published journals to offer a guide to the Christian life for his followers. The early journals conveyed to readers the wonders they could expect to accompany the born-again life. The edited ones implicitly downplayed the enthusiastic experiences, advising readers not to put much emphasis on dreams, spiritual impressions, or the notion that they could receive reliable guidance in the moment from the Spirit of God. By the mid-1740s, Whitefield had begun his own process of sorting out the balance between spiritual humility, and walking in step with the Spirit.[34]

The itinerant did not forget about the latter half of that balance, however, and critics for the rest of his career would still lament his emphasis on the work of the Spirit in his own ministry, and in the lives of believers generally. For example, after Whitefield visited Harvard again in the mid-1740s, Edward Wigglesworth, Harvard's Hollis Professor of Divinity, spoke on the biblical office of evangelist. The anti-revivalist Wigglesworth contended that evangelists were 'a sort of officer peculiar to the apostolic age', and that evangelists had passed with the end of that era, and the formation of the scriptural canon. 'The itinerants and exhorters', including Whitefield, 'who have once and again overrun this, and the neighboring provinces and colonies, were no evangelists in the scripture sense of the word, as some of them pretended to be', Wigglesworth argued. The Professor cited

---

[32] Marsden, *Jonathan Edwards*, pp. 285-86; Jonathan Edwards, *A Treatise Concerning Religious Affections*, in John E. Smith, Harry S. Stout, and Kenneth P. Minkema (eds), *A Jonathan Edwards Reader* (New Haven, CT: Yale University Press, 1995), pp. 141, 143, 147.

[33] Kidd, *George Whitefield*, p. 205.

[34] Rack, *Reasonable Enthusiast*, pp. 115-16; D. Bruce Hindmarsh, *The Evangelical Conversion Narrative: Spiritual Autobiography in Early Modern England* (Oxford: Oxford University Press, 2005), pp. 109-10.

Whitefield's 1745 *Letter to the Rev. the President, and Professors, Tutors, and Hebrew Instructor, of Harvard-College in Cambridge*, in which the itinerant confirmed that he regarded his traveling ministry as legitimate because he was working as an evangelist, not a local pastor. Wigglesworth had hoped that the chaos and separations caused by the Great Awakening had sufficiently demonstrated the dangers of Whitefield's kind of ministry, but 'the length of a few years seems to have worn out all remembrance of past calamities', he lamented.[35]

Wigglesworth also criticized Whitefield for saying that the Spirit assisted him in his speaking. Such assistance, to Wigglesworth, entailed a claim to 'infallible guidance', and also ended with the time of the apostles and biblical authors. 'If any man pretends to speak as the Spirit gives him utterance, or to be under the immediate direction of the Spirit of God in his speech and preaching; you may conclude him to be a bold deceiver, or a man given over to strong delusions.' Of course, Whitefield never suggested that he spoke with infallible authority, only that the Spirit directed and encouraged him – as the Spirit would do for any converted believer. Critics such as Wigglesworth were not convinced by this difference. When a prominent minister claimed to speak with the aid of the Spirit, he must somehow be implying that the Spirit had granted him apostolic authority, Wigglesworth concluded. Wigglesworth was a proponent of a stark break between the operations of the Spirit during the time of the apostles, and the operations during the time of the church and codified Scripture – a doctrine that later observers would call 'cessationism'. Even after Whitefield moderated and quieted his claims about the Spirit's work, critics still objected to his concept that the Holy Spirit had an active role in guiding believers in the post-apostolic era.[36]

In one of his best-selling works of the 1760s, *Observations on Some Fatal Mistakes, In a Book Lately Published, and Entitled, The Doctrine of Grace*, Whitefield explained his more chastened position on the work of the Spirit. This pamphlet was written in response to an attack on Methodism by William Warburton, the Bishop of Gloucester. Contradicting Warburton and similar antagonists, Whitefield posited that the Spirit had an indispensable ongoing role in the life of the individual believer, and in the work of the Kingdom of God. 'The Holy Ghost, like its almighty purchaser, is the same today as he was yesterday', Whitefield wrote, and

---

[35] Kidd, *George Whitefield*, pp. 223-24; Edward Wigglesworth, *Some Distinguishing Characters of the Extraordinary and Ordinary Ministers of the Church of Christ* (Boston, MA: Thomas Fleet, 1754), pp. 9, 11, 14; Whitefield, *Letter to the Rev. the President, and Professors, Tutors, and Hebrew Instructor, of Harvard-College in Cambridge* (Boston: S. Kneeland and T. Green, 1745), p. 16.

[36] Wigglesworth, *Some Distinguishing Characters*, p. 30; Thomas S. Kidd, 'The Healing of Mercy Wheeler: Illness and Miracles among Early American Evangelicals', *William and Mary Quarterly*, 3rd series, 63.1 (January, 2006), p. 149. Wigglesworth's idea that even gifts such as evangelism stopped with the apostolic period is a stronger kind of cessationism than one would typically find today. Cessationists commonly hold that the 'sign gifts', including healings and tongues, have ceased, but not others employed in the normal operations of the church.

'he is now, as well as formerly, in the use of all instituted means, appointed to convince the world of sin, of righteousness, and judgment [John 16.8]'. Warburton assumed that any talk of the work of the Spirit entailed dangerous enthusiasm. But to Whitefield, seeking the 'supernatural influences of the Blessed Spirit' was not enthusiasm, it was a component of normal, biblical Christianity.[37]

Even in the tempered decades of his later ministry, Whitefield insisted that the Holy Spirit played a critical role in conversion, regeneration, sanctification, and the precipitation of revival. Not only did the Spirit convince the 'world of sin, of righteousness, and judgment', but the Spirit opened the minds of believers 'that they may understand the Scriptures'. The Spirit also cleansed and renewed the hearts of the elect in order to make them fit for eternity with God. Anglican critics, Whitefield asserted, denigrated the 'standing and ordinary operations of the Spirit'. The formation of Christ-like character was utterly dependent on the work of the Spirit: faith, hope, and love were 'exotics; planted originally in heaven, and in the great work of the new birth, transplanted by the Holy Ghost … into the hearts of all true believers'. Because depravity was so deeply entrenched in every human heart, divine intervention was needed. Without such intervention – which God worked by the Spirit – 'our understandings cannot be enlightened, our wills subdued, our prejudices and enmity overcome, our affections turned into a proper channel, or, in short, any one individual of the apostate fallen race of Adam be saved'. Here Whitefield's Calvinism undergirded his sense of people's utter dependence on the power of the Spirit to renovate their moral characters.[38]

Several years later, shortly before his last visit to America, Whitefield defended several Methodist students who had been expelled from Oxford, and opened his argument with an even more forceful statement of the Holy Spirit's importance. 'The mission of the HOLY GHOST is the one grand promise of the New, as the coming of JESUS CHRIST was the great promise of the Old Testament dispensation.' Whitefield believed that the crux of the Anglican authorities' problem with students like these was the students' Spirit-filled religion. As he often reminded Anglican officials, the ordination ritual required the candidate to affirm that he was 'inwardly moved by the Holy Ghost'. But if students like these were to be expelled, Whitefield posited the question might be better worded, 'Do ye trust that ye are NOT inwardly moved by the Holy Ghost?'[39]

So moderation did not erase Whitefield's convictions about the Spirit's centrality to a vital life of faith, but it did smooth the rough edges of his expectations about the Spirit's work and guidance. We may not have appreciated enough how much that emphasis on the Holy Spirit drove Whitefield's early experiences as a born-again

---

[37] Kidd, *George Whitefield*, p. 234; George Whitefield, *Observations on Some Fatal Mistakes* (Edinburgh: John Traill, 1763), pp. 6-8; Whitefield to W—P--, Esq., Dec. 30, 1766, in *Works*, III, p. 343.

[38] Whitefield, *Observations on Some Fatal Mistakes*, pp. 8, 11, 18.

[39] George Whitefield, *A Letter to the Reverend Dr Durrell* (London: J. Millan, 1768), pp. 1, 26-27.

believer, and how much the work of the Spirit undergirded Whitefield's success as a revivalist. Evangelicals across the world continue to struggle today with tensions over the manifestations and ministry of the Holy Spirit in the church, and in revival. One can see this especially in global perspective, as the vibrant churches of the Global South emphasize dreams, visions, healings, and often speaking in tongues. Perhaps we need guidance on these matters from both the brash young Whitefield, whose converted state was marked most notably by an affective, revelatory sense of the Spirit's presence, and the reflective Jonathan Edwards (and an older Whitefield), who remained convinced that Holy Spirit would precipitate any true conversions or revivals, but who wanted to test conversion or awakening by examining the fruit that a true work of the Spirit must cultivate.

We might also note that, however applicable David Bebbington's quadrilateral may be to English-speaking evangelicals across three centuries, the beginnings of evangelicalism were marked by a new emphasis on the Holy Spirit. Moderate evangelicals have always tended to worry about the excesses of a focus on the ministry of the Spirit. Especially in the past century, the evangelicals with a distinguishing focus on the Spirit have tended to branch off into self-consciously charismatic, or denominationally Pentecostal churches. But at the birth of the evangelical movement, the work of the 'Holy Ghost', along with the experience of conversion, were the two most determinative marks of what made an evangelical Christian an evangelical. This emphasis is seen clearly in the life and ministry of George Whitefield, the most well-known transatlantic evangelical leader in the eighteenth century.

CHAPTER 12

A Microcosm of the Community of the Saints: John Erskine's Relationship with the English Particular Baptists, John Collett Ryland and his Son John Ryland, Jr

Jonathan Yeager

Halfway through his *Memoir of the Rev. Charles Nisbet*, the Presbyterian clergyman and professor of ecclesiastical history at Princeton Theological Seminary, Samuel Miller paused to reflect on one of Nisbet's correspondents from Scotland. Miller wrote,

> But of all Dr. Nisbet's correspondents in Great Britain, the most persevering and punctual was the venerable Dr. Erskine, of Edinburgh, one of the most pious and public spirited men of his day. That gentleman probably maintained a more extensive correspondence with American clergymen than any other European Divine. And probably, no private man on the other side of the Atlantic ever sent so many books gratuitously to this country as Dr. Erskine. He probably had twenty or thirty correspondents in different parts of the United States; and it is believed that almost every letter he wrote was accompanied by a package of books.[1]

Miller was referring to the Scottish Presbyterian minister John Erskine (1721–1803), who is one of the best examples of an early evangelical who participated in the transatlantic Republic of Letters. He maintained contact with dozens of individuals in America, Britain, and Western Europe throughout the eighteenth century and, as Miller rightly postulated, nearly all Erskine's letters were accompanied with literary packets.[2] Erskine can be placed within what Susan O'Brien has called 'a transatlantic community of saints', an intricate network of evangelicals who sought to promote the revivals on both sides of the Atlantic.[3] In their letters to one another, eighteenth-

---

[1] Samuel Miller, *Memoir of the Rev. Charles Nisbet, D.D.: Late President of Dickinson College* (New York, NY: R. Carter, 1840), p. 194.
[2] See chs 7 and 8 in Jonathan Yeager, *Enlightened Evangelicalism: The Life and Thought of John Erskine* (New York, NY: Oxford University Press, 2011).
[3] Susan O'Brien, 'A Transatlantic Community of Saints: The Great Awakening and the First Evangelical Network, 1735–1755', *The American Historical Review* 91 (1986), pp. 811-32.

century evangelicals were keen to recommend specific religious literature, circulate devotional material, and discuss theological issues despite their denominational differences.[4] But it is important to note that this elaborate network did not wane after the 1750s. Instead, it continued to build throughout the eighteenth century and beyond.

A microcosm of the community of the saints can be seen in the letters written by Erskine to the English Particular Baptists, John Collett Ryland (1723–92) and his son, John Ryland, Jr (1753–1825) in the last quarter of the eighteenth century.[5] The close connection that formed between these men was based on a shared theological conviction and desire to disseminate religious publications, especially the works of Jonathan Edwards. An analysis of Erskine's correspondence with the Rylands reveals the extent of these interests and, in particular, the extraordinary number of texts recommended, promoted, and dispersed between them.

Of the more than ninety extant letters from Erskine to the Rylands, the first six were written primarily to the father, beginning on November 1, 1779. We don't know if the elder Ryland communicated with Erskine prior to that date, but there is evidence that the two might have been in touch much earlier. John Collett Ryland was born at Bourton-on-the-Water in 1723. After experiencing conversion in 1741 at a revival that overtook his hometown, he sought the spiritual guidance of the Baptist minister Benjamin Beddome, who had studied under Bernard Foskett at the Bristol Academy. Beddome encouraged Ryland to follow his footsteps and seek further theological training under Foskett at Bristol, which he did from 1744 to 1745. After his time at the Bristol Academy, Ryland accepted the call to become pastor of the Baptist church at Warwick, remaining there until 1759, after which time he moved to Northampton, where he served for twenty-six years as a schoolteacher and minister at the Baptist church at College Lane. He resigned his pastorate at Northampton to his son John Ryland, Jr, in 1786, moving to Enfield outside of London where he lived until his death in 1792.[6]

Scholars typically associate John Collett Ryland with the high Calvinism of his fellow Particular Baptists John Gill and John Brine.[7] Gill and Brine were two of the

---

[4] O'Brien, 'Transatlantic Community of Saints', p. 813.

[5] Unless otherwise stated, Erskine's letters to the Rylands are housed at the Edinburgh University Library, special collections, E.99.14.

[6] On Ryland, see James Culross, *The Three Rylands: A Hundred years of Various Christian Service* (London: Elliot Stock, 1897), pp. 9-66; Peter Naylor, 'John Collett Ryland (1723–1792)', in Michael A.G. Haykin (ed.), *The British Particular Baptists, 1638–1910* (3 vols; Springfield, MO: Particular Baptist Press, 1998–2003), I, pp. 186-201; William Newman, *Rylandiana: Reminiscences Relating to the Rev. John Ryland, A.M. of Northampton* (London: George Wightman, 1835); H. Wheeler Robinson, 'A Baptist Student – John Collett Ryland', *Baptist Quarterly* 3.1 (1926), pp. 25-33; W.T. Whitley, 'J.C. Ryland as Schoolmaster', *Baptist Quarterly* 5.3 (July, 1930), pp. 141-44.

[7] Roger Hayden, *Continuity and Change: Evangelical Calvinism among eighteenth-century Baptist ministers trained at Bristol Academy, 1690–1791* (Chipping Norton: Roger Hayden and The Baptist Historical Society, 2006), pp. 70-71; Michael A.G. Haykin, *One*

leading Baptist theologians of the day who taught that since only the elect could be saved ministers should not offer the gospel to the unregenerate for fear that they would futilely seek divine salvation.[8] Although the stringent theology of Gill and Brine has often been identified as the cause for the declension of Baptist churches during the first half the eighteenth century, the high Calvinism of Ryland did not deter his church at Warwick from growing in size from roughly thirty members to over 200 during his tenure. Even though Ryland appreciated the theology of Gill and Brine (the 'great John Brine') he also esteemed moderate Calvinists such as Philip Doddridge, James Hervey, and Jonathan Edwards.[9]

Hervey appears to have been an important link between Erskine and John Collett Ryland. When his father died in 1752, Hervey became rector of Collingtree and Weston Favell. His residence in Northamptonshire allowed him the opportunity to develop a friendship with John Collett Ryland, who completed *The Character of the Rev. James Hervey* in 1790, long after the Anglican evangelical's death on Christmas day 1758. Ryland greatly respected many of the works of Hervey, notably his posthumous *Eleven Letters to Mr. John Wesley* (1764), also published as *Aspasio Vindicated* at Edinburgh around the same time.[10] Hervey's *Eleven Letters* surfaced as an unauthorized response to John Wesley's *A Preservative against Unsettled Notions in Religion* (1758), in which the Methodist leader publicly chided his younger colleague for defending the Calvinistic notion of imputed righteousness. Although supposedly with his dying breath Hervey insisted to his brother that no one publish the *Eleven Letters*, it came to print anyway in 1764 with several subsequent editions following in England, Scotland, and America.[11] No one can be certain who spearheaded the surreptitious first edition of Hervey's *Eleven Letters*. Complicating matters is the fact that Hervey circulated the manuscript among several of his friends, among them John Collett Ryland.[12] It seems significant that it was Erskine

---

Heart and One Soul: John Sutcliff of Olney, His Friends and His Times (Darlington: Evangelical Press, 1994), pp. 17-24, '"A Habitation of God, Through the Spirit": John Sutcliff (1752–1814) and the Revitalization of the Calvinistic Baptists in the Late Eighteenth Century', *Baptist Quarterly* 34 (1992): 304-19; D. Bruce Hindmarsh, *The Evangelical Conversion Narrative: Spiritual Autobiography in Early Modern England* (New York, NY: Oxford University Press, 2005), pp. 301-306.

[8] Hayden gives a useful summary of the 'Modern Question' debate among Particular Baptists in *Continuity and Change*, pp. 186-94. See also Geoffrey F. Nuttall, 'Northamptonshire and *The Modern Question*: A Turning-Point in Eighteenth-Century Dissent', *Journal of Theological Studies* 16.1 (April, 1965), pp. 101-23.

[9] Haykin, *One Heart and One Soul*, pp. 69-73.

[10] Hayden, *Continuity and Change*, p. 73.

[11] For a summary of these events, see Jonathan Yeager, 'John Wesley's Conflict with James Hervey and Its Effects in Scotland', *Journal of Religious History* 34.4 (December, 2010), pp. 398-413.

[12] See the letters from Hervey to the elder Ryland from 1755 to the end of 1758, in John Collett Ryland, *The Character of the Rev. James Hervey* (London: W. Justins, 1790), pp. 34-97.

who published the first edition of *Aspasio Vindicated* at Edinburgh. But as there are no extant letters between Erskine and Ryland until the end of 1779, we are left to wonder if their friendship commenced as a result of a joint pursuit to defend the doctrine of imputed righteousness while undermining Wesley.

What is certainly not conjecture is that Erskine's relationship with the elder Ryland was primarily based on a love of books. If he had not contacted the English Particular Baptist minister until the late 1770s, Erskine might have chosen the opportunity to initiate a correspondence after reading Ryland's *Contemplations on the Beauties of Creation* (1777), praising the author in his November 1779 letter for his 'amazing conformity' in his 'views and impressions as to zeal for propagating the gospel'.[13] Less than two years later, Erskine told Ryland that he had subscribed to the second and third volumes of the *Contemplations*.[14] Interestingly, from reading the *Contemplations*, Erskine affiliated the elder Ryland with his evangelical colleagues, the Baptists Robert Hall, Sr, and Caleb Evans, referring to all three as being 'raised up to plead for the great truths of the gospel and for vital holiness'.[15] Admittedly, Erskine's Presbyterian ecclesiology was not entirely congruent with that of the English Particular Baptists (most obviously on the issue of baptism), but overall he believed that any differences they had were minor, and would not threaten what he assumed to be a united effort to spread the gospel message.

With his extensive knowledge of books and access to booksellers' catalogs, Erskine took the liberty of supplementing Ryland's established reading for divinity students, suggesting the addition of John Flavel's *Token for Mourners* (1674), described as 'the best book of the kind I ever read'.[16] Erskine provided a more extensive list of books for students in his letter to Ryland on November 2, 1781 in which he recommended specific titles on exegesis, pastoral theology, practical divinity, biblical commentaries, speculative theology, foreign perspectives on Calvinism, and biographical introductions to eminent ministers.[17]

Within his letters, Erskine made it clear to the elder Ryland that he wished to be kept abreast of the latest publications by other English Particular Baptists, and alerted to which booksellers he could contact for acquisitions.[18] For his part, Erskine

---

[13] Erskine to Ryland Sr, November 1, 1779.

[14] Erskine to Ryland Sr, February 27, 1781. Erskine also subscribed to Robert Hall, Sr's *Help to Zion's Travellers: being An Attempt to remove various Stumbling Blocks out of the Way, relating to Doctrinal, Experimental, and Practical Religion* (Bristol: William Pine, n.d. [1781]).

[15] Erskine to Ryland Sr, October 19, 1781.

[16] Erskine to Ryland Sr, November 1, 1779.

[17] For the full list of authors and works, see the table in Yeager, *Enlightened Evangelicalism*, pp. 176-78.

[18] In his letter to Ryland, Sr, on February 27, 1781, Erskine wrote, 'I should wish from time to time to be informed not only of larger books but of smaller doctrinal or practical sermons or tracts by yourself and the worthy ministers with whom you are connected, and of the bookseller in London from whom they may be commissioned.' See also Erskine's letter to John Collett Ryland on October 19, 1781.

promised to do the same. But as the relationship between Erskine and the Rylands developed, the original agreement evolved into an exchange of books, rather than simply recommendations. Over the course of two decades, Erskine received from Ryland, Sr, and his son the latest Northamptonshire Baptist Association circular letters as well as pamphlets and books by Abraham Booth, Hugh and Caleb Evans, Andrew Fuller, John Rippon, the Rylands, Thomas Scott, Samuel Stennett, and John Sutcliff.

Erskine seemed especially interested in Fuller's theology. Periodically, he received several publications by Fuller from the younger Ryland, beginning with *The Nature and Importance of Walking by Faith* (1784), which arrived shortly after it came to print.[19] Erskine enjoyed reading *The Gospel of Christ Worthy of All Acceptation* (1785), remarking in a letter in August 1786 that even after a second reading of it, Fuller's reasoning on the duty of the unconverted to believe in Christ 'appears to me as conclusive as ever'.[20] Erskine thanked Ryland, Jr, for his diligence in forwarding the polemical Philip Withers' *Philanthropos, Or a Letter to the Revd. Andrew Fuller, in Reply to His Treatise on Damnation* (1785), adding the comment that 'Dr. Withers performance is an oddity ... the book will be little read', and Dan Taylor's *Observations on the Rev. Andrew Fuller's Late Pamphlet, Entitled, 'The Gospel of Christ Worthy of All Acceptation'* (1786).[21] In 1787, Erskine mentioned reading Fuller's *Defence of a Treatise, Entitled, The Gospel of Christ Worthy of All Acceptation; Containing a Reply to Mr. Button's Remarks, and the Observations of Philanthropos* (1787) 'with great satisfaction ... especially the last part of it, which answers Philanthropos', but was glad to hear that the debate would not continue with further publications.[22] Years later in 1793, Erskine commended Fuller's *Calvinistic and Socinian Systems Examined and Compared* (1793), telling Ryland, 'I think it much the usefulest book which has been published against Dr. Priestley's Socinian tenets.'[23] As evidence of his high regard for the book, Erskine dispatched copies to 'The Hague Society for the Defense of Christianity Against Its Present Day Adversaries', a society formed in 1785 as a response to the Dutch publication of Joseph Priestley's *History of the Corruptions of Christianity* in 1782, in addition to the Utrecht divinity professor and correspondent, Gijsbert Bonnet.[24] Even near the

---

[19] Erskine to Ryland, Jr, June 18, 1785. Erskine acknowledged receiving the second edition of Fuller's *The Nature and Importance of Walking by Faith* (s.l.: s.n., 2nd edn, 1791) from Ryland, Jr, in his letter on October 3, 1791.

[20] Erskine to Ryland Jr, August 21, 1786.

[21] Erskine to Ryland Jr, August 19, 1786. In his letter on May 22, 1786, Erskine told Ryland, Jr, that he had William Button's *Remarks on a Treatise, Entitled, The Gospel of Christ Worthy of All Acceptation* ([London]: Printed for J. Buckland 1785) and a pamphlet by John Brine, but it is unclear whether he obtained these from Ryland, Jr.

[22] Erskine to Ryland Jr, August 20, 1787.

[23] Erskine to Ryland Jr, October 1, 1793.

[24] Yeager, *Enlightened Evangelicalism*, pp. 193-95.

time of his death, Erskine made it a point to read Fuller's latest evangelical contribution, *The Gospel Its Own Witness* (1799).[25]

At the beginning of the 1780s Erskine's correspondence with the Rylands shifted to one that favored the son. The connection between Erskine and Ryland, Jr, burgeoned into a relationship that involved the regular exchange of letters until the Scotsman's death in 1803. While calculating a comprehensive list of texts that Erskine sent to the younger Ryland would be virtually impossible due to the fragmented condition of many of the manuscripts, we can estimate that in the eighty-six extant letters the young Baptist minister received approximately 400 titles, averaging over four publications with each letter. As one might expect, Erskine typically forwarded the literature that Ryland would have had difficulty obtaining. From consulting the number of identifiable works that Erskine sent to Ryland at the end of this article, one can see that the bulk of these consisted of Scottish and American sermons and pamphlets.

As a wealthy Scottish laird and bibliophile living in Edinburgh, Erskine had easy access to bookshops that specialized in religious texts, and could afford to send countless publications gratuitously to his correspondents. His favorite bookseller-publishers were William Gray and his daughter Margaret, who established a shop in Edinburgh at the Royal Exchange, across from St Giles' Church. Margaret worked for her father until he passed away at some point before her wedding to William Galloway on April 11, 1785, at which time she continued the family business as the sole proprietor until her death in 1794.[26] Erskine acted as a consultant to the Grays, whom he convinced to publish Scottish editions of works by evangelical authors, most notably Jonathan Edwards. Since Ryland, Jr, had expressed a desire to be informed of the publishing of Edwards' writings, Erskine often gave updates on the stages of production during the years in which the Grays, and a brief successor named John Galbraith, produced *A History of the Work of Redemption* (1774, 1788, 1793), *Practical Sermons* (1788), *Twenty Sermons* (1789), *Miscellaneous Observations on Important Theological Subjects* (1793), and *Remarks on Important Theological Controversies* (1796). Importantly, Erskine introduced his young Baptist correspondent to Jonathan Edwards, Jr, and allowed Ryland to participate in the editing process of some of Edwards, Sr's 'Miscellanies'.

The influence of Jonathan Edwards on the younger Ryland's transition from high to moderate Calvinism cannot be underestimated. By his own admission, Ryland struggled to come to terms with the high Calvinism that dominated his youth.[27] A precocious boy, he supposedly could read parts of the Bible in Hebrew at age five and the entire New Testament in Greek by the time he turned nine. Three years after his conversion experience at age fourteen and baptism, Ryland joined his father as co-pastor of the Baptist church at Northampton in 1781, becoming the sole minister

---

[25] Erskine to Ryland, Jr, December 10, 1799.

[26] Yeager, *Enlightened Evangelicalism*, pp. 166-67.

[27] Timothy Whelan, 'John Ryland at School: Two Societies in Northampton Boarding Schools', *Baptist Quarterly* 40.2 (April, 2003), pp. 90-116.

in 1786 when his father moved to Enfield. He remained at Northampton until 1793 when he moved to Bristol to become the pastor of the Broadmead Baptist church and principal of Bristol Academy.[28] Through a mentoring relationship that he established with the evangelical Anglican John Newton, but more importantly by studying the theology of Jonathan Edwards, Ryland gradually found peace in preaching the gospel to all.[29]

The elder Ryland had been reading Edwards as early as the 1740s. He owned a copy of *The Distinguishing Marks of a Work of the Spirit of God* (1741), signing and dating the book in 1742.[30] It is likely that Ryland, Jr, became acquainted with Edwards through his father. They had in their possession 1765 editions of Edwards' *Life of Brainerd* (curiously published by William Gray at Edinburgh) and Hopkins' *Life of Jonathan Edwards*.[31] The younger Ryland had the *Life of Brainerd* bound in 1776 and wrote on the inside cover that this book 'he prizes above almost all others'.[32] As many scholars have pointed out, the interest that Ryland, Fuller, and Sutcliff had in studying Edwards' theology contributed to the transformation of the English Particular Baptists into a more evangelistic denomination by the end of the eighteenth century.[33] When Erskine casually posted Edwards' *Humble Attempt to*

---

[28] Culross, *Three Rylands*, pp. 69-91; Grant Gordon, 'John Ryland, Jr. (1753–1825)', in Hayken (ed.), *British Particular Baptists*, II, pp. 78-95, and 'The Call of Dr John Ryland Jr', *Baptist Quarterly* 34.5 (January, 1992), pp. 214-27; John Ryland, *Pastoral Memorials: Selected from the Manuscripts of the Late Revd. John Ryland, D.D. of Bristol: With a Memoir of the Author* (2 vols; London: B. Holdsworth, 1826–28), 'Memoir &c.' (which appears in both volumes), I and II, pp. 1-61.

[29] Michael A.G. Haykin, '"The Sum of All Good": John Ryland, Jr. and the Doctrine of the Holy Spirit', *Churchman* 103.4 (1989), pp. 332-53.

[30] Hayden, *Continuity and Change*, p. 87. Hayden suggests that it was Benjamin Beddome who first introduced Edwards to Ryland.

[31] See Hayden, *Continuity and Change*, pp. 77-78 and D. Bruce Hindmarsh, 'The Reception of Jonathan Edwards by Early Evangelicals in England', in David W. Kling and Douglas A. Sweeney (eds), *Jonathan Edwards at Home and Abroad: Historical Memories, Cultural Movements, Global Horizons* (Columbia, SC: University of South Carolina Press, 2003), pp. 207-10.

[32] The original copies are held at Bristol Baptist College.

[33] L.G. Champion, 'The Theology of John Ryland: Its Sources and Influences', *Baptist Quarterly* 28.1 (January, 1979), pp. 17-29, and 'Evangelical Calvinism and the Structures of Baptist Church Life', *Baptist Quarterly* 28.5 (January, 1980), pp. 196-208; Keith S. Grant, 'Plain, Evangelical, and Affectionate: The Preaching of Andrew Fuller (1754–1815)', *Crux* 48 (2012), pp. 12-22; Michael A.G. Haykin, 'Great Admirers of the Transatlantic Divinity: Some Chapters in the Story of Baptist Edwardsianism', in Oliver D. Crisp and Douglas A. Sweeney (eds), *After Jonathan Edwards: The Courses of the New England Theology* (New York, NY: Oxford University Press, 2012), pp. 197-207, and 'Jonathan Edwards and His Legacy', *Reformation & Revival* 4 (1995), pp. 65-86; Thomas J. Nettles, 'Edwards and His Impact on Baptists', *Founders Journal* 53 (Summer, 2003), pp. 1-18; and Gerald L. Priest, 'Andrew Fuller's Response to the "Modern Question": A Reappraisal of *The Gospel Worthy of All Acceptation*', *Detroit Baptist Seminary Journal* 6 (Fall, 2001), pp. 45-73.

Promote Explicit Agreement and Visible Union of God's People in Extraordinary Prayer for the Revival of Religion and the Advancement of Christ's Kingdom on Earth (1748) with his letter to Ryland on March 15, 1784, it is doubtful that he had any idea of the enormous effect that this book would have on the Northamptonshire Baptist Association, igniting the so-called 'Prayer Call of 1784', which led to the formation of the Baptist Missionary Society in 1792.

Ryland willingly loaned his copy of the *Humble Attempt* to Fuller and Sutcliff, both of whom had already become familiar with the American Congregationalist – in particular his *Freedom of the Will* (1754), which profoundly influenced Fuller's theology as he came to terms with implications of Edwards' definition of natural and moral ability as it related to preaching the gospel.[34] Shortly after perusing the *Humble Attempt*, Ryland and his friends determined to meet regularly to pray for the revival of religion. Fuller subsequently spoke at the Northamptonshire Association meeting at Nottingham in June of the same year on walking by faith, and encouraging his audience to band together in united prayer for a general awakening of God's Spirit. Sutcliff then proposed that the Baptist Association churches set up a consistent time to come together in prayer for revival. The participating sixteen congregations agreed to meet and pray for one hour on the first Monday evening of the month. Sutcliff drafted the 1784 circular letter for this united prayer effort, and five years later attempted to strengthen the movement by assisting in the publishing of a 1789 edition of Edwards' *Humble Attempt* at Northampton.[35]

As the years went by, Erskine kept the younger Ryland informed of his plans to partner with Jonathan Edwards, Jr, in publishing some of his father's manuscripts. Erskine convinced the son to transcribe Edwards, Sr's *History of the Work of Redemption*, sending the manuscript to Edinburgh to be published by William Gray in 1774. But the American Revolution disrupted Erskine's efforts to publish more of Edwards' writings, forcing him to wait until after the war ended to produce additional works. Throughout the late 1780s Erskine updated Ryland on the prospect of publishing Edwards' manuscripts. Erskine wanted some of the remaining manuscripts to be published in Northampton and some at Edinburgh, 'where greater care would be taken to do them cheap, and correct than if the matter was trusted to London booksellers, whose carelessness and selfishness I well know'.[36] Erskine

---

[34] See Chris Chun, *The Legacy of Jonathan Edwards in the Theology of Andrew Fuller* (Leiden: Brill, 2012); and Peter J. Morden, *Offering Christ to the World: Andrew Fuller (1754–1815) and the Revival of Eighteenth Century Particular Baptist Life* (Studies in Baptist History and Thought, 8; Milton Keynes: Paternoster, 2003).

[35] David W. Bebbington, 'Remembered Around the World: The International Scope of Edwards's Legacy', in Kling and Sweeney (eds), *Jonathan Edwards at Home and Abroad*, pp. 183-84; Haykin, *One Heart and One Soul*, pp. 156-69, and 'John Sutcliff and the Concert of Prayer', *Reformation & Revival* 1 (1992), pp. 66-88; Ernest A. Payne, *The Prayer Call of 1784* (Edinburgh: The World Mission of the Church: Scotland's Week of Witness, 1942).

[36] Erskine to Ryland, Jr, August 20, 1787. Here, Erskine was reflecting on what he determined to be the exorbitant prices charged by Margaret Gray's former London partner,

hoped to publish Edwards' books at prices affordable to the middling and lower ranks, but came to realize that Ryland did not have the financial means or influence to secure a Northampton printer for such a large project.[37] It would be left to Erskine to convince Margaret Gray to publish more manuscript editions at Edinburgh.[38]

After the war between America and Great Britain concluded in 1783, Margaret Gray reprinted Edwards' *Sermons on Various Important Subjects* in 1785, and three years later in 1788 published a smaller edition (duodecimo) of *A History of the Work of Redemption*. In April of 1788 an elated Erskine reported to Ryland 'the agreeable news that President Edwards' manuscript sermons are arrived safe' and 'will soon be set to the press, and probably published by November at furthest'.[39] By August of the same year, Erskine could mention that about half of what became Edwards' *Practical Sermons* (1788) had been printed. The following year, Margaret Gray agreed to publish Edwards' *Twenty Sermons*, a series of discourses originally printed at Hartford in 1780 during the war. As early as August 1790, Erskine learned that Gray contracted with Edwards, Jr, to print more of his father's writings.[40] By July 1792 Erskine was relaying information to Ryland that the next set of manuscripts had arrived the previous month.[41] This edition became Edwards' *Miscellaneous Observations on Theological Subjects* (1793). Erskine was generally pleased with the volume, but questioned the wisdom of including large numbers of extracts in it that related to the deistical controversy. Wanting a second opinion, Erskine made arrangements for the manuscript to be sent to Ryland at Northampton. Ryland then made some changes, which Erskine and Margaret Gray adopted before setting the type for print.[42]

When Margaret Gray died in mid-1794, Erskine scrambled to find a publisher for the next volume of Edwards' manuscripts. He decided to give Gray's apprentice John Galbraith the opportunity, writing to Ryland that 'As he is a young bookseller and of a small stock, I wish he may meet with that sale, which may encourage him to

---

Charles Dilly, who was selling an edition of Hopkins' *Life of Jonathan Edwards* for five shillings, even though Edinburgh subscribers could purchase the same book for three shillings less. See Erskine to Ryland, Jr, August 19, 1786.

[37] In Erskine's letter on November 5, 1787, he apologized to Ryland, Jr, saying, 'I never thought of your running any risk in the publication of President Edwards' manuscripts. I only meant that if any bookseller undertook them, some of them might be printed under your revisal of the sheets, a proper allowance being made for that trouble. I image your printer at Northampton was a man of enterprise, who would willingly patronize so good a design.'

[38] Ryland did, however, manage to publish Edwards' manuscript sermon on Revelation 14.2 in the *Biblical Magazine*, edited and printed by J.W. Morris. See the extract published in *The New-York Missionary Magazine, and Repository of Religious Intelligence; for the Year 1802*. Volume 3 (New York, NY: Cornelius Davis, 1802), p. 299.

[39] Erskine to Ryland, Jr, April 26, 1788.

[40] Erskine to Ryland, Jr, August 9, 1790.

[41] Erskine to Ryland, Jr, July 7, 1792.

[42] Erskine to Ryland, Jr, November 27, 1792, and Erskine to Ryland, Jr, July 8, 1793.

other similar undertakings.'[43] Galbraith co-published Edwards' *Remarks on Important Theological Controversies* (1796) with an up-and-coming publisher named Archibald Constable, who would later become famous for a spectacular bankruptcy in 1826 that involved Sir Walter Scott. Erskine later determined that Galbraith was incompetent and chose not to pursue any additional publications with him.[44] The younger Edwards had by 1795 moved to Colebrook, Connecticut, before moving to Schenectady, New York, in 1799 to serve briefly as the President of Union College before his death in August 1801. With the death of the Grays, a lack of confidence in Galbraith, and the constant traveling and early death of Edwards, Jr, Erskine ceased direct involvement in publishing more of Edwards' writings.

From examining Erskine's correspondence with the Rylands we can see that evangelicals participated in the Republic of Letters that pervaded the eighteenth century. A mutual high regard for Calvinism, religious literature, and the writings of Jonathan Edwards solidified the connection between a Scottish Presbyterian clergyman and two English Particular Baptist ministers. Erskine corresponded with the Rylands for at least twenty-three years, exchanging hundreds of texts with them, and providing constant updates on the dissemination of works by key evangelical authors. The relationship between Erskine and the Rylands thus represents a microcosm of the community of the saints.

Works Sent by Erskine to John Ryland, Jr[45]

January 14, 1782

William Hobby, *Self-Examination in It's* [sic] *Necessity and Advantages Urged and Applied* (Boston, 1746)

March 30, 1782

Charles Chauncy, *A Compleat* [sic] *View of Episcopacy* (Boston, 1771)

April 25, 1782

Benjamin Colman, *Souls Flying to Jesus Christ Pleasant and Admirable to Behold* (Boston, 1740; London, 1741; Glasgow, 1742)

Samuel Finley, *Christ Triumphing, and Satan Raging* (London, Philadelphia, and Edinburgh, 1741; Boston, 1742)

Thomas Prince, *Extraordinary Events the Doings of God* (Belfast and Boston, 1745; London, Belfast, and Edinburgh, 1746; Boston, 1747)

---

[43] Erskine to Ryland, Jr, December 30, 1795.

[44] Erskine to Ryland, Jr, October 25, 1796.

[45] If the exact year and place of publication of the titles that Erskine sent is unknown, all possible editions are provided.

Joseph Bellamy, *The Great Evil of Sin, as It Is Committed against God* (Boston, 1753)

Jonathan Parsons, *The Doctrine of Justification by Faith Asserted and Explained* (Boston, 1748)

Richard Elvins, *True Justifying Faith Producing Evangelical Obedience* (Boston, 1747)

Mather Byles, *The Glorious Rest of Heaven* (Boston, 1745)

John Foot, *A Discourse, Delivered January 8th, 1769, Occasioned by the Death of Mr. Joseph Hall, Jun.* (New Haven, 1769)

Charles Chauncy, *The New Creature Described and Considered as the Sure Characteristick* [sic] *of a Man's Being in Christ* (Boston, 1741; Edinburgh, 1742)

Samuel Hopkins, *Sin, Through Divine Interposition* (Boston, 1759, 1773; Edinburgh, 1773)[46]

'Letter 13', no date

Thomas Foxcroft, *Divine Providence Adored and Justified in the Early Death of God's Children and Servants. A Sermon Preached ... of the Death of the Reverend Mr. William Waldron* (Boston, 1727; Edinburgh, 1746)

Erskine sends 'a volume of sermons by Boston ministers on early piety, which as appears by the 2nd volume of Mr. [Thomas] Prince's *Christian History* were accompanied with an extraordinary awakening'

Erskine also sends '4 single sermons, which I cut out from a volume of pamphlets I lately purchased'

March 15, 1784

Jonathan Edwards, *Humble Attempt to Promote Explicit Agreement and Visible Union of God's People in Extraordinary Prayer for the Revival of Religion and the Advancement of Christ's Kingdom on Earth* (Boston, 1748)[47]

Jonathan Dickinson, *A Defence of Presbyterian Ordination* (Boston, 1724)

Thomas Foxcroft, *The Ruling and Ordination power of Congregational Bishops, or Presbyters Defended* (1724)

Gilbert Tennent, *The Blessedness of Peace-Makers* (Philadelphia, 1765)

August 31, 1784

William Gordon, *The Doctrine of Final Salvation Examined and Shews to Be Unscriptural: In Answer to a Pamphlet Entitled Salvation for All Men Illustrated and Vindicated as a Scriptural Doctrine* (Boston, 1783)

---

[46] Erskine also includes an additional copy of Hopkins' work for Robert Hall, Sr.

[47] Erskine comments, 'I know not if there is another copy in Scotland.'

Erskine also sends 5 unnamed 'political sermons, or pamphlets of an old date'[48]

June 18, 1785

Jonathan Edwards, *Sermons on Various Important Subjects* (Edinburgh, 1785)
Thomas Prince, *Dying Exercises of Mrs. Deborah Prince* (Edinburgh, 1785)
Thomas Prince, *Six Sermons by the Late Thomas Prince* (Edinburgh, 1785)
Erskine also sends four proposals for publishing Jonathan Edwards' life and posthumous sermons at Glasgow[49]

November 29, 1785

Samuel Spring, *The Nature and Importance of Rightly Dividing the Truth* (Newburyport, 1784)
Eden Burroughs, *The Profession and Practice of Christians Held Up to View By Way of Contrast to Each Other* (Windsor, VT, 1784)
Andrew Croswell, *A Letter to the Reverend Alexander Cumming; Attempting to Shew Him, that It Is Not Blasphemy to Say, No Man Can Love God, While He Looks on Him as a God Who Will Damn Him* (Boston, 1762)

May 22, 1786

Samuel Wales, *The Dangers of Our National Prosperity; and the Way to Avoid Them* (Hartford, 1785)
Erskine also sends four unnamed pamphlets

August 19, 1786

Erskine sends twenty-two New England pamphlets[50]
Erskine also sends Thomas Snell Jones, *Mankind Accountable Creatures. A Sermon Occasioned by the Death of the Right Honourable the Lady Viscountess Glenorchy* (Edinburgh, 1786)

November 19, 1786

Erskine sends his own *Theological Dissertations* (London, 1765) for Ryland, Jr's 'friend'

---

[48] Only one of the five sermons he specifically mentions, Amos Adams, *Ministerial Affection Recommended ... At the Ordination of the Rev. Mr. Caleb Prentice* (Boston, 1769).

[49] Samuel Hopkins, *The Life and Character of the Late Reverend, Learned, and Pious Mr. Jonathan Edwards* (Glasgow, 2nd edn, 1785).

[50] Erskine states that the pamphlets will acquaint Ryland 'with the characters of many of the Connecticut clergy, and the state of both of true and false religion among them'.

Erskine also sends '5 small American publications for yourself'

February 15, 1787

James Bannatyne, *Mistakes about Religion, Amongst the Causes of Our Defection from the Spirit of the Gospel* (Edinburgh, 1737, 1738)

James Fraser, *A Treatise on Justifying Faith. Wherein is Opened the Grounds of Believing, or the Sinner's Sufficient Warrant to Take Hold of What is Offered in the Everlasting Gospel* (Edinburgh, 1749)

David Osgood, *The Unsearchable Riches of Christ. Sermon at the Installation of Rev. Peter Thacher* (Boston, 1785)

Elhanan Winchester, *An Attempt to Collect the Scripture Passages in Favour of the Universal Restoration, as Connected with the Doctrine of Rewards and Punishments* (Providence, 1786)

Two copies of Charles Nisbet, *Address to the Students of Dickinson College* (Carlisle, PA, and Edinburgh, 1786)

May 14, 1787

Joseph Bellamy, *The Law, Our School-Master* (New Haven, 1756) – originally sent by Bellamy for Erskine's 'Baptist correspondent'

Erskine also sends '10 pieces from America'

August 20, 1787

Andrew Croswell, *A Second Defence of the Old Protestant Doctrine of Justifying Faith. Being a Reply to the Exceptions of Mr. Solomon Williams, Pastor of a Church in Lebanon, against a Book, Entitled, What is Christ to Me, If He Is Not Mine?* (Boston, 1747)

Solomon Williams, *A Vindication of the Gospel-Doctrine of Justifying Faith, Being an Answer to the Revd Mr. Andrew Croswell's Book, Intitled* [sic], *'What is Christ to Me, If He Is Not Mine?'* (Boston, 1746)

Theophilus Hall, *The Most Important Question, Considered and Answered; or, A Saving Faith, Scripturally Explained* (New Haven, 1760)[51]

John Barclay, *The Assurance of Faith Vindicated from the Misrepresentations of Sandeman and Cudworth* (Edinburgh, 1774)

Samuel Spring, *Christian Knowledge, and Christian Confidence Inseparable* (Newburyport, 1785)[52]

---

[51] Erskine comments, 'I hope few in Connecticut would have wrote in so odd a manner, confounding faith with its concomitant graces and effects.'

[52] Erskine comments, 'I am sorry that a pious and able Calvinist should in some places express himself so inaccurately e.g. p 6 where he says that to know God is to keep his command and p 28 he who is more concerned for himself than for the souls of his children

Erskine also sends 'a piece of dying advice' by the Burgess Oath Seceder and professor of divinity, John Brown

November 5, 1787

Erskine sends '10 American (mostly Connecticut) pamphlets, and [George] Thomson's treatise chiefly sent on account of the extracts from Davenant and Usher'

February 15, 1788

Jared Eliot, *The Two Witnesses: or, Religion Supported by Reason and Divine Revelation* (New London, CT, 1736)

James Fisher, *Christ Jesus the Lord Considered as the Inexhaustible Matter of Gospel-Preaching. In a Sermon at the Ordination of the Reverend Mr. James Mair* (Edinburgh, 1741)

Erskine also sends 'a small collection' of some of Ralph Erskine's first publications, 'which I am told were much blessed when preached and first printed'

May 15, 1788

Erskine sends 'two small New England books by Lee and Williams and three American pamphlets'

August 16, 1788

Erskine sends 'a few good Sermons stitched together by Tennent whose ministry was so blessed'

November 8, 1788

Jonathan Edwards, *Two Dissertations Concerning the End for Which God Created the World; and the Nature of True Virtue* (Edinburgh, 1788)[53]

Joseph Huntington, *A Plea Before the Ecclesiastical Council at Stockbridge, in the cause of Mrs. Fisk, Who Was Excommunicated by the Reverend Pastor and Church in That Place, for Marrying a Man Whom They Called Immoral and Profane* (Norwich, CT, 1780; Boston, 1782)

---

and the great family of mankind, is destitute of benevolent concern. Surely one duly affected with eternity, must be habitually wretched, if his concern for the soul of every other equalled his concern for his own.'

[53] Erskine comments that Edwards' book is 'published here at 1 shilling which is not half the price of the edition of that on moral virtue strangely published without President Edwards name'. This is a reference to the anonymous *Essay on the Nature of True Virtue* (London: W. Oliver, 1778).

Erskine sends discourses by Andrew Croswell, 'Porter',[54] and two sermons by 'Baucus'[55]
Erskine also sends three sermons by Thomas Foxcroft

February 20, 1789

James Fraser, *A Treatise on Justifying Faith* (Edinburgh, 1749)
Hugh Cunningham, *A Short Explanation of the Ten Commandments, Designed for the Use of Sunday Schools* (Edinburgh, 1789)
Erskine also sends an unnamed sermon by Morgan Edwards

May 13, 1789

Erskine sends 'A volume of Mr. Ralph Erskine's last published sermons' and an unnamed Dutch book on the atonement, which William Carey translated

August 12, 1789

Henry Ainsworth, *Two Treatises by Henry Ainsworth* (Edinburgh, 1789)

August 31, 1789

Erskine sends 'a paper very incorrectly published from which you will have [a] general view of Dr. [William] Mcgill's exceptionable writing'

October 27, 1789

Edwards Fisher, *The Marrow of Modern Divinity*, with notes by Thomas Boston (several editions)
Erskine sends another copy of Henry Ainsworth's *Two Treatises by Henry Ainsworth* (Edinburgh, 1789) and a second copy of James Fraser, *A Treatise on Justifying Faith* (Edinburgh, 1749)
Erskine also sends three copies of a work by William McGill

February 9, 1790

James Robe, *Narratives of the Extraordinary Work of the Spirit of God, at Cambuslang, Kilsyth, &c* (Glasgow, 1790)
Erskine sends 'the piece by Mr Kennedy, which you wanted'[56]

---

[54] Probably Eliphalet Porter.
[55] Isaac or Charles Backus.
[56] Presumably Hugh Kennedy's *A Short Account of the Rise and Continuing Progress of a Remarkable Work of Grace in the United Netherlands* (London, 1752).

Erskine also sends '4 old pamphlets by Seceding Ministers'

July 13, 1790

John Erskine, *Sketches and Hints of Church History, and Theological Controversy*, volume 1 (Edinburgh, 1790)

John Erskine, *Letters Chiefly Written for Comforting Those Bereaved of Children or Friends* (Edinburgh, 1790)

Erskine also sends '2 old pieces by Mr. James Hogg, minister at Carnock, which probably you have not seen'

October 18, 1790

Peter Allinga, *The Satisfaction of Christ, Stated and Defended, against the Socinians ... Faithfully Translated from the Dutch, by Thomas Bell* (Glasgow, 1790)

John Jamieson, *Socinianism Unmasked ... Occasioned by Dr. McGill's Practical Essay on the Death of Jesus Christ* (Edinburgh, 1787, 1790)

William Campbell, *An Examination of the Bishop of Cloyne's Defence of His Principles* (Belfast and Dublin, 1788)

Samuel Seabury, *An Address to the Ministers and Congregations of the Presbyterian and Independent Persuasions in the United States of America. By a Member of the Episcopal Church* (New Haven, 1790)

Erskine also sends 'Three single American Sermons by Austin, [Levi] Hart, and [Timothy] Pitkin'[57]

April 19, 1791

Uzal Ogden, *The Theological Preceptor; or Youth's Religious Instructor* (New York, 1772)

James Hog, *A Casuistical Essay upon the Lord's Prayer Wherein Divers* [sic] *Important Cases, Relative to the Several Petitions, Are Succinctly Stated and Answered* (Edinburgh, 1705)

Erskine sends 'A volume of pamphlets, all by Mr. [Thomas] Foxcroft, Boston, except the last' and 'A volume of pamphlets' by James Hog

Erskine also sends unnamed pamphlets by Benjamin Colman, Robert Shirra, and Andrew Moir

July 9, 1791

John McKnight, *Six Sermons on Faith* (1790)

---

[57] Pitkin's discourse must be *A Sermon, Preached at New-Cambridge, in Bristol, February 12th, 1789* (Hartford, 1790).

Erskine also sends 'a volume of old sermons, all except the 2 by Smith, of Boston ministers'

October 3, 1791

Thomas Blackwell, *Ratio Sacra, or an Appeal unto the Rational World, about the Reasonableness of Revealed Revelation* (Edinburgh, 1710)
Erskine also sends six unnamed American pamphlets

December 30, 1791

Two copies of William Cooper, *A Reply to the Religious Scruples against Inoculating the Small Pox, in a Letter to a Friend* (Edinburgh, 1791)
Erskine sends '3 late American sermons, which were in Mr. [Levi] Hart's packet to me and 3 older pamphlets which were in Dr. [Jonathan] Edwards [Jr's]' and 'a volume of bound pamphlets in which you will find 4 of the first sermons preached before our Scots society,[58] which were published'

April 7, 1792

Erskine sends unnamed sermon by Thomas Foxcroft and others

August 23, 1792

Solomon Stoddard, *The Safety of Appearing at the Day of Judgment, in the Righteousness of Christ* (Edinburgh, 1792)

November 27, 1792

Moses Hemmenway, *A Discourse Concerning the Church; in Which the Several Acceptations of the Word Are Explained and Distinguished; the Gospel Covenant Delineated* (Boston, 1792)
John Searl, *A Funeral Sermon Delivered at Newbury-Port, Dec. 30. 1770. Occasioned by the Death of Mrs. Phebe Parsons, Consort of the Rev. Jonathan Parsons* (Boston, 1771)
John Murray, *The Happy Voyage Completed, and the Sure Anchor Cast. A Sermon, Occasioned by the Universally Lamented Death of Capt. Jonathan Parsons* (Newburyport, MA, 1785)

March 13, 1793

John McKnight, *Six Sermons on Faith* (1790)

---

[58] The Society in Scotland for the Propagation of Christian Knowledge (SSPCK).

Charles Backus, *The Faithful Ministers of Jesus Christ Rewarded. A Sermon, Delivered at the Ordination of the Rev. Azel Backus to the Pastoral Care of the Church in Bethlem, April 6, 1791* (Litchfield, CT, 1791)

Jonathan Eames, *Walking with God, Considered and Improved ... Occasioned by the Decease of the Rev. John Tucker* (Newburyport, MA, 1792)

Two copies of William Cooper, *A Reply to the Religious Scruples against Inoculating the Small Pox, in a Letter to a Friend* (Edinburgh, 1791)

July 8, 1793

John Erskine, *The Fatal Consequences and the General Sources of Anarchy* (Edinburgh, 1793)

John Webb, *Some Plain and Necessary Directions to Obtain Eternal Salvation: In 6 Sermons* (Boston, 1729)

Peter Thacher, *A Sermon Preached to the Society in Brattle Street, Boston ... And Occasioned by the Death of the Hon. James Bowdoin* (Boston, 1791)

Benjamin Colman, *The Faithful Ministers of Christ Mindful of Their Own Death ... A Sermon Preached ... upon the Death of the Learned and Venerable Solomon Stoddard* (Boston, 1729)

Jonathan Dickinson, *A Sermon, Preached at the Opening of the Synod at Philadelphia, September 19, 1722* (Boston, 1723)

Jonathan Dickinson, *The Danger of Schisms and Contentions with Respect to the Ministry and Ordinances of the Gospel, Represented in a Sermon Preached at the Meeting of the Presbytery at Woodbridge, October 10th, 1739* (New York, 1739)

October 1, 1793

Erskine sends two Latin commentaries on the Heidelberg Catechism written by Dutch authors

February 4, 1794

Samuel Hopkins, *A New Edition of Two Discourses* (Bennington, VT, 1793)

James McGregor, *Letter to the General Associate Synod* (Paisley, 1793)

Erskine also sends four unnamed American pamphlets

April 8, 1794

James Fraser, *Memoirs of the Life of the Very Reverend Mr. James Fraser of Brea ... Written by Himself* (Edinburgh, 1738; Aberdeen, 1776)

Erskine also sends an almanac from last year

June 15, 1794

Erskine sends three unnamed American pamphlets

August 22, 1794

Two manuscripts by Jonathan Parsons, one of which is *Manna Gathered in the Morning* (Boston, 1751) – 'It has been printed but I cannot procure the printed copy'[59]

Erskine also sends six additional undetermined works

December 12, 1794

John Anderson, *A Discourse on the Divine Ordinance of Singing Psalms* (Philadelphia, 1791)

Erskine also sends a sermon on a passage in Psalms by 'Williams'

March 12, 1795

Erskine sends '5 late American pieces', including William Linn's *Discourses on the Signs of the Times* (New York, 1794) and Samuel Langdon's *Remarks on the Leading Sentiments in the Rev'd Dr. Hopkins System of Doctrines* (Exeter, NH, 1794)[60]

June 18, 1795

John Asplund, *The Universal Register of the Baptist Denomination in North America, for the Years, 1790, 1791, 1793, and Part of 1794* (Boston, 1794)

William Romaine, *An Earnest Invitation to the Friends of the Established Church* (Edinburgh, 1795)

July 20, 1795

Erskine sends '5 American pamphlets received last week'

---

[59] Erskine comments on the second manuscript, 'The 2nd several sermons on revival of religion, which were transcribed for me by one of his family, and which I have endeavored in vain to persuade different booksellers here to publish. I think it may be usefuler in your hands than mine.'

[60] Erskine states that the other three unnamed publications are by Arminians.

July 28, 1795

Benjamin Trumball's ordination sermons[61]
Peter Thacher's ordination sermons[62]
Erskine also sends 'Mason's fast'[63] and a convention sermon preached by William Smith

October 6, 1795

Erskine sends '5 pamphlets lately received from New York'

December 30, 1795

John Rodgers, *The Faithful Servant Rewarded ... Occasioned by the Death of the Rev. John Witherspoon* (New York, 1795)
Dionysius van de Wijnpersse, *A Proof of the True and Eternal Godhead of Our Lord Jesus Christ ... Translated from the Dutch, by Thomas Bell, Minister, Glasgow* (Philadelphia, 1795)[64]
Erskine also sends sermons by 'Williams and Tyler'

March 17, 1796

Erskine sends 'four late pamphlets'

July 20, 1796

Account of the Proceedings and Debate, in the General Assembly of the Church of Scotland, 27th May 1796; on the Overtures from the Provincial Synods of Fife and Moray, Respecting the Propagation of the Gospel Among the Heathen (Edinburgh, 1796)
The United States Christian Magazine (1796)
Thomas Walker, *An Alarm to the Church of Scotland on the Apparent Prevalence of a Worldly Above a Spiritual and Religious Interest in Her Supreme Judicatory* (Edinburgh 1771)

---

[61] Trumbull's ordination sermons include those on Nehemiah Prudden (Springfield, MA, 1783), Thomas Holt (Worcester, 1790), Lemuel Tyler (New Haven, 1793), Aaron Woodward (New Haven, 1794), and Reuben Moss (New Haven, 1793).

[62] Thacher's ordination sermons include those on William Frederick Rowland (Exeter, NH, 1790), Elijah Kellogg (Portland, ME, 1788), and Thomas Cushing (Boston, 1794).

[63] Probably, *A Form of Prayer to Be Used at St. Philip's and St. Michael's, Charleston ... Being Appointed by Proclamation for a General Fast and Humiliation before Almighty God* (Charleston, SC: Printed by Timothy and Mason, 1793).

[64] On Wijnpersse's text, Erskine states that it was 'published at the expense of 15 ministers and private Christians chiefly for distributing gratis in some parts of America and Scotland in danger of antitrinitarian errors.'

John Erskine, *A Narrative of the Debate in the General Assembly of the Church of Scotland, May 25, 1779. Occasioned by Apprehensions of an Intended Repeal of the Penal Statutes Against Papists* (Edinburgh 1780)

August 3, 1796

John Gillies, *A Supplement to Two Volumes (Published in 1754) of Historical Collections* (Edinburgh, 1796)
Erskine sends 'five other late publications'

October 25, 1796

Erskine sends '6 American pamphlets'

March 2, 1797

Robert Balfour, *Liberal Charity Stated and Recommended on the Principles of the Gospel. A Sermon Preached before the Society in Scotland for Propagating Christian Knowledge* (Edinburgh, 1789)
James French, *The Effectual and Universal Influence of the Cross of Christ: A Sermon Preached before the Glasgow Missionary Society, November 8, 1796* (Glasgow, 1796)
'Tyler's answer to Paine'[65]
George Lawson, *Considerations on the Overture, Lying Before the Associate Synod* (Edinburgh, 1797)
Alexander More, *Select Sermons of Mr. Alexander Morus ... Translated from the French* (Edinburgh, 1797)

June 6, 1797

John Erskine, *Sketches and Hints of Church History*, volume 2 (Edinburgh, 1797)[66]
The Missionary Magazine (Edinburgh, 1796-1813), numbers 1–6 and 10–12[67]

June 12, 1798

John Erskine, *Dr. Erskine's Reply to a Printed Letter, Directed to Him by A.C.; in Which the Gross Misrepresentations in Said Letter of His Sketches of Church History, in Promoting the Designs of the Infamous Sect of the Illuminati, Are Considered* (Edinburgh, 1798)

---

[65] Possibly, Royall Tyler, *The Algerine Captive* (2 vols; Walpole, NH, 1797).
[66] Erskine comments, 'you will probably find many particulars of the history of Popery in the present century not generally known.'
[67] Erskine believes Ryland possesses numbers 7–9.

Erskine also sends '7 American pamphlets'

August 8, 1799

Peter Thacher, *A Sermon Preached June 12, 1799, before His Honor Moses Gill, Esquire, Lieutenant Governor and Commander in Chief* (Boston, 1799)
Erskine also sends '7 American pamphlets'

October 26, 1799

Erskine sends 'a paper by a Mr. Wilson who went from Scotland, soon after the peace to the American states, settled a few years at New York as Dr. Roger's colleague, removed thence on account of bad health to Charleston, South Carolina, and soon returned to Scotland'

December 10, 1799

Erskine sends '2 bound books, 8 new, and 9 old pamphlets of which 3 are incomplete'

March 30, 1800

Erskine sends '3 American pamphlets of which the sermons by Tappan and Adams are the best'

April 21, 1800

Erskine sends '7 American pamphlets', which includes Jedidiah Morse, *A Sermon, Delivered at the New North Church in Boston ... May 9th, 1798, Being the Day Recommended by John Adams, President of the United States of America, for Solemn Humiliation, Fasting and Prayer* (Boston, 1798)[68] and 'Porter's funeral sermon'[69]

June 18, 1800

Erskine sends '6 American pamphlets'

---

[68] On Morse's sermon, Erskine states that it 'contains very interesting accounts of the insidious conduct of the French to the Americans, and of the societies of the Illuminati corresponding with France in the American states.'

[69] Presumably, Eliphalet Porter's *A Sermon, Delivered to the First Religious Society in Roxbury, June 16, 1799. Occasioned by the Death of His Excellency Increase Sumner, Esq. Governor of the Commonwealth of Massachusetts* (Boston, 1799).

September 1, 1800

Erskine sends '4 American [and] 2 Scots publications, and a Massachusetts Almanac 1799 in which you will find lists of ministers, seminaries of learning, &c. in that state'[70]

August 13, 1801[71]

John Erskine (ed.), *Religious Intelligence and Seasonable Advice from Abroad* (Edinburgh, 1801)

John Glas, *Remarks on Modern Religious Divisions. By a Late Minister of the Church of Scotland* (Edinburgh, 1801)

Erskine also sends '7 American pamphlets which I hope won't be disagreeable'

January 26, 1802[72]

Erskine sends '4 American pamphlets and 3 collections of religious intelligence from abroad'[73]

March 5, 1802

The New York Missionary Magazine, 'in which I'm sorry a letter from me to Dr. [John] Rodgers only intended for private information has been inserted'[74]

Erskine also sends 'three other American pamphlets', and 'a short account of Dr. Evans prefixed to a new edition of his Christian temper,[75] but of which I got a few copies stitched separately for those who have former editions'

May 18, 1802

Erskine sends '7 American pamphlets'

---

[70] One of the Scottish works is John Anderson's *The Scripture Doctrine of the Appropriation Which is in the Nature of Saving Faith, Stated and Illustrated* (Edinburgh, 1797).

[71] Isaac Mann Autograph Collection at the Beinecke Rare Book and Manuscript Library, Yale University, OSB MSS 46:1:18.

[72] Isaac Mann Autograph Collection at the Beinecke Rare Book and Manuscript Library, Yale University, OSB MSS 46:1:18.

[73] John Erskine (ed.), *Religious Intelligence and Seasonable Advice from Abroad* (1801). Erskine comments, 'It has now near half a year since I have received anything of importance from America, otherwise a 4th collection would have appeared.'

[74] An extract of Erskine's letter to Rodgers can be found in *The New York Missionary Magazine*. Volume 2 (New York, NY: Cornelius Davis, 1801), pp. 232-33.

[75] John Evans, *The Christian Temper* (1801).

'Letter 90', no date

Erskine sends '9 American pamphlets'

December 1802

Erskine sends 'six late pamphlets, which I hope won't prove disagreeable'

CHAPTER 13

The East African Revival and British Evangelical Spirituality, from the 1930s to the 1950s

Ian M. Randall

In October 1937, W.H. Aldis, chairman of the Keswick Convention, held annually in the English Lake District, wrote to Joe Church, a medical missionary in Ruanda (now Rwanda): 'I am writing to thank you for your help during the recent Convention ... We were all deeply impressed with the story you had to tell of God's wonder-working in Ruanda, and I pray that this revival movement may continue and deepen.'[1] The 'story' was about the East African Revival, as it is usually called. Part of that story was that evangelical missionaries from England brought to Africa the spirituality which had nurtured them, but were challenged and changed by what they experienced through African Christians. In this study aspects of Revival experiences from the 1930s to the 1950s will be examined.[2] Joe Church was a central figure, gathering a very large amount of material about the Revival, and his book, *Quest for the Highest*, contains his perceptions.[3] The beginnings were associated with two medical doctors, Len Sharp and Algie Stanley Smith, who met at Cambridge University in 1908, and went together to Uganda in 1921. Wider revival began in the 1930s.[4] Studies of evangelicalism and of revival have been central to David Bebbington's work: his analyses have exercised a shaping influence and have been determinative in my own research and writing. Thus the present study relates to themes Bebbington has probed so convincingly. Also, Cambridge University, where he studied, figures largely in the Revival story. In 1936 Church described his outlook

---

[1] W.H. Aldis to John ('Joe') E. Church, 28 July 1937, JEC 3/2/41. The Joe Church papers are held in the Cambridge Centre for Christianity Worldwide. The archive references are all JEC. I am indebted to Dr Emma Wild-Wood, Director of CCCW, and Dr Lucy Hughes, who was the Archivist, for their significant help.

[2] 'Revival' with a capital 'R' means the East African Revival. The 1950s as an end point for this study represents a time when the Revival had produced a massive East African movement.

[3] J.E. Church, *Quest for the Highest: A Diary of the East African Revival* (Exeter: The Paternoster Press, 1981).

[4] H.H. Osborn, *Fire in the Hills* (Crowborough: Highland Books, 1991), pp. 23-35, 71-82.

as 'the C.I.C.C.U. [Cambridge Inter-Collegiate Christian Union] one. In fact I am their own missionary.'[5]

The first scholarly study of the East African Revival which analysed the movement in relation Keswick was in 1978, by Brian Stanley. At that time Stanley could speak of the 'little which has been written' about the Revival. What had been done fell into two categories: there were evangelical accounts which narrated the course of the Revival from evangelical perspectives, and there was work by historians, sociologists, and anthropologists who interpreted it 'almost exclusively in terms of categories drawn from African traditional religion and society'. Stanley's carefully constructed argument was that the Revival was an 'African initiative within a European interpretation'.[6] In recent years the Revival has received greater scholarly attention, especially through the work of Emma Wild-Wood, Kevin Ward, Derek Peterson, and Jason Bruner.[7] Peterson sees the Revival as an East African dissenting movement rejecting traditional societal allegiances. He does not deal with Keswick in his work.[8] Jason Bruner gives attention to Keswick, and part of his thesis is that the Revival should not be defined in terms of Keswick spirituality.[9] Kevin Ward refers to Bebbington's identification of four evangelical characteristics – conversionism, activism, Biblicism, and crucicentrism – and sees the Revival as clearly fitting into the category of an evangelical movement, but contends that the Revival was 'a complex phenomenon which cannot be wholly confined to any single category'.[10] This study aims to investigate some dimensions of that complexity by focusing on aspects of evangelical spirituality.

---

[5] Joe Church to Bishop Cyril Stuart, 23 February 1936, JEC 3/1/6.

[6] See Brian Stanley 'The East African Revival: African Initiative within a European Tradition', *Churchman* 92.1 (1978), pp. 9-10. The standard evangelical account at that time was Patricia St John, *Breath of Life: The Story of the Ruanda Mission* (Norfolk Press: London, 1971). A book-length scholarly account of the Revival was produced in 1975 by C.E. Robbins, 'Tukutenderaza: A Study of Social Change and Sectarian Withdrawal in the Balokole Revival' (PhD diss., Columbia University, 1975), but this has never been published.

[7] For a survey of literature, see Emma Wild-Wood, 'The East African Revival in the Study of African Christianity', in Kevin Ward and Emma Wild-Wood (eds), *The East African Revival: History and Legacies* (Farnham: Ashgate, 2012), pp. 201-12.

[8] Derek R. Peterson, *Ethnic Patriotism and East African Revival* (Cambridge: Cambridge University Press, 2012).

[9] Jason Bruner, 'The Politics of Public Confession in the East African Revival in Uganda, ca 1930–1950' (PhD diss., Princeton Theological Seminary, 2013).

[10] Kevin Ward, 'The Revival in an African Milieu', in Ward and Wild-Wood, *The East African Revival*, pp. 188-89. For the evangelical characteristics, see D.W. Bebbington, *Evangelicalism in Modern Britain: A History from the 1730s to the 1980s* (London: Routledge, 1995), pp. 2-17.

Keswick and East Africa

The roots of the connection between Keswick and East Africa are to be found in the late nineteenth century. In 1893 a 'Keswick Convention' was held in Kampala, Uganda. One of those present was George Pilkington, who was with the Church Missionary Society (CMS). Pilkington's biography was written by C.F. Harford-Battersby, whose father was one of the founders of Keswick in 1875. The later nineteenth century was a time when the 'fresh spirituality' of the Keswick message of full sanctification 'induced many to offer for missionary service'.[11] Pilkington experienced personal revival and this in turn affected others. In 1896, while on furlough in Britain, he spoke at Keswick about 'the work of the Holy Spirit' in his own life and that of the Ugandan church.[12] It was at the Keswick Convention in 1910 that Sharp and Stanley Smith dedicated themselves to missionary work, and the Ruanda Mission, which took shape in the 1920s to support their work, saw itself as operating within the framework of Keswick spirituality. From mid-1929 the Mission spoke of its commitment to working 'on Bible, Protestant and Keswick lines'. Almost all the early missionaries were products of CICCU and participated in student camps at Keswick.[13] In 1950, a report of the Ruanda Mission Conference recalled that from the beginning 'God had entrusted the Ruanda Mission with the task of cherishing and preaching the message of the victorious life as preached at Keswick'.[14]

Sharp and Stanley Smith established a hospital in the Kigezi district of Western Uganda, because of political difficulties in entering Ruanda, a Belgian colony, but in 1928 Joe Church took charge of what was then an unfinished hospital in Gahini, Ruanda.[15] Although Joe's father was an Anglican clergyman, Joe's personal experience of Christ came when he was a student at Cambridge. From Cambridge he went to Bart's Hospital in London, qualifying as a doctor in 1926. Joe Church later recalled that it was in 1920, when he found himself – to his own surprise – helping with a Children's Special Service Mission (CSSM) in Whitby, that he had experienced evangelical conversion. He found himself praying using a song the children sang, 'Cleanse me from my sin Lord; Put thy power within, Lord.'[16] His involvement, from this point, in CICCU, meant he was introduced to the Keswick spirituality which flourished among its members and which more broadly was

---

[11] Bebbington, *Evangelicalism*, p. 179.

[12] C.F. Harford-Battersby, *Pilkington of Uganda* (London: Marshall Bros, 1899), pp. 225, 251.

[13] *Ruanda Notes* 29 (July, 1929), p. 3. See Stanley, 'The East African Revival', p. 10. In 1937 Joe Church was chaplain to the Cambridge Camp at Keswick.

[14] 'Report of the Missionaries Conference held at Gahini, October 28–November 1, 1950', JEC 3/7/4.

[15] Medical personnel represented a high proportion of the missionaries of the Ruanda Mission.

[16] H.H. Osborn, *Pioneers in the East African Revival* (Winchester: Apologia Publications, 2000), p. 55.

shaping 'the prevailing pattern' of evangelical piety.[17] A popular book in CICCU at that time, *How to Live the Victorious Life*, by an 'Unknown Christian' (the author was Albert Richardson, who had been a CMS missionary),[18] was one of the influences on Church's spirituality. He commented on this book, 'It proclaims the glorious fact that victory may and ought to mark the daily life and witness of God's children – not in a dim and distant future but here and now.'[19] This was the spiritual vision Church took to Gahini and began to see fulfilled.

In 1930 Joe Church and Decie Tracey were married in Kampala. They had met while both were medical students.[20] Alongside his medical work, Joe Church received an Anglican lay preacher's licence, affirming his wider ministry in East Africa as a speaker. In January 1932, missionaries with the Ruanda Mission were invited to the conference for CMS missionaries in Uganda. The Ruanda Mission, although having its own Home Council, operated under the auspices of the CMS. Kevin Ward argues that the CMS 'desperately needed to convince conservative evangelicals in England that they still wholeheartedly welcomed such people as missionaries', given the exodus of conservative evangelicals from the CMS in 1922 to form the Bible Churchman's Missionary Society (BCMS).[21] Church, well aware of the tensions over the broader theology present within the CMS, believed 'God was going to unite us more deeply through revival'. Bishop Cyril Stuart, as Assistant Bishop of Uganda, organised the 1932 CMS conference. He and Church knew each other from Cambridge (where Stuart had been chaplain and lecturer at Ridley Hall), and from the Whitby CSSM.[22] The relationship between Stuart (Bishop from 1934) and Church later became fraught for a time: from 1942 to 1944 Stuart withdrew Church's licence to preach.[23] Following the CMS conference the Churches came home to Cambridge for a year. Their base was where Joe's father was vicar, Fen Ditton, 'known to all rowing men of Cambridge' – as Joe Church, the keen sportsman, noted – because 'the famous Ditton Corner and Paddock formed part of the Rectory garden and grounds'. For Church it was important to connect with CICCU members who were praying for him. More widely, he began to seek the formation of a 'Revival Prayer Fellowship' in England.[24]

---

[17] Bebbington, *Evangelicalism*, p. 151.

[18] Albert E. Richardson, *How to Live the Victorious Life* (London and Edinburgh: Marshall Bros, [1921]).

[19] Katharine Makower, *The Coming of the Rain: The Life of Dr. Joe Church. A Personal Account of Revival in Rwanda* (Carlisle: Paternoster Press, 1999), p. 27.

[20] Joe and Decie had five children. I am grateful to one of their sons, Robin, and his wife, Joan, for their memories of East Africa.

[21] Kevin Ward, 'Revival, Mission and Church in Kigezi, Rwanda and Burundi', in Ward and Wild-Wood (eds), *The East African Revival*, pp. 16-17.

[22] Church, *Quest*, p. 88.

[23] Bishop Stuart to Joe Church, 9 October 1942, JEC 4/1/6. Church wrote on the letter, 'Stuart's rocket to me'. Church spoke of being 'broken' by Stuart's action: Joe Church to Roy Hession, 9 December 1950, JEC 5/6/31.

[24] Church, *Quest*, p. 90.

After the Churches returned to Gahini in April 1933, they found a desire there for fresh spiritual initiatives. African staff at the hospital began building prayer huts, and Geoffrey Holmes, another missionary at Gahini, encouraged supporters of the Ruanda Mission to ask God for 'a deep outpouring of His Holy Spirit'.[25] In May 1933 Church spoke of a 'real work of the Spirit' going on.[26] At the end of 1933 a Convention took place in Gahini, covering (over five days) topics which mirrored Keswick emphases: sin, the holiness of God, new birth, repentance, faith, the Holy Spirit, sanctification, and the second coming of Christ. At the end of the Convention at an extra meeting, and following some 'formal prayers', unexpected, open confession of sins took place. This was seen as sparking a 'flame' of revival.[27] Meanwhile there were developments in Kigezi, where Laurence Barham, who had trained for Anglican ministry at Ridley Hall, was head of Kigezi High School, Kabale. Barham (later Bishop of Ruanda and Burundi) had been invited to teach Hebrew and Aramaic in Cambridge, but had felt a missionary call. His wife, Julia Leakey, who trained at Goldsmith's College, London, was influential in areas of spiritual guidance.[28] Meetings took place in Kabale in 1933 which Stanley Smith saw as something new: those arranging them had 'no other purpose then to get a fresh vision of God and of their own hearts'.[29] Church averred that he and Barham shared 'the essential basis of real revival', namely 'the teaching about the atonement and the power of the blood of Jesus as shown in the Scriptures'.[30] In 1935 a large-scale Keswick-style Convention was held in Kabale, setting the pattern for many subsequent events.[31] A few months later Stuart (now Bishop), approached Church about a mission in Mukono, where Bishop Tucker Theological College was located. In reply, Church set out his conviction, one that had grown 'as the years have gone by in the mission field', that 'the source of power' for any such work lay in 'the Keswick Message'.[32]

The hope that the Keswick 'blessing' might spread more widely in East Africa was reflected in a letter that Archdeacon Arthur Pitt Pitts, the Ruanda Mission Field

---

[25] Geoffrey Holmes, *Ruanda Notes* 44 (January–March, 1933), p. 19; Church, *Quest*, pp. 97-98.

[26] Joe Church, *Ruanda Notes* 44 (April–June, 1933, letter of 30 May 1933), p. 22.

[27] Lindesay Guillebaud, *A Grain of Mustard Seed* (London: Ruanda Mission, 1959), pp. 55-56.

[28] For Lawrence and Julia Barham, see Osborn, *Pioneers*, pp. 153-90. Julia was a sister of the archaeologist and anthropologist, Louis Leakey. Her counsel was so valued that she became known as 'sister of Jesus': Osborn, *Fire in the Hills*, p. 107.

[29] A.C. Stanley Smith, *Road to Revival: The Story of the Ruanda Mission* (London: CMS, 1946), p. 56.

[30] Church, *Quest*, p. 84.

[31] Colin Reed, *Walking in the Light* (Brunswick East, Victoria: Acorn Press, 2007), pp. 20-1. In 1931 Barham had expressed his belief in 'a big new blessing' in Kabale, as well as opposing the view that missionary work was 'one long CSSM': *Ruanda Notes* 39 (Oct.–Dec. 1931, 28 November 1931), p. 12.

[32] Joe Church to Cyril Stuart, 23 February 1936, JEC 3/1/6.

Leader, wrote (from Kabale) to Joe Church. He asked what could be done in Kenya: 'We may never have such a chance again in our lives. A chance of lighting a whole Colony with the blessing, and great will be our responsibility if we fail now.'[33] As a result, a visit from the Ruanda team took place in 1937, with meetings held in Nairobi, Weithaga, and Kabete, among other places. Plans were then made for the first Kenya Keswick to be held in 1938. Church wrote to J.F. Rownthwaite, who was appointed the Kenya African Keswick Secretary, about holding – as part of the meetings – an African Refresher Course. Church proposed bringing fifteen senior Africans 'who we know have made a stand for Revival, and who we know God is using. They are scattered throughout Uganda and Ruanda, and are mostly Senior English speaking Africans, who in most cases know Swahili too I think.' Church explained that 'we have a certain plan which we have used before at such Conventions', but added, 'God is not tied to any fixed plans and schemes.'[34] The Kenya Keswick, which was held at Kikuyu, was reported on by Church. He believed he had 'never known the messages go home with such tremendous force'. His expectation that 'plans and schemes' might alter proved correct. Whereas the usual procedure was to invite individuals to raise their hands to indicate their response, African team members urged that to 'check emotionalism' there be no invitation. Some Europeans disagreed, but the African view prevailed.[35] The Africans were looking for spontaneous rather than structured responses. The 1930s saw Keswick being re-shaped in a variety of ways in the African context.

Fellowship and Revival

The evangelical experiences that missionaries brought from England were to find new expressions through African encounters. A crucial meeting which took place in September 1929 in Kampala between Joe Church and Simeoni Nsibambi (and which was often recounted) indicated some of the new spiritual energy that was to exercise a profound influence. Nsibambi's father was a chief in Uganda's most dominant ethnic group, the Buganda, and Simeoni was educated at the CMS-founded Mengo High School, Kampala, and King's College Budo, which sought to replicate famous English public schools. After the First World War, Nsibambi was decorated for distinguished service and became Health Officer in the Bugandan king's government.[36] Christianity had exercised a significant influence in Buganda from the 1880s onwards. Hastings speaks about a movement involving 'conversion at the heart of society'.[37] But there was a growing feeling in the 1920s that fresh spiritual impetus was now needed. Albert Cook, director of Mengo (CMS) Hospital, lamented

---

[33] Archdeacon Arthur Pitt Pitts to Joe Church, 14 December 1936, JEC 1/2/2.
[34] Joe Church to J.F. Rownthwaite, 26 May 1938, JEC 1/2/14.
[35] Church, *Quest*, p. 158.
[36] Osborn, *Pioneers*, pp. 15-16.
[37] Adrian Hastings, *The Church in Africa, 1450–1950* (Oxford: Oxford University Press, 1994), p. 383.

in 1931 that missionaries had 'lost their fire', and African Christians 'were being pulled away by growing wealth, racial feelings and bad habits'.[38] Nsibambi was one of those in the early-mid 1920s who, in the Pilkington tradition, sought deeper knowledge of God. He spoke of finding literature from Britain about 'the ministry of the Holy Spirit', and how 'The reading of my Bible led me to complete commitment, and God filled me with the Holy Spirit'.[39] Biblicism marked Nsibambi's spirituality.

Joe Church wrote a long letter to CICCU about the encounter with Nsibambi. Prior to this meeting, Nsibambi had heard Church speaking, at a Bible class in Kampala, about 'surrendering all and coming out for Jesus'. In Church's account, following that meeting Nsibambi 'had done so, and had great joy in the Lord'. However, he still felt 'something was missing' – in himself and the Uganda church.[40] The Bible class was run by Mabel Ensor, a CMS missionary who came to Mengo as a nurse but whose gifts in teaching and evangelism were recognised. Nsibambi joined her class in 1927. Ensor became frustrated by Ugandan Anglican spiritual life and resigned from the CMS.[41] Although part of Church's report to CICCU suggests that Nsibambi did not know about deeper spiritual experience until he heard about it from Church, this is at odds with Nsibambi's own account and also the perception in 1926 of the Bishop of Uganda, John Willis, who recognised Nsibambi's special gifts and invited him to start prayer meetings. At these, Nsibambi experienced 'deep times of prayer'.[42] What seems to have been the case was that Church and Nsibambi found they had the same spiritual aspirations. Their shared biblicism led them to spend several days together in study, using the Scofield Reference Bible to look at 'the filling of the Spirit'. This profound experience of fellowship, at that time very rare between missionaries and Africans, involved them praying together to 'quit all sin in faith'. Joe Church subsequently spoke of how, in this period of new discovery, God gave him 'a share of the power of Pentecost'.[43]

Several younger Africans became significant for this new movement. One was Nsibambi's younger brother, Blasio Kigozi, a school teacher who was head of the Evangelists' Training School in Gahini, and who had a burning desire to follow in the footsteps of the pioneer Muganda evangelist, Apolo Kivebulaya.[44] Yosiya

---

[38] William B. Anderson, *The Church in East Africa, 1840–1974* (Dodoma: Central Tanganyika Press, 1972), p. 123.

[39] Osborn, *Pioneers*, p. 17.

[40] Church, *Quest*, pp. 67-68.

[41] John V. Taylor, *The Growth of the Church in Buganda* (London: SCM Press, 1958), pp. 98-99.

[42] Osborn, *Pioneers*, p. 17.

[43] Church, *Quest*, p. 68. The Scofield Reference Bible's notes are often associated with dispensational premillennialism, but Brian Stanley points out that the notes also use Old Testament typology to point to the cross of Christ and spiritual experience: Stanley, 'East African Revival', pp. 11-12.

[44] Kevin Ward, '"Tukutendereza Yesu": The Balokole Revival in Uganda', in Zablon Nthamburi (ed.), *From Mission to Church* (Nairobi: Uzima Press, 1995 [reprint]), p. 115. For Kigozi, who died prematurely of fever in 1936, see J.E. Church, *Awake!: An African Calling:*

Kinuka, who was the son of cattle owners of the Ankole tribe and was Gahini's senior hospital assistant, had been a strong critic of Kigozi, but when Kinuka visited Nsibambi in Kampala his life was turned round. Kinuka had 'never seen such a fervent Christian before'. Whereas Kinuka had been blaming others for problems at the hospital, Nsibambi told him to examine his own heart. 'My sins', Kinuka testified, 'became like a burden upon my back, and I yielded to Christ'.[45] Teams committed to spiritual renewal took shape at Gahini. These 'Bible Teams', as they were initially called, were new: they were characterised by 'simplicity, spontaneity and above all fellowship'.[46] Where the Revival spread, 'Fellowship Meetings' – marked by singing, sharing and Bible study – developed, often meeting two or three times a week.[47] African-European fellowship deepened: at Kabale Lawrence and Julia Barham began to work closely with Ezekieri (later Canon) and Losira Balaba. It was initiatives by Lawrence Barham and Ezekieri Balaba that led to the powerful Kabale Convention in 1935 – in which Nsibambi, Kigozi, Kinuka and Church participated – and out of such experiences Church was able to assure Bishop Stuart that he could offer a team for a Mukono mission which had 'a united aim'. Church suggested to Stuart that Barham and African leaders, lay and ordained, speak on typical Keswick subjects.[48] Stuart, in reply, told Church he was increasingly concluding that it was the Keswick message 'which is needed to carry conviction of sin'.[49] The Revival saw this message being embodied in communities marked by authentic fellowship.

The theme of fellowship continued to be central. Writing in 1938, F.J. Rownthwaite, in Kenya, agreed with Church about the importance of 'fellowship with our African brothers in Christ, even to the point of ignoring racial barriers', and expressed his belief that if missionaries could 'conquer the racial barrier' then revival would be 'very near indeed'. The Keswick motto, 'All One in Christ Jesus', was taking new forms.[50] One African leader who came to the fore in this period was William Nagenda, whose wife, Sala, was a sister of Nsibambi's wife, Eva, and of Kigozi's wife, Katharine. William was from a prominent Buganda family, was well educated and worked for the government. Bishop Stuart wrote to Church in 1936

The Story of Blasio Kigozi (London: CMS, 1937). For Kivebulaya, see Emma Wild-Wood, 'Powerful Words: Reading the diary of a Ganda Priest', *Studies in World Christianity* 18.2 (2012), pp. 134-53.

[45] An extended testimony from Kinuka is in *Ruanda Notes* 51, 2 December 1934, pp. 23-26.

[46] Guillebaud, *Mustard Seed*, p. 57.

[47] Emma Wild (Wild-Wood), '"Walking in the Light": The Liturgy of Fellowship in the Early Years of the East African Revival', in R.N. Swanson (ed.), *Continuity and Change in Christian Worship* (Woodbridge: The Boydell Press, 1999), pp. 420-21.

[48] Joe Church to Bishop Cyril Stuart, 23 February 1936, JEC 3/1/6.

[49] Bishop Stuart to Joe Church 3 March 1936, JEC 3/1/17.

[50] F.J. Rownthwaite to Joe Church, 4 June 1938, JEC 1/2/17. See Max Warren, *Revival: An Enquiry* (London: SCM Press, 1954), p. 39. Warren speaks about a 'demonstration of the power of God to establish right human relationships'.

about Nagenda and others who had vowed to 'resist sin' and had begun to preach around Entebbe. Four had asked about training for ordination.[51] By 1939 the members of teams with a sense of committed fellowship included Ernesti Nyabagabo and Ezekeili Balaba, who were teaching in Kigezi; Elisafati Matovu, a trader; Erica Sabiti, a clergyman (later Archbishop of Uganda, Rwanda and Burundi); and Nagenda, whom Bishop Stuart assigned to Gahini as chaplain. Most team members were in their twenties or thirties. The Revival fellowship across East Africa continued to expand and cross boundaries and borders. Tribal distinctions were seen as being 'swept away in a way we have never seen before'.[52] In Kenya and Tanganyika (now Tanzania) there was also pan-denominational revival, among Presbyterian, Methodist, Mennonite, and Lutheran churches. In April 1939 a team from Buganda and Kigezi spent six days in Bugufi and Katoke, Tanganyika. Lionel Bakewell, an Australian CMS missionary and head of the Katoke Teacher Training College, said, 'Some of us have seen the Saviour as we never saw Him before.'[53]

There were, however, strains in fellowship. Writing to 'Kiru', editorial secretary of the Ruanda Mission, Church took the view in 1938 that whereas Africans were 'insistent on a deep and open fellowship based on 1 John ch. 1' ('if we walk in the light ... we have fellowship with one another'), with 'fellowship meetings' now common, there had been 'some disunity' among European missionaries.[54] But significant changes were taking place. Evelyn Cafe, a CMS missionary at the Mengo Girls School, told Church in 1940 that she had attended a meeting of the *balokole* (the Luganda term – 'saved ones') and been dramatically affected. For years she had 'gone more and more into Liberalism' in theology, but now, she testified, the Bible 'speaks to me on every page that I read and [Keswick] hymns and choruses which I've scoffed at as being sentimental, now express what I genuinely believe and experience'.[55] Disunity over 'liberalism' caused a major crisis in 1941 at the Theological College, Mukono, where Nagenda and other *balokole* were receiving ordination training. John Jones, the College Warden, who was averse to revivalism, felt his theology and authority were being criticised and undermined by the *balokole*. The upshot was that Nagenda and twenty-five other students were expelled.[56] On 1 November 1941 Stuart wrote to them: 'I have received the report of the Warden of Mukono and it hurts me a lot. We are brought to great shame ...' He begged each 'to leave your sin and to return to the College humbly to obey all the rules of the Warden.'[57] John V. Taylor saw Stuart's 'unshakeable patience' as helping to avoid a

---

[51] Bishop Stuart to Joe Church, 3 March 1936, JEC 3/1/7.
[52] Lawrence Barham, cited by Osborn, *Fire in the Hills*, p. 89.
[53] Lionel Bakewell circular letter, 29 April 1939, JEC 1/3/10.
[54] Joe Church to Edith Hall (known by her African name, 'Kiru'), the editorial secretary of the Ruanda Mission, 29 December 1938, JEC 3/4/9.
[55] Evelyn Cafe to Joe Church, 2 September 1940, JEC 3/4/39.
[56] See Kevin Ward, 'Obedient Rebels: The Relationship Between the Early "Balokole" and the Church of Uganda: The Mukono Crisis of 1941', *Journal of Religion in Africa* 19.3 (1989), pp. 194-227.
[57] Bishop Stuart letter, 1 November 1941, JEC 3/5/19.

Church schism over Mukono,[58] but Stuart's stance meant Europeans in 'fellowship meetings' felt closer to Africans than to other Europeans.

In the light of events at Mukono, missionaries who had co-operated in teams with Africans felt they had to respond. On 15 November Church wrote a long and detailed letter to Stuart stating that many of the dismissed students 'are personally known to me and have worked on and off with me for years in a number of evangelistic teams'. Church had 'grown to love and trust them'. The Revival – which was spreading not only in Ruanda, Burundi, Uganda, Kenya, and Tanganyika, but also Southern Sudan and the Belgian Congo – had, Church said to Stuart, 'blessed the African Church' and 'blessed the missionaries'; the result was that many missionaries 'can bear witness to the fact that they have been helped by the life and fellowship of these "saved" (Balokole) Christians'.[59] A meeting was convened in Kabale on 16–17 December 1941 to think and pray about a fuller response and in the 'Report of a Meeting of some C.M.S. Missionaries & Africans at Kabale' sympathy was expressed for the Bishop and the Mukono Warden, but it was considered that the College was aiming to 'crush' the *balokole* and to 'exclude their message of Repentance and Revival from the Worship and teaching of the College'. The Kabale statement did not seek to refute the 'untrue, or grossly exaggerated' accusations made against the students, but focused on prayer, testimony, and the encouragement of 'faith in the word of God'. Of the twenty-three identified as present at the Kabale meeting, ten were Africans and thirteen were Europeans, with seven of the twenty-three being women.[60] It was through members of this group that the East African Revival would influence British evangelicalism.

Cleansing, Brokenness and the Cross

Writing in March 1940 to Bill Butler, a CMS missionary who had a period teaching at Mukono (and was to become an Archdeacon), Joe Church urged him to resist any dilution of the 'full preaching of the gospel of Grace, and the full preaching of the Blood of Jesus in atonement'.[61] In similar vein, the Ruanda Mission group at Kabale in December 1940 stated that 'the message of the perpetual cleansing and power of the Blood of Jesus' was 'the heart and centre of the message we are called to preach'.[62] The message was also sung, as in the signature song of the Revival, *Tukutendereza Yesu* ('We praise you, Jesus'). This was a song in Keswick's *Hymns*

---

[58] John V. Taylor, *The Growth of the Church in Buganda* (London: SCM Press, 1958), p. 104; cf. Gordon Hewitt, *The Problems of Success: A History of the Church Missionary Society*, Volume 1 (London: SCM Press, 1971), pp. 240-41.

[59] Joe Church to Bishop Stuart, 15 November 1941, JEC 3/5/22.

[60] 'Report of a Meeting of some C.M.S. Missionaries & Africans at Kabale (Dec. 16–17, 1941)', JEC 3/5/10. See Ward, '"Tukutendereza Yesu"', pp. 119-20. Ward suggests that the Statement ('Memorandum') was printed and circulated at the instigation of Leslie Lea-Wilson, a tea planter.

[61] Joe Church to Bill Butler, 10 March 1940, JEC 3/4/25.

[62] 'Report of a Meeting ... at Kabale (Dec. 16–17, 1941)', JEC 3/5/10.

of Consecration and Faith and was translated into Luganda.[63] It continues, 'Jesus, Lamb of God, Your blood cleanses me, I praise you, Saviour.'[64] In common with wider evangelicalism, crucicentrism characterised the Revival. Over time, 'Tukutendereza' was used to express a kind 'absolution' of sin 'in the Lord's name'.[65] There was a particular stress (again, 1 John 1) on the blood of Christ for spiritual 'cleansing' and victory over sin. In 1938 Martin Capon, Principal of the CMS Theological College in Limuru, Kenya, wrote to Cecil Bewes (later Africa Secretary of the CMS) about study he was undertaking of 1 John. In this context Capon related to Bewes how some Africans had been using language 'tending towards what seemed to me unscriptural teaching about holiness, in a word "eradication" instead of "counteraction" ... partly due', he added, 'to lack of knowledge of some of the finer points of English involved'. These terms were also finer points of Keswick theology. Capon was tempted to dismiss the Africans as 'pig-headed ignoramuses', but, he acknowledged, 'it began to dawn on me what they were after, namely that I was in danger of watering down my witness to the possibility of complete victory'.[66]

Another link made in the East African context was between the cross and personal 'brokenness'. This can be illustrated from Joe Church's family. Bill and Howard, Joe's brothers, both became missionaries in East Africa. Bill Church, also a doctor at Gahini, confessed in *Ruanda Notes* in 1934, 'I have the natural tendency of the British to be reserved and stand-offish. These and several other things hinder us, and me especially.'[67] Howard and Lizzo Church were serving with CMS at Kabete, near Nairobi, and in 1941 Lizzo wrote to Joe and Decie Church to tell them that she had come to an 'understanding of the meaning of victorious life and with it the experience of "breaking"'. She was indebted to them and to William Nagenda, who had helped her and Howard to see that 'often we just gas trivialities when all the time we could be really helping other Christians'.[68] A year later Algie Stanley Smith, writing notes in preparation for the Annual Conference of the Ruanda Mission, confessed, 'I once criticized the Africans for seeming to speak of nothing but the Cross ("almost ad nauseam" I said) and I deeply regret it. I see now that every doctrine and every experience must be illuminated by the "beams that shine from Calvary".' As well as giving testimony, he commended a book by a pioneer

---

[63] James Mountain and Mrs. Evan Hopkins (eds), *Hymns of Consecration and Faith* (London: Marshall Bros, 1902), No. 201.

[64] This song spread across East Africa, Kevin Ward, 'The East African Revival of the Twentieth Century: The Search for an Evangelical African Christianity', in K. Cooper and J. Gregory (eds), *Revival and Resurgence in Christian History* (Woodbridge: The Boydell Press, 2008), p. 369.

[65] Ward, '"Tukutendereza Yesu"', p. 131.

[66] Martin Capon to Cecil Bewes, 9 October 1938, JEC 1/2/40.

[67] Bill Church, *Ruanda Notes* 48 (Jan.–March 1934, 27 February 1934), p. 22.

[68] Lizzo Church to Joe and Decie Church, 11 August 1941, JEC 1/2/54.

missionary to North Africa who was influenced by Keswick, Lilias Trotter, who died in 1928, *Parables of the Cross*.[69]

'Breaking' at the cross could, however, lead to results deemed by the Revival teams to be unacceptable. In 1939, when Church was speaking at Katoke, he illustrated his message by drawing a picture of Christ on the cross and a man kneeling at the foot of the cross.[70] Later in the year, Lionel Bakewell wrote that prayer by one of the Africans for 'an open manifestation of the Spirit's power' was being answered in dramatic ways.[71] In March 1940 Bakewell confessed to Church that he had realised his 'deep seated sort of superiority complex over Africans'. He decided to ask them what was 'hindering' him. This was, he said, a 'breaking process'. Bakewell's experience resulted in his leading teams to other places and seeing people 'broken down'. But extended periods of singing in some meetings included unwelcome noises: people 'singing different things or the same things in different keys or with a strangled sort of voice'. Bakewell tried to warn against 'frenzy or hysteria', while admitting it was 'difficult to explain that in Swahili'. Overall, Bakewell believed there was a 'work of the Holy Spirit'.[72] This view was emphatically not shared by George Chambers (an energetic Australian evangelical), Bishop of Central Tanganyika, who visited Katoke. Chambers, writing to Church, described 'cryings, screamings, shoutings' in meetings, and spoke of 'a shame and scandal on the name of Christ'.[73] By May 1940 Chambers was gratified to tell Church, who shared Chambers' concerns, that Bakewell 'has followed my guidance and is restraining the excesses'. Unfortunately, Chambers added, 'the whole of his staff is against him'.[74] Bakewell confirmed to Church, 'My name is mud.'[75]

The episode illustrates differing perceptions of spiritual experience. This was highlighted again in 1945 at an Alliance Convention for European missionaries held at Mutaho, in Burundi, which drew together English, American, Canadian, Danish, and Swedish missionaries from Anglican, Methodist, Baptist, Quaker, and Holiness denominations. One speaker was a Swedish Pentecostal. At this conference, Church (testifying later) said he felt he still had too much 'reserve' and 'old school tie'. He asked for prayer and the laying on of hands. Others were similarly stirred.[76] It soon became evident, however, that African leaders, who had not been at Mutaho, were unimpressed. Nagenda and others thought missionaries from the Ruanda Mission

---

[69] 'The Annual Conference of the Ruanda Mission, 1942', JEC 3/7/2.

[70] Lionel Bakewell, circular letter, 29 April 1939, JEC 1/3/10.

[71] Lionel Bakewell to Joe Church, 28 October 1939, JEC 1/2/19.

[72] Lionel Bakewell to Joe Church, 22 March 1940, JEC 1/3/35.

[73] Bishop George Chambers to Joe Church, 8 April 1940, JEC 1/3/37. For an examination of ecstatic experiences in the Revival, see Benjamin J.D. Udy, 'Ecstatic Spirituality in Kigezi, Ruanda and Western Tanganyika, c. 1933–1940: Censorship, Control and the Ruanda Mission' (MA diss., University of Durham, 2013).

[74] George Chambers to Joe Church, 7 May 1940, JEC, 1/3/45.

[75] Lionel Bakewell to Joe Church, 15 May 1940, JEC, 1/3/47.

[76] Joe Church, circular letter, 25 July 1945, JEC 1/8b/7.

had been 'led astray', compromising the message of brokenness at the cross.[77] Lawrence Barham reported to Joe Church that Nagenda had written to Lawrence to ask, 'How far have you got with your Holy Spirit error?'[78] In the light of this potential division, a joint testimony was issued, signed by seven Ruanda missionaries: Joe and Decie Church, Godfrey and Phyllis Hindley, Peter Guillebaud, Ruth Pye-Smith, and Jane Cooper. They explained that some missionaries at Mutaho thought 'Revivalists' were 'testifying to defeat' through stressing brokenness. They saw a need for 'a testimony to a definite second work of grace and to the filling of the Holy Spirit'. The seven signatories wrote, 'It was not wrong to seek for a fresh filling, but it was wrong to imply that there was something special about this one.' There had been consequent confusion. The letter concluded, 'We are truly repentant.'[79]

Not all the Ruanda missionaries agreed with the sentiments in the joint testimony. Len and Esther Sharp did not accept that there had been any compromise. Esther wrote to Church in November 1945, invoking Keswick spirituality: 'As a Mission', she said, 'we stand on the Keswick platform.' She continued, 'The teaching of Keswick is a true and balanced doctrine of the estimable value of the Cross and of the benefits purchased for us there by the Holy Son of God.' She was wary of following the Africans in their negative reaction to Mutaho.[80] In similar vein, Algie Stanley Smith asked who was leading the Revival – Africans or Europeans? 'If the latter, why do they so often go back on their experiences and decisions, apparently at the dictates of the African leaders?'[81] Yet early in 1945, at a Ruanda Mission Council Meeting, Stanley Smith had answered a question about the issue of leadership by Europeans or Africans in this way: 'It is fair to say that the strongest <u>direct</u> influence on the African Church comes from Africans.' Europeans, he said, were rightly in the background.[82] The much-used motto card to illustrate 'brokenness', with its prayer 'Help me to bow the neck and die' – connecting with Christ who 'bowed His Head' on Calvary – came from a dream shared publically in July 1945 by Kilimenti Semugabo. In August, a Convention in Kabale, with Nagenda and Festo Kivengere (later Bishop of Kigeze) as major speakers, attracted huge crowds, up to 15,000.[83] Numbers at this African Convention far exceeded those at Keswick. The strength of African influence on the Revival was evident in a number of ways in the mid-1940s.

---

[77] Godfrey Hindley to Joe Church and Lawrence Barham, 11 August 1945, JEC 1/bb/10.
[78] Lawrence Barham to Joe Church, 26 August 1945, JEC 1/8b/12.
[79] Open letter from Ruanda Missionaries, 24 September 1945, JEC 1/8b/17.
[80] Esther Sharp to Joe Church, 1 November 1945, JEC 1/8b/21.
[81] Stanley Smith to Joe Church, 12 December 1945, JEC 1/8b/22.
[82] 'A Summary of Answers to Questions at the Council Meeting, Jan. 15th 1945', JEC 5/3/1.
[83] Church, *Quest*, pp. 216-21. See also J.E. Church, *Jesus Satisfies?* (London: Ruanda Mission, [1955]). There was an earlier booklet, *Jesus Satisfies*, published in 1946 after the first Kabale Convention. A second Convention was held in 1955.

In 1947 a tour of Britain by a Revival team created a considerable impact. William Nagenda and Yosiya Kinuka were the two Africans on the team, and Nagenda kept a diary recording their visits: a CICCU event at Tyndale House; meetings in London with the Worldwide Evangelisation Crusade (WEC); and opportunities to be at the Keswick and Southport (Wesleyan holiness) Conventions. Nagenda spoke of evangelical leaders he met, of testimonies he and Yosiya gave in churches, and of challenges to their hearers to 'walk in brokenness and daily cleansing'.[84] Lawrence Barham addressed the Keswick audience, stressing the way the Revival had brought 'a new revelation of the blood of Christ to cleanse from sin and bring victory'. Church, who had been asked to speak to young people at Keswick, took as his outline prayerfulness, brokenness, fullness, openness, and oneness.[85] One person profoundly affected by the Revival team's message in 1947 was Roy Hession, an effective evangelist with the National Young Life Campaign. He and his wife Revel invited a team to speak at a large conference for young people in Matlock, Derbyshire, on 'Revival is here for you – now?' The team, led by Barham, spoke about their failures and weaknesses in Africa and of God's grace.[86] Later Hession heard Nagenda and Kinuka, whose ministry he found 'if anything, more penetrating and helpful' than that of the Europeans. Hession described how he and his wife found 'Jesus showing Himself to us again'.[87] From the later 1940s travelling Revival teams went to Europe, India, North America, and Brazil. Brian Stanley writes of the message reaching 'to all corners of the globe'.[88] In this process, British evangelicals were being affected, as they heard powerful presentations from the African context of the cross in spiritual experience.

Walking in the Light

Along with the message of the cross that characterised the message of the East African teams, there was a strong emphasis in Revival circles on confession of sins and 'walking in the light'. In the early Revival experiences, Church was struck that an African, who would not want 'to repent of his sins before his fellows', was doing precisely that.[89] However, Karanja sees confession as 'an integral part of African

---

[84] William Nagenda, diary account, JEC 1/5/22.

[85] Letters from George Duncan and W.H. Aldis to Joe Church, 16 June and 21 June 1947, JEC 5/4/43 and 5/4/44; Church, *Quest*, p. 227.

[86] Roy Hession, *My Calvary Road: One Man's Pilgrimage* (London: Hodder & Stoughton, 1978), pp. 111-12.

[87] Hession, *My Calvary Road*, pp. 119-23.

[88] Brian Stanley, *The Global Diffusion of Evangelicalism* (Nottingham: IVP, 2013), p. 82. For more on the global impact, see Richard K. MacMaster and Donald R. Jacobs, *A Gentle Wind of God: The Influence of the East African Revival* (Scottdale, PA: Herald Press, 2006). This book is particularly valuable for the way it traces the impact of the revival in North America, and especially among Mennonites. I am grateful to Don Jacobs for the email correspondence I have had with him.

[89] Joe Church, *Ruanda Notes* 48 (Oct.–Dec. 1933), p. 20.

religion and culture'; thus confession was 'culturally' as well as 'biblically' mandated.[90] In the British context the sins were often connected with inter-personal relationships. Stanley Smith saw the period before the outbreak of the Second World War as one of 'deepening unity' in relationships in the Ruanda Mission.[91] In January 1938 a three-day gathering was arranged at short notice at Elfinsward, an Anglican conference centre in Haywards Heath, Sussex, for those being challenged by the message of the Revival. Several Ruanda missionaries were involved in the conference, and others present included Harold Earnshaw Smith, who became a central evangelical figure as Rector of All Souls Church, Langham Place, London; Godfrey Buxton, who ran the WEC Missionary Training Colony in London; and George Ingram, a CMS missionary in India who had a deep interest in prayer. Reginald Webster, General Secretary of the Ruanda Mission, affirmed a 'Revival Prayer Fellowship' in England, since 'our Mission has a vital message based on the experiences of God's grace which may be widely used at home'. At the final communion service of the conference there was time for open prayer and also for putting things right with others. The first one to do this was Webster himself, who asked forgiveness from someone else in the chapel.[92] This was the experience of walking in the light.

Later in the year, Martin Capon discussed with Cecil Bewes whether the Swahili and Kikuyu words for 'confess', as in 1 John 1, would always be understood as 'confession in front of people' unless 'confess in secret to God' was explained. Joe Church disagreed: his copy of this letter has 'No' written in the margin.[93] However, Church did believe public confession was at times necessary. Often this was associated with the initial experience of conversion, expressing 'severance from traditional society' and commitment to 'the Revival fellowship'.[94] Nsibambi's preaching included memorable evangelical conversionist phrases: in Luganda, *Ekibi kibi nnyo*, 'Sin is bad, very bad', and *ekisa*, 'grace'.[95] The message was of repentance, putting things right, and forgiveness. This applied to relationship with God and with other people. Thus when Bakewell turned against the ecstatic experiences at Katoke, Church's worry was broken relationships. Bakewell wrote in scathing terms of how 'the Bible has been combed for texts about people falling down on their faces, and these have been used to justify rolling about when one receives the Holy Spirit'.[96] Although Church supported Bishop Chambers' desire to check spiritual extravagances, the problem for Church was that in following Chambers' advice Bakewell 'fell into his old "schoolmastery" habits', and forfeited

---

[90] John Karanja, 'Confession and Cultural Dynamism in the Revival', in Ward and Wild-Wood (eds), *The East Africa Revival*, p. 147; cf. Bruner, 'The Politics of Public Confession in the East African Revival in Uganda'.

[91] Stanley Smith, *Road to Revival*, p. 84.

[92] Church, *Quest*, p. 150.

[93] Martin Capon to Cecil Bewes, 9 October 1938, JEC 1/2/40.

[94] Stanley, 'The East African Revival', p. 15.

[95] Osborn, *Pioneers*, p. 30.

[96] Lionel Bakewell to Joe Church, 18 May 1940, JEC, 1/3/52.

fellowship. Church encouraged reconciliation and 'walking in the light', and was happy to report that 'Bakewell saw his mistake in just condemning it all and set about to put it right and repent'.[97] The result was that when Bakewell left Katoke he did so with a sense of peace.[98]

One issue the Revival had to confront was the emphasis placed on open 'sharing' within the interdenominational, evangelistic Oxford Group, led by an American Lutheran, Frank Buchman. In England, in 1920, Buchman made contact with CICCU. Buchman recommended to students the book that helped Joe Church, *How to Live the Victorious Life*.[99] Soon Buchman's 'First Century Christian Fellowship' (as it was then called) was centred on Oxford – hence the Oxford Group.[100] The Oxford Group grew rapidly and spread internationally in the 1930s.[101] Its influence was felt in East Africa, with an Oxford Group house-party held at Bishop Stuart's house in Kampala in 1936. Joe Church attended, but felt that a 'deeper foundation' in 'the atonement and the blood of Jesus' was needed.[102] Joe Church wanted biblical teaching emphasised, and 1938 saw the publication of his widely-read *Every Man a Bible Student*, which had a particular emphasis on the 'Victorious Life' as understood by Keswick.[103] Roland Pittway, who was with the CMS in Kenya, told Church in January 1938 that he and one of his African colleagues had spent five hours with two Oxford Group leaders, Dr Anderson and Irving Benson, 'but we did not get very far'. Pittway said they 'do not seem at all prepared to put Christ and the shed blood in the forefront of their message'.[104] The Oxford Group accommodated varied theological viewpoints. Lizzo Church, however, explained to Joe in March 1938 that she believed God was using any 'keen' fellowships, including the Group.[105] There was not a united Revival position on this issue.

In a later letter, in August 1938, Lizzo described some missionaries 'getting fussed' about the Oxford Group, and went on, 'We are not bothered about that any longer. It's just fellowship in Christ we want and Revival and real love for each other instead of the heavy "tick-offs" etc.'[106] Howard Church explained that he and Howard Guinness, who worked for Inter-Varsity Fellowship (IVF, of which CICCU

---

[97] Joe Church report, 10 July 1940, JEC 1/3/53.

[98] Lionel Bakewell to Joe Church, 27 July 1940, JEC 1/3/54.

[99] Philip Boobbyer, *The Spiritual Vision of Frank Buchman* (Philadelphia, PA: Penn State University Press, 2013), p. 180 n. 98.

[100] I.M. Randall, *Evangelical Experiences: A Study in the Spirituality of English Evangelicalism, 1918–1939* (Studies in Evangelical History and Thought; Carlisle: Paternoster Press, 1999), pp. 238-39.

[101] See D.W. Bebbington, 'The Oxford Group between the Wars', in W.J. Sheils and Diana Wood (eds), *Voluntary Religion* (Oxford: Blackwell, 1986), pp. 495-507.

[102] Church, *Quest*, p. 136.

[103] J.E. Church, *Every Man a Bible Student* (London: Ruanda Mission, 1938).

[104] Rowland Pittway to Joe Church, 24 January 1938, JEC 1/2/44.

[105] Lizzo Church to Joe Church, 30 March 1938, JEC 11/2/1. Both 'Group' and 'Groups' were terms used.

[106] Lizzo Church to Joe Church, 2 August 1938, JEC, 1/2/25

was a part), had spent time together recently and found they 'had both been led along similar lines' owing to contact with the Oxford Group. He continued, 'We both felt what you [Joe] and many others feel, that what is needed in the Keswick crowd is a fellowship along Group lines. The sort of fellowship you tried to get going in the C.I.C.C.U.' Howard saw a 'lack of true fellowship in our crowd', but was encouraged that 'We seem to be getting something much deeper going in Ruanda, especially of late.'[107] Joe Church agreed about the 'deeper' work going on in Ruanda, but he did not want this to be seen as 'Oxford Group' spirituality.[108] Church was also hearing reports of Group 'guidance' (a common Oxford Group theme) that were worrying. He was told that an Oxford Group mission had been planned for Maseno, but two weeks before the start most of the team felt guided instead to go to South Africa. Of the remainder, one had fever, one 'got stuck in the mud' while travelling, and ultimately only one member appeared.[109] In the latter part of 1938 Martin Capon consulted with others about the Oxford Group. He was wary of using the word 'sharing' for confession, since it could confuse 'the Keswick world' and the Oxford Group.[110] For Capon, the 'place of closest fellowship is normally in Keswick circles'. He told Church he could not join the Oxford Group but was ready to work with Groupers, although they seemed 'vague about fundamental doctrines'. He explained that to join the Oxford Group 'would be to add my testimony, for what it might be worth, to positions and methods with which I do not agree'.[111]

From 20 to 27 August 1939 a conference was held in Kampala on 'Spiritual Re-Armament' (the Oxford Group took the name Moral Re-Armament). As well as an Oxford Group team, Bishop Stuart, Martin Capon and his wife Mary, Joe Church, Bill Butler, and Howard and Lizzo Church took part.[112] Later in the year Joe Church seemed to be employing Oxford Group terminology, saying that he had 'not felt guided to write to Kiru or Webster lately'.[113] Martin Capon, writing in December 1939, acknowledged that he and Mary wanted to keep 'up to the highest' (a Revival concept) since only then would the Oxford Group 'accept "sound doctrine" (!) from us'. The Capons had found Oxford Group witness 'challenging, especially the uncompromising attitude to sin – not "big sins" only'. Martin spoke of 'hindrances to the Holy Spirit' as including 'little things which perhaps we thought were only "temperament" and so not wrong'.[114] These sentiments echoed the Revival, but the language of 'temperament' reflected the more contemporary Oxford Group approach. The Capons connected their own approach, however, with Revival teaching about 'going to any sort of person who has been wronged and making an

---

[107] Howard Church to Joe Church, 2 August 1938, JEC 1/2/26.
[108] Church, *Quest*, p. 177.
[109] Carey Francis to Joe Church, 11 Sept 1938, JEC 1/2/32.
[110] Martin Capon to Cecil Bewes, 9 October 1938, JEC 1/2/40.
[111] Martin Capon to Joe Church, 3 November 1938, JEC 1/2/43.
[112] 'Spiritual Re-Armament', 20–27 August 1939, JEC 3/4/41.
[113] Joe Church to Dora Skipper, 9 November 1939, JEC 3/4/23.
[114] Martin Capon to Joe Church, 19 December 1939, JEC 11/2/5; Martin Capon report, 1939, 1/2/50.

apology – such would seem to be what God has been telling us, and our mandate for this simple prescription is in 1 John 1'.[115] Writing to Bill Butler in 1940, Joe Church said he did not feel 'guided' to join the Oxford Group, although the Group had helped him. He warned against 'we who represent the Keswick, C.S.S.M. outlook' being 'criticizers or ostracizers'.[116] Writing in reply, Butler was pleased that two African team members, one of them Nagenda, were 'led' to attend large Oxford Group meetings in Nairobi and spoke to Oxford Group members who had 'never heard quite that point of view'. The Revivalists had 'been blessed and also made a blessing'.[117]

In England, conservative evangelicals, often associated with Keswick and the IVF, were by this time sharply distinguished from evangelicals who felt at home in the Oxford Group and other broader movements. Instead of 'walking in the light' together, evangelicals were 'walking apart'.[118] Within Anglicanism, this was highlighted through the launch in 1928 by the 'liberal evangelical' Anglican Evangelical Group Movement (AEGM) of the Cromer Convention, an alternative to Keswick.[119] As an indication of this bifurcation, Joe Church's expectation was that Bishop Stuart's 'spiritual home' was Cromer, not Keswick.[120] It was largely through more conservative evangelical channels that the spirituality of the Revival flowed. In 1945, answering a question about the 'Revival Group' appearing to dominate in East Africa, Stanley Smith instanced other evangelical movements with limited objectives: Keswick, CSSM, Crusaders, and the IVF, and advocated 'a free recognition of the Balokole as a Pietist movement in the Ugandan Church'.[121] In the following year, at an IVF Conference for Theological Students, with 150 attending, Martin Capon was asked by Martyn Lloyd-Jones, minister of Westminster Chapel, London, and a moving force in the IVF, to recount his personal experience of the Revival to conference leaders. Capon spoke of the impact of Africans such as Nsibambi and Nagenda – who once said to Capon, 'You've not seen the cross.' Capon explained how profound encounters in Africa had taken him from a 'cold' experience to brokenness, fullness, openness, and oneness. Evidently impressed, Lloyd-Jones asked Capon to address the whole conference.[122] Lloyd-Jones, who was deeply interested in revival, extended an open invitation to Nagenda and others to Westminster Chapel, and this 'led to many visits'.[123] It was in these ways that 'light' was spread.

---

[115] Mary and Martin Capon, 'Report on Kenya, 1939', 1/2/45.
[116] Joe Church to Bill Butler, 10 March 1940, JEC 3/4/25.
[117] Bill Butler to Joe Church, 30 March 1940, JEC, 11/2/16.
[118] Bebbington, *Evangelicalism*, ch. 6, pp. 181-228.
[119] For the AEGM and Cromer, see Randall, *Evangelical Experiences*, ch. 3, pp. 46-69.
[120] Bishop Stuart to Church 3 March 1936, JEC 3/1/7.
[121] 'A Summary of Answers to Questions ... 1945', JEC 5/3/1.
[122] Martin Capon, report, 25 December 1946, JEC 5/4/36. For Lloyd-Jones' approach to revival, see I.M. Randall, 'Lloyd-Jones and Revival', in Andrew Atherstone and David Ceri Jones (eds), *Engaging with Martyn Lloyd-Jones* (Nottingham: Apollos, 2011), pp. 91-113.
[123] Church, *Quest*, p. 229.

Spreading the Message

From the mid-1940s the message of the East African Revival began to spread more extensively in Britain. In 1945 Stanley Smith defined this message as the new birth, the efficacy of the cross of Christ, death to self, the surrendered life and fellowship, and he advocated a 'spirituality marked by Christ-centredness, humility, faith, the "burning heart" (zeal), the "merry heart" (joy) and the "unruffled heart" (peace)'.[124] In 1946 Jim Brazier (then Archdeacon and later Bishop of Rwanda and Burundi) wrote of how the church in Ruanda had been 'revived by the power of the Holy Spirit' in a way that had not happened in England.[125] After the team visit to Britain in 1947, Revival conferences began to multiply, in typical evangelical activist fashion. Gordon Hindley wrote to Church about a conference at which, he said, 'there was light such as I have never seen anywhere let alone in England'; for him it was 'like the old days at Gahini'.[126] In 1950 Roy and Revel Hession produced *The Calvary Road*, which became the most widely-read book expounding the Revival's spirituality. Norman Grubb, General Secretary of the WEC, wrote the introduction to *Calvary Road* and spoke of how encounter with those touched by the Revival had taught him about the implications of 'walking in the light', and brought willingness to 'break' and 'confess'.[127] Grubb, whose sympathies were wide-ranging and who admired the Oxford Group,[128] became a major supporter of the Revival. In 1952 he wrote *Continuous Revival*.[129] These books did much to spread the message. In December 1950 Church wrote to Hession to encourage him about *The Calvary Road*. Already 36,000 copies had been sold: there is, said Church, a 'great hunger for Revival'.[130] In 1953 Church spoke how 'the testimony of what God is doing in East Africa has gone far and wide', and highlighted *The Calvary Road*.[131]

Some in the Keswick constituency, however, had reservations. In July 1948 Peter Marrow, who was then Vicar of Christ Church, Surbiton, wrote to Church about recent experiences relating to Keswick. Marrow had studied at Magdalene College, Cambridge, and then trained for Anglican ministry at the BCMS College in Bristol. His curacy was at a leading evangelical centre, St Paul's, Portman Square, London. Although Marrow was able to report to Church that Fred Mitchell, who had become Keswick chairman following the death of W.H. Aldis, was 'influenced somewhat by the message of the Ruanda team', other Keswick leaders took a different view. Donald Grey Barnhouse, a Presbyterian minister from Philadelphia, USA, who was a

---

[124] 'A Summary of Answers to Questions ... 1945', JEC 5/3/1.

[125] Church, *Quest*, p. 222.

[126] Godfrey Hindley to Joe Church, undated, but probably January 1949, JEC 5/5/56.

[127] Norman Grubb, introduction to Roy and Revel Hession, *The Calvary Road* (London: CLC, 1950), pp. 8-9.

[128] I.M. Randall, *Entire Devotion to God: Wesleyan Holiness and British Overseas Mission in the Early Twentieth Century* (Ilkeston: The Wesley Fellowship, 1998), pp. 21-22, 24.

[129] Norman Grubb, *Continuous Revival* (London: CLC, 1952).

[130] Joe Church to Roy Hession, 9 December 1950, JEC 5/6/31.

[131] Joe Church, *Ruanda Notes*, Feb.–April 1953, 26 January 1953, p. 15.

Keswick speaker in 1948, told Marrow that there had been discussion among speakers and Keswick Council members about future Keswick speakers and that Marrow's name had been mentioned, but the view expressed was that Marrow was 'spoiling' his ministry by being 'lined up with the Ruanda message'. This negative perception was confirmed in a letter from Colin Kerr, who was the influential Vicar at St Paul's, Portman Square, who told Marrow it was time the Revival 'got away from the Cross and entered more into resurrection life'.[132] While Marrow was disappointed that such criticisms were coming from Keswick, he and others had no intention of toning down the Revival message.

A few months after the Keswick Convention of 1948, Revival conventions began to be launched in various centres. At St Paul's Church, Cambridge, for example, a banner, 'Britain Needs Revival', was displayed, advertising a convention for the beginning of term, 1948. Among those heading up 'Revival Teams of Witness' were a number of Anglican clergy and their wives, such as Peter and Barbara Marrow, Fred and Constance Barff (Fred had studied in Cambridge and then at Wycliffe Hall, Oxford), Philip and Lucy Ridsdale, who were CMS missionaries in Uganda – in Philip's case following Joe Church's call in 1937 to Cambridge students to consider Uganda – and Howard and Lizzo Church.[133] As part of the spread of the message, conventions organised by Roy Hession in Matlock, Abergele, Clevedon, and Southwold played an important role. Joe Church told Hession in 1950 of the 'certainty' he had of being linked with Hession 'in seeking Revival in England and indeed, the world'.[134] Church urged Hession in 1955 to seek the Holy Spirit's work when addressing those with fixed views: Church instanced 'rigid' Calvinists, Baptists and 'P.B.s' (members of the Plymouth Brethren).[135] There was also a concern to see new movements in local parishes, such as St Andrew's, Histon, where Philip Knight was Vicar, and St Matthew's, Fulham, where Peter Johnston was Vicar.[136] But such work was often challenging. Howard Church wrote in 1957 to friends, 'The job here [Sparkbrook, Birmingham] is a tough one.' He spoke of the church, which served a parish of 10,000 people, as 'more a clique than a living outgoing fellowship.'[137] The contrast with East Africa was stark.

For some, the desire for revival meant that they embraced the charismatic movement as it developed in the 1960s. As early as 1936, Joe Church included 'glossolalia', along with 'dreams, visions, falling down in trances', as outward signs

---

[132] Peter Marrow to Joe Church, 27 July 1948, JEC, 5/5/83.

[133] Church, *Quest*, p. 228. I am grateful to Dr Andrew Atherstone of Wycliffe Hall, Oxford, for information about a number of Anglican clergy mentioned here. Philip Ridsdale was Bishop in the Congo in the 1970s.

[134] Joe Church to Roy Hession, 9 December 1950, JEC 5/6/31.

[135] Joe Church to Roy Hession, 25 October 1955, JEC 5/6/33.

[136] Peter Johnston was Vicar of Islington in the 1960–70s and as convener of the annual Islington Conference was an important evangelical spokesman in Anglicanism.

[137] Howard Church, writing from Christ Church, Sparkbrook, for friends, 4 December 1957, JEC 9/3/44.

of the Spirit's work.[138] In 1939 Lionel Bakewell spoke in tongues,[139] but at that time the 'Pentecostal' approach was 'a road not taken'.[140] However, in the later 1950s, new links began to be forged. In 1957 George Ingram, a retired CMS missionary in India who had an interest in the East African movement, began Nights of Prayer for Worldwide Revival. These were held each month in London, and they contributed to the beginnings of the charismatic movement in Britain.[141] Revel Hession, writing 1958, noted the influence of Arthur Wallis' book on revival, *In the Day of Thy Power* (1956), but she was worried about 'an undue emphasis on the value of all night prayer'. She also found some of the meetings 'full of striving'. Revel was concerned, too, that Stanley Voke, minister of Bethesda Baptist Church, Sunderland, who worked with the Hessions, was seeking 'something more' and that this produced instability.[142] Voke's personal testimony to revival was that he had been 'an energetic, proud, tense pastor of a large church' – his congregation numbered 700 – but that he 'lived a life of inward defeat'. It was at the Abergele conference that he saw 'two pathways, one of unbrokenness, the other of brokenness and repentance, the first a lonely way ending in darkness and ruin, the second a way of fellowship leading into light', and later, in Uganda, Voke was deeply impressed by African Christians 'whose faces all shone with joy'.[143] In the early 1960s he would speak of his hope that evangelicals could blend several spiritual emphases, including the Ruanda Revival, charismatic experience, Keswick, and the IVF.[144]

Finally, the Revival message was seen as stimulating mission. In 1937 Church began to explore with Wilson Cash, General Secretary of the CMS, the idea of a 'Uganda Seven', like the 'Cambridge Seven' missionaries who had gone to China in the 1880s. Church hoped that he might recruit from CICCU.[145] He also kept the Keswick leadership informed, since he believed that the missionaries needed 'some experience of leadership in mission work and some very definite experience of the Keswick message of full sanctification'.[146] However, he felt that he was up against 'a vast body of the "Cromer" type' seeking 'to water down the distinctive message for which the "Seven" stands'.[147] Writing at length in 1953 to Max Warren, who succeeded Cash as the CMS General Secretary, Church recalled that he used to

---

[138] Church, *Quest*, pp. 130-31.

[139] Lionel Bakewell to Joe Church, 28 October 1939, JEC 1/3/19.

[140] Peterson, *Ethnic Patriotism*, p. 123.

[141] Peter Hocken, *Streams of Renewal* (Carlisle: Paternoster Press, 1997), pp. 70-78.

[142] Revel Hession to Joe Church, 5 December 1958, JEC 5/6/39.

[143] Stanley Voke, quoted in Hession, *My Calvary Road*, pp. 133-34; Stanley Voke, *Walking His Way* (Otley: Righteous Books, 1996), p. 28. I am grateful to my colleague Dr Chris Voke for material on his father.

[144] I.M. Randall, 'Baptist Revival and Renewal in the 1960s', in Cooper and Gregory (eds), *Revival and Resurgence*, p. 349, citing Stanley Voke to Alec Steen, 2 December 1964.

[145] Joe Church to Wilson Cash, General Secretary, CMS, 14 June 1937, JEC 3/2/10. Algie Stanley Smith's father was one of the 'Cambridge Seven'.

[146] Joe Church to W.H. Aldis, 22 October 1937, JEC 3/2/43.

[147] Joe Church to Kenneth Hooker, 12 May 1938, JEC 3/3/9.

speak to Warren – who was then Vicar of Holy Trinity, Cambridge – about his missionary scheme. Church noted that only two of the hoped-for 'Seven' reached East Africa, Bill Butler and Philip Ridsdale. Church's letter gave an account of the story of the Revival to assist Warren with a book he was writing.[148] A year later the massive Billy Graham campaign in London gave fresh impetus to evangelism in Britain. Church wondered if the Revival teams had 'been a little bit carried away by the success of Billy Graham's methods, especially Roy [Hession] ... God is showing us that we are not to copy Billy Graham, we know the way quite well, it's the way of brokenness and daily repentance that really matters'. The order, said Joe, was that 'revival leads to evangelisation', not 'evangelisation will lead to revival'.[149] One leading Revival figure who did become involved with Billy Graham's work was Festo Kivengere. Laurence Barham, writing in 1956, hoped that Kivengere, who was then in England, would 'learn to distinguish between those who want him for his witness & those who want him as an addition to the travelling circus'.[150] The spirituality of the Revival was missional, but in undertaking mission there was a deeply-felt desire that the Revival message should not be diluted.

Conclusion

In 1950 a Ruanda Missionaries Conference held at Gahini recalled the blessing that had started at Gahini and how 'the wind of God had carried us beyond where we thought our boundaries would have been'.[151] The shaping of the Revival took place in the African context, with the energy coming largely from African leadership. Missionaries contributed to this movement from their experience of Keswick spirituality, but Keswick thinking was re-moulded. Those involved in the Revival, Africans and Europeans, searched together and served together, as equals. Within the process of exploration, the Oxford Group offered its own approach. For some Anglican leaders, the emergence of a 'Revival Fellowship', with a distinctive message, was an unwelcome development. In 1942 Bishop Stuart wrote to Joe Church to say that he did not object to Keswick's message – 'I seldom preach anything else myself' – but he alleged that 'the message that you and your friends now preach is a corruption of Keswick'.[152] Those who were committed to the Revival did not believe they had a corrupted message. Rather they believed they were learning important lessons from being in fellowship with Africans and through

---

[148] Joe Church to Max Warren, 6 September 1953, JEC 9/2/25. Warren was writing *Revival: An Enquiry* (1954). Another would-be 'Uganda Seven' missionary was Raymond Turvey, later a leading Anglican evangelical. He was deemed medically unfit for overseas service: Raymond Turvey to Joe Church, 16 July 1938, JEC 3/3/16.

[149] Joe Church to Berthe Ryf, Switzerland, 16 July 1954, JEC 1/7/35.

[150] Lawrence Barham to Joe Church, 17 October 1956, JEC 6/2a/40.

[151] 'Report of the Missionaries Conference held at Gahini, October 28–November 1, 1950', JEC 3/7/4.

[152] Bishop Stuart to Joe Church, 9 October 1942, JEC 4/1/6.

Africans giving direction.[153] The emphases that came from East Africa spread through teams of Africans and Europeans, and had significant effects internationally. In Britain, Revival conventions were launched. Local churches were affected. Stanley Voke could say of his congregation's life in 1954, 'At present there is so much blessing, and such deep fellowship with so many.'[154] Books were important: the themes contained in *The Calvary Road* lay at the heart of the missional spirituality of George Verwer and Operation Mobilisation, the global movement he founded.[155] Those British evangelicals who embraced the spirituality of the Revival saw in it a powerful embodiment of boundary-crossing fellowship, brokenness at the cross, and commitment to walking together in the light.

---

[153] Mark Noll, 'The East African Revival', in *The New Shape of World Christianity* (Downers Grove, IL: IVP Academic, 2009), p. 184.

[154] Stanley Voke to Roy Hession, 27 May 1954, JEC 9/4/44.

[155] Ian Randall, *Spiritual Revolution: The Story of OM* (Milton Keynes: Authentic, 2008), pp. 43, 105, 107.

CHAPTER 14

American Evangelical Transformation in the Aftermath of World War II

Mark A. Noll

The history of evangelicals in the United States since the mid-twentieth century is complicated because of the complexity of events on the ground, but also because of complexities of definition. Particularly amid intense focus on evangelical political involvement over the last decades, clear and consistent usage for the word 'evangelical' has been rare. My contribution in honor of a historian who has demonstrated the virtues of clear and consistent scholarship to the highest possible degree attempts to sort out the definitional issue to which David Bebbington has made such a significant contribution. It then attempts an account of the significant transformation of American evangelicalism from the era of the Second World War, with a special focus on developments in the 1950s. The chapter closes with an assessment of those developments that relates them to broader patterns in American history and broader questions of Christian integrity.[1]

Dilemmas of Definition

Among historians, it has become standard in the United States and Canada to define 'evangelicals' along two overlapping trajectories. First, with an eye to the past, 'evangelical' designates the churches and voluntary organizations descended from Protestant renewal movements of the eighteenth century that still maintain major emphases of those movements. The inheritance of John and Charles Wesley, George Whitefield, Jonathan Edwards, and other well-known progenitors has proliferated in an incredible diversity of institutional forms, but it remains identifiable as the quest for 'true religion' more or less as defined by these great revivalists of the eighteenth century. In the United States, many entire denominations and large sections in other

---

[1] As another way of honoring the leadership of David Bebbington in so many valuable enterprises that have promoted the history of evangelicals, this chapter is revised from a paper prepared for a conference he organized in London in 2009. It also adapts some material first published as 'Where We Are and How We Got Here' (fifty years of evangelical history), *Christianity Today* October 2006, pp. 42-49, 'Protestant Evangelicals and Recent American Politics', *The Journal of American and Canadian Studies* [Sophia University, Japan] 25 (2007), pp. 3-18, and 'Jesus and Jefferson', *The New Republic* 9 June 2011, pp. 35-39.

groups continue to be marked by this historical tradition. They include the Southern Baptist Convention (about sixteen million members); Wesleyan and Holiness groups like the Church of the Nazarene (about one million members) and the Salvation Army (several hundred thousand members); Pentecostal bodies like the Assemblies of God (at about four million members, a denominational grand-child of the Wesleyan revival); scores of smaller Baptist, Presbyterian, Church of Christ, Methodist, and Episcopalian or Anglican denominations; new organizations like the network of Calvary Chapels and the Vineyard Association; and tens of thousands of independent local churches. Several older mainline Protestant denominations with strongly revivalist roots – like the United Methodists (seven million members), the Presbyterian Church (USA) (two and a half million members), or the Disciples of Christ (about one million members) – were once thoroughly within this evangelical tradition, but have moved to one degree or another away from it. To make things more complicated, quite a few denominations that did not participate in Anglo-American revivals have nonetheless passed through experiences that now result in their self-designation as evangelicals, including some Mennonites, some Lutherans, some in the Dutch Reformed denominations, and some Quakers.

The second angle that is important for definition is doctrinal. Evangelicals have consistently been identified by their convictions. David Bebbington's well-known four-fold statement of these convictions highlights the Bible (or reliance on Scripture as ultimate religious authority), conversion (or an emphasis on the New Birth), activism (or energetic, individualistic engagement in personal and social duties), and crucicentrism (or focus on Christ's redeeming work as the heart of true religion).[2] The Bebbington definition has been widely adopted because it is specific enough to establish meaningful boundaries, yet flexible enough to take in a wide range of movements and groups with genuine similarities. In the United States, since the early twentieth century, one might say that self-described *fundamentalists* have held to these four convictions most strictly or most militantly, generic *evangelicals* have held them more flexibly, *denominational evangelicals* have held them in the shape prescribed by specific ecclesiastical traditions, and *pentecostals* or members of *charismatic* movements have shared these characteristics but also stressed the special gifts of the Holy Spirit, like healing and speaking in tongues.

The two prongs of definition – through history and by conviction – produce a relatively coherent subject for analysis and assessment. The need for these two angles of vision, when trying to construct an historical narrative, is indicated by two examples from North American experience. In 1996 an extensive cross-border survey put Bebbington's four convictions to use in asking numerous questions of a large number of Canadians and Americans.[3] Almost one-third of all Americans

---

[2] D.W. Bebbington, *Evangelicalism in Modern Britain: A History from the 1730s to the 1980s* (London: Routledge, 1989), pp. 2-17.

[3] The survey was conducted by the Angus Reid polling organization with guidance on the questions provided by the late George Rawlyk of Queen's University, Kingston, Ontario; the figures used here from that survey were prepared by Lyman Kellstedt, Emeritus Professor of

affirmed all four of Bebbington's characteristics, and about one-eighth of all Canadians. Yet among the Americans whom the survey could identify as evangelicals on the basis of the four Bebbington traits, almost one-fifth were Roman Catholics; in Canada, it was one-third. From this survey, and other proliferating evidence, it is obvious that in North America the great gulf that once divided evangelical Protestants and Roman Catholics is shrinking; a minority of Catholics now look like evangelicals by conviction. Yet for writing a connected evangelical history, it makes sense to treat the story of Protestant evangelicals as one thing and the more recent appearance of Catholics who share evangelical traits as another.

In the second example, this same 1996 survey found that more than one-eighth of all Americans who could be identified as evangelicals by the Bebbington characteristics were African Americans. In the United States, white evangelical church-goers and black Protestant church-goers affirm just about the same basic convictions concerning religious doctrines and moral practices. But for well-established historical reasons concerning the discriminatory treatment of African Americans, black Protestant political behavior and social attitudes are very different from those of white evangelicals. If in terms of both historical descent and religious convictions, most black Protestants could also be considered evangelicals, the history of racial attitudes has driven a sharp social wedge between them and white evangelicals. In the American case, it thus makes sense both to recognize the similarities shared by these two groups but also to realize that narratives about their historical development will be substantially different.

Conditions c.1950

After World War II the situation for American evangelicals was changing fast – internationally and domestically; politically, socially, and culturally. Whether evangelicals were up to the challenges of a rapidly changing world was an open question. The nation seemed to have moved beyond evangelical influence, and evangelical Christianity itself was in a fragmented state.

In the country at large, the number of evangelical adherents was actually quite large, and it was growing. Along with Catholics, Jews, and Protestants of all sorts, evangelicals rode a wave of expansion on the back of a post-war economic boom. But if evangelicals were in the vanguard of numerical advance, their situation as a whole was far from propitious. The churches that were expanding most rapidly (Southern Baptists, Seventh-day Adventists, Church of God in Christ, Nazarenes, Assemblies of God, and independents) occupied a negligible place in national consciousness. The large northern denominations (Methodists, Congregationalists, Episcopalians, Presbyterians, Baptists, and Lutherans), which had long played a central role as arbiters of the nation's public life, still included many evangelicals. But in the 1920s and 1930s theological conservatives had lost their dominant place

---

Political Science at Wheaton College. They are explored further in Mark A. Noll, *American Evangelical Christianity: An Introduction* (Oxford: Blackwell, 2001), pp. 29-43.

in most of these denominations, and by the 1950s 'mainline Protestantism' was well on the way to an amorphous theological identity.

Besides evangelical elements in the Protestant mainline, there remained many other outposts of evangelical strength: Baptist denominations of several kinds; self-described fundamentalist associations and individual congregations; burgeoning Pentecostal networks; ethnic Mennonites, Lutherans, and Christian Reformed; a variety of African American church families; even a few Hispanic-American and Asian-American bodies. But these outposts were largely unconnected with each other. Beneath the Mason-Dixon Line evangelicals in rich variety dominated the landscape, but the South's institutionalized racism made it very difficult for its religious strength to influence the rest of the country.

By the mid-twentieth century, in other words, it was clear that the United States' Protestant Era was over. Whether mainline, evangelical, fundamentalist, or liberal, the Protestantism that had once done so much to shape American life was in recession. In retrospect, the intra-Protestant quarrels of the early twentieth century – the fundamentalist-modernist controversies – had weakened all Protestant factions at the same time that several non-Protestant forces were gaining strength in American society.

The controversies of the early-twentieth century had exacted a special toll on Protestant intellectual life. By the 1950s Christian influence of any sort was rare in the nation's leading universities, serious publishing, or first-level discussions of public policy. Fundamentalists had lost the battles against evolution and the higher criticism of Scripture and so had angrily opted out of the mainstream academy. Modernists had made their peace with the dominant paradigms of the secular university but were left with little that was explicitly Christian to offer in that setting. The mass of Protestants, situated between fundamentalist and modernist polarities, included many capable intellectuals, but few working in the academy with self-conscious Christian goals and fewer still eager to identify themselves as evangelicals.

It was similar with the era's cutting-edge media. A few evangelical groups, like the Salvation Army, had pioneered use of the cinema, but by the 1920s and 1930s this increasingly influential form of cultural communication was controlled by forces hostile or indifferent to evangelical concerns. It was the same with television, still something of an experiment but rapidly coming to assume a dominant presence in the nation's economy, living rooms, and psyche. A very occasional Christian presence could be glimpsed on television, like the effective programs of Bishop Fulton Sheen, but as a Catholic the Bishop offered scant reassurance to Protestants that the new medium could be put to Kingdom use. Only on radio had evangelicals like Aimee Semple McPherson (Los Angeles radio station KFG), Charles Fuller (The Old Fashioned Revival Hour), Walter Maier (The Lutheran Hour), and the Moody Bible Institute network held their own, but with the rise of television, radio was becoming a niche medium in contrast to the nation-wide and pervasive presence of the tube.

In publishing, several active denominational presses were producing books that promoted traditional Christian teaching. But as late as 1945 there were hardly any publishers who had positioned themselves to serve a general evangelical constituency.

In politics it was almost the same story. Apart from nearly universal support for the United States' stand against communism, a burst of interest in the new state of Israel (driven more by apocalyptic speculation than on-site analysis), and simmering agitation against the liquor trade, evangelicals as a national force were all but invisible. Some of that invisibility arose from the effect of evangelical principles demanding separation from the world. More came from evangelical conformity to the regional, racial, and economic interests of the Democratic or Republican parties. Where evangelicals were politically active, concentration on local issues prevented broader involvement.

Sadly, evangelical political passivity extended to the nation's greatest enduring moral problem – race. In the early 1950s, far more than half of the nation's African Americans were still prevented by law or custom from voting, and the nation's armed forces had been recently integrated only because Russian propagandists made capital out of the plight of segregated blacks in the supposed 'home of the free'. The landmark Supreme Court decision of 1954, *Brown v. Board of Education*, had, in principle, abolished school segregation. But Congress was finding it very difficult to pass legislation for implementing a systematic plan of racial integration. No such legislation had been enacted since the 1870s, and prospects for change remained uncertain. As if to underscore how difficult it would be to alter the racial habits of the centuries, in 1956, ninety-six white Southern congressmen from the eleven states of the former Confederacy issued a well-publicized 'Southern Declaration of Constitutional Principle'. It was a Manifesto that defended segregation, criticized non-Southerners for their own hypocrisy concerning race, and defied federal efforts at altering Southern race traditions. Individual white evangelicals could be found both contributing to the Southern Manifesto and working to pass the civil rights bill that eventually became law in 1957. But on matters of race, there existed no evangelical consensus, no national mobilization, and not even an awareness that coercive discrimination against African Americans contradicted evangelical moral norms even more than it did American national ideals.

World War II, by galvanizing the nation morally as well as militarily, had prompted a general upsurge of religion. But this religion was more a vague patriotic theism than a sharply focused particular faith. As argued in Will Herberg's insightful book from 1955, *Protestant, Catholic, Jew*, a generic advocacy of 'Judeo-Christian values' was as much a substitute for individual faiths like evangelical Protestantism as an extension of them.[4]

Evangelicalism was by no means dead in 1950. Yet if large numbers of evangelicals still existed, their general impact was considerably less than the sum of

---

[4] Will Herberg, *Protestant, Catholic, Jew: An Essay in American Religious Sociology* (Garden City, NY: Doubleday, 1955).

their parts. The capacity to shape national mores or to influence national agendas in politics, the media, or intellectual life seemed spent. Proposals for internal revitalization were unclear. Prospects for intra-evangelical relationships that could break through regional, denominational, and racial barriers were uncertain. Perceptive observers in the late 1940s would have been justified in predicting increasing fragmentation, increasing irrelevance, and therefore decreasing visibility for America's evangelicals. Some might have anticipated selected outposts of evangelical strength fueled (especially in the race-divided South) by resistance to the secularizing trends of national life. Few could have predicted what actually happened.

Resurgence, by the Numbers

What happened was a multifaceted resurgence. In the United States the last six decades have witnessed more evangelical numbers, wider evangelical connections, stronger evangelical institutions, and broader evangelical influence than any reasonable observer at mid-century could have anticipated. This story shares some features with the recent history of evangelicals in Canada, especially a heightened sense of national evangelical identity. But in Canada the evangelical numbers have been much smaller, ancient racial tensions have not played a major role, and evangelical social engagement has been less aggressive. The American evangelical story is likewise similar in some respects to the British, though with such complex differences that it would require a separate consideration to treat them with even minimal justice.

Evangelical resurgence can be treated objectively by the numbers and almost as objectively by noting the cultural re-engagement that, on many fronts, brought evangelicals back into American public life. It is, of course, more difficult to explain the causes of numerical growth and to evaluate the character of cultural re-engagement.

Concerning a post-war numerical expansion of evangelicals there can be no doubt. Between 1935 and 2000, the number of individual US congregations identified as Congregationalist, Episcopal, Methodist, Disciples of Christ, Baptists in the North, or from the main Presbyterian denominations shrank, in some cases precipitously. By contrast, the number of congregations identified as Southern Baptist, Holiness (like the Church of the Nazarene, and the Salvation Army), Churches of Christ, Mennonites, Seventh-day Adventist, or from conservative Presbyterian denominations at least doubled. The number of Pentecostal and nondenominational congregations – as also the number of Mormon and Jehovah's Witness congregations and worship centers of non-Christian religions – grew much faster than that.[5]

---

[5] This compilation is from Nancy T. Ammerman, 'American Evangelicals in American Culture: Continuity and Change', in Steven Brint and Jean Reith Schroedel (eds), *Evangelicals and Democracy in America* (New York, NY: Russell Sage Foundation, 2009),

Partly driven by evangelical political activity, survey researchers have increasingly paid careful attention to the size of national religious constituencies. The most reliable of these surveys, which are usually based on the respondents' church affiliation, conclude that about 26% of the American electorate identifies with mostly white evangelical Protestant churches, and another 6–8% with African-American Protestant churches.[6] For white Protestants, this 26% represents an increase from about 22% as of the early 1970s. Other surveys have indicated that over 40% of all individuals at religious services in the United States during any given week are found in identifiably evangelical churches.[7]

Of particular note in the recent demography of American religion has been the emergence of megachurches, which are defined by the Hartford Institute for Religious Research as Protestant congregations with an average attendance of approximately 1,800 or more per week. In a 2011 listing the Hartford Institute counted 1,361 of these congregations. The count in 1990 was only 350. Seventy-one percent of these megachurch congregations describe themselves as evangelical, another 13% as charismatic or Pentecostal, and an additional 4% as missional. Again, to suggest differences between the United States and Canada, whose megachurches are also included on the Hartford Institute's list, in 2008 there were more Protestant congregations with an average weekly attendance of 2,000 or more in Atlanta, Georgia (seventeen), than in all of Canada (twelve). In that 2008 accounting, fifty-five congregations were tabulated with weekly attendance averaging 10,000 or more. Of these mega-megachurches twenty-six were nondenominational, eight were Southern Baptist, five part of the Calvary Chapel network, and five belonged to Pentecostal denominations. None were from the mainline Protestant denominations.[8]

To summarize the statistical picture, the number of people attending evangelical churches has risen steadily since the 1950s, and the increase has been found disproportionally in Baptist, Pentecostal, and especially nondenominational congregations.

---

pp. 51-52. It aligns closely with similar enumerations provided in Mark A. Noll, *God and American Politics: A Short History* (Princeton, NJ: Princeton University Press, 2008), p. 162.

[6] E.g., Andrew Greeley and Michael Houk, *The Truth about Conservative Christians: What They Think and What They Believe* (Chicago, IL: University of Chicago Press, 2006); and Pew Forum on Religion and Public Life, 'U.S. Religious Landscape Survey' (Washington, DC: Pew Forum, 2008).

[7] John H. Evans, 'Where is the Counterweight?: Explorations of the Decline in Mainline Protestant Participation in Public Debates over Values', in Brint and Schroedel (eds), *Evangelicals and Democracy in America*, p. 224, which puts to use Mark Chaves, *Congregations in America* (Cambridge, MA: Harvard University Press, 2004).

[8] Hartford Seminary Foundation, Hartford Institute for Religious Research, http://hirr.hartsem.edu/megachurch/megachurch-2011-summary-report.htm, 13 March 2013. For the 2008 report, http://hirr.hartsem.edu/megachurch/database.html, accessed 28 May 2009.

Causes and Effects

Causes and effects are more obscure than statistics, but it is nonetheless possible to chart a sequence for this post-war evangelical resurgence. First in time was a new wave of voluntary organizations that reinvigorated evangelicals in the middle part of the twentieth century as the formation of the American Board of Commissioners for Foreign Missioners, the American Bible Society, and similar foundations had done in the early-nineteenth century. This new effervescence of evangelical entrepreneurialism was rooted in fundamentalist or independent initiatives of the 1920s and 1930s, but it was consolidated during World War II, and then took off in the post-war boom of wealth, higher education, and upward mobility. Usually without denominational identification, without sanction from the universities, without much public recognition, and usually without carefully constructed organizational charts, this new wave of voluntary activity was brimful of energy. A partial listing of the new agencies and institutions includes Intervarsity Christian Fellowship (1938), the Summer Institute of Linguistics (1934) with Wycliffe Bible Translators (1942), Young Life (1941), the National Association of Evangelicals (1942), the Navigators (incorporated 1943), Youth for Christ (1944), Fuller Theological Seminary (1947), Campus Crusade for Christ (1951), World Vision (1953), and the Fellowship of Christian Athletes (1954). These new organizations were pure-bred evangelical in their commitment to traditional Christian faith. But they were also pure-bred evangelical in expressing those commitments independently, focused on need, and with organizational creativity. They have contributed greatly to reconstructing the infrastructure of contemporary American evangelicalism, especially by paving the way for the rise of independent nondenominational churches as an ever more significant part of evangelical life. Such churches are, in effect, an ecclesiastical expansion of the independent-mindedness that first came to expression in the parachurch.

A second set of important factors in the post-war evangelical resurgence relates to national history more broadly, especially the emergence of the United States as a military super-power and as an engine of unprecedented material affluence. As the United States' global presence increased from the first test of the hydrogen bomb through the Korean War and to the settlement of the Suez Canal crisis in 1956, so too did its economic expansion advance at breakneck speed. Much of the initial evangelical entrepreneurialism of the recent past came from missionary and development efforts related to the experience of service men and women overseas during World War II and the Korean War. The rapid growth of evangelical missionary activity in the post-war years was very much part of the United States' leadership in the Cold War, its rejection of the nation's historic isolationism, its increasing commitment to global trade, and the increasing amounts of money that evangelicals could donate to missionary work – though understanding the exact relationship of these factors awaits the appearance of a Brian Stanley or an Andrew Porter who can sort out issues of empire and missionary service for the US as these historians have done so well for an earlier British empire.[9] Internationalism has continued to be a major feature of American evangelical life, as symbolized by the Billy Graham Associations' sponsorship of the 1976 World Congress on Evangelization at Lausanne and the rapidly accelerating congregation-to-congregation missionary outreaches of recent years.[10]

At home, the post-war boom in new-home construction and the rapid growth of suburbia, which were fueled by the massive interstate highway system inaugurated under President Eisenhower, created an automobile culture and unusual freedom of individual movement. Evangelical voluntarism, independency, and nondenominationalism flourished in an environment made to order for entrepreneurs and built to move people, products, and ideas rapidly from place to place. In these terms, it is not facetious to regard President Eisenhower as a key early figure in the history of American megachurches.

The United States' post-war economic boom also supported the rapid diffusion of television as the most popular means of popular communication. In 1950, less than a tenth of American homes possessed a television set, in 1956 more than three quarters.[11] The impact of television on religious movements has been too little studied. For evangelicals, television hastened a process of national interconnection, with more people from more parts of the country aware of evangelists like Billy Graham and Oral Roberts because of their effective broadcast ministries and their ability to raise funds for exploiting the nation's free trade in television accessibility. Television also made Hollywood and New York styles of professional entertainment into a national norm that soon was setting the standard for Christian worship in many evangelical churches. Only five weeks before the evangelical magazine *Christianity Today* made its debut in 1956, Elvis Presley appeared for the first time on television's Ed Sullivan Show (Sunday night, 9 September) where he wowed – or outraged – the entire nation with renditions of 'Don't Be Cruel' and 'Hound Dog'. Few of the evangelicals who missed Elvis on TV – because they were attending Sunday evening service – could have guessed that within a few decades the music of public worship in their own churches would look and sound more like Elvis Presley on the Ed Sullivan Show than the Sunday evening worship they attended in 1956. Television was one of the main reasons for this rapid change.

A third immensely important development in the recent history of evangelicals in America was the civil rights movement. It began in African American churches during the 1930s and 1940s when more and more black Americans began to apply biblical faith in an all-righteous God, which had sustained them through deserts of

---

[9] Brian Stanley, *The Bible and the Flag: Protestant Missions and British Imperialism in the Nineteenth and Twentieth Centuries* (Leicester: Apollos, 1990); A.N. Porter, *Religion Versus Empire?: British Protestant Missionaries and Overseas Expansion, 1700–1914* (New York: Manchester University Press, 2004).

[10] Robert Wuthnow, *Boundless Faith: The Global Outreach of American Churches* (Berkeley, CA: University of California Press, 2009).

[11] *Historical Statistics of the United States: Colonial Times to 1957* (Washington, DC: Bureau of the Census, 1960), pp. 488, 491.

slavery and segregation, to the structural racial injustices of ordinary American life. When civil rights reform was advanced by the 1954 Supreme Court decision *Brown v. Board of Education*, white evangelicals mostly remained ambivalent: they could recognize strong biblical convictions in the black church folk who were driving the revolution, but they were also frightened by influences like the pacifism of Mahatma Gandhi and the socialism of A. Philip Randolph that also shaped the movement. In addition, an unreflective acceptance of the racist status quo, which evangelicals shared with most of their white contemporaries, remained very strong.

Without much white evangelical support, the civil rights movement nonetheless moved ahead with the 1957 civil rights bill, and then the landmark legislation of the mid-1960s: civil rights (1964), voting rights (1965), and open housing (1968). By the late 1960s, white evangelicals, even in the South, were beginning to accept the inevitability of civil rights for blacks, and a few intrepid evangelicals, like Frank Gaebelein of Stony Brook School, actively joined in the struggle. It was, however, President Lyndon Johnson, Dr Martin Luther King, Jr, and a host of African American leaders and followers who pushed the revolution through.

The spin-off effects for American evangelicals were nonetheless immense. In the first instance, evangelical acceptance of civil rights principles did not mean that evangelicals embraced the means that had been used to secure those principles. That means was federal power, which soon expanded into many other areas of life beyond civil rights. Sociologists Robert Wuthnow and Steve Bruce have demonstrated how resentment against intruding national authority – especially on issues concerning sexuality, the family, and public schools – fueled the political mobilization of evangelicals and eventually attached them to the Republican party, as putatively the party of small government.[12] Evangelical political engagement was propelled by this resentment at the expansion of central government authority, which was in turn a direct result of the civil rights struggle.

But once legally enforced racism was gone, the great impediment that had restricted the influence of Southern religion to only the South was also gone. Stripped of racist overtones, Southern evangelical religion – the preaching, the piety, the sensibilities, and above all the music – became much easier to export throughout the country. Billy Graham had earlier shown how attractive a non-racist form of affective Southern evangelicalism could be. As historians Grant Wacker and Darren Dochuk have demonstrated, evangelical sons and daughters of the South (Pat Robertson, D. James Kennedy, Jerry Falwell, Anita Bryant, even Jimmy Carter and Bill Clinton) found it much easier to export the gospel sensibilities of their region once the battle for civil rights was won.[13] For reviving and defining recent American

---

[12] Steve Bruce, *The Rise and Fall of the New Christian Right: Conservative Protestant Politics in America, 1978–1988* (New York, NY: Oxford University Press, 1988); Robert Wuthnow, *Red State Religion: Faith and Politics in America's Heartland* (Princeton, NJ: Princeton University Press, 2012).

[13] Grant Wacker, 'Uneasy in Zion: Evangelicals in Postmodern Society', in George M. Marsden (ed.), *Evangelicalism and Modern America* (Grand Rapids, MI: Eerdmans, 1984); Darren Dochuk, 'Evangelicalism Becomes Southern, Politics Becomes Evangelical: From

evangelicalism as a whole, the expansion of Southern influence throughout the nation has made a great difference.

At the same time that revived voluntarism, participation in the post-war economic boom, and reaction to the civil rights movement redirected evangelical life, still other changes were altering the shape of weekly worship and the constitution of congregations that met for worship. Among the most important of these developments was the charismatic movement, which began in the 1950s but which burst into prominence in the following decade. It promoted several emphases of classical Pentecostalism, but in typical American fashion as a spiritual smorgasbord to sample as individuals chose. Charismatic emphases on personal conversion, physical healing, speaking in tongues, participation in small group fellowships, and freshly written songs offered a range of open possibilities rather than formal ecclesiastical requirements. Lay organizations, like the Full Gospel Business Men's Fellowship, International, founded as a nondenominational association by Demos Shakarian in California in 1952, were especially effective in expanding the charismatic constituency.

Effects of the movement included greater concern for the specific work of the Holy Spirit, but even more a general turn toward subjective spirituality, especially in churches where Pentecostal teachings were alien. In a post-war world of increasing mobility, rapid population growth, suburban sprawl, and accelerated pace of life, teaching about the presence of the Spirit – as Comforter, Guide, Counselor – found real traction. In the week-to-week life of congregations, the influence of the charismatic movement was most visible in the great changes in church music that accelerated from the early 1960s. Almost all these changes were related to some combination of charismatic influences, the expanding influence of Southern evangelicalism, and the new influence of television.

A further development that boosted charismatic influences while also working to transform public worship was the Jesus Movement of the late 1960s and early 1970s. It was a particularly visible instance of voluntary and charismatic vitality. The Jesus People foreswore suits and ties. They penned lyrics beyond number to be sung with guitar and even drums. They imported new vocabularies from pop culture that were completely foreign to Protestant traditions in order to connect with young people disillusioned by the corporate rat race or the Vietnam War. They cooperated with a number of energetic young pastors, like Chuck Smith of Calvary Chapel in Costa Mesa, California, who were committed to becoming all things to all restless youth that by all means they might save some. They were wild, they were unconventional, but they were also obviously evangelical.

The short career of the Jesus People should not blind observers to the wide-ranging significance of the movement. From the 1920s to the 1950s, American evangelicals had tended to view popular culture as an enemy – to save the gospel it

---

FDR to Ronald Reagan', in Mark A. Noll and Luke Harlow (eds), *Religion and American Politics: From the Colonial Period to the Present* (New York, NY: Oxford University Press, 2nd edn, 2007); see also n. 21 below.

was necessary to flee the world. In the late 1960s, the Jesus People treated popular culture as a potential friend – to spread the gospel it was necessary to use what the world offered. The fact that leaders of the movement displayed a firm commitment to scriptural values while rejecting the licentious practices of the counter-culture reassured the broader evangelical world that, strange as they might seem, these Jesus People were OK. As historian Larry Eskridge has shown, the Jesus People demonstrated that a potent antidote to sex, drugs, and rock-n-roll music could be offered by the Bible, the Spirit, and rock-n-roll music.[14]

If the charismatic and the Jesus Movement changed the style of evangelical worship, the Immigration and Nationality Act of 1965 changed who showed up for church. Since the loosening of immigration restrictions in 1965, the United States has once again become, as it was a century before, the most ethnically diverse nation on the planet. Conventional wisdom understands that the dramatically increased presence of Hindus, Buddhists, Sikhs, Muslims, and other faiths has created unprecedented religious pluralism. But as sociologist R. Stephen Warner and others have pointed out, the new immigration has been surprisingly – even overwhelmingly – Christian.[15] Among the new immigrants, Christian adherence is often higher than in the immigrants' country of origin; and in the United States, Christian churches have become favored places for social organization even for immigrants who were not believers in their original lands. Warner has called the outcome of recent immigration 'the de-Europeanization of American Christianity'. Because so many of the Hispanic, Korean, Nigerian, Chinese, Eastern European, Filipino, Ghanaian, and Brazilian newcomers are evangelicals, often of a Pentecostal cast, the result has also contributed to the re-evangelization of America. The impact of these new evangelicals has been particularly strong on campus ministries, in the academy, and with the growth of evangelical congregations in the nation's urban centers.

Cultural Adaptation in the Mid-1950s

The major post-war developments and changes all pointed in one direction, which was the willingness – whether expressed consciously as a decision or simply taken for granted as a natural fact of life – to embrace broader currents of American culture. That engagement with broader cultural patterns has enjoyed a long evangelical history.

Since its beginning in the revivals of the eighteenth century, evangelicals everywhere had been characterized by their effort to combine traditional religion with cultural adaptability. Evangelicals are properly identified by the doctrines they affirm and the moral practices they encourage in direct descent from the revivals of the eighteenth century and, in many cases, from the Protestant Reformation. But in

---

[14] Larry Eskridge, *God's Forever Family: The Jesus People Movement in America* (forthcoming).

[15] R. Stephen Warner and Judith G. Wittner (eds), *Gatherings in Diaspora: Religious Communities and the New Immigration* (Philadelphia, PA: Temple University Press, 1998).

most places, especially the United States, they have also been marked by an unusually sensitive responsiveness to contemporary cultures, which has led to an unending series of innovations in organizational models, strategies of communication, appeals to the public, and much more.

Evangelicalism has been at its best theologically and its most effective culturally when continuity with doctrinal tradition has balanced sensitive response to surrounding circumstances. In the eighteenth century, John Wesley, himself a politically conservative Anglican, nonetheless sensed the need for new forms of organization and new modes of religious expression to respond to what historians have called 'the invention of the individual'. The result was small groups, a more lively and personal hymnody, and extensive lay recruitment that made Methodism the fastest growing Christian movement of the century, and positively influenced the whole world of English-speaking Protestantism, including those who disagreed with specific points of Wesley's theology.

During the 1920s and 1930s, evangelicals had in fact shown considerable cultural creativity – by setting up publishing networks outside the denominations, producing radio programs with broad popular appeal, and organizing youth activities for the public square. But the era was also defined by a defensive mentality that deployed doctrine and requirements of life-style piety to fend off threats from the world. Into the period of World War II, separatism triumphed over engagement among many evangelicals. Things changed in the mid-twentieth century as evangelicals once again began to run on the two tracks of tradition and innovation. Re-engagement with main currents of American life was the common theme, and from every point on the compass.[16]

Among the signal events from the mid-1950s that altered the force fields of evangelical history was one of the most powerful Christian stories in modern times. Early in 1956, five young missionaries who had ventured deep into the Amazonian jungle to evangelize the Woarani tribes people were slain by the ones they were trying to convert. (The word 'Auca', which means 'savage', is a pejorative to be avoided.) Such attacks had taken place before – indeed, quite regularly – in the history of evangelical missions. This time, however, the after-effects were startling. The story of the missionaries' sacrifice was featured not only in the pulpit and the pages of Christian periodicals. But the story of the missionaries' selfless dedication and their widows' Christ-centered fortitude was also broadcast widely by American secular media – first with a photoshoot in *Life* magazine followed soon thereafter by an article in *Reader's Digest*, then on television's *This Is Your Life*, and finally in the bestselling *Through Gates of Splendor* that was published by Harper, a major New York press.[17]

---

[16] The best treatment for these middle decades of the century is Joel A. Carpenter, *Revive Us Again: The Reawakening of American Fundamentalism* (New York, NY: Oxford University Press, 1997).

[17] I am indebted to Kathryn Long and her forthcoming book on the Woarani for this information; see Long, 'In the Modern world, but Not of It: The 'Auca Martyrs',

Nothing like this level of positive attention to evangelicals had been seen in American mainstream media for more than a generation. Nothing like such evangelical skill at engaging and exploiting the mainstream media had been witnessed since the heady days of D.L. Moody sixty years earlier. The missionaries had died attempting to spread the old story of Jesus and his love; their testimony was being communicated through the most up-to-date media that contemporary America could offer.

Significantly, *Through Gates of Splendor* was written by Elisabeth Elliot, widow of one of the missionary martyrs. It was the first in Elliot's extensive series of books that came to include other missionary memoirs, novels, devotional reflections, and social commentary. With Rachel Saint, sister of another of the missionaries, Eliot returned to the Woarani. Aided by Dayuma, a formidable Woa woman, the missionaries began to translate the Scriptures and establish a beachhead for the gospel, only short years after the killings took place. Elisabeth Elliot, Rachel Saint, and Dayuma were not feminists. But they were exercising the kind of public 'agency' for which modern feminists appealed. Without setting out to be pioneers, they were nonetheless showing the way to an evangelical female activism that led on to a bulging roster of influential public figures, including political organizers Beverly LaHaye and Diane Knippers, authors on feminist themes Nancy Hardesty and Letha Scanzoni, and (as outsiders heeded by evangelicals) the Catholic political figure Phyllis Schafly and the Eastern Orthodox author Frederica Mathews-Green. Some of these influential evangelical women, including Elisabeth Elliot, have been social as well as doctrinal conservatives. But their activity was geared to realities of contemporary life and they made themselves heard through the strategies of contemporary media.

Two other events from about the same time also testified to shifting directions. Both concerned Billy Graham.[18] The first was the new magazine, *Christianity Today*, that appeared in October 1956. By assembling the personnel, brokering the financing, and hammering away at the need, Billy Graham had been the key figure in starting *Christianity Today*. In words of an early appeal he stressed how 'a religious magazine ... that will reach the clergy and lay leaders of every denomination presenting truth from the evangelical viewpoint' could help overcome the 'confused, bewildered, divided, and almost defeated' condition of evangelicals in the United States.[19] Graham's influence came from where authority has always arisen in evangelical circles – namely, from his power as a preacher. Beginning in 1944, as the first full-time employee of Youth for Christ, then through break-out campaigns in

---

Evangelicalism, and Postwar American Culture', in Daniel H. Bays and Grant Wacker (eds), *The Foreign Missionary Enterprise at Home* (Tuscaloosa, AL: University of Alabama Press, 2003).

[18] For reflective assessment of Graham's long career, a particularly helpful article is Grant Wacker, 'Billy Graham's America', *Church History* 78 (2009), pp. 489-511.

[19] The quotations in this and the next paragraph are from an address that Billy Graham delivered in 1955 that proposed the creation of *Christianity Today*; personal copy in my possession courtesy of Harold Myra, former publisher of the magazine.

Los Angeles (1949) and Great Britain (1954), Graham had established himself as an unusually fresh, straightforward, and also convincing voice for traditional evangelical faith.

That his interests also extended to a magazine like *Christianity Today* was, however, unusual. Since the late nineteenth century, it had become customary for evangelicals to pose an antithesis between pious preaching and formal intellectual labor. Graham wanted the magazine to function differently. He had similar concerns for several new evangelical seminaries – Fuller near Los Angeles, Gordon-Conwell near Boston, and Trinity near Chicago – that received substantial support from Graham and the circles he influenced. He hoped *Christianity Today* would act as a forum uniting disparate evangelical movements, but that it would also provide evangelicalism with a measure of theological depth alongside savvy social analysis. In this attempt he was joined by the founding editor of the magazine, Carl F.H. Henry, and a host of other intellectually ambitious younger evangelical scholars. They shared Graham's desire for disseminating biblical expositions and evangelistic messages, but also for 'discuss[ing] current subjects ... from the evangelical viewpoint' (as Graham put it), taking a stance above sectarian in-fighting, shunning arguments over the details of prophecy, standing 'for social improvement', and advancing political opinions from the center – and all together in one place under a generic evangelical auspices.

By trying to strengthen evangelicalism with biblical content brought into engagement with public issues, world affairs, and the life of the mind, *Christianity Today* marked a new evangelical openness to the intellectual life. Like much else from the mid-1950s it was a harbinger of things to come. Intellectual life among evangelicals has strengthened considerably in subsequent years, especially in the academic study of philosophy and to a lesser extent in history, sociology, law, and other disciplines. While anti-evolution still exerts a great pull for evangelicals, while literature and the visual arts suffer from relative neglect, and while evangelicals share fully in their nation's intellectual *Drang nach Unten*, there now exists a small but functioning evangelical intelligentsia that continues to expand upon the pioneering work of Billy Graham and Carl F.H. Henry.[20]

Graham's action as an evangelist, even as he was starting up *Christianity Today*, was also unusually significant. In 1957, Graham mounted a preaching campaign in New York City that represented his most ambitious project of that sort to date. As it turned out, the meetings drew tremendous crowds, including one gathering of 92,000 at Yankee Stadium. There were also many life-changing decisions for Christ. But this New York campaign also solidified a decisive break with the past. In New York City, Graham clarified a strategy he had been developing for some time: he would cooperate with whoever would cooperate with him, including mainline Protestants whom other evangelicals considered dangerously liberal. When fundamentalist

---

[20] A recent update is provided in Mark A. Noll, 'Postscript: How Fares the Evangelical Mind?', in *Jesus Christ and the Life of the Mind* (Grand Rapids, MI: Eerdmans, 2011), pp. 151-67.

critics challenged him on this strategy, Graham stood firm. Soon thereafter Graham expanded his ecumenicity to include selected Roman Catholics, a move that had been all but unimaginable only shortly before.

The result, which many others besides the Billy Graham Evangelistic Association also supported, was a clearer distinction between separatistic and intentionally narrow fundamentalism and more open, intentionally outgoing evangelicalism. That distinction has not always been recognized by outsiders, but it has been crucial for the history of theologically conservative American Protestants. It draws a straight line from Graham to such later figures as Bill Hybels (founding pastor of the Willowcreek Community Church in South Barrington, Illinois, with a weekly attendance in 2011 of 24,200), Rick Warren (best-selling author and pastor of the Saddleback Valley Community Church in Lake Forest, Orange County, California, with a weekly attendance of 18,800), and Tim Keller (founding pastor of Redeemer Presbyterian Church in New York City that has built a constituency of lawyers, businesspeople, artists, and entrepreneurs with a weekly attendance of 5,200). Those who continued to call themselves fundamentalists would seek to protect the gospel by separating from the world, evangelicals would seek to promote it by engaging the world. In that effort, the latter put to use whatever means modern America made available.

At the same time that planning was proceeding for Graham's New York campaign and that the *Christianity Today* editorial team was starting its work, another event of far-reaching significance was taking place in suburban Chicago, but completely out of the spotlight. On his daily commute by train to work at Moody Press in Chicago, Kenneth Taylor began in 1956 to paraphrase passages from the King James Version of the Bible that he could read at night with his family. They had complained about difficulties in understanding the KJV, and Taylor, with the kind of evangelical initiative that had become common after the War, was doing something about it. His efforts led eventually to the immensely popular *Living Bible*, which for a few years in the mid-1970s accounted in its various editions for nearly half of all Scriptures sold in the United States.

Taylor, with his devotion to the Bible, exemplified a classic evangelical commitment. Just as classically evangelical was his willingness to launch out on his own without waiting for someone else's approval; his creation of a major new organization (in this case, Tyndale House Publishers) to institutionalize his creativity; and his disregard for traditional church structures (the Revised Standard Version of 1952 was rejected by many evangelicals precisely because it was sponsored by the National Council of Churches). The evangelical break from the King James Version, which has gone on from Taylor's *Living Bible* to the immensely popular *New International Version* and several other million-selling modern translations, represents a momentous shift in the history of evangelicalism. Although strong loyalty to the King James Version remains in some evangelical circles, the willingness to modernize the biblical language of faith was perhaps the clearest indicator that a new era had dawned.

Assessment

Although few observers in the mid-1950s could have realized it, the course pursued by the Woarani missionary families, Elisabeth Eliot, Billy Graham, *Christianity Today*, and Kenneth Taylor anticipated the major evangelical developments of coming years. Traditional evangelical convictions remained important – missionary proclamation of the gospel abroad, committed evangelization of the lost at home, passionate fidelity to the Bible, and (in the case of *Christianity Today*) careful exposition of classical Christian teaching alongside principled Christian assessment of current events.

But also central was deliberate adaptation to the norms of contemporary American culture. These evangelicals embraced the modern media, instead of treating them as an evil. They set theological battles of former eras aside in order to communicate with as many contemporaries as possible. They considered women fully capable of active public service. They forsook traditional theological language and traditional versions of the Bible in an effort to bring the substance of Scripture to generations for whom traditional vocabularies had become irrelevant. They set out boldly – as in Washington, DC, where *Christianity Today* was located in its early years – to engage contemporary world affairs, politics, culture, and the arts with the historical truths of Christian faith.

Since the 1950s, the history of American evangelicals has taken unexpected turns, with none more eventful than the large scale involvement of many evangelicals in politics. Political re-engagement was only one part of evangelical reorientation in the 1950s, but it eventually became so widely noticed as to obscure other important developments. That re-engagement actually began before World War II, especially among 'plain folk' migrants to California from the south and southwest. When these Bible-believers encountered the strains of California's sprawling suburbs, the activism of the state's labor organizers, the California tradition of grass-roots political organization, and what they perceived as a growing communist menace, they began to mobilize for traditional values in family, workplace, and government.[21] In the post-war period, those California organizations began to connect up with similar groups throughout the country. In the 1970s, they started to coalesce as a political movement. Yet, intriguingly, the first overt national political mobilization of evangelicals was called into being by moderates and liberals committed to civil rights, distressed about the United States' roll in Vietnam, and worried about the domination of consumerism.[22]

---

[21] A fine treatment of this pre-history of the New Religious Right, see Darren Dochuk, *From Bible Belt to Sunbelt: Plain-Folk Religion, Grassroots Politics, and the Rise of Evangelical Conservatism* (New York, NY: W. W. Norton, 2011).

[22] David R. Swartz, *Moral Minority: The Evangelical Left in an Age of Conservatism* (Philadelphia, PA: University of Pennsylvania Press, 2012).

Soon, however, a more broadly based right-wing drift exerted itself.[23] Widely reported events like a controversy over school texts in West Virginia, a dispute over a campaign for gay rights in Florida, and an effort to remove the tax exemption of Bob Jones University in South Carolina for violations of civil rights laws exerted a politicizing effect. Visible leaders like Francis Schaeffer, Jerry Falwell, and Pat Robertson expanded their ministries from soul-winning and discipleship-training to politics. After initial indifference to the *Roe v. Wade* decision of 1973 that legalized abortion (it was at first viewed as a Catholic matter), evangelicals soon became active campaigners in the pro-life cause. Evangelicals had given an unusual measure of support to Jimmy Carter in the presidential election of 1976, in large part because of his reputation as a Bible-reading and Sunday-School teaching Baptist. But disillusionment followed when Carter showed his Baptist credentials more by insisting on separation of church and state than by promoting the family-friendly policies that evangelicals supported. After savvy efforts at reaching out to evangelical communities, President Ronald Regan (1981–89) solidified the recent identification of white evangelicals with conservative elements in the Republican Party.

The process that led American evangelicals to look like the Republican Party at prayer has been the focus of an immense literature. For whatever it is worth, my own judgment about evangelical politicization has been expressed recently in a comment by John Turner, a young historian who was assessing a book on what the Christian Right had contributed positively to American democracy: 'Despite its recent (and not unprecedented) obituaries, the Christian right will probably remain a significant part of the American political landscape for the foreseeable future. It will therefore also remain an albatross for American evangelicalism. The Christian Right may possess underreported democratic virtues, but it has been a public relations disaster, especially because of the need for incendiary rhetoric to raise money and mobilize volunteers.'[24]

For broader purposes, it is important to realize that the attention to evangelical politics has obscured recent engagement of significant evangelical elements in business, publishing, public administration, professional and amateur sports, and even the entertainment industries.[25] Specific histories for those broader engagements are only now being written.[26] But the trajectory from what began to occur in the immediate post-war years is clear.

---

[23] Amid the great number of shallow or panicked treatments of this recent history, a perceptive exception is Daniel K. Williams, *God's Own Party: The Making of the Christian Right* (New York, NY: Oxford University Press, 2010).

[24] John Turner, 'Civility and Boldness', *Books & Culture: A Christian Review*, May–June 2009, p. 19.

[25] D. Michael Lindsay, *Faith in the Halls of Power: How Evangelicals Joined the American Elite* (New York, NY: Oxford University Press, 2007).

[26] See especially Axel Schäfer, *Countercultural Conservatives: American Evangelicalism from the Postwar Revival to the New Christian Right* (Madison, WI: University of Wisconsin

The sharpest general assessments of this recent evangelical history have been made by those who ask – not how successful American evangelical re-engagement has been – but how faithful to the Christian gospel. Always for evangelicals, the ultimate test should be whether adaptability for the sake of effectiveness has sustained or undermined fidelity to the gospel for the sake of the truth.

As it happens, some secular and evangelical commentators agree about the negative effects of this engagement. Alan Wolfe, a sociologist with secular commitments, has written, for example, 'Evangelicals, so successful at planting new churches and watching them grow, had made a Faustian bargain with America's secular culture. They would give up a fire-and-brimstone insistence on the ubiquity of sin in favor of Oprah-style confessionalism.'[27] Wolfe's words specify a more general indictment offered by evangelical theologian David Wells: 'When the consumer is allowed to be sovereign in Church, the Church is abdicating its responsibility because it is allowing truth to become displaced by spiritual and psychological desire.'[28]

Even those like myself, who think that evangelical politicization and evangelical ease with consuming culture have led, in Christian terms, to as much danger as progress, may nonetheless resist going all the way with Wolfe and Wells in their analyses. Since World War II, the many varieties of American evangelical Christianity have been active in many more venues than just the political. American evangelicals remain rough hewn, uncoordinated, simplistic, populist, low-brow, and entrepreneurial. Yet in these very earthly vessels those with eyes to see may still discover many treasures of the gospel.

Press, 2011), and *Piety and Public Funding: Evangelicals and the State in Modern America* (Philadelphia, PA: University of Pennsylvania Press, 2012).

[27] Alan Wolfe, 'The Territory of Belief', *The Chronicle of Higher Education* 28 July 2006, p. B11.

[28] David F. Wells, *Above All Earthy Pow'rs: Christ in a Postmodern World* (Grand Rapids, MI: Eerdmans, 2005), pp. 302-303.

Socio-Political Studies

CHAPTER 15

British Evangelicals and the United States of America, c.1775–c.1820

Emma Macleod

William Wilberforce told the eighteenth anniversary meeting of the British and Foreign Bible Society on 1 May 1822

> I know ... that so long as the infirmities and bad passions of men remain, there will be differences, arising from ambition, or the jealousies one country may entertain of another; but here we have a principle in operation, which tends all the while gradually and imperceptibly, but surely, to unite the good of both communities, and make them love one another as brethren, and to concur in endeavouring to promote peace and concord among men. As the differences we have had with that country have been peculiarly painful to me, so, I doubt not, there is now a principle at work, which will promote the most lasting agreement.[1]

Just as those who have studied the political aspect of the transatlantic association have largely tended either to concentrate on the eighteenth-century colonial nexus, on the war of separation, or on the nineteenth-century post-colonial relationship, so historians of the transatlantic Evangelical connection have not generally scrutinised it at the hinge, at the moment of transition, that is, in the decades following American independence.[2] This essay examines what British Evangelicals thought of the new American republic in the decades following its separation from the British

---

[1] *Wesleyan-Methodist Magazine*, 2nd series, 1 (August, 1822), p. 526.
[2] Comparison and contrast has more often been the focus than relationship. But see Charles I. Foster, *An Errand of Mercy: The Evangelical United front, 1790–1837* (Chapel Hill, NC: University of North Carolina Press, 1960); Richard Carwardine, *Transatlantic Revivalism: Popular Evangelicalism in Britain and America, 1790–1865* (Studies in Evangelical History and Thought; Milton Keynes: Paternoster, 2006 [1978]); Louis Billington, 'British and American Methodisms grow apart', in R.A. Burchell (ed.), *The End of Anglo-America* (Manchester: Manchester University Press, 1991), pp. 113-36; George A. Rawlyk and Mark A. Noll (eds), *Amazing Grace: Evangelicalism in Australia, Britain, Canada and the United States* (Montreal: McGill-Queen's University Press, 1994); Mark A. Noll, David W. Bebbington and George A. Rawlyk (eds), *Evangelicalism: Comparative Studies of Popular Protestantism in North America, the British Isles, and Beyond, 1700–1990* (Oxford: Oxford University Press, 1994).

Empire. It also explores what they may have contributed to the wider British understanding of America at that time.

It is argued here that British Evangelicals did not respond much more uniformly to the American Revolution, on the basis of theology or ecclesiology, than British political commentators did on the basis of political ideology. Following David Bebbington's argument that Evangelicals were not only highly influential in shaping the wider culture in which they operated, but were substantially moulded *by* that culture,[3] this essay shows that, just as British political opinion on the formation of the new republic ranged broadly from great admiration, through sympathy and regret, to unqualified disapproval, so, too, did Evangelical opinion on the United States range from high regard to severe criticism. They were, like other British writers, divided over the new United States of America; and so, rather than inserting a united argument or position into the British conversation about America post-independence, they contributed particular concerns, or, we might say, a distinctive thread. This spectrum of Evangelical views also meant that the generally very positive nineteenth-century British Evangelical attitude towards its American counterpart was already becoming infused with a degree of caution that perhaps had not existed previously, and with a growing awareness that Evangelicalism on the other side of the Atlantic was similar in theology, but different in culture. As David Hempton has suggested, 'the history of the early republic is ... indissolubly linked with the spread of populist forms of evangelical religion'.[4] It is therefore not surprising that British Evangelical views of the United States were thoroughly bound up with their opinions of American Evangelicals.

Was national separation influential in sowing some of the seeds of divergence, or would they have emerged anyway? British Evangelicals may have been slower to identify Americans as different than other British writers, and they may have retained a sense of family longer, while other Britons acquired a clear perception of American difference and identity from the War of Independence.[5] Did the relationship between Evangelicals help to restrain the widening of the gap between Britain and the United States after 1783? David Bebbington has also argued convincingly that the impact of the transatlantic Evangelical relationship was far more influential for British Evangelical life and practice than was the American

---

[3] David W. Bebbington, *Evangelicalism in Modern Britain: A History from the 1730s to the 1980s* (London: Unwin Hyman, 1989); see also his 'Evangelicalism and British Culture', in Stewart J. Brown, Frances Knight and John Morgan-Guy (eds), *Religion, Identity and Conflict in Britain: From the Restoration to the Twentieth Century* (Farnham: Ashgate, 2013), pp. 105-19.

[4] David Hempton, *Methodism: Empire of the Spirit* (New Haven, CT: Yale University Press, 2005), p. 24.

[5] P.J. Marshall, 'Presidential Address: Britain and the World in the Eighteenth Century: II, Britons and Americans', *Transactions of the Royal Historical Society*, 6th series, 9 (1999), pp. 8-13; Carwardine, *Transatlantic Revivalism*, p. 198.

Revolution.[6] The transatlantic experience of revival earlier in the eighteenth century and its ramifications thereafter, and the mutual context of the Enlightenment, he contended, did more to shape the nature of British Evangelicalism than did the separation of the thirteen American colonies from the British Empire. The relationship between Evangelicals in Britain and America continued, of course, to be enormously important for British Evangelical attitudes towards the new United States of America and American Evangelicals, irrespective of the Revolution. Yet the divergences between American and British Evangelicalism which developed over the course of the nineteenth and twentieth centuries – manifesting themselves as differences in denominations, in theological emphases, in cultural context, and in education of ministerial candidates[7] – may already have been fostered by the rupture of the Revolution, despite the undoubtedly close association of Evangelical circles and their similar and strongly held convictions of the gospel imperatives.

This essay suggests that British Evangelicals *both* perceived Americans, increasingly, as different from themselves *and* retained a sense of family and of family likeness. It proposes that both sympathy and caution are evident in their views on the American Revolution itself, before arguing that they displayed a variety of attitudes to the new United States in the post-revolutionary period, ranging from defence, admiration and a desire to cooperate, to disappointment and criticism; and it suggests that this range of reactions can be explained at least partly by differences in the national contexts in which British and American Evangelicals operated as early as the post-revolutionary decades.

I

The depth and breadth of the Anglo-American Evangelical relationship in the several decades preceding the American Revolution is well established. Rooted in seventeenth-century Puritan emigration and early eighteenth-century revival, by the mid-eighteenth century this relationship was manifested in close personal friendships, transatlantic evangelistic activity, correspondence networks, publishing connections and continuing emigration.[8] Already preachers were reading sermons

---

[6] David W. Bebbington, 'The Democratization of British Christianity: The Baptist Case', in Anthony R. Cross (ed.), *Ecumenism and History: Studies in Honour of John H.Y. Briggs* (Carlisle: Paternoster Press, 2002), p. 279.

[7] David W. Bebbington, 'Evangelicalism in Modern Britain and America: A Comparison', in George A. Rawlyk and Mark A. Noll (eds), *Amazing Grace: Evangelicalism in Australia, Britain, Canada and the United States* (Montreal: McGill-Queen's University Press, 1994), pp. 183-212, at pp. 196-99.

[8] There is a huge literature on this area, but see, for instance, B.R. Wilson, 'American Religion: Its Impact on Britain', in A.N.J. Den Hollander (ed.), *Contagious Conflict: The Impact of American Dissent on European Life* (Leiden: Brill, 1973), 233-63; Colin Bonwick, 'English Dissenters and the American Revolution', in H.C. Allen and Roger Thompson (eds), *Contrast and Connection: Bicentennial Essays in Anglo-American History* (London: Bell, 1976); Carwardine, *Transatlantic Revivalism*; Susan O'Brien, 'A Transatlantic Community

from across the Atlantic, and adopting such features as extemporaneous preaching, itinerancy, and so on in imitation of each other.[9] Susan O'Brien pointed out that this did not mean that Evangelicals in Britain and America thought as one even before 1776, nor did they always understand or even take much interest in the internal disagreements and divisions of each other, although they were aware of them because of the volume of Evangelical publications that crossed the Atlantic in both directions. 'But what they most wanted from the publishing network was a sense of the shared', because 'the idea of a widespread work of God mattered greatly in itself'.[10] O'Brien's thesis is that a common theology and active individuals such as George Whitefield were crucial to the sense of transatlantic Evangelical union before 1776, but that it was sustained by the emergence and expansion of advertising, publishing and distribution networks.

British Evangelical reactions to the American Revolution also form familiar territory, but reviewing them with a fine grain raises interesting questions. James Bradley's major study of English Dissenting politics at the time of the American Revolution concludes that, though not all of them were politically radical, the vast majority of them were clearly pro-American during the Revolution; that there was an impressive degree of Dissenting unity in England on the American Revolution; and that they led all the opposition petitions on America except perhaps in London. He acknowledges that 'there was nothing uniquely "Nonconformist" about English pro-Americanism', and he argues that in fact the majority of English pro-Americans were Anglican, including a relatively small number of Low Church clergy, but that Dissenting support for the colonists was more consistent than Anglican backing, and took the lead. He does not generally distinguish between the political behaviour of Evangelical and 'rational' Dissenters, except to note in conclusion that 'the great majority of pro-American Dissenters were orthodox trinitarians', a judgement he reinforces in a later study.[11] His argument is based on the political sympathies of

---

of Saints: The Great Awakening and the First Evangelical Network, 1735–1755', *American Historical Review* 91 (1986), 811-32; Bebbington, *Evangelicalism in Modern Britain*; Noll, Bebbington and Rawlyk (eds), *Evangelicalism: Comparative Studies*; H.M. Davies, *Transatlantic Brethren: Rev. Samuel Jones (1735–1814) and his Friends: Baptists in Wales, Pennsylvania and Beyond* (Bethlehem, PA: Lehigh University Press, 1995); Jonathan M. Yeager, *Enlightened Evangelicalism: The Life and Thought of John Erskine* (New York, NY: Oxford University Press, 2011).

[9] Joanna Cruickshank, 'The Sermon in the British Colonies', in Keith A. Francis and William Gibson (eds), *The Oxford Handbook of the British Sermon 1689–1901* (Oxford: Oxford University Press, 2012), pp. 513-29 (pp. 516-17); Wilson, 'American Religion', p. 235.

[10] Susan O'Brien, 'Eighteenth-Century Publishing Networks in the First Years of Transatlantic Evangelicalism', in Noll, Bebbington and Rawlyk (eds), *Evangelicalism: Comparative Studies*, p. 52.

[11] James E. Bradley, *Religion, Revolution and English Radicalism: Nonconformity in Eighteenth-Century Politics and Society* (Cambridge: Cambridge University Press, 1990), pp. 121, 124, 410-11, 423, and 'The Religious Origins of Radical Politics in England, Scotland,

English Dissenters for the position of the rebellious American colonists – opposition to hierarchy and church establishment, a belief in the right of consent, psychological (if not always actual) exclusion from public affairs, and the conviction, which suited them, that the Americans were, like themselves, 'chiefly Dissenters and Whigs'[12] – and on their motivation to criticise the British government provided by their own socio-economic status. Various other studies demonstrated that there is a great deal of evidence of Dissenting and Established Church Evangelical pro-Americanism during the Revolution.[13]

On the one hand, however, Dissenting enthusiasm for the Revolution can be complicated. Colin Bonwick and Hywel Davies both argue that 'at no point did Dissenters encourage American separatism', rather, Dissenters deeply regretted the American seizure of independence and saw it as a last resort forced on the Americans by British government policy. Robert Hall, the Baptist pastor of Cambridge, wrote in 1793, 'Had [the Dissenters'] remonstrances been regarded [by government], the calamities of that war had never been incurred'.[14] Moreover, as Bradley himself shows, Dissenting support for the Revolution was far from universal.[15] Davies even suggests that 'the majority of Baptists in England and Wales did not actively support the American cause' and that Baptist support for the Revolution was overstated after the war, probably from a desire to safeguard the transatlantic Baptist connection in the face of political separation.[16] Furthermore, many British Evangelicals were constrained in what may have been deep affection for their American Evangelical brethren by their desire either not to appear to be

---

and Ireland, 1662–1800', in James E. Bradley and Dale Van Kley (eds), *Religion and Politics in Enlightenment Europe* (Notre Dame, IN: University of Notre Dame Press, 2001), pp. 187-253 (p. 192).

[12] Joseph Priestley, *An Address to Protestant Dissenters of all Denominations on the Approaching Election of Members of Parliament with Respect to the State of Public Liberty in General and American Affairs in Particular* (London: Joseph Johnson, 1774), p. 3. Cf. the importance of the 'Madoc myth' for Welsh Baptists: Davies, *Transatlantic Brethren*, pp. 171-72.

[13] E.g., Bonwick, 'English Dissenters and the American Revolution'; Colin Bonwick, *English Radicals and the American Revolution* (Chapel Hill, NC: University of North Carolina Press, 1977); Henry Ippel, 'Blow the Trumpet, Sanctify the Fast', *Huntingdon Library Bulletin* 44 (1980), pp. 43-60, and 'British Sermons and the American Revolution', *Journal of Religious History* 12 (1982-3), pp. 191-205; Paul Langford, 'The English Clergy and the American Revolution', in Eckhart Hellmuth (ed.), *The Transformation of Political Culture: England and Germany in the Late Eighteenth Century* (Oxford: Oxford University Press, 1990), pp. 275-307; Rena Denton, 'Enlightened Thought Devised from Biblical Principles', in Robert D. Cornwall and William Gibson, *Religion, Politics and Dissent, 1660–1832* (Farnham: Ashgate, 2010), pp. 51-63 (pp. 52-53).

[14] Bonwick, 'English Dissenters and the American Revolution', pp. 103-107 (p. 104); Robert Hall, *Apology for the Freedom of the Press* (1793), in O. Gregory (ed.), *The Works of Robert Hall* (6 vols; London: Holdsworth and Ball, 1831–32), III, pp. 153-54.

[15] Bradley, *Religion, Revolution and English Radicalism*, pp. 398-99.

[16] Davies, *Transatlantic Brethren*, pp. 119-25, quotation at pp. 119-20.

disloyal to the British government or, indeed, not to be disloyal to it. John Rogers of London, for instance, was one of the many Dissenters who was willing to criticise the government's policy on America, but not to support American independence.[17]

And indeed, Bonwick asserts that 'a good many' Dissenters actually condemned rebellion in the colonies, and that there was 'no solid cohort of Dissent' on the issue.[18] In 1775 Caleb Evans, the leading Baptist minister in Bristol and himself a convinced pro-American, rejected the accusation that Baptists were disposed to defend rebellion by stating with regret that there were 'too many Calvinists and Baptists' on both sides of the Atlantic who supported the British government.[19] Bradley notes that Evangelical pastors such as L.L. Peters of Newport, Gloucestershire, John Martin, the Calvinistic Baptist pastor in Grafton Street, Soho, Henry Hunter of Little St Helens, London, John Rippon of Southwark, Job Orton of Kidderminster, and John Handasyds of Newcastle, as well as the pamphleteer, Israel Mauduit, and the MPs Joseph and Thomas Lockyer of Ilchester, and Sir Henry Hoghton, all preached or published in defence of the government's cause.[20] And, since the concern here is with Evangelicals in the round and not just Dissenters, most Methodists can be added to these Dissenters in opposition to the American separation: famously, John Wesley published two pamphlets in support of the government and against the colonists, even if his private opinion was less certain.[21] These argued that republicanism was a despotic form of government destined to cause unhappiness among its citizens. Furthermore, many British Evangelicals took a quietist line during the Revolution and did not take political sides – for example, the Baptist Joseph Jenkins of Wrexham, and the Anglican John Newton.[22] Neither were British Evangelicals often converted by the American example to political republicanism in the modern sense, or to social levelling. The political reformism of English Dissenters, as Bonwick put it, was more remarkable for its moderation than its subversiveness.[23]

On the other hand, Dissenting leadership of British pro-Americanism can also be queried. The Scottish Popular Party's sympathy for the American Revolution shows that, at least in Scotland, even momentum from Dissenters was not required. It also

---

[17] Bradley, *Religion, Revolution and English Radicalism*, p. 123.

[18] Bonwick, 'English Dissenters and the American Revolution', pp. 90-91.

[19] Davies, *Transatlantic Brethren*, p. 119; Caleb Evans, *A Reply to the Rev. Mr. Fletcher's Vindication of Mr. Wesley's Calm Address* (Bristol: W. Pine, 1775), pp. 85-86.

[20] Bonwick, *English Radicals and the American Revolution*, pp. 86-87; Bradley, *Religion, Revolution and English Radicalism*, pp. 123-24.

[21] David Hempton, *Methodism and Politics in British Society, 1750–1850* (London: Hutchinson, 1984), p. 45.

[22] Davies, *Transatlantic Brethren*, pp. 122-23; Ippel, 'British Sermons and the American Revolution', pp. 201-202. Cf. Deryck Lovegrove, 'English Evangelical Dissent and the European Conflict 1789–1815', in W.J. Sheils (ed.), *The Church and War: Papers Read at the Twenty-First Summer Meeting and the Twenty-Second Winter Meeting of the Ecclesiastical History Society* (Oxford: Oxford University Press, 1983), pp. 263-76.

[23] Bonwick, 'English Dissenters and the American Revolution', p. 107.

suggests that the transatlantic Evangelical network built up from the 1730s, supplemented by church politics at home, may have been as significant in British Evangelical support as the genuine political sympathy with the American rebels that Bradley identified, although conforming Evangelicals were often as suspicious as Dissenters that a government made up of sinful humans did not deserve implicit trust, and criticised the British government for its American policies.[24] John Erskine, minister of Old Greyfriars in Edinburgh, was one of the earliest to predict a war between Britain and America, and his trenchant criticism of British government policy on America even earned him an accusation of treason in the *Edinburgh Magazine and Review* in 1776. It is likely that his particularly strong transatlantic relationships, built up over three decades of correspondence and book circulation, were much more important than political considerations in his inability to oppose the Americans when they separated from the British Empire.[25] Nor was Erskine a lone figure in Church of Scotland Popular Party circles – other leading Evangelicals such as John Gillies and William Porteous in Glasgow, William Thom in Govan, Charles Nisbet in Montrose, and, most famously, John Witherspoon in Paisley (President of Princeton College, 1768–94), were all firm pro-Americans.

British Evangelicals therefore represented the political spectrum on the American Revolution, even if it was weighted in their case towards support for the Americans; and pro-Americanism was neither limited to nor dependent upon English Dissent, although English Dissenters were undoubtedly very active and very influential. Nor was British Evangelical pro-Americanism based only or even mainly on political sympathy, but it also stemmed from spiritual and ecclesiastical affection. The transatlantic Evangelical network constituted a community which transcended the ruptures of 1776 and 1783, but it would be surprising if, in Evangelical circles as in political, commercial and family networks, the disagreements caused by the crisis did not resonate in the post-revolutionary relationship.

II

So far, so familiar. After 1783, there is certainly substantial evidence of British Evangelical sympathy with the new American republic as well as respect and affection for American Evangelicalism in particular. They admired American politicians, they respected the American experiment in government, they compared the American state favourably with the British polity, and they praised the relative egalitarianism of American society.[26] The Baptist preacher Robert Robinson, who had consistently criticised British policy in America, was delighted and a little star-

---

[24] Yeager, *Enlightened Evangelicalism*, p. 156.

[25] Yeager, *Enlightened Evangelicalism*, p. 141; John R. McIntosh, *Church and Theology in Enlightenment Scotland: The Popular Party, 1740–1800* (East Linton: Tuckwell Press, 1998), pp. 157-60.

[26] Bonwick, 'English Dissenters and the American Revolution', pp. 92, 95-96; Davies, *Transatlantic Brethren*, pp. 181, 185-86.

struck when he entertained General Joseph Reed, Dr John Witherspoon and an American diplomat to tea in his Cambridge home on their fund-raising tour to support Princeton College in June 1784.[27] British Evangelicals often associated the United States with liberty, and opposition to its foundation with illiberal 'toryism'. Robert Hall, in 1793 contrasting Pitt the Younger unfavourably with his father, who had been 'the vehement opposer of the American War', counted the son 'the rallying point of toryism, the type and symbol of whatever is most illiberal in principle, and intolerant in practice'.[28] All this was reinforced in the British context of the economic struggles and the political repression of the 1790s, when America featured frequently in 'signs of the times' literature as a fulfilment of optimistic biblical prophecy. According to the Monmouthshire Baptist Morgan John Rhys, America was now literally a 'new world', where 'justice had been established by God ... and government was as good as any on earth'. The war against revolutionary France was part of God's judgement of Britain for its many sins, and Rhys urged his readers to escape its immoral and illegitimate government by emigrating to the 'vast, free and fruitful' land of America, an asylum of liberty which was under God's blessing as surely as Britain was under his wrath. Rhys himself emigrated to the United States in August 1794.[29]

The United States was particularly important to Evangelical Dissenters as well as 'rational' Dissenters in Britain, as this potential asylum from religious oppression at home, and as a model for the religious liberty that they did not possess in Britain and which was a central tenet of Dissent.[30] Theophilus Harris, another Welsh Baptist, composed a very detailed balance sheet when he was deciding to emigrate to America in 1793, in which he came to the following conclusion:

> There the prospects are truly pleasing, her inhabitants are far remov'd out of the reach of tyranny and oppression, every one may sit under his own vine and his own fig tree in quiet, and the rational pleasures of the soul are enjoy'd in their purity ... In most, if not all of the States, there is no established religion[;] religion, as it ought to do, stands upon its own basis unconnected with the state, and the greatest encouragement is given to freedom of enquiry and the propagation of truth ... Who then would continue to wade in filth and corruption in such a deprav'd Country as Britain? Who would not wish to go and taste those sweets of liberty and peace freely offer'd to every honest character in America?[31]

British Dissenters were delighted by Jefferson's Virginia Statute for Religious Freedom in 1786 and by similar statutes in other American states. As James

---

[27] Gina Luria Walker, '"Brief Encounter": Robert Robinson and the Right to Private Judgement', *Enlightenment and Dissent* 24 (2008), pp. 54-70 (pp. 55, 57-60).
[28] Hall, *Apology for the Freedom of the Press*, p. 82.
[29] Davies, *Transatlantic Brethren*, pp. 14, 181, 184-87 (pp. 185-86).
[30] Bradley, *Religion, Revolution and English Radicalism*, p. 139.
[31] John Hammond Moore, 'Theophilus Harris's Thoughts on Emigrating to America in 1793', *William and Mary Quarterly*, 3rd series, 36.4 (October, 1979), pp. 602-14 (p. 613).

Bicheno, the radical Baptist pastor of Newbury, put it in 1794, the United States had shown the fallacy of the insistence on the need for an established religion.[32] And yet, the Popular Party of the (Established) Church of Scotland had also felt some identity with the American campaign for political and religious liberty, since they supported the freedom of congregations to call their own ministers, and since MPs who were members of the Church of Scotland, as non-Anglicans still had to take communion in the Church of England annually to be allowed to take up their seats in Westminster.[33] The American example showed that religious liberty did not lead inexorably to anarchy; in fact, it could even improve human behaviour. The Methodist, John Kingston, recorded in his travel journal, published in 1799, that he had noticed that

> as the Legislature knows no man better or worse for his religious creed; so the idea prevails, that all good men are equal, and according to their respective abilities, qualified to discharge the duties of civil society. This principle has a happy tendency to suppress the natural tyranny of the human heart.[34]

These British perceptions of the extent of religious liberty in America were not always absolutely accurate, but they did show what their writers wished to believe was true of the United States, a model in this respect of what they hoped to see come to pass in Britain.[35] Under the influence of the Enlightenment, religious freedom was coming to be seen as a natural right of man; and, inspired by the American example, some politically radical Dissenters began to believe that political representation was required to safeguard religious freedom.[36] It is true that often the politically radical Dissenters were liberal theologically (in England and Wales, frequently Unitarians, or heterodox Presbyterians on the way towards Unitarianism). But orthodox Baptists with radical politics included Robert Robinson and Robert Hall of Cambridge, Thomas Davis of Reading, Mark Wilks and Rees David of Norwich, Caleb Evans of Bristol, James Hinton of Oxford, and William Winterbotham of Plymouth, and James Murray of Newcastle was an orthodox Presbyterian of clearly radical politics.[37]

---

[32] James Bicheno, *The Signs of the Times: or, The overthrow of the papal tyranny in France, the prelude of destruction to popery and despotism; but of peace to mankind* (London: Parsons, Paternoster Row, 3rd edn, 1794), p. 12.

[33] McIntosh, *Church and Theology in Enlightenment Scotland*, p. 8; Robert Kent Donovan, 'The Popular Party of the Church of Scotland and the American Revolution', in Richard B. Sher and Jeffrey R. Smitten (eds), *Scotland and America in the Age of Enlightenment* (Princeton, NJ: Princeton University Press, 1990), pp. 81-99.

[34] Extract from 'Memoirs of the Life of Mr John Kingston, Preacher of the Gospel', published in the *Wesleyan-Methodist Magazine* 22 (1799), pp. 264-65.

[35] Bonwick, 'English Dissenters and the American Revolution', pp. 101-102.

[36] H.T. Dickinson, *Liberty and Property: Political Ideology in Eighteenth-century Britain* (London: Weidenfeld and Nicolson, 1977), pp. 202-203.

[37] Walker, '"Brief Encounter"'; C.B. Jewson, *Jacobin City: A Portrait of Norwich in its Reaction to the French Revolution* (Glasgow: Blackie, 1975), esp. pp. 26-27, 29, 52, 63-64, 68-70, 79-80, 138; Timothy Whelan, *Politics, Religion and Romance: The Letters of*

On the other hand, some British Evangelicals were warier of American politics and applauded them on the grounds of their moderation rather than because of their progressive nature. The Anglican Evangelical periodical, the *Christian Observer*, was happy to record 'a degree of soundness in the public sentiment of Americans' indicated by evidence that sympathy for the politics of William Godwin was a charge to be repudiated.[38] It was confident, too, that America would be 'sound' in international politics, and would resist Bonaparte's pressure to cave into his demands after his purchase of Louisiana from the Spanish in 1802.[39]

British Evangelicals widely admired American church vitality and growth. The *Christian Observer* commended the example of the Connecticut legislature in circulating Bibles throughout its state, and its promotion of school and family worship.[40] It was widely believed among British Methodists that 'in the "fine and improving" United States the Methodist Church was "likely to become the most extensive and pure in the Universe"'.[41] Accounts of American evangelistic tours, camp meetings and revivals were published in Britain from the 1790s, with exhortations to emulate them in Britain;[42] as the Rev. W. Ward said, reporting to the annual meeting of the Auxiliary Society for the London (Methodist) District in 1821 on 'a great out-pouring of the HOLY SPIRIT' in 'the Continent of America': 'If these things be done in America, why may not we seek and expect similar visitations in other countries?'[43] Even before steamship travel made transatlantic crossings easier from the late 1820s, American ministers visited Britain and Ireland, most famously John McGee in 1797–1803, and 'Crazy' Lorenzo Dow in 1798–1807, whose tour in Britain encouraged native revivalistic Methodism, and prompted the foundation of Primitive Methodism.[44]

Benjamin Flower and Eliza Gould Flower, 1794–1808 (Aberystwyth: National Library of Wales, 2008); Michael Durey, 'William Winterbotham's Trumpet of Sedition: Religious Dissent and Political Radicalism in the 1790s', *Journal of Religious History* 19.2 (1995), pp. 141-57; Emma Macleod, 'Civil Liberties and Baptists: William Winterbotham of Plymouth in Prison and Thinking of America', *Baptist Quarterly* 44.4 (October, 2011), pp. 196-222; John Robert Parnell, 'Baptists and Britons: Particular Baptist Ministers in England and British Identity in the 1790s' (PhD diss., University of North Texas, 2005), pp. 68-172; Denton, 'Enlightened Thought Devised from Biblical Principles'.

[38] *Christian Observer*, 1 (1802), p. 127.
[39] *Christian Observer*, 2 (1803), p. 117.
[40] *Christian Observer*, 3 (1804), p. 445.
[41] Carwardine, *Transatlantic Revivalism*, p. 103, quoting J. Hawtrey to J. Emory, 4 August 1820, and A. Clarke to J. Emory and others, 6 February 1832, MS Collection, Rose Memorial Library, Drew University, Madison, NJ.
[42] E.g. in the *Wesleyan-Methodist Magazine, passim*.
[43] *Wesleyan-Methodist Magazine*, 44 (1821), p. 475.
[44] Raymond L. Cohn, 'Transatlantic U.S. Passenger Travel at the Dawn of the Steamship Era', *International Journal of Maritime History* 4.1 (1992), pp. 43-64; Carwardine, *Transatlantic Revivalism*, pp. xiii-xiv; Wilson, 'American Religion', p. 237; Hempton, *Methodism and Politics*, p. 94.

There is some evidence of the continuation of a long-held British sense of responsibility for those who had previously been their colonists, and perhaps a desire to maintain British Christian influence over the new United States. It has been suggested that this was a particularly Anglican impulse, emerging naturally from groups such as the Society for the Propagation of the Gospel in Foreign Parts, which had been founded by the Church of England in 1701 to help minister to the American colonists, though it had swiftly expanded its remit to British colonies worldwide.[45] It was, though, also present in the Welsh 'Madoc' fever which gripped the imagination of William Richards, and which sent John Evans out in the 1790s as a missionary to the 'Welsh Indians', or the Padouca tribe, based near the head of the Missouri.[46] It was tactful of Mr Armstrong of Boston, speaking to London Methodists in 1821, to remark, 'it may please you to know, that British Christians are there considered as our elder brethren, and we are treading in your steps ...'[47]

A stronger theme, however, was the British Evangelical desire to cooperate with American Evangelicals in the post-independence era. Evangelicals in both places shared a sense of election as peoples; and 'the idea of a widespread work of God' still 'mattered greatly in itself' to them.[48] Many Evangelicals continued to think of themselves as members of a transatlantic community, which was manifested in transatlantic correspondence, publication, migration and mission, both denominational and interdenominational, and in the recognition of shared challenges.[49] A great deal of informal transatlantic correspondence was carried on between Evangelicals, but John Rippon's *Baptist Annual Register* was founded in 1790 in a deliberate effort to restore, enlarge and formalise transatlantic Baptist correspondence interrupted by the war, and it published circular letters by regional Baptist associations on both sides of the Atlantic, as the *Wesleyan-Methodist Magazine* did for its own denominational constituency.[50] American Methodist membership statistics were included in the *WMM* immediately after the British figures; American delegates were regularly reported therein as having attended the annual meeting of the Auxiliary Society for the London District. The extent of

---

[45] Robert G. Ingram, 'From Barbarism to Civility, from Darkness to Light: Preaching Empire as Sacred History', in Francis and Gibson (eds), *Oxford Handbook of the British Sermon*, pp. 481-96 (pp. 484, 489-92); Rowan Strong, 'Eighteenth-Century Mission Sermons', in Francis and Gibson (eds), *Oxford Handbook of the British Sermon*, pp. 497-512.

[46] Davies, *Transatlantic Brethren*, pp. 254-58.

[47] *Wesleyan-Methodist Magazine*, 44 (1821), p. 475.

[48] Kathleen Wilson, 'The island race', in Tony Claydon and Ian McBride (eds), *Protestantism and National Identity: Britain and Ireland c.1650–c.1850* (Oxford: Oxford University Press, 1998), pp. 265-90 (pp. 284-85); O'Brien, 'Eighteenth-Century Publishing Networks', p. 52.

[49] J.F. Maclear, 'The Idea of "American Protestantism" and British Conformity, 1829–1840', *Journal of British Studies* 21.1 (Fall, 1981), pp. 68-89 (p. 75); Carwardine, *Transatlantic Revivalism*, p. xiv; Davies, *Transatlantic Brethren*, p. 278.

[50] Davies, *Transatlantic Brethren*, pp. 125-31, 141-60.

reporting on American affairs in these periodicals testifies to the continued British Evangelical appetite for it. British Evangelicals referred regularly in their writings to American Evangelical authors, published American essays in their collections, and published British editions of American Evangelical works.[51]

Richard Carwardine noted a growing confidence among American Evangelicals, and a concomitant lessening sense of dependence in their partnership with their British counterparts; and it is also true that their British counterparts treated the Americans as equals, if not leaders in mission and evangelism.[52] Richard Watson, one of the Secretaries of the British Wesleyan Missionary Society, told its annual meeting that 'The American Christians are coming forward in a most astonishing manner; they make the most surprising calculations; their designs are gigantic and overwhelming.'[53] The *Christian Observer* admired the evangelistic missions and medical advances offered to the American Indian tribes, as well as the missions to the uncouth back settlements which were currently being cleared and settled in the states of New York, Vermont, Pennsylvania, and Connecticut.[54] Evangelical impetus towards mission and, in the post-French Revolutionary world, overseas mission, was able to mitigate American insularity and give transatlantic Evangelicals a common purpose in mission to the non-European and non-Anglophone world. Methodists – whose organisation was 'built for mobility' – were particularly deliberate in cultivating partnership and a sense of common purpose in mission.[55] In Newcastle in 1814 a Methodist Missionary Society was formed, directly inspired by Methodist successes in the United States as well as in the West Indies.[56] But there was also the cooperation of the nondenominational British and Foreign Bible Society (B&FBS, established in 1804 by the Clapham Sect) with nascent and rapidly multiplying Bible Societies in America from 1809, a cooperation which continued through the War of 1812 without serious interruption:

> While the destructive sword was unsheathed, and the sound of the trumpet and the din of war were heard abroad, Christians of various denominations at home, were employed in making unprecedented exertions, to illuminate mankind with the word of God.[57]

---

[51] Robert Hall, *Modern Infidelity Considered* (1799), in Gregory (ed.), *Works*, I, pp. 13-80 (pp. 58-60), on Jonathan Edwards; Henry Moncrieff Wellwood (ed.), *Account of the Life and Writings of John Erskine* (Constable: Edinburgh, 1818), pp. 321, 328, 484-85.
[52] Carwardine, *Transatlantic Revivalism*, pp. 29, 56.
[53] *Wesleyan-Methodist Magazine* 43 (1820), p. 550.
[54] *Christian Observer* 1 (1802), pp. 533, 536, 809-10.
[55] Hempton, *Methodism: Empire of the Spirit*, p. 21.
[56] *Wesleyan-Methodist Magazine* 37 (1814), pp. 555-56; Carwardine, *Transatlantic Revivalism*, pp. 29, 32-33, 38-40.
[57] *Wesleyan-Methodist Magazine* 37 (1814), p. 699; Foster, *An Errand of Mercy*, pp. 105-14. The American Bible Society was formed to organise them in 1816, but British grants to American Bible Societies were continued throughout the war years of 1812–15.

Indeed, the *WMM* regularly reprinted B&FBS reports with pleasure and admiration, so that the cooperation was interdenominational as well as transatlantic. Hence its quotation of Wilberforce, mentioned at the start of this chapter, in 1822, asserting his confidence that, despite painful differences between Britain and America in the past, in overseas mission there was now 'a principle at work, which [would] promote the most lasting agreement' between Evangelicals in both America and Britain.[58]

There was, therefore, a great deal of British Evangelical respect and affection for American Evangelicalism, as well as sympathy with the new American republic. Yet this transatlantic Evangelical admiration was not uniform. British Evangelicals were not averse to criticising Americans. They were highly critical of the American institution of slavery, which we might expect, but also of American religious practices.

It is perhaps possible to distinguish between Evangelicals in Britain and the rational Dissenters whom Anthony Page has helpfully examined, trying to answer the question why, as convinced abolitionists, they were so sensitive about criticising the new republic in America on this issue.[59] By contrast, British Evangelicals were blunt and inflexible in their criticisms. 'It is impossible to be temperate and to pursue this subject through the various considerations of policy, of morals, of history, natural and civil', wrote William Winterbotham in 1795.[60] 'Slavery', wrote a correspondent to the *WMM* in 1819, 'is justly styled "the leprosy of the United States" – a foul blotch which more or less contaminates the entire system, in publick and private, from the President's chair to the cabin of the hunter.'[61] In their own campaign to have the institution of slavery made illegal in the British West Indies and all British dominions, they were perplexed by Evangelical toleration of American slavery, and they showed considerably less understanding of the difficulties that their American counterparts had in trying to maintain church unity, than the rational Dissenters did of the difficulties that liberal American politicians did in trying to establish national unity, in the face of deep divisions over slavery.[62] Dr Olinthus Gregory, the editor of Robert Hall's collected *Works*, added a note to Hall's *Address on the State of*

---

[58] See n. 1.

[59] Anthony Page, '"A Species of Slavery": Richard Price's Rational Dissent and Antislavery', *Slavery and Abolition* 32.1 (2011), pp. 53-73; Anthony Page, 'Rational Dissent, Enlightenment and Abolition of the Slave Trade', *Historical Journal* 54.3 (2011), pp. 741-72.

[60] William Winterbotham, *An Historical, Geographical, Commercial, and Philosophical View of the American United States, and of the European Settlements in America and the West-Indies* (4 vols; London: Ridgway, Symonds and Holt, 1795), III, p. 110.

[61] *Wesleyan-Methodist Magazine* 42 (1819), p. 859.

[62] Carwardine, *Transatlantic Revivalism*, p. 43; Billingon, 'British and American Methodisms grow apart', pp. 122-23; Davies, *Transatlantic Brethren*, pp. 216-31. Slavery continued to be a major cause of Nonconformist disillusionment with American religion into the 1840s: Maclear, 'The Idea of "American Protestantism" and British Conformity', pp. 88-89.

Slavery in the West India Islands, from the committee of the Leicester Auxiliary Anti-Slavery Society (1824):

> The Slave population of the United States in America, in 1830, amounted to 2,010,436; being increased threefold since the year 1790! This is an anomalous result, with which those in Great Britain who admire America, her free institutions, and her missionary spirit, are exceedingly perplexed.[63]

The Anglican *Christian Observer* went so far as to suggest that a black rebellion in the South in 1802 had been incited by white Americans.[64] Yet it distinguished between the slave states and individuals on the one hand, and the federal government and constitution on the other: it praised the federal constitution for opposing slavery, and the progress made by the American government towards the abolition of the slave trade.[65]

Perhaps more surprising is British Evangelical criticism of American Evangelicalism itself so early in the relationship between Britain and the United States. Anglicans, and Church of Scotland clergymen, did not approve of disestablishment in the United States. Charles Nisbet, minister in Montrose till 1785 when he emigrated to become President of Dickson College in Pennsylvania, was widely critical of the religion that he found in America; one of his most persistent claims was that the poor state of religion in Pennsylvania arose from the lack of constitutional support for it, so that ministers depended on the voluntary contributions of their people, which tended not to be a reliable source of support. And the lack of a state supported church allowed the multiplication of many sects, which he dubbed 'anythingarians' and 'nothingarians'.[66] In fact, British Evangelicals of all denominations professed anxiety regarding the growth of irreligion in America, attributing it to growing prosperity and to the influx of irreligious immigrants as well as to the lack of an established Church.[67]

The separation of American from British Methodism was bound to encounter some bumps in the road, though in fact there was much continuity and cooperation, as we have seen.[68] Even British Methodists were divided over American revivalism

---

[63] Robert Hall, *Address on the State of Slavery in the West India Islands, from the committee of the Leicester Auxiliary Anti-Slavery Society* (1824), in Gregory (ed.), *Works*, III, pp. 298-326 (p. 306).

[64] *Christian Observer* 1 (1802), p. 543.

[65] *Christian Observer* 3 (1804), pp. 184, 678-79.

[66] James H. Smylie, 'Charles Nisbet: Second Thoughts on a Revolutionary Generation', *Pennsylvania Magazine of History and Biography* 98 (April, 1974), pp. 189-205 (pp. 200-202); cf. S.J. Brown, 'Chalmers, Thomas (1780–1847)', *Oxford Dictionary of National Biography* (Oxford University Press: Oxford, 2004); and Thomas Chalmers, *On the Use and Abuse of Literary and Ecclesiastical Endowments* (1827), in *Works of Thomas Chalmers* (25 vols; Glasgow: Collins, 1836-42), XVII, pp. 112-15, 180-80, for a later but similar diagnosis.

[67] E.g. *Wesleyan-Methodist Magazine*, 22 (1799), p. 313.

[68] E.g. *Strictures on the Substance of a Sermon preached at Baltimore in the State of Maryland, before the General Conference of the Methodist Episcopal Church, on the 27th of*

and did not universally admire it; there were those who thought its emotionalism was 'theologically unsound and socially distasteful'.[69] The Anglican *Christian Observer* also objected to the nature of the Kentucky revival of 1801 and the Presbyterian revival in Pennsylvania in 1803, and it took issue with the editors of the *Evangelical Magazine* for their uncritical admiration of these revivals. Large crowds of up to 20,000 people, it said, had necessitated the attendance of several preachers, so that people could wander from one to the other, 'creating an appearance of confusion and disorder', an appearance which was reinforced by the phenomenon of people falling down both in services and afterwards; the length of services of worship, often extending to several days, also puzzled the periodical's writers. They doubted whether it was legitimate to ascribe to 'the God of order and wisdom, such wild and disorderly effects' as these, and suggested that such phenomena were more likely to have been stimulated by the devil, otherwise known in Scripture as 'the Deceiver' of the world. It was relieved to be persuaded that 'these disorders are considered in much the same light by the discerning part of the religious world in America'.[70]

Some more politically conservative British Evangelicals, such as David and Joseph Kinghorn, father and son, Baptist preachers in Newcastle and Norwich, disapproved of the American constitutional system. David Kinghorn wrote to his son in 1794 that 'England is almost infinitely preferable to [A]merica', since in America there were 'too many restless spirits, and jarring interests ... to permit them to live long in peace'. Joseph was of the opinion that when George Washington died, state disputes and litigation would increase and result in political turmoil. Although he was prepared to admire the freedom of political expression in America, he concluded, 'I am however quite of your opinion [of] the future prospect of America – not the most pleasing.'[71]

Evangelicals in Britain were sometimes critical, however, less from fundamental disapproval of the United States and its institutions and more as a result of the disappointment of their high hopes for it. Just as radical political reformers in Britain needed the United States to succeed as a model republic, so many British Evangelicals very much wanted America to embody their image of piety and freedom from political corruption, and so they were all the more sharply critical when it fell short of these idealised standards.[72] Nisbet had agreed to emigrate to

---

December 1784: at the ordination of the Rev. Francis Asbury, to the Office of Superintendant, by Thomas Coke LLD, Superintendant of the said Church. By a Methodist of the Church of England (London: G. Herdsfield, 1785).

[69] Billington, 'British and American Methodisms grow apart', pp. 114-20, quotation at p. 117.

[70] *Christian Observer* 1 (1802), pp. 667-70; *Christian Observer* 3 (1804), 55-56, 187-88, 371-73, 640-43: quotations from 1 (1802), pp. 667, 670; 3 (1804), p. 641.

[71] David Kinghorn to Joseph Kinghorn, 18 October 1794; Joseph Kinghorn to David Kinghorn, 7 October 1794; Joseph Kinghorn to David Kinghorn, 4 November 1794. Kinghorn correspondence in Box 4/3/1, Angus Library, Regents Park College, Oxford, and quoted in Parnell, 'Baptists and Britons', pp. 201-202.

[72] Davies, *Transatlantic Brethren*, pp. 187-88.

Pennsylvania because of his admiration for America's resistance to British 'tyranny', but he did not think that the United States had lived up to its initial promise. He came to believe that it was corrupt, anarchic, and much less admirable than he had supposed. It lacked of men of learning, leisure, talent for government and public spirit; instead, it was rife with party spirit and factional interests; it placed too much emphasis on popular sovereignty; it had been radicalised by way of the French Revolution, which it had itself been partly responsible for fomenting; and it was plagued by constant revolts (by students, or over whisky, or by slaves).[73] He became cynical about the American experiment and accused its people of 'an over-weaning Conceit of themselves, or an extravagant opinion of their own wisdom', to the extent that they construed the Bible heretically thus: 'In the Beginning the Sovereign People created Heaven & the Earth'.[74] Less forcefully, but more sententiously, the *Christian Observer* thought that the American government had displayed 'very low ideas of morality' in its swift acquisition of Louisiana from France in 1803 without regard, in its opinion, for due process and justice. It was also shocked that Alexander Hamilton had been seconded in his illegal duel with Aaron Burr by Judge Nathaniel Pendleton.[75]

Evangelicals were distressed by the rupture of the War of 1812, which caused some mutual irritation. British Methodists were described as arrogant anti-republicans most often during these years and, in turn, they expressed fear that the conflict was distracting Americans from spiritual priorities. Joshua Marsden, a Methodist missionary detained by the war in New York on his way home to England from Bermuda, wrote to the Methodist Missionary Committee in October 1813:

> The present war is not favourable to religion in this country. Political discussions swallow up every other kind of conversation, and are the whole gospel and study of thousands, both in and out of the church of Christ. Alas! ... In this city ... [a] great part of the community are professing people, but the present unhappy contest throws every thing into confusion. My earnest prayer is, that the Lord may speedily send peace to the two nations.[76]

---

[73] David W. Robson, 'Anticipating the Brethren: The Reverend Charles Nisbet critiques the French Revolution', *Pennsylvania Magazine of History and Biography* 121.4 (October, 1997), 303-28 (p. 305).

[74] Smylie, 'Charles Nisbet: Second Thoughts on a Revolutionary Generation', pp. 195, 200; Mark A. Noll, 'Revival, Enlightenment, Civic Humanism, and the Evolution of Calvinism in Scotland and America, 1735–1843', in Rawlyk and Noll (eds), *Amazing Grace*, pp. 73-107 (pp. 99-100).

[75] *Christian Observer* 3 (1804), pp. 62, 570.

[76] Joshua Marsden to the Methodist Missionary Committee, 26 October 1813, published in the *Wesleyan-Methodist Magazine* 37 (1814), pp. 315-17 (p. 316); Carwardine, *Transatlantic Revivalism*, pp. 30, 32. Cf. also Richard Pope in the *Wesleyan-Methodist Magazine* 41 (1818), p. 788, on the effects of the war on religious vitality between Montreal and the American border.

The Anglicans at the *Christian Observer* were more politically partial. They were happy to have been convinced, 'not that our enemies are in the wrong, but that we are in the right' and that 'we have acted throughout with ... moderation'. They claimed that American complaints regarding British navigation practices were a mere smokescreen for what was really an American 'lust of conquest, joined to an envy of British greatness'.[77] And they were offended by what they identified as readiness on the part of the United States to forget what it owed to Britain, and to cast its lot on the side of Britain's enemy, Napoleonic France:

> It is impossible to turn to the United States of America, without feelings of poignant regret, and even of deep disgust. To think that a nation sprung from our own loins, inheriting, in its boast at least, our love of liberty; speaking the language, and transcribing into its code, the institutions of freedom; should have selfishly refused to take any part in vindicating the general cause of the civilized world, would have been of itself no light subject of disappointment. But could it have been believed, prior to the ignominious fact; – will posterity believe, that such a nation, so descended, and so constituted – before the generation had quite passed away by whom her own independence had been gallantly achieved – should have become so absorbed by the one mean, sordid, selfish passion of commercial cupidity, as not only to throw her hopes and wishes into the scale which carried the fortunes of the grand enemy of the freedom, and independence, and happiness of the world; but to place her sword also on the same side, with the avowed purpose of weighing down to the ground that very power whose gallant bearing alone had hitherto furnished a rallying point for the hopes and prayers of the oppressed nations of the earth?[78]

British Evangelical responses to the United States were, naturally, shaped by their own political identities, whether conservative or liberal, as well as by their Evangelical identity.

III

While there was, therefore, a great deal of respect for and desire to collaborate with their American Evangelical brothers and sisters, this did not mean uncritical or universal approval of the new republic or of Evangelicalism within it by British Evangelicals. When Joshua Marsden was finally released to sail home, he was full of gratitude for the kindness of New York Methodists to him during his enforced stay; and yet at the same time (in the same paragraph!) pretty sharp in his criticisms:

> Thank God I am at last delivered from bondage; I have passed through a *democratic wilderness* of briars and thorns, but I am escaped 'as a bird from the fowler's snare'. Never did party spirit so embitter the sweets of life, and poison the streams of social happiness, as in the United States of America.

---

[77] *Christian Observer* 12 (1813), pp. 63, 127.
[78] *Christian Observer* 12 (1813), pp. 749-50.

I am now at sea, and my ears are no longer stunned with crabbed discussions.[79]

Clearly, it was possible for Evangelicals to disagree profoundly with American politics and yet to treasure the spiritual link. But there was also a developing awareness that Evangelicalism on the other side of the Atlantic was perhaps similar in theology, but different in culture. While this recognition of variation had much to do with British Evangelicals' own political environment and their individual political dispositions, it may also be at least partly explained by the contexts of the separate development of national identity, and of separate spiritual development, on either side of the Atlantic.

America, in this pre-steam era, was still seen by Joshua Marsden and others as 'the ends of the earth', and the physical distance mattered.[80] Moreover, it was developing fast as a nation in its own right, with its own national character, and the sense of special destiny that marked it out from the corruptions of the Old World, just as British national identity was being indelibly marked by the experience of resisting the French Revolution and Napoleon Bonaparte over twenty-two years and thereby having its conviction reinforced that it was 'the true Israel of God' for the times.[81] These national settings marked Evangelicals in Britain and the United States, and affected British views of America and of their counterparts there. The Scottish Evangelical leader, Henry Moncrieff Wellwood, put it this way,

> The final decision of the question has ... demonstrated to the conviction of all impartial men ... that the immediate and the remote consequences of the American war have gone equally beyond the anticipations of those who defended, and of those who condemned it, as well as of those who laboured to mediate between them, or to moderate their hostility.[82]

Ted Campbell's proposal that a broader examination of what Evangelical literature made it across the Atlantic would reveal a great deal, is convincing; for one thing, it would help to demonstrate more substantially the nature of much of what was actually known in Britain about American Evangelicalism at this time.[83]

Secondly, the development of Evangelical religion in both countries was separate. While it had been common for defeat in the War of American Independence to have been explained in sermons as divine chastening as a result of Britain's imperial greed

---

[79] *Wesleyan-Methodist Magazine* 38 (1815), p. 302.

[80] *Wesleyan-Methodist Magazine* 38 (1815), 308.

[81] Davies, *Transatlantic Brethren*, p. 14; Carwardine, *Transatlantic Revivalism*, p. 3; Marshall, 'Presidential Address'; Eliga H. Gould, 'A Virtual Nation: Greater Britain and the Imperial Legacy of the American Revolution', *American Historical Review* 104.2 (1999), pp. 476-89; Dror Wahrman, 'The English Problem of Identity in the American Revolution', *American Historical Review* 106 (2001), pp. 1236-62; Wilson, 'The island race'.

[82] Wellwood (ed.), *Account of the Life and Writings of John Erskine*, p. 281.

[83] Ted. A. Campbell, 'Evangelical Institutionalization and Evangelical Sectarianism in Early Nineteenth-Century Britain and America', in Rawlyk and Noll (eds), *Amazing Grace*, pp. 108-23 (pp. 121-22).

and oppression, or of the British people's self-indulgence in luxury and corruption, this did not lead preachers to urge imitation of the religion of the vindicated Americans.[84] The advance in America of voluntarism rather than parish religion, and of popular religion over church membership and discipline and clerical authority, was not diametrically opposed to British Evangelicalism, which was, as David Bebbington and others have argued, not universally authoritarian and staid, *pace* Nathan Hatch, while many American Evangelicals were similarly troubled by uncontrolled religion.[85] But British Evangelicalism was, normally, *relatively* more organised, more subject to the clergy, more staid and socially conservative; and its increasing momentum and energy in the decades after the American Revolution mounted relatively gradually by contrast with the periods of extraordinary revival experienced in the United States. It was much harder for British Primitive Methodists to operate, amidst social criticism and harassment, than it was for their American counterparts, who did not have a strong Anglican establishment with which to contend.

It would have been remarkable if transatlantic differences had not influenced British Evangelical attitudes towards their American counterparts. Just as British political attitudes towards the United States of America combined an ambivalent mix of admiration and mystification, so British Evangelical attitudes combined respect and a deep desire to associate and cooperate with American Evangelicals, with criticisms of American toleration of slavery, and some discomfort with the levels of religious and political diversity and disorder apparent in the new republic. Evangelicals were therefore to be found adding their voices to the conservative, liberal and radical positions in the British debate on the new United States of America.[86] Yet their most distinctive contribution was their enthusiasm for cooperation with Americans in missionary enterprises inside and outside the United States. In this they added weight to the stance of those liberal politicians who viewed the United States as a force for good in the world and a natural ally for Britain, and who favoured a close Anglo-American relationship on the basis of shared values, despite their differences.[87] While the national and spiritual cultures in which British

---

[84] Warren Johnston, 'Preaching, National Salvation, Victories, and Thanksgivings: 1689–1800', in Francis and Gibson (eds), *Oxford Handbook of the British Sermon*, pp. 261-74 (p. 270); G.M. Ditchfield, 'Sermons in the Age of the American and French Revolutions', in Francis and Gibson (eds), *Oxford Handbook of the British Sermon*, pp. 275-88 (p. 280).

[85] Nathan O. Hatch, *The Democratization of American Christianity* (New Haven, CT: Yale University Press, 1989); Bebbington, 'Democratization of British Christianity', and 'Evangelicalism in Modern Britain and America'; Campbell, 'Evangelical Institutionalization'. See also Valerie Honeyman, '"That ye may judge for yourselves": The Contribution of Scottish Presbyterianism towards the Emergence of Political Awareness amongst Ordinary People in Scotland between 1746 and 1792' (PhD diss., University of Stirling, 2012).

[86] Emma Macleod, *British Visions of America, 1775–1820: Republican Realities* (London: Pickering and Chatto, 2013).

[87] Macleod, *British Visions of America*, pp. 124-25.

and American Evangelicals operated were different, the theological and spiritual ties which bound them were substantial; and British Evangelicals looked forward to the time when the transatlantic separation would be removed and when, 'as there was but one Shepherd, there would be only one sheepfold'.[88]

---

[88] Earl of Harrowby, Lord President of Council, at the fourteenth anniversary meeting of the British and Foreign Bible Society, 6 May 1818, reported in the *Wesleyan-Methodist Magazine* 41 (1818), p. 547.

CHAPTER 16

Hands Joined in Brotherhood: The Rise and Decline of a Movement for Faith and Social Change, 1875–2000

David Killingray

Christian organisations rise and fall. Institutions once common cease to exist and are little known to a later generation. One such was the Pleasant Sunday Afternoon (PSA) or Brotherhood Movement, with the motto, 'One is your Master, even Christ, and all ye are Brethren', that grew within the Nonconformist churches in the late nineteenth century. By 1912 it claimed more than 400,000 members and had the support of leading Nonconformist clergy and lay-people as well as prominent figures in the Labour and Liberal Parties. David Bebbington, as would be expected, devoted several pages to the PSA/Brotherhood in his doctoral thesis, but other than two semi-official brief histories the movement has not yet found a devoted historian.[1]

The PSA was started by John Blackham, a Sunday school teacher and deacon in the Ebenezer Congregational Church, West Bromwich, in 1875. Influenced by Dwight L. Moody and Ira D. Sankey's meetings in Birmingham, Blackham was concerned that young men ceased to attend church. His solution to help 'reclaim the lapsed masses' for the Christian faith and for the church was to offer a meeting that was 'brief, bright and brotherly'. Held on Sunday afternoons the meetings were informal affairs with a Bible reading, one or two hymns, a solo, a ten minute talk, and a prayer.[2] The idea caught on and by 1885 there were 10,000 men gathering in similar meetings within the Birmingham area.[3] There were links with the local

---

[1] David Bebbington, 'The Nonconformist Conscience: A Study of the Political Attitudes and Activities of Evangelical Nonconformists, 1886–1902' (PhD diss., University of Cambridge, 1975), pp. 32-40. J.W. Tuffley, *Grain from Galilee: The Romance of the Brotherhood Movement* (London: Headley Bros, 1935); A.E.H. Gregory, *Romance and Revolution: The Story of the Brotherhood Movement 1875–1975* (Sevenoaks: Hodder & Stoughton, n.d. [c.1975]).

[2] See an account by Blackham in *The P.S.A. Reporter and Record for Stockport and District* 1 (March, 1892), pp. 1-3; *PSA Leader* June 1898, pp. 98-100; and *Brotherhood Outlook* July 1923, pp. 89-90, 'John Blackham: An Appreciation'. David Killingray, 'The Pleasant Sunday Afternoon Movement: Revival in the West Midlands, 1875–90?', in Kate Cooper and Jeremy Gregory (eds), *Revival and Resurgence in Christian History: Studies in Church History,* Volume 44 (Woodbridge: Boydell & Brewer, 2008), pp. 262-74.

[3] Earlier there had been similar meetings for working men, e.g., the Rev. H.S. Brown, Baptist minister in Liverpool in 1854, began a PSA style meeting that attracted mainly skilled

YMCA, through its secretary Reginald Hodder, and PSA work was extended first to Derby and then to Nottingham and Leicester. In 1890 Blackham addressed the annual Assembly of the Congregational Union meeting in Birmingham on 'The spread of the PSA movement'. This encouraged the growth of new societies as members moved to another part of the country or as clergy and church members caught the vision of how working men might be contacted and held by the church. Starting a new society was often attended by extensive publicity; for example the class started by the Rev. A. Holden Byles at Tabernacle Church, Hanley, Staffordshire, in 1890, was promoted by use of large posters and the distribution of 10,000 handbills for ten days and also by door to door visitation.[4]

By the mid-1890s the movement had spread to other parts of the country, predominantly under Nonconformist patronage, mainly in Congregational, Wesleyan, and Baptist churches, although there were a few Anglican clergy who were sympathetic supporters. The greatest strength in membership was in the Midlands, Lancashire, and Yorkshire. Similar development in London was hindered by its more mobile population, although 'Men's Own' meetings, similar in purpose to but initially not associated with the PSA, had been founded in the metropolis, for example at Edinboro' Castle by Dr Barnardo, John Clifford's Institute at Westbourne Park, Paddington, founded in 1885, and that led by F.B. Meyer at Christ Church, Lambeth ('Meyer's Lambs' as they were called). The first London PSA was at Tottenham, founded in 1888; the largest was the 1,200 strong Men's Meeting at Charles Vine's Ilford Congregational Church. A later major men's meeting was created by Silvester Horne at Whitefield's Chapel, Tottenham Court Road, in 1903.[5] PSA work existed in the major Scottish cities (Henry Drummond played a significant role in Glasgow[6]), but it was less well established in the counties of north east and south west England. Much of Wales, where men continued to attend chapel, was not

---

labourers, and by the Rev. John Clifford, at Praed Street Chapel, London, in 1859, who spoke of being there to 'save souls and bodies and to increase social good'. See David Thompson, 'John Clifford's Social Gospel', *Baptist Quarterly* 31.5 (January, 1986), pp. 199-217. F.B. Meyer, following his encounter with D.L. Moody in the 1870s, made the evangelism of the 'submerged masses' one of his major goals, see Ian M. Randall, *Spirituality and Social Change: The Contribution of F.B. Meyer* (Studies in Evangelical History and Thought; Carlisle: Paternoster Press, 2003), p. 233. According to the *PSA Leader* March 1906, p. 33, the Ashton-under-Lyne PSA meeting was 'a very old class that had been in existence for fifty years and was doing PSA work before the PSA was started'.

[4] A. Holden Byles, *The P.S.A.: What it is, and how to start it* (London: James Clarke, 1891), pp. 22-24. PSA *Leader* November 1902, p. 166.

[5] C. Silvester Horne, *The Institutional Church* (London: James Clarke, 1906), p. 186, 'The Men's Meeting was a new type of church that would compete with the music hall and the theatre and in which all classes and races would feel at home.'

[6] George Adam Smith, *The Life of Henry Drummond* (London: Hodder & Stoughton, 1900), pp. 462-63. Smith wrote, 'I do not think he sufficiently realised the danger which the P.S.A. movement involves, of leading its members away from the family aspects of religion; yet, it is certain that, as in other places, so here, the meetings attracted a large number of men, who would otherwise not have attended a religious service ...'

natural PSA country; branches developed in the early 1900s mainly confined to the towns of the south. The vast majority of PSA societies were in urban areas including rural towns, for example King's Lynn which had a strong and vibrant meeting.[7] Work also flourished in some village chapels.[8] Members were mainly drawn from 'artisans and office or shop assistants',[9] although there were a good number of societies where rough clad labouring men sat alongside middle class members.

Each society, or class as they were usually called in the West Midlands, was autonomous.[10] The term 'brotherhood', widely used in a variety of Christian contexts on both sides of the Atlantic, was adopted by the Leamington Spa class early in the 1890s. It was a term that also appealed to the Rev. J.K. Nuttall at George Street Chapel in Liverpool, and to Meyer at Christ Church, Lambeth.[11] In the early years of the twentieth century the Brotherhood Movement, as increasingly it was called, had 250,000 members meeting in over 1,200 societies organised in regional federations. In 1906 a national federation was formed, there was a co-operative publishing house, and international work was promoted vigorously from 1909 onwards in the Dominions and colonies, the USA, France, and Belgium.

The PSA movement was an important element of late nineteenth-century Nonconformist activity attempting to reach the working classes alienated from Christianity, to arrest the decline in church attendance, and also to find answers to widespread acute social and economic distress.[12] It was similar in aim to other contemporary institutions and ideas, for example the Salvation Army, the city Settlements, and Hugh Price Hughes' 'Forward Movement' at West London Mission. For example, the Rev. R.F. Horton argued in 1893 that the 'Forward Movement' was 'to bring the vast uncared-for masses back to God', while his fellow Congregationalist J. Guinness Roger wrote that 'What I understand ... by the Forward Movement is some action inspired by devoted loyalty to the Master for bringing men to faith in Him ... [with] one aim ... the conversion of souls to Jesus

---

[7] I am grateful to Roger Ottewill for sharing with me his work on PSA/Brotherhood in Hampshire.

[8] 'Brotherhood in the villages', a paper given to the 7th Annual Brotherhood Conference, Manchester, 1908.

[9] Report in *Christian Commonwealth* 2 October 1907, p. 12. One indication that PSAs appealed to better-off working men were the holidays advertised. In the 1890s these tended to be walking holidays in the Lake District – 'Pleasant Summer Holidays' – accompanied by 'a University man' who would associate with the men and give lectures, at the cost of 30 shillings, *Brotherhood* June 1893, p. 22; later in the next decade this had extended to holidays in France and even a cruise in the Norwegian fjords.

[10] Byles, *The P.S.A.*, provides a description of the organisation and management of a PSA class.

[11] W.Y. Fullerton, *F.B. Meyer: A Biography* (London: Marshall, Morgan & Scott, 1929), p. 108.

[12] Hugh McLeod, *Class and Religion in the Late Victorian City* (London: Routledge, 1974), p. 80, wrote that the PSA represented 'all that was original and fresh in nonconformity'.

Christ ... The process of change is from within outward, not from the outside inward.'[13]

Why did the PSA, with its temperance, anti-gambling, and evangelistic message appeal to many working men, and also to women who, from the early 1890s, met in parallel sisterhoods? The attraction of the PSA was its informality, often meeting not in the church of the parson and the pew but in a hall or custom built institute. Men attired in working clothes could gather in warm friendly surroundings, not forbidden to cheer and laugh, and they could enjoy free entertainment attended by cheap tea and food. It offered, as was intended, an alternative to the pub and the music hall and consequently met the approval of many working class women who saw only material and social benefit if their men attended. And direct benefits were offered in the form of clothing, boot, and coal clubs, sick and dividend societies, labour bureaux for the unemployed, self-improvement through books, savings' banks, ambulance classes, plus music, sports and recreation.[14] Despite their avowed evangelical purpose the PSAs met with criticism from Sabbatarians who viewed them as 'direct agents of secularisation'.[15]

Regular attendance at PSA meetings was rewarded by book prizes although this was usually funded by a weekly subscription of one penny.[16] From the early 1890s, perhaps even earlier, different aims began to appear within the PSA movement between those who argued that its purpose was the regeneration of souls and those who inclined to a social gospel that aimed at physical transformation. The social gospel was viewed with considerable suspicion by certain evangelical Nonconformists who saw PSAs as being divisive and inherently hostile to church growth.[17] Some evangelicals reacted to the idea of a 'pleasant Sunday afternoon', not

---

[13] See C. Oldstone-Moore, *Hugh Price Hughes: Founder of a New Methodism, Conscience of a New Nonconformity* (Cardiff: University of Wales Press, 1999), ch. 5; K.S. Inglis, *Churches and the Working Classes in Victorian England* (London: Routledge and Kegan Paul, 1963), pp. 79-85. R.F. Horton, *British Weekly* 9 February 1893, p. 259; J. Guinness Rogers, *The Forward Movement and the Christian Church* (London: James Clarke, 1893), pp. 4, 8, 12, 14 (Rogers' italics).

[14] The *P.S.A. Magazine* 1, 1 December 1891, provides insight to PSA work and classes in Nottingham.

[15] *The Bolton Chronicle* 3 November 1888, quoted by John Wigley, *The Rise and Fall of the Victorian Sunday* (Manchester: Manchester University Press, 1980), p. 139.

[16] Leonard Smith, *Religion and the Rise of Labour: Nonconformity and the Independent Labour Movement in Lancashire and the West Riding, 1880–1914* (Keele: Ryburn, 1993), pp. 54-55, argued that these were books likely to encourage the spread of socialist ideas, whereas the majority of books advertised and recommended as prizes were religious, fiction, travel, biography, and works encouraging self-improvement. On books and self-improvement, see James Munson, *The Nonconformists: In Search of a Lost Culture* (London: SPCK, 1991), pp. 63-65.

[17] See D.M. Thompson, 'The Emergence of the Nonconformist Social Gospel in England', in K. Robbins (ed.), *Protestant Evangelicalism in Britain, Ireland, German and America c.1750–c.1950: Essays in Honour of W.R. Ward* (Oxford: Basil Blackwell, 1990), pp. 225-80.

because they were against enjoyable worship but because they feared that the social activities of the PSA inclined towards liberal theology. Widespread use of phrases such as 'the brotherhood of all under the fatherhood of God' as the goal of Christianity only helped confirm their fears that this was a slippery theological slope. Undoubtedly men were converted through PSAs, the initial work in the Midlands indicating something of a religious revival;[18] individual lives were changed and, it was claimed, 'tens of thousands of homes today are little paradises on earth that used to be the centres of squalid misery'.[19] Although the PSA and Brotherhood claimed to be above politics, the social issues addressed in many meetings could readily be identified with the progressive economic and social agendas espoused by sections of the Liberal Party and socialists. Rooted in the language of Christianity and founded in Nonconformist churches, many PSA and Brotherhood societies increasingly offered the ideas of the social gospel that could only be realised by political action.[20]

In 1913 the Brotherhood Movement claimed over 300,000 members with as many again regularly attending meetings. The commitment was to international brotherhood and attempts were being made to advance the cause into Germany from bases in Belgium and France. The message was avowedly anti-war, many leaders being firmly pacifist. As part of its optimistic programme in the United Kingdom a home missionary campaign was planned for Autumn 1914 but cancelled when war broke out. In early May 1915 the Rev. Andrew Clark, rector of the village of Great Leighs in Essex, confided in his diary,

> I am told that the 'foreman' at 'The Warren' in Little Leighs parish is all that is offensive – an offensive Radical, an offensive 'Chapelite', and offensive 'Brotherhood', and that he comes into Great Leighs and makes very offensive speeches saying that the authorities are sending out our poor lads to certain slaughter, and that the Germans are winning all along the line, and will win thoroughly.[21]

The Great War dashed for many the ideal of Christian 'brotherhood' and it also disillusioned many socialists who had believed that international working class solidarity would prevent war. By 1919 the Brotherhood Movement was reduced to 100,000 members. The optimism of some was not reduced as was evident from the

---

[18] For a Nottingham PSA, see Robert Mellors, *How Two Thousand Men Have Been Won* (Nottingham: J. Bell, 1893). The impact of the PSA at Belgrave Independent Chapel, Leeds, established by Richard Westrope in 1890, is briefly described in J.W. Dixon, *Pledged to the People: A Sketch of Rev. Richard Westrope and Congregational Aggressive Work in Leeds* (Leeds: J. Whitehead, 1896), and analysed in Gerard Charmley, 'Richard Westrope and Belgrave Chapel', *Journal of the United Reformed Church History Society* 9.4 (2014), pp. 207-25.

[19] Harry Jeffs, *The Good New Times* (London: James Clarke, 1908), p. 124.

[20] *PSA and Brotherhood Journal*, November 1907, pp. 261 and 271, John Hay's call to the Liverpool conference that it was 'a time for action, for deeds, not words'.

[21] James Munson (ed.), *Echoes of the Great War: The Diary of the Reverend Andrew Clark 1914–1919* (Oxford: Oxford University Press, 1988 [1985]), p. 60.

claims made at the International Brotherhood Conference in London in 1920.[22] But the liberal theological and secularising trends, very evident in the Movement from about 1906 onwards, were now more pronounced. Although leading evangelicals such as John Clifford gave strong support to the Brotherhood, there were many Christians who saw it as having deserted the true way of faith. Although 'to bring people to Christ' remained a foundation principle, the prevailing idea nationally and in many societies was of social improvement and of the 'Christ values in life'.[23] In the 1930s the Movement could still claim 115,000 members in Britain, organised in thriving local societies and represented by a national conference, and with confident energy for a five year crusade that each member should 'win one more' member. War in 1939 again hit at the ideals and the organisation of Brotherhood. Further decline followed and many branches closed as the social programmes of early societies were now met by welfare state provision. By the end of the twentieth century the Brotherhood, more correctly an elderly 'Sisterhood', numbered c.2,000 members in branches across the country.

The PSA and the Brotherhood Movement are frequently mentioned in studies of late nineteenth and early twentieth century British ecclesiastical and socio-political history although it is surprising that so little attention has been given to their influence in evangelising the working classes and their relationship as pressure groups on the policies of the Liberal and Labour parties. The autonomy of each society makes for scattered material but there were regular local and national journals, beginning with the *PSA Gazette* and moving to the *Brotherhood Outlook*, a range of books and other publications, memoirs, branch records in local archives, and much comment in the contemporary ecclesiastical and secular press. One wonders why these Movements have been marginalised when thirty years ago Hugh McLeod wrote of Brotherhood that 'In its heyday, between about 1890 and 1914, it was the most representative, and one of the largest bodies of working-class Christians in London'.[24]

The term 'brotherhood' was widely used on both sides of the Atlantic in the nineteenth and twentieth centuries, and not only in Christian contexts.[25] Several similarly named but smaller bodies in Britain in the years 1893–1910 can cause

---

[22] Basil Mathews (ed.), *World Brotherhood* (London: Hodder & Stoughton, 1920).

[23] J.W. Tuffley, *The Sowers* (London: Brotherhood Movement, 1937), p. 31. In this 'comprehensive survey of the Brotherhood Movement', ch. 3 is headed 'Must I be a Christian?' A.S.D. Birch of Sheffield feared that the PSA was 'adrift', no longer out to convert but merely to provide a pleasant afternoon, *Danger Signals* (Norwich, n.d. [c.1893]), reported in the *Sheffield & Rotherham Independent* 13 December 1893, p. 2.

[24] McLeod, *Class and Religion*, p. 65.

[25] From 1787 'Am I not a man and a brother' had been the appeal of the shackled black slave on Wedgwood's cameo, symbol of the abolitionist movement. Elihu Burrit formed the League of Universal Brotherhood in 1846, a transatlantic pacifist body which collapsed in Britain with the onset of the Crimean War. In 1893 Leighton Williams and Walter Rauschenbusch helped form 'The Brotherhood of the Kingdom', an important influence for the social gospel in the United States and beyond.

confusion. First, the Society for the Furtherance of the Brotherhood of Man was established in Somerset in April 1893 by the Quaker Catherine Impey.[26] A month later in Aberdeen, Impey met with Isabella Mayo and the two women reconstituted this as the Society for the Recognition of the Brotherhood of Man (SRBM). The main purpose was to oppose racial discrimination, and particularly lynching in the United States, the focus of Impey's monthly paper *Anti-Caste*, published from Street, Somerset, since 1888. The two women set about establishing branches in Scotland and England, but almost immediately disaster struck. Impey committed a silly indiscretion which Mayo refused to forgive and the new Society was torn apart, continuing as two weakened bodies both claiming the mantle of the SRBM. Most branches adhered to Mayo with those in the West Country identifying with Impey. A new monthly journal for the Mayo wing of the SRBM, *Fraternity*, was edited by J.S. Celestine Edwards from the Caribbean island of Dominica; the mast head showed clasped black and white hands whereas the PSA/Brotherhood's badge showed two white hands clasped. Early in the next century the SRBM became the League of Universal Brotherhood, and continued to campaign for black civil rights.[27]

Second, there was J. Bruce Wallace's Brotherhood Church, founded in 1892, 'which stood for socialism and untheological religion'.[28] Third, John Clifford's Christian Socialist League, founded in 1894 on the principle that 'we believe God is the Father of all men, and that all men are consequently brethren', transformed itself into the Christian Social Brotherhood four years later. Clifford was president, and the new body's declared aim was 'to bring the teaching of Christ to bear directly' on social problems.[29] Confusion in name is compounded by major figures, such as

---

[26] On Impey, see Caroline Bressey, *Empire, Race and the Politics of Anti-Caste* (London: Bloomsbury, 2013).

[27] See Vron Ware, *Beyond the Pale: White women, Racism and History* (London: Verso, 1992), Part 4; Jonathan Schneer, *London 1900: The Imperial Metropolis* (New Haven, CT: Yale University Press, 1999), pp. 204-12.

[28] Starting in April 1887, Wallace had published, from Limavady, a weekly paper called *Brotherhood* 'designed to help the peaceful evolution of a juster and happier social order'. Later (1894) it became 'a magazine of social progress'. In a 'summary of methods advocated in Brotherhood' were land nationalisation, 'home colonisation' to help the pauper population, total abstinence from alcohol, 'simplicity of life with a view to generous service', 'co-operation rather than competition', all leading to the 'socialisation of capital' and a 'commonwealth of comfortable workers'. See *Brotherhood*, September 1888, pp. 57-59. By July 1900 there were three Brotherhood churches in London, and eleven groups, ten in London, and one in Hereford. On the Labour Church, see Inglis, *Churches and the Working Classes*, ch. 6. According to Robert Moore, *Pit-Men, Preachers and Politics: The Effects of Methodism in a Durham Mining Community* (Cambridge: Cambridge University Press, 1974), pp. 171 and 225, but without supporting references, the Labour Church, unlike John Trevor's Socialist Sunday schools, had anarcho-Christian pacifist and utopian leanings. On the latter, see Stephen Mayor, *The Churches and the Labour Movement* (London: Independent Press, 1967).

[29] Peter d'A. Jones, *The Christian Socialist Revival 1877–1914* (Princeton, NJ: Princeton University Press, 1968), pp. 28-29 and 346-47. By early 1892 the *Christian Socialist* had

Clifford and the Rev. F.B. Meyer, acting simultaneously as patrons for different brotherhood bodies, with a handful of members of the PSA/Brotherhood also belonging to these much smaller brotherhoods.

Theological Direction and Integrity of Purpose

Blackham's original idea of attracting men was avowedly evangelical: that acceptance of Christ as Saviour would transform men inwardly and thus outwardly. This remained his consistent view as the PSA grew and increasingly embraced a different set of priorities as the Brotherhood Movement. The diversity of membership and societies meant that spiritual and social purpose differed from one class to another. Classes occasionally rivalled one another for members, their appeal depending on programmes, emphasis, and also facilities. Some remained firmly evangelical in purpose with emphasis on Christ the Redeemer, the Bible as the inspired word of God, and the importance of prayer. These classes were more likely to use Sankey's *Sacred Songs and Solos* rather than H.A. Kennedy's *Sunday Afternoon Song Book*, compiled and published in 1892, or, after 1909, the *Brotherhood Hymn Book*. Other classes, perhaps the majority, placed more emphasis on the need for social action and the necessity to challenge economic and political institutions to bring about social change. The theological and political pressures for a social gospel agenda were considerable, dictated by the need to address acute poverty, unemployment and deprivation, and those pressures came from within the church and also from without. The direction taken by a class to some extent depended upon the individual leader. This was often the minister of the church with which the class was associated, although it called for a bold, determined, and imaginatively gifted leader to retain the loyalty of a group of men fed merely on a diet of traditional Christian teaching. The ideas of temperance and a deep hostility to gambling remained at the heart of Brotherhood thinking. Many PSA branches had Institutes that offered an environment that sought to compete with the attractions of the pub – a reading room, perhaps a smoking room, provision of non-alcoholic drinks, as well as an area for meetings and music making. Blackham's belief was that Christian conversion would empower men so that they could begin to challenge and change their environment and by self-help also their economic and social condition. Education had an integral role, thus the prominence of Adult Bible Classes in the Birmingham area and books as prizes. The spiritual and the practical had to be balanced, but vital was a man's spiritual change of heart that then led to the cultivation of new habits of diligence, sobriety, and thrift.

Getting the balance right was difficult. There were regular complaints in the pages of the *PSA Leader* that some societies placed an 'exaggerated stress and a

---

been incorporated into Wallace's *Brotherhood*. The Christian Social League adopted Wallace's *Brotherhood* as its official organ. Percy Walden, the Revs C. Fleming Williams, Richard Westrope, and Silvester Horne were all members of the Christian Social Brotherhood.

misinterpretation ... on the word "pleasant", and some provided an afternoon entertainment with songs, recitations, and orchestral pieces, with a hymn or two, reading and prayer, and an address thrown in'.[30] F.B. Meyer, President of the PSA at Christ Church, and also President of the Free Church Council, writing in the *Free Churchman*, argued that if he were to begin again he would adopt the title of 'Men's Own' or 'Men's Brotherhood' instead of the PSA, 'as in many cases it had fallen beneath the high standard designed by its founder'.[31] The wide gulf that existed between individual Brotherhood meetings in London, and elsewhere, is well illustrated by a meeting addressed by the theosophist Mrs Annie Besant at Grafton Street Congregational Church; the Rev. E.W. Lewis, who chaired the gathering, arguing that 'he rejoiced in the breadth of the Men's Meeting platform ... available to every sincere man and woman who had a message to convey'.[32]

Blackham, along with many evangelicals, saw PSAs providing an inviting threshold to the church. Men would be converted and then move to church membership.[33] But how men should receive Christ as Redeemer and what conversion actually meant to them was more widely interpreted probably by the majority of those associated with Brotherhood. The Kingdom of God was to be experienced in improved social conditions and the elevation of human dignity. As evangelicals Meyer and Clifford believed in the social gospel but they continued to give pre-eminence to the regeneration of souls. J.K. Nuttall, Congregational minister of a Liverpool church, summarised this in mid-1898: the aim was 'the salvation of the men', regeneration rather than mere reformation by 'Christ's saving and sanctifying power, and that men should then join the church'.[34]

The spiritual focus of PSAs was in part connected with those who exercised control over a particular society or branch. PSAs might or might not be attached to or integrated with a church. Some societies met in a church hall while others built their own Institutes or Brotherhood halls. There was a strong antipathy by many working men to parsons and particularly to pew rents, an alienation that embraced not only the Established Church but also Nonconformist places of worship that increasingly seemed to cater only for the respectable middle classes. Debate continued whether PSAs should be integrated with churches, have a loose attachment, or be independent. When the Rev. J.G. Gascoigne left Nuneaton Congregational Church and the PSA that he had founded, the deacons demanded to take control in the name of the church. The result was the departure of a large number of men from the class and the church.[35]

The gulf between those who argued for the original integrity of spiritual purpose and the more liberal-minded who demanded practical religion began to widen in the

---

[30] *PSA Leader*, March 1904, p. 35.
[31] F.B. Meyer, 'How to work a PSA', *The Free Churchman*, March 1904, pp. 55-56.
[32] *PSA Leader*, July 1907, p. 163.
[33] E.g., Byles, *The P.S.A.*, pp. 13 and 28.
[34] *PSA Leader*, June 1898, p. 86.
[35] Reported in the *PSA Leader*, April 1903, p. 54.

mid-1890s and increasingly so during the first decade of the twentieth century. At the 1909 conference in Cardiff, William Ward, the national president, warned of the threat of schism between those who advocated the 'old gospel' and those intent on advancing the cause of the social gospel. 'As we get a firm grasp of the eternal teaching of the Carpenter of Nazareth, we are convinced that it contains those principles of life and conduct which alone will give a solution to every social problem ... social salvation'.[36] However, as Kenneth D. Brown argues, when he got on to the atonement he was far less specific, suggesting that 'We will not ... stultify ourselves by limiting our ideas concerning this great theme ... we will seek to be permeated with its spirit'.[37] These divisions within the Movement can be illustrated by C. Fleming Williams, Congregational minister at Stoke Newington, who had moved from orthodoxy to a deep concern for solving the housing question, and by J.E. Wakerley, a Wesleyan at West Ham, who argued that the spiritual should always take precedence over the social. By 1914 two prominent Brotherhood leaders, Harry Jeffs and Herbert Evans, could state that the Movement's 'theology reduces itself to acceptance of the Fatherhood of God, the Brotherhood of Man, and the obligation of each man to recognize the family relationship and to work out in practice the moral logic of that relationship', the first phrase being the very slogan adopted for Trevor's Labour Church at a socialist congress in 1896.[38] This move away from a christocentric position continued during the Great War. In 1920 the *Brotherhood Outlook* could report without comment that a Spiritualist Brotherhood and Sisterhood had existed for the past year in Brighton.[39]

It was perhaps not surprising then that, in early 1919, John Clifford, who had remained close the Brotherhood Movement, failed to persuade a group of Free Church ministers to put aside their theological objections and to support the Movement. Tom Sykes, national secretary of the Movement, recalled leaving the meeting: 'We both of us came away with an oppressive sense of failure. The streets were cold and wet with the slush of a thaw. Gripping my arm he [Clifford] said, "Sykes, some ministers care no more for men than this slush"'.[40] Ten years later in October 1930, the Movement published and distributed 'The Challenge of Brotherhood', a statement that it believed to be the 'true purpose of Christian

---

[36] See text in William Ward, *Brotherhood and Democracy* (London: P.S.A. Brotherhood Publishing, 1910), pp. 164-66. Earlier in the book Ward had written, 'In the gradual development towards a perfect humanity the Brotherhood Movement represents the latest, though by no mean, the last phase.' See pp. 123-24.

[37] Ward, *Brotherhood*, p. 174; and Kenneth D. Brown, 'Nonconformist Evangelicals and National Politics in the Late Nineteenth Century', in John Wolffe (ed.), *Evangelical Faith and Public Zeal: Evangelicals and Society in Britain 1780–1980* (London: SPCK, 1995), p. 144.

[38] Harry Jeffs and Herbert Evans, *Social Workers Armoury: What a Brotherhood Man Can Do* (London: Brotherhood Publishing House, 1914), pp. 1-2. Jones, *Christian Socialist Revival*, p. 317.

[39] *Brotherhood Outlook*, August 1920, p. 143.

[40] James Marchant, *Dr. John Clifford* (London: Cassell, 1924), p. 209.

Brotherhood'. This declared that the Movement was 'actively associated with Christian churches, but eager to proclaim from a common platform, a gospel of social service and sanctified manhood'. Although the old motto was retained, Jesus Christ was only mentioned halfway through the document, the emphasis then being in 'recognising that the springs of character need ever to be touched by the transforming power of the Divine'.[41] As J.W. Tuffley, the general secretary, put it in the mid-1930s, the concern was with 'Christ values in life ... the expression of which is often unconscious either of the label "Christian" or that they are related to what we term "the service of Christ"'. Later in the same book Tuffley's answer to the question 'Must I be a Christian?' was fairly open-ended.[42]

Mixed Meetings

Meetings similar to the PSA but specifically for women developed in the 1880s. These gatherings, known as 'Pleasant Monday Evenings' (PME) or 'Pleasant Tuesday Evenings' (PTE), by the early 1890s were being referred to as 'Sisterhoods'. Some PSA meetings were mixed, a subject of some concern to those who saw the original purpose to reach and transform men and which they freely aired in the pages of the monthly *PSA Leader*. For example, by the early twentieth century the largest mixed meeting in London was the Congregational Church, Dawes Road, Fulham, which had a membership of 800.[43] The anxiety was that a mixed gathering would divert attention away from the spiritual aspects of the meeting towards the social. Ebenezer Goold, the editor of the *PSA Leader*, reported F.B. Meyer as saying that too often the PSA meeting had 'become a mixed gathering of men and women for little else than a social meeting in which the moral and religious elements are overpowered by the solos, recitations and other pleasantries'.[44] This echoed the condemnation by some Anglican clergy that PSA meetings fostered religious observance without moral effort, although such views need to be seen in the context of the hostility of many in the Established Church towards the Free Churches. Nevertheless the majority of PSA/Brotherhood meetings remained separate and a parallel Sisterhood developed integral to what became known as the Brotherhood and Sisterhood Movement. Addressing the Albert Hall conference of the London federation in 1912, Meyer as president, began with the words 'Sisters and Brothers', and most other speakers followed suit.[45]

---

[41] Gregory, *Romance and Revolution*, pp. 36-37.
[42] Tuffley, *The Sowers*, p. 31 and ch. III.
[43] *PSA Leader*, March 1904, p. 35.
[44] *PSA Leader*, April 1904, p. 57. See also E. Goold, 'The P.S.A. Movement', in R. Mudie-Smith (ed.), *The Religious Life of London* (London: Hodder & Stoughton, 1904), p. 321.
[45] Fullerton, *Meyer*, p. 114.

Autonomy or Federation?

Each PSA society or class was autonomous. Representatives met annually from 1893 when the first national conference was held in the Memorial Hall, Farringdon Street. Thereafter the annual conference met at different venues. Local federations were also created, early on for Lancashire, Yorkshire, and Warwickshire, and later for the London federation. As local organisations individual PSAs carried little weight. The Movement lacked a national structure to give voice to the issues that concerned it. The need for a representative national union or council was raised during the 1890s but met with little support.[46] In 1900 Blackham sent a letter 'to all the known PSAs and kindred societies asking whether they thought an annual conference or a National Federation would best serve the highest interests of the movement'. The response showed that ten to one favoured the continuation of a conference. However, during the next few years demands grew at the grassroots level for a national federation which, argued Ebenezer Goold, would give 'the Greater Brotherhood ... [a] formal and concrete existence'.[47] F.B. Meyer and John Clifford both favoured a central body; Meyer thought that it would help to focus attention on the original spiritual task of the movement. Local federations in Yorkshire, Lancashire, Warwickshire, and South Wales endorsed a central organisation while the Leicester federation revived a scheme for unity, first proposed in 1896, which met with widespread approval. This was discussed in late 1905.

John Blackham was the obvious candidate as national president. In the discussions for federation, held at Carr's Lane, Birmingham, in September 1905, to which he was party, Blackham did not demur and he agreed to be head of the national body.[48] However, when the decision was publicly announced he suddenly stated, via an interview in the *Christian World*, that the proposal went 'much further in the direction of Federation than I am prepared to go', that he would not support societies joining, and that he withdrew his name as future president. He feared centralisation would stifle the freedom of individual societies, create an unwieldy council, and lead to an 'independent PSA sect'. But, as was clear from his *Christian World* interview, his ideal of the PSA was being challenged. No longer was the Bible and evangelicalism in the first place, and he viewed with anxiety 'the mischievous tendency in some quarters to use the P.S.A. platform for social and political propaganda'.[49] Ebenezer Goold, the national secretary, along with L. Clayton Ridge and James Branch, MP, respectively secretary and president of the London federation, argued strongly that F.B. Meyer should become national president. This was what happened and Blackham continued to give loyal but less prominent service to the movement as an honorary vice president.

Probably Blackham's fears for the future direction of the PSA movement were justified. Despite the presence of prominent evangelicals in the leadership, the

---

[46] See the Editorial in the first issue of *The PSA Magazine* 1, 1 December 1891, p. 4.
[47] *PSA Leader*, April 1904, p. 57.
[48] *PSA Leader*, October 1905, pp. 145-49, 153-57.
[49] *Christian World*, 8 February 1906, p. 11, and 15 February, p. 4.

Brotherhood became more liberal in its theology. The 'Fundamental principles' might still proclaim the purpose to 'win men for Jesus Christ' but his divine kingship was beginning to take a less important place in the ambitions of many societies in preference for building the kingdom of God on earth. Although Brotherhood had its own official journal, a successor to the *PSA Leader*, the *Official Year Book 1911– 1912*, stated that *Christian Commonwealth*, R.J. Campbell's 'New Theology' weekly that proclaimed itself as the organ of the 'World Wide Progressive Movement in Religion and Social Ethics', was also 'the recognized weekly medium of the PSA Brotherhood Movement'.[50] Blackham, who died in 1923, must have thought his fears were realised when Silvester Horne, in his presidential address in 1913, called the Brotherhood Movement 'A New Protestantism'. 'It is a return to what is primitive and fundamental. It is an impressive challenge to all those complexities of doctrine and ritual that have obscured the divine ends for which Christianity exists, and would have destroyed the essential power of Christianity itself were it not indestructible'.[51]

Brotherhood and Politics

The PSA and Brotherhood consistently declared that it was 'non sectarian and knows no party politics'. This was generally so, although a profound hostility to the drink trade and gambling, the vices that clearly brought ruin to many families, meant that those were political issues always on the PSA agenda.[52] As an organisation catering predominantly for working class men the PSA had an interest in those issues espoused by progressive radical Liberals and socialists: the minimum wage, working conditions, industrial diseases, housing, old age pensions, and the impact of war and imperialism.[53] Will Crooks, the labour leader and Liberal-Labour MP, was associated with an East London PSA organised by the Poplar Labour League.[54] Many PSAs campaigned at the local level and inevitably this was political activity even if it did not involve open support for one political party or another. For example, PSA members were exhorted to participate in the municipal elections in County Durham in 1907, and seven years later Jeffs and Evans indicated how Brotherhood members might get elected to Boards of Guardians, to education

---

[50] *Brotherhood Year Book 1911–12* (London: Brotherhood Publishing House, 1911), p. 233.

[51] C. Silvester Horne, *The Brotherhood Movement: A New Protestantism* (London: Brotherhood Publishing House, 1913).

[52] Temperance or abstinence was always a contentious issue. Many Free Church people advocated the latter, e.g., at Meyer's Christ Church, Lambeth, the PSA had a 'Teetotal Corner' and a 'Consecration Corner', Fullerton, *Meyer*, p. 111. *Fifty Doctors Against Alcohol: A Call to National Defence* (London: Brotherhood Publishing House, 1912), fifty addresses given to the Brotherhoods and PSAs in Birmingham, 23 July 1911.

[53] Francis Herbert Stead, Congregational minister who led the Brotherhood group at the Browning Centre in London's Walworth Road, helped lead the campaign for old age pensions; F.H. Stead, *How Old Age Pensions Began to Be* (London: Methuen, 1909).

[54] George Haw (ed.), *Christianity and the Working Class* (London: Macmillan, 1906).

committees, and to local authorities.[55] William Ward, president in 1909, firmly stated that the franchise was in the hands of the working classes and it was important to 'get men to look upon the use of their vote as a religious act'.[56] Brotherhood was not 'party political' but, as Smith argues, it 'provided a kind of halfway house between religion and politics'. In the Hyde area of Manchester, and elsewhere, its ward organisation made it a useful tool for Labour electoral agents.[57] In many areas the PSA leaned towards the Independent Labour Party or the Labour Party, which inevitably created problems with those members who were Liberals. Silvester Horne, who was elected as Liberal MP for Ipswich in 1910, ran a successful 'political' PSA at Whitefield's Chapel, one aim being to counter Keir Hardie's attempts to 'sour the workmen'.[58] When Arthur Henderson, the deputy leader of the Labour Party and an active Brotherhood member, became president in 1914, his critics feared that he was trying to link together the two bodies.

Goold, writing in 1904, stated that the introduction into London PSA meetings of 'discussions on social and political problems ... tended to wrangling rather than to brotherliness, and the meetings came to grief'.[59] Some PSAs were certainly political and active in promoting Christian Socialism, for example the London PSA classes in Canning Town and in Hackney which had close connections with Wallace's Brotherhood church.[60] The Rev. M. Duffill, of Whitefield's Tabernacle, Leonard Street, who became honorary secretary of the PSA London federation, actively supported Wallace's Brotherhood church, speaking at its opening in Southgate in December 1892.[61] At the Rye Hill Baptist Church, Newcastle-upon-Tyne, the Rev. Walter Walsh ran 'a church for the people' with a 'People's Open Platform' on which spoke the socialists Ben Tillett and Thomas Mann, and the Liberal-Labour MP Sam Woods.[62]

Meyer at Christ Church, Lambeth, said that at Brotherhood meetings 'I never talked politics or economics, but always Jesus Christ, and there were conversions by the score'.[63] However, in his national presidential address at Liverpool in September 1907, he urged social and political activism and declared that 'Socialism is the

---

[55] Jeffs and Evans, *Social Worker's Armoury*, p. 4.

[56] Ward, *Brotherhood and Democracy*, pp. 163-64.

[57] Smith, *Religion and Labour*, p. 69. See further K.D. Brown, 'Non-conformity and the British Labour Movement: A Case Study', *Journal of Social History* 8 (Winter, 1975), pp. 113-20.

[58] W.B. Selbie (ed.), *Charles Silvester Horne* (London: Hodder & Stoughton, 1920), p. 191.

[59] E. Goold, in Mudie-Smith, *Religious Life of London*, p. 321.

[60] *Brotherhood*, March 1893, p. 29, referring to a recent 'Conference' with open discussion on 'social questions' held on Sunday afternoons in the Brotherhood churches at Southgate, West Croydon, and Walthamstow.

[61] *Brotherhood*, January 1893, p. 9.

[62] *Plain Talk* [Bradford] 20, November 1893, p. 308

[63] Fullerton, *Meyer*, p. 111.

expression of the human quest for Brotherhood'.[64] Later in the year, at the Mechanics Hall, Bradford, he spoke on 'Socialism of the best sort', telling the audience that the churches had failed because they had 'allied themselves with the classes rather than the masses'.[65] This did not in itself associate the Brotherhood Movement with the political left but inevitably ideas like this, aired by a variety of speakers at PSA meetings throughout the country, helped stimulate sympathy if not support for the parties of the left. John Clifford, who identified with Christian socialism, invited Labour leaders to address PSA meetings at Westbourne Park, while the *PSA Leader* made great moment of Lloyd George speaking there in early 1907.[66] Leading Labour and trade union leaders gave their support to the PSA and Brotherhood, the most notable after Arthur Henderson being Will Crooks and Keir Hardie. In mid-1910 Hardie was the headline speaker for a Brotherhood crusade to Northern France and Belgium.[67]

PSA sensitivity on certain political issues became more pronounced after the Tory victory at the general election in early autumn 1900, an administration that the *PSA Leader* described as 'the worst government in living memory'.[68] Many PSA members opposed the terms of the 1902 Education Act and also the Licensing Act of 1904.[69] In conflicts between labour and employers it was not surprising that PSA societies tended to give vocal if not active support for men against masters. Various PSA societies, and certainly the *PSA Leader*, raised condemnatory voices of Chinese labour in South Africa, the Congo atrocities, and certain imperial issues. The South African War, 1899–1902, divided Liberals, Nonconformists, the working classes and also PSA members. Brotherhood implied an inherent hostility to warfare and the production of weapons, rhetoric easy to promote when directed against imperial campaigns, the Russo–Japanese conflict, or the Balkan wars, but less easy to maintain when it threatened British jobs or ran counter to popular notions of patriotism and national security.

The Great War and After

The idea that international Brotherhood, and socialist fraternity, could prevent war was common rhetoric as the arms race intensified. In 1912–13 there was much talk of the Brotherhood Movement extending from France and Belgium into Germany.

---

[64] *PSA and Brotherhood Journal*, October 1907, pp. 220-23.
[65] *PSA and Brotherhood Journal*, December 1907, pp. 309-10.
[66] *PSA Leader*, January 1907, p. 10.
[67] *PSA Leader*, June 1901, pp. 165-67.
[68] *PSA Leader*, June 1903, p. 88. 'Never perhaps, in the history ... since Parliament was free ... has there been such a swift and easy descent to the bad old times of privilege, priestly tyranny, and the re-forging of fetters, as these early years of the new century are witnessing. Trade unions and working people can get no relief from this decrepit Government that lives only to bestow doles on landlords and parsons, and to hand over the education of children to the priests.'
[69] *PSA Leader*, July 1903, pp. 100-101.

When war broke out in August 1914 the Brotherhood response was predictable. 'This is not a people's war', stated the national journal. '**Our duty**, – We must show to the German nation that, while we are battling against Kaiserism and all that it represents, we want to be as brothers to those of German nationality …'[70] Opposition to the conflict steadily changed as once passive sentiments became resigned to combating German warmongering,[71] and Harry Jeffs warned speakers at society meetings 'to be guarded and not purport to speak on behalf of the whole Brotherhood Movement about war and peace'.[72] Unrealistic was the plaintive voice in 1915 in the pages of the *Brotherhood Journal* urging that a deputation be sent to explain to the Kaiser the spirit of the Brotherhood movement! A major role of the Movement during the war was providing relief for refugees in France, Belgium, and Serbia. The war dealt a serious blow to the idea of brotherly accord. Many Brotherhood members died in action, societies shrank in number, classes closed, and by 1920 the Movement had declined to 100,000 members.

However, despite the war the spirit of internationalism resurfaced after 1918. The Brotherhood supported the nascent League of Nations and organised a World Brotherhood Federation and an international gathering at the City Temple in September 1919.[73] In the unstable economic conditions of the 1920s the Brotherhood sought to co-operate with government, employers and unions in finding industrial peace. Unemployment was a major concern; there was co-operation with the National Unemployed Workers Committee in 1924, and three years later the Movement proposed a National Service Corps under the Ministry of Labour. The Mond-Turner meetings between the Trade Union Congress and employers to discuss industrial 'rationalisation' in 1928–29 owed something to Brotherhood input. Brotherhood ideas can be traced not only in the renamed monthly journal, *Brotherhood Outlook*, but also in the annual Clifford Lectures, the first being given by John Clifford in 1920, and delivered by prominent figures in political and social life.[74] The Sisterhood, reorganised in 1918, was active in social welfare schemes for young women. Adult education was another interest although in the view of Basil Yeaxlee, who had given a Clifford lecture, most PSAs had programmes that were 'popular', the equivalent of 'the American Sunday newspaper'.[75] In the 1920s–30s prominent politicians and church people were closely associated with Brotherhood –

---

[70] *Brotherhood Journal*, September 1914, pp. 273-74.

[71] *Brotherhood Journal*, April 1915, pp. 106-108. Blackham opposed the war, see *Brotherhood Journal*, May 1915, p. 146.

[72] *Brotherhood Journal*, June 1915, p. 107

[73] Mathews, *World Brotherhood*. The first meeting of the Assembly of the League of Nations was reported in *The Times* 13 November 1920, p. 13, under the headline 'The Ideal of the League. Universal Brotherhood'.

[74] Clifford's lecture was 'The Gospel of World Brotherhood according to Jesus'. Other lecturers included Stanley Baldwin, Josiah Stamp, A.V. Alexander, Isaac Foot, J.Y. Simpson, and Dick Sheppard.

[75] Basil Yeaxlee, *Spiritual Values in Adult Education*. Volume 2 (London: Oxford University Press, 1925), p. 80.

Viscount Snowden, Isaac Foot, Margaret Bondfield, Dick Shepherd, Maude Royden, Hugh Redwood, Arthur Henderson, Josiah Stamp, Dick Shepppard, Charles Raven, and G. Campbell Morgan. The social and international issues that occupied Brotherhood were similar to those of earlier decades but given greater urgency by the Depression and growing militarism in Europe and Asia.

Who are 'Brothers'?: Colour and Race

In an age when African and black peoples were popularly viewed as exotic, the Brotherhood stands out as a body that welcomed them into membership, provided hospitality and also a public platform. Prominent leaders of PSA/Brotherhood, such as Meyer, opposed racial discrimination,[76] and the very idea of 'brotherhood' that brought together men of different social classes also implied that all men, irrespective of origin or colour, were to be regarded as fellows. This seems to have applied in Britain but not in the colonies and South Africa where Brotherhood branches conformed to local racist practice. In Britain an educated black person, whether from Jamaica or Africa, was often welcomed to a church or Christian meeting because they were perceived to represent an example of the transforming power of the gospel. Three prominent black men from the Caribbean, J.S. Celestine Edwards, the Rev. H. Mason Joseph, and Henry Sylvester Williams, were active in or connected to the SRBM and its successor the League of Universal Brotherhood, and their presence attracted other black people.

Black speakers addressed PSA meetings, a class was started in Freetown, Sierra Leone, in the early 1890s, and the Rev. Samuel Coker, on his return home to Lagos, started a Brotherhood meeting.[77] Members of both the black and 'Coloured' South African deputations to London in 1909, to protest to the Imperial Government at the exclusion of non-Europeans from equal terms in the new Union constitution, attended the Brotherhood national conference at Cardiff in September that year.[78] The following month the *Brotherhood Journal* stated that 'we stand for the principle of universal brotherhood. To us a man with a black skin is as much a brother as a

---

[76] See F.B. Meyer, *A Winter in South Africa* (London: National Council of Evangelical Free Churches, 1908).

[77] *Sierra Leone Times* 5 March 1892; *PSA and Brotherhood Journal*, May 1909, p. 133, and August 1909, p. 234.

[78] *PSA and Brotherhood Journal*, October 1909, pp. 338-39. The African and Coloured deputations were led by W.P. Schreiner, and they were joined in London by other unofficial black spokesmen. Some were Congregationalists and they had close contact with the London Missionary Society, the Aborigines' Protection Society, and the active support of W.T. Stead, editor of *Review of Reviews*, Keir Hardie, and other leading members of the Labour and Liberal parties. The Cardiff conference took place 18–22 September; the deputation sailed for Cape Town on 21 September. See André Odendaal, *Vukani Bantu: The Beginnings of Black Protest Politics in South Africa to 1912* (Cape Town: David Philip, 1984), ch. 9.

man with a white skin.'[79] D.D.T. Jabavu, a black South African, and later a distinguished educationalist, was the principal violinist in the Hampstead Brotherhood orchestra in north London.[80] As Harry Jeffs wrote, 'the Brotherhood Gospel sweeps away the frontier between race and race. In the family of one Father there is no longer "stranger and foreigner", for all are brothers.'[81]

Robert Hill, the authority on Marcus Garvey, the Jamaican founder of the Universal Negro Improvement Association (UNIA), suggests that the Brotherhood Movement helped to shape what became known as 'Garveyism'. Garvey was in Britain in 1913–14, and Hill asks the question, 'If the doctrine known as "Garveyism" was predicated upon the principles of brotherhood and confraternity, where did it originate?' He then argues that 'Garvey discovered the power inherent in the idea of the brotherhood in Britain during the winter of 1913–14', and that 'the roots of the "strange" admixture of universalism and nationalism in Garvey's evolving racial philosophy' was 'an ideological debt owed … to … the Brotherhood movement in the twilight of Edwardian England'.[82] However, Hill's claim, which is not altogether new, is a tenuous supposition, based on a number of statements made by Garvey about his experience in Britain and on the similarity of language and terminology adopted by the UNIA to that of the Brotherhood Movement. What is lacking is firm evidence that Garvey had contact with any of the several strands of Brotherhood while he was in Britain. It does seem likely that he met Charles Garnett, the secretary of the League of Universal Brotherhood, which might go some way in explaining how Garnett came to chair two of Garvey's meetings in London in 1928. Additionally it also needs to be stressed that the idea of 'brotherhood' was a constant and common currency among groups as diverse as Muslims, Hindus, Theosophists, trade unionists, socialists, anarchists, freethinkers, as well as Christians.

In 1914 a further black deputation from the newly formed South African Native National Congress (SANNC), the future African National Congress, arrived in London to protest at the African Land Act. The principal spokesman was Sol Plaatje. The five men, all Christians (three of whom had been in London in 1909), were mission educated, fluent and articulate in English, and previously involved with improvement societies, backgrounds that brought them close to the ideas and ideals of the Brotherhood Movement. Thus they were warmly welcomed when they visited the London offices of the Brotherhood at 37 Norfolk Street, their group photograph being published in the August issue of the *Journal* along with an article by Sol

---

[79] *PSA and Brotherhood Journal*, October 1909, p. 338. Earlier (September 1909, p. 278) the *Journal* reported Ladipo Oluwolu, a medical student from Nigeria, had spoken at the Hoylake PSA in 1909, 'and that that Society, anyhow, makes no distinction of creed or colour'.

[80] *APO* (Cape Town), November 1913.

[81] Harry Jeffs, 'The Brotherhood Movement as a missionary force', *Universal Brotherhood*, January 1912.

[82] Robert A. Hill, '"Comradeship of the More Advanced Races": Marcus Garvey and the Brotherhood Movement in Britain, 1913–14', *Small Axe* 40 (March, 2013), pp. 50-70, quotations from pp. 62 and 70.

Plaatje, 'An Appeal to the British Brotherhood: Shall injustice be sanctioned under the British flag?'[83] The *Brotherhood Journal* denounced the racist policies of the new Union of South Africa and urged London to intervene. This ultimately fruitless message was promoted by Plaatje, and the other members of the deputation, at various Brotherhood meetings up and down the country.[84] Plaatje said that he knew that he felt at home in a Brotherhood meeting when he attended one that was chaired by an African American. The deputation returned home empty handed. Plaatje remained in Britain, for some of the time a guest in the London home of William Cross, a member of the Southall Brotherhood.[85]

On his return to South Africa in 1917 Plaatje devoted more of his time to Brotherhood work than to the SANNC. He established a branch in Kimberley, 'The Diamond Fields Men's Own Brotherhood', using as a meeting hall an old tram shed given by De Beers.[86] Brotherhood branches had been formed in South Africa, at Pietermaritzburg, Durban, and elsewhere, before Union in 1910, but these were White groups. Plaatje's branches referred to themselves as 'native' or 'Bantu'. Back again in Britain with an African deputation in 1919–20, Plaatje spoke at Brotherhood meetings, as did one of his colleagues, Richard Selope-Thema.[87] He also addressed the International Brotherhood Congress in London in September 1919, and, as an elected member of the International Federation, helping to draft the new constitution the 'Brotherhood Challenge', a document calling upon nations and peoples to unite to construct a post-war world of peace and amity.[88]

One outcome of Plaatje's visit was the formation in June 1920 of a British based South African Bantu Brotherhoods Committee, 'to help to develop Brotherhood work among the South African natives by helping to erect, furnish and maintain meeting halls in some South African centres where regular Brotherhood and Sisterhood work could be conducted'.[89] In 1920 Plaatje travelled to Canada

---

[83] *PSA and Brotherhood Journal*, August 1914, p. 225, and November 1914, pp. 224-27.

[84] Plaatje spoke at over 150 meetings mainly in 1914–15. For a chapter on 'The Brotherhood', and the places where the South Africans spoke, see Sol T. Plaatje, *Native Life in South Africa* (London: P.S. King, 1916), ch. 18.

[85] For Plaatje, and also William Cross, see Brian Willan, *Sol T. Plaatje: South African Nationalist* (London: James Currey, 1984).

[86] Brian Willan, 'Sol Plaatje, De Beers and an Old Tram Shed: Class Relations and Social Control on a South African Town, 1918–19', *Journal of Southern African Studies* 4 (1978), pp. 195-215. Willan, *Plaatje*, pp. 218-21.

[87] See Richard Selope-Thema, 'From Cattle Herding to Editor's Chair', unpublished biographical sketch, MS, School of Oriental and African Studies Library, London.

[88] Willan, *Plaatje*, pp. 248-49. For Plaatje's address to the Congress, see Mathews, *World Brotherhood*, pp. 90-95. Plaatje was there with the Cape Union delegation along with the Rev. H.R. Ngcayiya and Mdani Xaba, then a student at Edinburgh.

[89] Historical Papers Research Archive, Johannesburg. A.B. Xuma papers. AD843 S38.2, 'South African Bantu Brotherhoods Committee' appeal notice, signed by the secretary Miss Irma Colenso of the well-known pro-Zulu family. The Committee was chaired by Sir Richard Winfrey, MP, the Vice-Chairman being W.B. Dixon, President of the Bedfordshire Brotherhood Federation, while Plaatje's friend William Cross, from the Southall

receiving financial help and hospitality from local Brotherhood branches. Back in South Africa the branches that he had helped to create languished and declined as a consequence of weak finances, poor management, and white hostility.[90]

In the inter-war years the Brotherhood Movement continued to protest at instances of colonial and racial oppression. Local branches received black speakers, for example Dr Harold Moody, founder of the League of Coloured Peoples, who collaborated with J.G. Beaumont of the Epsom branch, in organising summer outings to the countryside for London's poor black children.[91] Moody, and the Indian Christian Shoran A. Singha, later to be Brotherhood president in the early 1950s, addressed the annual conference in Nottingham in June 1933.[92] John A. Barbour-James, a retired civil servant, originally from British Guiana, and a member of the Acton Brotherhood for twenty-five years, introduced an annual Africa Sunday 'when the platform is occupied by brethren from different parts of Africa'.[93] The Malvern Link Brotherhood also had a Black member.[94]

And Further ...?

Clearly what is needed is a detailed study of the PSA and Brotherhood Movement during the period from 1875 to the 1930s. This would examine and analyse the Movement's influence nationally and regionally with comparative studies of urban and rural areas. A major question to be addressed is what impact did PSA/Brotherhood have on the religious life of Britain? It seems evident that it did contribute to evangelicalism in late nineteenth-century Britain, but to what extent and how effectively. The changing focus and purpose of the Movement, that move away from Blackham's evangelical vision, raised questions at the time as to whether Brotherhood classes should be attached to a church, as many Wesleyans thought, or autonomous bodies not associated with denominationalism. Further, were classes to be sectarian or non-sectarian, and were they to be democratic institutions, as Blackham intended, or subject to dominance by leaders who saw them as vehicles for socialism or a moral theism? Another question is how Brotherhood meshed and co-operated with other Nonconformist 'outreach' organisations, for example, the uniformed Salvation Army and the Boys' Brigade, and with Christian Endeavour, another large organisation which has been neglected by historians. The Brotherhood

---

Brotherhood, served as treasurer. Plaatje and his wife were described as 'Missioners in South Africa'.

[90] Willan, *Plaatje*, pp. 294-95. The African American Southern Syncopated Orchestra, which included a youthful Sidney Bechet, gave a concert at the Kingsway Hall, London, to raise funds for Plaatje's Brotherhood work; *Brotherhood Outlook*, September 1920, p. 157, and October 1920, p. 175.

[91] See *The Keys* [journal of The League of Coloured Peoples] 1, 2 (October 1933), pp. 24-25.

[92] *Brotherhood Outlook*, July 1933, p. 119.

[93] *Brotherhood Outlook*, May 1933, p. 78.

[94] *Brotherhood Outlook*, December 1933, p. 234, central photograph.

Movement offers a rich field of study and research with an abundant and varied range of sources.

CHAPTER 17

Taking Leave of Gladstone

John Wolffe

Alongside his seminal contributions to the historiography of evangelicalism, David Bebbington has throughout his career been fascinated by the life and thought of William Ewart Gladstone, as a leading politician, but above all as an intellectual and Christian thinker. In an early article Bebbington clearly demonstrated the natural links between Gladstone studies and his other interests in evangelical Nonconformity.[1] In subsequent decades he has published a 'religious biography' of Gladstone, co-edited a collection of essays to mark the centenary of the statesman's death, and written a detailed monograph tracing the development of his ideas from the 1830s to the 1890s.[2] Gladstone's religion had received some literary attention in the immediate aftermath of his death,[3] but this lapsed after the First World War, and Bebbington's work has made a major contribution to a revival of interest in the subject, alongside the work of scholars such as Eugenio Biagini, Perry Butler, Boyd Hilton, Peter Jagger, Colin Matthew, and Jonathan Parry.[4]

Bebbington and others have traced Gladstone's religious development from his early evangelicalism, through the strong sympathy with the Oxford Movement that coincided with his early adulthood, to the more liberal Anglo-Catholicism that characterised his maturity and old age. His evangelical affinities remained, however, as was apparent in his enduring appeal to Nonconformists, for religious as well as political reasons, and while his *Impregnable Rock of Holy Scripture* (1890) was by no means fundamentalist, it sought to rebut radical criticism. As Bebbington has shown, Gladstone's central literary preoccupation in his closing years, after his final

---

[1] D. Bebbington, 'Gladstone and the Nonconformists: A Religious Affinity in Politics', in D. Baker (ed.), *Church, Society and Politics* (Studies in Church History, 12; Oxford: Basil Blackwell, 1975), pp. 369-82.

[2] David W. Bebbington, *William Ewart Gladstone: Faith and Politics in Victorian Britain* (Grand Rapids, MI: Eerdmans, 1993); and David Bebbington and Roger Swift (eds), *Gladstone Centenary Essays* (Liverpool: Liverpool University Press, 2000); David Bebbington, *The Mind of Gladstone: Religion Home and Politics* (Oxford: Oxford University Press, 2004).

[3] George W.E. Russell, *Mr Gladstone's Religious Development* (London: Rivingtons, 1899); D.C. Lathbury, *Correspondence on Church and Religion of William Ewart Gladstone* (2 vols; London: John Murray, 1910).

[4] For a bibliography, see Bebbington, *Mind of Gladstone*, pp. 319-22.

retirement from the premiership in 1894, was the defence of traditional Christian orthodoxy.[5]

Against that background, this chapter will examine reactions to Gladstone's final illness and death, aged eighty-eight, from cancer and heart failure, at his home, Hawarden Castle in North Wales, on Ascension Day, 19 May 1898. He had been seriously ill for several months, and his terminal condition had become public knowledge in late March. Hence his personal struggle was conducted very much in the public eye, and seen by many, not least the dying man himself, as a final test of the integrity and power of his Christian witness.

Although Gladstone lived almost to the close of the Victorian age, expectations of his deathbed were still shaped by an earlier ideal of the 'good death', inspired by evangelicalism, in which a patient surrounded by those close to them was able to make a final decisive profession of faith in Christ, thus inspiring the onlookers with confidence in the eternal salvation of the deceased and with hopes of heavenly reunion. Needless to say, few patients were in practice sufficiently strong or lucid at the last to deliver fully on these expectations. Other high-profile deaths in the same period manifested diverse realities. Two strongly contrasting cases, those of the Duke of Clarence in 1892 and of David Livingstone in 1874, may be taken to exemplify two influential models, the 'bad death' and the 'heroic death'. Prince Albert Victor, Duke of Clarence and Avondale, elder son of the Prince of Wales, died from influenza at Sandringham in Norfolk on 14 January 1892, aged only twenty-eight. Not only the Prince's age but his circumstances induced an acute sense of unfulfilled promise: he had recently become engaged to Princess Mary of Teck, and had he lived he would in due course have succeeded to the throne. Moreover, his death had occurred in delirium after a relatively short illness. Sir Edward Hamilton, Gladstone's private secretary, who was later to take charge of the funeral arrangements for his former employer, wrote of Clarence's death, 'It really is too sad. Indeed if all the fates had been set to devise the saddest of occurrences, they could scarcely have selected an event more tragic or more calculated to arouse universal gloom.'[6]

The missionary and explorer David Livingstone died in a hut at Ilala in Central Africa on 30 April 1873 having succumbed to exhaustion, piles and dysentery in the midst of his final obsessive endeavour to find the source of the Nile. His body was found kneeling by his bed, as if in prayer, and was brought back to England for burial through the devotion of his African followers. At one level Livingstone's death could appear a 'bad' one: it was relatively untimely – he was only sixty – with his life's work seemingly unfulfilled, and he died in lonely and uncomfortable conditions. However the image it assumed was rather a heroic one. Livingstone's

---

[5] Bebbington, *Mind of Gladstone*, pp. 216-56.

[6] British Library, Additional Manuscript [hereafter BL Add MSS] 48657 (Sir Edward Hamilton's Diary), f. 29, 14 January 1892, quoted by John Wolffe, *Great Deaths: Grieving, Religion and Nationhood in Victorian and Edwardian Britain* (The British Academy Postdoctoral Fellowship Monographs; Oxford University Press, Oxford, 2000), p. 208.

readiness not only to spend his life in the perceived service of Africa, but to accept a death in circumstances far removed from those of the conventional 'good death', appeared an act of ultimate self sacrifice.[7] A similar point might be made about General Gordon's at Khartoum in January 1885, but here the issue was complicated by the lack of a body, or hard information about the manner of Gordon's death when the city fell to the forces of the Mahdi.[8]

Gladstone's great rival Benjamin Disraeli died in London aged seventy-six on 19 April 1881. Disraeli's situation differed from Gladstone's in that as he was a decade younger and as his underlying condition, bronchitis, was not obviously terminal, hopes of recovery remained until a late stage in his illness. He was also a widower, dying in a recently rented London house, without family around him, and without the strong and explicit Christian ethos that characterised Gladstone's life and deathbed. These factors tended to make his death appear more of a shock and the process of dying less serene.[9]

Gladstone himself was, of course, no stranger to death, and had indeed composed lengthy memoranda relating to the four closest family bereavements that he had experienced, the deaths of his mother in 1835, his father in 1851, and of the two children who predeceased him, his daughter Jessy, aged four, in 1850 and his son William Henry in 1890. The three earlier memoranda, as analysed by Pat Jalland, show Gladstone's hopes for ideal 'good' deaths brought into tension with messy and sometimes distressing realities. The results were sometimes mildly comical, as when the family prematurely gathered round Anne Gladstone's bed were told by the sick, but not yet dying patient, 'You all give me the idea that this is my last hour, but I have no such notion …'[10] Sometimes though the disjunction added to the pain of bereavement, as even Gladstone's robust Christian faith struggled to make sense of the acute suffering young Jessy experienced as she was dying from meningitis.[11]

By the time William Henry Gladstone died in 1890 following an operation to investigate a brain tumour, his father's response to death had mellowed. Even though the circumstances once again failed to conform to the ideal of the good death, insofar as it occurred as an unforeseen result of surgery, without any opportunities for farewells or professions of faith, it was still seen as providential:

> the Doctors saw that a stage had been reached, on the verge of other stages: of physical agony, loss of speech etc I believe that we were mercifully led on to the interception of these evils and that he was spared the at least temporary and seeming loss of the most precious gifts, without which human nature sinks below itself.

---

[7] Wolffe, *Great Deaths*, pp. 138-45.

[8] Wolffe, *Great Deaths*, p. 146.

[9] Wolffe, *Great Deaths,* pp. 157-58; Robert Blake, *Disraeli* (London: Methuen, 1969), pp. 746-49.

[10] Pat Jalland, *Death in the Victorian Family* (Oxford: Oxford University Press, 1996), p. 166.

[11] Jalland, *Death in the Victorian Family*, pp. 167-8.

Gladstone went on to praise his son's 'free acceptance of the Divine Will' and readiness to 'answer to the loving discipline which his Father in Heaven had ordained for him'. He concluded by quoting Psalm 24 and affirmed the hope of resurrection in the words of Romans 6.8 and the final stanza of J.H. Newman's 'Lead Kindly Light': 'And with the morn those angel faces smile/Which we have loved long since and lost a while.'[12] On other hand, while Gladstone could see the hand of God in William's relatively painless death, he continued to believe that pain could have positive moral and spiritual consequences. In 1894 he wrote, defending the doctrine of atonement against the criticisms of the freethinker Annie Besant,

> Be it remembered that pain, though it is not lawfully to be inflicted, except for wrong done, is not in itself essentially evil. It has been freely borne, again and again, by good men for the sake of bad men, and they have borne it sometimes with benefit to the bad men, always with benefit to themselves. Pain indicates, it may be, a relation to evil; but it is so far from being absolutely an evil, that it may be relatively and conditionally a good, as being the instrumental cause of good.[13]

Such thoughts, one can infer, were very much in his mind some three years later as he faced his own painful terminal illness.

Gladstone's approach to death may be considered in three phases. First there was a period of withdrawal from life, from early 1894 to late 1897. He had remained in remarkably good health and vigour well into his eighties, forming his last government at the age of eighty-two, and only resigning, aged eighty-four, when it became clear that deteriorating sight and hearing were reducing his fitness for office.[14] During the next two years, however, it seemed that a consciousness of mortality was leading him to seek a closure in his public and personal life. He retired from Parliament at the general election of 1895, made his final will in late 1896, and on his eighty-seventh birthday on 29 December that year wrote the last entry in the diary he had kept on a daily basis since he started it as a schoolboy more than seventy years before. He reflected on his long life, and noted that his health was still fairly good, and that he was blessed with a thriving family life. Still he continued, significantly, 'old age is appointed for the gradual loosening and succeeding snapping of the bonds'.[15] He began to appear ready for death. In the early autumn of 1897 when an enthusiastic friend said to him 'you'll live ten years to come', he commented 'I do trust that God in his mercy will spare me that'.[16]

---

[12] BL Add MS 46269, ff. 150-51. For a rather different reading of this document, see Jalland, *Death in the Victorian Family*, p. 184.

[13] W.E. Gladstone, 'True and False Conceptions of the Atonement', *The Nineteenth Century* 211 (September, 1894), p. 322.

[14] John Morley, *The Life of William Ewart Gladstone* (2 vols; London: Edward Lloyd, 1908), II, pp. 559-63.

[15] Quoted by Morley, *Gladstone*, II, p. 572.

[16] Morley, *Gladstone*, II, p. 574.

Second, there was a phase of struggle and anguish, from November 1897 to March 1898. Chronic nasal congestion and neuralgia on the side of his face were the first – as yet undiagnosed – symptoms of cancer, but the rapid deterioration of his sight to the point where he could no longer read was particularly distressing for a man who had always derived enormous pleasure from his books and scholarship. There were also attacks of breathlessness, indicating that his heart was weakening. He became depressed. He spent part of the winter in Cannes in the south of France, but the warmer climate did not have any beneficial effect and the facial pain continued. Helen Gladstone, who accompanied her parents to Cannes, wrote anxiously to her sister recording his intermittent symptoms and his consequent mood swings.[17] He returned in England in February concerned that he was becoming a burden to his family and expressing 'a fervent wish that he might go to sleep and not wake again'.[18] On 24 February, with his doctors still insisting that he was suffering only from chronic catarrh, he confided in his daughter Mary Drew, who had been urging him to try to return to his normal occupations. She recalled, that he

> related the history of the last 3 months, the terrible battle with pain, and his utter collapse and defeat. It seemed impossible while listening to this heart rending story, to believe that the Doctors would be right. I was only too thankful to believe it then, and <u>alas</u> I hardened my heart, and withheld from him that passion of sympathy with which it was bursting.

His anguish was heightened by concern for his aged wife, agreeing that she would find life very difficult without him, and adding that 'his prayer now would be that they might die together'.[19]

Gladstone went to Bournemouth in late February and stayed there for much of March 1898, hoping for benefits from its relatively balmy climate, which was a transitional one between the south of France and his home at Hawarden. His facial pain, however, increased further. Although already being given morphine, his nights were very disturbed, but he remained capable of occasional 'brilliant flashes of talk'. Music appeared to soothe him: Mary Drew would play the piano softly to him for hours at a time and professional musicians also called to play for him.[20] On 13 March his own doctor noticed a swelling above the gum 'which caused the gravest apprehensions', and called in a leading cancer specialist, Sir Thomas Smith. Smith saw the patient on 18 March and gave a terminal diagnosis, pronouncing the tumour

---

[17] BL. Add MSS 46,231, ff. 153-61, Helen Gladstone to Mary Gladstone Drew, 22 December 1897, 30 January 1898.

[18] Colin Matthew, 'Gladstone's Death and Funeral', *The Historian* 57 (Spring, 1998), p. 20; Dudley W.R. Bahlman, *The Diary of Sir Edward Walter Hamilton 1885–1906* (Hull: University of Hull Press, 1993), p. 351 (19 February 1898); BL Add MSS 46,521 Helen Gladstone to Mary Drew 30 January 1898.

[19] BL Add MSS 46269, Mary Drew's record of Gladstone's illness, ff. 15-16, 24 February.

[20] BL Add MSS 46269, ff. 16-18, 24 February, 6 March, newspaper cutting.

malignant and judging that Gladstone only had a few weeks to live. Gladstone himself was clearly informed of the diagnosis which 'he received with perfect serenity, and with an unutterable sense of relief, and thankfulness'.[21]

Third, there was a final phase of resignation, from the giving of the terminal diagnosis on 18 March 1898 to Gladstone's death exactly two months later. Central to his state of mind, and to that of all around him, with the exception of his wife, was the calm acceptance that there was no prospect of recovery and that treatment would only be palliative. An operation was discussed, but apparently only in the hope that it might relieve the pain, rather than provide a cure. However, despite Gladstone's age his general physical condition appeared remarkably resilient, and his decline in strength was a very gradual one. The cancer did not prove particularly aggressive, and he accordingly lived somewhat longer than Smith originally anticipated. However, it still sapped his strength. The heavy use of morphine in the last two months hastened this process. Symptoms of heart failure increased, and at the end at least, nitro-glycerine was used to relieve them. In the event the immediate cause of death was to be not the cancer but circulatory collapse.[22] Once hope of recovery was abandoned there was a change in management of the patient. Whereas since the autumn Gladstone had been kept in mild locations, first Cannes and then Bournemouth, on 22 March he travelled home to Hawarden in North Wales, where the spring was likely to be much cooller. Now that he was acknowledged to be dying, there was evidently felt to be no point in keeping him where the risk of chest infection might be reduced, and his known wish to die at home was regarded as paramount. At this date the idea of hospitalization would have been inconceivable for someone of Gladstone's wealth and social standing, although nurses were employed to ensure that the family were spared the practical burden of care. As Mary put it starkly, 'On Tuesday March 22nd, he came home to die.'[23] Moreover strong doses of morphine were now used to alleviate the pain, meaning that he became much more comfortable, albeit inevitably drowsy and disorientated.[24]

The situation was also made public. While the statement released through the Press Association was not explicit, it was clearly intended that people should read between the lines:

> Mr Gladstone's medical advisers have for some time felt anxious about the continuance of the neuralgic pains. Certain changes in the symptoms of late made a consultation with a surgeon necessary. It was decided that Mr Gladstone would not derive benefit from a further stay at Bournemouth, and he was advised to return to Hawarden.

---

[21] BL Add MSS 46269, f. 17, 13, 18 March.
[22] BL Add MSS 46269, f. 22, 23-29 March; f. 28, 30 April–May, f. 33, 17 May.
[23] BL Add MSS 46269, f. 17.
[24] BL Add MSS 46269, f. 22, 23–29 March. Mary Drew's notes regarding the use of morphine appears at variance with Matthew's statement that Gladstone 'refused to take many opiates'. It may well be though that, as with modern cancer patients, efforts were made to manage his medication so that he could enjoy periods of lucidity.

Journalists readily made their own conclusions explicit, as in a report, on 28 March, that 'It is no news, we fear, to say that Mr. Gladstone's illness must necessarily be fatal, and in a comparatively short time.'[25] Far from ignoring or denying such reports as the illness progressed, the family confirmed them: thus in a letter published in *The Times* on 29 April, Helen Gladstone wrote,

> I do not think there is anything to say about Mr. Gladstone's health beyond what is generally known – namely, that he is seriously ill, and that we cannot hope for his recovery; but that, the progress of his illness being very slow, he will probably remain with us for some time.[26]

Understandably Mrs Gladstone, to whom he had been married for fifty-eight years, was slower than others to accept the inevitable. When Sir Thomas Smith came to Hawarden for a further consultation on 24 April, he spent time with her and 'with the utmost tact and tenderness spoke in a way that made her gradually realize the state of things'.[27] As late as 9 May though, although she was reported to be gradually realizing the 'the hopelessness of his state', she was still trying to persuade herself 'that the end is far off'.[28] At the last though even she was reconciled to the situation, and on 17 May was reported to have been with him all day, 'entirely herself and brave while realizing all'.[29]

During this final phase the sense of closure and leave taking became stronger as the dying man's world became ever narrower. In her account of the illness, Mary Drew recorded his last attendance at church on 6 March, the last time he went into the garden, on 10 April, the last time he came downstairs for dinner with the family, on 18 April, and the last time he got out of bed, on 14 May.[30] Gladstone himself was consciously valedictory in his words to those who saw him off from Bournemouth station: 'God bless you and this place, and the land you love.'[31] Once he had settled back at Hawarden, there was a steady stream of visits from members of his extended family, friends and colleagues, which assumed the quality of ritual final farewells.[32] He was still capable of mustering great dignity and eloquence as in his dictated response to a message from his beloved Oxford:

> There is no expression of Christian sympathy that I value more than that of the ancient university of Oxford, the God-fearing and God-sustaining university of Oxford. I

---

[25] BL Add MSS 46269, ff. 17v-18, press cuttings.
[26] *The Times* 29 April 1898, p. 9.
[27] BL Add MSS 46269, f. 28, 24 April.
[28] Bahlman, *Diary of Sir Edward Hamilton*, p. 352, 9 May 1898.
[29] BL Add MSS 46269, f. 54, Memoir by Harry Drew (Gladstone's son-in-law).
[30] BL Add MSS 46269, ff. 16, 25, 26, 32.
[31] Morley, *Gladstone*, II, p. 575.
[32] Matthew, 'Gladstone's Death', p. 20; *The Times* 30 April 1898, p. 12, 7 May 1898, p. 11 and *passim*; BL Add MSS 46269, f. 52, Harry Drew Memoir, 29 April; Morley, *Gladstone*, II, p. 576.

served her, perhaps mistakenly, but to the best of my ability. My most earnest prayers are hers to the uttermost and the last.[33]

The openness of the family, and the great fame of the dying man, ensured that there was considerable public interest in his illness. It showed not the excitement and suspense that came from expectation of possible recovery (as had been the case with Disraeli's deathbed in 1881), but rather a fascination with the manner in which the great man was dying. A French newspaper, while deploring the general tendency of the press to pry into private life, wrote on 3 April that this case was an exception in which publicity was justified:

> There are lives that have unfolded magnificently in the bright light of day, for the welfare of humanity, for the accomplishment of progress, for the achievement in this world of an ideal of justice and liberty. Such lives must not be allowed to end in silence and indifference ... In this waiting for death there is an incomparable calm and serenity. It is the evening of a fine day. A whole people, indeed, the whole world, follows this last struggle with an intense sympathy.[34]

Daily bulletins were issued, even though for several weeks the slow progress of the illness meant that there was actually little to report. These were nevertheless followed with widespread interest: a young Jewish boy reported that he had 'looked in the paper every day to see how he was'.[35] A dying old man in Derby was continually asking his nurse for news of Gladstone.[36] Eventually, in mid-May, when Gladstone's condition became critical, the family decided to issue at least two bulletins a day.[37]

While the severe pain Gladstone had experienced in the early months of his illness was mitigated towards the end, particularly by the use of morphine, it still gave rise to considerable anguish, both for the patient himself and for his family and friends. Sir Edward Hamilton thought it 'too inexpressibly sad to think that so painful an end should be in store for that great man at so advanced an age'.[38] Throughout his illness Gladstone expressed the wish that he might die soon. In addition to the pain one can infer that there was considerable psychological anguish for a man who had remained very active into advanced old age, and who now felt unable to occupy himself. His wish for death and his expectation of it was apparent on 4 April when he believed his last hours near, and summoned all the family to

---

[33] Quoted Morley, Gladstone, II, p. 576.

[34] *Bulletin de L'Étranger* 3 April 1898, cutting in BL Add MSS 46269, f. 20 (author's translation).

[35] St Deiniol's Library, Hawarden, Glynne-Gladstone MSS [hereafter G-G MSS] 1037, Leonard Stern to Mrs Gladstone.

[36] G-G MSS 1038, Flora Holden, 2 June 1898.

[37] *The Times* 16 May 1898, p. 11.

[38] Bahlman, *Diary of Sir Edward Hamilton*, p. 351, 22 March 1898.

gather round him.[39] On 21 April, he again, according to Mary Drew, 'felt the hand of death' and refused all food.[40] Even in late April, he was still suffering enough to revert to the idea of an operation, but Smith apparently persuaded him against it. Mary, listening at the door, recalled that her father asked Smith 'wistfully, longingly, how soon the end might come. No one who heard it could ever forget the "Thank God" with which he greeted the assurance that it would not now be long delayed.'[41] On 18 May, the day before he died, Mary was struck by his 'most intense weariness, the most pathetic heartbreaking yearning for release'.[42]

The Christian convictions of Gladstone and his family were fundamental in their ability to come to terms with the imminence of his death, and above all in providing a framework to make sense of the physical suffering. Gladstone's conviction of divine providential purpose and of the reality of an afterlife that would transcend the limitations of material human experience explain his easy acceptance of his fate and the eagerness with which he anticipated it.[43] Moreover, others saw the perceived patience and resignation with which he bore his suffering as a triumphant vindication of his religious convictions. Such an idea was conveyed to Mary Drew in a letter from her friend Frances Balfour, which greatly comforted Gladstone when it was read to him:

> If he realises at all that the way he is bearing his cup of suffering is helping many a one towards the belief that the Christian religion can be enough to support the human being through all the trials of this life, he himself would be the last to wish that it should pass from him. It is after all a wonderful privilege to be chosen as a standard bearer.[44]

Another correspondent developed a similar theme:

> Now he is given, in love, the surest and most fruitful opportunity, more influential even, than when he was Prime Minister, [a] larger audience than that even in the great Market Place at Edinburgh, and a more attentive one, awed, silent, reverent, under the silent eloquence and individual interest of suffering, So it is all God's Love, and it will crown the life, and the life's work, bringing it all in simplicity just to the foot of the Divine Cross.[45]

Sometime in mid-April Gladstone himself spoke to his son-in-law Henry Drew of his 'yearning for Rest, the longing for Release, the burden of physical existence, the heaviness of the Dispensation', but then continued,

---

[39] BL Add MSS 46269, f. 24, 4 April, quoted by Jalland, *Death in the Victorian Family*, pp. 184-85.
[40] BL Add MSS 46269, f. 27.
[41] BL Add MSS 46269, ff. 27-28.
[42] BL Add MSS 46269, f. 33.
[43] For an overview of Gladstone's religious life, see Bebbington, *William Gladstone*, pp. 224-45.
[44] BL Add MSS 46269, f. 23, 31 March.
[45] BL Add MSS 46269, f. 25, 4 April.

But I remain totally unshaken in my resolute belief in the wisdom and will of God. Do not think me unhappy – the consolations are wonderful, the wealth of prayer which is being offered up for me is the greatest possible comfort.[46]

When George Russell visited Gladstone on 10 May and knelt to receive his parting benediction he felt 'that I had been on the Mount of Transfiguration, and had seen a glimpse of paradise through the Gates Ajar'.[47]

As the end approached, the Anglican monk Father Ignatius wrote to Gladstone that 'The eyes of the Church and of the world rest lovingly upon you – you are sending us daily such messages of faith and blessing that our hearts rejoice more than ever in Him who is thus sustaining you'.[48] Henry Scott Holland, Canon of St Paul's and a personal friend, counselled him to let his life's work fall from his hands 'and give it back to God, and do this with Thanksgiving'.[49] A Norfolk clergyman hoped that Gladstone would muster the strength to send a final message proclaiming 'his unchangeable faith in a Personal God, and an incarnate Saviour', but those closer to him evidently felt that this testimony was already being effectively proclaimed.[50]

Christian language and rituals surrounded the deathbed and were an evident source of comfort for the patient and his family. On 31 March G.H. Wilkinson, the Bishop of St Andrews, celebrated Holy Communion in Gladstone's bedroom.[51] Mrs Gladstone read daily psalms and prayers with him.[52] The music played to him included hymn tunes, which he sometimes asked his children and grandchildren to sing for him.[53] As he lapsed into unconsciousness in the last few days, his son Stephen Gladstone, and his son-in-law, Harry Drew, both clergymen, said prayers beside the bed.[54] It was reported that his last articulate words were 'Our Father', interpreted as an attempt to say the Lord's Prayer.[55] As Gladstone died early on the morning of 19 May, Stephen, with a stentorian voice and superb self-command and sense of timing managed to finish reading the commendatory prayer just as his father ceased to breathe. His sisters went from the death chamber to attend early morning communion at the parish church. It was Ascension Day, timing the family regarded as supremely appropriate.[56]

---

[46] *Sermons Preached in Memory of the Rt. Hon, W.E.Gladstone in Hawarden Parish on Sunday after Ascension Day, 22 May 1898* (London: Cassell, 1898), p. 23.
[47] Russell, *Gladstone's Religious Development*, p. 62.
[48] G-G MSS 1040, 10 May 1898.
[49] G-G MSS 1040, not dated.
[50] G-G MSS 1037, J.R. Baldwin, 18 May 1898.
[51] BL Add MSS 46269, f. 22.
[52] BL Add MSS 46269, f. 31, 9 May.
[53] BL Add MSS 46269, f. 31, 13 May.
[54] BL Add MSS 46269, f. 55, 18 May.
[55] Thomas Fuller Bryant, *The Death of Gladstone: A Sermon Preached in the Wesleyan Methodist Chapel, Alford, Lincolnshire* (Alford: T.A. Bellamy, 1898), p. 7.
[56] BL Add MSS 46269, f. 34, 19 May; Matthew, 'Gladstone's Death', p. 20.

The sense of Gladstone's last weeks as a triumphant testimony to Christianity was maintained in commentary after his death. This was the clear message of the sermons preached in Hawarden parish on the following Sunday by four of his relatives, his sons-in-law, Harry Drew and Edward Wickham, the Dean of Lincoln, and his nephews Arthur Lyttelton, then Vicar of Eccles, and Edward Talbot, formerly first Warden of Keble College, and now Bishop of Rochester. Talbot took as his text Luke 9.51, 'He stedfastly set His face to go to Jerusalem', and characterised Gladstone as following Jesus's own example in steadfastly setting his face to go to his death. Thus the last weeks, Talbot thought,

> not only crowned the life, they have laid bare its secret, and we have seen the whole energy of a life's self-discipline bestow itself with the concentration which one has said was almost his most striking quality, and in the strength of an unfaltering faith, to the great business of complete submission to pain and death.[57]

In similar vein, Wickham preached on 2 Timothy 4.7, 'I have fought a good fight. I have finished my course. I have kept the faith.' Wickham applied these words of the apostle Paul both to Jesus whose earthly life had reached its conclusion with the ascension, and to Gladstone whose life had been 'brought to its beautiful and honoured end amongst us'. Wickham saw his Christian submission to 'the very pain and distress of the last months' as preaching a sermon 'more eloquent than even his own tongue could have uttered'.[58] Drew saw Gladstone's 'months of untold suffering, borne with such noble fortitude, and with such sublime and trustful patience' as a testimony to the triumphant message of the ascension.[59] Lyttelton acknowledged that some might see the pain and suffering of the final months as a 'cruel mystery', but pointed out that Gladstone himself had written of the positive value of pain as a stimulus to self-sacrifice and had spoken of his illness as 'a fresh trial, a new discipline, a final preparation'.[60]

Other clergy, both in sermons and in letters to the family, expressed similar views. Malcolm MacColl, Gladstone's ardent erstwhile supporter and publicist, believed that his 'Christian endurance of suffering' had revealed his character to the world in a new and complete manner and that he had 'done as much good by the manner of his death as by the activity of his life'.[61] Nor was such a view the monopoly of the clergy: Sir George Otto Trevelyan observed that 'it is singular how whatever one's creed, the more the body failed the greater impression he gave of the victory of the spiritual over the material.'[62] It also figured prominently in letters of sympathy sent to the family by members of the general public. For example, a Nottingham woman felt that 'he showed the world how a Christian should die', and a Devon farmer

---

[57] *Sermons Preached in Hawarden Parish*, p. 44.
[58] *Sermons Preached in Hawarden Parish*, pp. 7-9.
[59] *Sermons Preached in Hawarden Parish*, p.21.
[60] *Sermons Preached in Hawarden Parish*, pp. 61-2.
[61] G-G MSS 1039, 29 May 1898.
[62] G-G MSS 1041, 19 May 1898.

praised the 'crowning triumph [of] the sweet patience, the Christian fortitude which ... he bore the sufferings of his closing hours'. A Bristol woman, although a member of the Primrose League, wrote that she had learnt to love Gladstone 'as an example of patience and marvellous submission to the divine Will.'[63] The Shirley (Southampton) Conservative Association acknowledged political difference, but paid tribute to Gladstone's 'high moral character, his fervent Christian belief [and] his patience under great suffering'.[64] The concluding lines of verses by the then well-known poet Lewis Morris, published in *The Times* the day after Gladstone's death, affirmed 'Thy changeless love of Man, thy trust in Heaven, Thy crown of Pain.'[65] A biography intended for boys published in 1899 dwelt on his manly courage in facing such 'wellnigh intolerable' pain.[66]

A further strand in the public response was the perception of that while Gladstone's social standing and his reputation as a statesman and scholar placed him on a remote eminence, every true Christian believer was his equal in the sight of God. This a Lincolnshire Wesleyan minister affirmed in a sermon 'in that which was most important we may be one with him by God's grace. His last experience ... is shared every hour by multitudes of lowly disciples.'[67] It was in the same spirit that the master of the Machynlleth Union workhouse wrote to Mrs Gladstone acknowledging that though people in his locality were poor and insignificant they were 'proud for the same Faith that your late companion in life clung steadfastly to the end'.[68]

Formal tributes were less explicit about Gladstone's suffering but struck a consistent note in highlighting his Christian character. In his eulogy in the House of Lords, the Marquess of Salisbury affirmed that 'He will leave behind him, especially to those who have followed with deep interest the history of the later years – I might almost say of the later months of his life – ... the memory of a great Christian statesman.' For Salisbury and others an emphasis on Gladstone's Christianity, while no doubt sincere, was also convenient as it was a matter of cross-party consensus that distracted attention from his more divisive political legacy. The image was also reinforced by arrangements for the funeral in Westminster Abbey on 28 May, in which the usual trappings of state ceremonial were severely curtailed in line with the family's wishes, so as not to be a distraction from the Christian tone of the proceedings. In particular the preceding lying-in-state in Westminster Hall had a stark simplicity, ornamented only with a cross and candlesticks, in striking contrast to the elaborate heraldic trappings that had surrounded the Duke of Wellington's coffin at the last public lying-in-state in 1852.[69]

---

[63] G-G MSS 1037, Mrs Richards, 19 May 1898.
[64] G-G MSS 1056, 1 June 1898.
[65] *The Times* 20 May 1898, p. 5.
[66] M.B. Synge, *Life of Gladstone: A Book for Boys* (London: Nelson, 1899), p. 7.
[67] Bryant, *Death of Gladstone*, p. 7.
[68] G-G MSS 1039, John Jones, 20 May 1898.
[69] For detailed discussion of the funeral arrangements, see Matthew, 'Gladstone's Death'; Wolffe, *Great Deaths*, pp. 180-91.

The intense public mood of May 1898 was not of course sustained, but there were ongoing echoes of the sentiments then expressed. Scott Holland preached on the first anniversary of Gladstone's death, reflecting that now that he was being taught the 'mysteries of Jesus' he would come to understand 'why the lovely peace of his old age was shattered by the awful discipline of pain'. Surely, Scott Holland suggested, 'he is nearer now, for all that he then endured to the pierced hands and to the wounded side'.[70] Gladstone's death also set a recent context for public response to the death of Queen Victoria at Osborne House on the Isle of Wight less than three years later on 22 January 1901, aged eighty-one. The realities were significantly different from Gladstone's: she had lapsed rapidly into a semi-vegetative state following an apparent series of strokes the previous week; she had little contact with her family or with clergymen during her final illness; the knowledge that she suffered significant discomfort from breathing difficulties was suppressed, and initially indeed, the Prince of Wales vetoed any public announcement that she was seriously ill. Nevertheless the public image of deep piety, Christian resignation, and close family life had much in common with that surrounding Gladstone's death and suggests perceptions were readily transferred.[71] It is an appropriate irony that Gladstone, who revered the monarchy despite Victoria's personal antipathy towards him, should have rendered this final posthumous service to the institution.

In the summer of 1903, as John Morley was working on the closing chapters of his monumental official biography, he was evidently unsure how to represent the final months of Gladstone's life. Prompted by her sister, Mary Drew, Helen Gladstone went to see Morley whom she found 'evidently nervous about our opinions'. He read to her 'some of the things he says at the beginning', presumably the passage in the Introduction to the biography in which he had explicitly stated that he was not attempting to cover Gladstone's history as 'theologian and churchman'.[72] She accepted the limitation as 'perfectly right'. Then

> we talked rather discursively about the last days and months and I think I said a few things or views that were more or less new to him ... One thing I had urged in writing that he should not speak of Father's end as gloomy or clouded: of course if he was going through it in detail there was all that dreadful pain and suffering, but spoken of as a whole, I am sure you and I feel the beauty and triumph far the most, all the suffering swallowed up in the victory.[73]

This passage is somewhat misunderstood by Pat Jalland in her book *Death and the Victorian Family*, where she suggests that the family persuaded Morley to 'sanitize' the death scene. Helen Gladstone's guidance did not entail a denial or obscuring of suffering, but rather stemmed from the family's perception that in an almost Christ-like manner her father's suffering has been 'swallowed up in victory'. However,

---

[70] Henry Scott Holland, *In Memoriam W.E .Gladstone* (London: Longmans, 1899), p. 19.
[71] Wolffe, *Great Deaths*, pp. 222-24.
[72] Morley, *Gladstone,* I, pp. 2-3.
[73] BL Add MSS 46,231, ff. 172-73, 2 September 1903.

recognizing that the agnostic Morley would, even with the best of intentions, be unable to do justice to this distinctively Christian conviction, she appears to have affirmed his sense that it was beyond his remit as a political biographer.[74] The result was that Morley condensed Gladstone's last weeks into one short paragraph, and emphasized not the Christian context of the death, but the beauty of the late spring morning: 'Nature outside – wood and wide lawn and cloudless far-off sky – shone at her fairest.' Nevertheless he acknowledged that Gladstone's illness had been a difficult one: he referred to 'months of distress', noted that 'his sufferings had been cruel', and recorded that 'At Hawarden he bore the dreadful burden of his pain with fortitude, supported by the ritual ordinances of his church and faith.'[75] Morley was not intending to sanitize Gladstone's deathbed, but rather appreciated that it held a spiritual significance in the eyes of Christians that he was not personally qualified to articulate.

Morley's account was nevertheless indicative of the new century's tendency to treat deathbeds not as the triumphant culmination of a life's spiritual journey, but rather as the inevitable but faintly embarrassing conclusion to a biographer's narrative. In that respect the Christian aura that surrounded Gladstone's final weeks was not, as some had hoped, an indication of national spiritual revival, but rather the last flowering of a tradition that was already somewhat dated, but was given new vigour by the fame of the dying man, and the profound Christian commitment he shared with those around him. It was a significant incident that complicates the usual portrayal of the *fin de siècle* as a period when the Victorian tide of faith began unmistakeably to ebb, but does not fundamentally change it. Nevertheless, it merits attention in confirming to posterity as it did to contemporaries, the integrity and consistency of Gladstone's Christian witness to the very end of his long life. It is also a case study that merits reflection in the context of early twenty-first century debates about the treatment of the terminally ill and the possibility of assisted dying. Modern medicine might have offered Gladstone the means to prolong his life for a few weeks, or conversely, in some legal jurisdictions, to have terminated it earlier when his suffering seemed unbearable. One strongly suspects, however, that he would not have chosen either option.

---

[74] Jalland, *Death in the Victorian Family*, pp. 185-86.
[75] Morley, *Gladstone*, II, pp. 574-76.

CHAPTER 18

Gardening for the Gospel: Horticulture and Mission in the Life of Robert Moffat of Kuruman

Brian Stanley

The Bebbington family traces its origins to the early fourteenth century and to the manor of Upper Bebington on the Wirral peninsula. By the seventeenth century the Bebbingtons were to be found in rather more humble circumstances living in the hamlet of Bunbury on the Cheshire plain.[1] Some twenty-four miles to the northeast of Bunbury lies what is now the Manchester commuter village of High Legh, on the main road between Knutsford and Warrington. High Legh today boasts both a garden centre and a Christian centre. The two apparently unrelated centres share a historical connection to one of the most remarkable Nonconformist missionaries of the nineteenth century. High Legh Garden Centre was developed from the nursery gardens of the prominent Cheshire landed family, the Cornwall-Leghs, where in 1813 a young Scottish gardener by the name of Robert Moffat found employment.[2] The Northwood Christian Centre in High Legh incorporates a former Independent Methodist chapel. The Methodist society who used to meet in that chapel first gathered in a farm cottage belonging to the Okell family; it was through the influence of this society in 1814 that Robert Moffat was converted to personal faith in Christ, giving some concern to his Presbyterian parents that he had succumbed to Methodist enthusiasm. Northwood Christian Centre pays due homage to Moffat on its website,[3] and Moffat's memory is perpetuated elsewhere in the village. The village has a street named after him, and since 2008 there has been an annual Robert Moffat Memorial ten kilometre race, jointly organized by the High Legh Community Association and a local running club, the Lymm Runners; the race was instituted by James Cavanagh, the son of the vicar at that time, a keen runner who had developed an interest in the village's former resident.[4] The churchyard of St Mary's Anglican chapel, formerly

---

[1] Eileen Bebbington, *A Patterned Life: Faith, History, and David Bebbington* (Eugene, OR: Wipf & Stock, 2014), p. 10.

[2] See http://www.highleghparishcouncil.gov.uk/local-info-indiv.php?id=71&name=Local %20History. On the Cornwall-Legh family, see Evelyn Lord, 'The Cornwall-Leghs of High Legh, Cheshire: Approaches to the Inheritance Patterns of North-West England', *Bulletin of the John Rylands University Library of Manchester* 73.2 (Summer, 1991), pp. 21-36.

[3] See http://www.northwoodchristiancentre.org.uk/pages/pv.asp?p=imcgb31.

[4] See http://www.highlegh10k.org.uk/?page_id=154.

the chapel of ease to the Cornwall-Legh family seat at East Hall, has in its grounds (or at least did have in 1949) a copper beech that Moffat is said to have planted during his time there.[5]

The two centres located within the single community of High Legh symbolize the close connection in Robert Moffat's life between his profession as a gardener and his vocation as a missionary of the gospel in the service of the London Missionary Society (LMS). Moffat was not simply a gardener who became a missionary – he was a missionary who remained a gardener and who always regarded his horticultural activities as integral to his work of evangelism and Christian discipleship. It is fitting that one of his biographies, by the distinguished Primitive Methodist missionary to southern Africa, Edwin W. Smith, should be entitled *Robert Moffat: One of God's Gardeners*.[6]

This article provides a welcome opportunity to express my immense gratitude to David Bebbington as someone who has not only profoundly influenced my academic career as a historian but has proved to be a faithful friend (as well as serving as an excellent best man at my wedding!). Since 2008 we have had in common residence in Scotland, not far from some of the locations featured in the early part of this article. Our wives now share a certain predilection for coffee shops in garden centres, and (for them, at least) gardening has come to form an important part of the Bebbington-Stanley friendship. In what follows I shall explore both the practical and the symbolic functions that horticulture and agricultural innovation fulfilled during the early years of Moffat's long missionary career at Kuruman, the station in the Northern Cape Province of South Africa with which his name will always be associated.

In particular, I shall consider here to what extent Robert Moffat saw the daunting task of creating a watered garden in the drought-ridden veldt of the interior of southern Africa as a parable of his spiritual vocation. As the American anthropologists Jean and John Comaroff have pointed out, missionary devotion to irrigation in southern Africa was not merely a practical strategy for survival and sustainability: it also carried a deeper symbolic meaning, reflecting the missionary desire to see what Moffat called 'the vast moral wastes' of Africa 'watered by the streams of life'.[7] That symbolic meaning was firmly grounded in biblical metaphor. The imagery found in many parts of the Old Testament that juxtaposes lush watered

---

[5] Raymond Richards, 'The Chapels of the Blessed Virgin Mary and St. John at High Legh, Cheshire with Some Account of the Cornwall-Legh and Egerton-Leigh Families', *Transactions of the Historic Society of Lancashire and Cheshire* 101 (1949), pp. 97-138 (p. 128); see also http://www.thornber.net/cheshire/htmlfiles/legh.html.

[6] Edwin W. Smith, *Robert Moffat: One of God's Gardeners* (London: Student Christian Movement, 1925). Smith dedicated the book to his wife, Julia, with the words 'NAMUSA, MY WIFE, ANOTHER GARDENER'.

[7] Robert Moffat, *Missionary Labours and Scenes in Southern Africa* (London: John Snow, 1842), p. 614, cited in Jean and John Comaroff, *Of Revelation and Revolution: Christianity, Colonialism, and Consciousness in South Africa*. Volume One (Chicago, IL: University of Chicago Press, 1991), p. 207.

gardens and the enveloping arid wilderness was readily translated into the physical ordering of mission stations. In early Victorian Britain Robert Moffat's Kuruman became the most widely celebrated example of what Protestant Christian missions were supposed to be capable of doing to transform and re-order supposedly 'primitive' and 'heathen' African agricultural economies in accordance with the principles of 'civilization'. Perhaps for that very reason, Moffat's stock among postcolonial historians of Africa has fallen to a low ebb, in comparison, for example, to the broadly favourable reputation still enjoyed by his near-contemporary John Philip or his son-in-law David Livingstone, whose equally undoubted enthusiasm for 'civilization' is seen, with some justice, as being at least in some measure redeemable by their often very vocal defence of African interests against white settlers or colonial adventurers.[8] Moffat could undoubtedly be an imperious character and he did not appear to have Livingstone's instinctive empathy for African cultures. Nevertheless, especially in his second period in Africa, from 1844 to 1870, when the growing power of the Boer republics in the southern African interior changed the whole political dynamics of the region, Moffat was far from quiescent in his advocacy of indigenous concerns.[9] He is undoubtedly overdue a scholarly assessment, not least on account of his contribution to an understanding of the role that horticultural innovation and water engineering had to play in enhancing the lives of African communities.

Robert Moffat was not, of course, the first Protestant to combine a career as a foreign missionary with dedication to horticulture. William Carey, as is well known, was an enthusiastic collector of Indian botanical specimens and a close associate of some of the leading Oriental naturalists of the day, notably William Roxburgh and Nathaniel Wallich, both of whom were superintendents of the East India Company's Botanic Garden in Calcutta.[10] He founded the Agri-Horticultural Society of India in 1820 and was elected a Fellow of the Linnean Society in 1823. Carey has given his name to several species of Indian plants and was one of the more important transmitters of botanical knowledge from Bengal to Britain. Carey was, however, a self-taught polymath for whom horticulture was simply one of a wide range of scientific, literary and cultural interests. He was not, of course, a gardener by

---

[8] See, e.g., the two scholarly, but strongly commendatory biographies by the late Andrew C. Ross of the University of Edinburgh, *John Philip (1775–1851): Missions, Race and Politics in South Africa* (Aberdeen: Aberdeen University Press, 1986); and *David Livingstone: Mission and Empire* (London: Hambledon, 2002).

[9] See Steve de Gruchy, 'The Alleged Political Conservatism of Robert Moffat', in John de Gruchy (ed.), *The London Missionary Society in Southern Africa: Historical Essays in Celebration of the Bicentenary of the LMS in Southern Africa 1799–1899* (Cape Town: David Philip, 1999), pp. 17-36. Steve de Gruchy was working on a biography of Moffat before his untimely death in a boating accident in 2010.

[10] On Carey as botanist, see Keith Farrer, *William Carey: Missionary and Botanist* (Kew: Carey Baptist Grammar School, 2005); also Sujit Sivasundaram, '"A Christian Benares": Orientalism, Science and the Serampore Mission of Bengal', *Indian Economic and Social History Review* 44 (2007), pp. 111-45.

profession, but a botanist by hobby and inclination. Carey's richly-stocked personal garden at Serampore was an object of love and a source of recreation, not a larder essential for his personal survival. Moffat, by contrast, gardened in order to live, labouring within an arid and isolated natural environment that was much less rich in flora than was Carey's Bengal. He is consequently remembered, not as a transmitter of non-European horticultural knowledge to Europe, but rather as an innovator who brought European techniques of irrigation and new crops to an African context. He is therefore less obviously appealing to current scholarly tastes than Carey, in that, unlike Carey, he appeared mostly to assume that useful horticultural knowledge was something that Europeans owned and had a duty to disseminate to non-Europeans. Moffat's twentieth-century biographers, including the missionary anthropologist Edwin Smith, note with some regret his apparent lack of interest in, or indeed sympathy for the religious rituals, customs and worldview of the Tswana (known to Moffat as Bechuana) peoples among whom he worked.[11] Nonetheless, his career serves to remind us that the place of agricultural development and even water engineering projects in Christian mission is not so recent an innovation as is often supposed; rather it has a history that stretches back to the earliest decades of the British Protestant missionary movement.

Robert Moffat was born in Ormiston, East Lothian, on 21 December 1795 into a United Presbyterian family. He learned his apprenticeship as a gardener at the age of fourteen at Polmont, near Falkirk, and in 1812 was appointed to his first job working in the gardens of the Earl of Moray at Donibristle, near Aberdour in Fife, overlooking the Firth of Forth. These were conveniently close to what had become the parental home in the port of Inverkeithing,[12] where his father had been appointed in 1811 to the post of His Majesty's Deputy Collector and Principal Coast Officer.[13] Moffat's post at High Legh was thus his second proper job. He worked there for only about a year. While at High Legh he noticed an advertisement for a meeting on behalf of the LMS to be addressed by William Roby (1766–1830), the leading Manchester Independent minister of Grosvenor Street Chapel and a founding member of the LMS. The notice was already out of date, but Moffat shortly afterwards heard Roby speak in Manchester and then summoned up the courage to seek out Roby in his home. Roby, an encourager and trainer of candidates for missionary service second in importance only to David Bogue,[14] took the young gardener under his wing as a hopeful prospect, and secured him a new job in Dukinfield, Manchester, situated nearer to his home so that this scantily educated

---

[11] Smith, *Robert Moffat*, p. 98; Cecil Northcott, *Robert Moffat: Pioneer in Africa 1817–1870* (London: Lutterworth Press, 1961), pp. 73-75.

[12] The *ODNB* article on Moffat confuses Inverkeithing with Inverness.

[13] Moffat Cottage, the Moffat family home, still stands in Heriot Street, Inverkeithing. The current occupant (in 2014) is a Baptist minister and church historian, Rev. Harry Sprange, who is a regular member of the Scottish Baptist History Project and the Christianity and History Forum (Scotland), both bodies started by David Bebbington.

[14] See *ODNB* and W. Gordon Robinson, *William Roby (1766–1830) and the Revival of Independency in the North* (London: Independent Press, 1954), p. 136.

young man could benefit from his tuition in theology. Moffat became a church member at Grosvenor Street Chapel. Roby would in due course be responsible for persuading the LMS Directors to rescind their initial decision in 1815 to decline Moffat's offer of missionary service on the grounds that they had received many other offers from those with 'the most promising acquirements'.[15] 'It is impossible for me to be grateful enough to God', Moffat wrote home to his parents, 'for such a friend as Mr. Roby. Truly his kindness, like that of a father, will not be easily obliterated from my mind'.[16] Moffat always carried with him on his travels in Africa a 460-page quarto manuscript in which he had copied from memory eighty of Roby's lectures on 'A System of Divinity' delivered in Roby's Manchester academy (which eventually became the Lancashire Independent College). The manuscript survives in the LMS archives in the School of Oriental and African Studies in London.[17]

At Dukinfield Moffat served in a nursery garden as under-gardener to James Smith. Smith and his wife, who were both committed evangelicals, he from an Independent background in Perthshire and she from an Anglican family in York. They were missionary enthusiasts. One of their three sons, John, became a pastor in Hulme in Manchester and later served with the LMS in Madras, before in 1843 being lost at sea in a shipwreck off the Indian coast.[18] Their eldest daughter, Mary, who was educated at the local Moravian school in Fairfield, would become Moffat's wife, though they did not marry until after she followed Moffat to South Africa in 1819, being married in St George's Church, Cape Town, on 27 December.[19] This was a marriage in which both parties shared a love of the gospel as well as a love for the soil.

The Moffats were appointed by the LMS to its station at Letakong (a name that the missionaries had Anglicised as Lattakoo) established in 1816 among the Thlaping, one of the nomadic Bechuana (now known as Tswana) Setswana-speaking peoples who inhabited the parched lands to the north of the Orange River that extend from what is now the Northern Cape Province of South Africa into Botswana. Letakong was situated on the Kuruman River, about ten miles from its source, the Eye of Kuruman, a remarkable spring located in a dolomite cave from which some four to five million gallons of clean water a day gushed forth to form a stream that flowed north-westwards towards the Kalahari desert. Sadly the watercourse frequently disappeared into the light sandy soil even before it reached Letakong.

---

[15] John S. Moffat, *The Lives of Robert and Mary Moffat* (London: T. Fisher Unwin, 3rd edn, 1885), p. 19.

[16] Robert Moffat to his parents, 23 September 1816, cited in John S. Moffat, *Lives of Robert and Mary Moffat*, p. 26.

[17] Robinson, *William Roby*, p. 118 n.; Northcott, *Robert Moffat*, p. 22; London, School of Oriental and African Studies (hereafter SOAS), CWM/LMS/Home/Odds, Box 25.

[18] James Sibree (comp.), *London Missionary Society: A Register of Missionaries, Deputations, etc. from 1796 to 1923* (London: London Missionary Society, 4th edn, 1923), p. 29, no. 271.

[19] John S. Moffat, *Lives of Robert and Mary Moffat*, p. 69; Smith, *Robert Moffat*, pp. 80-81.

'Our present station', wrote Robert to his elder brother Alexander in Inverkeithing on 26 February 1822, 'is miserable, both for the Bootchuanas [Bechuanas] as well as for us. Daily irrigation is requisite to procure a very scanty supply of vegetables, which has failed us this year'.[20]

The LMS missionaries had constructed a ditch to divert what intermittent water the river supplied to water their own gardens. Irrigation was a technique hitherto unknown to the Thlaping, but their women soon got the idea and began cutting trenches to divert the missionaries' water into their own gardens. Moffat and the existing missionary, Robert Hamilton, had to take turns in going out each day – or sometimes under cover of night – with a spade to re-establish the flow in the direction of their homes, but this game of horticultural tit-for-tat went on indefinitely. The water supply was frequently so curtailed that poor Mary Moffat had to dispatch the bed linen on a journey of a hundred miles to be washed.[21] Furthermore, what vegetables they did manage to grow – cabbages, peas, carrots and kidney beans[22] – were liable either to be stolen by the people or to be trampled by the oxen whenever the gardens were left untended. Mary wrote in confession to her parents in February 1822 that 'After our hearts had both been often excessively pained at Robert being obliged to spend so much time in the garden, we have had four dishes of vegetables out of it this year.'[23] Robert expressed his own intense frustration at the meagre results gleaned from these early years of hard labour: 'Our time was incessantly occupied in building, and laboring frequently for the meat that perisheth; but our exertions were often in vain, for while we sowed, the natives reaped'.[24] The depressing paucity of the horticultural harvest was, if anything, exceeded by the entire absence of a spiritual one: 'The Batlaping', notes John Smith Moffat's biographical study of his parents, 'continued indifferent to the gospel, and unbelieving of anything beyond the things of time and sense.'[25]

In response to the repeated frustrations experienced at Letakong, the Moffats began to contemplate moving eight miles up-river to a new site close to the Eye of Kuruman itself, where there was fertile valley ground and a guaranteed supply of water. Like most Nonconformist missionaries of his day, Robert Moffat was a committed disciple of the principles of self-support that would later be taken up by the Evangelical Anglican Henry Venn, Honorary Clerical Secretary of the Church Missionary Society from 1841 to 1872, and incorporated into his famous 'three-self'

---

[20] Isaac Schapera (ed.), *Apprenticeship at Kuruman: Being the Journals and Letters of Robert and Mary Moffat* (London: Chatto & Windus, 1951), p. 60.

[21] For a commentary on Moffat's battles with the Thlaping women over water, see Comaroff and Comaroff, *Of Revelation and Revolution*, p. 208.

[22] Schapera (ed.) *Apprenticeship at Kuruman*, pp. 71, 105.

[23] Schapera (ed.) *Apprenticeship at Kuruman*, p. 60, n. 1.

[24] Robert Moffat, *Missionary Labours and Scenes*, pp. 285-87 (p. 285).

[25] John S. Moffat, *The Lives of Robert and Mary Moffat*, p. 107.

formula.²⁶ Moffat's ambition for the new mission community was that it should be entirely self-sufficient in food: supplies from the far south were extremely expensive to haul by ox-wagon, and painfully slow in coming.²⁷ Just as medical missions would subsequently develop from a pragmatic recognition that missionaries were more likely to survive in oriental or tropical climates if some of them possessed at least a modicum of medical expertise, the first experiments in agricultural mission were pioneered out of a concern for simple survival of the missionaries themselves.

By January 1824 Moffat was able to inform the LMS Secretary, George Burder, that he had purchased from the Thlaping paramount chief Mothibi an extensive 550-acre site for a new mission station at Kuruman for the modest expenditure of forty pounds of beads, which he described as being equivalent to about £5.²⁸ The land was then divided into twelve lots, three for missionary houses, and nine for indigenous employees of the mission. Work began on the construction of a dam and major irrigation canal, two miles long, six feet wide, and two feet deep, which would supply each of the homes and their gardens. Khoikhoi ('Hottentot') labourers were brought up from the LMS station at Bethelsdorp in the Eastern Cape to do the work, but proved unreliable. The LMS Director and missionary John Philip, who visited Kuruman in September 1825, reported that Moffat and Hamilton had received even less assistance in the construction work from the Thlaping, 'who were not sufficiently impressed with the importance of the undertaking to take any part in it. Until they saw the water running into the ditch, they deemed it impossible, and treated the attempt with ridicule.'²⁹ Writing in 1885, J.S. Moffat supplied a cruder, more racially stereotyped explanation, namely that 'the Bechwanas knew little about work'; whatever the true reason for the hesitation of the Thlaping, the missionaries, with the help of a mason named Millen, had to do much of the construction work themselves, a remarkable feat of civil engineering accomplished by manual labour in day-time temperatures that could reach 120 degrees fahrenheit.³⁰

---

²⁶ On Venn's indebtedness to Nonconformist models of self-support, see C. Peter Williams, *The Ideal of the Self-Governing Church: A Study in Victorian Missionary Strategy* (Leiden: E. J. Brill, 1990), pp. 25-26, 50-51.

²⁷ Northcott, *Robert Moffat*, p. 111.

²⁸ Schapera (ed.) *Apprenticeship at Kuruman*, p. 113. However, a letter from the LMS to the Colonial Office in 1886 said that the land had been purchased for goods to the value of £50, 'that sum being at the time, and for many years after, ample payment for a tract of poor and uncultivated wilderness in a region totally unknown to Europeans'; Schapera (ed.) *Apprenticeship at Kuruman*, p. 189. The size of the site is mentioned by Nancy Jacobs, 'The Flowering Eye: Water Management in the Upper Kuruman Valley, South Africa, c.1800–1962', *Journal of African History* 37.2 (July, 1996), pp. 237-60 (p. 241).

²⁹ John Philip, *Researches in South Africa; Illustrating the Civil, Moral, and Religious Condition of the Native Tribes: Including Journals of the Author's Travels in the Interior; Together with Detailed Accounts of the Progress of the Christian Missions, Exhibiting the Influence of Christianity in Promoting Civilization* (2 vols; London: James Duncan, 1828), II, p. 113.

³⁰ John S. Moffat, *Lives of Robert and Mary Moffat*, p. 133.

The results of all this construction activity greatly impressed John Philip on his visit to Kuruman. The station's regular ordered lines and well watered community seemed to him a striking visual embodiment of 'the spirit of improvement' that Christian missionaries longed to see take hold among the African populace:

> With very great labour, the missionaries have succeeded in erecting a neat row of houses in the bottom of the valley; to each house is attached a large garden, enclosed with a neat fence. The gardens have been laid out, by Mr Moffat, with much taste; and, from his knowledge of horticulture, they have been stocked with a variety of seeds and edible roots. In front of the houses, and at a distance of, perhaps, forty feet, is the canal by which the water has been led out from the river. Across this water-channel is a wooden-bridge, leading to each house. Within ten feet of the house is the garden, from which it is entered by a gate; and along the whole line of the fence, the space between it and the water-course is planted with willows and poplars.[31]

The newly laid out and more effectively irrigated gardens soon began to yield fruit, vegetables, and corn of high quality, despite occasional attacks from invading hordes of locusts. By December 1827 Mary Moffat was able in a letter to inform her brother, James Smith, that

> We are now reaping wheat and barley on the place ... We are also eating fine potatoes, the produce of our own garden; a great blessing to me, as I was beginning to feel seriously the want of vegetables and the warm weather, having a large strong child to nurse, not being able to wean him for want of milk. We have also a prospect of plenty of grapes and figs and some peaches, everything of the kind growing very luxuriantly here.[32]

The irrigation scheme soon began to benefit the whole community. One year later, Mary, writing to her brother again, was able to tell him that the local poor people were reaping good crops of wheat and tobacco in their own little gardens, and sowing maize for the season ahead. 'The temporal affairs of the station are very prosperous.' Such agricultural change was a sign that 'Civilization is advancing', while their own personal gardens were 'becoming beautiful. The fruit which is just ripening is very abundant; indeed, I am astonished to see what the willing earth yields in so short a time.'[33]

In an environment in which severe drought remained endemic, the luxuriance of Kuruman's produce became a potent symbol of the flowering of Christian civilization in a 'heathen' wilderness. In a letter written in February 1834 Moffat described to William Ellis, one of the LMS Secretaries, how the season's drought had been marked by almost 'one perpetual blaze of solar fire ever since the

---

[31] Philip, *Researches in South Africa*, II, pp. 114-15.

[32] Mary Moffat to John Smith, 6 December 1827, in Schapera (ed.), *Apprenticeship at Kuruman*, p. 271. The nursing infant was Robert junior, born in January 1827.

[33] Mary Moffat to John Smith, 30 December 1828, in Schapera (ed.), *Apprenticeship at Kuruman*, p. 292.

commencement of summer ... The wind sometimes felt like flame & the earth seemed ignivomous [vomiting fire].' Yet, despite the ferocity of the heat and the duration of the drought, Moffat reported that his irrigation scheme had secured 'a good harvest of wheat ... about 3 times the quantity of last year'. Kuruman, he observed, had become 'a comparitive [sic] Goshen to the surrounding country', a biblical storehouse of plenty set in a dry and thirsty land.[34]

It had taken some time for the agricultural fecundity that was increasingly being demonstrated at Kuruman to be paralleled by spiritual growth. Despite the idyllic scene he had described in September 1825, John Philip had noted that as yet the people did not 'see the importance of eternal things', with only forty regularly attending divine worship.[35] However, within a few years the mission had its first candidate for baptism and an initial group of eager inquirers. In the same letter of December 1828 in which Mary described to her brother the encouraging signs of advancing civilization and the ripening of the abundant fruit in her gardens, she also reported that a former run-away slave named Arend, not a local, had become a candidate for baptism. 'He is an industrious pushing man', she observed in what was clearly intended to be a compliment, 'and we have reason to believe that he will be a good example, and that ere long there will be some of our poor people inclined also to come out and be separate.'[36] Arend and his three children were baptized on 1 May 1829, when he assumed the Christian names of Aaron Joseph.[37] The baptismal service in the temporary chapel that had been erected at Kuruman, at which the Moffats' own son Robert was also baptized, was well attended and was marked by a quite unanticipated outpouring of weeping among the women, children, and – most unusually for the Tswana – even the men. Moffat's enthusiastic recollection in his *Missionary Scenes and Labours in Southern Africa* (1842) of this 'revival' – the term is used in the index entry referring readers to these events – records that 'we were favoured with the manifest outpouring of the Spirit from on high. The moral wilderness was now about to blossom. ... The simple Gospel now melted their flinty hearts ... Our temporary little chapel became a Bochim – a place of weeping.'[38] Late-night and early-morning prayer meetings were now organized in homes, and by June 1829 there were six more candidates for baptism. Aaron was a builder and thatcher by trade, and he began to construct a schoolhouse that would also serve as a permanent chapel. On the first Sunday in July, the six, who included Aaron's wife, were baptized in the new chapel. Moffat felt that the long awaited spiritual harvest for which he had prayed was now ripening to fruition; he first alluded to, and then directly cited the words of the psalmist, 'We were as those that dreamed, while we

---

[34] SOAS, CWM/LMS South Africa Incoming Correspondence, Box 14A, Folder 2, Jacket F, Robert Moffat to William Ellis, Kuruman, 3 February 1834.

[35] Philip, *Researches in South Africa*, II, p. 115.

[36] Mary Moffat to John Smith, 30 December 1828, in Schapera (ed.), *Apprenticeship at Kuruman*, p. 292.

[37] *LMS Report* (1830), p. 85, cited in Schapera (ed.), *Apprenticeship at Kuruman*, p. 292.

[38] Robert Moffat, *Missionary Labours and Scenes*, pp. 496-97, 623. On Bochim as a place of weeping for ancient Israel, see Judges 2.1-5.

realized the promise on which our souls had often hung. "He that goeth forth and weepeth, bearing precious seed, shall doubtless come again with rejoicing, bringing his sheaves with him."[39]

Moffat's account in *Missionary Scenes and Labours in Southern Africa* of this modest but significant spiritual breakthrough took the opportunity to drive home the theoretical point beloved of early nineteenth-century English evangelicals (as opposed to Scottish Presbyterian Moderates) – that true 'civilization' could only follow, and not precede the conversion of the heart to Christ[40] – and went on to describe how the new converts had indeed adopted Western dress and begun to use Western furniture, with the women and girls learning to handle needle and thread in order to make their new European garments:

> The same Gospel which had taught them that they were spiritually miserable, blind, and naked, discovered to them also that they needed reform externally, and thus prepared their minds to adopt those modes of comfort, cleanliness, and convenience which they had been accustomed to view only as the peculiarities of a strange people. Thus, by the slow but certain progress of Gospel principles, whole families became clothed and in their right mind.[41]

In point of fact, however, the causal sequence of conversion and civilization was not quite so clear-cut as Moffat and strict evangelical theory maintained. It may not be wholly coincidental that the evangelistic breakthrough came hard on the heels of the demonstrable success of the irrigation project at Kuruman, and indeed also in the wake of an uncharacteristically wet rainy season after which 'the fields and gardens teemed with plenty, such as had not been experienced for several years'.[42] In 1845–47 Moffat's son-in-law David Livingstone would find to his cost that an unusually protracted and uncannily localized drought that had uniquely affected the Bakwena group of the Tswana, among whom he was then resident, would be interpreted as clinching evidence that he was a wizard who had bewitched the clouds to prevent them yielding their promised rain.[43] Among the Thlaping in 1829 Moffat may have been reaping the benefit of the converse, as the exceptionally abundant rain could be taken to signify the blessing of the ancestral spirits on his presence and the wisdom of his teaching. Moffat rather gave the game away when he assured his British readers that 'The ancient ramparts of superstition had been broken through by our

---

[39] Robert Moffat, *Missionary Labours and Scenes*, pp. 498-500 (p. 500). Moffat is citing Psalm 126.1 and 6.

[40] See Brian Stanley, 'Christianity and Civilization in English Evangelical Mission Thought, 1792–1857', in Brian Stanley (ed.), *Christian Missions and the Enlightenment* (Grand Rapids, MI/Cambridge, and Richmond: Eerdmans/Curzon Press, 2001), pp. 169-97.

[41] Robert Moffat, *Missionary Labours and Scenes*, pp. 502-505 (p. 505).

[42] Robert Moffat, *Missionary Labours and Scenes*, p. 558.

[43] See Brian Stanley, 'The Missionary and the Rainmaker: David Livingstone, the Bakwena, and the Nature of Medicine', *Social Sciences and Missions* 24.2-3 (2014), pp. 145-62.

converts, *and many others'*, when they proved eager to adopt the new crops that he had introduced – maize, wheat, barley, peas, potatoes, carrots, and onions – with the men, who traditionally in Tswana society would never have deigned to be seen doing the women's work of digging the gardens, now displaying anxiety to obtain for their own use ploughs, harrows, spades, and mattocks.[44] Such innovation was not restricted to converts or even inquirers, although any change there was to the customary restriction of gardening to the female gender seems to have been slow and limited; as late as the 1860s, Moffat was still noting in his journal that it was 'considered below the dignity of the man to dig or cultivate the ground'.[45] The message that men ought not to leave the gardening entirely to their wives was proving to be, and perhaps still remains, one of the harder sayings of the gospel.

Two letters from Mary and Robert Moffat, each written on 30 December 1828, both suggest that the initial attraction to Christianity of those who had made their residence at Kuruman owed at least as much to the visible (and edible) fruits of civilization as the process of civilization owed to the leaven of the gospel. As we have seen, Mary's letter to her brother James reported *both* that 'civilization' as evidenced by agricultural innovation was already advancing and that the very first convert, who was an outsider to the Thlaping, was seeking baptism. Robert's letter of the same date, written to his own brother Richard in Inverkeithing, similarly reported that 'It is pleasing to see the progress the natives residing with us are making in civilization. One person stands a candidate for baptism, and being a person possessed of a little influence his example and zeal may through the divine blessing prove useful to others.'[46] What is beyond dispute is the unqualified enthusiasm of both Robert and Mary Moffat for the introduction of European ways, whether in agriculture, dress, or moral codes. For the Moffats, in contrast to many later missionaries in Africa, there was little or no tension between the gospel and European civilization.

As a member of Grosvenor Street Independent Chapel in Manchester, Robert Moffat would almost certainly have sung the hymn by the most celebrated hymn writer of the Independent tradition, Isaac Watts (1674–1748), in which Watts famously employed decidedly horticultural language to express the dissenting idea of the true church as a gathered congregation:

We are a Garden wall'd around,
Chosen and made peculiar Ground,
A little Spot inclos'd by Grace
Out of the World's wide Wilderness.

---

[44] Robert Moffat, *Missionary Labours and Scenes*, pp. 558-59 (my italics).

[45] SOAS, CWM/LMS Africa Personal, Box 4, Robert Moffat Papers, Notebook of Robert Moffat on 'Charms', n.d. [1860s].

[46] Schapera (ed.), *Apprenticeship at Kuruman*, p. 290.

> Like Trees of Myrrh and Spice we stand,
> Planted by God the Father's Hand;
> And all his Springs in Sion flow,
> To make the young Plantation grow.[47]

From 1833 the gradual availability of scripture portions in Setswana, translated by Moffat, became an attraction, prompting a hunger for literacy in the schools he had established at Kuruman and the surrounding villages. Enthusiasm for reading soon translated into enthusiasm for the message itself: Moffat records that 'We were visited at this time with refreshing showers of Divine blessing, and very considerable accessions were made to the number of believers.'[48] In 1838 Moffat was able to report 'great accessions' to the church at Kuruman. The numbers learning to read had risen markedly, and the infant school was giving 'great satisfaction'. Spiritual progress was matched in the material sphere:

> The people made rapid advances in civilization; some purchasing wagons, and breaking in their oxen for those labours which formerly devolved on the female sex. The use of clothing became so general, that the want of a merchant was greatly felt, to supply the demands for British commodities.[49]

By the end of Moffat's first period of service in Africa in 1843 the Kuruman mission had become a topographical representation of that dissenting spiritual picture of the church as a covenanted and fruitful community of clearly professed believers, bounded by clear lines of demarcation and visibly different from the surrounding barren environment. Although most members of the community had been quicker to believe the gospel of irrigation than the gospel of the water of life, a growing number were making the connection between the two. However, the total membership of the Kuruman church appears not to have exceeded seventy in Moffat's lifetime.[50] Some European visitors to the station, being more easily impressed by the numerous signs of 'civilization' than by the more limited evidence of adoption of Christianity, now described Kuruman in terms reminiscent of Watts' hymn. Thus in 1839 Captain William Cornwallis Harris, an East India Company engineer and an enthusiast for big game hunting, published his impression of Kuruman as 'a lovely spot in the waste by which it is completely environed'; it was a 'speck of civilization, seeming as though it had been accidentally dropped into the

---

[47] Isaac Watts, first two stanzas of 'The Church the Garden of Christ', cited in Donald Davie, *A Gathered Church: The Literature of the English Dissenting Tradition, 1700–1930* (London and Henley: Routledge & Kegan Paul, 1978), pp. 28-29.

[48] Robert Moffat, *Missionary Labours and Scenes*, p. 571.

[49] Robert Moffat, *Missionary Labours and Scenes*, p. 605.

[50] Northcott, *Robert Moffat*, p. 315.

very heart of this wide wilderness'.[51] A new missionary arriving in 1866 described Kuruman as 'the loveliest mission station I have seen ... The trees in front of the building are thick with a beautiful foliage: over the garden wall hang clusters of rich red pomegranates and within the gardens fruit and vegetables in abundance are ready for gathering.'[52]

Robert Moffat is surely one of the clearest exemplars of the second – and arguably the least studied – point of the famous 'Bebbington quadrilateral': activism. Like many other nineteenth-century evangelicals, he was always unimpressed with what he judged to be the modest extent of his own busyness in the cause of the gospel in the light of the constant and sobering proximity of eternity. On his sixty-seventh birthday, on 21 December 1862, he wrote in his journal

> My birth day [sic] 67 years old. How old to have done so little. I might have done much. I always hope each returning year to do more than the past. I must try thro' divine help to try again tho' I have neither the strength of body nor mind I once had & who is to see the close of another year? The last of my life has been eventful & warning. There have been many deaths in Mission families & now another Mrs Thomas & her youngest.[53]

In fact Moffat would soldier on at Kuruman until March 1870, though his strength was failing. Robert and Mary left South Africa for the last time in June 1870. Mary died within a few months of their return to England. Robert lived till August 1883.

Despite his characteristic self-deprecation, Moffat was in fact extraordinarily industrious in his missionary vocation as church-planter, Bible translator (he was the first to translate the Bible into Setswana, completing the task in 1857) and horticulturalist. But his activism was more than simply a by-product of his absorption with his divinely appointed commission. In Robert Moffat's case the virtues of hard manual labour in agricultural cultivation – and for *men* in particular – became an integral part of his personal embodiment of the Christian gospel and its attendant values of 'civilization' to the Tswana. As Edwin Smith put it in his biography,

> By precept and example he taught his converts to labour. He knew full well that neither God nor man can do anything with idle folk. Day by day he worked under a burning sun, in the saw pit, at the anvil, in the garden. He taught the Bechuana how to make use of their wonderful spring to irrigate their fields and how to use the manure of their

---

[51] Captain William Cornwallis Harris, *The Wild Sports of Southern Africa; Being the Narrative of an Expedition from the Cape of Good Hope, through the Territories of the Chief Moselekatse, to the Tropic of Capricorn* (London: John Murray, 1839), p. 45.

[52] SOAS, CWM/LMS, Africa South Incoming Letters, Box 34, John Brown to LMS, 2 February 1866, cited in Jacobs, 'The Flowering Eye', pp. 241-42.

[53] SOAS, CWM/LMS Africa Personal Robert Moffat Papers, Box 4, Notebook 1860-8, Journal entry for 21 December 1862. Moffat refers to the death of Mrs Anne Thomas (née Morgan), who died at Inyati on 10 June 1862; Sibree (comp.), *Register of Missionaries*, p. 71.

cattle-kraals to fertilize the soil. At a much later period he could say, 'When I went out there was but one plough in the country, now there are thousands.' He introduced, and taught the natives to cultivate, various kinds of grain and fruit – wheat, barley, peas, potatoes, and so on. He encouraged them to substitute spades and mattocks for their old tools.[54]

However, it would be unfair to Moffat to suggest that he never moved beyond the conventional European view of the African male as a lazy bounder who left all hard work to the women. In his letter to William Ellis in 1834 he reflected on the probable connection between the relentlessly hot climate, the inhabitants' chronic undernourishment, and the apparent lack of energy that seemed to differentiate the Tswana from the indigenous inhabitants of other mission fields (including, so he had read, Ellis' own former field of the South Seas Islands). Nevertheless, he also commented on the underlying resilience of the Tswana in terms that are considerably more complimentary than those that characterize some of his writing for publication to a British readership:

> There is however something in their character which in the estimation of everyone raises them far above their southern neighbours. They have been accustomed to habits of industry & economy from their early years & would find means of living where others would starve & I believe they would rather die of hunger than eat the seeds or grain intended for next year's sowing. We anticipate a new & superior race with a new generation that is among those on & in the vicinity of Missionary stations.[55]

Robert Moffat should not be interpreted simply as an unthinking advocate of Western civilization and ways. Indeed, the nineteenth-century missionaries who laid the greatest emphasis on what they termed 'civilization' were the closest in spirit and purpose to those today who proclaim the necessity for Christian mission to be wedded to 'development'. As a gardener himself, Moffat was an astute observer of the African natural environment, including its geology,[56] and one who could pass intelligent observations that have a surprisingly modern ecological ring to them. Reflecting in *Missionary Labours and Scenes in Southern Africa* on the fact that 'the whole country north of the Orange River lying east of the Kalagare [Kalahari] desert, presented to the eye of an European something like an old neglected garden or field', he attributed the widespread desertification of the landscape to the Tswana tendency to 'cut down every species of timber, without regard to scenery or economy' in order to build their houses and fences. This systematic deforestation was the cause of the endless succession of droughts and drying up of previously abundant springs, and Moffat had done his best to persuade 'the more acute thinkers among the people' of the connection.[57] Even such perceptive observations have failed to impress some

---

[54] Smith, *One of God's Gardeners*, p. 148.

[55] SOAS, CWM/LMS South Africa Incoming Correspondence, Box 14A, Folder 2, Jacket F, Robert Moffat to William Ellis, Kuruman, 3 February 1834.

[56] See John S. Moffat, *Lives of Robert and Mary Moffat*, pp. 370-71.

[57] Robert Moffat, *Missionary Labours and Scenes*, pp. 330-33 (pp. 330 and 332).

modern scholars. The environmental historian Richard Grove has accused Moffat of holding 'an inflexible and pre-conceived environmental religion'. Moffat's description of one of the species of trees so widely destroyed, the *acacia giraffe* tree, as being so old that 'one might be led to conclude that they sprung up immediately after the flood, if not before it'[58] leads Grove to speculate that Moffat saw the 'neglected garden' as 'possibly' the Garden of Eden, and the Tswana's destruction of trees as somehow of a piece with the transgressions which led to Noah's flood.[59] Grove's suggestion is too ingenious to be taken seriously – if Moffat indeed supposed, as he may well have, that there had been divine judgment on deforestation in southern Africa, it had taken the form of a withdrawal of rain, not a catastrophic superfluity of it. However, he certainly believed that human sinfulness had gravely affected the natural environment, and that therefore it was an appropriate missionary goal to seek to reverse the process. An environmental dimension to Christian mission is neither a novelty of the late twentieth and twenty-first centuries nor a mere duplication of secular development trends. Robert Moffat gardened for the sake of the gospel, and he reaped a not insignificant harvest.

---

[58] Robert Moffat, *Missionary Labours and Scenes*, p. 331.

[59] Richard Grove, 'Scottish Missionaries, Evangelical Discourses and the Origins of Conservation Thinking in Southern Africa 1820–1900', *Journal of Southern African Studies* 15.2 (1989), pp. 163-87 (p. 170).

CHAPTER 19

How Evangelical Biblicism Saved Western Civilization

Timothy Larsen

The title of this chapter somewhat playfully echoes that of a bestselling book, *How the Irish Saved Civilization*.[1] The context of that story is the fall of the Roman Empire and with it classical civilization. The Greeks and Romans had developed a high intellectual culture and strong structures for education – for the transmission and expansion of knowledge. Then Rome was conquered by illiterate, barbarian tribes. In the resulting disruption, the transmission and preservation of knowledge was radically curtailed. *How the Irish Saved Civilization* is about the ways in which monks maintained the art of literacy and a commitment to education and the preservation and copying of manuscripts.

Much ground was gained in the thousand years between the fall of the Roman Empire and the Reformation and yet, from the perspective of what comes thereafter, what is noticeable is how far there was yet to go. Here is a snapshot of culture before the rise of Protestantism. Despite the fact that the only Bible to which they had access was the Latin Vulgate and that one of their primary duties was saying the Latin Mass, many medieval priests did not even know Latin and therefore were functionally illiterate when it came to the world of learning and sometimes completely illiterate. An English bishop surveying his priests in 1551 found that when they were asked where in the Bible one could find the Ten Commandments, a popular guess by his befuddled clergy was Matthew's Gospel.[2]

There were a range of social and technological factors that would lead to a rise of literacy rates in the seventeenth century and thereafter – not least developments in printing that greatly increased access to books. Nevertheless, a significant factor was distinctly theological, namely a Protestant commitment to the conviction that lay people should nurture their spiritual lives through reading or hearing portions of

---

[1] Thomas Cahill, *How the Irish Saved Civilization: The Untold Story of Ireland's Heroic Role from the Fall of Rome to the Rise of Medieval Europe* (New York, NY: Doubleday, 1995). An earlier version of this chapter was published as Timothy Larsen, 'Literacy and Biblical Knowledge: The Victorian Age and Our Own', *Journal of the Evangelical Theological Society* 52.3 (September, 2009), pp. 519-35. It also shares in common some material that has been published in Timothy Larsen, *A People of One Book: The Bible and the Victorians* (Oxford: Oxford University Press, 2011).

[2] David Daniell, *William Tyndale: A Biography* (New Haven, CT: Yale University Press, 1994), p. 78.

scripture daily. One thinks of William Tyndale's famous ambition to make the contents of the Bible familiar even to 'a boy that driveth a plough'. Tyndale's dream would become a widespread vision for Protestants in the English-speaking world. It is important to recall that it is not self-evident. For centuries thereafter society was divided by a strong sense of class distinctions. There was a real concern that a person might be made unfit for his or her station in life by exposure to the ways of those at a higher rung on the ladder. It became impermissible to argue that literacy would raise anyone above their station, however, because the gift of literacy was defined – specifically and precisely due to Bible-reading – as so beneficial to the spiritual life that it should be bestowed as universally as possible.

My own primary area of research is Victorian Britain and thus I shall focus on it but, following David Bebbington's fine example, this will also be a transatlantic piece. Bebbington has aptly named the Victorian era among the English-speaking peoples as the age of 'the dominance of evangelicalism'.[3] Even historians in other subfields beside religion agree with this. Boyd Hilton, for example, has demonstrated how evangelicalism shaped social and economic thought in the nineteenth century.[4] In his unrivalled definition of evangelicalism, Bebbington has identified biblicism as one of the movement's distinguishing marks.[5] Putting these things together, what we discover is that the Victorians had an astonishing commitment to reading and understanding the Bible because a dominant evangelical ethos had taught them to value knowledge of the scriptures.[6] The purpose of this chapter is to put on display the cultural impact of evangelical biblicism and to reflect on its significance.

In the nineteenth century, evangelical Protestants were very active spreading literacy. Many people have at least heard the term 'Sunday school', but when we think of it today we imagine specifically religious instruction. Sunday schools, however, were originally schools. There were no state schools and poor children often worked what we would consider adult jobs. In the early Victorian period – in a landmark piece of humanitarian legislation – the law graciously limited the work week of children to twelve hours a day six days a week. This meant that Sunday was their one day to learn. Sunday schools were funded by churches with the goal of teaching poor children to read. This was for their spiritual good – factory and mine owners and other employers by and large did not see any economic advantage to their labor force being literate.

The textbook for learning to read was the Bible. This was near universally true. The schools that existed were overwhelmingly sponsored by a church or a pan-

---

[3] David W. Bebbington, *The Dominance of Evangelicalism: The Age of Spurgeon and Moody* (Downers Grove, IL: InterVarsity Press, 2005).

[4] Boyd Hilton, *The Age of the Atonement: The Influence of Evangelicalism on Social and Economic Thought, 1785–1865* (Oxford: Clarendon Press, 1998).

[5] D.W. Bebbington, *Evangelicalism in Modern Britain: A History from the 1730s to the 1980s* (London: Unwin Hyman, 1989), pp. 2-17.

[6] For an exploration of how large the scriptures loomed in nineteenth-century Britain, see Larsen, *A People of One Book*.

denominational organization and they also made the Bible their core textbook. Even in independent, working-class schools the Bible was still the standard book used for learning to read.[7]

Once state education was established, the Bible retained a place in the core curriculum during the nineteenth century. Even after universal state education was enacted in 1870 the Bible retained a fundamental place in schooling throughout the Victorian age. No less a figure than the polemical man of science and sceptic T.H. Huxley – who coined the word 'agnosticism' and was known as Darwin's bulldog – voted for the London School Board resolution on the core curriculum for elementary school children that named the Bible first, and only thereafter listed reading, writing, and arithmetic.[8]

It is worth illustrating this scriptural formation with a few individual case studies. Catherine Mumford (1829–90) became well known as the co-founder of the Salvation Army under her married name of Catherine Booth. She was raised as an earnest Methodist. Not from a socially elite family, her father was a coach builder. Catherine did not receive any formal schooling until she had reached the age of twelve and, even then, it was all over within two years. Her home schooling, however, was centered on the Bible. She was already reading it by the age of five. Before she reached the age of twelve and was sent off to school, she had 'read the sacred Book from cover to cover eight times through'.[9] Keep in mind that this was done with no other intention than general learning and evangelical piety. Her parents had no schemes for her to become a minister, nor did she harbour any such aspirations. In fact, by her own subsequent reckoning, she was not even converted yet. This continuous, energetic, systematic study of scripture represents simply a normal course that the education of a precocious child might take in Victorian Britain. Nor did her voracious consumption of the Bible slacken as Catherine progressed through her teen years. Here is her primary New Year's resolution for 1848 when she was eighteen years old:

> above all, I am determined to search the Scriptures more attentively, for in them I have eternal life. I have read my Bible through twice during the last sixteen months, but I must read it with more prayer for light and understanding. Oh, may it be my meat and drink! May I meditate on it day and night! And then I shall 'bring forth fruit in season, my leaf also shall not wither, and whatsoever I do shall prosper.' [Psalm 1:2-3][10]

The result, not unexpectedly, was that Catherine Mumford thoroughly appropriated the biblical text. To take a telling example, even when describing seaside Brighton

---

[7] Phil Gardner, *The Lost Elementary Schools of Victorian England: The People's Education* (London: Croom Helm, 1984), p. 177.

[8] For his defense of the view of that Bible was essential to education, see Thomas Henry Huxley, *Critiques and Addresses* (London: Macmillan, 1873), pp. 33-55.

[9] F. de L. Booth-Tucker, *The Life of Catherine Booth: The Mother of The Salvation Army* (2 vols; London: Salvationist Publishing, 3rd edn, 1924), I, p. 15.

[10] Booth-Tucker, *Life*, I, pp. 52-53.

as a teenager on vacation, she reached eccentrically to the Old Testament to evoke the scene: 'I have just returned from the beach. It is a lovely morning, but very rough and cold. The sea looks sublime. I never saw it so troubled. Its waters "cast up mire and dirt" [Isaiah 57:20], and lash the shore with great violence.'[11]

If choosing someone destined to become the Mother of the Salvation Army somehow seems like a rigged sample, Victorian Britain's most famous atheist leader might serve as a counterweight on the other end of the spectrum. Charles Bradlaugh (1833–91), the president of the National Secular Society, became a household name through his ultimately successful campaign to become the first Member of Parliament who was an avowed atheist. His beginnings were humble, however, being raised in a poor family in London.[12] His parents were nominally Anglican, but not regular churchgoers. Bradlaugh's formal schooling, begun when he was seven years old, ended before he had reached his eleventh birthday. This education was steeped in scripture. Indeed, extraordinarily, everything that has survived of his school work is explicitly biblical, although these works were certainly retained merely as examples of his achievements rather than because of their theme – the last one is his ten-year old effort on the 'Death of Absalom' from 2 Samuel 18.[13] These pieces were clearly intended to demonstrate to his parents that he was learning to write with a clear hand. In other words, his penmanship lessons were scriptural ones. The point is not that it is ironic that the nation's preeminent atheist leader was raised on the Bible, but rather that it was well nigh inevitable.

In addition to standard patterns of general education, the biblical literacy of the Victorians was also buoyed up by mass exposure to scripture as a component of pursuing a life of piety. Daily Bible readings in the home circle and as an individual were widespread practices. Today, meaty, expositional sermons and daily Bible reading are often thought of as evangelical traits. Evangelicalism, as has been said, did indeed dominate Victorian culture. And evangelicals did insist that to be a good Christian meant to follow a way of life that included reading the Bible every day. The Methodist minister, William Cooke, in the *Juvenile Instructor*, for example, insisted that youths must never shirk this duty. He helpfully recommended that on particularly busy days, although they could not cut their Bible reading, they were free to decide to spend less time eating or sleeping.[14]

Nevertheless, it is important to underline that these religious practices were pursued across the Christian spectrum in the nineteenth century. Theological liberal Anglicans also shared these values. For example, although Florence Nightingale was so theologically liberal that she would not formally consent to the belief that the

---

[11] Booth-Tucker, *Life*, I, p. 48 (I have added the reference in brackets).

[12] Charles Bradlaugh, *The Autobiography of Mr. Bradlaugh: A Page of his Life* (London: Austin, 1873).

[13] Bishopsgate Institute, Bishopsgate Library, London, Bradlaugh Papers, Bradlaugh 18/B, 'Death of Absalom', 1843.

[14] William Cooke, *Explanations of Difficult Portions of Holy Scripture, &c., in 565 Queries and Answers* (reprinted from the *Juvenile Instructor*) (London: Henry Webber, 1866), p. 12.

Bible was a unique source of revelation and even asserted that its teaching was sometimes wrongheaded, she nevertheless read the Old and New Testaments earnestly every day, both by herself and aloud to her servants.[15] One can find these habits across the denominations – for example, daily Bible readings were widespread among both Quakers and Unitarians.

The Bible, therefore, was the common cultural currency of the Victorians. There are only two kinds of eminent Victorian authors – the kind who have had a whole book written about their use of scripture and the kind who are ripe for such attention. Christina Rossetti is one of the most celebrated poets of the Victorian age. A scholar has produced a 256-page concordance of biblical allusions in her poetry.[16] Such a concordance could profitably be compiled for any Victorian poet, I suspect. The poet P.B. Shelley was one of the first public atheists in Victorian elite culture. Irreligion and biblical illiteracy, however, do not correlate in this period and therefore there is a whole book on *Shelley and Scripture*.[17] There are, of course, books on the Bible and the most famous Victorian writer of them all, Charles Dickens.[18] This premier Victorian novelist took his religion in his stride, disliked zealous and dogmatic Christians, and left his wife for a mistress. Nevertheless, Dickens so assumed that every Victorian should know the contents of the Bible that he even wrote his own harmony of the four Gospels as a tool for the education of his own children.[19] To glance across the Atlantic for a moment, Harriet Beecher Stowe's *Uncle Tom's Cabin* (1852) became the bestselling novel in American history.[20] Reading it to today, one is struck by the fact that the dialogue includes discussions of the correct interpretation of specific biblical texts. Its sales were superseded, however, by an even more biblically-charged work of fiction: Lew Wallace's *Ben-Hur: A Tale of the Christ* (1880), making it the bestselling novel in nineteenth-century America.[21] Pick up an annotated edition of any Victorian novel and the notes will include biblical allusions that it never occurred to the author would ever need elucidating.

The content of the scriptures also loomed large in the visual arts. The Pre-Raphaelites – the main, new, trendy school of art – were deeply biblical.[22] Not

---

[15] Lynn McDonald (ed.), *Florence Nightingale: An Introduction to Her Life and Family* (The Collected Works of Florence Nightingale, 1; Waterloo, ON: Wilfrid Laurier University Press, 2001), p. 703.

[16] Nilda Jiménez (compiler), *The Bible and the Poetry of Christina Rossetti* (Westport, CT: Greenwood Press, 1979).

[17] Bryan Shelley, *Shelley and Scripture: The Interpreting Angel* (Oxford: Clarendon Press, 1994).

[18] Janet L. Larson, *Dickens and the Broken Scripture* (Athens, GA: University of Georgia Press, 1985).

[19] Charles Dickens, *The Life of Our Lord* (London: Associated Newspapers, 1934).

[20] Harriet Beecher Stowe, *Uncle Tom's Cabin* (New York, NY: Harper, 1852).

[21] Lew Wallace, *Ben-Hur: A Tale of the Christ* (New York: Harper, 1880).

[22] Michaela Giebelhausen, *Painting the Bible: Representation and Belief in Mid-Victorian Britain* (Aldershot: Ashgate, 2006).

content with merely a biblical theme and title, Holman Hunt even had the frames of his paintings inscribed with scriptural texts. *The Scapegoat*, for example, has Isaiah 53.4 written out on the top of the frame, balanced by Leviticus 16.22 on the bottom.[23]

I am confident that one could dive at random into any sources left by the Victorians and find that they contain biblical allusions which assume their audience possessed a scriptural knowledge base. This would hold true from the sublime to the mundane, from the religious to the anti-religious to the purely secular in the sense of given over exclusively to the practical issues of life. The recorded speech of any event would do – a trade union conference or a murder trial – or any person, whether prostitute or parliamentarian. I tried such a random sounding myself once. In an idle moment in the library of Trinity College, Cambridge, the thought occurred to me that the international industrial show, the Great Exhibition of 1851, was such an iconic Victorian moment that I wondered if it reflected the culture's biblical saturation. I looked up the official Great Exhibition catalogue, but did not even need to open it: on the cover was written out the words of Psalm 24.1.[24] If you are not yet convinced, I would encourage you to make any such experiment yourself: 'Seek and ye shall find.'

With biblical literacy so pervasive in Victorian popular culture, it is perhaps unsurprising that there was a snobbish backlash by certain members of the social and intellectual elite. This response was most thoroughly articulated by the poet and literary critic, Matthew Arnold (1822–88), in his influential book, *Culture and Anarchy* (1869). Arnold exuded disdain for the hordes of evangelical, Bible-toting Baptists and Congregationalists whose influence in Victorian society was waxing strong. Arnold claimed that an ideal culture is one that balances what he labelled 'Hebraism' and 'Hellenism'. Hebraism is the earnest, biblicist Christianity of the evangelical middle classes. One needs a certain amount of that, of course, in order to sustain sound morality. Victorian society had too much of it, however, which meant that it was squeezing out Hellenism, a high culture sensibility that revels in the most exquisite human achievements as exemplified in the philosophical, literary, and artistic accomplishments of ancient Greece and Rome. Arnold offers this thought experiment: imagine Virgil on the Mayflower.[25] It is apparent that this cultured soul would not have found his Puritan fellow-travelers diverting company, therefore, there is something wrong with the Puritan spirit – a spirit which Arnold finds

---

[23] For photographs of Hunt's frames, see Judith Bronkhurst, *William Holman Hunt: A Catalogue Raisonné* (2 vols; New Haven, CT: Yale University Press for the Paul Mellon Centre for Studies in British Art, 2006).

[24] *Official Catalogue of the Great Exhibition of the Works of Industry of All Nations, 1851, By Authority of the Royal Commission* (London: Spicer Brothers, 1851). Some years after my little sounding, a monograph (which I had the pleasure of peer-reviewing) was published which helpfully documents many more scriptural connections: Geoffrey Cantor, *Religion and the Great Exhibition of 1851* (Oxford: Oxford University Press, 2011).

[25] Matthew Arnold, *Culture and Arnold: An Essay in Political and Social Criticism* (London: Smith, Elder, 1897 [1869]), p. 19.

thriving in his own day, with the evangelical Baptist preacher, Charles Haddon Spurgeon, serving as a readily identifiable embodiment of it.[26] The specific weakness of the Hebraists is their inordinate attachment to scripture: 'The book which contains this invaluable law *they* call the Word of God, and *attribute* to it, as I have said, and as, indeed, is perfectly well known, a reach and sufficiency coextensive with all the wants of human nature.'[27] In other words, Arnold assumed that if people were not attending to their Bibles so much they would be reading more Plato, Virgil, and Shakespeare, and thereby have a richer civilization. Arnold occasionally even lets slip his disdain for the Bible itself.[28] A telling quotation is the following one which begins with his mockery of the scripture-lover who praises

> A man's sticking to the one thing needful, – *he knows*, says Hebraism, *his Bible!* – whenever we hear this said, we may, without any elaborate defence of culture, content ourselves with answering simply: 'No one, who knows nothing else, knows even his Bible.'[29]

Arnold's dictum echoes down the decades to the present. In this literary tradition, biblical knowledge is actually a way of signaling that someone is ignorant. The quintessential representation of this move is *Inherit the Wind*, a 1955 Broadway play that became in 1960 an influential, award-winning film, and has since often been staged as well as generating three additional film versions (1965, 1988, and 1999). In *Inherit the Wind*, Matthew Harrison Brady represents the ignorance of the biblically literate, although even he is portrayed as a cut above the real grassroots Bible-thumpers. The dramatic center of this courtroom play is the cross examination of Brady done by Henry Drummond, the latter representing Hellenism in Matthew Arnold's terms. This scene begins,

> Drummond: Am I correct sir, in calling on you as an authority on the Bible?
> Brady: I believe it is not boastful to say that I have studied the Bible as much as any layman. And I have tried to live according to its precepts.
> Drummond: Bully for you. Now, I suppose you can quote me chapter and verse right straight through the King James Version, can't you?
> Brady: There are many portions of the Holy Bible that I have committed to memory.
> Drummond: I don't suppose you've memorized many passages from the *Origin of the Species*?
> Brady: I am not in the least interested in the pagan hypotheses of that book.
> Drummond: Never read it?
> Brady: And I never will.
> Drummond: Then how in perdition do you have the gall to whoop up this holy war against something you don't know anything about? How can you be so cocksure that

---

[26] For his identification of Spurgeon as a one of the Hebraisers, see Arnold, *Culture*, p. 131.
[27] Arnold, *Culture*, p. 105.
[28] Arnold, *Culture*, p. 142.
[29] Arnold, *Culture*, p. 113.

the body of scientific knowledge systematized in the writings of Charles Darwin is, in any way, irreconcilable with the spirit of the Book of Genesis?
Brady: Would you state that question again, please?[30]

In this exchange, Brady's knowledge of the Bible is presented as the visible and outward sign of his inner, fundamental ignorance. The key words of Drummond's final question in this excerpt are 'you don't know anything' which are immediately validated by Brady's inability even to comprehend the question and which has already been signaled by his confession of having memorized many passages from the scriptures. The play is depicting the Scopes Trial and Brady is a fictionalized version of William Jennings Bryan. In reality, Bryan had studied thoroughly the text of Darwin's *On the Origin of the Species* but, marching on from Matthew Arnold, the impression is given that study of the Bible means having no general knowledge or wider culture so the play has Brady boastful about his ignorance of Darwin's celebrated tome. When Drummond's probing questions push Brady to think, the strain is so great that he breaks under it, the sign that he has lost control of his reasoning faculties being that he starts chanting the names of books of the Bible. This display of biblical memorization amply reveals that nothing further can be learned in such a scripture-infested environment and the judge has no alternative but to call for a recess.[31]

The dissemination of this trope may be witnessed in what became the most popular show on American television just a couple years after *Inherit the Wind* was released as a feature film, *The Beverly Hillbillies*. Winning eleven Emmys and setting a new ratings record, this TV sitcom ran for almost a decade (1962–71) and has never been decommissioned from re-run land. A running joke throughout the series is that these hillbillies have scant formal education, do not read, fail to appreciate or even understand high culture, and are usually literally illiterate. This, once again, is signaled by a display of biblical knowledge: the two male members of the family are named Jedidiah and Jethro. These names reflect such a depth of familiarity with the Hebrew scriptures that I am confident that nine out of ten literary critics today would not be able to trace these allusions back to their specific, biblical source from memory. In a strangely twisted way, the careful scrutiny of an ancient text that these naming choices reveal are intended as shorthand for the fact that these are uncultured, illiterate, and ignorant people.

My own dictum is the inversion of Matthew Arnold's. You will recall that he asserted, 'No one, who knows nothing else, knows even his Bible.' I would like to submit for investigation the following thesis, 'A western culture where people don't read their Bibles is one in which they probably don't read much else either.' I will not belabour the most obvious sense in which this is true, namely that the illustrious literary and artistic inheritance of western culture assumes scriptural knowledge and becomes progressively more obscure, incomprehensible, and inaccessible the less

---

[30] Jerome Lawrence and Robert E. Lee, *Inherit the Wind* (New York, NY: Bantam Books, 1965), pp. 76-77.

[31] Lawrence and Lee, *Inherit*, pp. 90-91.

biblical literacy one has. Northrop Frye emphasized that the Bible is 'the Great Code' for understanding English literature.[32] Frye discovered this when he tried to teach undergraduates the poetry of John Milton and of William Blake: 'I soon realized that a student of English literature who does not know the Bible does not understand a good deal of what is going on in what he reads: the most conscientious student will be continually misconstruing the implications, even the meaning.'[33] Likewise, many of the most celebrated visual artists of the western tradition – Michelangelo and Rembrandt, for example – count on viewers being familiar with the biblical subject matter that they are depicting. Rather than this specific advantage of biblical literacy – that it decodes our own cultural inheritance – what I want to explore in this chapter is a much more sweeping claim. My argument is that Bible reading serves as the gateway – arguably the indispensable gateway – to advanced literacy and high literary culture for a western society – and thus it is vital to the preservation of civilization.

First, however, we need briefly to contrast our own times with those of the Victorian age in terms of biblical literacy. I personally would rather live now than at any time in the past, not least the Victorian age. This chapter is not intended to present it as an ideal time, or even as the good old days. Much has improved since then, not only in other spheres such as gender equality and medical advances, but even in the specific areas of universal education, mass basic literacy, access to books, and admirable spiritual sensibilities. The biblical knowledge of the Victorians is simply evoked as a standard that a culture can attain and one that has significant consequences for literacy in the widest and deepest senses of that word.

The difference in general levels of biblical literacy between my lifetime and the Victorian age may be illustrated by an emblematic moment. In 1985 perhaps the most collaborative project to date in the history of the American pop music industry occurred as a charity fundraiser for African famine relief, the recording of the specially written song, 'We Are the World'.[34] This hit sold millions of copies and won Grammy awards for Song of the Year, Best Pop Performance by a Group, and Record of the Year. There is no telling how many people were involved in this project behind the scenes, but over forty celebrity singers and musicians took part including Bob Dylan, Diana Ross, Billy Joel, Tina Turner, Paul Simon, Kenny Rogers, Stevie Wonder, Willie Nelson, Dionne Warwick, Ray Charles, Bruce Springsteen, and Bette Midler. Nevertheless, the lyrics of the song (written by Michael Jackson and Lionel Richie) exemplify basic biblical illiteracy, containing as they do this line, 'As God has shown us by turning stones to bread.'[35] The Bible, of course, shows the exact opposite: Jesus resisted the Satanic temptation to turn stones

---

[32] Northrop Frye, *The Great Code: The Bible and Literature* (New York, NY: Harcourt Brace Jovanovich, 1982).

[33] Fry, *Great Code*, p. xii.

[34] David Breskin, *We are the World* (New York: Perigree Books, 1985).

[35] Berskin, *We are the World*. (There is no pagination in this volume, but the lyrics are printed in it.)

into bread (Matthew 4.3-4). This mistake is particularly egregious as the Gospels are the most well-known books of the Bible. It is inconceivable that any group of Victorians – however personally irreligious they all might have been – could have let a project go forward without noticing and correcting such an elementary error in biblical knowledge. Moreover, it has been demonstrated that biblical literacy has continued to decline yet further since 1985. Gallup polls have tracked this descent to a current 'record low'. Not even able to get started with the canon in either Testament, most Americans now cannot name the first book of the Bible and half cannot name even one of the four Gospels.[36] Stephen Prothero, Professor of Religion, Boston University, highlighted this in a 2007 article in the *Los Angeles Times* which was bluntly entitled, 'We live in the land of biblical idiots'.[37]

When George W. Bush gave his first inaugural address, he made one biblical allusion. Again, it was to the most familiar part of the Bible, the Gospels – to the Story of the Good Samaritan, to be specific. He said, 'And I can pledge our nation to a goal: When we see that wounded traveler on the road to Jericho, we will not pass to the other side.' It just bewildered most people as so many Americans are no longer biblically literate enough to understand such allusions. Even the political commentator that was covering the speech for CBS quite cheerfully confessed that he had no idea what it meant. Most anyone in the nineteenth century would have been able to explain what such a reference meant by the time they were eight years old.

Nor should we fail to face how much this impoverishes us. Great orators such as Abraham Lincoln, John Bright, W.E. Gladstone, and Martin Luther King, Jr, drew on the rich storehouse of scripture in the confidence that their hearers would grasp the resonant allusions they were making. What common cultural resources could an orator today draw on with confidence that her hearers would understand? Are these resources too shallow or trivial to bear the weight of speaking profoundly to vital matters of state and society?

So what do I mean by the claim that mass Bible reading serves as the gateway to a society marked by advanced literacy? To begin at the most fundamental level: *first, the habit of daily Bible reading creates a culture in which people read regularly.* A Pew Research Center reported in 2014 that 'the number of non-book-readers has nearly tripled since 1978'.[38] In reports issued in 2004 and 2007, the National Endowment for the Arts provided alarming, statistical evidence to demonstrate that Americans are losing the habit of regular reading.[39] 43.4% of adults reported that

---

[36] Stephen Prothero, *Religious Literacy: What Every American Needs to Know – and Doesn't* (New York, NY: HarperSanFrancisco, 2007), p. 30.

[37] Stephen Prothero, 'We live in the land of biblical idiots', *Los Angeles Times* 14 March 2007.

[38] 'The Decline of the American Book Lover', *Atlantic* 21 January 2014 (accessed on-line at www.theatlantic.com).

[39] *Reading at Risk: A Survey of Literary Reading in America* (Research Division Report, 46; Washington, DC: National Endowment for the Arts, 2004; *To Read or Not to Read: A*

they did not read a single book in the entire previous year.[40] Positively, these reports correlate regular, voluntary reading with other vital outcomes including achieving as a student and employee and contributing constructively as a citizen and member of society. I am putting forward the hypothesis that one of the factors that is sustaining a culture of readers in society today is religious motivation that results in a way of life which includes reading the Bible. This motivation – even when found amongst those in other traditions such as Roman Catholicism – in turn is, at the very least, an indirect debt to evangelical biblicism. It is suggestive that the book industry has observed in recent years that, although the population at large is reading fewer books, the market for religious books is actually growing.[41] I think it is likely that what this is reflecting is that while many other people are losing the reading habit, a segment of religious people are maintaining it through a culture of scripture reading.

Certainly, Victorians who were raised on the Bible often caught the reading habit more generally. This is brilliantly revealed in Jonathan Rose's *The Intellectual Life of the British Working Classes*. Rose shows that the deeply evangelical and biblicist chapel culture of Wales also created a community of avid readers. This culture of reading was so strong that these tough, working-class men would boast to one another that they had read every book in the library.[42] This connection was being made even by contemporary observers. The Victorian evangelical Congregational minister, Thomas Binney, averred,

> The religious man becomes of necessity a thinker and a reader ... He is the student of a Book which is adapted to expand and elevate the mind, to fill it with great thoughts, to inspire it with noble purposes, to exercise the imagination, to strengthen the judgment, and to teach the true philosophy of life; he gets by the study of it mental power, from the effort required by some of its parts; – acuteness and caution, from patient comparison of passage with passage, which mutually interpret and modify each other ... He may increase his library, – and probably will; he may enlarge his acquaintance with the educated and accomplished, and greatly augment his knowledge by conversation; and he may improve his taste by what meets his eye of the elegant and the beautiful ...[43]

Secondly, the practice of Bible reading creates a culture in which people read proficiently. There is a crisis of the level of reading capability in our culture today. A 2003 study revealed that 'only 5% of high school graduates are proficient readers'. *For those with a bachelor's degree, the statistic is 31%!*[44] Moreover, the bar for

---

Question of National Consequence (Research Report, 47; Washington, DC: National Endowment for the Arts, 2007).

[40] *Reading at Risk*, p. 4.

[41] *Book Industry Trends 2007* (New York, NY: Book Industry Study Group, 2007).

[42] Jonathan Rose, *The Intellectual Life of the British Working Classes* (New Haven, CT: Yale University Press, 2001), p. 251.

[43] T. Binney, *Is It Possible to Make the Best of Both Worlds?* (London: James Nisbet, 17th edn, 1870), pp. 80-81.

[44] *To Read or Not to Read*, pp. 61, 65.

proficiency is not high. In this study, a person was considered a proficient reader if he or she could successfully perform such tasks as comparing the viewpoints in two different newspaper editorials or infer what the purpose of an event described in a magazine article was.[45] Anyone who reads the Bible and has learned to comprehend it could approach such a test with complete confidence. I have no doubt that Catherine Booth could have passed it at the age of eleven, making her a more skilled reader before she had ever gone to school than most American university graduates are today! Victorian newspapers assumed that their readership possessed a higher reading level than newspapers today do. In short, a society of Bible-readers is also a society of proficient readers.

Thirdly, the practice of Bible reading creates a culture in which people are able to read books from a variety of different genres. The Bible is a collection of scores of different documents reflecting a variety of different genres. Sometimes even within the same book of the Bible there is more than one genre. These genres include history, law, poetry, drama, lament, proverbs, epistles, royal records, genealogies, parables, stories, speeches and songs, not to mention more explicitly religious genres such as prophecies and apocalyptic writings. Americans are also losing the habit of reading across genres. Only 12% reported that they had read any poetry at all during the previous year.[46] The Victorians would have been baffled by the twentieth-first century category of the ostensibly literate people who can assert flatly, 'I don't read poetry.' The Victorian mass reading public avidly consumed books in a range of genres, including novels, poetry, philosophy, and history. I am positing a connection. As one old coal miner and wide reader reminisced in the mid-twentieth century,

> It is true that our fathers, in Wales, taught us a religion of cast-iron dogma, which, according to all the theories, should have made us obscurantists, inhabiting a very small world. But it did not ... I defy any child of ordinary intelligence to read the Bible constantly (in the Authorized Version) without acquiring a genuine literary taste, a sense of style, and at least a feeling for the beauty of words. Before I was twelve I had developed an appreciation of good prose, and the Bible created in me a zest for literature.[47]

Fourthly, the practice of Bible reading creates a culture in which people are able to read ancient texts despite the otherness of the past. In addition to losing the habit of reading across genres, we are also losing the habit of reading across time. In 2007, the British charity World Book Day conducted a survey of the books 'the nation cannot live without'.[48] It released the list of the top 100. With the sole exceptions of Shakespeare and the Bible itself, the oldest items were all from the nineteenth century and the majority of the books on the list were written in living memory including such instant classics as *The Hitch Hiker's Guide to the Galaxy, The Da*

---

[45] *To Read or Not to Read*, p. 63.
[46] *Reading at Risk*, p. 3.
[47] Rose, *Intellectual Life*, pp. 239-40.
[48] Their website is www.worldbookday.com.

Vinci Code, *Notes From a Small Island*, *Bridget Jones's Diary*, and *His Dark Materials*. In short, Britain has developed a reading culture that apparently can usually reach no further into the past than to Jane Austen. In marked contrast to the biblical knowledge that infused the bestselling novels of the nineteenth century, thus far the twenty-first century's smash hit is not a tale of the Christ but rather the erotic, *Fifty Shades of Grey* (2011), by the British author E.L. James.[49]

Likewise, on a recent visit to my local public library, in Wheaton, Illinois, I noticed on the reference desk a pile of hand-outs for patrons which offered a list entitled '100 Best English Language Books' as selected by the Modern Library Board. The English-language restriction makes one wonder why works in translation were not to be commended to American readers, but at least that limitation is acknowledged. More fundamentally, the list is actually an attempt to identify the best English-language *novels* published *since 1900*. The Modern Library Board reveals these restrictions on a separate page on its website, but the prominent list itself is simply entitled '100 Best Novels', thereby trading the English-language disclosure for a genre one and continuing to hide the chronological one.[50] There is no fine print disclosure on the list from my library: it is a sign of the times that a public library could not notice something odd about a purported list of '100 Best English Language Books' that did not even include Shakespeare. Indeed, perhaps even much of the twentieth century is now considered too remote. In 2011, *Time* magazine offered the 'All-TIME 100 Best Nonfiction books' list.[51] All-TIME, it turns out, is a pun on the name of the magazine which also serves to mislead the reader. The fine print says that it is 'the 100 best and most influential written in English since 1923'. That last date is particularly curious – it seems that even the first quarter of the twentieth century is now too remote for readers today to bother about. Maybe the cut-off date is actually closer than that. Anne Trubek, a Professor of English at Oberlin College, has recently recommended that her colleagues stop assigning *The Catcher in the Rye*. When asked for a rationale, she said nothing at all about the literary merits or demerits of this novel, but rather observed, 'It was published in 1951 and it's not so contemporary anymore.'[52]

This can be contrasted with the list of the 100 best books compiled by Sir John Lubbock which working-class Victorians used to guide their reading choices. It began, of course, with the Bible and was followed by the *Meditations* of Marcus Aurelius, Epictetus, Aristotle's *Ethics*, and Confucius.[53] It is a stunning list – ranging across the genre, the centuries, and the globe.

Once again, Matthew Arnold should be inverted. If the masses do not read their Bibles it is not at all likely that they will read Aristotle or Horace instead. On the

---

[49] E.L. James, *Fifty Shades of Grey* (New York, NY: Vintage, 2011).

[50] Their website is www.randomhouse.com/modernlibrary.

[51] 'All-TIME 100 Best Nonfiction books', *Time* 17 August 2011 (accessed on-line at http://entertainment.time.com).

[52] Cory Franklin, 'Let's not turn our YouTubing backs on the classics', *Chicago Tribune* 15 September 2008, Section 1, p. 23.

[53] John Lubbock, *The Pleasures of Life* (London: Macmillan, 1899), pp. 89-93.

other hand, someone who has mastered the Bible is far less likely to be overwhelmed by other ancient texts: they have learned to swim in the otherness of the past. The Victorians' love of classics was actually nurtured by their love of the Bible. This connection is explicit in nineteenth-century lives across the social spectrum all the way from the Prime Minister, William Gladstone, down to the Welsh miners.[54] Arnold might have been right that Virgil would not have appreciated the company of the Pilgrim Fathers, but he was certainly wrong if he assumed that these Puritans would not have appreciated the works of this classical Roman poet. There is no surviving list of what few books the Mayflower Pilgrims were able to take with them in the limited space they had, but we know that one of them was Caesar's *Commentaries*, and if they had come across a copy of the *Aeneid* stowed away below deck they would certainly have thanked the Almighty for this blessed boon.[55] This is no less true for Arnold's representative contemporary 'Puritan', Charles Haddon Spurgeon. Although he never attended college, this populist evangelist learned both Greek and Latin, built up a personal library of over 12,000 volumes, and gave this advice to earnest, working-class evangelicals who aspired to preach the gospel with power, 'The acquisition of another language affords a fine drilling for the practice of extempore speech ... I know of no better exercise than to translate with as much rapidity as possible a portion of Virgil or Tacitus, and then with deliberation to amend one's mistakes. Persons who know no better, think all time thrown away which is spent upon the classics.'[56]

Victorian labourers raised on the Bible did not know that they were supposed to find Homer and Pliny difficult, irrelevant, and distastefully high-brow, so they eagerly bought the penny editions which publishers produced for folks of their limited means and consumed them delightedly.[57] Once again, standing Arnold on his head, I believe if a scientific survey was done today it would show a clear correlation between students of Greco-Roman classics and Bible readers. The vast majority of English-speakers today who read classical Greek authors in the original language undoubtedly initially learned Greek from a desire to read the New Testament. Latin, of course, has an important place in the life of the Catholic Church, but many people might not be aware of a fascinating commitment to it among conservative Protestants. It is positively trendy for evangelical children who are being homeschooled to learn Latin (as well as to read texts from across the centuries and genres). This commitment has moved into private evangelical Protestant schools as well. My children all attend our local public schools and are thus far innocent of ancient languages, but if I were to prioritize them learning Latin I could have them tutored by some of the homeschooled evangelical teenagers in our town who I know

---

[54] For the interaction between Gladstone's study of the Bible and his study of classics, see David Bebbington, *The Mind of Gladstone: Religion, Homer, and Politics* (Oxford: Oxford University Press, 2004).

[55] Azel Ames, *May-Flower and Her Log* (Boston, MA: Houghton, Mifflin, 1901), p. 217.

[56] C.H. Spurgeon, *Lectures to My Students*, First Series (London: Passmore and Alabaster, 1875), p. 160.

[57] Rose, *Intellectual Life*, p. 400.

have become competent in that language. Or I could send them to nearby Covenant Classical School – a Christian school which is committed to graduating students who are biblically-literate and which teaches Latin as part of the core curriculum.

It might be objected that I am presenting an idealized picture, that Bible reading does not typically yield such fruits. The stereotype of the ignorant fundamentalist cannot be so easily dispelled. My argument, however, is not that Bible reading always produces such results, but only that Bible reading does a far better job of producing these fruits in mass western culture than is being and perhaps can be done without it. In the national consciousness, the Scopes Trail essentially pitted the level of learned culture of the poor folks of Rhea County, Tennessee, against that of the journalists and critics of our cosmopolitan centers. This is always the way: the Beverly Hillbillies contrasted poor, uneducated southerners with elite and privileged west coast families; Matthew Arnold put his Oxford education up against that of men of trade who had never had the opportunity to go to a university. My point is that I am confident that if you took ordinary people from the same geographical area who have the same level of education and wealth and work the same jobs, the Bible readers will be significantly more likely to be proficient and literary readers than those who are not. Their co-workers on the factory line who do not read the Bible are not electing to read Dante or Plato instead, but rather are more apt to watch *Sex and the City* or play *Grand Theft Auto V: Witness Torture*. Those who do study scripture, however, are far better equipped to read the *Divine Comedy* or Plato's *Republic* than those who do not, and would be more likely actually to do so and would be much easier to encourage to do so. Wallace Shawn, in his play *The Designated Mourner*, gloomily imagines a time in the near future when there is no one left on earth 'who could read John Donne'.[58] As long as there is a subculture of committed Bible readers in the world, that fate need not be feared, and as long as there is an evangelical movement its commitment to biblicism will help to make sure that is so.

I have now presented the main argument I wanted to make in this chapter. It could be developed in other directions as well. For example, arguably the Victorians readily memorized poems and soliloquies because they were taught as a spiritual discipline to learn holy scripture by heart, and perhaps a mass culture of literary memorization cannot be sustained without this religious practice. The decline in literacy in recent decades is generally attributed to the rise of television, computer games, the internet, and other forms of entertainment and electronic media. This connection is obviously correct, but it is not necessary to assume that our culture is powerless in the face of such forces. The National Endowment for the Arts is alarmed by the decline in literacy, but it is not defeatist. Rather, it has issued a 'call to action'.[59] Stephen Prothero recommends reversing our society's religious illiteracy through required courses in schools and colleges.[60] This proposal has merit, but the

---

[58] Wallace Shawn, *The Designated Mourner* (London: Faber and Faber, 1996), p. 53.
[59] *To Read or Not to Read*, p. 6.
[60] Prothero, *Religious Literacy*, pp. 126-48.

NEA study makes a compelling case for the claim that school requirements are insufficient and only the habit of *voluntary* reading can produce a culture of proficient readers.[61] What would it take to reverse the decline in regular reading? The motivation of a faith commitment is something that is powerful enough to mobilize ordinary people to make a habit of serious reading even in an image-driven age. Perhaps there is no other motivation that could create a mass culture of reading ancient texts today – or even a mass culture of proficient or literary reading. If you care about the future of literacy, read proficiency, high culture, and knowledge of the literary treasures of past ages, you just might want to think about writing a well-crafted thank you note to someone you know who is helping to guide ordinary people into the habit of regular Bible reading. And feel free to throw in a classical allusion if you wish.

---

[61] *To Read or Not to Read*, pp. 55-66.

Bibliography of the Writings of David William Bebbington[1]

1972

'The Life of Baptist Noel: Its Setting and Significance', *Baptist Quarterly* 24.8 (October, 1972), pp. 389-411
'R.H. Tawney as a Historian', *The Christian Graduate* 25.2 (1972), pp. 52-56

1975

'Gladstone and the Nonconformists: A Religious Affinity in Politics', in D. Baker (ed.), *Church, Society and Politics* (Oxford: Basil Blackwell, 1975), pp. 369-82

1976

'Gladstone and the Baptists', *Baptist Quarterly* 26.5 (January, 1976), pp. 224-39

1977

R.J. Bauckham and D.W. Bebbington, *History and Christianity: A Bibliography* (Leicester: Universities and Colleges Christian Fellowship, 1977)
A History of Queensberry Street Baptist Church, Old Basford, Nottingham (Nottingham: Privately printed, 1977)
'Politics and Philanthropy: The Social Concern and Political Activity of Lord Shaftesbury', *Third Way* 1.15 (1977), pp. 13-16
'C.H. Spurgeon, William Carey and William Wilberforce', in T. Dowley (ed.), *The History of Christianity* (Tring: Lion Publishing, 1977 [rev. edn, 1990]), pp. 529, 548, 651

1979

Patterns in History (Leicester: Inter-Varsity Press, 1979/Downers Grove, IL: Inter-Varsity Press, 1980)
'The City, the Countryside and the Social Gospel in Late Victorian Nonconformity', in D. Baker (ed.), *The Church in Town and Countryside* (Oxford: Basil Blackwell, 1979), pp. 415-26

---

[1] The Bibliography is arranged by sole-authored and co-authored monographs, edited and co-edited volumes, chapters in books, articles in journals, contributions to dictionaries and encyclopedias, and internet contributions.

1980

'Baptist M.P.s in the Seventeenth and Eighteenth Centuries', *Baptist Quarterly* 28.6 (April, 1980), pp. 245-62

1981

'Baptist M.P.s in the Nineteenth Century', *Baptist Quarterly* 29.1 (January, 1981), pp. 3-23
'Baptist Members of Parliament, 1847–1914', *Baptist Quarterly* 29.2 (April, 1981), pp. 51-64

1982

The Nonconformist Conscience: Chapel and Politics, 1870–1914 (Allen & Unwin, London, 1982)
'Religion and National Feeling in Nineteenth-Century Wales and Scotland', in S. Mews (ed.), *Religion and National Identity* (Oxford: Basil Blackwell, 1982), pp. 489-503

1983

'Baptists and Politics since 1914', in K.W. Clements (ed.), *Baptists in the Twentieth Century* (London: Baptist Historical Society, 1983), pp. 76-95
'Evangelicals and Reform: An Analysis of Mass Socio-Political Action', *Third Way* 6.5 (1983), pp. 10-13
'The Gospel in the Nineteenth Century', *Vox Evangelica* 13 (1983), pp. 19-28
'History for Theology and Mission', *Faith and Thought* 110.1–2 (1983), pp. 69-78
'Thomas Chalmers: Man, Churchman and Social Theorist in Early Nineteenth-Century Scotland', *Schools Scottish Studies Review* 1.2 (1983), pp. 21-26

1984

'The Persecution of George Jackson: A British Fundamentalist Controversy', in W.J. Sheils (ed.), *Persecution and Toleration* (Oxford: Basil Blackwell, 1984), pp. 421-33
'Evangelicals and the Role of Women, 1800–1930', *Christian Arena* 37.4 (1984), pp. 19-23
'Nonconformity and Electoral Sociology, 1867–1918', *The Historical Journal* 27.3 (1984), pp. 633-56

1986

'Baptist M.P.s in the Twentieth Century', *Baptist Quarterly* 31.6 (April, 1986), pp. 252-87
'The Oxford Group between the Wars', in W.J. Sheils and D. Wood (ed.), *Voluntary Religion* (Oxford: Basil Blackwell, 1986), pp. 495-507

1987

'Evangelicals and Class in Britain', *Third Way* 10.4 (1987), pp. 10-14
'Historical Background', in *Religion in Scotland* (Edinburgh: HMSO, 1987), pp. 3-6

1988

D.W. Bebbington (ed.), *The Baptists in Scotland: A History* (Glasgow: Baptist Union of Scotland, 1988)
'The Advent Hope in British Evangelicalism since 1800', *Scottish Journal of Religious Studies* 9.2 (1988), pp. 103-14
'A Rising Tide [Anglican Evangelicals since the Second World War]', *Third Way* 11.4 (1988), pp. 14-16
'Elizabeth Fry and C.H. Spurgeon', in J.D. Woodbridge (ed.), *Great Leaders of the Christian Church* (Chicago, IL: Moody Press, 1988), pp. 313-15 and 334-38
'History', in S.B. Ferguson and D.F. Wright (eds), *New Dictionary of Theology* (Leicester: Inter-Varsity Press, 1988), pp. 307-308
'History and the Human Condition on the Other Side of 1984', *Christianity and History Newsletter* 2 (1988), pp. 8-14
'The Philosophical Climate and Mission to Students', *Forum for the Association of Christians in Higher Education* 2 (1988), pp. 4-18

1989

Evangelicalism in Modern Britain: A History from the 1730s to the1980s (London: Unwin Hyman, 1989/Grand Rapids, MI: Baker Book House, rev. edn, 1992/London: Routledge, rev. edn, 1993)
'Evangelical Christianity and the Enlightenment', *Crux* 25.4 (1989), pp. 29-36
'Religion and Society in the Nineteenth Century', *The Historical Journal* 32.4 (1989), pp. 997-1004

1990

Patterns in History: A Christian Perspective on Historical Thought (Grand Rapids, MI: Baker Book House, 1990)
'Baptists and Fundamentalism in Inter-War Britain', in K. Robbins (ed.), *Protestant Evangelicalism: Britain, Ireland, Germany and America, c.1750–c.1950* (Oxford: Basil Blackwell, 1990), pp. 297-326
'Evangelical Christianity and Modernism', *Crux* 26.2 (1990), pp. 2-9
'Evangelical Christianity and Romanticism', *Crux* 26.1 (1990), pp. 9-15
'History and Theory', *History* 75.244 (1990), pp. 257-61
'How Moody Changed Revivalism', *Christian History* 9.1 (1990), pp. 22-25
'What Lutherans can Teach Evangelicals (and vice versa)', *Reformed Journal* 40.2 (1990), pp. 24-25
'George (Fielden) MacLeod and Donald (Oliver) Soper', in K. Robbins (ed.), *The Blackwell Dictionary of British Political Life in the Twentieth Century* (Oxford: Basil Blackwell, 1990), pp. 285-86 and 382

1991

Patterns in History: A Christian Perspective on Historical Thought (Leicester: Inter-Varsity Press, 1991)
'Evangelical Christianity and the Enlightenment', in M. Eden and D.F. Wells (ed.), *The Gospel in the Modern World* (Leicester: Inter-Varsity Press, 1991), pp. 66-78
'The Baptist Conscience in the Nineteenth Century', *Baptist Quarterly* 34.1 (January, 1991), pp. 13-24
'Evangelicalism in Modern Scotland', *Scottish Bulletin of Evangelical Theology* 9.1 (1991), pp. 4-12
'The Political Force [C.H. Spurgeon]', *Christian History* 10.1 (1991), pp. 38-39

1992

Evangelicalism in Modern Britain: A History from the 1730s to the 1980s (Grand Rapids, MI: Baker Book House, rev. edn, 1992)
Victorian Nonconformity (Bangor: Headstart History, 1992)
'The Secularization of British Universities since the Mid-Nineteenth Century', in G.M. Marsden and B.J. Longfield (ed.), *The Secularization of the Academy* (New York, NY: Oxford University Press, 1992), pp. 259-77
'History and the Gospel in our Culture', *Epworth Review* 19.2 (1992), pp. 57-66
'William Wilberforce', in J.D. Woodbridge (ed.), *More than Conquerors* (Chicago, IL: Moody Press, 1992), pp. 240-44
'What does the future hold for Evangelicals?', *Aware* 71.1 (1992), pp. 4-5

1993

Evangelicalism in Modern Britain: A History from the 1730s to the 1980s (London: Routledge, rev. edn, 1993)
William Ewart Gladstone: Faith and Politics in Victorian Britain (Grand Rapids, MI: Eerdmans, 1993)
'Holiness in Nineteenth-Century British Methodism', in W.M. Jacob and N. Yates (ed.), *Crown and Mitre: Religion and Society in Northern Europe since the Reformation* (Woodbridge: Boydell Press, 1993), pp. 161-74
'Martyrs for the Truth: Fundamentalists in Britain', D. in Wood (ed.), *Martyrs and Martyrologies* (Oxford: Basil Blackwell, 1993), pp. 417-51
'Revival and Enlightenment in Eighteenth-Century England', in E.L. Blumhofer and R. Balmer (ed.), *Modern Christian Revivals* (Urbana, IL: University of Illinois Press, 1993), pp. 17-41
'Baptist Thought, British Evangelicalism', in A.E. McGrath (ed.), *The Blackwell Encyclopedia of Modern Christian Thought* (Oxford: Basil Blackwell, 1993), pp. 25-26 and 41-42
'Lord Balfour of Burleigh, Arthur James Balfour, Conventions, Enlightenment, Evangelicalism, William Ewart Gladstone, Robert Hall, Moral Re-Armament, William Robertson Nicoll, (Sir) Robert Peel, Preaching: themes and styles: the modern era, Seamen's Missions, Charles Haddon Spurgeon, George Armstrong

Young', in N.M. de L. Cameron *et al.* (eds), *Dictionary of Scottish Church History and Theology* (Edinburgh: T.&T. Clark, 1993), pp. 53, 209, 294-95, 306-308, 363-64, 387-88, 607, 627, 651, 670-71, 764, 790 and 902-903

1994

M.A. Noll, D.W. Bebbington and G.A. Rawlyk (eds), *Evangelicalism: Comparative Studies of Popular Protestantism in North America, the British Isles and Beyond, 1700–1990* (New York, NY: Oxford University Press, 1994)

'Evangelicalism in its Settings: The British and American Movements since 1940', in M.A. Noll, D.W. Bebbington and G.A. Rawlyk (eds), *Evangelicalism: Comparative Studies of Popular Protestantism in North America, the British Isles and Beyond, 1700–1990* (New York, NY: Oxford University Press, 1994), pp. 365-88

'Evangelicalism in Modern Britain and America: A Comparison', in G.A. Rawlyk and M.A. Noll (eds), *Amazing Grace: Evangelicalism in Australia, Britain, Canada and the United States* (Grand Rapids, MI: Baker Books/Montreal and Kingston: McGill-Queen's University Press, 1994), pp. 183-212

'Catholic emancipation, Clapham Sect, Disestablishment, Evangelicalism, Methodism, Nonconformity, Oxford Movement, Quakers, Test and Corporation Acts, repeal of, Wilberforce, William', in J. Belchem and R. Price (eds), *A Dictionary of Nineteenth-Century World History* (Oxford: Blackwell Publishers, 1994), pp. 105, 129-30, 169-71, 209-11, 377-78, 425-26, 441-42, 508-509, 608 and 658

1995

'The Decline and Resurgence of Evangelical Social Concern, 1918–1980', in J. Wolffe (ed.), *Evangelical Faith and Public Zeal: Evangelicals and Society in Britain, 1780–1980* (London: SPCK, 1995), pp. 175-97

'Spurgeon and the Common Man', *Baptist Review of Theology* 5.1 (1995), pp. 63-75

'Trends in British Church History', *Studia Historiae Ecclesiasticae* 21.2 (1995), pp. 57-70

'Clapham Sect, Shaftesbury, Lord, Wilberforce, William', in D.J. Atkinson and D.H. Field (eds), *New Dictionary of Christian Ethics and Pastoral Theology* (Leicester: Inter-Varsity Press, 1995), pp. 235, 785 and 892-93

1996

'Towards an Evangelical Identity', in S. Brady and H. Rowdon (ed.), *For Such a Time as This: Perspectives on Evangelicalism, Past, Present and Future* (London: Scripture Union, 1996), pp. 37-48

'Spurgeon and British Evangelical Theological Education', in D.G. Hart and R.A. Mohler (ed.), *Theological Education in the Evangelical Tradition* (Grand Rapids, MI: Baker Book House, 1996), pp. 217-34

'The Holiness Movement in British and Canadian Methodism in the Late Nineteenth Century', *Proceedings of the Wesley Historical Society* 50.6 (1996), pp. 203-28

'Missionary Controversy and the Polarising Tendency in Twentieth-Century British Protestantism', *Anvil* 13.2 (1996), pp. 141-57

'Scottish Cultural Influences on Evangelicalism', *Scottish Bulletin of Evangelical Theology* 14.1 (1996), pp. 23-36

1997

Evangelical Conversion, c.1740–1850 (North Atlantic Missiology Project; Cambridge: University of Cambridge, 1997)

'Canadian Evangelicalism: A View from Britain', in G.A. Rawlyk (ed.), *Aspects of the Canadian Evangelical Experience* (Montreal and Kingston: McGill-Queen's University Press, 1997), pp. 38-54

1998

Atonement and Empire, 1880–1914 (North Atlantic Missiology Project; Cambridge: University of Cambridge, 1998)

'Gladstone and Grote', in P.J. Jagger (ed.), *Gladstone* (London: Hambledon Press, 1998), pp. 157-76

'Of this Train, England is the Engine: British Evangelicalism and Globalization in the Long Nineteenth Century', in M. Hutchinson and O. Kalu ed.), *A Global Faith: Essays on Evangelicalism and Globalization* (Sydney: Centre for the Study of Australian Christianity, 1998), pp. 122-39

'Henry Drummond, Evangelicalism and Science', *Records of the Scottish Church History Society* 28 (1998), pp. 129-48

1999

'Gospel and Culture in Victorian Nonconformity', in J. Shaw and A. Kreider (ed.), *Culture and the Nonconformist Tradition* (Cardiff: University of Wales Press, 1999), pp. 43-62

'Henry Drummond, Evangelicalism and Science', in T.E. Corts (ed.), *Henry Drummond: A Perpetual Benediction* (Edinburgh: T.&T. Clark, 1999), pp. 19-38

'Science and Evangelical Theology in Britain from Wesley to Orr', in D.N. Livingstone, D.G. Hart and M.A. Noll (ed.), *Evangelicals and Science in Historical Perspective* (New York, NY: Oxford University Press, 1999), pp. 120-41

2000

Holiness in Nineteenth-Century England (Carlisle: Paternoster Press, 2000)

D.W. Bebbington and R.E. Swift (eds), *Gladstone Centenary Essays* (Liverpool: Liverpool University Press, 2000)

'Gladstone and Homer', in D.W. Bebbington and R.E. Swift (ed.), *Gladstone Centenary Essays* (Liverpool: Liverpool University Press, 2000), pp. 57-74
'Evangelical Conversion, c.1740–1850', *Scottish Bulletin of Evangelical Theology* 18.2 (2000), pp. 102-27
'William Ewart Gladstone', in J. Powell (ed.), *Biographical Dictionary of Literary Influence: The Nineteenth Century, 1800–1914* (Westport, CT: Greenwood Press, 2000), pp. 175-77

2001

'Episcopalian community, Missions at home, Religious life: Evangelicalism', in M. Lynch (ed.), *The Oxford Companion to Scottish History* (Oxford: Oxford University Press, 2001), pp. 234-35, 422-23 and 515-16
'Mission in Scotland, 1846–1946', in D. Searle (ed.), *Death or Glory?* (Edinburgh: Rutherford House, 2001), pp. 32-53

2002

D.W. Bebbington (ed.), *The Gospel in the World: International Baptist Studies* (Studies in Baptist History and Thought, 1; Carlisle: Paternoster Press, 2002)
'The Democratization of British Christianity: The Baptist Case, 1770–1870', in A.R. Cross (ed.), *Ecumenism and History: Studies in Honour of John H.Y. Briggs* (Carlisle: Paternoster Press, 2002), pp. 265-80
'The Evangelical Revival in Britain in the Nineteenth Century', *Kyrkohistorisk arsskrift* (2002), pp. 63-70
'Christianity (Evangelical)', in C. Partridge (ed.), *Dictionary of Contemporary Religion in the Western World* (Leicester: Inter-Varsity Press, 2002), pp. 195-97

2003

T. Larsen, D.W. Bebbington and M.A. Noll (eds), *Biographical Dictionary of Evangelicals* (Leicester: Inter-Varsity Press, 2003)
D.W. Bebbington and T. Larsen (eds), *Modern Christianity and Cultural Aspirations* (Lincoln Studies in Religion & Society, 5; London: Sheffield Academic Press, 2003)
'Atonement, Sin and Empire, 1880–1914', in A. Porter (ed.), *The Imperial Horizons of British Protestant Missions, 1880-1914* (Grand Rapids, MI: Eerdmans, 2003), pp. 14-31
'The Dissenting Political Upsurge of 1833–34', in D.W. Bebbington and T. Larsen (ed.), *Modern Christianity and Cultural Aspirations* (London: Sheffield Academic Press, 2003), pp. 224-45
'Evangelism and Spirituality in Twentieth-Century Protestant Nonconformity', in A.P.F. Sell and A.R. Cross (ed.), *Protestant Nonconformity in the Twentieth Century* (Carlisle: Paternoster Press, 2003), pp. 184-215
'Holiness in the Evangelical Tradition', in S.C. Barton (ed.), *Holiness Past and Present* (London: T.&T. Clark, 2003), pp. 298-315

'Remembered Around the World: The International Scope of Jonathan Edwards's Legacy', in D.W. Kling and D.A. Sweeney (ed.), *Jonathan Edwards at Home and Abroad: Historical Memories, Cultural Movements, Global Horizons* (Columbia, SC: University of South Carolina Press, 2003), pp. 177-200

'Revival and Enlightenment in Eighteenth-Century England', in A. Walker and K. Aune (ed.), *On Revival: A Critical Examination* (Carlisle: Paternoster Press, 2003), pp. 71-85

2004

The Mind of Gladstone: Religion, Homer and Politics (Oxford: Oxford University Press, 2004)

'Contrasting Worldviews in Revival: Ferryden, Scotland, in 1859', in G.R. Treloar and R.D. Linder (ed.), *Making History for God* (Sydney: Robert Menzies College, 2004), pp. 347-66

'Evangelicals, Theology and Social Transformation', in D. Hilborn (ed.), *Movement for Change: Evangelicals and Social Transformation* (Carlisle: Paternoster Press, 2004), pp. 1-19

'Le protestantisme évangélique anglo-saxon au xix e siècle. Un résau international de convertis', in S. Fath (ed.), *Le Protestantisme Evangélique: Un Christianisme de Conversion* (Turnhout: Brepols Publishers, 2004), pp. 39-56

'Moody as a Transatlantic Evangelical', in T. George (ed.), *Mr Moody and the Evangelical Tradition* (London: T&T Clark International, 2004), pp. 75-92

'Evangelical Theology in the English-Speaking World during the Nineteenth Century', *Scottish Bulletin of Evangelical Theology* 22.2 (2004), pp. 133-50

'Henry Drummond, Edward Miall, D. L. Moody, James Orr, William Pennefather', in H.C.G. Matthew and B. Harrison (eds), *The Oxford Dictionary of National Biography* (Oxford: Oxford University Press, 2004)

2005

The Dominance of Evangelicalism: The Age of Spurgeon and Moody (Downers Grove, IL: Inter-Varsity Press, 2005)

'The Free Church M.P.s of the 1906 Parliament', in S. Taylor and D.L. Wykes (ed.), *Parliament and Dissent* (Edinburgh: Edinburgh University Press, 2005), pp. 136-50

'Evangelical Historiography: An Interview with David Bebbington', *Brethren Archivists and Historians Network Review* 3.2 (2005), pp. 82-102

'Gladstone's Christian Liberalism', *Christianity and History Bulletin* 2 (2005), pp. 11-17

'The News from Rhosllanerchrugog', *Books & Culture* 11.3 (2005), pp. 36-39

'Nonconformity', in website, Liberal Democrat History Society (2005)

2006

D.W. Bebbington, with K. Dix and A. Ruston (eds), *Protestant Nonconformist Texts:* Volume 3. *The Nineteenth Century* (Aldershot: Ashgate Publishing, 2006)

'The Growth of Voluntary Religion', in S. Gilley and B. Stanley (eds), *The Cambridge History of Christianity: World Christianities, c.1815–c.1914* (Cambridge: Cambridge University Press, 2006), pp. 53-69

'The Place of the Brethren Movement in International Evangelicalism', in N.T.R. Dickson and T. Grass (eds), *The Growth of the Brethren Movement: National and International Experiences* (Milton Keynes: Paternoster Press, 2006), pp. 241-60

'Gladstonian Liberalism according to Gladstone', *Journal of Liberal History* 52 (2006), pp. 14-19

'History', in C. Campbell-Jack and G.J. McGrath (eds), *New Dictionary of Christian Apologetics* (Leicester: Inter-Varsity Press, 2006), pp. 320-22

2007

Congregational Members of Parliament in the Nineteenth Century (Cambridge: United Reformed Church History Society, 2007)

'The Reputation of Edwards Abroad', in S. Stein (ed.), *The Cambridge Companion to Jonathan Edwards* (Cambridge: Cambridge University Press, 2007), pp. 239-61

'Baptist Members of Parliament: A Supplementary Note', *Baptist Quarterly* 42.2 (April, 2007), pp. 148-61

'Contrasting Worldviews in Revival: Ferryden, Scotland, in 1859', *Evangelical Review of Theology* 31.1 (2007), pp. 43-59

'Evangelicals and Public Worship, 1965–2005', *Evangelical Quarterly* 79.1 (2007), pp. 3-22

'The Evangelical Conscience', *Welsh Journal of Religious History* 2 (2007), pp. 27-44

2008

'Gladstone and the Classics', in L. Hardwick and C. Stray (eds), *A Companion to Classical Receptions* (Oxford: Blackwell, 2008), pp. 86-91

'Culture and Piety in the Far West: Revival in Penzance, Newlyn and Mousehole in 1849', in K. Cooper and J. Gregory (ed.), *Revival and Resurgence in Christian History* (Woodbridge: Boydell Press, 2008), pp. 225-50

'Eschatology in Evangelical History', in R. Rook and S. Holmes (eds), *What are we Waiting for?: Christian Hope and Contemporary Culture* (Milton Keynes: Paternoster, 2008), pp. 75-86

'Evangelicalism and Cultural Diffusion', in M. Smith (ed.), *British Evangelical Identities Past and Present:* Volume 1. *Aspects of the History and Sociology of Evangelicalism in Britain and Ireland* (Milton Keynes: Paternoster, 2008), pp. 18-34

'Introduction', in K. Cooper and J. Gregory (ed.), *Revival and Resurgence in Christian History* (Woodbridge: Boydell Press, 2008), pp. xv-xviii
'J.C. Ryle, 1816-1900', in A. Atherstone (ed.), *The Heart of Faith* (Cambridge: Lutterworth Press, 2008), pp. 101-10
'Response', in M.A.G. Haykin and K.J. Stewart (eds), *The Emergence of Evangelicalism: Exploring Evangelical Continuities* (Nottingham: Inter-Varsity Press, 2008), pp. 417-32

2009

The Very Essence of Evangelicalism: The Islington Conference (Melbourne: Ridley College, 2009)
'Methodism and Culture', in W.J. Abraham and J.E. Kirby (eds), *The Oxford Handbook of Methodist Studies* (Oxford: Oxford University Press, 2009), pp. 712-29
'Response: The History of Ideas and the Study of Religion', in A. Chapman, J. Coffey and B.S. Gregory (eds), *Seeing Things Their Way: Intellectual History and the Return of Religion* (Notre Dame, IN: University of Notre Dame Press, 2009), pp. 240-57
'Revival and the Clash of Cultures: Ferryden, Forfarshire, in 1859', in D.W. Roberts (ed.), *Revival, Renewal and the Holy Spirit* (Milton Keynes: Paternoster, 2009), pp. 65-94
'Evangelical Trends, 1959-2009', *Anvil* 26.2 (2009), pp. 93-106
'Revivals, Revivalism and the Baptists', *Baptistic Theologies* 1.1 (2009), pp. 1-13
'Unitarian Members of Parliament in the Nineteenth Century', *Transactions of the Unitarian Historical Society* 24.3 (2009), pp. 153-75
'Unitarian Members of Parliament in the Nineteenth Century: A Catalogue', *Transactions of the Unitarian Historical Society* 24.3 (2009), pp. 1-88
'Evangelicalism and Fundamentalism in Britain' (2009), Summary of Project in Religion and Society Programme funded by AHRC and ESRC, http://www.eauk.org/efb/conference-information.cfm

2010

Baptists through the Centuries: A History of a Global People (Waco, TX: Baylor University Press, 2010)
The Nonconformist Conscience: Chapel and Politics, 1870-1914 (London: Routledge, new edn, 2010)
'Evangelicalism', in D. Fergusson (ed.), *The Blackwell Companion to Nineteenth-Century Theology* (Chichester: Wiley-Blackwell, 2010), pp. 235-50
'The Union of Hearts Depicted: Gladstone, Home Rule and *United Ireland*', in D.G. Boyce and A. O'Day (eds), *Gladstone and Ireland: Politics, Religion and Nationality in the Victorian Age* (Basingstoke: Palgrave Macmillan, 2010), pp. 186-207
'The Problem of Pleasure: Sport, Recreation and the Crisis of Victorian Religion' (2010), Reviews in History (review no. 960), http://www.history.ac.uk/reviews/review/9602011

2011

Victorian Nonconformity (Eugene, OR: Wipf and Stock/Cambridge: Lutterworth Press, 2nd edn, 2011)
'Calvin and British Evangelicalism in the Nineteenth and Twentieth Centuries', in I. Backus and P. Benedict (eds), *Calvin and His Influence, 1509–2009* (New York, NY: Oxford University Press, 2011), pp. 282-305
'The King James Bible in Britain from the Late Eighteenth Century', in D.L. Jeffrey (ed.), *The King James Bible and the World it Made* (Waco, TX: Baylor University Press, 2011), pp. 49-69
'Lloyd-Jones and the Interwar Calvinist Resurgence', in A. Atherstone and D.C. Jones (eds), *Engaging with Martyn Lloyd-Jones: The Life and Legacy of 'the Doctor'* (Nottingham: Inter-Varsity Press, 2011), pp. 38-58
'British Baptist Crucicentrism since the Late Eighteenth Century', *Baptist Quarterly* 44.4 (October, 2011), pp. 223-37, and 44.5 (January, 2012), pp. 278-90
'Christian Higher Education in Europe: A Historical Overview', *Christian Higher Education* 10.1 (2011), pp. 10-24

2012

Victorian Religious Revivals: Culture and Piety in Local and Global Contexts (Oxford: Oxford University Press, 2012)
'Conscience and Politics', in L. Husselbee and P. Ballard (eds), *Free Churches and Society* (London: Continuum, 2012), pp. 45-64
'Foreword', in R. Quinault, R. Swift and R.C. Windscheffel (eds), *William Gladstone: New Studies and Perspectives* (Farnham: Ashgate, 2012), pp. xv-xvi
'Gladstone's Preaching and Gladstone's Reading', *Nineteenth-Century Prose* 39.2 (2012), pp. 113-36

2013

D.W. Bebbington and D.C. Jones (eds), *Evangelicalism and Fundamentalism in the United Kingdom during the Twentieth Century* (Oxford: Oxford University Press, 2013)
D.W. Bebbington and M. Sutherland (eds), *Interfaces: Baptists and Others: International Baptist Studies* (Studies in Baptist History and Thought; Paternoster: Milton Keynes, 2013)
'Baptists and Fundamentalism in Inter-war Britain', in D.W. Bebbington and D.C. Jones (eds), *Evangelicalism and Fundamentalism in the United Kingdom during the Twentieth Century* (Oxford: Oxford University Press, 2013), pp. 95-114
D.W. Bebbington and D.C. Jones, 'Conclusion', in D.W. Bebbington and D.C. Jones (eds), *Evangelicalism and Fundamentalism in the United Kingdom during the Twentieth Century* (Oxford: Oxford University Press, 2013), pp. 366-76
'The Discipline of History and the Perspective of Faith since 1900', in R. Lundin (ed.), *Christ across the Disciplines: Past, Present, Future* (Grand Rapids, MI: Eerdmans, 2013), pp. 16-34

'Evangelicalism and British culture', in S.J. Brown, F. Knight and J. Morgan-Guy (eds), *Religion, Identity and Conflict in Britain: From the Restoration to the Twentieth Century* (Farnham: Ashgate, 2013), pp. 105-19

'The Evangelical Discovery of History', in P.D. Clarke and C. Methuen (eds), *The Church on its Past* (Woodbridge: Boydell Press, 2013), pp. 330-64

'F.F. Bruce: A Review Article', *Brethren Historical Review* 9 (2013), pp. 43-48

'Foreword', in P.J. Lalleman, P.J. Morden and A.R. Cross (eds), *Grounded in Grace: Essays to Honour Ian M. Randall* (London: Spurgeon's College and Baptist Historical Society, 2013), pp. xv-xvii

'Foreword', in T. Cupit, R. Gooden and K. Manley (eds), *From Five Barley Loaves: Australian Baptists in Global Mission, 1864–2010* (Preston: Mosaic Press, 2013), pp. ix-x

'Foreword', in A. Yeh and C. Chun (eds), *Expect Great Things, Attempt Great Things: William Carey and Adoniram Judson, Missionary Pioneers* (Eugune, OR: Wipf & Stock, 2013), pp. xiii-xiv

D.W. Bebbington and D.C. Jones, 'Introduction', in D.W. Bebbington and D.C. Jones (eds), *Evangelicalism and Fundamentalism in the United Kingdom during the Twentieth Century* (Oxford: Oxford University Press, 2013), pp. 1-12

D.W Bebbington and M. Sutherland, 'Introduction', in D.W. Bebbington and M. Sutherland (eds), *Interfaces: Baptists and Others. International Baptist Studies* (Milton Keynes: Paternoster, 2013), pp. xv-xvii

2014

The Intellectual Attainments of Evangelical Nonconformity: A Nineteenth-Century Case-Study (Friends of Dr Williams's Library Sixty-Fourth Lecture; London: Dr Williams's Trust, 2014)

'The Context of Methodist Missions: Global Evangelicalism in the Nineteenth Century', *Proceedings of the Wesley Historical Society* 59.6 (2014), pp. 227-44

'Evangelicalism and British Culture', in N.T.R. Dickson and T.J. Marinello (eds), *Culture, Spirituality and the Brethren* (Troon: Brethren Archivists and Historians Network, 2014), pp. 25-38

'Foreword', in B.R. Talbot (ed.), *A Distinctive People: A Thematic Study of Aspects of the Witness of Baptists in Scotland in the Twentieth Century* (Milton Keynes: Paternoster, 2014), pp. xi-xii

'The Islington Conference', in A. Atherstone and J. Maiden (eds), *Evangelicalism and the Church of England in the Twentieth Century* (Woodbridge: Boydell Press, 2014), pp. 48-67

'Nineteenth-Century British Baptist Attitudes towards the Relations of Church and State', *Pacific Journal of Baptist Research* 9.1 (2014), pp. 8-21

'The Spiritual Home of W.E. Gladstone: Anne Gladstone's Bible', in J. Doran, C. Methuen and A. Walsham (eds), *Religion and the Household* (Woodbridge: Boydell Press, 2014), pp. 343-53

'The Context of Methodist Missions: Global Evangelicalism in the Nineteenth Century' (2014), http://www.methodistheritage.org.uk/missionaryhistory-historyproject.htm

'Evangelical Christianity and Romanticism', *Crux* 26.1 (1990), pp. 9-15, http://www.theologicalstudies.org.uk/pdf/crux/26-1_009.pdf (2014)

'Evangelical Christianity and Modernism', *Crux* 26.2 (1990), pp. 2-9, http://www.theologicalstudies.org.uk/pdf/crux/26-2_002.pdf (2014)

'Methodist spirituality, 1800-1950', in compact disc, *Great was the Company of the Preachers: Methodist Missionary Society History Project Conference* (2005), (republished online at http://www.methodistheritage.org.uk/missionary history-historyproject.htm, 2014)

General Index

Abington, L.J. 36, 37, 40, 49
able [ministers] 51, 64, 69-72, 73, 74, 75, 77
Aborigines' Protection Society 335n
Adams, Amos 242n
Adcock, Rachel 22
African Inland Mission 169n
Ainsworth, Henry 245
Aitken, Thomas 155
Akroyd, Mary 37
Aldis, W.H. 255, 273
Alexander, A.V. 334n
Alford, Timothy 97
Allan, Fanny 165
Allinga, Peter 246
Althusser, Louis 172, 175
American Board of Commissioners for Foreign Missioners 285
Amos, Bessie 133
Anabaptists 33
Anderson, Dr 270
Anderson, John 163, 166n, 249, 253n
Andrewes, Lancelot 18
Angus, Joseph 101, 114
Annales 178
Arab World Ministries 166n
Arianism 195, 213
Arminianism 24, 63, 192, 195, 208, 209
Arminians 224, 249n
Armstrong, Mr of Boston 309
Arnold, Matthew 48, 374, 375, 376, 381, 383
Arnott, Jack 165
Arthington, Robert 150
Arthur, J.W. 169
Ash, John 61, 62
Ashman, Herbert 125, 129
Ashworth, James 43
Asplund, John 249
Assemblies of God 280

atheism 372
atonement 58, 65, 68n, 77, 109, 343
Atterbury, Bishop 196
Aylward, Gladys 163

Backus, Charles 248
Bacon, Ernest 110, 111
Bacon, John 40
Bacon, John Jr 40n, 48
Bagster, George 36n
Bagster, John (the older) 35
Bagster, John (the younger) 36n
Baird, Elizabeth 165 (Mrs E. Dick) 165
Bakewell, Lionel 266, 269, 270, 275
Balaba, Ezekieri 262, 263
Balaba, Losira 262
Baldwin, Stanley 334n
Balfour, Frances 348
Balfour, James 155
Balfour, Robert 251
Bannatyne, James 243
baptism 32, 34, 36, 58, 74, 170
  believer's/believers' baptism 3, 79n, 101, 104, 105, 107, 109, 115, 116, 118
  infant baptism 15, 28, 30
  Paedobaptists 101
Baptist Annual Register 309
Baptists xviii, xx, xxi, 3, 4, 15, 21, 38, 40, 41, 42, 50-77, 78, 82, 80, 97, 115, 122, 123, 124, 129, 143, 144, 153, 178, 180, 181, 182, 232, 233, 234, 266, 274, 279, 280, 281, 283, 303, 306, 307, 320, 374
  American Baptist Foreign Missionary Union 167, 168
  American Baptist International Ministries (Northern American Baptist Convention (USA)) 167
  Baptist Board, the 60

Baptist Historical Society xiv, xv, xxi
Baptist Home Missionary Society (Canada) 165
Baptist Industrial Mission 165, 166, 168
Baptist Mission Press, Calcutta 159
Baptist Missionary Society 52, 89n, 134, 139, 140, 141, 146, 147, 148, 150, 152, 153, 154-62, 238
Baptist Society in London for the Encouragement and Support of Itinerant (and Village) Preaching, the 44
Baptist Sunday School Union 89
Baptist Union of Great Britain and Ireland xiv, 52, 90, 103, 110, 111, 119, 121, 129, 140
Baptist Union of Scotland 147, 153, 154
Baptist World Alliance 182
Baptist Zenana Mission 157
Bristol Baptist Academy/College 50-77, 129, 142, 143, 232
Bristol Education Society 50, 51, 61, 65, 67, 69, 70n, 72
Bristol Tradition, the 50-77
English Baptist Mission, Sianfu, Shensi 158, 160
French-speaking Baptist churches 89n
General Baptist Association 39
General Baptists 60
German Baptists 88
Gospel Standard Baptists 98
Grace Baptist Mission 88, 89, 96
Grace Baptists 79n, 95
Metropolitan Association 92, 97
New Connexion General Baptists 35n, 39, 67
New Zealand Baptist Union 181, 182
Northamptonshire Baptist Association 59n, 235, 238
Northern Baptist Education Society 73

Particular Baptist Fund 44
Particular Baptists 22, 52, 63, 77, 119, 232, 234, 237, 240, 304
Pentre Baptists 61
Rawdon Baptist College 161n
Scottish Baptists 145-71
Southern Baptist Convention 279
Southern Baptists 280, 284
Strict Baptist Mission 88, 89
Strict Baptist Theological Institute, Bury 89
Strict Baptists 78-98
Suffolk and Norfolk Association of Strict Baptist Churches 78-98
Suffolk and Norfolk Baptist Home Missionary Society 98
Suffolk Baptist Union 89
Suffolk Strict Baptists 82
Barbour-James, John A. 338
Barclay, John 243
Barff, Constance 274
Barff, Fred 274
Barham, Julia (née Leakey) 259, 262
Barham, Laurence 259, 262, 267, 268, 276
Barnado, Dr 320
Barnhouse, Donald Grey 273
Barr, Martin Sr 48
Baxter, Richard 15, 26-33, 34
Bayle, Pierre 27
Baylor University xiii
Beale, Frederick 162
Beale, Hannah 162
Beaumont, J.G. 338
Beaumont, William 24
Bebbington, David W. xiii-xxi, 1-11, 52, 76, 78, 126, 173, 174, 175, 176, 177, 183, 187, 188, 213, 219, 230, 255, 278, 279, 280, 319, 340, 354, 355, 366, 370
Bebbington, Eileen xiii
Bebbington, Harold Leech 1, 2
Bebbington, Madge 3, 4
Bebbington, William 2, 3, 4, 7, 8

General Index 401

Bechet, Sidney 338n
Beddome, Benjamin 61, 232
Beddome, John 55, 57, 59
Beddome, Samuel 46n
Begg, Thomas D. 165
Bellamy, Joseph 241
Bendalow, John 165
Benson, Irving 270
Bentley, Michael 175
Benzie, Jean 161
Berge, B.-J. 89
Besant, Annie 327, 343
Bethel, Stanley 158
Betts, Emily 130
Bewes, Cecil 265, 269
Biagini, Eugenio 340
Bible, the 51, 369-84
Bible Churchman's Missionary Society 258
Bible Societies 310
    American Bible Society 285
Bible Women 134, 138, 143
Bible Women's Mission 135, 138
Bicheno, James 306, 307
Bill, Samuel 166n
Billy Graham Evangelistic Association 286, 293
Binney, Thomas 379
Birrell, Catherine 157
Bishop Tucker Theological College 259
Bisset, Mary 158
Black, Adam 162
Black, Marion 162
Blackham, John 319, 320, 327, 330, 331, 338
Blackwell, Thomas 247
Blair, Robert 194
Blake, William 377
Blanchard, John 96
Bland, S.K. 89
Bloch, Marc 178
Bob Jones University 295
Bogue, David 357
Bondfield, Margaret 335

Bonnet, Gijsbert 235
Bonwick, Colin 303, 304, 305
Booth, Abraham 62n, 235
Booth, Catherine 371, 380
Booth, William 3
Boston, Thomas 195, 245
Bowman, George 163
Boyce, Sarah 218
Boys' Brigade 338
Bradlaugh, Charles 372
Bradley, James E. 303, 305
Bradley, Samuel 46
Brady, Matthew Harrison 375
Braid, Annie (Mrs A. Fanston) 165
Brainerd, David 75, 209
Braithwaite, George 57, 62
Branch, James 330
Braudel, Fernand 178
Brazier, Jim 273
Brazil Mission 165
Brethren 6
Briggs, John H.Y. xiv, xv, xxi, 225
Bright, John 378
Brine, John 60, 62, 232, 233
British and Foreign Bible Society 37, 148, 165, 168, 299, 310, 311
British Wesleyan Missionary Society 310
Brotherhood 3
Brown, Bladwin 42
Brown, Bryan 94
Brown, Callum xvi
Brown, Catherine 163
Brown, Charles 155
Brown, James D. 169
Brown, Jean 194
Brown, John 244
Brown, Kenneth D. 328
Brown, Kenneth xvi
Brown, W. Roundsfell 147
Brown, William 155
Bruce, Steve 287
Bruner, Jason 256
Bryan, Keith 158
Bryan, William Jennings 376

Bryant, Anita 287
Buchan, Mary 169
Buchman, Frank 270
Bultmann, Rudolf 177
Bunyan, John 16
Burder, George 360
Burger, Ronna 28
Burgoyne, Emily 101
Burke, Kenneth 18, 19, 20
Burnet, Bishop 213
Burnet, Robert 165
Burns, Jabez 39
Burr, Aaron 314
Burrit, Elihu 324n
Burroughs, Eden 242
Bush, George W. 378
Butler, Bill 264, 271, 272, 276
Butler, Joseph 220
Butler, Perry 340
Butt, Clara 142
Byles, A. Holden 320
Byles, Mather 241
Byrom, John 201

Café, Evelyn 263
Calabar College 155
Calvinism 24, 59, 63, 79, 98, 100n, 107, 109, 110, 188, 194, 195, 201, 208, 209, 210, 224, 229, 233, 236, 240
Calvinists 191, 194, 196, 214, 274
Cambridge Inter-Collegiate Christian Union xiv, 256, 258 261, 268, 270, 271, 275
Cambridge Seven, the 275
Cambuslang revival 201, 222, 223
Cameron, George 155
Cameronians 204
Campbell, Archibald 192
Campbell, R.J. 331
Campbell, Ted 316
Campbell, William 246
Campus Crusade for Christ 285
Capon, Martin 265, 269, 271, 272

Carey, Hilary 152n
Carey, William 59n, 67, 146, 245, 56, 357
Carlyle, Alexander 191, 194
Carlyle, William 191, 194, 201
Carter, Jimmy 287, 295
Carwardine, Richard 310
Cash, Wilson 275
Cessationism 228
Chalmers, Grace 165
Chambers, George 266, 269
Charismatic Movement, the 288
Charismatics 279
Charlesworth, Vernon 106
Chauncy, Charles 240, 241
Chiesley, Rachel 197
Children's Special Service Mission 257, 258, 272
China Inland Mission 154, 162, 163, 164, 165, 171
Chisholm, Thomas 165
Christian and Missionary Alliance 165
Christian Endeavour 338
Christian Institute, the 96
Christian Observer 310, 312, 313, 314, 315
Christian Reformed 281
Christian socialism 333
Christian Socialist League 325
Christian Union Universities Mission 168, 169
Christianity Today 292, 293, 294
christology 90, 195
church membership 15, 32, 33n, 34
Church Missionary Society 148, 149, 169n, 257, 258, 261, 263, 264, 265, 269, 270, 274, 275, 359
  Church Missionary Society Theological College, Limuru, Kenya 265
Church of Christ 279
Church of England 3, 6, 17, 40, 42, 90, 94, 129, 180, 201, 210, 309

General Index 403

Anglicanism 302, 309, 312
Anglican Church Missionary Society 167
Anglican Evangelical Group Movement 272
Anglicans 124, 138, 201, 233, 266, 279, 320, 354, 372
Anglo-Catholicism 340
Church of God in Christ 280
Church of Scotland 145, 147, 149, 150, 168, 307, 312
    Church of Scotland Jewish Mission 167n, 168
Church of the Nazarene 279, 283
Church, Decie 265, 267
Church, Howard 265, 270, 271, 274
Church, Joe 255, 257, 258, 260, 261, 262, 263, 264, 265, 266, 267, 269, 270, 271, 272, 273, 274, 276
Church, Lizzio 265, 270, 271, 274
churches (local)
    Aberchirder Baptist Church 155
    Academy Street Baptist Church, Aberdeen 155
    Adelaide Place Baptist Church, Glasgow 155, 156, 161
    Airdrie Baptist Church 170
    Alcester (Aulcester) Baptist church 57, 58n
    Anstruther Baptist Church 164
    Barnoldswick Baptist Church 62n
    Bellshill Baptist Church 170
    Bengeworth Baptist Church 57
    Bethesda Baptist Church, Ipswich 84, 97
    Bethesda Baptist Church, Sunderland 275
    Bourton-on-the-Water Baptist Church 61, 232
    Bridlington Baptist Church 57
    Bristo Baptist Church, Edinburgh 156, 159, 160, 165, 167, 171
    Brixton Independent Church 42
    Broadmead Baptist Church, Bristol 53, 55, 56, 57, 60, 62, 65, 67, 69, 70, 122, 143, 237, 304
    Broughty Ferry Church of Scotland, Dundee 162
    Buckingham Baptist Church, Bristol 128, 129
    Calvary Chapel 279, 284, 288
    Cannon Street Baptist Church, Birmingham 75
    Carr's Lane, Birmingham 330
    Charlotte Baptist Chapel, Edinburgh 160, 161, 163, 164, 165, 166, 167, 168, 169, 170, 171
    Chipping Sodbury Baptist Church 65n
    Christ Church, Lambeth 320, 327, 332
    Church Street Baptist Church, Blackfriers 42
    Church Street New Connexion Baptist Church, Marylebone 39
    Church Street, Blackfriers (Upton Chapel) 36n, 40, 42, 49
    Coate Baptist Church 72
    College Lane Baptist Church, Northampton 232
    Cornwall Road Baptist Church, Bayswater 101
    Counterslip Baptist Church, Bristol 124-29, 130, 131, 132, 133, 134, 135, 136, 137, 138, 139, 140
    Crown Terrace Baptist Church, Aberdeen 156, 169, 170
    Dalkeith Baptist Church 166, 168
    Dawes Road Congregational Church, Fulham 329
    Dennistoun Baptist Church, Glasgow 155, 167, 169, 171
    Devonshire Square Baptist Church, London 57
    Dublin Street Baptist Church, Edinburgh 161

Dumfries Baptist Church 159
Duncan Street Baptist Church,
    Edinburgh 155, 156, 157, 158,
    169, 170, 171
Dundas Street Congregational
    Church, Glasgow 162
Dunoon Baptist Church 156, 159
Eagle Street, London 36n, 56
Ebenezer Congregational Church,
    West Bromwich 319
Edward Street New Connexion
    Baptist Church, Dorset Square 39
Elgin Baptist Church 170
Exeter Baptist Church 55n
Forfar Baptist Church 170
Fraserburgh Baptist Church 161
Gartley United Free Church,
    Aberdeenshire 162
George Street Chapel, Liverpool 321
Gilcomston Park Baptist Church,
    Aberdeen 156, 158, 163, 164,
    165, 166, 167, 168, 169, 170
Gorgie Baptist Church, Edinburgh
    160, 170
Grafton Street Baptist Church, Soho
    304
Gray's Walk Baptist Chapel,
    Lambeth (Regent Chapel) 42, 49
Grosvenor Street Independent
    Chapel, Manchester 357, 358,
    364
Grovelands Baptist Chapel, Reading
    113n
Grundisburgh Baptist Church 90
Hamilton Baptist Church 160
Hammersmith Baptist Church 36, 61
Harper Memorial Baptist Church,
    Glasgow 169
Hawick Baptist Church 164, 169
Hebden Bridge Baptist Church 73
Henley in Arden Baptist Church 55
High Blantyre Baptist Church 157,
    161

Hillhead Baptist Church, Glasgow
    155, 160, 164, 169, 170, 171
Hoetown Mission Hall 158
Hopeman Baptist Church 169
Horlsey Baptist Church,
    Gloucestershire 65n
Horsley Baptist Church 61
Horsleydown, Southwark 55
Ilford Congregational Church 320
Islington Baptist Church 136
John Street Baptist Church, Glasgow
    155, 159, 170
Kelso Baptist Church 163, 168
Kelvinside Baptist Church, Glasgow
    161
Keppel Street Baptist Church,
    London 36n
Kilmarnock Baptist Church 160, 165
Kirkintilloch Baptist Church 164,
    168
Leith Baptist Church, Edinburgh 157
Leslie Baptist Church, Fife 155, 156
Little Wild Street Church, London
    35, 36, 55, 56, 66, 101
Lodge Street Congregational Church,
    Bristol 142
Longton General Baptist Church 40,
    49
Lowestoft Baptist Church 92
Maidstone Baptist Church 61
Marshall Street Baptist Church,
    Edinburgh 156, 157, 159, 168,
    170
Maxwelltown Baptist Church,
    Dundee 156, 171
Maze Pond Baptist Church, London
    42, 43, 44n, 45, 46, 52n, 63n
Melbourne Hall, Leicester 119
Metropolitan Tabernacle/New Park
    Street Chapel, Southwark 41,
    100, 101, 102, 103, 104, 105,
    106, 107, 109, 110, 112, 113,
    114, 115, 116, 117, 118, 120, 121

General Index

Mitchell Street Baptist Chapel, London 40
Morningside Baptist Church, Edinburgh 156
Morningside Congregational Church, Edinburgh 162
Motherwell Baptist Church 158, 169, 170, 171
Northampton Baptist Church 61, 62, 236, 237
Northwood Christian Centre 354
Norwich Baptist Church 92
Nottingham Baptist Church 56
Nuneaton Congregational Church 327
Old King Street Baptist Church, Bristol 124n
Orangefield Baptist Church, Greenock 155, 158, 163, 169
Osset Baptist Church, Yorkshire 161n
Queen's Park Baptist Church, Glasgow 160, 164, 167, 168
Partick Baptist Church, Glasgow 166
Pershore Baptist Church 47, 62
Perth Baptist Church 157
Pill Baptist Church, near Bristol 124n
Pithay, the, Bristol 52, 66, 125
Pittenweem Baptist Church, Fife 163
Plymouth Baptist Church 54n, 55n
Port Glasgow Baptist Church 166
Praed Street Baptist Church, Paddington 39
Queensberry Street Baptist Church, Nottingham xiv, 2, 3, 10
Red Cross Street Baptist Church, London 63n
Rome Baptist Church, Italy 89
Rothesay Baptist Church 160
Rutherglen United Free Church 162
Rye Hill Baptist Church, Newcastle-upon-Tyne 332
Sanday Baptist Church, Orkney 170
Scarborough Baptist Chapel 44

South Leith Baptist Church, Edinburgh 161, 165, 168
Springburn Baptist Church, Glasgow 159
Springburn United Free Church 162
St Andrews Baptist Church 156, 157, 159, 170
St Andrews Street Baptist Church, Cambridge 303
St Austell Baptist Church 38
St Paul's Episcopal Church, York Place, Edinburgh 157
Stirling Baptist Church 159
Tabernacle Church, Hanley 320
Taunton Baptist Church 60n
Tillicoultry Baptist Church 168
Totterdown Baptist Church, Bristol 127
Tower Street Mission, Bristol 134, 140
Trowbridge Baptist Church 60n
Tyndale Baptist Church, Bristol 122, 123, 124-29, 130, 131, 132, 133, 134, 136, 137, 139, 140, 141, 143
Unicorn Yard Baptist Church, London 67
Union Grove Baptist Church, Aberdeen 158
Victoria Place Baptist Church, Paisley 164
Victoria Street Baptist Church, Galashiels 163
Viewfield Baptist Church, Dunfermline 158, 160, 165, 168, 171
Ward Road Baptist Church, Dundee 157
Warwick Baptist Church 232, 233
Wellington Baptist Church 60n, 61
West Baptist Church, Perth 158, 159
West Croydon Baptist Church 100, 101n, 103, 109, 110, 113, 115, 116, 119, 121

Westbourne Park Baptist Church, Paddington (Praed Street Chapel) 320, 333
Westray Baptist Church, Orkney 155, 166
Whitefield's Chapel, Tottenham Court Road, London 63, 320, 332
Willowcreek Community Church 293
Wishaw Baptist Church 155, 156, 158, 163, 167
Churches of Christ 156
City Temple, London 334
Clapham Sect, the 310
Claridge, G.C. 157
Claridge, Helen 157
Clark, Andrew 323
Clark, Elizabeth 158
Clark, Ena 165
Clark, James 158
Clark, Margaret 223, 224
Clarke, Adam 48
Clarke, Samuel 195, 196
Cliff, Mr 43
Clifford, John 39, 320, 324, 325, 326, 328, 330, 333, 334
Clift, Miss 169
Clinton, Bill 287
Clipsham, E.F. 62
Close, Julia 128
closed communion 79n
Coade, Eleanor 40, 48, 49
Coffey, John xx
Coker, Samuel 335
Colenso, Irma 337n
Collect, Mary 161
Collins, A.H. 181
Collins, May 158
Collins, Pastor 88
Collins, Samuel 85, 90
Collins, William 73n
Colman, Benjamin 240, 246, 248
Columbian College 73n
Comaroff, Jean 355

Comaroff, John 355
Comenius, Jan Amos 205
confessions 58n, 59
Congo-Balolo Mission 167
Congregationalists 3, 36, 42, 61, 78n, 124, 148, 280, 283, 320, 321, 328, 335, 374, 379
    Congregational Union of Scotland 152
Constable, Archibald 240
Contento, Paul 163
conversion 1, 21, 27, 62, 64, 69, 77, 101, 219, 220, 221, 224, 229, 363
Cook, Albert 260
Cooke, William 372
Cooper, Jane 267
Cooper, John 44n, 46n
Cooper, Mr 169
Cooper, Mrs 169
Cooper, Pastor 88
Cooper, William 247, 248
Cotham, Isaac 44n
Counterslip Gospel Mission Band 140
Countess of Huntingdon 202, 204, 205, 211, 212
Coutts, Marjory 166
covenant of grace 86
Covenanters 208
Cowie, Nurse 169
Cowley, Mary 158
Craig, John 163
Crew, Alice 134, 137, 138, 140
Crockett, Bryan 25
Cromer Convention 272
Crooks, Will 331
Cross, William 337n
Croswell, Andrew 242, 243
Cruickshank, A.H. 169
Crusaders 272
Cuff, William 120n
Cunningham, Hugh 245
Cunningham, James 169
Cushing, Thomas 250n

General Index 407

Cuthbertson, Janet 166

Darwin, Charles 371, 376
Davenport, James 224, 225, 227
David, Rees 307
Davidson, James 169
Davidson, Mrs James 169
Davidson, Randall 145
Davies, Hywel 303
Davis, Thomas 307
Dawson, Norah 128
Day, Mary 131
Day, Robert 61
Dayuma 291
Deism 203, 206
Dewar, A. 152
Dick, Gladys 170
Dickinson, Jonathan 241 248
Dickson College, PA 312
Dickson, Herbert 166
Dingwall, Mrs William 170
Dingwall, William 170
Disciples of Christ 279, 283
dispensational premillennialism 261n
Disraeli, Benjamin 342, 347
Dissent 302, 305
Dissenters 27, 33, 35, 36, 37, 39, 40, 42, 46n, 49, 53, 61, 195, 212, 221, 303, 304, 305, 307, 311
Dixon, W.B. 337n
Dochuk, Darren 287
Dod, John 23
Doddridge, Philip 202, 212, 233
Dodds, Margaret (Mrs Chalmers) 170
Donne, John 18, 383
Dorcas Society/societies 134, 135, 137, 140, 143
Dore, Bannister 45
Dore, James 44n, 45, 47, 63n
Dorward, Alan 163
Doulton, Frederick 42, 44
Doulton, Henry 42
Doulton, John 42
Dovey, E. 163

Dovey, Ian 166
Dow, Lorenzo 308
downgrade controversy 110-12, 129
Dowson, Henry 89
Draper, Mrs T. 166
Draper, T. 166
Dresser, Madge 123
Drever, Thomas 166
Drew, Henry 348, 349, 350
Drew, Mary 344, 345n, 348, 352
Drew, W. 181
Drummond, Henry 320, 375, 376
Duffill, M. 332
Dunan, Anne 15, 16
Duncan, Jessie 155
Duncan, Moir 155
Duncan, Mr 170
Duncan, Mrs 170
Dunscombe, Thomas 72
Durkheim, Emile 178
Dutch Reformed 279
Dyke, Daniel 73n

Eadie, Annie 158
Eadie, William 158
Eames, Jonathan 248
East African Revival 255-77
East Windsor, CT 216
East, Jane 128
East, William 128
Eaton, George 65
Ecclesiastical History Society xiii
ecclesiology 178, 234
ecumenism 187
education 50, 51, 56, 68, 70, 71, 99
Edward, Charles 211
Edwards, Ethel 157
Edwards, G.K. 157
Edwards, J.S. Celestine 325, 335
Edwards, Jonathan 75, 76n, 207, 209, 215, 216, 217, 220, 225, 226, 227, 230, 232, 236, 237, 238, 239, 240, 241, 242, 244, 278
Edwards, Jr, Jonathan 236, 238, 239, 247

Edwards, Morgan 245
Edwards, Sarah 143
Eekhout, Rebecca 155
Egypt General Mission 167
Elder, Lawrence 170
Eliot, Jared 244
Elliot, Elisabeth 291, 294
Ellis, Sarah 166
Ellis, William 361, 367
Elmslie, Mrs 164
Elton, G.R. 175
Elvins, Richard 241
Enlightenment, the xvii, 10, 174, 187, 188, 194, 204, 212, 213, 307
Ensor, Mable 261
Episcopalians 279, 280, 283
Erasmus 22, 24
Erskine, Anne 188n
Erskine, Ebenezer 188n, 195, 198, 200, 201
Erskine, Frances 210, 211
Erskine, James 187-214
Erskine, John 188n, 190, 231-54, 305
Erskine, Jr, James 202
Erskine, Ralph 188n, 195, 200, 201, 244, 245
eschatology 28, 178
Eskridge, Larry 289
Evangelical 64, 66, 67, 69, 72, 77
Evangelical Anglicanism 40
Evangelical Calvinism 67
Evangelical Magazine 313
Evangelical Nonconformity 340
Evangelical Revival, the 57, 67, 77, 187, 188, 189, 191, 200-12, 204, 205, 206, 207, 210, 212, 214
Evangelical Union of South America 159n, 166
Evangelicalism xvi, xvii, xviii, xix, 10, 50, 52, 53, 60, 66, 76, 77, 109, 175, 176, 187, 188, 200n, 204, 207, 212, 213, 214, 219, 220, 258, 265, 278-96, 282, 288, 290, 292, 293, 295, 296, 300, 316, 317, 330, 338, 340, 369-84
Evangelicals 36, 73n, 121, 143, 146, 204, 206, 210, 213, 215-30, 232, 234, 268, 269, 276n, 277, 278, 279, 280, 282, 283, 284, 289, 294, 296, 291, 299-318, 374, 379, 382
Evangelical Quadrilateral xvi, 52, 76, 219, 220, 230, 256, 366
   activism xvi, 52, 58, 65, 219, 256, 273, 279, 366
   ethical activism 68
   biblicism xvi, 52, 58, 63, 65, 66, 68, 70, 219, 256, 261, 279, 369-84
   conversionism xvi, 52, 66, 219, 256, 269, 279
   crucicentrism xvi, 52, 58, 64, 66, 68, 72, 77, 109, 219, 223, 256, 265, 266, 279
evangelism 81, 300
Evangelists' Training School, Gahini 261
Evans, Caleb 234, 235, 304, 307
Evans, Caleb 50, 52, 58, 60, 61, 64n, 66-69, 70, 71, 72, 73, 74, 75, 76, 77
Evans, Herbert 328
Evans, Hugh 50, 52, 54n, 57, 59, 61, 64-66, 67, 69, 70, 74, 75, 76, 77, 235
Evans, John (of Northampton) 61
Evans, John (of Pentre) 61
Evans, John 253, 309
Evans, Sarah (née Browne) 66
Ewing, John 157

Falwell, Jerry 287, 295
Fawcett, John 73
Fellowship of Christian Athletes 285
Fergusson, Elizabeth 158
Finley, Samuel 240
First Century Christian Fellowship 270
Fischbacher, Lily (Elizabeth) 163
Fisher, Edwards 245
Fisher, James 244
Fison, Lilias 166

General Index

Flavel, John 234
Fleming, Euphemia 158
Fleming, William 158
Fletcher, John 24
Flight, John 45, 46, 47, 48
Flight, Joseph 46, 47, 48
Flight, Samuel 47
Flight, Thomas 44, 45, 46, 47, 49
Foley, Allice 128
Folgham, Selina 43
Foot, Isaac 334n, 335
Foot, John 241
Forsyth, Robert 155
Forty, Henry 73n
Forward Movement 321
Foskett, Bernard 54-62, 73n, 77, 70, 232
Foxcroft, Thomas 241, 246, 247
Francis, Benjamin 61, 65
Franklin, Benjamin 217
Fraser, J.G. 181
Fraser, James 243, 245, 248
Freckleton, T. 39
Free Church Council 327
Free Church of Scotland Jewish Mission 167n
Free Church of Scotland Mission 169
Free Churches 329
French, James 251
French, Roland J. 84
Frye, Northrop 377
Full Gospel Business Men's Fellowship, International 288
Fuller Theological Seminary 285
Fuller, Andrew 62n, 67, 76, 235, 236, 237
Fuller, Charles 281
Fuller, William 61n
Fullerism 79
Fullerton, William Young 113, 118
Fundamentalism 293
Fundamentalists 279, 281, 293

Gaebelein, Frank 287
Galbraith, John 236, 239, 240
Galbraith, Maisie 170
Gardiner, Colonel 211
Gardiner, Margaret 158
Garrard, L.R. 97
Garrioch, Lydie 166
Garvey, Marcus 336
Gascoigne, J.G. 327
Gast, Philip 136
Gast, Susanna 136
Gaube, Joseph 55n
George Washington University 73n
Gibb, G.W. 163
Gibb, Margaret 163
Gibbons, Thomas 61
Gibson, Julia 130, 131
Gifford, Andrew 56
Gifford, Andrew 62, 63, 67
Gill, John 55, 60, 232, 233
Gill, Moses 252
Gillam, Ann 47
Gillam, Mrs 47
Gillam, Thomas 47
Gillespie, Katherine 16
Gillies, John 251, 305
Girling, Edwin 155
Girling, Kate 155
Gladstone 7
Gladstone, Anne 342
Gladstone, H.H. 87
Gladstone, Helen 344, 346, 352
Gladstone, Stephen 349
Gladstone, William Ewart xiv, xviii, 340-53, 378, 382
Gladstone, William Henry 342, 343
Glas, John 253
Glenesk, Alfred 158
Glenesk, Edith 158
Glover, Anna 133, 134, 135
Glover, Dorothy 122, 123, 129, 134, 135, 136, 141, 143, 144
Glover, Richard 124, 129, 133, 139, 140
Glover, T.R. 129
Godwin, William 308
Goffman, Erving 18, 19, 20

Goold, Ebenezer 329, 330
Gordon, General 342
Gordon, Mary (May) 158
Gordon, William 241
Gordon-Conwell College 292
Gospel Missionary Society 169
Gotch, Frederick 129, 139, 142, 143
Gotch, Katherine 140
Gover, Alice 130
Grace 58, 59, 62, 69n, 71, 107
Graham, Billy 276, 286, 287, 291, 292, 293, 294
Grange, Lady (Rachel) 197, 198, 203, 204
Grass, Tim xix, xx, 98
Gray, George 170
Gray, Laura 166
Gray, Margaret 236, 238n, 239
Gray, William 236, 237, 238
Great Awakening, the 215, 216, 219, 220, 222, 224, 225, 226, 228
Great Ejection (1662) 3
Green, James 43, the
Green, James Sr 43
Green, Sarah 43
Green, Stephen 43
Green, Valentine 46
Greenman, Sarah 133
Gregory, Helen (Ella) 159
Gregory, Olinthus 311
Grose, W.H. 38, 49
Grove, Richard 368
Grubb, Norman 273
Guillebaud, Peter 267
Guinness, Harry 167n
Guinness, Henry Grattan 159n
Guinness, Howard 270
Gurney, John 46n
Gurney, Joseph 46n, 63
Guy, C.A. 92

Haddon, Ann 129
Hague, Mr 44

Hall, Jr, Robert 67, 76, 303, 306, 307, 311
Hall, Sr, Robert 62n, 234
Hall, Theophilus 243
Hamilton, Bessie 166
Hamilton, Edward 341, 347
Hamilton, Robert 359, 360
Handasyds, John 304
Hannam, June 123, 143
Hardestry, Nancy 291
Hardie, Keir 332, 335
Harford-Battersby, C.F. 257
Harris, Howell 202, 205, 209, 210
Harris, Theophilus 306
Harris, William Cornwallis 365
Harrison, Edward 57, 62
Harrison, James 169
Harrison, Mary 167
Harrobin, Mrs 164
Hart, Levi 246, 247
Hartford Institute 284
Hartley, John 156
Harvard College 227, 228
Harvey, Charles 39
Harvey, George 156
Harwood, Edward 60, 67
Hasler, John 159
Hasler, Marion 159
Hastings, Adrian 260
Hatch, Nathan 317
Hay, Christina 170
Hayden, Roger 59, 75
Heart of Africa Mission 165, 167, 168, 169
Heath, Job 46n
Helsinger, Elizabeth 134
Helwys, Thomas 3
Hemmenway, Moses 247
Henderson, Arthur 332, 335
Henderson, George 170
Henderson, Susan (Mrs Dickson) 167
Henry, Carl F.H. 292
Henry, Elsie 167

General Index 411

Herberg, Will 282
Hern, Enid 167
Hervey, James 233
Hession, Revel 268, 273, 275
Hession, Roy 268, 273, 274, 275, 276
Hicks, William Joynson 91
Higgs, William 106, 113
high Calvinism 62 87, 232, 233
high Calvinists 98
High Church Anglicanism 187
Hill, Robert 336
Hill, Rowland 36
Hilton, Boyd 340, 370
Hindley, George 273
Hindley, Godfrey 267
Hindley, Phyllis 267
Hindmarsh, Bruce 222
Hinmers, J. 36, 37
Hinton, James 307
Hinton, John 36n
historicism 174
historiography 174, 175, 177, 178
history 172-83
Hoad, Jack 91n
Hobby, William 240
Hodder, Reginald 320
Hogg, James 246, 247
Hoghton, Henry 304
Holiness groups 279
Holiness tradition 266, 268, 283
Holland, Henry Scott 349, 352
Holmes, Geoffrey 259
Holt, Thomas 250n
Holy Spirit 215-30
Hope, Thomas 203, 204
Hopkins, Mark 111
Hopkins, Samuel 241, 248
Horne, Sylvester 320, 326n, 331
Horsburgh, Olive 159
Horsburgh, Peter 159
Horton Academy 73
Horton, R.F. 321
Huber, Alice 170
Hunt, Holman 374

Hunter, Henry 304
Hunter, Robert M. 113n
Huntingdon, Joseph 244
Hus, Jan 205
Hussey, Samuel 133
Hussey, Susan 133
Hutcheson, Francis 199, 207, 213
Hutchinson, Colonel 3, 9
Hutton, James 201, 208, 209
Huxley, T.H. 371
Hybels, Bill 293
hymn-singing 90, 91

Ibbotson, Robert 21, 22
Idealism 174, 175, 176
Ignatius, Father 349
immersion 58n
Impey, Catherine 325
independency 121
Independent Labour Party 332
Independents 3, 78n, 101, 204, 357, 364
India and Ceylon General Mission 168
India General Mission 168
Ingle, Agnes 161
Ingle, Laurence 161
Ingram, George 269, 275
Inter-Varsity Fellowship 270, 272, 275, 285
itinerancy 65, 77
Ivimey, Joseph 47, 55, 56, 63

Jabavu, D.D.T. 336
Jack, Miss 170
Jackson, Alverey 62n, 67
Jagger, Peter 340
Jalland, Pat 352
James, E.L. 381
Jamieson, John 246
Jardine, John 159
Jarvis, F. 160
Jeffs, Harry 328, 334, 336
Jenkins, Herbert 61
Jenkins, Joseph 304
Jesus Movement 288, 289

Jesus People 289
Jewitt, Llewellyn 36, 46
Johnston, Archibald 194
Johnston, Mrs 170
Johnston, Peter 274
Jones, Edwin 133
Jones, Emma 133
Jones, John 263
Jones, Martha 42
Jones, Morgan 61
Jones, Thomas Snell 242
Jope, Caleb 55, 56n
Joseph, H. Mason 335
Joseph, Nelie 157
Julian of Norwich 20
Jynam, Charles 38

Kabale Convention 262
Karanja 268
Katoke Teacher Training College 263
Keach, Benjamin 55
Keeble, Neil 26
Keene, Henry 44n
Keller, Tim 293
Kellogg, Elijah 250n
Kellstedt, Lyman 279n
Kennedy, D. James 287
Kennedy, H.A. 326
Kennedy, Mr 245
Kerr, Colin 274
Kerr, William 210
Kerrigan, George 167
Keswick Convention 255, 256, 257-60, 265, 266, 267, 268, 270, 271, 272, 273, 274, 275
Keswick spirituality 256, 257, 259, 267, 276
Kiffin, William 73n
Kigozi, Blasio 261, 262
Killingray, David xv, xix
Kilsyth revival 201
King James Version (Authorized Version) 293, 375, 380
King, Gordon 159

King, Jr, Martin Luther 287, 378
King, Mary 159
King, W. 170
Kinghorn, David 313
Kinghorn, Joseph 76, 313
Kingston, John 307
Kinuka, Yosiya 261, 262, 268
Kirkland, Agnes 159
Kirkland, Margaret 159
Kirkland, Robert 156, 159
Kitterell, Peter 55, 56
Kivebulaya, Apolo 261
Kivengere, Festo 276
Knee, Henry 125, 133
Knee, Mary 133, 135, 138
Knight, Joseph 39
Knight, Philip 274
Knippers, Diane 291
Kuruman 354-68
Kyles, David 159
Kyles, Helen 159

Labour Party 319, 324, 332, 335
LaHaye, Beverly 291
Lamont, Susie 170
Lancashire Independent College 358
Langdon, Samuel 249
Langdon, Thomas 73
Lap, Margaret 222, 224
Larsen, Timothy xiii, xv, xvi, xvii, xviii, xix
Latin Vulgate 369
Latitudinarianism 187, 201, 213
Law, Georgina M. 170
Lawson, Dugald 163
Lawson, George 251
Lawson, Jeannie 163, 164
Le Clerc, Jean 207, 213
Leakey, Louis 259n
Leet, Miss 161
Lefebvre, Georges 178
Lewis, E.W. 327
Liberal Party 319, 324, 333, 335
Lincoln, Abraham 378

General Index

Lindsay, Fanny 191
Lindsay, Francis 204
Lindsay, James 170
Linn, William 249
Linton, John 169
Little, Elizabeth 157
Living Bible 294
Livingston, David 356, 341, 363
Llewelyn, Thomas 61, 65
Lloyd-Jones, Martyn 272
Lochhead, Elsie 170
Locke, John 192, 196, 213
Lockhart, Ella 157
Lockhart, George 193, 197
Lockyer, Thomas 304
Logan, Allan 193
Logan, D.R. 170
Logan, Margaret 159
London City Mission 148
London Confession (1688) 52
London Confession (1699) 60n
London Missionary Society 36n, 166, 335, 355, 357, 358, 359, 360
Lord's Supper 2
Lubbock, John 381
Luther, Martin 205
Lutherans 263, 270, 279, 280, 281
Lynch, Kathleen 22, 24, 25
Lyttelton, Arthur 350

M.K. 15, 21-25, 33
MacBeath, Andrew 160
MacBeath, Emmie 160
MacColl, Malcolm 350
MacGregor of Balhaldy 200
Mackenzie, George 163
MacLaren, Alexander 101, 107, 120
Maclaurin, Colin 206
MacLaurin, John 201, 206
Macleod, Emma xiv, xv, xix
Maida, Bolster 163
Maier, Walter 281
Mair, Alex 164
Mair, Janet 164

Maitland, Annie 155
Malcolm, C. 170
Malcolm, Mrs C. 170
Mann, Thomas 332
Manning, Samuel 48
Manson, Christina 160
Marchant, James 39
Marrow Men 204
Marrow, Peter 273, 274
Marrow, Barbara 274
Marsden, George xvii, 217
Marsden, Joshua 314, 315, 316
Martin, John 304
Martindale, Clarice Evelyn 1, 7
Marxist theory of history 173, 174
Mason, C.J. 37
Mason, Miles 36n
Mathews-Green, Frederica 291
Matovu, Elisafati 263
Matthew, Colin xvi, 340
Matthewson, Glendoline 160
Matthewson, William 160
Mauduit, Israel 304
Maus, Katherine Eisaman 17
Mayer, Elijah 36
Mayer, Eliza 130
Mayer, Joseph 36
Mayo, Isabella 325
McCulloch, William 201, 223
McCurrach, Mr 156
McCurrach, Mrs 156
McGee, John 308
McGregor, James 248
McIntyre, Mr 167
McIntyre, Mrs 167
McKay, Dr 169
McKilligan, Miss (Mrs Bernard) 170
McKnight, John 246, 247
McLean, Archibald 146
McLeod, Elizabeth 152
McLeod, Ella 157
McLeod, Hugh 126, 324
McNaughton, Angus 161
McPhail, Miss (Mrs Myres) 167

McPherson, Aimee Semple 281
McVicar, Marjorie 154, 156, 157
Mellers, Dame Agnes 4
Mellors, Robert 3, 4, 6
Mennonites 263, 268n, 279, 281
Mentalitiés 175, 178, 180, 181, 182
Methodists 141, 149, 220, 221, 233, 263, 266, 279, 280, 283, 307, 308, 310, 314, 315, 354, 371, 372
   Calvinistic Methodists 188n, 208
   Methodism xix, xx, 228, 290, 308, 312
   Methodist Missionary Society 310, 314
   Methodist New Connexion 36, 37
   Primitive Methodism 308
   Primitive Methodists 3, 317
   United Methodist Missionary Society 148
   United Methodists 3, 279
   Wesleyan Arminians 213
   Wesleyan Methodists 3, 129, 279, 320, 328, 338, 351
Meyer, F.B. 320, 321, 326, 327, 329, 330, 332, 335
Mile End Academy 66
Mill, Alex 161
Miller, Samuel 231
Miller, William 157
Milne, Jeannie 160
Milne, Margaret 170
Milne, Robert 167
Milne, William 160
Milne, William 156
Milton, John 15, 17
Milton, John 377
Minister(s) 50, 51, 55, 69, 71, 72, 74, 75
ministry 50, 53, 55, 57, 64, 65, 68, 70
mission 59n, 65, 77, 88, 109, 110, 135, 139-41, 145-71
Mission Africa (Qua Iboe Fellowship) 166n
Mission at Anand 166
missionaries 68, 354, 359

Mitchell, Fred 273
Mitchell, W. 170
moderate Calvinism 57-61, 67, 233
Modern Question, the 233
Modernism xvii, 174, 175
Modernists 281
Moffat, Alexander 359
Moffat, J.S. 360
Moffat, Jr, Robert 362
Moffat, Mary 359, 361, 364, 366
Moffat, Robert 354-68
Monta, Susannah Brietz 25
Moody Bible Institute 281
Moody, Dwight L. 291, 319
Moody, Harold 338
Moon, James 167
Moravians 192, 201, 202, 205, 206, 208, 209, 212, 213, 225
Morden, Peter J. xiii
More, Alexander 251
Morgan, G. Campbell 335
Morley, Francis 37
Morley, John 352, 353
Morris, Glyn 3
Morris, Lewis 351
Morse, Jedidiah 252
Morton, Elizabeth 130
Moss, Reuben 250n
Mumford, Catherine 371
Munne, Phillip 29
Murdock, William 170
Murray, James 307
Murray, John 247
Murray, Mr 170
Murray, Mrs 170
Myles, Margaret 170

Nagenda, Sala 262
Nagenda, William 262, 263, 265, 267, 268, 272
National Association of Evangelicals, the 285
National Young Life Campaign 268
Navigators, the 285

Nazarenes 280
Neale, James 36
Neave, David 170
Neave, Mrs David 170
Neill, Michael 24
New International Version 293
Newbury, Mary 167
Newman, John Henry xiv, 343
Newton, James 52, 61, 66, 72n, 237, 304
Nightingale, Florence 372
Nisbet, Charles 243, 305, 312
Nisbet, John 170
Noble, Mrs Peter 156
Noble, Peter 156
Noll, Mark xvii, xviii
Nonconformists xx, 3, 4, 17, 55, 90, 91, 122, 123, 124, 129, 149, 319, 322, 333, 338, 340, 354, 359
Nonconformity xviii, xx, 15, 16, 18, 26n, 27, 36, 37, 41, 84, 135, 141, 302, 311n, 320
Norman, Mrs 139
North Africa Mission 166
Northampton, MA 215, 216, 225
Nsibambi, Simeoni 260, 261, 262, 269
Nuttall, Geoffrey F. 26, 188
Nuttall, J.K. 321, 327
Nyabagabo, Ernesti 263

O'Brien, Susan 231, 301
Ogden, Uzal 246
Oldfield, Grace 164
Oldham, Ann 127
Oldrieve, Frank 156
Oliver, Kelly 18, 20
Olney, Thomas 120
Olney, William 106, 113, 114
Oncken, J.G. 88
open communion 21, 103
Operation Mobilisation 277
ordinances 58, 59
ordination 57n, 218
original sin 28
Orton, John 304

Osgood, David 243
Oulton, John 61
Oxford Group spirituality 271
Oxford Group, the (Moral Re-Armament) 270, 271, 272, 273, 276
Oxford Movement, the 340

Page, Anthony 311
Page, Dr 23
Pandian, T.B. 88
Pannenberg, Wolfhart 177, 178
papists 204
Parry, Jonathan 340
Parson, Robert 41n
Parsons, Jonathan 241, 249
particular redemption 57n, 84, 209
Passmore, Elizabeth 128
Pastors' College Evangelical Association 109, 113, 116, 119n
Pastors' College, The/Spurgeon's College xiv, 85n, 99, 102, 103, 104, 107, 109, 112, 113, 114, 116, 117, 118, 119, 121, 160
Paterson, Annie 161
Paterson, Donald 161
Paterson, Hugh 190
Payne, Ernest A. xiv
Pearce, Samuel 67, 76
Pendleton, Nathaniel 314
Pentecostals 266, 279, 284
performance 15, 16, 17, 18, 19, 20, 22, 24, 33, 34
Peters, L.L. 304
Peterson, Derek 256
Philadelphia Education Society, the 73n
Philip, John 356, 360, 362
Phillips, Jacob 35, 36
Phillips, John 55n
Pierson, Arthur T. 112, 113, 114, 115, 116, 118
pietism 187, 272
piety 51, 219
Piggott, John 55
Pike, G. Holden 99, 100, 109, 114, 115

Pilgrim Fathers, the 382
Pilkington 261
Pilkington, George 257
Pitkin, Timothy 246
Pitts, Arthur Pitt 259
Plaatje, Sol 336, 337, 338n
Pleasant Monday Evenings 329
Pleasant Sunday Afternoon (Brotherhood Movement) 319-39
Pleasant Tuesday Evenings 329
Plymouth Brethren 274
Polglase, Eliza 129
Polglase, Sarah 129, 137
Poole, Kristen 15
Porteous, Robert 164
Porteous, William 305
Porter, Andrew 285
Portland Chapel 101, 107
positivism 174, 175, 176
postmillennialism 187
Postmodernism 175
Potter, John 202, 213
Powell, Thomas 40
Powell, Vavasor 21, 22
Prayer Call (1784) 238
preaching 59, 64, 65, 67n, 68, 69, 75n, 77, 215
predestination 209
Presbyterians 3, 60, 112, 113, 118, 152n, 193, 231, 240, 263, 273, 279, 280, 283, 293, 307, 354, 363
   American Presbyterian Mission 167
   Presbyterian Church (USA) 279
   Presbyterian Church in Scotland 145
   Presbyterianism 234
   Scottish Presbyterians 205, 206, 213
   United Presbyterians 357
Price, Seymour J. 42
Priestley, Joseph 235
Prince, Thomas 240, 241, 242
Princeton College 305, 306
Princeton Theological Seminary 231
Protestant Dissenting Deputies 44

Prothero, Stephen 378, 383
providence 176, 177, 178
Prudden, Nehemiah 250n
Puritanism 15, 24, 187, 188, 206
Puritans xvii, 15, 205, 213, 374, 382
Pye-Smith, Ruth 267

Quakers 3, 35n, 123n, 129, 143, 204, 266, 279, 325

Randall, Ian M. xiii
Randolph, A. Philip 287
Ranyard, Ellen 138
Rauschenbusch, Walter 324n
Raven, Charles 335
Ravis, Eliza 137
Raw, Mary 157
Rawden, Yorkshire [Rawdon] 61
Rawlyk, George 279n
Redwood, Hugh 335
Reece, Emily 140
Reed, Joseph 306
Reformers xvii
Regan, Ronald 295
Regions Beyond Missionary Union 159, 166n, 167, 168, 169
Reid, Ella (Mrs Bristow) 170
Reid, Mary 168
Religious liberty 91
Religious Tract Society 37
Revised Standard Version 293
revival(s) 215, 218, 219, 220, 224, 230, 238, 255, 260, 276
Rhys, Morgan John 306
Richards, William 309
Richardson, Albert 258
Richardson, Miss (Mrs Taylor) 168
Ridge, L. Clayton 330
Ridgley, Thomas 196
Ridgway, E.J. 36, 37
Ridgway, John 37
Ridgway, William 36, 37
Ridsdale, Lucy 274

General Index 417

Ridsdale, Philip 274, 276
Rippon, John 52, 56, 59, 61, 66, 72n, 76, 304, 309
Ritchie, Mary 168
Robe, James 201, 209, 245
Roberts, Aida (Mrs Hill) 171
Roberts, Howard 171
Roberts, L. (Mrs Amner) 171
Roberts, Oral 286
Robertson, Douglas 164
Robertson, Isabella (Mrs Ball) 171
Robertson, Pat 287, 295
Robinson, Arthur 124, 139, 141
Robinson, E.S. 124
Robinson, Edward 125, 129, 139, 141, 142
Robinson, Katherine 139, 140, 141, 142, 143
Robinson, Robert 44n, 305, 307
Roby, William 357, 358
Rodger, Isabel 160
Rodgers, John 250, 253
Roger, J. Guinness 321
Rogers, Ann 160
Rogers, Hester Roe 218
Rogers, John 304
Rogers, Joseph 156
Rogers, Thomas 54n, 55n
Romaine, William 249
Roman Catholic Church 382
Roman Catholicism 379
Roman Catholics 3, 129, 280, 293
Romanticism xvii, 10, 174
Rose, Jonathan 379
Ross, Ellen 130
Ross, Ina 163
Rossetti, Christina 373
Rowland, William Frederick 250n
Rownthwaite, J.F. 260, 262
Roxburgh, William 356
Royden, Maude 335
Ruanda Mission 257, 258, 263, 266, 269
Ruanda Revival 275
Rushbrooke, John 98

Russell, George 349
Ryland, John C. 35n, 231-54
Ryland, Jr, John 67, 231-54

Sabiti, Erica 263
sacrament(s) 2, 31
Sailors' Mission 168
Saint, Daniel 207
Saint, Rachel 291
Salters' Hall 60
salvation 58, 62, 67n, 69, 233
Salvation Army, the 3, 279, 281, 321, 338, 371, 372
Sampson, Richard 54n
Samuel Jones 55n
Sandon, John 46
Sankey, Ira D. 319, 326
Savidge, Margaret 162
Scanzoni, Letha 291
Schaeffer, Francis 295
Schafly, Phyllis 291
Schreiner, W.P. 335n
Scollay, Thomas 156, 157
Scott, Adam 168
Scott, Adam 168
Scott, Jean 171
Scott, Jonathan 36
Scott, Thomas 235
Scottish Moderatism 187
Scottish Seceders 188n, 200, 204
Seabury, Samuel 246
Searl, John 247
Secession Church 195
Selleck, Nancy 17n
Selope-Thema, Richard 337
Selwyn, George August 178
Semugabo, Kilimenti 267
Separatists 3, 17
Seventh-day Adventists 280, 283
Seward, William 220
Shakespeare, John H. 120n
Shakespeare, William 15, 25, 381
Shakarian, Demos 288
Sharp, Annie 164

Sharp, Esther 267
Sharp, Len 255, 257
Shawer, Miss (Mrs Longlands) 171
Shawn, Wallace 383
Shelley, J.B. 39
Shelley, P.B. 373
Shepherd, Dick 335
Sheppard, Dick 334n, 335
Shields, John 162
Shirley, James 24
Sibbes, Richard 205
Simpson, J.Y. 334n
Simson, John 195, 196, 199, 204, 207
Singha, Shoran A. 338
Sisterhood Movement 329, 334
Skepp, John 60
slavery 311, 312
Smith of Boston 247
Smith, Adelaide D. 171
Smith, Alex 168
Smith, Algie Stanley 255, 257, 265, 267
Smith, Christina 160
Smith, Chuck 288
Smith, Colin 168
Smith, Donald 156, 160
Smith, Edwin W. 355, 357, 366
Smith, George Adam 320
Smith, Harold Earnshaw 269
Smith, James 361
Smith, John 359
Smith, Karen E. 142
Smith, Mrs Alex 168
Smith, Mrs F.L. 128
Smith, Thomas 344, 346
Smith, Timothy L. xvii
Smith, William 250
Smyth, John 3
Snowden, Viscount 335
Soane, John 36
Society for International Ministries 167n
Society for the Propagation of the Gospel 148, 151n
Society for the Propagation of the Gospel in Foreign Parts 309

Society for the Recognition of the Brotherhood of Man 325
Socinianism 235
South American Evangelical Mission 166n
South American Missionary Society (Patagonia Missionary Society) 165
South American Missionary Society 168
South[ern] Morocco Mission 166
Southport Convention 268
Speedie, George 168
spirituality 255-77
Spring, Samuel 242, 243
Spurgeon, Charles Haddon 41, 85n, 99-121, 129, 375, 382
Spurgeon, Eliza (née Jarvis) 101
Spurgeon, James Archer 99-121
Spurgeon, John 101, 107
Spurgeon, Thomas 113, 114, 115, 116, 117, 120
Staddon, F.O. 90
Staley, Benjamin 44n
Stamer, Lovelace 38
Stamp, Josiah 334n, 335
Stanley, Brian 256, 261n, 285, 355
Stark, James 164
Stark, Robert 168
Staughton, William 73n
Stead, Francis Herbert 331n
Stead, W.T. 335
Steadman, William 73, 76
Steedman, Robert 168
Steel, Arthur Y. 171
Steinbach, Susie L. 130, 143
Stennett, Joseph 66
Stennett, Samuel 67, 235
Stephens, A.E. 168
Stephens, Mrs A.E. 168
Stepney College/Regent's Park College 101
Stewart, C. 168
Stewart, Kenneth J. xvii
Stewart, Mrs C. 168
Stewart, Nellie 168

General Index 419

Stiff, Ebenezer 41
Stiff, James 41, 49
Stiff, Robert 41
Stiff, William 41
Stiles, Martha 136
Stirling University xiii, xiv, 6
Stock, Eugene 149
Stocker, Thomas Medland 38
Stockwell (Spurgeon's) Orphanage 99, 102, 103, 105, 106, 112, 120
Stoddard, Solomon 247
Stone Chapel, Leeds 73
Stott, Margaret 156
Stowe, Harriet Beecher 373
Street, Leonard 332
Stuart, Bishop 262, 264, 270, 276
Stuart, Cyril 258, 259
Stubbs, C.M. 168, 169n
Sudan Interior Mission 167
suffrage 142, 143
Summer Institute of Linguistics, the 285
Sunday School Union 37, 90
Sunday schools 3, 92, 95, 135, 137, 370
Sutcliff, John 44, 67, 75, 76, 235, 238
Sweet, Leonard 133
Swiss, Mary Ann 130
Sykes, Tom 328

Tait, Ruth 160
Talbot, Edward 350
Taylor, Abraham 189, 196
Taylor, Dan 67, 235
Taylor, Hudson 162, 163
Taylor, John V. 263
Taylor, Kenneth 293, 294
Taylor, Michael 90
teleology 173, 174
temperance 141n
Tennent, Gilbert 209, 225, 241, 244
tent meetings 78-98
Terrett, Sarah 141n
Terrill, Edward 53-54, 56, 70, 122
Thatcher, Peter 248, 250, 252
Theological College, Mukono 263, 264

Thom, William 305
Thomas, Fred 162
Thomas, Joshua 56n, 59
Thomas, Timothy 47
Thomas, William 54n
Thompson, E.P. 172, 173, 175
Thompson, Hamlet George 164
Thompson, Josiah 67
Thomson, George 244
Thomson, W.S. 156
Thoroton Society, the 5
Tidball, Derek xvi
Tillett, Ben 332
Tombes, John 15, 26-33, 34
Tomkins, Benjamin 46n
Tommas, John 52n
Tooke, H.D. 92
Townsend, Charles 129
Tracey, Decie 258
tragicomedy 15, 24, 25, 33
Trevelyan, George Otto 350
trinitarianism 60, 67, 205
    anti-trinitarianism 194, 250n
Trinity Evangelical Divinity College 292
Trinity, the 57
Trotter, Lilias 266
Trubek, Anne 381
Trumball, Benjamin 250
Tuffley, J.W. 329
Turner, James 75
Turner, John 295
Turvey, Raymond 276n
Twaddel, Robert 171
Tyler, Lemuel 250n
Tyler, Royall 251n
Tyndale House, Cambridge 268
Tyndale Mission 137, 139
Tyndale, William 370

Unevangelised Fields Mission 168
Union College, New York 240
Unitarians 123n, 143, 307, 39, 42, 60
United Free Church of Scotland 146, 147, 149, 150, 152, 166

Universal Negro Improvement
  Association 336
Upton, James 40
Urquhart, Alec 1, 7
Urquhart, Clarice Vera 1, 2, 3, 7, 8
Urquhart, Roy 1
Urquhuart, Mary 164
Urquhurt, David 164

Vaux(e), Thomas 54
Vaux, Dorothy (Terrill) 54
Venn, Henry 359
Verwer, George 277
Vine, Charles 320
Vineyard Association 279
Voke, Stanley 275, 277
voluntarism 288

Wacker, Grant 287
Wakerley, J.E. 328
Walden, Percy 326n
Wales, Samuel 242
Walker, Catherine 160
Walker, Henry 21, 22
Walker, Thomas 250
Wall, James 46
Wallace, J. Bruce 325
Wallace, Lee 373
Wallace, William 160
Waller, Gordon 5
Wallich, Nathaniel 356
Walpole, Robert 196
Walsh, Walter 332
Warburton, William 228
Ward, Kevin 256, 258
Ward, W. 308
Ward, W.R. 188, 211
Ward, William 328, 332
Warner, R. Stephen 289
Warren, Max 275, 276
Washington, George 313
Watkins, Edmund 61
Watkins, Owen 24
Watson, Agnes 155n, 156

Watson, James 156
Watson, Nicholas 18, 20
Watson, Richard 310
Watt, Helena 156
Watts, Isaac 196, 221, 364, 365
Watts, John 42
Weaver, John 32
Webb, Elizabeth 128
Webb, John 248
Webster, Alexander 201, 210
Webster, Reginald 269
Wedgwood, Josiah II 37
Weir, Lizzie B. 169
Wells, David F. 296
Wellwood, Henry Moncrieff 316
Welsh Revival 1904 3
Wesley, Charles 189, 202, 203, 204, 205,
  209, 211, 214, 278
Wesley, John 189, 205, 208, 209, 210,
  214, 217, 220, 221, 233, 278, 290,
  304
Wesley-Methodist Magazine 309
Western Association 59, 60, 75
Westminster Confession 205, 214
Westrope, Richard 326n
Whelan, Timothy D. 44
White, Edith 171
White, Hayden 175
Whitefield, George 63, 200, 201, 202,
  203, 206, 208, 209, 210, 211, 215-
  30, 278, 302
Whitefield, John 222
Whitridge, John 36
Whittington, Harry 171
Wickham, Edward 350
Widgery, Jessie 131
Wigglesworth, Edward 227, 228
Wijnpersee, Dionysius van de 250
Wilberforce, William 299, 311
Wild-Wood, Emma 256
Wileman, Charles 39
Wileman, Henry 39, 40, 49
Wileman, James 39
Wilkes, John 199

Wilkes, Mrs 169
Wilkinson, Allan 169
Wilkinson, G.H. 349
Wilks, Mark 307
William of Orange 3
Williams, C. Fleming 326n, 328
Williams, Charles 111
Williams, Christabel 164
Williams, George 60
Williams, Henry Sylvester 335
Williams, Leighton 324n
Williams, Solomon 243
Williamson, Joan 161
Williamson, W.R. 159n
Willis, John 57, 261
Willison, John 224
Wills, Miss (Mrs McKay) 169
Wilson, Alex 164
Wilson, Ann 157
Wilson, Elizabeth 171
Wilson, Georgina 171
Wilson, Jean 161
Wilson, Linda xviii
Wilson, Mr 252
Wilson, Robert 36
Wilson, William 161
Winchester, Elhanan 243
Winterbotham, William 307, 311
Wishart, Jr, William 199
Wishart, Mary 171
Withers, Philip 235
Witherspoon, John 305, 306
Wodrow, Robert 189, 194, 195, 196, 197, 214
Wolfe, Alan 296
Wolffe, John xvi
Women's Liberal Association 142
Women's Missionary Auxiliary 160
Wood, Anthony 32
Woods, Sam 332

Woodward, Aaron 250n
Worgan, Hannah 127
World Congress on Evangelization 286
World Council of Churches xiv
World Missionary Conference (1910) 145
World Vision 285
Worldwide Evangelisation Crusade 165, 268, 269, 273
Worthern, W.B. 18, 19, 20
Wright, George 86
Wuthnow, Robert 287
Wyatt, Benjamin 36
Wycliffe Bible Translators, the 285
Wylie, Anne 223, 224
Wylie, Greta 157

YMCA 320
Young Life 285
Young, Andrew 157
Young, C.B. 162
Young, Charlotte 157
Young, George 161
Young, Leonora 161
Young, Ruth 162
Youth for Christ 285, 291
Yuille, George 154, 155, 156, 156, 157, 158, 160, 161, 162, 163, 164, 169, 170, 171
YWCA 142

zeal/zealous [ministers] 51, 57, 69, 74, 75, 99
Zenana Mission(s) 139n, 140, 142, 143, 155, 157, 159
Zenana Society 137
Zinzendorf, Count Nickolaus Ludwig von 188, 189, 201, 202, 204, 205, 207, 208, 209, 212, 214

www.ingramcontent.com/pod-product-compliance
Lightning Source LLC
Chambersburg PA
CBHW071225290426
44108CB00013B/1295